Theory
and
Practice
of
PSYCHOLOGICAL
————————TESTING

FRANK S. FREEMAN

CORNELL UNIVERSITY

Theory and Practice of
—— PSYCHOLOGICAL
———————— TESTING

Third Edition

Holt, Rinehart and Winston

NEW YORK

Printed in the United States of America

TO *E.W.F.*

PREFACE

Emphasis in this edition again is placed on the psychological foundations of tests and on the psychological aspects of interpreting and evaluating test findings, while the statistical aspects are not neglected. A good deal of illustrative test material, therefore, has been incorporated, as in the first two editions.

This edition includes two major additions: a chapter on the historical background of psychological testing and one on elementary statistical concepts. I believe that students, especially graduate students, should have the perspective provided by an historical introduction to the subject. Better still, they should consult specialized books and original sources. That students should understand certain statistical concepts goes without saying. The chapter on statistics attempts to provide that understanding. Preferably, students should have a prior course in statistics, designed to give them insights through working on a large number of varied kinds of problems. For students who have had such a course, this chapter on statistical concepts can serve as a refresher; for others it should provide the information necessary to understand the statistical terms and data in the text.

The sections on reliability and validity have been considerably expanded; materials throughout have been brought up to date; some tests have been eliminated from discussion and others, which seem to be more useful in the presentation, have been added; much more attention has been given to multiple factor batteries. The fact that very few tests developed in countries other than the United States are included is not an index of their quality or number. Space and redundancy were the determinants.

Projective tests again are given an appreciable amount of space; for, though opinions vary concerning their value, projective tests are of primary importance in current psychological practice, research, thinking, and controversy. Students of the general subject of psychological testing, especially those whose major interests do not include clinical psychology, should be familiar with projectives as well as with other types of instruments. A bibliography has been appended to each chapter to provide additional sources of information about the tests and more readings for advanced students.

I am indebted, of course, to the individuals and publishers who provided materials and who readily granted permission to reproduce these. I am indebted, also, to several psychologists who contributed valuable suggestions for this revision; especially to Dr. Harold H. Abelson.

F. S. F.

Ithaca, New York
1962

CONTENTS

LIST OF TABLES

Theory
and
Practice
of
PSYCHOLOGICAL
————— TESTING

I.

HISTORICAL BACKGROUND

Uses of Psychological Tests

Psychological tests have been devised and are used primarily for the determination and analysis of individual differences in general intelligence, specific aptitudes, educational achievement, vocational fitness, and nonintellectual personality traits. Tests also have long been used for a variety of psychological, educational, cultural, sociological, and employment studies of groups rather than for the study of a particular individual. Among these studies of groups, the following have been most common and include the most important fields of investigation: the nature and course of mental development; intellectual and nonintellectual personality differences associated with age, sex, and racial membership; differences that might be attributed to hereditary or to environmental factors; differences among persons at different occupational levels and among their children; intellectual and other personality traits of atypical groups such as the mentally gifted, the mentally retarded, the neurotic, and the psychotic.

Psychological tests, especially those of general intelligence and of specific aptitudes, have had very extensive use in educational classification, selection, and planning, from the first grade (and sometimes earlier) through the university. Prior to World War II, schools and colleges were the largest users of psychological tests. During and after World War II, however, so many types of tests were administered to so many men and women in all branches of the military services that the armed forces, along with educational institutions, must now be regarded as the major users of psychological devices.

When tests are used for the determination and analysis of an individual's intellectual abilities or nonintellectual traits, the purpose might be to provide educational and vocational guidance; to place an individual in a special class for superior pupils or in one for the mentally retarded; to discern weaknesses in order to provide remedial instruction; or to discover causes, intellectual or otherwise, which might account for behavior problems in school.

In clinics, psychological tests are used primarily for individual diagnosis of factors associated with personal problems of learning, behavior, attitudes, or specific interpersonal relations.

In business and industry, tests are helpful in selecting and classifying personnel for placement in jobs that range from the simpler semiskilled to the highly skilled, from the selection of filing clerks and salespersons to top management. For any of these positions, however, test results are only one source of information—though an important one.

The foregoing discussion emphasizes the fact that psychological tests and testing play a significant role in a wide variety of situations and can significantly affect the lives of many persons. But even though they are significant educational, vocational, and diagnostic assets today, psychological tests did not begin to assume appreciable significance until about 1910–15.

The Nineteenth Century

Although the fact that persons differ in intellectual and other psychological characteristics had been apparent to observers for many centuries, it was only about a hundred years ago that these differences were first studied scientifically and subjected to measurement and objective evaluation.

Francis Galton (1822–1911) was the first scientist to undertake systematic and statistical investigations of individual differences. He was preceded, before the middle of the nineteenth century, by other men who are important in the history of psychology; but these men, who belonged to one of two groups, were not concerned with devising means of measuring individual differences. Some were nonexperimental, speculative psychologists who were concerned largely with problems of the dualism of mind and matter, the nature of ideas, intellectual "faculties," and classical associationism. Others, though experimentally oriented, directed their attention to general problems and theories rather than to variations and differences in human abilities.

Among these was Ernst Heinrich Weber (1795–1878), educated as an anatomist and physiologist, who experimented on weight discrimination, vision, hearing, and the "two-point threshold" of the skin. He is best remembered for his quantitative experimental approach to psychological problems and for what we know as Weber's law.[1] Gustav Theodor Fechner (1801–87), who started his career in physics and chemistry, was basically concerned with the application of the exact methods of the natural sciences to the study of man's "inner world," that is, the relations of mental processes to physical phenomena. Johannes Müller (1801–58), a professor of physiology, was especially interested in the physiology of the senses and in reflex action. In his significant experiments in space perception, he attempted to reconcile the opposed theories of "nativism" versus "empiricism." William Hamilton (1788–1856) and James Mill (1773–1836) were concerned with reformulating more completely and rigorously the classical association theory.

One of the most significant writers in psychology at mid-nineteenth century was Alexander Bain (1818–1903), who was Professor of Logic, Mental Philosophy, and English Literature in Aberdeen University. His two most distinguished works were *The Senses and the Intellect* (1855) and *The Emotions and the Will* (1859). Bain's approach was principally through physiology; he utilized, organized, and interpreted findings of the German experimentalists in a systematic restatement of associationism. Perhaps Bain's most important contribution was his pioneering effort to contain the entire range of human experience within a system of psychology.

Although Wundt's principal work was done somewhat later than Galton's, he is significant not only for his actual contributions but also as an example of nineteenth-century neglect of differential psychology. Wundt (1832–1920), who established the first laboratory of psychology, in 1879, at Leipzig University, employed physiological methods and introspection in his and his students' research. He held that ". . . a genuinely psychological experiment involved an objectively knowable and preferably a measurable stimulus, applied under [specific] conditions, resulting in a response objectively known and measured. But there were certain intervening steps which [could be known only] through introspection, sometimes supplemented by instrumentation" (31, p. 161). Thus, Wundt's method emphasized the necessity of knowing and stating con-

[1] This law states that the least added difference of a stimulus that can be noticed is a constant proportional part of the original stimulus.

sciously experienced events as they are related to objective and measurable stimuli and responses. For Wundt, introspection became the most important method of the experimental psychologist. These methods he applied to experimental study of vision, hearing, reaction time, psychophysical problems,[2] and to the analysis of word associations. It is interesting to note that one of Wundt's students from the United States, James McKeen Cattell (1860–1944), was impressed by the range of individual differences he found in his experiments. Although he was discouraged by Wundt from pursuing the subject, he persisted in doing so for many years.

These several examples will suffice to indicate the major interests of nineteenth-century psychologists, from which the pioneers in psychological testing had to break away. Yet the work of these early psychologists did significantly influence the types of testing first used in experimental work on individual differences.

Interest in the Mentally Deficient

In France, during the first half of the nineteenth century, interest in more accurate differentiation among individuals with regard to mental abilities was stimulated by a number of men, of whom two of the outstanding will be mentioned: Jean Esquirol (1772–1840) and Édouard Seguin (1812–80). They were concerned with mental deficiency and mental disease (14, 37).

Esquirol, in the first place, made explicit the distinction between mental deficiency and mental illness. These abnormal conditions were at that time generally undifferentiated and confused.[3] He also distinguished among the several levels of mental deficiency. Esquirol spoke of the "weak-minded" and of several grades, or levels, of "idiocy"; the former term he applied to what, for many years now, has been called "moronity" (and probably also includes borderline cases), while the latter term refers to the current terms "imbecility" and "idiocy." These groups, however, were not precisely defined or delineated, although Esquirol did attempt unsuccessfully to distinguish and classify mentally deficient individuals on the basis of physical measurements, especially size and formation of the

[2] Psychophysics is the study of the relation between the physical attributes of the stimulus and the quantitative attributes of sensation.

[3] Esquirol's distinction, essentially the one that has been current since then, is now widely understood: namely, that mental deficiency is a condition of seriously subnormal mental development due to congenital causes or to accidental causes occurring during early childhood, whereas mental illness (psychosis) is a severe disorder which may be marked by progressive impairment of mental functions and behavior, and by personality disintegration.

skull. It remained for Binet and his collaborator, Simon, to devise the first standard scale of intelligence and behavioral criteria that would differentiate the three levels of mental deficiency: *moron, imbecile,* and *idiot.*

Esquirol did, however, correctly discern the fact that development and use of language is one of the most useful and valid psychological criteria for differentiating levels of mental deficiency. This observation is of historical interest because for many years now the development, use, organization, and interpretation of verbal materials has been regarded by numerous psychologists as one of the major aspects—in some instances, *the* major aspect—of mental ability. Especially noteworthy among these psychologists is the late Lewis M. Terman, about whose work much more will be said in subsequent chapters.

Seguin is noteworthy for his pioneering work and methods in the training of mental defectives. He was placed in charge of a school for this purpose in 1842, after having had his own small school for the training of mental defectives for five years. Seguin believed that with appropriate help these individuals could improve in behavior, in utilization of their limited mental capacity, in their economic adequacy, and in their personalities generally. In 1846, his book on the treatment of mental defectives appeared (37). Like Esquirol, he attempted to find a basis for distinguishing between idiocy and imbecility, and between these and "backwardness." In 1848, Seguin migrated to the United States where, as in France, he stimulated interest in the study and training of mental defectives. His methods emphasized the development of greater sensory sensitivity and discrimination and of improved motor control and utilization.

Both Esquirol and Seguin are of significance to us because of their efforts to establish psychological criteria upon which to base differentiations among levels of mental deficiency; and, as will be seen later, it was this problem which provided the strongest original motive force to the testing movement after 1900. Seguin, furthermore, is noteworthy for his Form Board, which carries his name and is part of several performance test batteries currently in use.

Francis Galton's Contributions

It is clear from the foregoing brief account that until the last quarter of the nineteenth century there was scant recognition of individual differences as a subject worthy of study and research by psychologists. This indifference, no doubt, retarded the development of psychological tests that would be necessary for their measurement. Galton, though interested in and influenced by the psychological work of his predecessors and contemporaries, was even more strongly influenced by the development of the biological sciences then ascendant among British scientists. Consequently, his efforts were devoted largely to investigations of individual differences more from biological interests than from psychological. In the introduction to his *Inquiries into Human Faculty* (1883), he states (18):

> My general object has been to take note of the varied hereditary faculties of different men, and of the great differences in different families and races, to learn how far history may have shown the practicability of supplanting inefficient human stock by better strains, and to consider whether it might not be our duty to do so by such efforts as may be reasonable, thus exerting ourselves to further the ends of evolution more rapidly and with less distress than if events were left to their own course.

This quotation is evidence of Galton's sustained interest in developing a science of genetics and eugenics. It also indicates a problem with which psychologists have since been concerned—the roles of heredity and environment (or, as Galton named them, "nature and nurture") in the development of man's intelligence. For the study of this problem, objective psychological tests have been indispensable.

Prior to the appearance of the volume mentioned above, Galton had published the results of his earlier studies in *Hereditary Genius* (1869), and *English Men of Science: Their Nature and Nurture* (1874). His *Inquiries into Human Faculty* was followed by *Natural Inheritance* (1889) and *Noteworthy Families* (1906), the last with Schuster. In addition to these larger works published during this period of about forty years, Galton produced numerous articles on the general subjects indicated by the titles of his books. At the same time, his statistical techniques for the analysis of data provided the basis for the elaborated, extended, and refined statistical methods used by such men as Karl Pearson, British biometrician, and Charles Spearman, British psychologist, who was one of the earliest and most noteworthy men to engage in the analysis of human abilities (38).

Galton not only stimulated investigations of individual differences; he also strongly influenced the direction of the experimental efforts to measure intelligence by means of tests of imagery and sensory discrimination. He devised a test for the measurement of the delicacy of weight discrimination; he invented what is now known as the Galton whistle for measuring sensitivity to high tones. In addition, he suggested devices for testing visual and auditory discriminations, reaction time, and muscular strength.

Galton assumed, apparently, that the simpler and measurable sensory capacities should be significantly correlated with intelligence. That this was his hypothesis is shown by the fact that as subjects for study he selected persons of extreme differences in mental ability in order to learn whether their differences in sensory discrimination corresponded with the known differences in their mental abilities. Although it has long since been learned that sensory and sensory-motor tests have very little value for the study of the higher and more complex processes called intelligence, Galton's work, nevertheless, did strongly affect the course taken by test experimenters until about 1900, when the influence of Alfred Binet, the French psychologist, was felt.

Binet's Contributions

It is impossible in a short space to present a full review and evaluation of the character, range, and importance of Alfred Binet's contributions to individual psychology. An attempt will be made, however, to indicate his supreme importance in the field of mental measurements and individual differences.

Young (48) has quite properly said that "the contribution of Alfred Binet stands supreme for its general originality and the fact that he synthesized the growing movement into his now well-known scale." Binet and his collaborators objected to the types of psychological testing which followed Galton's work, on the ground that they were too simple in nature and would contribute little to the understanding of differences in the complex and higher mental processes; for it is in these higher processes that individual differences are most marked, and it is these which distinguish individuals most significantly and characteristically in daily activity; whereas it is in the simpler sensory and motor processes that persons differ least. Binet was quite ready to admit that the simpler processes lent themselves to more precise measurement and, therefore, yielded more nearly constant results. Yet his interests were strongest in individuals rather than in the study of sensations or ideas. Thus he was ready to sacrifice the greater quantitative precision of sensory-motor tests in order to obtain a more nearly accurate study of the integrated mentality of the individual. He argued that in the measurement of the higher functions, the greatest precision, though desirable, was not as essential as in measuring the simpler functions, because of the very fact that individual differences are more marked in the former. Binet made it clear, however, that his proposed scale would not measure in a physical sense, in the same way, for example, that a line is measured. It would, however, yield "a classification, a hierarchy among diverse intelligences; and for the necessities of practice this classification is equivalent to a measure" (2, p. 40). He and his collaborators were interested, consequently, in

establishing the extent and nature of variations of the mental processes
from one individual to another, and in the determination of the interrelations of the various processes *within* the individual. Binet and Henri
(a collaborator) proposed, therefore, to study the following functions:
memory, the nature of mental images, imagination, attention, comprehension, suggestibility, esthetic feeling or appreciation, moral sentiments,
muscular strength and strength of will, motor skill, and visual judgment.
These are, they believed, "faculties" which differ much from one individual to another and are such that knowledge of their state for an
individual gives us a general idea of this person and permits us to distinguish him from other individuals within the same milieu. Here we
have the beginnings of the tests which a few years later proved so useful
in the construction of Binet's scales.

The range and number of publications coming from Binet and his collaborators were remarkable (45). They—especially Binet—interested
themselves in and investigated an unusual variety of problems relevant to
individual psychology including such matters as handwriting, head
measurements, physical growth, physiognomy, and palmistry. Yet his
abiding interest was in the problems of measuring intelligence and in differentiating between the mental level of one person and another.

The Binet-Simon Scale.   In 1904 a practical situation arose in
which Binet had an opportunity to apply his principles with regard to
the differentiating of individuals and to make a great contribution to the
study of individual differences in mental ability. The French Minister of
Public Instruction appointed a commission to recommend means of edu-
cating subnormal children in the schools of Paris because these children
were unable to profit from regular instruction. The plan, therefore, was
to eliminate subnormal children from ordinary schools and to give them
instruction in a special school. Admission was to be determined by a
medical and a psychological examination. Obviously, the first device
needed was an objective means of selecting those of subnormal mentality.
Subjective opinions were worse than useless; for not only was there disagreement among different "experts," but serious injustices might result
in some cases. It was to meet this problem that the first intelligence scale
was constructed. This first one is known as the 1905 Binet-Simon scale
(4, 5). In it we find the fundamental concept underlying all tests that
measure the mentality of children. This principle is that we may identify
differences in mental development—in degree of brightness or dullness—
with differences in the levels of development as represented by the average capacities of children of various ages.

In the construction of their first scale, Binet and Simon limited themselves to the definite and practical problem of creating a device with

which school children's intellectual abilities might be measured, and with which the normal might be distinguished from the subnormal. They devoted their efforts to the evaluation and the quantitative determination of "general intelligence," that is, intellectual level, and to comparisons with normal children. They recognized that the determination of *special aptitudes* was a matter for later investigation. In fact, that very problem has been studied rather intensively within more recent years.[4]

Binet's first scale (1905), which he himself tested in Paris, was also tried out by other psychologists in Europe. As a result of these trials and consequent suggestions and criticisms, a second and considerably revised scale was constructed and appeared in 1908. Again, other psychologists collaborated by using this new scale in their own countries: Decroly and Degand in Belgium, Goddard in the United States, Bobertag in Germany, and Ferrari in Italy. Binet took account of their findings and criticisms. As a result of these and his own investigations, he published another revised scale in 1911. This was Binet's final contribution to the field of mental testing, for he died the same year.[5]

Binet, the synthesizer and the originator, provided the original major impetus to the study of individual differences by means of standardized tests. Since 1911, revisions and adaptations of his scale have been made in a number of countries. Most later developments have been expansions, modifications, and improved standardizations of the 1911 scale. Understandably, the principal interest for some years following Binet was in the identification and classification of mentally defective individuals.

Developments in the United States

Early Experiments. One of the most important of the early American psychologists in the study of individual differences was James McKean Cattell (1860–1944), a man much younger than Galton, but still his contemporary. "It was Cattell," says Professor R. L. Thorndike, "[who] . . . was perhaps the first rebel from within the ranks of psychologists . . . to set his face against the narrowness of the Wundtian School where . . . individual diversities were hidden in averages, or even discarded as erroneous. . . . Cattell was bold enough to declare, in reference to reaction times, that . . . 'The individual difference is a matter of special interest.' Wundt opposed any study of individual differences in themselves" (48, p. 32).

The term "mental tests" was first employed by Cattell in a publication

---

[4] Binet and Simon excluded from consideration those persons who had suffered mental disorganization; that is, the dements.
[5] Binet's scales are examined in some detail in Chapter 8.

of 1890 in which he described tests then being used in his laboratory in
the University of Pennsylvania (11). Cattell's tests were of memory, imagery, keenness of eyesight and of hearing, afterimages, color vision, color
preferences, perception of pitch and of weight, perception of time intervals, sensitivity to pain, rate of perception and of movement, accuracy of
hand movement, and reaction time.

The last of these was the most important of his early contributions to
differential psychology; for much of the subsequent interest in reaction-
time experiments is attributable to Cattell's work (20). One of the most
direct methods with which certain of the simpler mental processes,
such as discrimination and choice, can be studied is the precise measurement of the time an individual requires to respond to a given stimulus
or to perform a specified act, usually a very simple one. Although many
experiments on reaction time followed those of Cattell, and although
these have added considerable information about speed of response to
some types of stimuli, they have not made significant contributions to
our understanding of higher, complex mental processes; for reaction time,
it has been found, has little or no value in estimating intellectual abilities.

The time factor in itself is a relatively minor aspect of most mental
tests, except in those devised specifically to measure speed of performance,
usually in a restricted type of activity for a specified purpose. A good example is the rate at which one can discern likenesses and differences between two sets of digits or letters of the alphabet—a form of clerical test.
However, Cattell justified his tests of sensory discrimination, motor activity, and simple reactions on the ground that his purpose at that time
was principally anthropometric; therefore, measurement of the senses
properly belonged within the scope of his research (12). He and his
collaborators realized that the more complex mental processes should be
measured; but they were also aware of the fact that much research and
analysis had yet to be done before adequate mental tests could be devised
for the measurement of these processes.

Other investigators in this country and abroad were experimenting
with psychological tests, following very much the same paths at those of
Galton and Cattell. Jastrow tried out tests of touch and cutaneous sensitivity, and tests of vision, memory, and reaction time (25). Gilbert used
measures of height, weight, and lung capacity; also tests of sensation,
rapidity of tapping, reaction time, memory, and suggestibility. Against
these he compared teachers' ratings of their pupils' mental abilities (22).

The importance of studying individual differences by objective scientific methods and through comprehensive research was emphasized as
early as 1895 when the American Psychological Association appointed a
committee of which Cattell was a member ". . . to consider the feasibility

of cooperation among the various psychological laboratories in the collection of mental and physical statistics" (12). Also, in 1896 the American Association for the Advancement of Science appointed a committee ". . . to organize an ethnographic survey of the white races in the United States" (12). Cattell, who was also a member of this committee, stressed the importance of including psychological tests in the survey and of cooperating with the committee of the Psychological Association.

The development of testing had assumed importance to educators at an early date. In 1899, President Harper of the University of Chicago ". . . recommended that a special study be made of the college student's character, intellectual capacity, and tastes by the questionnaire method" (10). Further, in 1909, a committee of the National Education Association presented a report regarding psychological tests for mentally deficient children (8). From the report, it appears that the tests were looked upon as applicable chiefly to the subnormal and to other exceptional children.

Revisions of the Binet. The great development in testing and studying individual differences in the United States occurred after Binet's work was made known. Goddard was the first to revise the Binet scales for use in this country. In 1911, he published his standardization of Binet's 1908 revision, with which he had been acquainted since 1909 (23). At that time, he was director of the laboratory of psychology at the Vineland (New Jersey) Training School for Feeble-minded Children. Thus, as in France under the guidance of Binet, the scale in this country was first used almost entirely for the study and selection of mentally deficient individuals. The Binet was made a part of the routine procedure at Vineland, and it was rapidly adopted for use by psychologists in other institutions.

Goddard and Kuhlmann, who in 1911 published a revision of Binet's 1908 scale, made the test known and were largely responsible for its early spread among clinical psychologists (30). Lewis M. Terman, who had already interested himself in psychological differences among individuals, brought the scale before the schools of the country. In 1912, he published a tentative revision of the Binet; in 1915, he completed this revision with collaborators. In 1916, he published *The Measurement of Intelligence,* which presented the scale in its revised form, its standardization and directions for administering and scoring, as well as brief explanations of the psychological justification for each part (41).

In 1937, a revised and much improved edition in two forms was published in collaboration with Maude E. Merrill (42). Inevitably, of course, another revision of the scale had to be prepared. This last edition appeared in 1960, again under the coauthorship of Terman and Merrill, although Terman had died in December, 1956 (43). The 1916 and 1937

editions have been widely used in clinics, schools, and other agencies; and
the 1960 edition, it is reasonable to assume, will also enjoy widespread
currency.

Group Tests.   Shortly after 1916, the most significant occurrence in psychological testing was the development of group tests. The
Binet and its several revisions are administered to each person singly, the
length of time required varying with the age, brightness, and responsiveness of the individual being tested. As a result, it is costly in time and
money to test large numbers of persons one by one, and in some instances
it is impossible to do so. Therefore, if many people are to be tested at
once, as is the case in the schools and the armed forces, a group test will
have distinct advantages if it yields sufficiently accurate and dependable
results.

Psychologists had already begun to study, by group tests, some of the
mental processes required in school work. So it was not a very long or
entirely new step to try devising a single scale in which a variety of items,
testing several mental processes, would be combined. This tendency in
group testing received its greatest impetus in 1917 with the entrance of
the United States into World War I. At that time the government agreed
with the views of a group of psychologists that it would be desirable to
examine the newly drafted men to determine their general mental capacity and vocational fitness by means of the best available psychological
methods. The need was a pressing one, and a group-testing method was
imperative. This army problem enlisted the interests and cooperation of
many psychologists, some of whom had already made contributions to the
field of measurements, and some of whom were already experimenting
with group methods. Pooling their efforts and resources, they emerged
with the well-known army tests, Alpha and Beta, the former being verbal
in content and the latter nonverbal.

With their army data, these psychologists opened up numerous fields
in which group tests might be used, and at the same time gave rise to a
number of controversial questions. Among these were the relative influence of heredity and environment, racial and national differences, occupational and regional differences, and the age at which maximum mental capacity is reached.

In the ensuing years, a large volume of research on these and other
problems was published. For present purposes, it is sufficient to note that
this use of tests in the army and the results achieved demonstrated the
possible values of group scales and supplied the impetus for their use in
other areas, especially in the schools (7, 32).

There are today a large number of group tests designed for use at educational levels from kindergarten to university. Of these, some are highly

reliable (see Chapter 4) and have reasonably good validity (see Chapter 5), whereas others do not withstand scrutiny and evaluation.

Performance Tests. Not long after the introduction of the Stanford-Binet scale, its emphasis upon language was criticized by some psychologists and educators. It was maintained that this scale, valuable though it is, needed to be supplemented by tests which do not require ability to deal with words, numbers, and abstract concepts. Accordingly, "performance tests" were developed to meet this criticism and to provide means of testing individuals with language handicaps, as well as the deaf, the blind, and others for whom an adequate rating could not be obtained with tests that depended largely on language, numbers, and abstractions.

A performance test provides a perceptual situation in which the subject manipulates items such as form boards, blocks, pictures, and disassembled objects instead of reasoning with symbols. Some psychologists apply the term also to "pencil-and-paper" tests that utilize nonverbal materials such as printed geometric forms, pictorial representations, printed cubes, substituting digits for symbols, and the like. It seems preferable, however, to designate these simply as "nonverbal" tests because they do not involve actual manipulation of objects as do performance tests. Both types of test materials, performance and nonverbal pencil-and paper, are now used extensively. Some scales, such as the Arthur and the Pintner-Paterson, are built entirely of performance materials; other scales combine one or both with verbal materials.

Aptitude Tests. Another type of instrument, the development of which received impetus in World War I, is the aptitude test. Each of these, unlike tests of general ability, is intended to measure an individual's ability to perform a task of a limited or specific kind, for example, clerical, mechanical, or musical aptitudes. Interest in and development of aptitude testing may be ascribed to several causes: the army's need, during World War I, to select men for tasks requiring specific skills; the desire, in vocational guidance and personnel assignment, to find the right person for a specific job; the opposition of some educators and psychologists to what they called the "super-faculty" of general intelligence; and the belief of some of them that only specific aptitudes, such as mechanical and clerical, could be satisfactorily measured.[6] As a matter

---

[6] Some psychologists prefer to avoid the use of the term "intelligence," and to speak, instead, of "general aptitude," "general ability," "scholastic aptitude," and the like. We shall continue to use the term "intelligence" because: (1) it has a long and respectable history in psychology; (2) many of the most important tests with which we shall be concerned are called tests of intelligence; (3) we shall have to deal with what psychologists have long called theories and definitions of intelligence; and (4) because there seems to be no merit in substituting the term "general ability" or "general aptitude" for "general intelligence." Furthermore, even those who would reject the term "intelligence" must and do use the concept of "intelligence quotient."

of fact, tests of general intelligence and those of specific aptitudes do not and need not stand opposed; they are supplemental.

Aptitude tests have been developed to predict educability and performance in music and drawing, in mechanical and clerical occupations, in engineering, in medicine and law, and in other areas as well. Others in this category are intended to evaluate aptitudes for the study of specific types of subject matter, such as science, foreign languages, and mathematics.

Occupational Interest Inventories. To supplement tests of aptitude and those of intelligence, several self-answering occupational preference questionnaires, or inventories, have been devised to provide information regarding an individual's interests in a variety of activities; for these, it has been found to have some relevance to and predictive value for certain broad vocational areas or for certain specific occupations.

Tests of Educational Achievement. Closely associated with the testing of aptitudes is the measurement of educational achievement and the construction of objective measures for that purpose. These are not designed primarily for prediction; instead, they are intended to measure the individual's actual learning in educational subject matter after a period of instruction. They have proved to be highly valuable in the determination of individual difficulties in learning, in the discovery of strong scholastic interests, in the discovery of special abilities or disabilities, and, in combination with other factors, in plotting the educational career of the individual child.

Educational achievement tests have other values as well: they provide objective measures of progress, as opposed to teachers' ratings that may be too subjective; they permit intergroup comparisons based on a reasonably objective determination; and they facilitate experimental evaluation of varied teaching methods.

Test Batteries. During World War II many test "batteries" [7] were constructed. Those that made use of specific aptitudes and subject-matter knowledge—especially the former—were most important. Batteries were devised for the selection and training of personnel in a great variety of assignments in the several branches of the armed forces: radio and radar operators, pilots, navigators, gunners, flight engineers, and other specialties (1). The development of these batteries in the armed forces stimulated research on and use of similar tests for the selection and training of personnel in civilian occupations.

Multifactor Tests. These, also called "differential aptitude tests," are relatively recent developments in psychological measurement and evaluation. Interest in them has increased markedly since about 1945,

---

[7] A "battery" of tests is a group of tests used in combination for a specified purpose.

although research on the subject began as early as the 1920's, when T. L. Kelley (28) and, later, L. L. Thurstone (44), published their work on *factorial analysis* of human abilities.[8] Factorial analysis provided the statistical tools for the development of multifactor tests, which isolate and measure relatively "pure" mental operations (factors) or "constellations" of closely related factors, rather than general intelligence or general ability. In other words *multifactor tests isolate the elements that constitute mental operations*. The psychological principle upon which these instruments are based is the theory that the factors, or elements, are relatively independent of one another; hence, it was concluded that they should be measured independently.

Multifactor scales were expected to be especially valuable in educational and vocational counseling because they consist of separate tests of numerical operations, space relations, form perception, name perception, verbal reasoning, rote memory associations, and others restricted in complexity and range of mental operations. Each factor, or test, is thought to have special educational and vocational relevance and predictive value in itself; and a combination of factors is thought to have predictive value for specific areas of learning or occupations. The use of multifactor scales, therefore, would yield a "profile"[9] of scores for each of the several factors or "constellation" of factors, rather than a general, over-all rating for the entire scale, such as those derived from the Stanford-Binet, the Wechsler, and numerous group tests. All of these will be described and evaluated in subsequent chapters.

Personality Tests

Efforts to evaluate and test nonintellectual traits of personality were apparent in the nineteenth century beginning with Galton in 1879 (17) and followed by Pearson (35), who devised questionnaires and rating scales. During the last decade of that century and the first of the twentieth, word-association tests were tried out by Jung of Switzerland (26, 27) and Kent and Rosanoff in the United States (29) in an effort to expose some of the "deeper" personality traits and, if possible, to assist in differentiating among the various mental disorders. Although word-association tests are still used today in psychological clinics and elsewhere in diagnosing personality traits, they are much less frequently employed than inventories and projective techniques.

[8] Spearman preceded both Kelley and Thurstone in making statistical analyses of human abilities; but he is not associated with the multifactor test movement.

[9] A psychological "profile" is a chart representing an individual's score or relative position in each of several types of performance, with separate scores made comparable by statistical treatment.

With widespread use of individual tests of intelligence in schools, clinics, and hospitals, it became increasingly clear that in some cases an individual's performance on a test, his successes and failures, and the content and quality of his responses, were not only evidence of intellectual functioning, but were also affected, in greater or lesser degree, by non-intellectual traits of personality. The recognition of this fact, in addition to the growing interest in the scientific and clinical study of personality per se, provided the stimulus for the development of the several varieties of personality tests. Personnel problems during World War I provided impetus for their growth as well.

Today the tests are used extensively for the analysis of desirable and undesirable traits in a wide range of civilian and military occupations. In addition, psychologists employ personality tests in studies of differences between subgroups within the same general society and of differences between various cultural, national, and racial groups.

The large current crop of personality tests now available varies in quality from those that are poorly conceived, inadequately validated, and therefore useless, to those having considerable value in the hands of competent psychologists.[10]

Rating Scales. The earliest device employed, the rating scale, is a means of obtaining the judgments of a number of respondents with reference to a limited number of traits of a given individual. They were tried out and used during World War I, well before they were formalized and scaled both by statistical methods and by psychological analysis of personality and behavior traits relevant to specified situations.

Self-Rating Inventories. The first self-report, questionnaire type of personality inventory is the Personal Data Sheet, devised by R. S. Woodworth for use in World War I and published in 1919. Employed with moderate success, its purpose was to identify men who would prove to be poor prospects for military service because of undesirable personality and behavioral characteristics. This questionnaire consists of a list of items in the form of questions about himself, to be answered by the individual. The aim of the questionnaire is to detect personality and behavioral symptoms that are regarded as indicative of maladjustment. The questions on the Data Sheet took the place of an individual interview. Men whose responses indicated a sufficient number of undesirable symptoms were later interviewed individually. The types of questions asked and the aspects of personality sampled were forerunners of many of those included, with very little modification, in subsequent inventories.

---

[10] Cf. O. K. Buros (9). In this volume, 145 personality tests of all types are critically reviewed.

Since the appearance of the Woodworth Personal Data Sheet, dozens of personality inventories, representing several different types, have been published. In general, the emphasis of the items—questions or statements—in these instruments is on what the individual respondent actually does in various kinds of situations and on how he feels about what he does in these situations. Relatively few of these inventories, however, have survived scientific analysis and practical use. Until the early 1930's these were, however, the principal instruments used to evaluate personality traits in a systematic and scientific, or quasi-scientific, manner (40).

Projective Tests. In the early 1930's a newer type of instrument became prominent in American psychology: the projective test of personality. This instrument is much more subtle than the self-rating inventory; it presents more or less equivocal, undefined ("unstructured") stimulus situations, usually in the form of pictures, inkblots, or incomplete sentences. Thus, the person being tested has a greater opportunity to impose upon the test his own private and particular personality traits than would be exposed by means of the questionnaire type of inventory.

The best known of the projectives is the Rorschach Inkblot Test, first published in Switzerland in 1921, although not introduced into the United States until the early 1930's. Rorschach, a Swiss psychiatrist, began his experimentation with inkblots as a means of stimulating and testing imagination. In the course of his work (1911–21), he perceived the possibilities inherent in the inkblot test as a device for differentiating among various kinds and traits of personalities. Although Rorschach's work on inkblots was the most extensive of any up to that time, he was not the first investigator to discern the possibilities of inkblots in psychological experimentation. As a matter of fact, these had been used for some years in psychological laboratories to study fertility of imagination and of invention [11] (46, part II). Since the introduction of what has come to be known as "the Rorschach," it has been extensively used in private psychological practice, in clinics, and in hospitals for diagnostic purposes; in business and industry for some types of personnel selection; in researches in cultural anthropology; and in researches on personality theory. Interest in and use of the Rorschach can be inferred from the huge number of professional publications on the subject, which did not begin to appear in appreciable numbers until about 1935.[12]

Another projective instrument of major importance is the Thematic Apperception Test, introduced by H. A. Murray and C. D. Morgan in

[11] Among those who early suggested the use of inkblots were Binet and Henri, in 1895.
[12] In O. K. Buros (9), 2297 publications are listed.

1935. This test consists of thirty rather ambiguous pictures, each on a separate card, and one blank card. The person being examined is asked to make up a story of his own for each picture. The psychological principle involved is that in his stories the examinee will, probably unwittingly, give expression to his needs, values, attitudes, and feelings about persons, situations, and the world around him, as well as to the pressures he is experiencing from sources outside of himself. This instrument, too, has been and is being widely used in a variety of psychological settings. While the number of publications on the TAT, as it is professionally known, is not so great as that on the Rorschach, it has, nevertheless, been the subject of many studies and researches.[13]

Since the appearance of the Rorschach and the TAT, a variety of other projective devices and techniques have been made available. Some of these are special adaptations of the two foregoing tests; others offer rather different approaches for the same general purpose, that is, to elicit responses which will reveal aspects and traits of personality that inventories and rating scales are incapable of eliciting. Since 1945 and to the present time, projective tests have occupied a position of primary importance in practical applications and in research.

The types of techniques for obtaining evaluations of aspects of personality thus far mentioned do not exhaust the list. Among other and more tenuous kinds of procedures used are storytelling and story completion, drawing and painting, and "situational tests," in which an individual's behavior is observed and rated in a setting that simulates reality (34). Contrived play activities, usually of one child who is being observed, are used for two purposes: to permit the child to project some of his inner traits and to serve as a form of psychotherapy. Sociometric methods, whereby an individual's social currency or acceptability is obtained from ratings made by his peers, is an adaptation and extension of the older rating scale (33).

Although all of these procedures are used in their appropriate settings, they are much less commonly employed in personality evaluations than are self-rating inventories, the Rorschach, and the TAT, because, being tenuous, they are not susceptible to standardization and objectification. To be sure, personality inventories and the more widely used projective tests present their own problems in standardization. However, progress has been and continues to be made with these and their development has proceeded far enough to provide sufficient common ground and research information, so that in the hands of qualified psychologists they are of value.

[13] In O. K. Buros, *op. cit.*, 610 publications are reported.

The Present Situation

Psychological tests of intelligence, whether based upon the theory of "general ability" or upon one of relatively independent factors (or aptitudes), and tests of specific aptitudes and skills are now at a reasonably advanced stage of development. This is so because they have been in the process of evolution and improvement for many years, a tremendous amount of research has been devoted to them by numerous psychologists, and they have been used in a variety of practical situations where their validity could be evaluated. Another reason is the fact that determination of the mental functions, or operations to be tested, though not simple, has not been as difficult as the determination by testing of nonintellective traits of personality.

Because "personality" is so all-inclusive a concept, and because its manifestations are often complex and covert, development and use of self-rating inventories and projective tests are as yet not on so secure a foundation as tests of mental abilities, of specific aptitudes and skills, and of educational achievement. In subsequent chapters, we shall discuss the principles upon which all of these types of tests are based, as well as their values and their limitations.

The great variety of psychological tests in existence has already been mentioned. The numerous uses to which they are put and the important part they may have in the determination of an individual's educational, vocational, or general welfare have been indicated. It is essential, therefore, that anyone who employs these tests in a professional capacity should understand the basic psychological and statistical principles upon which they rest. It is necessary that everyone—teachers, psychiatrists, guidance counselors, personnel administrators—who interprets the results of test findings should be familiar with their essential theory as well as with the meanings of the technical terms.

Since the end of World War I, the use of psychological tests has continuously increased, because they are needed and because they have improved steadily. Education in the United States has become more nearly universal; individuals of inferior and those of seriously deficient mental abilities are being retained in public schools much longer than was the case in earlier years. Thus, the range of intelligence found in schools extends from the very low to the highest levels, making it essential that each individual's educational potential and promise be known as accurately as available psychological means permit. The general increase in years of schooling, not to speak of the tremendous growth in numbers of students, has extended to college and university, so that the importance of knowledge of individual variations in mental ability at higher educational levels has also grown.

Educational and vocational guidance, at all levels, have consequently assumed increasing significance. With the availability of standardized tests, even with their defects, guidance has been placed upon a more objective basis, instead of remaining a matter of subjective, perhaps even casual, advice.

For many years schools and, now more recently, colleges and universities have been concerned with the learning difficulties of individuals. Are these difficulties due to inferior general intelligence? Or are they due to specific disabilities, as in reading or spelling? Or to defective perception of spatial relations? Or perhaps to defects of the visual-motor function? Is an individual's lack of aptitude in shopwork attributable to inferior manual dexterity? Is the individual's learning impaired or retarded by poor ability for recall of rote or meaningful materials although his level of general ability might otherwise be adequate for learning? Answers to these and other important educational problems have been provided or at least facilitated by the use of psychological tests.[14]

The types and numbers of occupations have multiplied, and specializations within the types themselves have increased. It is unnecessary to detail the vocational changes and developments that have taken place with technological and scientific developments, but it does seem necessary to point out that for purposes of psychological testing and vocational guidance, occupations designated by the same name are not necessarily identical in regard to skills, knowledge, specialized functions, and interests involved. For example, there are various factors that combine in different ways to create not a single, unitary aptitude called "mechanical"; but, rather, there are several different aspects of mechanical aptitude, although all have something in common. "Engineering aptitude" is not a single, unitary function either. There are differences in requirements for learning and achieving proficiency in civil, mechanical, electrical, and chemical engineering, although, of course, their requirements are not mutually exclusive. Nor is "clerical aptitude" a single, unitary function. The fact that each of these general areas of training and employment is complex and divisible gives increased significance to psychological testing and insightful guidance.

Tests of personality are being used in some business and industrial organizations in the selection of management personnel, whereas in certain professions, tests are utilized in selecting individuals to be educated for

[14] We are assuming throughout, of course, that tests are administered and interpreted by qualified professional persons. More will be said on this matter in subsequent chapters.

practice in them. These professions include medicine, in which there have been researches on desirable personality traits of medical students. Some engineering schools would like to identify those nonintellectual traits that distinguish the successful from the unsuccessful students of the profession. Psychologists are desirous of determining personality characteristics of the more promising students of clinical psychology. Some religious denominations require that candidates for admission to their theological schools take tests of nonintellectual personality traits as well as of mental ability.

Finally, there is the whole area of "mental health," to which so much attention has been given since the termination of World War II. Schools and colleges are concerned over individuals who present more than ordinary degrees of personality difficulties or of problems of behavior. Numerous bureaus of child guidance have been established within school systems; there are mental health clinics in many sections of the country; federal hospitals (for example, of the Veterans' Administration) have psychological divisions, as do many state and some private hospitals. In all of these settings, psychological testing of all types, especially involving nonintellectual personality traits, is one of the established practices. And it is not uncommon for private welfare agencies to have on their staffs psychologists whose work consists of psychological diagnosis by means of tests, or of the practice of psychotherapy, which is often based upon or facilitated by diagnostic testing, or of both. Also, many psychologists in private practice make diagnostic testing a significant or a major part of their work.

This brief account of the current role and extent of psychological testing should be sufficient to emphasize the development of this branch of psychology since its relatively modest beginnings, shortly after the turn of the twentieth century, when the principal purpose of testing was the identification and special schooling of mentally deficient children.

References

1. *Aviation Psychology Program in the Army Air Forces.* Reports numbers 1–19. Washington, D.C.: U.S. Government Printing Office, 1947–48.
2. Binet, A. *The Development of Intelligence in Children* (translated by E. S. Kite). Vineland, N.J.: Training School, 1916.
3. Binet, A., and V. Henri. La psychologie individuelle. *L'Année Psychologique,* 1896, *2,* 411–465.
4. Binet, A., and T. Simon. Sur la necéssité d'établir un diagnostic scientifique des états inférieurs de l'intelligence. *L'Année Psychologique,* 1905, *11,* 163–190.

5. Binet, A., and T. Simon. Methodes nouvelles pour le diagnostic du niveau intellectuel des anormaux. *L'Année Psychologique*, 1905, *11*, 191–244.

6. Boring, E. G. *History of Experimental Psychology* (2nd ed.). New York: Appleton-Century-Crofts, Inc., 1950.

7. Brigham, C. C. *A Study of American Intelligence*. Princeton: Princeton University Press, 1923.

8. Bruner, F. G., E. Barnes and W. F. Dearborn. Report of the committee on books and tests pertaining to the study of exceptional and mentally deficient children. *Proceedings of the National Education Association*, 1909, *7*, 901–914.

9. Buros, O. K. (ed.). *Fifth Mental Measurements Yearbook*. Highland Park, N.J.: The Gryphon Press, 1959.

10. Carothers, F. E. Psychological examinations of college students. *Archives of Psychology*, 1921, no. 46.

11. Cattell, J. McK. Mental tests and measurements. *Mind*, 1890, *15*, 373–381.

12. Cattell, J. McK., and L. Farrand. Physical and mental measurements of students of Columbia University. *Psychological Review*, 1896, *3*, 618–648.

13. Ebbinghaus, H. Über eine neue Methode zur Prüfung Geistiger Fähigkeiten und ihre Anwendung bei Schulkindern. *Zeitschrift für Psychologie*, 1897, *13*, 401–459.

14. Esquirol, J. E. D. *Des maladies mentales considérées sous les rapports médical, hygienique, et médico-legal*. Paris: J. B. Bailliere, 1838. 2 vols.

15. Galton, F. *Hereditary Genius*. London: Macmillan & Co., 1869.

16. Galton, F. *English Men of Science: Their Nature and Nurture*. London: Macmillan & Co., 1874.

17. Galton, F. Psychometric experiments. *Brain*, 1879, *2*, 149–162.

18. Galton, F. *Inquiries into Human Faculty and Its Development*. London: Macmillan & Co., 1883.

19. Galton, F. *Natural Inheritance*. London: Macmillan & Co., 1889.

20. Garrett, H. E. *Great Experiments in Psychology*. New York: Appleton-Century-Crofts, Inc., 1951.

21. Gilbert, J. A. Researches on the mental and physical development of children. *Studies from the Yale Psychological Laboratory*, 1894, *2*, 40–100.

22. Gilbert, J. A. Researches upon school children and college students. *University of Iowa Studies in Psychology*, 1897, *1*, 1–39.

23. Goddard, H. H. A revision of the Binet scale. Vineland, N.J.: *The Training School Bulletin*, 1911, *8*, 56–62.

24. Huey, E. B. The Binet Scale for measuring intelligence and retardation. *Journal of Educational Psychology*, 1910, *1*, 435–444.

25. Jastrow, J. Some anthropometric and psychologic tests on college students: A preliminary survey. *American Journal of Psychology*, 1891–1892, *4*, 420–428.

26. Jung, C. G. The association method. *American Journal of Psychology*, 1910, *21*, 219–269.

27. Jung, C. G. *Studies in Word Association* (translated by M. D. Eder). London: William Heinemann, Ltd., 1918.

28. Kelley, T. L. *Crossroads in the Mind of Man*. Stanford, Calif.: Stanford University Press, 1928.

29. Kent, G. H., and A. J. Rosanoff. A study of association in insanity. *American Journal of Insanity*, 1910, *67*, 37–96, 317–390.

30. Kohs, S. C. Annotated bibliography of the Binet-Simon scale. *Journal of Educational Psychology*, 1914, *5*, 215–224, 279–290, 335–346.

31. Murphy, G. *An Historical Introduction to Modern Psychology*. New York: Harcourt, Brace & World, Inc., 1929.

32. National Academy of Sciences. *Memoirs*. Washington, D.C.: U.S. Government Printing Office, 1921, *15*.

33. Northway, M. L. A method for depicting social relationships by sociometric testing. *Sociometry*, 1940, *3*, 144–150.

34. Office of the Strategic Services Staff. *Assessment of Men*. New York: Holt, Rinehart and Winston, Inc., 1948.

35. Pearson, K. On the laws of inheritance in man. *Biometrika*, 1904, *3*, 131–190.

36. Peterson, J. *Early Conceptions and Tests of Intelligence*. New York: Harcourt, Brace & World, Inc., 1926.

37. Seguin, E. *Idiocy: Its Treatment by the Physiological Method*. New York: Bureau of Publications, Teachers College, Columbia University, 1907.

38. Spearman, C. General intelligence objectively determined and measured. *American Journal of Psychology*, 1904, *15*, 201–292.

39. Stern, W. *Über Psychologie der individuellen Differenzen*. Leipzig: Barth, 1900.

40. Symonds, P. M. *Diagnosing Personality and Conduct*. New York: Appleton-Century-Crofts, Inc., 1931.

41. Terman, L. M. *The Measurement of Intelligence*. Boston: Houghton Mifflin Company, 1916.

42. Terman, L. M., and M. E. Merrill. *Measuring Intelligence*. Boston: Houghton Mifflin Company, 1937.

43. Terman, L. M., and M. E. Merrill. *Stanford-Binet Intelligence Scale*. Boston: Houghton Mifflin Company, 1960.

44. Thurstone, L. L. *The Vectors of the Mind*. Chicago: University of Chicago Press, 1935.

45. Varon, E. J. The development of Alfred Binet's psychology. *Psychological Monographs*, 1935, *46*, no. 3.

46. Whipple, G. M. *Manual of Mental and Physical Tests*. Baltimore: Warwick and York Incorporated; 1914, part I, Simpler Processes; 1915, part II, Complex Processes.

47. Yoakum, C. S., and R. M. Yerkes. *Army Mental Tests*. New York: Holt, Rinehart and Winston, Inc., 1920.

48. Young, K. The history of mental testing. *Pedagogical Seminary*, 1924, *31*, 1–48.

2.

ELEMENTARY STATISTICAL CONCEPTS

Construction of psychological and educational tests requires the use of statistical methods, as does a sound evaluation of the results obtained with these devices. Those who administer tests and those who evaluate the findings must, therefore, understand the meanings of the basic statistical concepts. It is the purpose of this chapter to present these concepts and their significance in the statistical treatment and interpretation of test results.[1]

Two Kinds of Statistics

Statistical methods and indexes are of two kinds: the *descriptive* and the *sampling*. The first are measures, or indexes, that show the principal characteristics of a set of data. When it is found, for example, that 65 percent of an entering college freshman class complete their course of study, this is a simple descriptive statistic for the group. When it is shown that of those individuals in the lowest decile group (lowest 10 percent) on a scholastic aptitude test only 40 percent complete the course of study, we have a somewhat more analytical, descriptive statistic. But it is desirable, in fact essential, to know the relationship between ranks on the

[1] Details of computational methods will not be presented, since the development of computational skills is not our purpose. For methods of computation, the student should consult any of the standard textbooks on statistics. Nor shall we be concerned with derivations of formulas.

test and achievement in college courses for the entire group. For this purpose, several different statistical methods are used, notably correlations. The coefficient of correlation, explained later in this chapter, is a much more complex statistic than is a percent; but it is still an index descriptive of the observed data for this one group.

These indexes do not *necessarily* hold for groups or individuals other than the ones actually studied. General predictions cannot be made from these data and their indexes; nor can they be applied to results that might be obtained from other groups, unless the statistical techniques of predicting from a sample are used. In that case, the characteristics of the groups *from* which, and *for* which, the predictions are being made must be considered. That is to say, not only are sampling errors calculated, but *comparability* of groups must be established.

Analysis of the *sampling error* of obtained data is the second type of statistical method. The purpose of determining sampling errors is to indicate the limits within which predictions can be made from one particular group to another and comparable group, or to predict from past to future performance of the one particular group. In other words, an answer is sought to this question: "How dependable are these obtained data for predictive purposes?" Analysis of sampling errors provides a statistical method of finding an answer.

Descriptive Statistics

The Normal Distribution Curve. This curve is of primary importance in the science of psychological measurement because it has been approximated so frequently by the scores of large unbiased samples of individuals on tests of intelligence, and on other psychological and educational tests as well. A generalized form of the normal curve is shown in Figure 2.1. The obvious properties of this curve (often called "bell-shaped") are that it has a single mode (high point), extends symmetrically

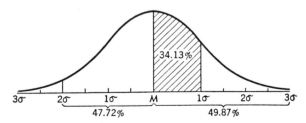

Fig. 2.1. Relationship between sigma distances and area included between ordinates in normal curve

in both directions (theoretically, without limit), and gradually approaches the base line as an asymptote. Interpreted in terms of frequency of cases, or of scores, this simply means that the scores are concentrated around the mid-point and gradually decrease in frequency as the distance from the center increases.

As will be seen in later chapters, normality of distribution is used as one criterion of the validity (see Chapter 5) of many tests of intelligence, a practice that emerged from early findings that the scores of such tests approximate the normal curve. What this curve signifies psychologically in respect to intelligence, for example, is that a large percentage of individuals are located at, or close to, the center of the distribution, and that farther up or down in the distribution, there are, respectively, fewer and fewer superior or inferior persons.

Skewed Distribution. If a set of scores or measures is distinctly asymmetrical—that is, when scores are relatively concentrated at one side or the other—there is a skewed distribution (Fig. 2.2). If such a curve were found for the scores of a representative group in the process of standardizing an intelligence test, it would indicate, depending upon the direction of skewness, that the test was too easy or too difficult for that group. In another instance, if a well-standardized test had been used, the skewed distribution might indicate that a selected group had been tested. The interpretation of a skewed distribution depends, therefore, (1) on the measure used and (2) on the group with whom it is used.

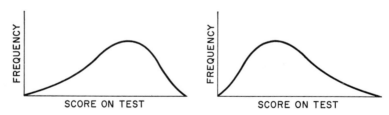

FIG. 2.2. Negatively skewed (left) and positively skewed distributions of test scores

The Frequency Distribution. The first step in ordering a set of data is to arrange them in a frequency distribution, that is, to put the scores into a systematic, condensed form that gives an over-all, comprehensible view of the entire set (Table 2.1). A frequency distribution is a table in which the total range of values is divided into class intervals of such a size as will make the table understandable, without distorting the over-all character of the data.[2] After the distribution table has been

---

[2] There are certain principles that are applied in plotting a frequency distribution. These are presented in textbooks on elementary statistics.

made, additional descriptive indexes, which will be discussed in this chapter, are calculated and a graph is plotted.

Tables 2.1 and 2.2 are illustrations, respectively, of an approximately symmetrical and an asymmetrical distribution. These tables are represented in Figures 2.3 and 2.4 (called frequency polygons).

TABLE 2.1

FREQUENCY DISTRIBUTION OF TEST SCORES

Scores	Frequencies
143–147	3
138–142	5
133–137	21
128–132	35
123–127	52
118–122	37
113–117	22
108–112	18
103–107	6
98–102	1
	$N = 200$

TABLE 2.2

A SKEWED FREQUENCY DISTRIBUTION

Scores	Frequencies
100–104	1
95–99	4
90–94	2
85–89	12
80–84	5
75–79	8
70–74	5
65–69	3
60–64	4
55–59	6
50–54	4
45–49	1
40–44	1
35–39	2
30–34	0
25–29	2
	$N = 60$

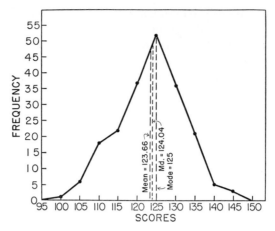

FIG. 2.3. Frequency distribution plotted from Table 2.1

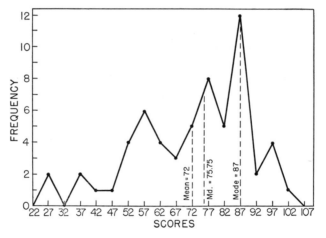

FIG. 2.4. Frequency distribution plotted from Table 2.2

THE MEAN. Two major types of indexes are calculated after the frequency table has been prepared: (1) the central tendencies—mean, median, and mode; and (2) the measures of variability, or dispersion, of the distribution. A measure of central tendency is a single value intended to represent one of the principal characteristics of the group studied. But any measure of central tendency (often referred to as an "average") has limited significance in itself, because it is derived from individual scores that may vary considerably. To say, for example, that the mean IQ (intelligence quotient) of a group of children is 115, tells us little about the characteristics of that group. It is essential, therefore, to accompany a mean or median by one or more measures of dispersion, discussed later in this chapter.

The *mean* is simply the total of all of the values in the distribution, divided by the frequencies (or number of cases).[3] The principal property of the mean is that every score, whether large or small, contributes its *proportionate* share to the result. At times this is a defect of the index, because a relatively small number of extreme scores will have an undue effect upon the mean, and thereby give a misleading impression of the group as a whole. The mean is particularly valuable, however, in deriving additional indexes, since it is rigorously defined mathematically and usually has the smallest sampling error.

THE MEDIAN. This is the middle value of the distribution, on each side of which fifty percent of the total number of values are located. Medians are of two kinds: counted and calculated. If the number of scores is not too large and if they have been arranged in order of increasing or decreasing size, finding the median is a simple matter of counting to find the central value.[4] If the number of cases is large, the median can be calculated from the frequency distribution. Counting from the top or bottom, we find the class interval in which the median case ($N/2$) falls. The exact value of this case is estimated by assuming that the scores within that class interval are evenly distributed. This method of estimating the median results in a relatively small error.

It is apparent that in deriving the median, every value, regardless of its size, is as important as any other value. It is, therefore, not affected by relative size or by extreme scores. This is its principal advantage, aside from the ease and simplicity of finding the counted median, and the relative ease of finding the calculated median. A secondary advantage is the fact that the meaning of the median is readily apparent.

THE MODE. This measure of central tendency simply indicates the most common value in a given distribution. In a frequency distribution, the mode is represented by the mid-point of the class interval having the greatest frequency. While a representative sample of a population is expected to yield only one mode in a set of measurements, it sometimes happens that a distribution of scores shows two modes (Fig. 2.5). Usually a bimodal curve is attributable to special characteristics of the group measured. Note that in Figure 2.5, the mean score is in, or close to, the center between the modes. In a normal, unimodal distribution, on the other hand, the mean *coincides* with the mode. In a curve that approximates the normal, the mean is close to the mode, as in Figure 2.3. The

---

[3] This is the kind of average taught generally in the fifth grade of elementary school.
[4] If the total number of cases is even, the two middle values are averaged.

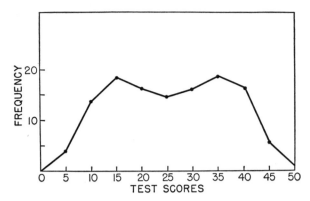

FIG. 2.5. A bimodal distribution

mode is of little value in psychological testing because it is not used in conjunction with other descriptive statistics.

COMPARISON OF MEAN, MEDIAN, AND MODE. The characteristics of the data and the purpose of the statistical analysis determine which one of these indexes will be used. Often, however, it is desirable to find two measures of central tendency as an indication of the effect produced by the distribution's skewness or other irregularity.[5]

The following two sets of scores illustrate conditions under which (1) mean and median are nearly identical and (2) they are markedly different. Consider the following nine IQs: 87, 88, 89, 90, 97, 98, 100, 110, 123. The mean is 98; the counted median is 97. Thus, it makes little difference whether one or the other is used to represent the group. By contrast, now consider the following values: 72, 73, 74, 75, 76, 77, 79, 81, 140. Here the mean is 83, whereas the median is 76. The mean in this instance is raised appreciably above the general run of scores. The median is, therefore, preferable as an index of central tendency. The mode, obviously, has no meaning in either instance. This illustration, of course, has been contrived; but it illustrates what can, and at times, does happen.

Measures of Variability or Dispersion. As already stated earlier in this chapter, an index of central tendency is insufficient as a description and characterization of a distribution of scores. Also, two sets of values for two groups of individuals might have the same, or nearly the same, means; but each set might have quite different dispersions of scores even so, one being much more variable than the other. It would, therefore, be a serious error to regard these two groups as com-

[5] A recent report states that the mean annual income of a "25-year class" of a large university is $50,000. The membership of that class includes a relatively small number of men who hold positions paying extraordinarily high salaries. These raise the mean to a level that is not representative of the class as a whole. The median would have been a preferable index.

parable. To assume, for example, that two groups of pupils are equivalent simply because both have mean IQs of 100 would be to overlook the possibility that one might have a range of 90–110, whereas the other's range might be 70–130. The educational and psychological characteristics of each group, as a whole, will differ significantly from those of the other. Figure 2.6 represents this situation.

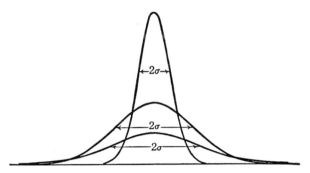

Fig. 2.6. Normal curves having identical means but different variabilities

RANGE.   This measure is the most obvious and readily observed index of variability. It is the difference between the lowest and the highest values in the set of scores. Although it is a useful index at times, its serious disadvantage is that it is determined by only the two extreme scores, even though most of the other scores in the distribution might be far removed from the extremes, for example, IQs of 50, 90, 95, 100, 103, 105, 106, 107, 110, 112, 140. If, on the other hand, the values varied continuously from 50–140, the range would be a more appropriate measure.

MEAN DEVIATION.   This index is derived by calculating the deviation of each score from the mean, without regard to plus or minus signs, and then finding the arithmetic mean of these deviations. All cases are thus taken into account. A small proportion of extreme scores will not appreciably distort the mean deviation; but it is subject to the same limitations as the mean value of the distribution. It can be a useful index, however, in two ways: (1) to compare two groups in regard to their variability (for example, does one fifth grade class vary more in arithmetical achievement than another?); (2) to find each individual's relative deviation from the mean of his group, through dividing each person's deviation by the mean deviation. In many situations, the mean deviation will suffice as an index of dispersion, particularly where no further statistical indexes are to be derived. It has the additional advantage of being easily calculated and readily understood.

STANDARD DEVIATION. This index of dispersion is the one most widely used because it is precisely determined mathematically, is a constant value of a normal curve, and is used in calculating other indexes, such as the coefficient of correlation, in transforming "raw scores" into "scaled," or weighted, scores (see p. 129), and in deriving the deviation intelligence quotient (see p. 133).

The standard deviation (SD) is computed by summing the *squared* deviation of each measure from the mean, dividing by the number of cases, and extracting the square root. The formula for the standard deviation will help to clarify the process of calculation:

$$SD = \sqrt{\frac{\Sigma(X - M)^2}{N}}$$

Σ is the symbol for summation; M represents the mean of the distribution; X represents each individual score; N represents the number of cases in the distribution.[6]

When the scores in a distribution are normally distributed,[7] the proportion of cases to be found within the SD ranges are as shown in Table 2.3 (see also Fig. 2.1).

TABLE 2.3

PROPORTION OF THE NORMAL DISTRIBUTION WITHIN GIVEN SD DISTANCES FROM THE MEAN *

Number of SDs	Percent of cases
1	68
1.5	87
2.0	95
2.5	99
3.0	99.7

* To the nearest whole number, excepting 3 SDs.

If an intelligence test, showing a normal or near-normal distribution, has a mean IQ and a standard deviation of 15, then 68 percent of the individuals tested have IQs between 85 and 115; 95 percent between 70 and 130; and 99.7 percent between 55 and 145. Only three cases in 1000 would be expected to fall outside the range of 55–145. It is apparent that the SD is valuable not only as an index that adds to the descrip-

[6] Squaring the deviations of each of the scores removes the plus and minus signs. It is obvious that if equal positive and negative deviations from the mean were added algebraically, the result would be zero; and there would be, apparently, no deviation.
[7] If the distribution is not entirely "normal," but is a satisfactory approximation, little error is introduced by using these same percentages.

tion of a group, but also that when it is translated into percentages it enables us to locate an individual relative to the whole group in terms of percentage of scores he surpasses in that group. Thus, the standard deviation ties in with percentile ratings, briefly defined later in this chapter, and more fully discussed in Chapter 6.[8]

QUARTILE DEVIATION. This index of variability, known also as the semi-interquartile range, is defined as half the spread of the middle 50 percent of the scores when these are arranged according to size or in a frequency distribution. It is found by using the following expression:

$$Q = \frac{Q_3 - Q_1}{2}$$

in which Q_3 is the point (or score) that is 75 percent up, and Q_1 is 25 percent up, from the bottom of the distribution. Thus, the highest and the lowest quarters are cut off, leaving the middle 50 percent. This simple device should be used only with the median (which can be represented by Q_2). While it has the advantages of being readily understood and not dependent on the type of distribution (normal, skewed, rectangular, etc.), it is not useful if statistical calculations are needed beyond it and the median. It is frequently employed, however, in representing various kinds of scores (intelligence test results, scores on educational achievement tests, school marks) for small groups.[9]

COMPARABILITY OF RATINGS. In addition to the several reasons already given for the use of measures of variability, there is still another very important one. Scores obtained on each of several different psychological or educational tests are not necessarily comparable. One test might have a maximum of 100, a mean of 75, and a standard deviation of 10; another a maximum of 200, a mean of 125, and an *SD* of 20. Obviously, identical scores on these two tests have different meanings.

For the most part, units of measurement in psychology and in education are not uniform throughout the scale, unlike units of physical measurement. Scores on psychological and educational tests, therefore, are more significant in terms of the *relative* rank they indicate than in terms of quantity.[10]

Measures of dispersion, especially the standard deviation, percentile and decile ranks, and other derived indexes, are essential in comparing an individual's scores on two or more tests. The obtained scores are translated into one of the derived indexes, so that an individual's *relative* performance on one may be compared with his performance on another.

[8] Standard scores, stanines, *T*-scores, and deviation intelligence quotients are indexes based upon the standard deviation. They are explained in Chapter 6.
[9] Percentile and decile ranks, which belong to the same "family" of indexes as quartiles, are explained in Chapter 6.
[10] This principle is further explained in Chapter 6.

Correlation

Meaning. It is frequently necessary to determine the degree of relationship that exists between sets of scores representing two or more traits or abilities, or between sets of scores obtained for other reasons. For this purpose, the statistical technique of correlation is used. As will be seen in Chapters 4 and 5, the use of this technique is basic in the determination of a test's soundness, represented in terms of reliability and validity.

For various scientific and practical reasons, educators and psychologists have wanted to know the extent of relationship between abilities in different school subjects (for example, arithmetic and reading comprehension), between ratings on a test of intelligence and course averages, between intelligence ratings of siblings, and between children's height and weight. Are high, mediocre, and low levels of ability in arithmetic associated with corresponding levels in reading comprehension or in other subjects of study? How well do intelligence-test ratings predict quality of performance in school work at any of the grade levels (particularly, now, at the college level)? Do siblings tend to be markedly similar in respect to intelligence level and other traits? How closely do the intelligence levels of children agree with those of their parents? For finding answers to these and many other questions, the correlational method has been universally employed, together with other types of statistical analysis.

Statistically, correlation is defined as the degree to which the paired scores of two (or more) sets of measures tend to vary together. The measure of the degree of concomitance is expressed as a *coefficient of correlation* that summarizes the relationship.

The Pearson product-moment coefficient, designated by the symbol r, is the one most frequently used and is the one meant, unless otherwise designated. This coefficient may be of any size from zero to $+1.00$ or to -1.00. The sign of the coefficient does not determine its significance; there are high, moderate, or low coefficients that are either positive or negative. Thus $+1.00$ indicates a perfect positive and -1.00 a perfect negative correlation. A coefficient of $+.20$ is low positive; one of $-.20$ is low negative. Complete lack of correspondence of the paired scores of the variables, that is independence of the traits or abilities being measured, is indicated by a zero coefficient. If, in general, scores in one variable tend to be associated with scores of the same, or approximately the same, relative size in the other variable, the measures will be positively correlated. If, on the other hand, there is, in general, an inverse relationship between the measured variables, the coefficient will be negative.[11] In the case of the Pearson coefficient, another requirement is that the relationship be linear.

TABLE 2.4

PAIRED SCORES CORRELATING .995

Student	Test score	Freshman average
A	192	93
B	183	82
C	181	80
D	178	79
E	176	75
F	174	75
G	173	74
H	170	69
I	165	64
J	158	59

Two simple tables of paired scores will illustrate different degrees of positive correlation. Note that in Table 2.4 the covariation of the paired scores is very close; in fact, they are almost identical, yielding a coefficient of .995. Figure 2.7, based on this table, shows the relationship graphically.

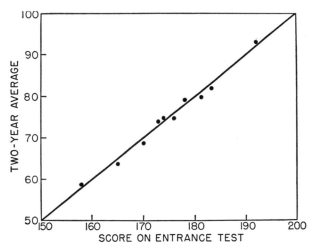

FIG. 2.7. Correlation chart. Each point represents an individual's position for test score and grades as listed in Table 2.4.

[11] The significance of correlation coefficients in estimating reliability and validity of tests is discussed in Chapters 4 and 5.

Each point, representing the position of one pair of scores, is on, or very nearly on, the diagonal line. If all points were located on the line, r would equal +1.00.

TABLE 2.5

PAIRED SCORES CORRELATING .65

Pupil	Test X	Test Y
A	89	38
B	86	40
C	83	46
D	82	28
E	79	40
F	76	34
G	75	30
H	74	36
I	72	28
J	63	24

By contrast, Table 2.5 and Figure 2.8 represent a correlation coefficient of .65. The difference between coefficients of .99 and .65 is graphically emphasized by comparing the locations of the points. In Figure 2.8 they are more widely scattered; there is much less agreement between the relative sizes of the scores in each pair.

The four charts in Figure 2.9 illustrate distributions of paired scores that would yield coefficients of four significantly different sizes: +1.00; .60; .40; and .00. The noteworthy characteristic of these charts is the extent to which the points (each representing one pair of scores) cluster about the diagonal or deviate from it. In chart *a*, all points are located in the squares (representing equivalent values of X and Y) through which the diagonal passes, thus indicating that each score X in any pair is of the same relative size as that other score Y in that pair. By contrast, as the coefficient decreases, the correspondence between the relative size of scores in a pair becomes less and less, until when $r = .00$ is reached, any score in one variable

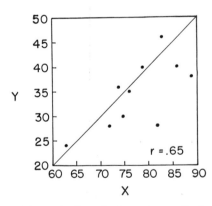

FIG. 2.8. Correlation chart. Each point represents an individual's position for test score and grades as listed in Table 2.5.

may occur with any score in the other. In this case, there is no demonstrable or necessary relationship between the two sets of measures of the traits or abilities tested.[12] Negative correlation coefficients of these same sizes would

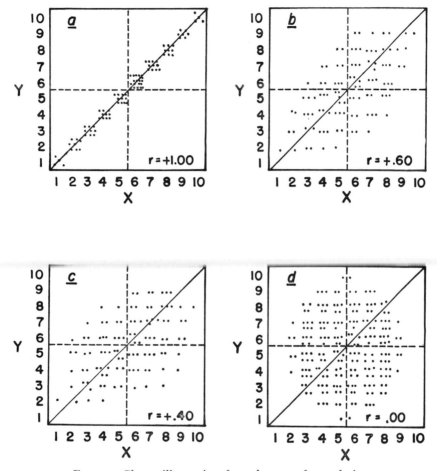

FIG. 2.9. Charts illustrating four degrees of correlation

be represented by trends along a line from the lower right to the upper left corner, thus indicating that scores above the mean in one variable

[12] This illustration was chosen so that the diagonal would correspond to an r of 1.00. The raw scores in each variable (X and Y) are divided by the standard deviation. The raw scores are thus reduced to comparable units; and the resulting standardized scores, as plotted, have the same standard deviation for each of the two variables. In instances where the scores have not been standardized, or where the means and variances of the two sets of scores are not equal, the points (representing paired X and Y scores) will fall on or along a line, but not necessarily a diagonal, if the scores are correlated.

tend, in varying degrees, to be associated with scores below the mean in the other.[13]

Error of Estimate. The fact that *r* varies from 0 to ±1.00 and looks like a percent has at times been erroneously interpreted to mean that it represents percentage of accuracy in making predictions, that is, the percentage of frequency with which paired scores are found to be correspondingly high, medium, or low (with steps between these three levels). That this interpretation is incorrect is readily apparent in the several figures illustrating correlations, all of which, except the +1.00 coefficient, show some "error" of estimate or prediction, since not all points of paired scores fall, in these instances, on the straight line. It may be said, however, that *r* is related, but not *proportional,* to the average amount of error made in predicting one set of measures from another.

A difference between an observed value and a predicted value is an "error of estimate." The standard deviation of these "errors" is known as the *standard error of estimate;* it is regarded as a measure of the accuracy of estimate. Generally speaking, the larger the *r,* the smaller the standard error of estimate. The equation for this index is:

$$SE_{(est)} = SD_y \sqrt{1 - r^2}$$

It is often more informative to know the standard error of estimate than it is to know the *r* alone. For example, in Table 2.5 the *SD* of test *Y* is 3.3. The correlation is +.65. When these values are substituted in the equation, the *SE* is 2.5. This is interpreted to mean that in this distribution two thirds of the "errors" will be within 2.5 (1 *SE*); 95 percent will be within 5.0 (2 *SE*); and 99 percent will be within 7.5 (3 *SE*).[14] Thus, the standard deviation of the distribution and its degree of correlation with the second variable determine the size of the error of estimate.

Although this statistical concept is not found in manuals of tests as often as are correlation coefficients, it occurs often enough to make it necessary that the student be familiar with its meaning.[15]

Sampling Statistics

Population Sampling. The statistical indexes discussed thus far describe the essential aspects of data obtained in a series of measure-

[13] The rank-difference correlation coefficient, designated by ρ (the Greek letter rho), is often used when the number of cases is small. Instead of indicating relative variability of paired scores, it indicates the extent to which the two scores of a pair agree as to relative rank. Partial and multiple correlations are explained in Chapter 5.

[14] This interpretation assumes that the errors of measurement are normally distributed and that the obtained scores for the two variables are also normally distributed.

[15] See also tables in Chapter 5 for further details on the predictive value of correlation coefficients of different sizes.

ments. These measures consist of a value for each individual in a selected group. The collected data are concerned only with this particular group; they do not necessarily bear directly on the problem of what the results might have been if other groups had been measured. This kind of statistical study is often valuable, indeed essential, in the study of a variety of educational and psychological problems when one is concerned only with a specific group. For example: What is the intelligence level of all children entering the first grade in a certain city in a particular year? What is the arithmetical ability of pupils finishing the sixth grade in the schools of this city? What is the correlation between their achievement-test scores in arithmetic and in reading comprehension?

For the general purposes of research, however, data are collected and analyzed in order to derive facts and principles that represent the general population being studied. The results obtained with any particular group, it is hoped, will approximate the results found for much larger representative groups. But data found for any specific group are regarded as an approximation to the facts, representative of the entire population, which (obviously) cannot be measured in its entirety in most types of problems.

The data obtained in any investigation represent a *sample* drawn from the total group that in statistical terms is called the *population* or the *universe*. A population may be a very broad, inclusive one, such as all children entering first grade in the United States in a given year. Or it may be narrowed down to any degree desired; for example, all entering first-grade children from families having incomes of $25,000 or more a year, living in cities of 1,000,000 or more inhabitants. The first requirement in undertaking a study involving the derivation of facts and principles applicable to a whole population is the selection of a representative sample of that population. There are two principal sampling methods: random (simple and unrestricted) and stratified (involving random sampling within specified groups).

RANDOM SAMPLING. This method is one whereby *each* member of the population under consideration has the same chance of being selected for study as any other. For example, it would require a most elaborate procedure to take a random sample of the whole population of the United States. Each name would have to be filed on a separate card; then the cards would have to be thoroughly and completely shuffled before the ones representing the sample were selected. If it could be assumed that the alphabetical listing of names was not related to the problem being studied, the procedure could be shortened by pulling every nth card from the filing case. Polling at street corners or using the classes of a selected school does not constitute random sampling. Whatever the method adopted, it is not random unless the definition of "random sampling" is satisfied.

The conditions of simple random sampling are not always fulfilled in psychological research because of difficulties inherent in dealing with large, diversified, and geographically scattered populations. When it is not feasible to obtain a satisfactory random sample, another method is available.

STRATIFIED SAMPLING.   This method is the commonly used alternative to simple random sampling and is superior to it. The total "population" to be studied is divided into a number of nonoverlapping categories which, if taken together, include all persons. Each characteristic selected in "stratification" should be relevant to the variable to be tested. This first step is followed by picking cases at random from *within each of the categories*. The number from each category is in the same proportion to the total number selected as that entire category is to the total population (the universe being studied). More specifically, this is called "proportionate stratified sampling" and is most frequently used in educational and psychological work. For example, if the economic status and educational levels of parents are related to the variable being studied, the stratified sample must include the correct proportions of children in the several economic levels, having correct proportions of parents at the different educational levels. The proportions would be determined by data in the national census. Within each subgroup, children would be drawn at random. To illustrate, all children in the communities selected for study whose parents are in the $4000-to-$5000 bracket and whose parents have both completed twelve years of schooling would have an equal chance of being included in the sample. The same principle holds for children in every subgroup designated as related to the variable. Note that *random sampling* is used *within* each subgroup.

Sampling Errors.   The basic problem in sampling statistics is to estimate the unknown values for the total population from the known values obtained with sample groups. If the total population has possibilities of a wide range of scores in the characteristic being measured, then a series of scores for group samples will fluctuate more than if the scores have possibilities of only a narrow spread. Also, if the number of individuals measured in a particular sampling is large, the probability is that its mean will be closer to the mean of the whole population than if the number is small. Stated otherwise, it is probable that there is some degree of error when means and other indexes are obtained from samplings; but the degree will depend, in part, upon the nature of the unit of measurement, the number of persons measured, and the adequacy with which these persons represent the total population.

An ideal situation is one in which the mean and the standard deviation in a particular set of measures are known for an entire specified population. The ideal, however, is never reached, except in instances where the population (or universe) is a restricted and relatively small one. For example, the range, mean, and standard deviation of annual incomes of all alumni of a given university who have been graduated 25 years or more. In lieu of the ideal condition, a number of different sample groups

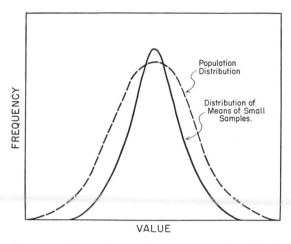

FIG. 2.10. Effect of sample size on sampling distribution of means

are measured. The *means* of these groups, will, theoretically, be distributed in the form of a normal curve. It is possible, then, to find the *mean of the means* and the *standard deviation of the means,* and thereby to estimate the probabilities that the mean for the whole population falls within one or more standard deviations in the distribution of the obtained means of the sample group. Figures 2.10 and 2.11 illustrate how *N*, the number of cases in the sample, affects the distribution of means; as the number in each group increases, the range of the means decreases; and, therefore, the precision of the estimated *population* mean is increased.

An explanation of the procedures used in estimating a total population's mean and *SD* from those obtained with a number of separate samples is not within the scope of this book. Nor is the converse of this: the estimation of whether the obtained mean and *SD* for a particular sample represent a random sample (within acceptable limits of error) or whether they represent a special group that differs in a systematic way from the total population. Details of these statistical techniques are avail-

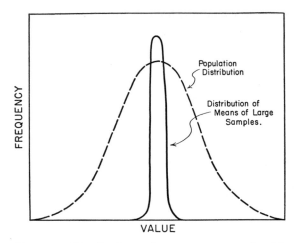

FIG. 2.11. Distribution of means compared with population distribution

able in textbooks on statistics. The purpose of this brief discussion is to call attention to sampling errors, which are important in the evaluation of the merits of psychological tests.

Sampling Errors of the Coefficient of Correlation. Since coefficients of correlation are based upon measurements of population samples, they, too, are subject to error. And, as in the case of means, the larger the sample, properly selected, the smaller is the error likely to be. The formula for the standard error of r follows.

$$\text{Standard error of } r = \frac{1 - r_p^2}{\sqrt{N - 1}}$$

N represents the number of cases in the sample; r_p represents the value of the coefficient for the entire population. Since that value is not actually known, statisticians have devised a neat method to obviate this difficulty. It is assumed that the *population coefficient* is zero but that the coefficients actually found for individual samples would not be exactly zero; instead, they would distribute themselves symmetrically on both sides of zero (positive and negative) and would take the form of a normal curve. Thus the mean of the distribution would be zero.

The coefficient for each group is substituted in the formula to find its standard error.[16] After calculating this index, the questions to be answered are these: Is the obtained coefficient, for this sample group, *significantly* different from zero? Does this coefficient represent only a

[16] The standard error is the standard deviation of the distribution of coefficients. Hence, it is interpreted in the same way as the *SD*.

ment, E. F. Lindquist (ed.). Washington, D.C.: American Council on Education, 1951, ch. 14.

3. McNemar, Q. *Psychological Statistics.* New York: John Wiley & Sons, Inc., 1949.

4. Walker, H. M. *Elementary Statistical Methods.* New York: Holt, Rinehart and Winston, Inc., 1943.

5. Walker, H. M., and J. Lev. *Statistical Inference.* New York: Holt, Rinehart and Winston, Inc., 1953.

6. Wesman, A. G. Better than chance. *Test Service Bulletin.* New York: The Psychological Corporation, 1953, no. 45.

3.

BASIC PRINCIPLES

Definition of Psychological Test

A dictionary definition of the verb "to test" states that it means the subjection to conditions that show the real character of a person or thing in a certain particular. It also has been stated that a test is a series of questions or exercises or other means of measuring the skill, knowledge, intelligence, or aptitude of an individual or group.

These definitions apply to all psychological tests; but psychological tests are more than these definitions indicate. A dictionary of psychological terms defines a psychological test thus: "A set of standardized or controlled occasions for response presented to an individual with design to elicit a representative sample of his behavior when meeting a given kind of environmental demand . . . it is now common usage to include as a test any set of situations or occasions that elicit a characteristic way of acting, whether or not a task, and whether or not characteristic of the individual's best performance. Thus even a self-inventory or an attitude survey is called a test" (3).

A concise definition then, is this: *A psychological test is a standardized instrument designed to measure objectively one or more aspects of a total personality by means of samples of verbal or nonverbal responses, or by means of behavior.* The key words in this definition are *standardized, objectively,* and *samples.* Their connotations and significance will be elaborated in the course of this and following chapters.

46

Although tests of general intelligence, specific aptitudes, educational achievement, and personality are designed for their own particular purposes, all of them have certain basic principles in common and have been constructed by certain common procedures. Nor are they mutually exclusive, for any combination of tests might be used in studying a specific individual or in attempting to solve a particular psychological problem, either practical or theoretical. But probably the most important use of tests has been their contribution to the analysis and description of an individual's characteristics; to the evaluation, prediction, and guidance of his education and behavior; and to sounder determination of his vocational preparation and selection.

Objectivity

The purpose of standardizing a test is to give it objectivity, that is, to devise an instrument that, so far as possible, will be free from subjective (personal) judgments regarding the ability, skill, knowledge, trait, or potentiality to be measured and evaluated. There are several elements, or aspects, that make a test objective. These are:

Everyone who administers the test does so according to a uniform and specified set of instructions.

The responses to test items are uniformly scored according to specific answers, or specimen answers, provided in a manual.[1]

Norms of performance are based upon a population sample that has been scientifically selected for the purposes of the particular test.

The mental activities or the personality traits to be tested are defined and specified, and the psychological rationale is given.[2]

The activities or traits to be tested have been selected on the basis of analyses of the operations or behaviors to be evaluated, upon the views of a number of experts, and upon information available from previous research.

The content of the test under construction is subjected to analysis by means of established techniques of test standardization.

Objectivity in Administering and Scoring. Each psychological test is administered under a prescribed set of procedures. These instructions prepare the respondent by means of introductory and explanatory remarks. The phrasing of instructions for presentation of each part (or at times, each item) is prescribed and time limits, if any, are set. Instructions are provided as to when directions should or should not be repeated, when

[1] In the case of projective tests, the responses are analyzed in accordance with certain given principles. In some instances, scores are added to the analyses; in others, they are not.

[2] This is not entirely true of all tests. It is true, however, of the sounder ones.

encouragement should be offered by the examiner or silence maintained, and when questions from the examinee should or should not be answered. If practice exercises are used, these are given in the manual, and usually in the body of the test itself. These prescriptions are intended to create conditions that are as nearly uniform as may be achieved for all persons taking the test. Thus, scores and ratings derived under these conditions are not subject to the individual judgment of the test administrator.

A key, provided with the test, is used to score the responses; or, as in the case of the Stanford-Binet and the Wechsler scales, the scoring criteria are defined, specified, and illustrated so that subjective judgments of individual examiners do not enter or are reduced to a minimum. By these means, an objective test provides uniformity in the scoring of responses as well as in methods of obtaining them, and results found by one competent examiner are comparable with those obtained by others.

The most objective kind of scoring is that of group tests, graded by hand with a stencil or by an electronic machine. When either of these means of scoring is used, a response is either right or wrong. The hand stencil can be used by a clerk who knows nothing about psychological testing, but who must be able to count correctly. The scoring machine, however, requires a skilled operator, but one who needs to know nothing about testing either; nor need she be able to count, since the machine performs that task.

While highly objective, neither of these methods is free of error. The clerk, scoring with a hand stencil, might make some mistakes. A score obtained with an electronic machine may be incorrect if the examinee did not make the necessary marks (with an "electronic pencil") exactly right.

In a later chapter the advantages and disadvantages of group testing and objective mass scoring will be discussed and compared with *qualitative* interpretations and evaluations of test responses, as discerned by a psychological examiner, especially when an individually administered scale is used.

A Representative Population Sample

Every test is designed for use with a specified *population,* or group. For example, a test of intelligence may be standardized for use with individuals from the age of 2 years through adulthood (Stanford-Binet); another, for ages 11 to 17 (Chicago Test of Primary Mental Abilities); another, primarily for adults (Wechsler Adult Intelligence Scale); still others cover different age ranges.

A test of scholastic achievement in a particular school subject may be intended for the first three grades; or for grades eight through twelve; or for college freshmen; or for other grade ranges, depending on the school subject and the prescribed scope.

Tests of specific aptitudes, similarly, are designed for specified populations. For example, one test of ability in art is designed for grades seven and above; one test of mechanical aptitude is to be used for ages 8 to 21; a law aptitude test is standardized for college students and others regardless of age, who are candidates for admission to a law school.

Rating scales, personality inventories, and projective tests are likewise intended for use with a specified segment of the total population. They may be designed for a selected age group; for particular occupations; for given educational levels; for one sex of limited age range; for the diagnosis of clinical cases, or for use with nonclinical populations as well.

In any event, whatever the traits or functions to be measured, whatever the range of ages or school grades, and whether for clinical or nonclinical groups, the test must be standardized on a group that is a representative sample of the total population for which it is intended. Each test must be constructed by actually sampling the performance or responses of an adequate group that is typical of its population.

The nature and the comprehensiveness of the test under construction will determine what factors are important in making a population sampling. In any instance, the sample should yield unbiased data on the population it purports to represent; and the sample should be large enough to provide statistically valid results for the traits or functions being measured by the test.

This means, of course, that the author of a test must decide at the outset with *which* group, with *what* segment of the population, his instrument is to be used. Then he must standardize his test on a population sample that is *stratified* according to relevant factors; and within each stratum the selection of cases should be adequate in number and of correct proportion in the total (13).

For example, if a psychologist is constructing a test of general intelligence for American children in the primary grades, ranging in age from 5 to 9 years, he will have to incorporate the following factors in obtaining his standardization population: age, sex, geographic area, parental occupation level, and type of community (urban, village, farm). The author of the test must decide, also, whether he will standardize his test entirely on a Caucasian population, or whether he will include non-Caucasian elements. If it is to be the latter, then the racial factor must be taken into account in obtaining the sample.

Since individuals within a representative sample of any given age vary widely in respect to mental abilities, some will reach only the levels of younger age groups while others will attain the levels of older groups. Thus, to ascertain the developmental level of the retarded, it is necessary to extend downward the chronological age of the standardization sample; and, conversely, it is necessary to extend upward the age limit for the superior. The validity of the results obtained with any psychological test will depend, in part, upon the adequacy and representativeness of the standardization population.

There are two major kinds of population sampling, as already explained in Chapter 2, and precautions must be taken to avoid obtaining a biased sample. It has been demonstrated that simple random selection very often fails to yield a representative group, so this sampling procedure should not be used for test standardization. On the other hand, stratified sampling is now commonly used in constructing psychological tests. The population to be tested is divided (ideally) into a number of nonoverlapping categories which, together, will represent the entire group. Then, as already explained in Chapter 2, individuals are selected at random *within each category*. The number drawn from each category must be of the same proportion in the *total sample* as that category is in the entire group under consideration.[3]

A two-category division, for example, male and female, would be the simplest case. In the stratified sampling, the two sexes would be represented in the same proportion as they occur in the whole group (the universe) from which the sample is being drawn. Similarly, if a test is to be constructed for a specified age range, the porportion of each category (sex, age, school grade, socioeconomic status, locale) would have to be determined for inclusion in the sampling. It is obvious that the problem of stratified selection becomes more complex and more difficult as the number of categories is increased. There are times, therefore, when authors of tests must be satisfied with close approximations to existing proportions.[4]

---

[3] Although the term "stratified sample" is well established, it is not entirely appropriate. Strata are layers, usually in a horizontal or near-horizontal plane, one superimposed upon another. It is obvious that the categories into which a universe is divided frequently fail to satisfy the definition of the word "strata."

[4] Throughout the discussion of stratified sampling, proportional representation has been emphasized. It should be noted that the precision of the estimated mean of a total population can sometimes be improved by another method, "disproportional sampling" and "optimal allocation." This method analyzes each stratum separately; then their results must be combined, by statistical techniques, to represent the population as a whole. For discussions of this method see R. Ferber, *Statistical Methods in Market Research.* New York: McGraw-Hill Book Company, Inc., 1949, Ch. 6; also, P. J. McCarthy, *Introduction to Statistical Reasoning.* New York: McGraw-Hill Book Company, Inc., 1957, 280 ff.

Sampling of Traits and Functions

Any given test measures a limited aspect of the person being examined, although some tests are much more restricted in scope than others. It is essential, therefore, that the test builder define the aspects he proposes to measure. After doing this, he must develop a series of test items that will best sample the traits or functions with which his test is concerned.

In developing a psychological test, it is impossible, and in fact unnecessary, to use an unlimited number of items. It is not necessary to attempt to present the individual being tested (called the "subject" or the "testee") with problems that will measure his responses for every conceivable situation involving a given trait or function. It is sufficient to get an adequate sampling of responses in a particular area or range of behavior, the assumption being that the sampling is representative of the whole.

Two kinds of sampling are actually involved in constructing a psychological test. First, the most relevant constituents of the *gross variable* (the broad, comprehensive trait or function) must be selected. Where, for example, the gross variable is general intelligence, the constituent parts in the test might be: *vocabulary, verbal comprehension, arithmetical problems, reasoning with practical problems, verbal and other analogies, perceptual organization,* and so forth. Second, the *operational levels* (that is, the actual items) must be selected: *which* arithmetical processes and at *what* levels, what kinds and which levels of words, what types and ranges of situations, which perceptual figures?

In following this procedure, psychologists are employing a well-known and widespread technique. If a chemist wishes to determine the quality of a shipment of milk, he takes small quantities here and there, combines these, and then analyzes a sample of the samples. If an agronomist wishes to analyze a given area of soil, he gathers small amounts from various spots. If a blood test is to be made, a very small quantity taken from one place is sufficient and representative of the entire stream. Numerous other illustrations can be found. So, too, with intelligence, specific aptitudes, personality traits, and school achievement. It has been said that psychological testing may be thought of, figuratively, as sinking shafts here and there within a given range in order to measure depth and evaluate quality.

Intelligence Tests. Specifically, for present purposes of illustration, *intelligence* may be defined in several ways: (1) capacity to integrate experiences and to meet a new situation by means of appropriate and adaptive responses; (2) capacity to learn; (3) capacity to carry on abstract thinking. Although psychologists differ in regard to which of these three aspects is the most important and which they would emphasize, the fact is that most tests of general intelligence probe and sample all three. The following types of items found in various current tests fall under one or more of these definitions; are constituent parts of the gross variable, general intelligence; and illustrate the operational aspect.

> Practical reasoning: "What's the thing for you to do when you have broken something which belongs to someone else?" (From the Stanford-Binet scale)
>
> Definitions of words: that is, concept formation
>
> Perceiving similarities and differences between objects. For example: "In what way are wood and coal alike?" "In what way are a baseball and an orange alike and in what way are they different?" (From the Stanford-Binet scale); that is, abstraction and generalization
>
> General information tests: assimilation and retention of experiences
>
> Arithmetical reasoning: reasoning with abstractions
>
> Supplying missing parts to pictures: perceptual analysis and integration
>
> Reproducing geometric figures from memory: visual imagery and organization
>
> Arranging a series of pictures in logical sequence: visual perception and reasoning
>
> Perception of form design: visual imagery and recall, perceptual analysis and organization
>
> Explanation of absurdities in given pictures: logical analysis of visual percepts
>
> Oral solution of practical problems orally presented: analysis and generalization
>
> Solving problems involving distances and directions (without use of paper and pencil): spatial orientation
>
> Deriving and giving the meanings from a prose passage: reasoning with abstractions

Another method of determining the component parts of the gross variable, *general intelligence,* is through "factor analysis," which will be discussed more fully in Chapter 7. According to one analysis, there are six such components, relatively independent of one another (17).

> 1. *Facility with numbers* (the four fundamental processes)
> 2. *Vocabulary* (word meaning)
> 3. *Space perception* (perceiving similarities of, and differences among geometric figures)
> 4. *Word fluency* (controlled word association)
> 5. *Reasoning* (insight into patterns of letters arranged in series)
> 6. *Memory* (immediate recall of discrete verbal materials)

Tests have been constructed on the basis of this analysis, items having been devised for each of the six categories.

Still another approach to analysis of test content is known as *construct validity* (see Chapter 5). This term means that a test measures what it claims to measure if the mental processes (activities) required by the test items sample well the *concepts,* or *constructs,* that the test is designed to measure. Obviously, when a test's author uses this approach, he must begin by selecting and defining the concepts to be included. To do this adequately requires insights into psychological operations and knowledge of the mental activities involved in the situations in which the test is to be used. For example, in one series of group tests of intelligence, using the principle of construct validity, intelligence is analyzed and the test items are based upon the following concepts (8):

> The tasks deal with abstract and general concepts.
>
> In most cases, the tasks require the interpretation of symbols.
>
> In large part, it is the relationships among concepts and symbols with which the examinee must deal.
>
> The tasks require the examinee to be flexible in his basis for organizing concepts and symbols.
>
> Experience must be used in new patterns.
>
> Power in working with abstract materials is emphasized rather than speed.

These concepts are then given form by determining which types or categories of materials should be employed. The authors of these tests decided on a nonverbal battery including *figure classification, number series,* and *figure analogies;* and on a verbal battery including *sentence completion, verbal classification, arithmetical reasoning,* and *vocabulary.*[5]

The next task, a difficult one, is the preparation and experimental selection of numerous individual *items* to give substance to each of these categories. This last task constitutes the technical aspects of test standardization, discussed in the next chapter.

The outline that follows is a further illustration of the trend among psychologists toward analysis of a gross variable into its component parts. In this instance, the investigator has set himself the task of testing reasoning (4).

Reasoning I
    a. manipulating symbols
    b. solving problems
    c. defining problems
    d. testing hypotheses

Reasoning II
    a. seeing rules or principles (induction)

[5] These and other types of materials are illustrated in subsequent chapters.

     b. seeing systems

     c. seeing trends

     d. seeing relations (educing relations)

     e. seeing identity of relationships

     f. analyzing forms

Reasoning III

     a. seeing common elements or properties

     b. classifying (in general)

     c. classifying forms

     d. educing correlates

Reasoning IV

     a. drawing inferences (deduction)

     b. syllogistic reasoning

Inspection of these four types of reasoning shows they are not independent of one another. Yet if it can be demonstrated that these types are sufficiently distinct and constitute reasoning in its several aspects, and if reasoning were to be measured according to this scheme, it would be necessary to devise items for each of the four types and for each subtype. Ultimately, too, research would have to demonstrate the validity of these types as tests of reasoning when compared with one or more external criteria.[6]

     Specific Aptitudes.   A specific aptitude test indicates the probable degree of successful learning and achievement in a particular and limited type of activity; for example, musical, graphic arts, mechanical, clerical, linguistic. A test intended to estimate a person's capacity in any specific area must include parts (called *subtests*) and items, sufficient in number and extensive enough in scope and level of difficulty to provide an adequate sampling upon which a prediction of subsequent learning and achievement may be based. Without comment on their merits at this point, three illustrations in the musical, clerical, and mechanical areas follow.

     The "Wing Standardized Tests of Musical Intelligence" (revised edition) include these seven aspects: chord analysis, pitch change, memory, rhythmic accent, harmony, intensity, and phrasing.

     The "Purdue Clerical Adaptability Test" (revised edition) includes six salient features that measure this aptitude: spelling, computation, checking, word meaning, copying, and reasoning.

     Since mechanical aptitude includes so many different kinds of performance and knowledge, each test in this area is limited in range and purpose. For instance, any one or a combination of some of the following

     [6] This would have to be done unless the author of the test is satisfied with construct validity (see Chapter 5).

aspects might be included in a test: knowledge of tools, knowledge of mechanical devices, manual dexterity, perception of spatial relations, knowledge of terms (mechanical vocabulary), rate and accuracy of tapping, mechanical comprehension, and reasoning. The "MacQuarrie Test of Mechanical Ability" includes several aspects: tracing (drawing a line through a series of broken lines), rate of tapping within a series of small circles, dotting (the same as tapping, but the circles are much smaller and irregularly spaced), copying simple jagged lines on a square of dots, location (matching parts of a large square with corresponding parts of a much smaller square), block analysis and block counting, and pursuit (following each of ten intertwined irregular lines). The first three parts are intended to measure rate and accuracy of eye-hand coordination, while the remaining four are devised to measure spatial perception (9). These tests do not make any demands upon any form of mechanical comprehension, information, or skill. It is MacQuarrie's view, apparently, that eye-hand coordination and spatial perception are basic and most significant in learning and functioning in certain mechanical occupations.

The tests of mechanical comprehension developed in the United States Air Force during World War II were of a different kind. These included: mechanical principles, requiring understanding of basic principles fundamental to the solution of mechanical problems; mechanical functions, requiring knowledge of tools and instruments and comprehension of the methods of machine operations; and mechanical movements, requiring ability to comprehend and follow the operation of moving parts of machines (5).

Personality Inventories. These tests must also be based upon samplings of the traits that the test's author proposes to evaluate. This is true even though so comprehensive a concept as "personality" is difficult to define, and even though nonintellective traits of personality are at times elusive. There are inventories, answered by the individual himself, that are intended to evaluate degrees of introversion–extroversion, neurotic tendencies, security–insecurity, anxiety, hypochondriasis, dominance–submission, adjustment to home and to school, and others. In each instance, the author of the test must define the area and traits and then provide questions or statements that represent the manifestations or symptoms of the trait. Some inventories are devised to evaluate a single bipolar characteristic (frequently called a "dimension"), such as security–insecurity (for example, the Maslow Inventory); others are multiple-trait inventories (for example, the Bernreuter).

The Maslow Security–Insecurity Inventory provides a useful illustration of the definition of a trait in terms of its syndrome; that is, the aspects that combine in one degree or another to create this bipolar trait. Maslow lists fourteen aspects of security, and the opposite pole of these fourteen as aspects of insecurity. The first three in each list are regarded as relatively prior, or causal, whereas the remaining eleven are consequent, or are effects produced in the course of an individual's development. The three causal aspects, at each pole, are as follows (10).

Security	*Insecurity*
1. Feeling of being liked or loved, of being accepted, of being looked upon with warmth.	1. Feeling of rejection, of being unloved, of being treated coldly and without affection, or of being hated, of being despised.
2. Feeling of belonging, of being at home in the world, of having a place in the group.	2. Feelings of isolation, ostracism, aloneness or being out of it; feelings of "uniqueness."
3. Feeling of safety, rare feelings of threat and danger; unanxious.	3. Constant feelings of threat and danger; anxiety.

The Bernreuter Personality Inventory is designed to evaluate degrees of six traits: neurotic tendency, self-sufficiency, introversion–extroversion, dominance–submission, confidence in one's self, and sociability (1). Each of these has to be defined and described. The rating on *self-sufficiency,* for example, is regarded as indicating the extent to which the individual prefers to be alone, asks for sympathy or encouragement, and tends to ignore the advice of others. In regard to *introversion–extroversion,* those scoring high on the scale (introverts) are said to be imaginative and to live within themselves, while those scoring low (extroverts) are said to worry rarely, to suffer seldom from emotional upsets, and rarely to substitute daydreaming for action.

In the case of each of these inventories, the characteristics of the traits to be evaluated are clarified by the actual items—questions and statements —included in the instrument, to which the individual is required to respond.

Projective Tests. The several types of projective tests of personality have had somewhat different origins. Rorschach, after whom the inkblot test is named, did not begin with a set of personality traits, arrived at through analysis of behavior, which he wanted to evaluate (see Chapter 25). As already noted in Chapter 1, inkblots had been used by psychologists for experimental purposes prior to Rorschach's use of them. He was interested in them, however, as providing a possible technique and type of stimulus that might be useful in the study of and differentiation among psychotics. Attribution of certain kinds of responses to certain personality characteristics resulted from Rorschach's own researches and those of others who followed him (14).

The Murray Thematic Apperception Test originated in a different manner (11). (See Chapter 25.) It derives from and is based upon the general theory of personality developed by H. A. Murray and his colleagues at the Harvard Psychological Clinic in studying "normal" persons. This projective test rests upon analyses of human needs and of the environmental forces (called "press") affecting human behavior. Murray lists twenty-six needs and sixteen environmental forces to be elicited by the series of ambiguous pictures, drawn for this purpose, constituting the Thematic Apperception Test. Among these needs are the following, cited for illustrative purposes (12):

Achievement: To work at something important with energy and persistence. To strive to accomplish something creditable. To get ahead in business, to persuade or lead a group, to create something. Ambition manifested in action.

Dominance: To try to influence the behavior, sentiments, or ideas of others. To work for an executive position. To lead, manage, govern. To coerce, restrain, imprison.

Intragression: To blame, criticize, reprove, or belittle [one's self] for wrongdoing, stupidity, or failure. To suffer feelings of inferiority, guilt, remorse. To punish [one's self] physically. To commit suicide.

Among the "press" listed and for whose presence the individual's test responses are analyzed, are these:

Affiliation (emotional): A person (parent, relative, lover) is affectionately devoted to the hero.[7]

Dominance (coercion): Someone tries to force the hero to do something. He is exposed to commands, orders, or forceful arguments.

Rejection: A person rejects, scorns, repudiates, refuses to help, leaves, or is indifferent to the hero. A loved object is unfaithful. The hero is unpopular or not accepted for a position. He is fired from his job.

At this stage, it is not our purpose to evaluate the abilities, aptitudes, and traits being measured or sampled by means of the tests. Our purpose is to indicate the several courses followed by psychologists in deciding upon the content of their tests.

Educational Achievement Tests. A test in this category is designed to measure an individual's understanding of, skill with, or information in a given subject of study—or all three. They may and do encompass almost the whole range of subjects taught in elementary and secondary schools, and some taught at the college level as well. In each instance, as in all other types, the scope of the test must be defined, the divisions

[7] The hero in each story is the central figure about whom the story is told in response to each picture. The theory is that the respondent identifies with the hero and through him reveals his own needs and the environmental forces affecting him.

of the subject must be determined, and the elements of each division must be adequately represented in the final version of the test; for its validity will depend upon the adequacy with which it samples its subject-matter field.

Tests of educational achievement are based primarily upon *content validity* (see Chapter 20). This term means that the effectiveness and value of a test—the extent to which it measures what it claims to measure—depend upon the comprehensiveness and soundness of the materials it includes. In this connection, the question to be answered is this: Are the areas covered and the choice of topics based upon a sound and expert analysis of what should be included? A satisfactory answer to this question will depend upon the expertness of the persons constructing the test.

In the first place, an educational achievement test must be based upon the stated objectives of instruction in that subject of study. For example, here are the objectives in the first course in secondary school algebra, as defined in one state. If these objectives are common throughout the United States, a test based upon them could be widely used. Otherwise, the test could be appropriately used only in schools that share the same objectives (16).

1. Acquisition of the basic vocabulary
2. Learning to translate quantitative statements into the language of algebra
3. Interpreting the solution of equations where they have significance and in using rules of equality and transformation
4. Solving general verbal problems using as a means of solution the table, graph, formula, and equation
5. Understanding of carefully considered concepts and principles which should lead to fundamental skills and techniques
    a. The four fundamental operations involving positive and negative numbers, algebraic monomials or simple polynomials, and algebraic fractions, mainly monomial denominators
    b. Special products and factoring, such as squaring a binomial, finding the product of the sum and the difference of two terms, factoring a polynomial containing a common monomial term, factoring trinomials of the form x^2 plus bx plus c, and factoring the difference of two squares
    c. Powers and roots involving the laws of exponents and their use, square roots of positive numbers, and fundamental operations involving radicals of the monomial type
6. The study of relationships and of dependence
    a. Interpreting tables of related number pairs
    b. Making graphs based on tables of related number pairs and using graphs in the solution of problems

    c. Using formulas as means of expressing relationship or dependence
    d. Equations involving the solution of equations of the first degree in one unknown, fractional equations, equations of the form ax^2 equals *b,* and simple radical equations
    e. Using equations in the study of proportion and of variables

The Stanford Achievement Test (Advanced Battery) includes subtests which are intended to measure pupils' progress in several aspects of English (6). These are as follows:

Paragraph meaning (involving some recall, but primarily interpretation)
Word meaning (involving definitions and, to some extent, reasoning)
Spelling
Language (involving capitalization, punctuation, knowledge of sentence structure, grammar, and usage)

Educational achievement tests are generally used to determine the learner's level of proficiency at the time of the examination. The results obtained with these devices are also useful in forecasting each individual's probable future level and quality of learning in the several subject-matter areas, and in diagnosing specific deficiencies and disabilities in school learning. The basic importance, therefore, of adequately conceived and satisfactorily standardized instruments of measurement is readily apparent.

Resemblance of Test Items to Actual Behavior or Experience

    Inspection of the types of test items already cited, and of those given in later chapters, shows that the degree of resemblance between the tasks presented by the items and actual behavior or traits to be discerned or predicted varies with the several kinds of instruments. *Tests of educational achievement,* because they are measures of actual learning in specific subjects of instruction, utilize items that are samples of acquired or developed skills. These tests seek to answer such questions as: How much information has the testee acquired in American history of a given period? How well can he perform arithmetical processes of a certain level of difficulty? How much does he know about punctuation or grammatical usage? In other words, educational achievement tests measure *directly* that which they are intended to represent.

    This is true, also, of some *aptitude tests,* as, for example, those in music that measure the several forms of sensory acuity, those in comprehension of mechanical principles, and those in law that present cases and problems of the sort studied in law schools. On the other hand, tests of spatial perception, speed and accuracy of eye-hand movements are *indirect* measures of some aspects of mechanical aptitude, since they are intended to provide signs or symptoms of a general type of functioning, rather than *direct* measures of an activity for which persons are being selected by means of the test.

Tests of general intelligence, with a few exceptions, are concerned with the forms, complexity, level of difficulty, quality, and at times, rate of mental activity, rather than with the specific content. When, for example, an author of an intelligence test uses problems in similarities and differences,[8] or synonyms–antonyms,[9] he is not concerned primarily with the particular objects or words being compared. What he wishes to test are the mental processes involved in reaching a correct answer. When an author decides to include rote or logical memory in his test, the particular series of digits or words (whether in a disconnected series or in a meaningful sentence) are unimportant as long as they meet certain elementary conditions, such as length and familiarity. What he wants to measure is "memory span," or "immediate recall," since this form of mental functioning is regarded as significant in the more general aspects of intelligence.[10]

The items in a subtest of general information, when included in tests of intelligence, are not selected because they are most worth knowing or deserving of more attention than others are. They are chosen in order to provide a measure of an individual's range of intellectual curiosity and activity and of his assimilation and retention of experiences; for these aspects are among those symptomatic of intellectual level and quality. Items in arithmetical reasoning are included to obtain evidence of complex reasoning ability with the use of abstractions, rather than to find out specifically and primarily the testee's proficiency in arithmetic.

All the types of subtests incorporated in tests of general intelligence should be similarly viewed. The fact that specificity of content is not of primary significance can be readily determined by comparing and noting the differences among the items of several different instruments, each of which is intended to measure the same mental functions and to serve the same purposes.

Personality inventories and *projective tests* present still different forms of content, so far as correspondence with actuality is concerned. Inventories consist of verbalizations of a variety of behavioral situations or of

[8] How are a pair of scissors and a knife alike, and how are they different?

[9] A word is presented, followed by five other words. The testee may be required to identify the one of the five that means the same, or nearly the same, as the first word. Or he may be required to select the one that means the opposite.

[10] Defects and distortions of memory are also significant in understanding and diagnosing certain personality problems (see Chapter 14).

[11] For example: Do you get upset easily? Do you have headaches frequently? Are you liked well enough at home so that you feel happy there?

conditions experienced.[11] Thus, they are representations of actual behaviors; but they are as close to actual behavior and experience as can be approached without observing a person in the behavioral situations themselves.[12] In projective tests, the closeness or remoteness of content materials varies with each instrument. The pictures presented in the Thematic Apperception Test are intentionally ambiguous. They are not designed to represent situations that might have been experienced by many persons taking the test. For example, one picture shows a young boy resting his head on his hands, looking at a violin lying on the table. Many of the T.A.T. pictures present situations which, if taken literally, are remote from actual experiences of most persons; others are thoroughly ambiguous, or even products of fantasy. The purpose of these pictures is not to offer situations representative of those actually experienced by testees but, rather, to present a variety of situations wherein each individual can impose his own interpretations. As a matter of fact, some of the projective tests portray animals rather than persons, the assumption being that the testee will more readily respond to animal pictures than to those of humans in these situations.[13] Then, by contrast, the Michigan Picture Test, for children, and the Symonds Picture–Study Test, for adolescents, represent a number of situations common to these age groups, the Michigan being more specific in its representation than the Symonds. The purpose of both is to elicit such responses to each situation as will reveal attitudes toward, feelings about, and values concerning persons, groups, and institutions in the environment.

The Rorschach Inkblot Test, by contrast with all others thus far mentioned, utilizes content materials that are completely unrepresentational. Inkblots are ordinarily not encountered in learning situations. They provide unfamiliar visual percepts upon which the respondent exercises his imagination; and the products of his imagination are analyzed for evidence of his personality characteristics.

In discussing and briefly illustrating the degree of similarity of test content to the actualities of learning, behavior and personality traits, the purpose is to demonstrate the several methods of obtaining psychological information, each depending upon the traits or functions to be assessed and upon the objectives to be served by each instrument.

---

[12] There have been experiments and observations in laboratories, playschools, school rooms, and elsewhere, in which certain conditions are simulated to evoke degrees of frustration tolerance, aggressiveness, conformity, leadership, etc. Some of these experiments have produced valuable results; others have suffered seriously from the fact that some actual vital situations are not transferable to a laboratory or other type of contrived setting.

[13] The Children's Apperception Test and the Blacky Pictures (see Chapter 26).

References

1. Bernreuter, R. G. *The Personality Inventory: Manual.* Stanford, Calif.: Consulting Psychologists Press, 1935–1938.
2. Carr, A. C., *et al. The Prediction of Overt Behavior Through the Use of Projective Techniques.* Springfield, Ill.: Charles C Thomas, 1960.
3. English, H. B., and A. C. English. *A Comprehensive Dictionary of Psychological and Psychoanalytical Terms.* New York: David McKay Company, Inc., 1958.
4. Guilford, J. P. *A Factor-Analytic Study of Reasoning Abilities.* Los Angeles: University of Southern California, June 1950, report no. 1.
5. Guilford, J. P. (ed.). *Printed Classification Tests.* Army Air Force Aviation Psychology Program Research Reports, No. 5. Washington, D.C.: U.S. Government Printing Office, 1947.
6. Kelley, T. L., *et al. Stanford Achievement Test.* New York: Harcourt, Brace and World, Inc., 1952.
7. Lorge, I. The fundamental nature of measurement. *Educational Measurement,* E. F. Lindquist (ed.). Washington, D.C.: American Council on Education, 1951, ch. 14.
8. Lorge, I., and R. L. Thorndike. *The Lorge-Thorndike Intelligence Tests.* Boston: Houghton Mifflin Company, 1957.
9. MacQuarrie, T. W. *MacQuarrie Tests for Mechanical Ability: Manual.* Monterey: California Test Bureau, 1943.
10. Maslow, A. H. *Security–Insecurity Inventory: Manual.* Stanford, Calif.: Consulting Psychologists Press, 1952.
11. Murray, H. A. *Explorations in Personality.* New York: Oxford University Press, 1938.
12. Murray, H. A. *Thematic Apperception Test: Manual.* Cambridge: Harvard University Press, 1943.
13. Parten, M. B. *Surveys, Polls, and Samples.* New York: Harper & Brothers, 1950.
14. Rorschach, H. (trans. by P. Lemkan and B. Kronenberg; W. Morgenthaler ed.). *Psychodiagnostics* (4th ed.). Berne, Switzerland: Hans Huber, 1942 (Grune and Stratton, Inc., U.S. distributor).
15. Stoddard, G. S. *The Meaning of Intelligence.* New York: The Macmillan Company, 1943.
16. Superintendent of Public Instruction. *Guide to Secondary Education in Oregon for School Years 1957–1959.* Salem, Ore.: State Education Department, 1957.
17. Thurstone, L. L., and T. G. Thurstone. *The Chicago Tests of Primary Mental Abilities.* Chicago: Science Research Associates, 1941, 1953.
18. Vaughn, K. W. Planning the objective test. *Educational Measurement,* E. F. Lindquist (ed.). Washington, D.C.: American Council on Education, 1951, ch. 6.

4.

TEST STANDARDIZATION: PROCEDURES AND RELIABILITY

The fundamental purpose of standardizing a psychological test is to establish its reliability and its validity at as high a level as possible. The techniques of establishing reliability and validity are discussed later in this and the following chapters. To begin with, the steps taken in devising a test will be explained.

Content

The first questions the author of a test must answer are these: Which abilities, aptitudes, proficiencies, or personality traits are to be measured? [1] Having determined that an instrument is to be constructed for the measurement or assessment of certain specified functions, behaviors, or traits, the author must then make his own analysis of their constituent elements or utilize analyses previously made by others and reported in the scientific literature on the subject. Examples of such analyses were given in the preceding chapter.[2] It often happens that specific job analyses must be made preparatory to devising a proficiency test.

[1] The fact is, of course, that the author of the contemplated test has answered this question for himself at the outset, having decided that an instrument was needed for one purpose or another.

[2] Methods of determining which elements are the most appropriate for inclusion are discussed further in later chapters in connection with definitions and theories of intelligence, the nature of specific aptitudes, aspects of personality, and the rationales of specific types of tests.

In other instances, considerable exploratory research, based originally upon psychological insights, must be carried out before it is possible to identify, even tentatively, the elements that should be included in a test.

The number and kinds of subtests and the nature of the individual items themselves will be determined in large part by the test author's theoretical position. For example, in devising a test of "general ability," his position with regard to the *general factor* will influence the content and structure of the test (see Chapter 7). The author's views regarding cultural influences will be another consideration (see, for example, the Davis-Eells test, Chapter 15). In devising a test of personality, especially the projectives, one's theory will influence the selection of traits to be assessed and the manner of assessing them (see Chapter 23). Testing for proficiency in specified jobs is the area in which theoretical differences play a minor role, if any, because both the available tests and the new ones being devised will be based upon a job analysis of the activities actually involved.

After he has decided which areas are to be tested, the author must prepare a large number of items to be used in the initial, or exploratory, stage of test construction. It might be necessary to begin with three or four times the number of test items that will be included in the final product. The exploratory and second stages of standardization will show that some items are of little or no value for the purposes of the test, while others will be eliminated from the final version because they are superflous even though, in themselves, they might be relevant to the purpose.

The actual kinds of items utilized will depend upon the nature and purpose of the instrument. Shall they be direct measures, as in the case of achievement tests? Or shall they primarily involve mental processes whose actual content is a secondary consideration, as in tests of general intelligence? Or shall they sample behavior, as do personality inventories? Or shall they evoke "signs" of personality traits, as do projective tests? [3]

After areas, age ranges, levels of difficulty, or kinds of traits to be studied are determined, the initial set of test items will be tried out on several relatively small groups to formulate and clarify instructions, to judge the clarity of item-phrasing, to learn whether each item evokes the kinds of responses expected, and to decide on time limits. It is also valuable to obtain the testees' introspective reports regarding the whole test and particular items in it.

Having taken into account the findings of the exploratory studies, the author can proceed to the preparation of a *preliminary form* for use with a large number of individuals who represent the universe for whom the instrument is intended. (The 1937 revision of the Stanford-Binet scale

[3] This aspect of test content is discussed in the preceding chapter.

went through seven versions before the satisfactory form was constructed.) Results obtained with the preliminary form will provide statistical data about the test as a whole and about each individual item. On the basis of these data, analyses can be made to determine the test's reliability and validity at this stage.

Other valuable statistical findings are range of individual differences among scores, norms and deviations of scores at each of the several ages or ability levels, difficulty level of each test item, and the degree to which each item or subtest discriminates between those who score high and those who score low on the test as a whole.[4] The data provided by this process will be used to prepare a revised version for further trial with another large stratified sample of the group.[5] For example, the Lorge-Thorndike test manual states: "The initial series of tryouts involved more than 6000 pupils. Each of 1200 different test items was tried out on 650 to 1000 of these pupils. Items were selected to yield an appropriate distribution of difficulties and to include only items with acceptedly high internal-consistency indices" (17).[6] The final norms are based upon results found with 136,000 pupils in forty-four communities in twenty-two states.

From this point on, the process is one of selection, rejection, addition, and refinement of items, and their placement in the scale in respect to difficulty level.[7] The ultimate purpose of this entire process of trial and improvement is to develop an instrument which will yield the maximum results in either assessment or prediction, or both, using a minimum number of test items.

Population

At the outset, too, the author of the test must define the group for whom the test is intended. For example, in devising measures of general intelligence or of "differential aptitudes" (specific areas of ability, such as facility with numbers or with words and spatial perception), the age range must be determined. Shall the test provide a scale appropriate for a wide range, as the Stanford-Binet does (2 years through adulthood); or for a moderate range, as does the Chicago Test of Primary Mental Abilities (ages 11 through 17); or for a narrow range as does the Cattell scale for infants and young children (ages two months to

---

[4] Reliability, validity, and item analysis are discussed in later sections.

[5] The term "large sample" does not indicate a fixed number. About 500 testees in the initial exploratory stages are desirable, if available. Much larger numbers are necessary for preliminary and final validation.

[6] Internal consistency is discussed under "Meaning of Reliability," later in this chapter.

[7] Determining difficulty of items and placing them in the scale accordingly is called *scaling.*

thirty months)? The age groups must then be subdivided according to the principle of stratified sampling, as explained in Chapter 2.

In the construction of tests of personality, age level is an important element. In tests of educational achievement, however, grade range or educational level, rather than age level, determines the difficulty and range of materials. This is the case also in tests of aptitudes or of proficiencies, where age range is less often a consideration than is the *level* of proficiency (or degree of skill) to be tested. In any event, the universe for whom the test is intended, and its subdivisions (strata), if any, must be determined. Then it is necessary to obtain a large enough sampling of this universe to try the test items at each of the several stages of its development.

Reliability

Meaning of Reliability. The two essential characteristics of a sound test are its *reliability* and its *validity*.

Whenever anything is measured, whether in the physical, biological, or behavioral sciences, there is some possibility of chance error. This is true of psychological tests as well. Variations of results obtained with the same test administered more than once, using the same persons as subjects, or within the parts of a test given only once, are due not only to chance factors, which should be eliminated so far as possible, but also to actual differences among the individuals taking the test and to whatever defects may be inherent in the instrument itself.

The reliability of a test is its ability to yield consistent results from one set of measures to another; it is the extent to which the obtained test scores are free from such internal defects as will produce errors of measurement inherent in the items and their standardization. These errors are not due to instability of the performances of the testees themselves or to chance factors. However, since individuals do not perform with complete consistency upon all occasions, and since chance cannot be entirely eliminated, the actual indexes of reliability obtained for psychological tests are the product of the interaction among true individual differences, defects of the instrument, and chance determinants.

The term *reliability* has two closely related but somewhat different connotations in psychological testing. First, it refers to the extent to which a test in *internally consistent,* that is, consistency of results obtained *throughout the test* when administered once. In other words, how accurately is the test measuring at a particular time?

Second, reliability refers to the extent to which a measuring device yields consistent results upon *testing and retesting*. That is, how dependable is it for predictive purposes? Obviously, if a test does not have a high degree of reliability when used more than once, it can have but limited value in predicting an individual's future performance or level of development.

The two aspects of reliability are intimately related; for if a test is not highly reliable when used upon a particular occasion (that is, internally consistent), it can have little predictive value.[8] Since one of the principal uses of psychological tests is for prediction and planning for the subsequent development and performance of individuals, a high degree of reliability is a *sine qua non* of a sound instrument. This statement applies also to tests that are to be used for research purposes, since the results obtained will not be any sounder than the research instrument itself.

Conditions Affecting Reliability. Reliability is not an all-or-none principle; it is a matter of degree. No test presently available is in itself perfectly reliable; scores for the same individuals, obtained on repeated testings, are not completely stable. Not only are there likely to be some different chance determinants in operation at different times, but it is quite normal for humans to vary in performance, generally within fairly narrow limits, from one occasion to another. Such variation is expected quite aside from changes that occur as part of the process of growth and development.

There are several possible sources of variation in performances on a test. This aspect of testing will recur frequently in subsequent discussions; but for the present, the most common of them may be listed as follows:

Actual, or "true," differences among individuals in the *general* traits or *general* abilities being measured

Differences in *specific* abilities required in a particular test; or *specific* disabilities in the functions being tested; for example, reading, manual dexterity

Skill in taking tests; being "test wise," or the converse

The "chance" acquisition of a particular piece of knowledge required in a test, for example, the meaning of an unusual word, such as *ambergris*, or unusual information, such as the name of the author of a little-known work (These would be poor test items.)

Effects of practice (previous test-taking) or coaching

Normal or expected fluctuations in performance from time to time

[8] In some individual cases, internal inconsistency is due to instability of, or inconsistencies within, the testee, rather than to defects of the test itself. This aspect of test interpretation is discussed in Chaper 14.

Personal characteristics of the testee: fluctuations of attention, motivation,
    health, energy level, emotional status

Physical conditions under which the test is taken: heat, light, ventilation

Unpredictable, or chance factors: noise, interference, broken pencil, mis-
    understanding of instructions

Fortunate guessing of answers

Competence of examiners and their agreement in scoring

Test results, ideally, should depend upon the extent to which the test measures the first two of these sources of variation; actually, however, co-efficients of reliability will be adversely affected by the nonsystematic operations of the others.

Standardization of a test aims to eliminate or reduce to a minimum its inherent defects. The conditions of testing and retesting should be as nearly optimal and consistent as possible; for reliability is in part a consequence of testing conditions, including strict adherence to pre-scribed instructions for administering, utilization of practice exercises (when included), accurate timing, elimination of noise, and general pro-visions for adaptation of individuals to the testing situation. Though *minor* fluctuations in an individual's performance from day to day can-not be eliminated, the reasons for any *major* fluctuations must be sought in the individual himself or in his environmental conditions, if the sources of serious discrepancies are to be understood.

Methods of Estimating Reliability. Methods of estimating re-liability fall into two general classifications: (1) *relative* reliability and (2) *absolute* reliability. The first of these is generally stated in terms of a coefficient of correlation, known as the *reliability coefficient.* This statistic indicates the extent to which individuals in a group maintain relatively consistent positions (scores) when two sets of measures are obtained and correlated, using the same test or its two equivalent forms. Relative re-liability is also reported at times, though infrequently, in terms of *analysis of variance.* The second method, absolute reliability, is stated in terms of the *standard error of measurement,* which is an estimate of the deviation of a set of obtained scores from their "true scores."

Several methods are used to derive the reliability coefficient. These are as follows:

(1) The same form of the test may be administered twice to the same group of individuals.

(2) Two separate but equivalent forms of the test may be administered to the same individuals.

(3) The test items of a single test are subdivided into two presumably equivalent and separately scored sets; the two sets of scores are cor-

related as though they were obtained from two equivalent forms or from two testings with the same form.

RETEST RELIABILITY USING A SINGLE FORM.[9]   When individuals are retested a number of times, they might undergo some changes as a result of repeated measurements, for example, because of practice effects, improvement in the skill of taking tests, and in their attitudes toward taking a test. In estimating reliability, therefore, it is necessary to limit the number of times an individual is examined with the same device. Hence, instead of frequent retesting of the same persons, data for a given test are obtained by increasing the number of individuals tested rather than by increasing the number of measures of each person.

Administering the identical test form twice has the obvious advantage of providing completely equivalent test content on both occasions. This is an essential consideration. Furthermore, it is, of course, less difficult to develop one form of a test rather than two.

However, this method also has its disadvantages. It is time-consuming. The experience of having taken the test the first time might result in some learning or improved skills, so that individuals on the second occasion are no longer "the same" in all respects as they were on the first. The first and second testings should take place within a week or two, in order to minimize the possible influences of intervening factors of developmental and chance changes. Even so, some psychologists hold that the brief interval of a week or two does not sufficiently reduce the possible effects of recall.

Yet, although the reliability coefficient might be somewhat too high when the same form of the test is used, the probable influence or importance of recall is not nearly so great as might be expected. In the first place, the number of test items in both individual and group tests is so large that it is extremely difficult to recall a significant number of them, especially when the persons taking the test are working under pressure and must rapidly shift attention from one problem to another.

---

[9] Currently, some psychologists prefer to use different terms to designate the several methods of estimating test reliability. Instead of speaking of the reliability coefficient and of retest reliability when using a single form, some prefer the term "temporal stability," while others prefer "coefficient of stability." When two equivalent forms of a test are used, or when a single form is divided into two equivalent halves, some prefer the term "coefficient of equivalence." Because the older term, "reliability coefficient," is the generic one and because, so far as the test itself is concerned, we are interested in *its* dependability but not in the influences of time as such, we shall use the older term while explaining the different methods. The equivalence of two forms or parts is a *precondition* of the test's reliability. Furthermore, the word "stability" is a different way of saying "reliability," but with a somewhat different emphasis. "Reliability" however estimated, is the preferable word, for we want to know how *dependable* test results are.

The results of two studies will illustrate this point. Thirty children, between the ages of 9 and 11, with IQs ranging from 96 to 114, were examined twice each with the 1937 Stanford-Binet scale, Form L. The tests were given a week apart to each child by two experienced examiners, each child being examined once by each of the psychologists. Upon completing the first examination, each child was told the correct answer or shown the correct solution to every item he failed, up through what is known as the "terminal year." [10] The purpose of this procedure was to learn how much would be retained from the first test and influence the results of the second. The correlation coefficient for the two sets of intelligence quotients was .89; the mean IQ increased by two points (from 103 to 105); and the total range was only slightly changed (92–117).

A second study was made with the Pintner Non-language Intermediate Test, using sixty-eight pupils in the sixth grade, ranging in IQ from 76 to 95. After the first testing had been completed and the booklets collected, the tester selected, for demonstration and explanation, two or three items from each of the subtests, representing the several levels of difficulty. For each of these items, the correct answer and the reason for it were given. The pupils were encouraged, also, to ask for the answers to any items they recalled and were doubtful about. Only a few questions were raised. A week after the initial test, the same groups were reexamined with the same form. The correlation coefficient for the two sets of intelligence quotients was .85.[11] Numerous investigations have demonstrated that, in general, longer intervals between repeated tests will result in lowering the reliability coefficient; that is, reliability is in part a function of the time elapsed. The following correlation coefficients are representative of those found for the stated intervals:

Immediate retesting (same day or next)	.90–.95
Retesting after 1 year	.85
Retesting after 2–2½ years	.80
Retesting after 5 years	.75–.80
Retesting after 9 years	.78

These are rather conservative indexes; some studies find closer correspondence of scores after appreciable intervals. For example, one study reports the following (7):

[10] Terminal year is the age level on the Stanford–Binet scale at which the testee fails all items.

[11] Both of the instances cited are unpublished studies. For several years, I have also made a practice of asking college seniors, within a few days (always within less than a week) of having taken the Graduate Record Examinations, to try to recall *specific* items in each of the several parts of these tests. Rarely has any student been able to do so. This result is to be expected from what is known about learning, recall, interference, and perseverance.

Age interval	r, boys	r, girls
6–10	.77	.74
7–10	.79	.76
8–10	.89	.83
9–14	.82 (both sexes)	

In still another research, the following results were obtained with the use of the Stanford-Binet scale (4).

Age at initial testing	Interval	r
4 years	6 years	.73
9 years	6 years	.87
11 years	6 years	.92

There are several reasons for the lowering of reliability coefficients as the time interval increases. If children are initially tested before 3 years of age, and retested after several years, the reliability coefficient will be misleadingly low because different functions and dissimilar mental operations are being sampled at the two age levels.[12] This fact, though true in a lesser degree when the first tests are given to children between the ages of 4 and 6, may account in part for the coefficient of .73 reported above for the group initially tested at the age of 4 with the Stanford-Binet scale. Another reason is that individual rates of mental growth and forms of mental development do not always progress uniformly, so that the greater the time interval, the greater will be the opportunities for idiosyncracies to affect test results. Furthermore, it is more difficult to motivate and hold the attention of young children. *Examiner reliability* is also a factor. If entirely competent examiners are used for both tests, as they should be, the discrepancies in scores will be minor. Numerous comparisons made in regard to this question have found correlations in the vicinity of .85–.90 for the same tests scored by two examiners, or for two scores derived by them from two separate examinations.

Reliability coefficients are affected, of course, by any defects or deficiencies inherent in the test itself in respect to content and scaling, with their consequent effects upon the range of scores at each of the several age levels. The question here is this: Are the standard deviations of the intelligence quotients the same, or nearly so, at all age levels, so that an individual who maintains his relative position in the group, over a period of time, will have the same IQ rating at all ages? If the dispersions of scores vary appreciably at different age levels, as they do with some tests, the reliability coefficients will be adversely affected.[13]

It is evident, then, that the reliability coefficient obtained by means of

[12] This problem is presented more fully in Chapter 13.
[13] This problem is discussed in Chapters 6 and 10.

retesting with the same form has its advantages and disadvantages. It will depend upon the quality of the instrument, the competence of the examiner, the characteristics of the individuals used in the study, and the circumstances under which the tests are given. Some of these aspects will be discussed in later sections of this chapter.

RETEST RELIABILITY USING EQUIVALENT FORMS.[14]   Estimating reliability by means of this method presents some of the same advantages and disadvantages as does the use of only one form. But using equivalent forms also has an advantage of its own: the possible effects of specific practice and recall are lessened, since the items in the two versions of the testing device are not identical. On the other hand, this method presents an additional problem in the construction and standardization of the second form, that is, the problem of making both forms truly equivalent. This means that both forms should meet all of the test's specifications as follows:

1. The number of items should be the same.
2. The kinds of items in both should be uniform in respect to content, operations or traits involved, levels and range of difficulty, and adequacy of sampling.
3. The items should be similarly *distributed* as to difficulty.
4. Both test forms should have the same degree of item homogeneity in the operations or traits being measured. The degree of homogeneity may be shown by intercorrelations of each item with subtest scores, or with total-test scores.
5. The means and the standard deviations of both forms should correspond closely.
6. The mechanics of administering and scoring should be uniform.

These are the ideal criteria of equivalent forms; but complete uniformity in all respects cannot be expected. It is necessary, however, that uniformity be closely approximated.

The purpose in having two forms of a test is to permit retesting without the disadvantages of using a single form. To achieve this purpose, it is essential to have alternate forms that may be reliably substituted for each other. The 1937 Stanford-Binet scale, for example, has Forms L and M. The content of each was derived from one and the same process of standardization. The correlation between these two versions at chronological age seven is .91. This index is typical of the relationship found at every age group (18, p. 44).

There are numerous individual and group tests that do not have alternate forms. Furthermore, the retest method, using either of the foregoing techniques, is more costly in time and energy, as well as presenting

---

[14] Sometimes called coefficient of equivalence.

the possible psychological disadvantages already discussed. Another technique has, therefore, been devised and is widely used.

SPLIT-HALF RELIABILITY. By means of this technique, which is used to find *internal consistency,* the items in a whole test are divided into two halves *which should be equivalent or very nearly so.* Thus, two scores —one for each half-test—are obtained for each individual by administering the test only once; and each score is treated as though it represented a separate form.

A prerequisite for using the split-half technique is that the items shall have been arranged in their order of increasing difficulty as determined by the percentage of individuals in the standardization group who have passed each (scaling). This fact rules out what would seem to be the first and obvious method; namely, taking the first half of the number of items, then the second half, from each of which a separate score is to be derived. It is obvious that these two parts would not be comparable in levels of difficulty, effects of cumulative fatigue, increasing or decreasing confidence, and external chance factors. In using the split-half method, the common practice is to make the division by taking the odd-numbered items as one part and the even-numbered as the other. The score is found for each individual for each half and the two sets of paired scores are then correlated.[15]

Some psychologists have suggested that each half of the whole be treated as a short form equivalent to the other half, and that they be administered on two different occasions, but within a short time of each other. This practice, of course, requires less labor compared with that needed to construct two full-length equivalent instruments; but it suffers from some of the disadvantages of giving two full-length alternates. The use of this method would be justified if the whole test were too long for a single occasion and, as a result, produced excessive fatigue in its later sections.

Selecting odd-numbered items as one half of the test and even-numbered items as the other half is justified on these grounds: items in most tests (as will be seen) are grouped according to type (number sequences, vocabulary, etc.) and are arranged according to difficulty, from easiest to most difficult. Thus, when this systematic arrangement is employed, the odd-even procedure yields close approximations to equivalent half-scores, because each half-score is based upon the same types of items and the same number of each type; and each half-score is based upon items that progress in difficulty in approximately the same degree. Consider the first ten items of a single type (known as a subtest), verbal analogies, for example. Numbers 1, 3, 5, 7, 9, as a group, are about as difficult as num-

---

[15] This method is also known as odd-even reliability.

bers 2, 4, 6, 8, 10—if they are graduated in difficulty from 1 to 10; for both the odd-numbered and the even-numbered include items from practically the entire range of difficulty represented from numbers 1 to 10.[16]

Since the correlation coefficient for the two sets of scores derived by this method is based upon subdivisions of the full test, each of which is half the length of the whole, a statistical formula (Spearman-Brown) is used to correct for the reduced lengths of the subdivisions from which the correlated scores have been determined. The reason for this correction is that the score of the whole test, being based upon a larger number of items, is a more adequate sampling of traits or functions and hence reduces the possible effects of chance solutions and accidental errors. The whole test is thus more reliable than its subdivisions; and the correction formula is intended to indicate what the reliability of the entire test would be, based upon what was found with the part scores.

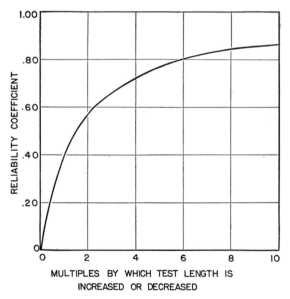

FIG. 4.1. Changes in reliability with changes in length of test, as predicted by Spearman-Brown formula. Unit length reliability is .40. From L. L. Thurstone, *The Reliability and Validity of Tests*. Ann Arbor, Mich.: Edwards Bros., Inc., 1935.

[16] Some psychological tests present special problems that do not lend themselves to this method, and these problems will be discussed, with the tests, in later chapters. Examples are the Stanford-Binet scale, self-report personality inventories, and projective tests.

An example will demonstrate how the Spearman-Brown formula operates. The generalized formula is:

$$r_n = \frac{nr}{1 + (n - 1)r}$$

in which r is the coefficient of reliability obtained between the parts of the divided test; r_n is the reliability of the test n times as long as half the original test.

In the method of odd-even reliability, n is 2, since the original test has been divided in two equal parts. Assuming then, that the odd-even coefficient r is .80, and substituting the values in the formula, the reliability of the whole test r_n is found to be .89. This estimated reliability coefficient for the test as a whole is the one usually reported in psychological research and in test manuals.

The Spearman-Brown formula may be used to estimate the effect upon reliability of a test of a given length if it should be increased by any multiple (3 or 4 times, for instance) or decreased by any fraction ($\frac{1}{2}$ or $\frac{1}{3}$). There is a point of diminishing returns, so to speak, beyond which the very small increase in the reliability coefficient, resulting from increase in length, does not warrant the extension of a test (see Fig. 4.1). Figure 4.2 illustrates increase in test reliability as the length of a test is doubled. This figure demonstrates what happens when reliability is calculated by the split-half method and then corrected by the Spearman-Brown formula.

Another formula that yields nearly the same results as the Spearman-Brown is available for estimating reliability by the split-half method. It is the following:

$$r_{tt} = 2\left(1 - \frac{SD_a^2 + SD_b^2}{SD_t^2}\right)$$

in which SD_a and SD_b are the standard deviations of the scores of the half-tests, and SD_t is the standard deviation of the scores of the whole test. The obvious advantage of this formula is that it is not necessary to correlate the half-tests themselves.

The split-half method of determining reliability can, under some circumstances, yield a coefficient that is somewhat higher than is warranted. In estimating reliability, an assumption is that the effects of chance factors are uncorrelated and, therefore, will cancel out one another. In using the split-half method, however, because both measures are obtained on a single occasion, fluctuations caused by temporary conditions within the testee or by conditions in the external environment will operate in the same direction, favorably or unfavorably, thus producing a higher coefficient than might be found otherwise.

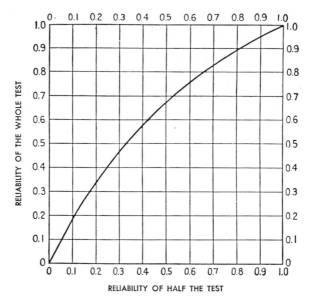

FIG. 4.2. Showing the increase in reliability of the whole-test scores as a function of the reliability of the half-test scores, when the Spearman-Brown formula is applied

The split-half technique might also yield higher reliability coefficients for *predictive* purposes than those found by retesting. The reason for this is that the former are not affected by the ordinary, day-to-day circumstances that cause normal fluctuations in performance.

In particular, the split-half method should not be used in estimating reliability of a pure "speed test," whose items are of the same degree of difficulty throughout and which, therefore, measures only rate of performance at the given level of difficulty. Since all items in the test are of equal difficulty, an examinee should do as well with any one item as with any other. Hence, to measure rates of performance and to differentiate among individuals, the time limit and the length of the test should be such that no one is able to complete all the items. Under the circumstances, except for chance errors in performance, the odd-even correlation should be +1.00 (perfect positive), because the test is, presumably, uniform throughout, and the psychological function being measured (speed) is operating uniformly on all items. It follows that the total scores on the odd-numbered items should equal those on the even-numbered items. One test manual, for example, reports an odd-even reliability coefficient of .99+, but the manual also reports a coefficient of .88 when the scores of two equivalent forms were used (5). The best procedure is to use the test-retest method with a "speed test."

Reliability of Homogeneous Items. Another method of estimating reliability of a test, based on a single administration (internal consistency) employs the Kuder-Richardson formula, named for its originators (15). The appropriate use of this method requires that all items in the test should be psychologically homogeneous; that is, every item should measure the same factor or a combination of factors in the same proportion as every other item. This is called "interitem consistency." A characteristic of interitem consistency is that every item in the test has a high correlation with every other one. As in the case of the split-half reliability method, this procedure is not affected by an individual's variations in performance from time to time. Again, like the split-half technique, it should not be used with speed tests. But if the items in the test are not highly homogeneous, this method will yield a lower reliability coefficient than does the split-half method.[17] The commonly used formula is the following:

$$r_{11} = \left(\frac{n}{n-1} \right) \left(\frac{SD_t^2 - \Sigma_{pq}}{SD_t^2} \right)$$

in which r is the reliability coefficient of the whole test

n is the total number of test items

SD is the standard deviation of the scores of the whole test; SD^2 is, of course, the variance of the total test

p is the percent of individuals passing each item

q is the percent of individuals not passing each item

Σ_{pq} is the sum of the products of pq (the product is found separately for each item).

THE STANDARD ERROR OF MEASUREMENT. This index of reliability is an estimate of the deviation of a set of obtained scores from their "true" scores. A "true" score is a value that is free from any chance factors and other errors of measurement. An individual's true level presumably remains constant from one measurement to another, but his obtained scores may vary to some extent from time to time. Theoretically, this kind of score represents an individual's true level of performance on the test being used. The true level of any individual would be represented by the average score (mean) of an unlimited number of measurements of that person, obtained with the measuring device in question, assuming that

[17] Kuder and Richardson have presented other formulas as well as the one given here. Other statisticians, also, have devised modifications and variants. The student who wants to study this technique should consult one of the textbooks on statistical methods used in psychology.

repeated testings have not changed the person. Since the standard error of measurement in psychological testing cannot be based upon a large number of repeated measurements of the same individuals because of practical difficulties, it is necessary to substitute a large number of individuals for whom only two sets of measures need be obtained. Thereby, the limits of the most probable true scores are found.[18]

The standard error of measurement is dependent upon the standard deviation of the distribution of obtained scores and upon the coefficient of reliability of the test from which the distribution of scores was obtained. The formula for determining the standard error of measurement is written:

$$SE_{(meas.)} = SD_x\sqrt{1 - r_{xx}}$$

in which SD_x is the standard deviation of the distribution of the obtained scores, and r_{xx} is the reliability coefficient of the test.

Assume that the standard deviation of a test (SD_x) is 12 IQ points and that its coefficient of reliability (r_{xx}) is .90. Substituting these values in the formula, we find that the standard error of measurement is approximately ±3.8 points. This statistic is interpreted as follows: assuming that the test scores are normally distributed and that the "errors of measurement" are similarly distributed, then approximately 68 percent of the obtained scores are *within* ±3.8 points of the true scores for the person measured. Otherwise stated, the odds are 68 out of 100 (or 68 to 32) that a particular individual's obtained score is in error by 3.8 points *or less*. Then, using the table of probabilities for standard deviation values, we can say, further, that the probabilities are 19 to 1 (95 in 100) that the error of measurement will be 7.6 points (twice the standard error of measurement), or less; and 99 to 1 that it will be 9.5 points (2½ times the standard error of measurement), or less.

Obviously, the higher the test's reliability coefficient, the smaller will be the error of measurement, and therefore the greater the dependability and the predictive value of the instrument. The standard error of measurement also provides a basis for estimating the probabilities that unequal scores for two or more individuals represent a true statistical difference,

---

[18] The true score as defined is a statistical concept. Whether or not it is consistent with a *psychological* conception of an individual's true score is a different matter. Assume, for example, that a pupil is capable of performance at, and does occasionally attain, an IQ level of 140. But for various *nonintellectual* reasons, his intelligence quotients, obtained by means of a large enough number of testings with the same instrument, average only 130. Psychologically, is his true score a 140 IQ, the level he is really capable of reaching, or is it 130 IQ, which represents only his average level of functioning? The answer is a matter of definitions; but to the clinician and the guidance counselor, the difference is an important consideration. The student should remember that what is statistically "true" may not be the psychological answer; it may be an artifact.

or whether the scores fall within a narrow enough range to be regarded as probable deviations from the same, or nearly the same, true scores.

Quite aside from any question of statistical significance, a psychologist who is experienced in administering, scoring, and interpreting tests—especially those individually administered, as is the Stanford-Binet—knows that no psychological significance attaches to a difference of a few points in intelligence quotients or percentile ranks.

As estimates of a test's dependability, the reliability coefficient and the standard error of measurement supplement each other. Since the size of the latter depends in part upon the former, the coefficient must always be found; it is regarded as an essential index of an instrument's value. While not all test manuals report standard errors of measurement, it too is now regarded as essential. Test authors are expected to include it; for the higher the reliability coefficient and the smaller the error of measurement, the greater will be the confidence attached to judgments and predictions based on the test's findings, provided, also, that the instrument is sufficiently valid.

If the error of measurement varies at different age levels or ability levels, the manual should report this fact, because sometimes a test measures with less error at some levels of the scale than at others. In that event, it is possible to estimate at which levels the standard errors of measurement are larger or smaller than that for the entire group. On the 1937 Stanford-Binet scale, for example, this index is 5.2 points for IQs above 130, but only 2.2 points for IQs below 70.

When this index is given in terms of test units (raw or weighted scores), it is not possible to compare directly the reliabilities of two or more such tests, because their units are rarely comparable. The coefficient of reliability, therefore, is the index used in making intertest comparisons. When the same derived index, as found by two or more different devices, is used (for example, the intelligence quotient), then their standard errors of measurement may be regarded as one basis of comparison.

Table 4.1 illustrates the extent to which the standard error of measurement depends upon the reliability coefficient and upon the standard deviation of obtained scores found for the group of persons tested.

ANALYSIS OF VARIANCE. As already stated, the degree of reliability of a test depends upon the extent to which variations in scores of the group are attributable to the true (that is, the actual) individual differences in the trait or the ability being measured and upon the extent of inaccuracies in measurement. A test is *unreliable* in proportion to the variations in results attributable to test inaccuracy, rather than to actual individual differences among members of the group. In group scores, the estimate of proportions of variations owing to each of the several sources of both

error and nonerror variation is technically known as "analysis of variance." [19]

In a study of test reliability by this method, the question is: What

TABLE 4.1

STANDARD ERRORS OF MEASUREMENT FOR DIFFERENT
VALUES OF THE RELIABILITY COEFFICIENT AND OF
THE STANDARD DEVIATION

SD	Reliability coefficient					
	.95	.90	.85	.80	.75	.70
30	6.7	9.5	11.6	13.4	15.0	16.4
28	6.3	8.9	10.8	12.5	14.0	15.3
26	5.8	8.2	10.1	11.6	13.0	14.2
24	5.4	7.6	9.3	10.7	12.0	13.1
22	4.9	7.0	8.5	9.8	11.0	12.0
20	4.5	6.3	7.7	8.9	10.0	11.0
18	4.0	5.7	7.0	8.0	9.0	9.9
16	3.6	5.1	6.2	7.2	8.0	8.8
14	3.1	4.4	5.4	6.3	7.0	7.7
12	2.7	3.8	4.6	5.4	6.0	6.6
10	2.2	3.2	3.9	4.5	5.0	5.5
8	1.8	2.5	3.1	3.6	4.0	4.4
6	1.3	1.9	2.3	2.7	3.0	3.3
4	.9	1.3	1.5	1.8	2.0	2.2
2	.4	.6	.8	.9	1.0	1.1

SOURCE: The Psychological Corporation.

factors may be important, and to what extent, in producing the obtained
differences of scores on two applications of the identical test (or of equivalent forms) to the same group of persons? First, because individuals
differ in any population sample, the analysis should estimate the extent
to which obtained differences in scores are due to true differences in the
functions being measured. Second, if there is some general improvement
of scores on the second test, it would be necessary to estimate the practice
effect. Third, to what extent are differences due to defects in the test
that will produce guessing and other chance responses (defects in content); or to errors in scoring; or to the testing environment? Because not

[19] *Variance* is defined as the mean of the squared deviations from the mean score of
the group. A measure of deviation is an index of the extent to which individual scores
of a group vary from the group's average score. Variance is the statistical term for
the square of the standard deviation (SD^2).

all elements contributing to variations in scores can be accounted for, those that cannot be separately isolated and analyzed are called "residual factors."

Analysis of variance is not ordinarily used as a method of reporting reliability of a psychological test. It is, however, an important research tool.[20]

Factors Affecting Reliability Estimates

Range of Ages. If a reliability coefficient is found with a group that has a relatively small variation of the trait or ability being measured, the coefficient will be relatively low. If the group has a wider range, the coefficient will be higher (see Fig. 4.3). Thus, a test having high reliability for a widely varying group does not necessarily have equal reliability for

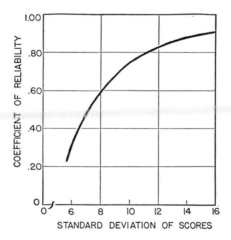

FIG. 4.3. Curve showing increase in test reliability as variability of a group increases

a group of persons who are significantly more homogeneous. One of the reasons for this fact is the nature of the correlation process and the elements in the correlation formula.

For illustrative purposes, suppose there is a group that is completely homogeneous in chronological age. Assume that everyone in the group is exactly 10 years of age. If they are an adequately representative sample of all 10-year-olds, the range in test scores will be from extremely low to

[20] Students who want to become familiar with this technique should consult one of the standard textbooks on statistical methods in psychology.

extremely high. In this instance, because there is no deviation (or range) at all in one of the measures (chronological age), the correlation coefficient for the two variables (test score and CA) will be zero.[21] Such an extreme instance rarely occurs, but it does demonstrate that when there are possibilities for wide variations in one measure (in this instance, the test score) and very restricted possibilities in the other (in this instance, the CA) the coefficient is lowered.

If the age range were two years instead of one, the coefficient of correlation would still be low, but not zero, because *in general* the members of the older group tend to have higher test scores than do those in the younger. But since there is a wide range of capacity within each group, and overlapping of capacity between the two age groups, the coefficient will be low.

A correlation coefficient reflects the *group* trends of the measures. As persons increase in age, mental capacity increases until maximum development is reached. The correlation coefficient will reflect this fact. But since there are wide differences in capacity within any age group, and since there is considerable overlapping of capacity even among rather widely separated age groups, the coefficient will be affected by these facts also. The result will be a coefficient lower than $+1.00$ (perfect correlation).

Thus, in correlational estimates of reliability, if the age range is wide, the group trends in scores (higher scores with higher ages) will have increased weight, as compared with a narrower age range in which the age trend has less weight. In interpreting a reliability coefficient of a test, therefore, it is necessary to know the range of ages upon which the test was standardized.

Range of Scores.   Just as, in the foregoing illustrations, correlation coefficients were shown to be lowered by homogeneity in chronological age, so in estimating reliability the coefficient will be lowered by restricting the group's range of variation in the trait being measured. An illustration will help to clarify this matter:

In Table 4.2 are shown the raw scores and rankings of twenty students on two forms of an arithmetic test. Looking at the two sets of rankings, we see that changes in rank from one form to the other are minor; the ranks shift a little, but not importantly. A coefficient computed from these data is very high: $r = .96$.

Now, however, let us examine only the rankings of the five top students. Though for these five students the shifts in rank are the same as before,

---

[21] Inspection of the product-moment correlation formula will show this to be the case:

$$r = \frac{\Sigma_{xy}}{N(SD_x \, SD_y)}$$

in which Σ_{xy} is the sum of products of the deviations of the paired scores; SD_x and SD_y are the standard deviations of the two sets of measures.

TABLE 4.2

RAW SCORES AND RANKS OF STUDENTS ON
TWO FORMS OF AN ARITHMETIC TEST

| | Form X | | Form Y | |
Student	Score	Rank	Score	Rank
A	90	1	88	2
B	87	2	89	1
C	83	3	76	5
D	78	4	77	4
E	72	5	80	3
F	70	6	65	7
G	68	7	64	8
H	65	8	67	6
I	60	9	53	10
J	54	10	57	9
K	51	11	49	11
L	47	12	45	14
M	46	13	48	12
N	43	14	47	13
O	39	15	44	15
P	38	16	42	16
Q	32	17	39	17
R	30	18	34	20
S	29	19	37	18
T	25	20	36	19

SOURCE: *Test Service Bulletin,* The Psychological Corporation, May 1952, no. 44.

the importance of the shifts is greatly emphasized. Whereas in the larger group Student C's change in rank from third to fifth represented only a 10 percent shift (two places out of twenty), his shift of two places in rank in the smaller top group is a 40 percent change (two places out of five). When the entire twenty represent the group on which we estimate the reliability of the arithmetic test, going from third on form X to fifth on form Y still leaves the student as one of the best in this population. If, on the other hand, reliability is being estimated only on the group consisting of the top five students, going from third to fifth means dropping from the middle to the bottom of this population—a radical change. A coefficient, if computed for just these five cases, is .50 (*rho*).[22]

Note that it is not the smaller number of cases which brings about the

[22] *Rho* represents the "rank-order" correlation coefficient. It approximates closely the product-moment coefficient *r*.

lower coefficient. It is the narrower range of talent which is responsible. A coefficient based on five cases as widespread as the twenty (e.g., Pupils A, E, J, O, and T, who rank first, fifth, tenth, fifteenth, and twentieth respectively on form X), would be at least as large as the coefficient based on all twenty students.[23] $[rho = +1.00]$

Furthermore, when the variation among testees is narrow, the correlation between two sets of scores may also be lowered by chance and minor psychological factors. Since individuals in such a group are closely clustered—that is, their true differences are small—the changes in scores and relative positions produced by extraneous factors are more significant than they would be in a widely divergent group.

This illustration makes clear the fact that reliability coefficients of a given test may vary as the composition of the tested group changes, even though the performances of the testees themselves are unchanged. Thus, reliability data may show that a test discriminates satisfactorily over a *wide* range of the trait or capacity measured; but reliability may still be inadequate where *finer* and *more precise* discriminations are necessary among individuals who vary within a narrow range.

The practical significance of range, and hence of ability, is this: in standardizing a test, its author must determine reliability with a group that is similar in average level of ability and in variations of scores to the group with whom the test is to be used. The examiner should select an instrument that, among other things, provides reliability data based upon a sampling of persons who resemble closely the group of individuals he desires to test.

The Time Interval Between Testings. When reliability estimates are based upon odd-even correlations or upon scores of two equivalent forms administered at a single sitting, the results are relatively uniformly affected by the examinee's physical condition and attitudes, and by prevailing environmental conditions. When two forms are administered in the same day, but several hours apart, it is unlikely that the physical conditions of the examinees will have changed significantly; nor will there be much opportunity for changes in basic attitudes, although conditions in general are not likely to be entirely uniform on both occasions.[24]

When there is a time interval, the retest results will be affected by the normally expected fluctuations in individual performances and by changes in environmental conditions. Thus, while reliability coefficients obtained

[23] From *Test Service Bulletin*, The Psychological Corporation, May 1952, no. 44.
[24] It is always possible that some individuals will be less motivated on the second testing. It is therefore essential that the second session should not come at a time of day when the testees are likely to be fatigued or impatient to leave.

at a single sitting, or in a single day, are most likely to estimate best the consistency of the instrument itself, they do not indicate stability of performance over a period of time as well as do coefficients obtained by the test-retest method, using a time interval. Conversely, the test-retest method is the more likely to underestimate the internal consistency of a test, because factors extraneous to it may affect the scores dissimilarly. The extent to which the accuracy of a test is underestimated by the test-retest method will depend upon the degree to which effective influencing conditions are inconsistent. If the time interval has been quite long, especially in the case of young children—perhaps three months or more—an individual's retest results may be influenced by peculiarities of his growth tempo, or by other more or less enduring conditions such as emotional experiences, which may affect persons of any age.

The Effects of Practice and Learning. Such effects will depend upon the content of the test, the length of the interval, and upon the examinee's experiences during the interval. For example, if some months have elapsed between two administrations of an educational achievement test, different pupils may have had different amounts and qualities of instruction during the period. The retest scores would, in part, reflect this difference; thus the correlation coefficient would not be solely a reliability coefficient. Or, in the case of a personality test, therapy or counseling may have modified an individual's attitudes, values, and behavior sufficiently to produce significant differences in test-retest results.

Reliability of Subtests. It has already been explained that, other factors being equal, the reliability of a test increases with increase in length, although not in direct proportion. This principle applies to those scales that consist of several different subtests, each of which utilizes a different kind of content. Nearly all group tests are of this kind, as are some of the individual scales (the Wechsler, for example). For these instruments, the total-test reliability is higher than that for each of the subtests. It is erroneous, therefore, to assume that the reliability coefficient for the whole may be applied to a part. For example, the Wechsler Intelligence Scale for Children yielded a full scale (nine subtests) reliability of .92 for a group of 200 children 7½ years of age, the coefficient having been calculated by means of the split-half technique. Yet, the reliabilities of the individual subtests for the same group of children ranged from a low of .59 to a high of .84 (21). It is obvious that the total score is a more dependable index of the abilities or the traits being measured than is any subtest score.

Consistency of Scores. This is a factor in evaluating test reliability. Some tests (such as the Stanford-Binet and, in particular, projective techniques) are not entirely objective in scoring, because the examiner at times finds it necessary to judge the correctness or quality of responses. For tests such as these, it is necessary to know the extent of agreement in scoring among competent psychologists who have scored the same sets of responses. Test authors usually report such data in their manuals; and in addition, other psychologists will have carried out and reported studies on this problem. Lack of agreement among scorers will adversely affect the reliability findings.

Which Method of Estimating Reliability Is Preferable? An answer to this question depends upon the problem at hand. Psychologists and educators want to know (1) the internal consistency of a test and (2) the predictive value of a test when it is subject only to the minor or accidental changes in conditions from day to day, rather than to fundamental permanent changes, or changes of long duration caused by learning, developmental idiosyncracies, or disturbing emotional experiences. To determine internal consistency, it is preferable to use the odd-even method or the test-retest method, the tests being given at one sitting or within one day (using equivalent forms). To estimate predictive value, the test-retest method is the preferable one, the tests being given within a week or two (using the same form or equivalent forms). Under testing conditions that are not too dissimilar, the results of the second method will not be far removed from those obtained with the first. A test manual should provide information regarding internal consistency and test-retest results.

Psychologists studying effects on mental operations and organization produced by psychotherapy, personality difficulties and disorders, serious emotional experiences, or basic personality changes with time use standardized tests for their purposes. Obviously, if their findings are to be meaningful, the testing devices must be reliable [25] (12).

References

1. Adkins, D. C., *et al. Construction and Analysis of Achievement Tests.* Washington, D.C.: U.S. Government Printing Office, 1947.
2. Adkins, R. M., and H. H. Remmers. Reliability of multiple-choice measuring instruments as a function of the Spearman-Brown prophecy formula. *Journal of Educational Psychology,* 1942, *33,* 385–390.
3. American Psychological Association. Technical recommendations for psychological tests and diagnostic techniques. Washington, D.C.: *Psychological Bulletin,* March 1954 supplement.
4. Bayley, N. Consistency and variability in the growth of intelligence from birth to eighteen. *Journal of Genetic Psychology,* 1949, *75,* 165–169.

[25] Fluctuations and inconsistencies in test performance because of the individual's own changed or changing traits are discussed in Chapter 14.

5. Bennett, G. K., *et al. Differential Aptitude Tests: Manual*. New York: The Psychological Corporation, 1952.

6. Davis, F. B. A note on correcting reliability coefficients for range. *Journal of Educational Psychology*, 1944, *35*, 500–502.

7. Ebert, E., and K. Simmons. *Psychometric Tests*. Washington, D.C.: Society for Research in Child Development, 1943, monograph no. 35.

8. Edwards, A. L. *Techniques of Attitude Scale Construction*. New York: Appleton-Century-Crofts, Inc., 1957.

9. Freeman, F. N., and C. D. Flory. *Growth in Intellectual Ability as Measured by Repeated Tests*. Washington, D.C.: Society for Research in Child Development, 1937, monograph no. 2.

10. Fruchter, B. *Introduction to Factor Analysis*. Princeton, N.J.: D. Van Nostrand Company, Inc., 1954.

11. Guilford, J. P. Factor analysis in a test-development program. *Psychological Review*, 1948, *55*, 79–94.

12. Harrower, M. *Personality Change and Development as Measured by the Projective Techniques*. New York: Grune & Stratton, Inc., 1958.

13. Hoyt, C. Test reliability obtained by analysis of variance. *Psychometrika*, 1941, *6*, 153–160.

14. Jackson, R. W. B., and G. A. Ferguson. *Studies on the Reliability of Tests*. Toronto: Department of Education Research, University of Toronto, 1941.

15. Kuder, G. F., and M. W. Richardson. The theory of estimation of test reliability. *Psychometrika*, 1937, *2*, 151–160.

16. Loevinger, J. A systematic approach to the construction and evaluation of tests of ability. *Psychological Monographs*, 1947, *64*, no. 285.

17. Lorge, I., and R. L. Thorndike. *The Lorge-Thorndike Intelligence Tests: Manual*. Boston: Houghton Mifflin Company, 1957.

18. Terman, L. M., and M. Merrill. *Measuring Intelligence*. Boston: Houghton Mifflin Company, 1937.

19. Thorndike, R. L. Reliability. *Educational Measurement*, E. F. Lindquist (ed.). Washington, D.C.: American Council on Education, 1951, ch. 15.

20. Thurstone, L. L. Psychological implications of factor analysis. *The American Psychologist*, 1948, *3*, 402–408.

21. Wechsler, D. *Wechsler Intelligence Scale for Children*. New York: The Psychological Corporation, 1949, 13.

5.

TEST STANDARDIZATION: VALIDITY

Definition

An index of validity shows the degree to which a test measures what it purports to measure, when compared with accepted criteria. The construction and use of a test imply that the instrument has been evaluated against criteria regarded by experts as the best evidence of the traits to be measured by the test. Selection of satisfactory validation criteria and demonstration of an appropriate degree of validity are fundamental in psychological and educational testing.

The first essential quality of a valid test is that it be highly reliable. If a reliability coefficient of a test is zero, it will not be correlated with anything. A test that yields inconsistent results (low reliability) cannot correlate well with a measure of another variable; in this instance, a criterion.

Psychologists, educators, guidance counselors, and personnel managers use test results for a variety of purposes: to estimate an individual's educational promise, to assist in solving learning problems, to select persons for jobs or for job training, to evaluate an individual's personality traits, and to assess personality traits before and after psychotherapy. Obviously, none of these purposes can be fulfilled, even partially, if the psychological instruments do not have a sufficiently high degree of validity.

Types of Validity

Operational and Predictive Validity. The terms "operational" and "operationalism" have considerable currency in contemporary psychological writings. "Operational" simply means that something pertains to an operation or a procedure. "Operationalism" is the principle, or doctrine, that propositions, concepts, constructs, and theories are given their meaning, in the last analysis, by the methods of observation or investigation used to arrive at them; that they have no other meaning than is yielded by the procedures or operations by which the things or processes to which they refer are known. "Prediction" is used here in its ordinary meaning: to forecast.

It is useful to recognize these two general types of validity, although they are not mutually exclusive. This is especially true at the present time, because much more attention is now concentrated on several forms of operational validity that are discussed in the following pages (for example, construct validity and factorial validity) than used to be the case.

"Operational validity" means that the tasks required by the test are adequate for the measurement and evaluation of certain defined psychological activities. For example, The Seashore Measures of Musical Talent are tests of *certain essential auditory aspects of musical talent,* but not of all aspects of "musical talent," which psychologically involves much more. In so far as the Seashore tests differentiate correctly among persons in regard to the specified auditory processes, they are *operationally* valid.

On the other hand, these measures have predictive validity to the extent that they are efficient in forecasting subsequent development of various degrees of skill and competence in the several aspects of music. Thus, the predictive validity of a test is the extent to which it is efficient in forecasting and differentiating behavior or performance in a specified area under actual working and living conditions.

Numerous other examples can be cited to illustrate the difference between predictive and operational validity. A pegboard test (placing small metal pegs into a perforated board) may measure manual and digital dexterity (operational), but it might be only slightly useful in predicting mechanical ability. Again, a word and number checking test may be quite satisfactory as a measure of perception of details (operational), but it might have limited value in predicting success as a secretary. A test of the four fundamental arithmetical processes might be valid for measuring proficiency in these (operational validity), but it might have very little value in predicting ability to learn algebra at the ninth-grade level.

Predictive validity is dependent, at least in part, upon the operational validity of the test. The reason is that the psychological operations required by the test were included because they were found essential for testing in certain actual situations. Hence, if the psychological operations, or the information, or the specific skills are not measured validly, predictions of later performance will be adversely affected.

Most tests must have predictive validity, as should be evident from the uses to which they are put. Possible exceptions are tests of educational achievement, when they are used solely for measuring specific learning during a specific period of time, without regard to future educational planning for the individuals examined. It is a fact, however, that results of educational achievement tests are most often used not only to determine an individual's level and quality of achievement in a subject of study, at a specified time, but also to plan his subsequent education.

Face Validity.   This is a term used to characterize test materials that *appear* to measure what the test's author desires to measure. That is, the test contains items that seem to be related to the variable being measured. The content of the test seems to be relevant to its stated purpose; and there is no further effort to confirm the assumption objectively. This, too, is an operational conception of validity, based upon subjective judgment.

This form of validity, now rejected, has been disparaged since more sophisticated procedures have been devised. As a matter of fact, however, face validity in the earlier days of test development was the criterion used by many competent psychologists *as a first step*. Validation of their test content at face value was not as capricious, haphazard, or casual as some critics have said. On the contrary, their content was based upon whatever psychological knowledge and insight could then be utilized.[1] Face validity was claimed most often with tests of educational achievement and of personality, and to a lesser extent with tests of specific aptitudes.

Tests have been validated at face value when there was urgent need for them, for example, when psychologists worked under pressure in the armed forces, or in the early stages of developing tests for use in selecting industrial and business personnel. Except in such instances, a claim of face validity is not sufficient to warrant the use of a test.

Tests of personality traits present an especially difficult problem in validation. Often in the past—and to some extent currently—authors of personality tests have used face validity. In this category, the sounder instruments, however, are validated against actual forms of behavior of a variety of individuals and against clinical diagnoses. However, these

---

[1] Of course, we do not have in mind the incompetents, charlatans, and popularizers of their own so-called tests.

validating criteria present difficulties because they are themselves based to an appreciable degree on the subjective judgments of the specialists making the diagnoses and the evaluations of behavior. These problems are discussed in detail in subsequent chapters.

Content Validity. As the name indicates, this form of validity is estimated by evaluating the relevance of the test items, individually and as a whole. Each item should be a sampling of the knowledge or performance which the test purports to measure. Taken collectively, the items should constitute a representative sample of the variable to be tested. At the same time, it is essential that the content not be compounded by introducing irrelevant problems and materials. For example, a test of spelling ability should not place any weight on rates of writing. A test of the four fundamental arithmetical processes should not be "contaminated" with demands upon reading ability. On the other hand, a test of ability to solve arithmetical problems must include reading comprehension.

Content validity is most appropriately applied only to tests of proficiency and of educational achievement, although such validity may be and should be supplemented by several types of statistical analysis. Validity of content, however, should not depend upon the subjective judgment of only one specialist. It should be based upon careful analyses, by several specialists, of instructional objectives and of the actual subject matter studied. For example, in constructing a test of American history, the specialists will examine textbooks and courses of study that they believe to be representative; they will determine which topics and facts are most significant, and what their relative weights in the whole test should be. Representative items will then be devised in collaboration with someone who is an expert in the writing of test items and in technical procedures of test construction.[2]

The validating process should not stop there. Statistical analyses should follow, for the purpose of: (1) determining which items discriminate best between individuals at the upper and the lower levels of performance; (2) determining the percent that answers each item correctly; (3) determining significance of increases in average scores from one school grade to the next; (4) determining for each item, or for each division (subtest), its correlation with educational progress and with general educational performance (school marks). Thus, content validation rests first upon an

[2] One university, for example, established a test bureau that was given the responsibility of preparing objective tests in each of several areas of study. Students were required to pass these tests before they were permitted to take courses in the upper division of the university. The staff of this bureau consisted of one or more specialists in each area for which measures were to be constructed, plus a number of specialists in test construction.

expert analysis of the materials to be sampled (the variable), and second upon the use of available statistical procedures to refine the original selection of items (16).

Factorial Validity. This method utilizes factor analysis techniques that are not within the scope of the present discussion. Factor analysis theory, however, is discussed in Chapter 7 in connection with theories of intelligence. Yet since factorial validation is a method used with some tests, students should be familiar with the general nature of the concept.

Most tests of mental ability and of personality sample a composite of behavior or of ability, such as verbal knowledge and facility, number facility and quantitative reasoning, memory span, and concept formation. Factor analysts maintain that these and others, especially when represented by a single composite index (such as mental age or intelligence quotient), are not "functional unities." Factorial analysts insist that they are not measures of a "pure" ability, that is, one type of ability uncomplicated by others. Thus, according to this theory, a test is said to have high factorial validity if it is a measure of one functional unity (for example, word knowledge) to the exclusion of other elements, as far as possible. The factorial process aims to identify, by the method of intercorrelations and further statistical analysis, a list of functional unities (also called "primary mental abilities") within a test and the weight contributed by each of these to total performance on the test. The ultimate goal is to devise tests, each of which will measure only one functional unity and be relatively independent of others (that is, show quite low intercorrelations). Such pure tests would then be used singly; or they might be used as subtests in a comprehensive measuring instrument. Even then, however, each subtest is scored and rated independently for the purpose of obtaining a psychological profile for each person.

These functional unities are identified by analyzing the intercorrelations among a number of separate, relatively restricted measures. If, for example, ten separate tests or separate types of test materials were administered to a large enough group of persons, each separate test score would be correlated with every other score. This will yield forty-five correlation coefficients.[3] Inspection of the table of coefficients can suggest that the tests they represent appear to group themselves into clusters, or functional unities, such as verbal facility, spatial perception, and memory span. But analysis by inspection is not sufficiently precise. Consequently, statistical techniques have been developed to analyze the table of correla-

---

[3] $\dfrac{10 \times 9}{1 \times 2} = 45$

tion coefficients and in this way identify the common factors that will account for the obtained coefficients.[4]

Since the original number of tests or types of materials will usually group themselves into clusters (factors), the number of factors will be smaller than the original number of tests. Factor analysis, therefore, is intended to reduce the number of variables, or test categories, needed to represent an individual's abilities or traits for specified purposes. It is a technique that yields clusters of correlations from which one can infer the existence of underlying variables. The psychologist must make the inference of their existence primarily on the basis of his psychological insights into the intellectual or behavioral processes involved in the tests included within each cluster of correlations.

Factorial validity, therefore, is determined by the weights (called "loadings") contributed to the total-test scores by each of the derived factors, as it is also by their relative independence of one another (low intercorrelations). Having deduced that certain *apparently* separate mental operations do, in fact, correlate well and tend to form a cluster, the tester may then devise more precise and more restricted sets of items for each of the factors and thus repeat the factorial analysis several times. He will thereby be able to construct a test in which each part (subtest) will be relatively distinct from the others, so far as kinds of mental activity are concerned.

The merit of factorial validity, in any given instance, will depend upon the appropriateness of the statistical procedure and upon the tester's initial psychological insights in selecting items, and also in the interpretation of his findings.

If validation stops at factorial validity, operational validity has been inferred. If the test has been validated against criteria of later performance in working situations, after factorial validity has been calculated, then we also have predictive validation. The principal contribution of factorial validation is this: instead of validating the total, undifferentiated instrument against external criteria, an effort is made to identify the component psychological elements and to establish their relative independence, and finally to correlate these elements separately against external criteria.

Such analysis into psychological unities, or elements, is of value when individuals are to be selected for specialized work or study and their performance predicted therein. For example, since mechanical aptitude is not a simple, unitary skill, it is valuable to be able to identify which

[4] An explanation of techniques of factorial analysis can be found in some of the textbooks on statistical methods in psychology. For a more comprehensive and detailed presentation, see (12).

psychological elements have most predictive value for a specified type of work. Mechanical work may involve a high degree of spatial perception in one situation but not in another; similarly with manual precision and speed, or comprehension of mechanical principles. Also, higher than average intelligence is desirable for the practice of both law and engineering. In the former, word knowledge and verbal concept formation are the more significant; in the latter, spatial perception and quantitative reasoning are more significant than word knowledge. Factorial analysis can assist in identifying the more restricted and immediately relevant aspects of ability required in a given occupation or activity.

Construct Validity. This is one of the newer operational conceptions of validity; it should be understood, first, in terms of the meaning of "construct." There are several parts to the dictionary's definition of the term: (1) a synthesis or ordering of elements or factors; (2) an object of thought which arises by synthesis or ordering of terms; (3) a product of the uniting of immaterial elements. The Englishes' dictionary of psychology states that a construct is "a concept formally proposed with definition and limits explicitly related to empirical data" (10). If this criterion of validity is applied in the development of a test, these definitions signify that the instrument's validity is to be judged by the extent to which it measures or assesses the psychological processes (mental operations) or the personality traits as defined and analyzed by the author of the test. Construct validity depends upon the degree to which the test items individually and collectively sample the range or class of activities or traits, as defined by the mental process or the personality trait being tested.

Construct validity differs from face and content validities in that under the first of these, each process or trait to be tested must be analyzed and made explicit, and each item in the test must belong to the process or trait in question. Thus, to devise a test of manual skill, a psychologist must learn, through analysis of the performances involved, what kinds of activities constitute manual skill.

Construct validity also differs from the others in so far as this conception implies (and assumes) that such a test has utilized previous research on the psychological characteristic being measured, and that the items of the test have been or are being subjected to refinement by means of factorial analysis or predictive validation in situations where the characteristic is in operation.

Construct validity of a given test might also be demonstrated by finding substantial correlations with other tests that have been shown to measure satisfactorily the mental processes or traits in question. For example,

The Lorge-Thorndike intelligence tests include several types of items which, over an appreciable period of years, have been accepted as sampling and measuring certain mental activities, such as interpretation of symbols, using words, numbers, and more or less abstract diagrammatical forms. If a self-rating personality inventory has been based on construct validity, each trait to be assessed has been analyzed (on the basis of actual cases) to determine the kinds of activities which exemplify the trait, and relevant items have been devised. For instance, in developing an inventory to assess the trait ("dimension") security–insecurity, a psychologist must answer these questions: What is the definition of the syndrome called security? What are the various specific forms of behavior manifested by persons who are diagnosed as "insecure" by counselors and clinicians? What are the opposites of these as manifested by individuals who are regarded as "secure"? Do the items in this inventory relate definitely and comprehensively enough to these specific forms of activity? Do the items, individually and collectively, differentiate between the markedly secure and markedly insecure? Do the test items also differentiate reasonably well among the several degrees of the trait, excluding the extreme groups?

If a test has a satisfactory degree of construct validity, the scores obtained with it should indicate the *status* of the testees at the time of examination. The psychologist may then interpret the obtained results primarily in terms of the mental processes or of the trait as defined and sampled, and with reference to the population sample upon whom the instrument has been standardized.

For example, if a sound "construct valid" test of mental ability has been administered, the findings can answer such questions as the following: How well does this individual now perform when dealing with abstract verbal concepts, standardized on a representative sampling of pupils in grades x, y, z? How well does this pupil perform on problems requiring organization and interpretation of quantitative symbols, standardized on a representative sampling of pupils in the same grades? At what grade or age level does the pupil perform when dealing with nonverbal forms requiring analysis and integration?

When a test of mechanical comprehension is being used, if it has construct validity, it will be properly scaled; it will be sufficiently comprehensive to serve its specified purpose. Its findings should, therefore, be able to supply an answer to this question: How well is each testee able to deal with a given range of problems representing mechanical comprehension at the specified levels of difficulty and in comparison with the performance of the standardization population?

In the case of a security–insecurity inventory that is said to have construct validity, its findings should answer this question: What degree of this trait is represented by a given range of scores if the norms were derived from scores based on ratings, by qualified observers, of responses in relevant situations?

This type of operational validity is employed, also, in devising aptitude tests in music and the graphic arts. These tests should be able to answer specific questions about an individual's capacities in the several psychological aspects on which learning and performance depend. These aspects have emerged from analysis of each of these arts by qualified artists themselves, in conjunction with psychologists who have used these as well as their own analyses of experimental tests, as in the case of the Seashore Measures of Musical Talent, and the Wing Standardized Tests of Musical Intelligence (see Chapter 19).

Tests of intelligence were initially based on certain ideas concerning which mental operations were most important in this complex mental process. These concepts were subjected to experimental trial, to further psychological and statistical analysis, and to practical use. As a consequence, the types of test materials underwent refinement in all instances and extension in some respects, but restriction or elimination in others. These results will become apparent in later chapters in which the tests and their contents are described and discussed.

Concurrent Validity. This is also one of the newer terms. Originally, psychologists spoke of validation with other tests, validation with a proficiency rating, validation with school grades, or, in the case of a personality test, validation with a recent diagnosis. At present, psychologists prefer the term "concurrent validity" to indicate the process of validating the new test by correlating it, or otherwise comparing it for agreement, with some present source of information. This source of information might have been obtained shortly before or very shortly after the new test was given.

New criteria of validity are not involved. For example, in standardizing a new group test of intelligence, its scores will be correlated with those on a sound, standardized achievement test, both being given within a short time of each other. Or, as frequently happens, the scores of the group test will be correlated with those obtained on the Stanford-Binet scale for a manageable but representative number of individuals.[5]

Cross Validation. This term refers to the process of validating a test by using a population sample other than the one on which the instrument was originally standardized. The reason for using this method is

[5] "Manageable" means that the number of individuals tested with the Stanford-Binet is necessarily much smaller than that to whom the group test is given, since the former is individually administered and time consuming.

that at times the original validity data may be spuriously high or low because of chance factors that produce a higher or lower correlation than is warranted. As a matter of fact, however, once a test is put to use in a variety of situations and by many different persons, it is being constantly cross-validated; and if it does not prove to have high enough value, its use will be or should be discontinued. It is sounder practice, however, to cross-validate a test before making it available for general use.

Validating Criteria

The problems of selecting and utilizing satisfactory validating criteria vary with the several types of tests.

In constructing *tests of intelligence* (general ability), a common practice is to use several of the following criteria: school marks, teachers' judgments of an individual's abilities, cumulative scholastic averages over a period of several years, number of school grades completed, chronological age, known groups, and other well-validated tests. The reasons for using these criteria are that:

Scholastic records provide evidence of mental ability even though affected by factors other than intellectual ability.

Teachers are in a position to evaluate individual ability with some validity, because they observe their pupils over a long period and are able to make interpupil comparisons.

Cumulative scholastic averages are more valid than marks or estimates of a single teacher, because they represent combined judgments of performance over a longer period of time.

On the whole, the more able persons complete more formal education; they reach higher levels in school and college.

As individuals grow older, their levels of intelligence increase until adult maximum is reached.

Definitely known groups, such as the gifted, somewhat superior, average, slow learning, and mentally deficient, should show significantly different levels of performance on a valid test.

A new test should correlate well with another instrument of proved validity that is intended for the same purpose.

The principal criteria in standardizing *tests of specific aptitudes* (such as mechanical, musical) are marks in training courses and differentiation of known groups possessing the aptitude in varying degrees. An example of known groups would be those working efficiently at each of several levels of a mechanical occupation and those in nonmechanical occupations. It is highly desirable, of course, to use degree of success of actual performance in the vocation as an ultimate criterion.

When criteria of actual performance on the job are used, they are usually ratings by supervisors, rate of production, and evaluation of the quality of the product. In managerial positions and in the professions—teaching, law, medicine, engineering—valid and uniform criteria of performance beyond the learning period are much more difficult, or at times impossible, to obtain. In standardizing an aptitude test, therefore, the most frequently employed criteria are grades and ratings in the training courses; that is, criteria of capacity to learn the given skill or the professional subject matter, since aptitude tests are used largely to select individuals to be educated in specified areas. Their use in employee selection, however, is not inconsiderable and has been increasing.

In *personnel work,* in business and industry, where specialized tests are used to select individuals for specific jobs, it is possible, indeed essential, to use actual production records or performance ratings as criteria of test validity. If, for example, a personnel department wants to know whether certain measures will identify the potentially best stenographers, the tests might be administered (1) to a group of employees of several quality levels to estimate the instrument's differentiating efficiency and (2) to newly employed personnel whose performance records, after an adequate period, would be correlated and otherwise analyzed against their test scores.

Devices used for this purpose are of two kinds. There are, first, the aptitude tests that sample the *psychological processes,* or operations, involved in the job, such as rate of tapping, digital precision, perception, and rate of learning new materials. Performance on such tests would be indicative of one's capacity to develop the skills or to acquire the knowledge needed for the work in question.

The content of the second kind of test consists of items which are *samples of the actual work* to be performed on the job. These are called *proficiency tests;* for example, some clerical jobs require speed and accuracy in simple arithmetical computations,[6] or knowledge of punctuation and English usage, or ability to read and interpret graphs. A test of stenographic proficiency should include rate and accuracy of copying and ability to spell.

Tests of educational achievement are ultimately validated against the educational criteria already discussed under content validity.

Criteria used in estimating validity of *personality tests*—inventories and projectives—were briefly presented in the discussion of face validity. In addition to these, several other techniques of validation are in use. These include matching interpretations of test results with case histories; com-

---

[6] The need for this particular skill seems to be rapidly disappearing with the increasing use of a variety of calculating machines.

paring results obtained after therapy with those obtained before; and temporary experimentally produced changes, when individuals are subjected to certain predetermined conditions in the laboratory.

Comparison of Types of Validation. As already stated, the basic purpose of any psychological or educational test is to determine each individual's present status, or to predict his future status with regard to specified types of mental functioning (including motor skills), personality traits, or learning.

A test's *content validity* indicates the extent to which it yields an adequate measure of achievement or performance in certain specified areas; as in measuring learning in a school subject, or in testing proficiency in the simple arithmetical calculations required in a clerical job.

A test's *construct validity* (including factorial validity) will indicate the psychological operations on the basis of which one's test performance may be explained and evaluated.

A test's *concurrent validity* indicates the extent of its agreement with other present criteria measuring similar psychological operations or traits.

It should be clear that content, construct, and concurrent validities are, in fact, evaluations of the extent to which the device estimates an individual's status at the time the test was administered. From the viewpoint of applied psychology, every test, whatever the type, must ultimately be shown to have predictive validity. Psychologists in applied fields, educators, and employers are usually interested in knowing present status as an indication of what may be expected subsequently. If a test of clerical proficiency or of arithmetical ability is given to a group, it is for the purpose of selecting those whose present status indicates satisfactory promise for future performance on the job. If a test of general intelligence is administered to school children or to college students, the results will be used for educational or vocational guidance at that time, or with a view to the future.

When testing on a large scale is undertaken, as in the armed forces, for purposes of screening on the basis of present status, determination of status is only the first step in eliminating those individuals whose test ratings show little or no promise. At the same time, the test serves to identify those who show adequate promise in the area tested.

If tests of intelligence, specific aptitudes, or personality traits are administered in a clinic, their purpose is not only to determine the person's status at that time, but to decide upon procedures to be followed with that individual in order to handle effectively the problem that brought him there.

A possible exception to the necessity of predictive validity is the educational achievement test administered at the end of a course of instruction for the purpose of measuring how much has been learned and for assigning grades. But this is by no means always the sole purpose served by achievement tests; for performance on them often provides the basis for selecting later courses of study. Thus, the predictive validity of a test is its most important characteristic; for, if high enough, it will indicate present status as well as being predictive.

Some theoretical psychologists would not place as much emphasis upon predictive validity. Their position is that when tests are used solely for research purposes, they are not concerned with prediction, but rather with the covariation of current variables. Although this is true, the research studies should still be of value in predicting future situations and findings under similar conditions.

Methods of Calculating Validity

Simple Correlation. The most frequently used technique of estimating validity is to correlate test scores with each criterion. A coefficient of a particular size cannot be specified as signifying, or not signifying, a satisfactory degree of validity. Whenever a coefficient is positive and has a small probability (or range) of error, it has some value. In some instances, coefficients of only $+.25$ have proved useful. In most cases, however, coefficients should be larger.

ERROR SCORES ON *STORE PERSONNEL TEST, FORM FS*

TRAINER RATINGS (SUM OF LEARNING ABILITY, WORKING SPEED, AND OVER–ALL FITNESS)

	56–54	53–51	50–48	47–45	44–42	41–39	38–36	35–33	32–30	29–27	26–24	23–21	20–18	17–15	14–12	11–9	8–6	5–3	2–0
12											2	2	1		1	1			
11									1		2		3	3	1	5	1		
10											3	1	3	1	1	2	2		
9									1		5	4	3	6	4	3	1		
8										1	4	4	2	2	2	2	1		
7											3	4	3	1	2	2	4		
6							2				2	6	2	1		2	1		
5								1	1		4	3		1	2	1	1		
4						1	1	3	1	1	1								
3		1				1	1	1			3			1	3				
2							1	1	1		1				1				
1												1							

FIG. 5.1. Chart for Pearson product-moment correlation between number of errors made by 155 grocery store trainees on Part II of the experimental Store Personnel Test, Form FS, and ratings made by the training staff. $r = .46$. SOURCE: The Psychological Corporation (25).

There are several ways of demonstrating validity by means of correlations. Figure 5.1 illustrates the simple correlation method. Test scores, shown horizontally, were correlated with instructors' ratings, shown vertically. The number in each cell shows how many individuals received the scores of that cell, as indicated on both axes. For example, two persons who made between 21 and 23 errors on the test were given trainer ratings of 12; then going to the bottom of the same column, we find that one person who also made between 21 and 23 errors had a trainer rating of 2. For this sampling of examinees, the coefficient is .46, which is well within the range of validity coefficients most often found for a single criterion in situations of this kind. One probable reason why the correlation is not higher is the subjectivity of ratings given by members of the training staff.

Table 5.1 presents another method of evaluating the efficiency of a cor-

TABLE 5.1

SELECTION RATIO

PROPORTION OF EMPLOYEES CONSIDERED SATISFACTORY = .50

r	.05	.10	.20	.30	.40	.50	.60	.70	.80	.90	.95
.00	.50	.50	.50	.50	.50	.50	.50	.50	.50	.50	.50
.05	.54	.54	.53	.52	.52	.52	.51	.51	.51	.50	.50
.10	.58	.57	.56	.55	.54	.53	.53	.52	.51	.51	.50
.15	.63	.61	.58	.57	.56	.55	.54	.53	.52	.51	.51
.20	.67	.64	.61	.59	.58	.56	.55	.54	.53	.52	.51
.25	.70	.67	.64	.62	.60	.58	.56	.55	.54	.52	.51
.30	.74	.71	.67	.64	.62	.60	.58	.56	.54	.52	.51
.35	.78	.74	.70	.66	.64	.61	.59	.57	.55	.53	.51
.40	.82	.78	.73	.69	.66	.63	.61	.58	.56	.53	.52
.45	.85	.81	.75	.71	.68	.65	.62	.59	.56	.53	.52
.50	.88	.84	.78	.74	.70	.67	.63	.60	.57	.54	.52
.55	.91	.87	.81	.76	.72	.69	.65	.61	.58	.54	.52
.60	.94	.90	.84	.79	.75	.70	.66	.62	.59	.54	.52
.65	.96	.92	.87	.82	.77	.73	.68	.64	.59	.55	.52
.70	.98	.95	.90	.85	.80	.75	.70	.65	.60	.55	.53
.75	.99	.97	.92	.87	.82	.77	.72	.66	.61	.55	.53
.80	1.00	.99	.95	.90	.85	.80	.73	.67	.61	.55	.53
.85	1.00	.99	.97	.94	.88	.82	.76	.69	.62	.55	.53
.90	1.00	1.00	.99	.97	.92	.86	.78	.70	.62	.56	.53
.95	1.00	1.00	1.00	.99	.96	.90	.81	.71	.63	.56	.53
1.00	1.00	1.00	1.00	1.00	1.00	1.00	.83	.71	.63	.56	.53

SOURCE: Taylor and Russell (32).

relation coefficient of validity. Assume that prior to the use of a test, 50 percent of the persons selected for a job proved to be satisfactory. These persons presently on the job constitute the criterion group with whom a certain test is being validated. In the top row of values are the selection ratios; that is, the percentage of new testees to be selected; namely, from 5 to 95 percent. If, for example, an employer has 50 applicants for 20 openings, the selection ratio is 40 percent. The smaller the percentage, the more stringent is the selection. In the column at the left are the possible validity coefficients. A validity of .oo, obviously, means that the test is useless and that the percentage of successes will be no greater than it was without testing.

If the validity coefficient is .25 and if the selection ratio is only .05 (only the highest 5 percent on the test are to be selected), then 70 percent of those chosen are likely to prove satisfactory. It can be said, therefore, that use of a test having a .25 validity coefficient has increased the probability of success to 70 percent in a situation where it was 50 percent before. The remainder of the table indicates the probable value of, and contribution made by, the test as the coefficient of validity increases.[7]

Table 5.2 is similar in purpose to Table 5.1, except that the former provides more detail regarding relations between a person's rating on the test and his prospects of success (26). Assume that the percentage of successes is 80, and percentage of failures is 20, on a given job. In that event,

TABLE 5.2

PERCENT OF SUCCESSFUL INDIVIDUALS IN EACH DECILE ON TEST SCORE

Standing on the test		When the total percent of failures is 20%, and				When the total percent of failures is 30%, and			
Percentile	Decile	$r = .30$	$r = .40$	$r = .50$	$r = .60$	$r = .30$	$r = .40$	$r = .50$	$r = .60$
90–99th	10	92%	95%	97%	99%	86%	91%	94%	97%
80–89th	9	89	91	94	97	81	85	89	92
70–79th	8	86	89	91	94	78	81	84	88
60–69th	7	84	86	88	91	75	77	80	83
50–59th	6	82	84	85	87	72	74	75	77
40–49th	5	80	81	82	83	70	70	70	71
30–39th	4	78	77	77	78	67	66	65	64
20–29th	3	75	73	72	71	63	61	59	56
10–19th	2	71	68	64	61	59	55	50	45
1– 9th	1	63	56	49	40	50	43	35	27

SOURCE: Psychological Corporation Test Service Bulletin, no. 45. By permission.

[7] Similar tables have been prepared for satisfactory proportions from .05 to .90 (32).

the probabilities are that individuals whose test scores place them in the highest 10 percent of the group (according to the norms of the test) may be expected to prove satisfactory in 92 cases out of 100 if the validity coefficient is as low as .30; and in 99 cases out of 100 if the coefficient is .60. By means of a table such as this, it is possible to make more accurate selections and predictions for the group as a whole, once the test's estimated validity is known. It is to be noted, however, that when validity coefficients are relatively low (.30–.40) and percent of failures is also relatively low (20–30 percent), the probabilities are about 50–50, or higher, that individuals whose test scores rank them in the lowest 20 percent of the distribution will be retained.

One of the principal uses of psychological tests in schools is to provide objective data for use in planning an individual's subsequent education and in predicting probable performance. Table 5.3 presents data obtained for this purpose.[8]

TABLE 5.3

CORRELATION BETWEEN TEST SCORES AND FOUR-YEAR GRADE AVERAGES

Test used	Practical arts	General	College preparatory	All
A.C.E.				
L	−.04	.27	.38	.51
Q	.12	.14	.46	.53
Total	.04	.25	.48	.58
D.A.T.				
VR	−.07	.39	.64	.66
NA	.27	.43	.66	.67
AR	.22	.27	.57	.54
SR	.29	.33	.47	.53
MR	.29	.24	.34	.43
CSA	.40	.12	.27	.31
Sp	−.03	.24	.48	.50
Se	.14	.37	.58	.64
N	50	91	104	245

SOURCE: H. G. Seashore (28). *A.C.E.* is Psychological Examination of the American Council on Education; *L* is its language (verbal) section; *Q* is its quantitative (mathematical) section. *D.A.T.* is the Differential Aptitude Tests: *VR* is verbal reasoning; *NA* is numerical ability; *AR* is abstract reasoning (using nonverbal materials); *SR* is space relations; *MR* is mechanical reasoning; *CSA* is clerical speed and accuracy; *Sp* is spelling; *Se* is sentences (language usage).

[8] In later chapters that deal with specific tests, or types, data on this aspect of testing will be encountered frequently.

Inspection of these coefficients shows that, with this group, the A.C.E. Psychological Examination has no predictive value for pupils enrolled in the practical arts curriculum and low predictive value for those in the general curriculum; but it has moderate predictive value for individuals in college preparatory courses. It is important to note, also, that the coefficients are appreciably higher for the group when treated as a whole. These data also demonstrate the importance of specifying the kinds of groups for whom a particular test has a certain degree of validity, rather than generalizing about it.

The data in Table 5.3 indicate that although the validity coefficients of the D.A.T. are appreciably higher than those of the A.C.E. test, they, too, are most significant for the college preparatory group. The D.A.T. coefficients also show that the subtests are not equally predictive.

Biserial Correlation. This statistic is used when one of the measures is given in terms of only two categories: for example "pass" or "fail," "satisfactory" or "unsatisfactory." The second measure, however, is given in terms of variable scores. In Table 5.4 the four groupings on the

TABLE 5.4

BISERIAL CORRELATION BETWEEN SCORES OF 52 EMPLOYED STENOGRAPHERS ON THE SEASHORE-BENNETT STENOGRAPHIC PROFICIENCY TEST AND THEIR SUPERVISORS' RATINGS ON STENOGRAPHIC ABILITY. $r_{bis} = .60$.

Test scores	Ratings on stenographic ability			
	Below average	Average	Above average	Excellent
19		1	3	2
18		3	3	5
17		1	2	2
16		1	—	2
15		8	5	
14		2	—	
13		3	—	
12		1	1	
11		—	—	
10	2	2	1	
9	—	—		
8	1	1		
Subtotals	3	23	15	11
Totals	26		26	
	(Group 1)		(Group 2)	

SOURCE: The Psychological Corporation.

basis of supervisors' ratings (below average, average, above average, excellent) have been reclassified into two categories (Groups 1 and 2) that have been correlated with stenographic proficiency test scores. The biserial coefficient of .60 indicates that the proficiency test has considerable value in identifying stenographers who will function at satisfactory or highly satisfactory levels.

Tetrachoric Correlation. This index is found when a coarse classification of two measures is adequate for the purpose at hand. When it is used, the ratings in *each* measure are grouped into only two classes, providing a fourfold table. The data in Table 5.4 have been so reclassified in Table 5.5, yielding a tetrachoric coefficient of +.60.

TABLE 5.5

FOURFOLD TABLE FOR COMPUTATION OF TETRACHORIC
CORRELATION COEFFICIENT

$r_{tet} = .60.$

Ratings

		3–5	6–8	
Test Scores	15–19	6 (11.5%)	19 (36.5%)	High on Test
	8–15	17 (32.7%)	10 (19.3%)	Low on Test
		Rated Low	Rated High	

SOURCE: The Psychological Corporation.

Whether one uses the finer classifications necessary for calculating the product-moment coefficient (the "simple" correlation), or the coarse groupings shown in biserial and tetrachoric calculations, will depend upon the nature of the data available and the purpose for which validation is to be used.

Since the tetrachoric correlation coefficient is much less accurate than the product-moment r, the former should be used only when approximations, not too precise, are satisfactory, or when the coefficient is computed from a very large number of cases, or where the original data are inherently dichotomous. The tetrachoric correlation is sometimes used because, with the aid of tables or nomographs, it is easier to compute than the product-moment coefficient.

Multiple Correlation.[9] This method is used when two or more measures are to serve as predictors. The scores of the measures are statisti-

[9] The statistical procedures involved in calculating the coefficient of multiple correla-

cally combined and correlated with a third measure to yield a single co-efficient of multiple correlation. Whereas the simple product-moment coefficient indicates the degree of relationship (or covariation) between paired scores of two sets of measures, the multiple-correlation coefficient shows the relationship between one set of scores (for example, college grades or proficiency ratings) and the composite of two or more sets of other measures (for instance, an intelligence test and college entrance ex-amination grades). The multiple-correlation coefficient provides an in-dex that represents the best combination of two or more measures for the purpose of predicting scores of a third variable. This coefficient indi-cates how well a certain composite of predictors (for example, average of high school grades and score on a scholastic aptitude test) will cor-relate with a criterion (for example, college grade averages). Although each of two tests, considered separately, might have a low or a moderate correlation with a criterion, the two scores will generally correlate higher, or quite significantly with the criterion, when treated as a composite. This is the case because the two tests in combination have more elements, or factors, in common with the criterion than does either test in itself. The following data provide an illustration: [10]

Variable 1 is college grade averages.

Variable 2 is scores on a scholastic aptitude test.

Variable 3 is high school averages.

$$r_{12} = .65$$
$$r_{13} = .52$$
$$r_{23} = .48$$
$$\text{Then } R_{1(23)} = .69$$

In this instance, when variables 2 and 3 are treated as a composite, the multiple-correlation coefficient has risen only slightly because variables 1 and 2 are already quite significantly correlated, and variables 2 and 3 are markedly correlated. R would have been higher if r_{23} had been signifi-cantly lower than it is.

In an instance such as the foregoing, some psychologists and educators would conclude that there is really no justification for considering both predictors, since the scholastic aptitude test itself correlates with the criterion about as well as the composite, as shown by the R of .69. This is true statistically because the increment in the coefficient may not be sig-nificant. This is a conclusion that could be accepted if we were in-

tion and the logic of the method are not within the scope of the present discussion. Stu-dents who want to learn the procedure and the logic should consult a standard textbook on statistics.

[10] The symbol for the coefficient of multiple correlation is R.

terested solely in group trends and group probabilities. But since an r of .65 and an R of .69 are both far removed from unity, there will be individual exceptions to any conclusions drawn from them; so that, if we are concerned with *individuals* in a practical situation, we will utilize as many sources of information as may be available that contribute information about the individuals tested.

Expectancy Tables. These provide a relatively simple, straightforward, and valuable method of estimating predictive efficiency of a test. Estimates are based upon the calculated probabilities that an individual who has a given test score will achieve a specified score or rating in the performance being predicted. We might ask, as examples, the following questions: What are the probabilities that a prospective college student scoring in the highest decile group on a scholastic aptitude (intelligence) test will remain in college a given number of terms? What are the probabilities that a child with an IQ of 80–85 will be able successfully to complete the work of the eighth grade? What are the probabilities that a candidate getting an average score on a stenographic proficiency test will achieve a rating of "excellent" or "above average" on the job? Appropriate expectancy tables are intended to answer similar questions.

Table 5.6 is an illustration in point. It presents part of a larger table representing all ten decile groups.

TABLE 5.6

DECILE RANK ON A SCHOLASTIC APTITUDE TEST
AND SEMESTERS COMPLETED
(IN PERCENTS)

		Terms [a]						
		2	3	4	5	6	7	8
Decile Rank	X	98	95	94	90	89	88	88
	VII	94	87	85	82	81	78	78
	VI	92	82	79	74	74	73	73
	II	85	71	66	61	59	57	56
	I	81	67	60	52	51	49	48

[a] Decile rank X is the highest; I is the lowest.

To take two items from Table 5.6, it can be said that the probability is that 88 in 100 of the students in the highest decile group on the scholastic aptitude test will complete their academic course, whereas only 48 in 100 of the lowest decile group will do so.

Table 5.7 illustrates the use of expectancy data in personnel selection. Inspection of this table shows that it may be used to indicate what percentage of individuals obtaining each of the several ratings on actually demonstrated stenographic ability may be found at each of the several levels on the proficiency test. It is also possible to calculate the percentages by rows (instead of columns) so as to indicate the converse: the frequencies of the several ability ratings within each of the score intervals of the proficiency test.

TABLE 5.7

EXPECTANCY TABLE SHOWING THE NUMBER AND PERCENT OF STENOGRAPHERS OF VARIOUS RATED ABILITIES WHO CAME FROM SPECIFIED SCORE GROUPS ON THE S-B STENOGRAPHIC PROFICIENCY TEST

($N = 52$, mean score $= 15.4$, $S.D. = 2.9$, $r = .61$;
score is average per five letters.)

Number in each score group receiving each rating on stenographic ability				Stenographic Proficiency Test scores	Percent in each score group receiving each rating on stenographic ability			
Below aver-age	Aver-age	Above aver-age	Excel-lent		Below aver-age	Aver-age	Above aver-age	Excel-lent
	4	6	7	18–19		17	40	64
	2	2	4	16–17		9	13	36
	10	5		14–15		44	33	
	4	1		12–13		17	7	
2	2	1		10–11	67	9	7	
1	1			8–9	33	4		
3	23	15	11		100	100	100	100

SOURCE: The Psychological Corporation.

Comparison of Tables 5.6 and 5.7 demonstrates that expectancy tables need not be uniform. The form and arrangement of data will depend upon the particular probabilities one desires to determine. But all expectancy tables for tests have this in common: they provide estimates of the probabilities that a certain level or quality of performance may be expected if the test score is known—that is, its validity in terms of probabilities in place of or, more often, in addition to a correlation coefficient.

Figure 5.2, a bar diagram, shows still another method of representing expectancy. Although three categories for elimination are shown, it is possible to estimate the percentages of elimination at each test level and, thus, to estimate the predictive efficiency of the battery of tests used in selecting candidates for pilot training. The term "stanine score" means a unit consisting of one-ninth of the total range of the standard scores of a test.[11] Thus, the percentage eliminated from among candidates whose scores placed them in the highest one ninth of the scores was only about 5 (about 4 percent for flying deficiency), nearly 80 were eliminated from among those in the lowest (approximately 70 percent for flying deficiency).

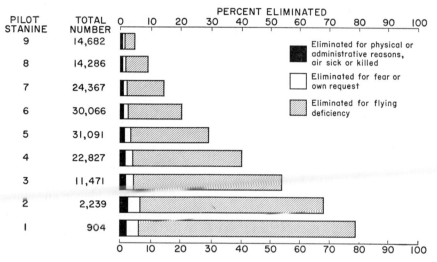

FIG. 5.2. Percentage of candidates eliminated from primary pilot training classified according to stanine scores on selection battery. Reproduced from *Psychological activities in the training command, Army Air Forces*, by the Staff, Psychological Section, Fort Worth, Texas. *Psychological Bulletin*. Washington, D.C.: American Psychological Association, Inc., 1945.

Cut-Off Score. This is a variation on the expectancy method. It is a test score used as a point of demarcation between examinees who will be accepted and those who will be rejected. For example, Table 5.8 shows several values from the Cornell index (a personality inventory) that might be taken as cut-off scores.

A low score on this inventory signifies fewer personality difficulties, hence it is more desirable. The table reads: "If a cut-off score of 7 on the

[11] "Stanine" is a condensation of "standard nine." The total *range of scores* is divided into nine equal units; the mean stanine is 5. The method was developed and the term was coined by psychologists in the United States Air Force during World War II.

TABLE 5.8

PERCENT OF PSYCHIATRIC REJECTS [a] AND ACCEPTS [a]
IDENTIFIED BY THE CORNELL INDEX

Cut-off level	400 rejects	600 accepts
7	86	28
13	74	13
23	50	4

[a] Based upon psychiatric interviews.
SOURCE: *Manual,* The Psychological Corporation.

Cornell index were used with this group of 1000 persons, 86 percent of
those who were rejected after the interview would have been rejected also
by the index; but 28 percent of those accepted after the interview also
would have been *rejected* by the index." The other percentages are read
in the same way. Since the higher scores in this instance are the less desirable, and if 7 is taken as the cut-off level, we mean that a score of 7, or
lower, would be necessary for acceptance. If 23 were the cut-off, then anyone with that score, or lower, would be acceptable. In this instance, the
cut-off score becomes less selective as it increases.

If we are using a test on which larger scores signify higher and more
desirable levels of the ability or trait being evaluated, then the cut-off
score becomes the more selective as it is increased. Table 5.9 is a case
in point.

TABLE 5.9

PERCENT OF SUPERIOR AND INFERIOR WORKERS IDENTIFIED BY
A PROFICIENCY TEST

	Superior workers		Inferior workers	
Cut-off score	Accepted	Rejected	Accepted	Rejected
20	100%	0%	80%	20%
25	90	10	60	40
30	80	20	40	60

The example shown in Table 5.9 is interpreted thus: If 20 were set as
the minimum acceptable score, then all examinees who proved to be
superior workers would have been employed; but so would 80 percent of
those who proved to be inferior workers.

It is clear that cut-off scores are especially useful in instances where many more candidates are available than there are places to be filled, so that the cut-off level may be made highly selective, and where one is not concerned primarily with the individual candidates as such, but rather with the places, jobs, or niches to be filled. The purpose in using cut-off levels is to identify a maximum number of potentially superior or desirable persons and, at the same time, to eliminate a maximum number of inferior or undesirable individuals. Since no test has perfect validity, and since the true potential of some persons may not be revealed by a single test, screening by means of cut-offs will not be perfect. Some desirable persons will be rejected, whereas some undesirables will be selected. Yet, cut-offs and other methods have a considerable advantage over subjective procedures previously employed; for they provide data for estimating with greatly increased objectivity and accuracy the chances of identifying the persons with the desired abilities or traits.

Differential Predictors. Some tests are adversely criticized, at times, because they do not predict *differentially;* that is, their predictive validity—especially in the form of correlation coefficients—is much the same for two or more types of criteria. For example, it may happen that scores on test A correlate $+.55$ with grades in college courses in the social sciences and the humanities, while the correlation is $+.45$ with grades in the physical and biological sciences. It would be argued by some, therefore, that the test is not useful as a selective instrument because the correlations are too close; it does not, they urge, differentiate. Or if test B correlates at $+.45$ with performance in one job category and $+.40$ with another, the same argument would be advanced.

This argument is misleading. While it is true that these instruments have not *differentiated* between the criteria in each instance, each test can still be useful as *one source of evidence* in making selections of students or workers. The adverse criticism fails to take into account the fact that human capacities, abilities, and skills—and to some extent, the personality traits being rated by means of inventories and projectives—are positively interrelated, and that psychological decisions and judgments should not be based upon scores alone. Study of "personality profiles" will demonstrate this point, as will the following illustration. In one university, these correlations were found:

r for grades in liberal arts college courses—freshman year—with general intelligence test score $= .48$

r for grades in engineering school courses—freshman year—with the same test of general intelligence $= .41$

Yet, of the 1400 students in liberal arts who were tested, nearly 90 percent of those in the highest decile group, and nearly 80 percent in the second highest graduated, while in the lowest and next to the lowest decile groups, only 48 percent, and 56 percent, respectively, graduated (after serious scholastic difficulty). Thus, while the two coefficients did not differentiate well between the group in liberal arts and that in engineering, the test was valuable in helping to estimate the probabilities of scholastic survival of individuals scoring at each of the several levels on the intelligence test.

Adverse critics also disregard the fact that achievement in education or on a job is a complex matter, involving not only intellectual, sensory, and motor capacities, but also motivational and personality factors. The view here expressed does not minimize the desirability of the efforts made to construct differential aptitude tests, which are evaluated in Chapter 17. The psychologists' task would be considerably simplified if human capacities and abilities were highly specific and specialized; but that does not appear to be the case.

Other Methods.   In later chapters it will become apparent that still other methods, in addition to those already explained, are used to estimate validity. Among these are the percentage who are successful, on a test or on individual items, in adjacent age groups and in groups of known ability (inferior, average, superior); the statistical significance of increases in scores from age to age; and closeness of the distribution of scores to the normal frequency curve. Also, in validating personality tests, the extent of agreement, among specialists, in scoring and in the interpretation of results is an accepted criterion.

There are instances, too, when very low correlations may be regarded as evidence of a test's validity. For example, if one constructs a test of mechanical aptitude, based upon the hypothesis that this is a special aptitude and, as such, is relatively independent of the mental operations measured as general intelligence, then in constructing the test of mechanical aptitude its author should, among other things, aim to devise an instrument that has a low or negligible correlation with tests of general intelligence.

Low correlations, or other evidence showing *absence* of agreement, obtained by means of a test, may be indicative of the test's validity in assessing personality traits; as, for instance, when a person has undergone successful psychotherapy and has been tested before and after therapy. In this case, appreciable changes in certain traits would be expected and should be shown by the test. On the other hand, if an individual's personality difficulties or disorders are known to have increased over a period of time, the test should, if valid, reflect these changes.

Item Analysis

With very few exceptions, psychological tests (other than some projective techniques) are made up of a large number of items. The

score on each item is added to the scores of the other items to obtain a subtest score or a total score, either or both of which are used in calculating
reliability and validity. Ultimately, however, the quality and merit of a
test depend upon the individual items of which it is composed. It is therefore necessary, in best practice, to analyze each item in the standardization
process in order to retain only those that suit the purposes and rationale
of the device being constructed. Item analysis is thus an integral part of
both the reliability and the validity of a test.

In evaluating items, two major aspects are considered: the *level of difficulty* of each and the *discriminative value* of each.

      Difficulty Level. This aspect is determined by the percentage
of individuals able to pass each item. In practice, if an item is to distinguish among individuals, it should not be so easy that all persons can
pass it; nor should it be so difficult that none are able to pass it.[12] It can
be demonstrated statistically that an item passed by 50 percent of a group
discriminates between more pairs of persons than does an item passed by a
smaller or larger percentage. For example, if an item is attempted by 100
individuals and passed by only 10, and if the testees are taken by pairs,
there are 900 (10 $\times$ 90) combinations in which that item can discriminate
between paired members of that group. If the item is passed by 50 in the
group, then the number of possible discriminations between paired individuals is 2500 (50 $\times$ 50), this being the largest number possible, as the
multiplication of any other proportions will show.[13] Obviously, not all
items in a scale are, or should be, so easy as to be passed by 50 percent of
the group. Some are included that are passed by large percentages and
some by small percentages, with many degrees between the extremes.

There is no formula for determining the exact distribution of item
difficulties. A common practice is to select some items whose difficulty
is at, or close to, the 50 percent level, and other items with a wide range
of degree of difficulty, in terms of percent passing. If all items selected
for inclusion in a test were at the 50 percent level of difficulty, the test
would, theoretically, simply divide the testees into two groups: those above
this predetermined dividing point and those below it. Such items would
not differentiate among the individuals in the group above the 50 percent
level, nor among those below it. Hence, for maximum differentiating efficiency, a test must contain items at various levels of difficulty as repre-

[12] Theoretically, it would be desirable that the test be so scaled that there is at least
one item that can be passed by all for whom the test is intended. For zero scores on
a particular test do not necessarily mean absolute zero capacity in the function being
measured; nor will all zero scores necessarily signify the same status. Conversely, it
would be desirable that a test be scaled upward to a level where no one for whom the
test is intended is able to pass the highest item. This aspect would require, of course,
that the test be constructed by a person superior to any of the intended testees.

[13] It is not to be assumed that "50 percent passing" is necessarily the best criterion in
placing an item in an age scale (like the Binet), as will be seen later.

sented by percentages passing. The final consideration will be the inclusion of items of such a range of difficulty as to yield the highest predictive index when compared with the criterion, allowing for the levels of the ability or trait to be measured and the degree of differentiation to be achieved.

In terms of difficulty, the discriminative value of a test item is the degree to which performance on it satisfactorily differentiates among individuals who vary in regard to the characteristic being measured. However, differences in percentages of individual passing items do not indicate differences in *amounts* of the characteristic. These percentages show only an *order* of item difficulty.[14]

Difficulty levels can be given also in terms of the standard deviation of the normal curve. Thus, if 84 percent of testees pass an item, it has a rank of -1 SD (one standard deviation below the mean). If an item is passed by 16 percent, its rank is $+1$ SD; if passed by 69 percent or by 31 percent, the ranks would be -0.5 SD or $+0.5$ SD, respectively.[15] Some psychologists prefer this index because the standard deviation is a property of the normal curve; but basically, like percentage passing, it is an index of relative rank.

Determination of difficulty levels is significant not only for a test's discriminative value; it is essential also if two equivalent forms of the instrument are to be devised, from the points of view of both degree of difficulty of each item and over-all range of difficulty.

In constructing a speed test, it is essential, obviously, that all items be of uniform difficulty or nearly so. Also, if a test is to serve only as a screening device to divide testees into two groups (pass-fail, satisfactory-unsatisfactory), it is necessary that a predetermined level of difficulty be selected, that items be of increasing difficulty up to that level, and that a number of items be concentrated at that level. If further differentiation is desired, it will be necessary, of course, to include increasingly difficult items.

Discriminative Value: Correlation.   Validity of items may be estimated by finding the biserial correlation coefficient of each item with the score of the subtest of which it is a part (such as arithmetical problems, similarities) to determine whether or not performance on it is consistent with performance on the *subtest* as a whole. For this purpose, each item is scored as "pass" or "fail"; or "plus" or "minus." This procedure assumes that all items in the subtest are expected to be relatively homogeneous in regard to the psychological operations or traits they are in-

[14] Meanings and interpretations of scores on psychological tests are discussed in Chapter 6.

[15] These percentages are based upon the standard deviation of a normal distribution curve. The table showing percentages of the distribution included within various fractions of the standard deviation are found in most textbooks on statistics.

tended to measure. Or, otherwise stated, success or failure on each item within the subtest is regarded as indicative, to some degree, of a specified kind of trait or mental operation, or of a similar combination of characteristics.

Successes and failures on each item may also be correlated with the total scores for the *whole* test. When this is done and an appreciable positive correlation is wanted, the assumption is that the items in *all the subtests* are expected to be relatively homogeneous in regard to characteristics measured. If the purpose of the scale is to measure relatively independent operations or traits by means of each of the subtests, neither the subtest scores nor the individual items within each subtest are expected to show a marked correlation with total-test scores.

The biserial correlation of performance on each item with its subtest scores and with total-test scores is found in order to identify, at each level of difficulty, items that will contribute most to the validity of the test as a whole. This is the process of establishing *internal validity*.[16]

Determining biserial correlations for all items is a long and laborious task, unless the work is done by calculating machines. It is not uncommon, therefore, to find that items have been correlated only with their subtest scores, followed by intercorrelations (product-moment) of the subtest scores with one another and with the total-test scores.

Discriminative Value: External Criteria. As emphasized throughout our discussion, it is essential that validity be determined, ultimately, by comparison of scores with one or more external criteria, after or during the process of internal item analysis. Thus, each item may be analyzed to determine whether it discriminates satisfactorily between a low and a high group, as classified under one or more of the external criteria detailed earlier in this chapter. As already stated, very few items should be within the ability range of all, or nearly all testees. Others should be of increasing selectivity. Some items should, of course, discriminate between two extreme groups, for example, the highest and lowest 10 percent of the population tested. But it is desirable to have items whose selectivity extends beyond these narrow boundaries; items that would also dependably distinguish between, for example, the highest one-fourth and the second-highest one-fourth and between the lowest one-fourth and the next-lowest one-fourth. Kelley has offered evidence indicating that most marked and significant discrimination between extreme groups is obtained when item analysis is based upon the highest 27 per-

---

[16] To begin with, before statistical analyses are made, the author of the test had employed the principle of "content validity" or of "construct validity." The statistical analyses refine and improve the original group of items that were devised according to either of these principles.

cent and the lowest 27 percent of the group. This method, however, provides only a crude item differentiation, since it does not provide a basis for differentiating among 50 percent of the population, the large middle group; see (15).

Using this method, one procedure would be to find what percentage of the highest 27 percent and what percentage of the lowest 27 percent passed each item; then, by statistical calculation, to determine if the difference between the two percentages is significant. The same method can be followed with other proportions as well. In fact, items may be analyzed with regard to a wide variety of group classifications. Each item might, for example, be analyzed with reference to high, average, low average, and low groups, classification being based upon total-test scores or upon external validating criteria.

Items should discriminate between some kinds of groupings but not others, depending upon the purpose of the test. For example, the items in a test of general intelligence should not favor either sex, whereas a personality inventory intended to evaluate degree of "masculinity" and "feminity" should discriminate sex differences. If a personality inventory is to differentiate among two or more clinical classifications or behavior syndromes, then here, too, items that show significant group differences in responses will be chosen. On the other hand, in constructing tests of intelligence, psychologists have emphasized that they should be "culture-fair"; that is, they should not favor some socioeconomic groups and be unfair to others.[17]

Speed Tests. Devices that are primarily tests of speed present a special problem. The position of each item in the series affects its *apparent* level of difficulty and its *apparent* validity, unless all individuals in the standardization group have had an opportunity to answer every item. In a speed test, all items should be of uniform, or nearly uniform, degree of difficulty. Having determined the level of difficulty desired, the best practice, then, is to correlate subtest scores and total-test scores with scores of criteria, under various time limits.

Validating Information

The objective of all validating procedures is to make the most useful selection of test types and test items from among those available, so as to yield the highest prediction of the criterion or criteria. To do this, the test's author must have insight into the psychological processes involved. In addition, he must write the test items clearly and precisely. Then the

[17] Techniques of item analysis, other than those here discussed, have been proposed (8, 21, 33).

ultimate decision on the criteria of validity in any area of testing rests upon the analytical judgments and agreement of qualified specialists, who evaluate the test's objectives and the groups for whom it is intended.

Anyone who uses a test professionally—and none but professionally qualified persons should—will want to know certain essential facts about the instrument's validation. The following information should be given in the test's manual:

The purpose of the test and the group or groups for whom intended.

The type of validation that has been employed: content, construct, concurrent, predictive, or a combination of these. Whichever one, or combination, has been used, should be explained and justified on the basis of either psychological or educational principles, or both.

The techniques used in item analysis.

The external validating criteria, if any; and the reasons for using them. Correlation coefficients, expectancy tables, and standard errors of measurment should be included whenever the data lend themselves to such treatment. The source of the external validating criteria should be stated: teachers' grades; objective achievement tests; supervisors' ratings; clinical diagnoses by psychologists or psychiatrists; other standardized tests.

The standardization sample of the population. The given information, where essential, should include age range, sex distribution, socioeconomic distribution, range of ability or trait variation, educational level, type of school.

Separate validity findings for different age groups, grade groups, ability groups, behavior syndromes, clinical groups, culture and subculture groups, and occupational groups. In fact, whenever membership in a particular group might produce differences, or whenever a test is intended to make group differentiations, separate validity findings should be provided.

Cross-validation data, if any; and the characteristics of the cross-validating groups.

Influence of any special factors, such as speed of work, auditory discrimination, color vision or visual acuity, manual dexterity, where these are not the primary concern of the test, but can influence the scores or ratings.

References

1. Barrett, D. M. Differential value of Q and L scores on the ACE psychological examination for predicting achievement in college mathematics. *Journal of Psychology,* 1952, *33,* 205–207.
2. Bechtoldt, H. P. Construct validity: a critique. *The American Psychologist,* 1959, *14,* 619–629.
3. Brogden, H. E. A new coefficient: application to biserial correlation and to estimation of selective efficiency. *Psychometrika,* 1949, *14,* 169–182.

4. Brown, H. S. Differential prediction by ACE. *Journal of Education Research,* 1950, *44,* 116–121.
5. Campbell, D. T. Recommendations for APA test standards regarding construct, trait, or discriminant validity. *The American Psychologist,* 1960, *15,* 546–553.
6. Clark, C. A. Developments and applications in the area of construct validity. *Review of Educational Research,* 1959, *29,* 84–105.
7. Cronbach, L. J. Processes affecting scores on "understanding of others" and "assumed similarity." *Psychological Bulletin,* 1955, *52,* 177–193.
8. Davis, F. B. Item analysis in relation to educational and psychological testing. *Psychological Bulletin,* 1952, *49,* 97–121.
9. Ebel, R. L. Obtaining and reporting evidence on content validity. *Educational and Psychological Measurement,* 1956, *16,* 269–282.
10. English, H. B., and A. C. *A Comprehensive Dictionary of Psychological and Psychoanalytical Terms.* New York: David McKay Company, Inc., 1958.
11. Freeman, F. S. Predicting academic survival. *Journal of Educational Research,* 1931, *23,* 113–123.
12. Fruchter, B. *An Introduction to Factor Analysis.* Princeton, N.J.: D. Van Nostrand Company, Inc., 1954.
13. Ghiselli, E. E. *The Validity of Commonly Employed Occupational Tests.* Berkeley, Calif.: University of California Publications in Psychology, 1949, *5,* no. 9.
14. Jessor, R., and K. R. Hammond. Construct validity and the Taylor anxiety scale. *Psychological Bulletin,* 1957, *54,* 161–170.
15. Kelley, T. L. The selection of upper and lower groups for the validation of items. *Journal of Educational Psychology,* 1939, *30,* 17–24.
16. Kelley, T. L., et al. *Stanford Achievement Test.* New York: Harcourt, Brace & World Inc., 1953.
17. Lennon, R. T. Assumptions underlying the use of content validity. *Educational and Psychological Measurement,* 1956, *16,* 294–304.
18. Loevinger, J. Objective tests as instruments of psychological theory. *Psychological Reports,* 1957, *3,* 635–694.
19. Meehl, P. E. *Clinical vs. Statistical Prediction.* Minneapolis: University of Minnesota Press, 1954.
20. Meehl, P. E., and A. Rosen. Antecedent probability and the efficiency of psychometric signs, patterns, and cutting scores. *Psychological Bulletin,* 1955, *52,* 194–216.
21. Mollenkopf, W. G. An experimental study of the effects on item-analysis data of changing item placement and test time limit. *Psychometrika,* 1950, *15,* 291–317.
22. Nisbet, J. T. Symposium: IV. Intelligence and age: retesting with twenty-four years interval. *British Journal of Educational Psychology,* 1957, *27,* 190–198.
23. Osborne, R. T., et al. The differential prediction of college marks by ACE scores. *Journal of Educational Research,* 1950, *44,* 107–115.
24. Owens, W. A. An empirical study of the relationship between validity and

internal consistency. *Educational and Psychological Measurement,* 1947, 7, 281–288.

25. The Psychological Corporation. *Test Service Bulletin,* New York: 1949, no. 37.
26. The Psychological Corporation. *Test Service Bulletin,* New York: 1953, no. 45.
27. Richardson, M. W. The interpretation of a test validity coefficient in terms of increased efficiency of a selected group of personnel. *Psychometrika,* 1944, 9, 245–248.
28. Seashore, H. G. Tenth grade tests as predictors of twelfth grade scholarship and college entrance status. *Journal of Counseling Psychology,* 1954, 1, 106–115.
29. Seashore, H. G. Cross-validation of equations for predicting CEEB-SAT scores from DAT scores. *Journal of Counseling Psychology,* 1955, 2, 229–230.
30. Staff, Psychological Section, Fort Worth, Texas. Psychological activities in the training command, Army Air Forces. *Psychological Bulletin,* 1945, 42, 37–54.
31. Super, D. E. The ACE psychological examination and special abilities. *Journal of Psychology,* 1949, 9, 221–226.
32. Taylor, H. C., and J. T. Russell. The relationship of validity coefficients to the practical effectiveness of tests in selection: discussion and tables. *Journal of Applied Psychology,* 1939, 23, 565–578.
33. Wesman, A. G. Effect of speed on item-test correlation coefficients. *Educational and Psychological Measurement,* 1949, 9, 51–57.

6.

INTERPRETATION OF TEST SCORES: QUANTITATIVE AND QUALITATIVE

An Index of Relative Rank

The raw score (that is, the actual number of units or points) obtained by an individual on a test does not in itself have much, if any, significance. One test may yield a maximum score of 150, another 200, and a third 300. Obviously, then, any point score on one of these tests is not directly comparable with the same number of points on either of the others; a score of 43 on one test cannot be directly compared with a score of 43 on another. Furthermore, the average scores of each of these will in all probability be different, as will the degree of variation of scores (called the *deviation*) both above and below the average. For example, the average (*mean*) score of the first test for a given age is, let us say, 90, with approximately the middle two thirds of the scores falling between 75 and 105. For the second test the mean is 120, with the middle two thirds of the scores between 100 and 140; while for the third test the mean is 180, with the range of the middle two thirds between 150 and 210.

It is clear that if scores obtained on each of several tests are to be compared, indexes must be used which will express the relative significance of any given score; or what is known as *relative rank*. In the example given above, assuming that all three tests are intended for the same group, the mean scores of 90, 120, and 180 have the same relative significance— that is, persons making these scores would be at the average in each. Similarly, scores of 75, 100, and 150 have the same relative significance in

their respective tests; for persons getting these scores would be one standard deviation below the means (averages), which signifies that their scores
surpass only about sixteen percent of all the scores made by the population sampling upon which the tests were standardized.

Innumerable other comparable points and scores could be selected for
illustration. Obviously, however, such score-for-score comparisons would
be extremely cumbersome and would, in each instance, have to be interpreted in terms of some common, meaningful index. Hence, to facilitate interpretation, sound psychological tests will provide tables of *age
norms,* or *grade norms,* or *percentile ranks,* or *decile ranks,* or *standard
scores,* depending upon the instrument's purpose. Other kinds of norms,
suitable to the test, should also be provided.

Norms

A norm is the average or typical score (mean or median) on a
particular test made by a specified population: for example, the mean intelligence test score for a group of 10-year-old children; the mean score
for a group of fifth-grade pupils on a test of arithmetic fundamentals.
Reference to a test's table of norms enables us to rank an individual
pupil's performance relative to his own and other age or grade groups.
For example, a child of 10 might have an intelligence test score that is
average for his own age, or for a population of 9-year-olds, or for those
who are eleven years of age. On a test of arithmetic fundamentals, a
fourth-grade pupil's score might be typical for his level, or for that of the
grade above or below.

Since it is desirable to locate an individual's score and relative rank not
only with reference to an average, but also with reference to other levels
in the scale, tables of norms should include the frequency distribution of
the scores, from which percentile ranks and standard scores may be readily
calculated, if they are not already provided in the test's manual.[1] (These
indexes are explained in later sections of this chapter.) Table 6.1 is an
illustration of this practice. From this, on the basis of his score, an individual's relative position may be readily determined with respect to his
own and other age groups. Table 6.1, as a type, is of additional interest
and value because it shows the range of scores within each age group, and
the extent of overlapping of scores from age to age, and between any two
age groups one might want to compare.

Table 6.2 represents another type of presentation. Here norms are

---

[1] For this reason, a table of norms presents not only the single value, the average, but
also a range of values representing the over-all performance of the group.

TABLE 6.1

THE FREQUENCY DISTRIBUTION OF SCORES FOR EACH AGE GROUP CHICAGO NONVERBAL EXAMINATION (VERBAL DIRECTIONS)

Score	Age								
	6–0 to 6–11	7–0 to 7–11	8–0 to 8–11	9–0 to 9–11	10–0 to 10–11	11–0 to 11–11	12–0 to 12–11	13–0 to 13–11	14–0[a] and above
180–184									1
175–179							1		9
170–174							0		9
165–169							1	5	21
160–164						2	1	6	49
155–159						1	6	11	70
150–154					1	0	5	18	86
145–149					0	5	13	16	129
140–144					3	5	19	35	114
135–139					1	12	20	29	130
130–134				2	8	16	31	35	175
125–129			1	2	14	18	41	37	190
120–124			0	7	18	35	58	52	172
115–119			1	9	18	36	41	45	145
110–114			3	19	33	36	24	30	122
105–109			6	15	43	30	37	29	122
100–104			11	29	35	41	28	21	95
95–99		2	27	27	41	22	17	14	62
90–94		6	22	45	42	26	10	11	44
85–89		12	40	32	29	13	10	11	19
80–84	2	11	37	37	19	7	4	3	24
75–79	3	23	43	33	20	7	6	4	12
70–74	7	32	29	19	8	3	2	2	14
65–69	16	47	33	21	5	3	1	4	11
60–64	12	56	27	8	4	2	1	1	3
55–59	29	43	20	4	4	1	0	4	6
50–54	43	45	12	4	1	0	0		4
45–49	31	32	7	0	1	1	2		2
40–44	35	23	9	3	1	1			2
35–39	26	16	6	1	1	1			0
30–34	26	16	3	0	0				0
25–29	22	10	3	1	0				1
20–24	18	6	1		1				1
15–19	21	6	2		0				
10–14	14	6	1		1				
5–9	6	4							
0–4	7	2							
Total	318	398	344	318	352	324	379	423	1844
Mean	41.1	56.7	75.3	89.0	99.3	110.0	118.5	122.8	125.6
SD	17.6	18.1	18.7	17.2	18.8	18.6	18.6	20.8	22.2

[a] This column includes the scores for both verbal and pantomime directions.
SOURCE: A. W. Brown et al. (2). By permission.

TABLE 6.2

AGE NORMS OF OTIS INTERMEDIATE EXAMINATION
(30-MINUTE TIME LIMIT)

Months	Years										
	8	9	10	11	12	13	14	15	16	17	18 or over
0	7	15	23	31	38	44	49	53	56	58	59
1	8	16	24	32	39	44	49	53	56	58	
2	8	16	24	32	39	45	50	53	56	58	
3	9	17	25	33	40	45	50	54	57	58	
4	10	18	26	34	40	46	50	54	57	58	
5	10	18	26	34	41	46	51	54	57	58	
6	11	19	27	35	41	46	51	55	57	59	
7	12	20	28	35	42	47	51	55	57	59	
8	12	20	28	36	42	47	52	55	58	59	
9	13	21	29	36	43	48	52	55	58	59	
10	14	22	30	37	43	48	52	56	58	59	
11	14	22	30	37	43	49	53	56	58	59	

SOURCE: A. S. Otis (14). By permission.

given, at monthly intervals, for the Otis Self-Administering Test of Mental Ability.

Table 6.3 illustrates the importance of providing separate norms and distributions of scores for each of several groups within a broad category. In this instance, though all had completed a college preparatory course and were college freshmen, there are differences among the several groups, some of them being quite significant. Inspection of the table shows that an identical score in each of the groups does not signify identical relative ranks. For example, a score of 119 gives a percentile rank of 37.5 in the B.A. group, 57.5 in the Business group, and 42.5 in the Engineering group (see the note under Table 6.3). This kind of table is essential for purposes of guidance and selection.

The characteristics of any table of norms will depend on a number of factors affecting the individuals who make up the group. For example, in standardizing a psychological test, the norm and the distribution of scores will be influenced by the representativeness of the population sample; that is, by the proportion from each sex, their geographic distribution,

TABLE 6.3

NORMS FOR COLLEGE FRESHMAN (MALE): COLLEGE QUALIFICATIONS TEST
ARRANGED ACCORDING TO TYPE OF CURRICULUM
(RAW SCORES)

Percentile [a]	B.A.	B.S.	Business	Nursing	Engineering
99	186–200	185–200	174–200	174–200	184–200
90	164–170	161–168	146–152	148–154	161–166
80	153–157	151–155	136–140	136–139	149–153
70	145–147	142–145	127–131	128–131	140–143
60	136–139	133–136	119–122	120–122	132–135
50	127–131	126–129	111–114	115–117	124–127
40	119–122	117–121	102–105	106–110	115–119
30	108–112	107–111	93–96	100–101	107–110
20	96–101	95–100	83–87	94–95	97–101
10	78–87	79–87	73–76	78–87	84–90
N	2359	3871	939	254	2576
Mean	126.6	125.1	111.9	115.7	125.1
SD	31.1	30.3	28.1	25.7	28.5

[a] Each percentile value in this table represents a range of percentile points of which the indicated percentile value is the mid-point. Thus the percentile value of 50 represents 47.5–52.5.
SOURCE: G. K. Bennett et al. (1). By permission.

their socioeconomic status, and their age distribution. In devising a test of educational achievement, factors influencing the normative data, in addition to the foregoing, are the quality of the schools and the kinds of curricula from which the standardization population is drawn. Norms of tests of aptitude (for example, clerical or mechanical) are influenced by the standardization population's degree of experience, the kind of work they have been doing, and by the representativeness of the group.

The point to be emphasized, therefore, is that tables of norms derived for each of several tests classified under the same name and intended for the same purposes are not necessarily comparable. Before deciding on the selection and use of a test, it is always necessary to know the characteristics of its standardization population. This information is essential in determining whether the instrument is appropriate in a given situation.

Percentile and Decile Ranks

Percentile Rank. An individual's percentile rank on a test designates the percentage of cases or scores lying below it. Thus, a person having a percentile rank of 20 (P_{20}) is situated above twenty percent of the group of which he is a member; or, otherwise stated, twenty percent of the group fall below this person's rank. A percentile rank of 70 (P_{70}) means that seventy percent fall below—and so on, for any percentile rank in the scale. In effect, this statistical device makes it possible to determine at which one-hundredth part of the distribution of scores or cases any particular individual is located. By this means a person's relative status, or position in the group, can be established with respect to the traits or functions being tested. And, as will be seen, psychological measurement, unlike physical measurement, derives its significance principally from relative ranks ascribed to individuals rather than from quantitative units of measurement.

A table of norms and frequency distribution often provides percentile ranks (see Table 6.3). Or, if the percentile ranks themselves are not given in a table, it is possible to calculate them easily from the frequency distribution.

The percentile method is a technique whereby scores on two or more tests, given in units that are different, may be transformed into uniform and comparable values. This method has the advantage of not depending upon any assumptions regarding the characteristics of the distribution with which it is used. The distribution might be normal, skewed, or rectangular. When a percentile rank is given for a particular individual, it refers to his rank in the specified group of scores from which it has been derived. On a test of reading comprehension at the fourth-grade level, for example, a percentile rank of 60 for a particular pupil is relevant to the group of pupils for whom the distribution of scores was found. Whether or not this same pupil would be rated at percentile 60 as a member of

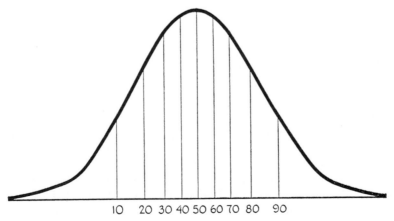

10   20 30 40 50 60 70 80   90

FIG. 6.1. Unequal distances between points on the base line of a normal curve by successive 10-percent divisions (deciles) of its area

another fourth-grade population will depend on the comparability of the two groups. His rating might be the same, or higher, or lower. (In this connection, consult Table 6.3, giving norms for college freshmen.)

Percentile points are based upon the number of scores (cases) falling within a certain range; hence the distance between any two percentiles represents a certain area under the curve; that is, a certain number of cases ($N/100$). Reference to Figure 6.1 shows that if percentages of the total area (total number of cases) are equal, the distances on the base line (range of scores) must be unequal, unless the distribution is rectangular (Fig. 6.2).[2] It is obvious from Figure 6.1 that differences in scores between

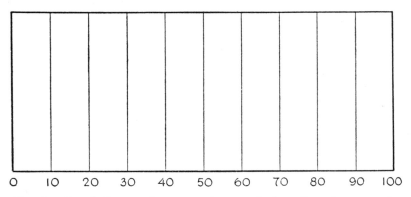

Fig. 6.2. Equal distances between points on the base line of a rectangle by successive 10-percent divisions (deciles) of its area

any two percentile points become greater as we move from the median (P_{50}) toward the extremes. Inspection of the curve shows, for instance, that the distance on the base line (representing scores) between percentiles 50 and 60 and the distance between 50 and 40 (these being at the center and equal) are smaller than that between any other intervals of ten percentile points. What this means in the practical interpretation of test results is that at, and close to, the median, differences in scores between percentile ratings are smaller in the measured characteristic than they are between the same percentile differences elsewhere on the curve. See, for example, the spread of the base line between 50–60, and that between 80–90, or 90–100. Yet each of these represents ten percentile points.

The percentile technique has the advantage of being easily calculated, easily understood, and of making no assumptions with regard to the characteristics of the total distribution. It answers the question: "Where does an individual's score rank him in his group?" Or: "Where does an individual's score rank him in another group whose members have taken the same test?"

[2] Occurrence of a rectangular distribution is extremely improbable.

Figure 6.3 is an example of the cumulative frequency curve, also known as the percentile curve. The cumulative frequencies are plotted, rather than the separate frequencies for each class interval. The points that are joined on the curve represent the upper limit of each interval. From such a curve it is readily possible to read off for any given value the percentile equivalent of its frequency distribution. Conversely, it is possible to read off the score equivalent for any given percentile.

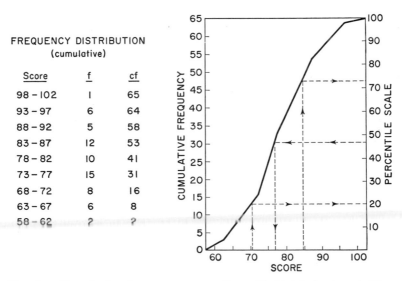

FREQUENCY DISTRIBUTION
(cumulative)

Score	f	cf
98 – 102	1	65
93 – 97	6	64
88 – 92	5	58
83 – 87	12	53
78 – 82	10	41
73 – 77	15	31
68 – 72	8	16
63 – 67	6	8
58 – 62	?	?

FIG. 6.3. Cumulative frequency curve. From E. F. Lindquist, *A First Course in Statistics*. By permission.

Decile Rank. The decile rank is the same in principle as the percentile; but instead of designating the one-hundredth part of a distribution, it designates the one-tenth part of the group $(N/10)$ in which any tested person is placed by his score. The term "decile" is used to mean a dividing point. "Decile rank" signifies a range of scores between two dividing points. Thus a testee who has a decile rank of 10 (D_{10}) is located in the highest 10 percent of the group; one whose decile rank is 9 (D_9) is in the second highest 10 percent; one whose decile rank is 1 (D_1), is in the lowest 10 percent of the group.

When the number of scores in a distribution is small, percentiles are not used, because there is little or no significance in making fine distinctions in rank. The decile-ranking method may be used instead.[3]

[3] When a rather coarse classification will serve the purpose, the quartile rank $(N/4)$ or the quintile rank $(N/5)$ may be used. As these terms indicate, they show, respectively, the one-fourth, or the one-fifth part of the distribution of scores in which an individual's score places him.

The Standard Score and Variants

Standard Score. The meaning of this index (Z) is less obvious than that of percentile and decile ranks, although it, too, designates the individual's position with respect to the total range and distribution of scores. The standard score indicates, in terms of standard deviation, how far a particular score is removed from the mean of the distribution. The mean is taken as the zero point, and standard scores are given as plus or minus. If the distributions of scores of two or more tests are approximately normal, standard scores derived from one distribution may be compared with those derived from the others.

The formula is:

$$Z = \frac{X - M}{SD}$$

in which X is an individual score, M is the mean of the distribution, and SD its standard deviation.

Assume, for example, that the mean IQ of a group is 100 and that the standard deviation is 14. In this distribution an individual reaching an IQ of 114 has a Z-score of $+1.0$. Another individual having an IQ of 79 has a Z-score of -1.5.

Standard scores must ultimately be given percentile values to express their full significance. Since the number of cases encompassed within a given number of standard deviations in a normal distribution is mathematically fixed, it is always possible to translate a Z-score into a percentile value. Thus, a person having a Z-score of $+1.0$, has a percentile rank of approximately 84; that is, his score surpasses 84 percent of the scores in

TABLE 6.4

PROPORTIONS OF CASES OR AREA UNDER THE CURVE,
CORRESPONDING TO GIVEN STANDARD SCORES

Z-score	Approximate percent of cases from the mean
.25	10
.50	19
.75	27
1.00	34
1.25	39
1.75	46
2.00	48
3.00	49.8

the group. The person having a Z-score of −1.5, has a percentile rank of approximately 7, surpassing only 7 percent of the scores. Table 6.4 shows several standard scores and their percentile values, for illustrative purposes. Figure 6.4 shows the percentage of scores (or cases) occurring above and below standard scores, with their corresponding percentile rank values.

As an index of relative rank, the standard score is preferred by some psychologists because it is a well-defined property of the normal curve, representing a fixed and uniform number of units throughout the scale.

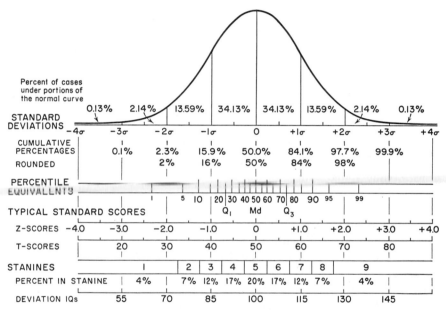

FIG. 6.4. The normal curve and derived scores. From H. G. Seashore *et al.* (15). Reproduced by permission.

Percentile and decile scores, on the other hand, are ranks in a group and do not represent equal units of individual differences.

The standard score principle has been utilized in deriving what is known as the *deviation intelligence quotient*. This index is explained in a later section of this chapter; and it will be discussed again in connection with two of the individual intelligence tests (Stanford-Binet and the Wechsler scales).

T-Score. A variant of the standard score, known as a *T*-score, was suggested by McCall (13). Using the *T*-score method, the mean is set at 50, whereas in terms of standard score, the value of the mean is zero. To obtain a *T*-score, the standard score is multiplied by 10 and then added to, or subtracted from, the mean T-score of 50. Thus, a standard score of $+1.00$ becomes a T-score of 60, while one of -1.00 becomes 40. In using this technique, the justified assumption is that nearly all scores will be within a range of five standard deviations from the mean. Since each SD is divided into ten units, the T-score is based upon a scale of 100 units, thus avoiding negative scores and, in most instances, fractions.

It should be clear that this index, found for any individual, is relevant only to the distribution of scores of the group from which the values have been derived and with which his score is being compared.

      Stanine.   Another variant of the standard score technique is called the stanine, a term coined by psychologists in the Army Air Force during World War II. According to this method, the standard population is divided into nine groups; hence, "standard nine" contracted to "stanine." Excepting the ranks of stanine 1 (lowest) and 9 (highest), each unit is equal to one half of a standard deviation. A score of 5 represents the median group, defined as those whose scores are within ± 0.25 SD of the mean; that is, a range of a half-sigma at the center of the distribution. A rank of stanine 6 represents the group whose scores fall between $+0.25$ sigma and $+0.75$ sigma (SD). The meanings of the other stanine rankings can be similarly determined in terms of standard deviations, except 1 and 9, as already stated, since the former represents all scores below -1.75 sigma, and the latter includes those above $+1.75$ sigma (see Fig 6.4).

This single-digit system of scores has certain advantages for machine computation; and it does eliminate plus and minus signs. Other than these considerations, it is difficult to find any advantage in its use in preference to the others already described.

In addition to understanding the meanings of the several indexes of variation described, it is essential to realize that basically all of them derive their significance from their relations to the *percentile* system. In other words, the psychologist and other users of test results will always want to have the answer to the question: "What is the *percentile equivalent* of a given standard score, or T-score, or stanine score?" Figure 6.4 presents the normal frequency curve with each of the several derived scores and their percentile equivalents, as well as the relative positions of several deviation IQs, which are explained later in this chapter.

Mental Age and Intelligence Quotient

      Mental Age.   This concept was introduced by Alfred Binet in 1908 in conjunction with the first revision of his scale. In this scale and in its later revisions, items are grouped according to age levels. For example, selected items, passed by a specified percentage of five-year-old children in the standardization sample are placed at the five-year level; items passed by a specified percentage of six-year-old children are placed at the six-year level.[4]

To determine mental age, in the 1908 scale, Binet adopted the following rule: the child was credited with the mental age of the highest year level in which he passed all test items, or all but one. To this basic level an additional year in mental age was added for every five items he passed in higher levels; but no fractional years were added for fewer than five items passed. The defect of this method was recognized, so that in his 1911 scale, Binet modified his procedure in order to permit the addition of a fraction of a year for items passed. In the Stanford-Binet revisions, the testee is credited with all items up through the age level at which he passes all. This is called the *basal year*. He is also credited with all items passed above the basal year. The sum of his basal plus the other credits, in terms of months, is his mental age.[5]

Mental age norms are also used with scales that are not arranged according to age levels. These are *point scales* that yield a score usually based on the number of items correctly answered. By means of a table of norms provided for the particular test being used, it is possible to assign an individual an age rating. Thus, on a point scale, an individual who, regardless of chronological age (CA), earns a score equal to the norm of the ten-year-old population sample, will have a mental age (MA) of ten, as determined by that test.

In determining mental age, whether by using an age scale or a point scale, an individual's performance on a standardized series of test items is being compared with the performance of the average group of a representative sample at successive age levels. Hence, we define mental age as the level of development in mental ability expressed as equivalent to the chronological age at which the average group of individuals reach that level. For example, a child having an MA of eight, has reached the level of the average group of eight-year-olds in the standardization group.[6]

At this point, our concern is only to define and clarify the mental age concept. There are several important psychological and measurement problems connected with this concept that are explained at several appropriate points in later sections.

[4] The question of placement of items in an age scale, according to percentage passing, is discussed in connection with the Binet scale and its revisions.

[5] In giving the test, the examiner continues upward in the scale until an age level is reached at which the individual fails all items. This is called the *terminal* year.

[6] The actual methods of determining mental age used by Binet and in revisions that followed are explained in Chapters 8, 9, and 10, in which the scales themselves are discussed.

Intelligence Quotient. The use of this index was first suggested by Stern (17) [7] and Kuhlmann (12) in 1912; but it was not actually employed as part of test findings and reports until 1916 when the first edition of the Stanford-Binet scale was made available. The intelligence quotient, the ratio of an individual's mental age to his chronological age, is found by the formula:

$$IQ = \frac{MA}{CA} \,(100)$$

The ratio is multiplied by 100 to remove the decimal.

An individual's IQ indicates *rate of mental development* or *degree of brightness.* If mental development keeps pace with one's life age,[8] the quotient is 100. If mental development lags, or is accelerated, the quotient will be less than or greater than 100, depending upon the degree of retardation or acceleration.

It is clear that mental age alone does not adequately represent an individual's mental capacity; for persons of different, at times widely different, chronological ages may and do reach the same mental age at a given time. One of the values of the IQ, therefore, is to reflect these age differences; hence it is defined in terms of rate of mental development and, as an attribute, degree of brightness.

In his volume accompanying the 1916 Stanford-Binet scale, Terman included a table showing the percentage of children at each of a number of IQ levels, each of which he gave a name; for instance, dull, normal, very superior. An individual whose test performance is normal for his chronological age earns an IQ rating of 100.

IQ range	*Terman's categories*
80–89	dullness
90–109	average intelligence
110–119	superior intelligence
120–140	very superior intelligence

As in any such table, the limits of each category were arbitrarily determined. These and similar categories are intended to serve only as guides in the interpretation of intelligence quotients and for purposes of statistical classification and analysis.

There are a number of problems associated with the interpretation and use of the IQ that are explained in later sections of this and other chapters. Our purpose at this stage is primarily to define and explain the meaning of the concept.

[7] In this publication, dated 1916, Stern refers to his suggestion of 1912.
[8] That is, until the age when maximum mental capacity is reached.

Deviation IQ. In later chapters dealing with the Stanford-Binet scale, and other scales, it will be seen that the standard deviations of intelligence quotients obtained by the relation MA/CA are not always of the same, or nearly the same, size at all age levels. For example, at one age level, *SD* might be 12; at another, 16; at still another, 18. The reasons for these differences are given in later chapters; but now it should be noted that differences such as these create problems and irregularities in the interpretation of the *relative* meaning of a given IQ. Thus, for example, in the first instance, an IQ of 88 (−1 *SD*) signifies a percentile rank of 16; in the second instance, an IQ of 84 has the same percentile equivalent; while in the third, an IQ of 82 also signifies a percentile rank of 16.

In order to overcome this difficulty, the "deviation IQ" is used with some tests. This index is an adaptation of the standard score (Z) technique. The method of determining the deviation IQ can be shown by using the Wechsler test's procedure as an illustration.[9] For each individual, the raw score is converted into a weighted score by using a conversion table. The mean weighted score of the group is given a deviation IQ value of 100; the *standard deviation* of the scores is equated with a deviation IQ value of 15. Thus, a person whose point score places him at −1 *SD* will have a deviation IQ of 85. One whose score is at −2 *SD* will have a rating of 70. Similarly, positive *SD* values will give ranks above 100: +1 *SD* equals 115 deviation IQ; +2 *SD* equals 130; and so forth. (See Figure 6.4.)

The 1960 revision of the Stanford-Binet scale also uses the deviation IQ, calculated by a different method; but the *basic principle* is the same. The principle is that an individual's intelligence quotient should be determined by the *relative* extent to which his score on the test deviates from the mean of his age group, and that an intelligence quotient of a given value should have the same *relative* significance throughout the age range. These ends are now achieved by using units of standard deviation as the basis; hence the name of the new index.

Making the mean score equal to a deviation IQ of 100 is readily understandable, since this value has long been conventional and is accepted as representing the average or normal. It also appears that the most probable standard deviation of intelligence quotients is 15–16, as found with the Stanford-Binet (which in many ways is regarded as a criterion); hence 15 has been taken to represent the standard deviation of the newer index. The choice of this value, therefore, was not an arbitrary one. Furthermore, the distribution yielded by a standard deviation of 15 points is very similar to the one to which psychologists and educators have become ac-

[9] The methods of calculating deviation IQs of the Stanford-Binet and the Wechsler scales are given more fully in Chapters 10 and 11.

customed, and in which values at each of the several levels have acquired qualitative significance in regard to mental ability and educational promise.

The deviation IQ, furthermore, is especially useful at age levels above 16 or 18 years. For these and older persons, the use of mental age and the formula for the ratio IQ (MA/CA) have been regarded as inappropriate and questionable by many psychologists. (This aspect of mental age is discussed in Chapter 10.)

It should be clear, from the materials thus far presented, that percentiles, standard deviations, standard scores, and intelligence quotients are intimately related. Whatever index is used, its principal significance is found in the relative rank it represents and in its psychological, educational, and vocational connotations.

Although the primary purpose of this section is to define and explain these concepts used in psychological testing, it is relevant here to emphasize the *qualitative* aspects of these indexes.

Qualitative Aspects

Assume that three boys, all of the same age, have been tested. Suppose that their intelligence quotients are 50, 100, and 150. Since these are numerical ratios (MA/CA × 100), it is natural to assume that they have a *quantitative* significance. So they do—for they indicate rate of mental development. But these quotients also have a *qualitative* significance—for, among other things, they indicate each boy's position in the "hierarchy of intelligence." If the measure of intelligence is valid, the boy having the IQ of 50 is seriously retarded and is in the lowest one percent of the population in respect to the psychological functions being tested; the boy with the IQ of 100 is the typical or average individual, midway up (or down) in the distribution of intelligence; and the boy having the IQ of 150 is very superior and belongs in the top percentile rank of the group.

Qualitative significance of the intelligence quotient can be illustrated further by asking this question: Is the brightest of these three boys one and one-half times as intelligent as the average boy, and three times as intelligent as the retarded one? This question cannot be answered in terms of numbers; it is impossible to say how many "times" more capable or less capable one is than the others, because *the IQ is not a percent.* But each of these quotients has certain connotations. In this example, the qualified school or clinical psychologist will be able to draw important inferences from each boy's IQ regarding rate and quality of school learning, extent and level of educability, vocational possibilities and levels, and probable types of interests.

The boy with an IQ of 50 probably will not be able to complete more than the second grade; the boy having the IQ of 100 should be able to complete twelve grades; the boy with an IQ of 150 will be able to progress in education as far as his interests and motives indicate. Obviously, too, the kinds of occupations that will be open to the first boy are very limited; those open to the second will be numerous; those open to the third will be practically unrestricted, so far as mental capacity is concerned. And the same may be said of the range of interests in general that will be within the scope of each. These facts are of educational and clinical significance, but at present there are no psychological or statistical means whereby one can calculate how many *times* more or less capable one person is than another.

Caution is necessary at this point. The inferences drawn in the preceding paragraph cannot be based solely upon the numerical IQ value without reference to the clinical features in the test performances or other factors not shown by the numerical index. We have assumed that there are no complicating factors and that the IQs are valid measures of the capacities and performances of the three boys. The boy with 150 IQ, however, *might be* an unstable personality who is failing in many or all of his school subjects. The boy with 100 IQ *might have been* penalized on the test by a language handicap. And the boy with an IQ of 50 *might* show a "scatter" (inconsistency and variation) of performance indicating emotional disturbance rather than intellectual impoverishment. Occasionally, also, it will be found that a high test rating *may be* attributable to an inconsistently high level of performance on one or a few types of subtests (for example, memory span or word knowledge), just as, conversely, it occasionally happens that a person's IQ is depressed by an inconsistently low performance on one or a few subtests. "Inconsistent" means that the individual's levels of performance on these few subtests differ markedly, in one direction or another, from the general and more consistent levels of his scores on the other subtests.

It is to be noted that the *possible* vitiating factors mentioned in the preceding paragraph are of the type to which the experienced and qualified psychological examiner will be alert. These precautions do not signify that all or most intelligence test ratings are affected by these and other contingencies.

Indexes Used with Educational Achievement Tests

Educational Age. The educational age index (EA) represents a pupil's average level of achievement in a group of school subjects, measured by means of standardized tests, and in terms of the average for various chronological ages in school. If, for example, a pupil's performance on the tests is at the average 12-year level, his EA is 12.

There is no fixed or uniform list of school subjects for which educational ages are obtained; therefore they are not all necessarily comparable. Furthermore, even if achievement in the same school subjects is measured, but with different tests, the EAs might still not be comparable because of possible differences in the standardization process.

Educational age is used, at times, to estimate the probable grade level at which a pupil's test performance places him, since the average age for each grade is known. This practice, however, is of doubtful merit. If a grade estimate or comparison is wanted, then grade norms should be used. These are provided by all the sound educational achievement tests.

Educational Quotient. As was to be expected, an "age" would be accompanied by a quotient. The educational quotient indicates, presumably, whether a pupil's knowledge of a group of school subjects is commensurate with his chronological age, or whether it is above or below the level to be expected of him for his age. The simple formula, therefore, is:

$$EQ = \frac{EA}{CA}(100)$$

the ratio being multipled by 100 to remove the decimal. It is hardly necessary to mention that the value of obtained educational quotients will depend upon the achievement test's reliability and validity.

Achievement Quotient. This index, AQ, the use of which was suggested in 1920 (7), is now rarely used.[10] It is found by dividing educational age by mental age (EA/MA). The reason for using MA as the divisor, instead of CA, is that the former is regarded as the more valid index of a pupil's learning capacity. Hence, it was believed, dividing EA by MA yields a quotient that indicates whether or not the individual is working up to his mental capacity, as found by the intelligence test. Although it is true that mental age is a more valid index of learning capacity and educational promise than chronological age alone, the AQ has some serious defects, which account for its virtual abandonment. First, it is erroneous to expect all mentally superior pupils to be at a level of educational achievement equal to their mental age, as the following example shows: assume that a superior child has completed the first grade at the age of 7; he has a mental age of 10, and, thus, an IQ of 143. To get an AQ of 100, he would have to earn an EA of 10. To obtain this EA, he must acquire, in one year of schoolwork, as much as

---

[10] Although this index is now in disuse, it is mentioned here because students will encounter it, from time to time, and because it has a place in the history of testing.

the ordinary child is expected to acquire in four. It is not probable that this will happen. To generalize this point: the superior child, especially in the lower school grades, has not had, and frequently does not have, the time and length of schooling necessary to learn the amount of subject matter necessary to equate EA with MA.

A second defect in using the AQ is that frequently the population samples upon which the educational achievement tests have been standardized are not comparable with those upon which the norms of the intelligence tests have been based. Generally, the former are less representative of the population and are dependent, of course, upon the quality of the schools in which the standardization process was carried out.

A third defect is the fact that many achievement tests do not differentiate as well among pupils as does a sound test of general intelligence. This fact tends to reduce the variability of the former and its correlation with the latter.

Currently, for the purpose of indicating a pupil's school achievement, the EA and EQ have value; but they should be supplemented by each individual's percentile rank within the distribution of scores for his grade. Since all sound tests cover a range of several grades, it is possible, if necessary, to compare any individual's score with the norms in grades above or below his own, for the purpose of finding his percentile rank within those other levels.[11]

Clinical Aspects

Scores, whether raw or converted, do not suffice for the complete interpretation of an individual's performances on psychological tests. The several aspects of test standardization thus far presented are concerned with the performance of *groups* of persons and with *average relationships* revealed by statistical treatment of results. It happens, however, that although certain types of test items meet some or most of the statistical requirements of validity, they are unsatisfactory as indicators of intelligence when used for clinical purposes. For example, on the Stanford-Binet scale, the percentage of adults able to repeat eight digits forward (*digit-span* test) is approximately the same as the percentage who can solve one of the more difficult reasoning problems. Yet, in clinical examinations, psychologists find some adult mental defectives who can pass the former test, although a mental defective can never succeed with

[11] At present, educational ages and grade norms have less significance than formerly as indexes of the quality and level of a child's educational achievement. This is the case because nearly all children and adolescents now remain in school much longer than they did formerly, and, regardless of quality or level of achievement in school subjects, are moved up through the grades. This practice, obviously, lowers the normative levels.

the latter. What this means is that statistical validation of a test item is not always sufficient; it must be supplemented by the pragmatic criterion of use with a wide variety of individuals in a variety of situations in order to show whether or not it has discriminative value among individuals at the several levels of ability.

Psychological tests, as already noted, are standardized on the basis of the performance of a representative population; and an individual's rating is determined by the relationship of his performance to that of a group as a whole. Thus we have the several "ages" (for example, mental age) and "quotients" (for example, intelligence quotient), percentile and decile ranks, and standard scores. Any useful test should yield one or more of these. In more recent years, however, without denying the usefulness and value of these indexes of relative status, increasing emphasis has been placed upon "patterns" of performance as clinical aids to psychological diagnosis and counseling.

A person's responses to tests are now frequently analyzed for the purpose of discovering whether he shows any special abilities or disabilities, whether there are marked discrepancies between responses on some types of materials as against responses on others, or whether certain psychological processes seem to be impaired or are markedly superior to others within the individual. A general contrast, for example, might be found between tests involving verbal materials and those which are nonverbal in character; the associative processes might be disturbed; memory or spatial perception might be found to deviate markedly in one direction or another from an individual's general level of capacity. Recent investigations have indicated that patterns of response may be useful in differentiating and diagnosing the several categories of maladjusted and abnormal personalities, as well as for discerning more clearly the mental defectives.

Also, it has been found that persons of equivalent general mental status may have different patterns of performance, or abilities, which in sum, nevertheless, give them much the same over-all and general ratings in terms of a single index (mental age, percentile rank). That is to say, it is possible for two persons to have test ratings that are *numerically* similar and yet have dissimilar "mental organizations," since the components of each total rating differ to a greater or lesser degree from those of the other.

If, therefore, the psychologist's concern is not primarily with group trends or averages, but rather with a particular individual, of course he will want to know the age level of performance and the consequent quotient; but he will also analyze the details of the individual's performance for the purpose of discovering that person's particular pattern or idiom, in order to discern his particular form of mental organization, specific evidences of retardation or disability, if any, and details of his development.

In more recent years there has been a partial shift in emphasis from almost exclusive concern with the analysis of abilities and methods of psychological measurement, as such, to an examination of individual performance and individual idiom, and to the individual as a functioning and dynamic unit. After all, any given test measures only a segment of a total personality; that segment is an integral part of the totality and is influenced by the whole. Hence, the psychologist who is concerned with insight into the nature of an individual's abilities must be able to *evaluate* a person's performance as well as *measure* it. The data and indexes derived from psychological tests are, for the most part, objectively determined; but their clinical use involves judgment, subjective assessment, and interpretation, based upon a variety of data from several sources. The experienced clinical examiner will supplement the test's numerical results with his observations of the testee's attitudes during the examination and the manner in which he attacks the problems of the test: his degree of confidence or dependence, his cooperativeness or apathy, his negativism or resentment, the richness or paucity of his responses. The individual test situation thus can be, in effect, an occasion for general psychological observations—really a penetrating psychological interview.

Ability not only to score a test but also to assess and interpret responses and to evaluate the individual's behavior during the examination is a clinical skill the psychologist develops from working with persons rather than with tests alone. However, for the practice of his skill he must, of course, thoroughly understand the psychological and statistical foundations and hypotheses upon which the tests are based.

A few specific instances of the *qualitative* analysis and interpretation of test responses will illustrate the kinds of observations that constitute the clinical aspects that supplement numerical scoring.

Word definitions are generally acceptable at a fairly elementary level; but they vary in level and quality from purely concrete, to functional, to conceptual or abstract. Differences in quality level are indicative of differences in modes of thinking. It also happens, at times, that some words are emotionally charged for the examinee, in which case his definition and behavioral response may be revealing.

Some test items permit the exercise of considerable freedom in response. These responses may reveal the examinee's attitudes, values, and modes of meeting life situations. In this category are test items that ask, "What is the thing to do when . . . ?" Or, "Why should we . . . ?" The subject's reactions to such items, the qualities of his verbalizations in making the responses, and the presence or absence of strong feelings reveal some of the nonintellective aspects of his personality.

The subject's specific comments while performing a task are of possible significance in regard to his attitude toward himself, or toward an authority figure (the examiner), or toward other individuals and institutions in his environment.

Responses to items or random comments may reveal hostilities and anxieties, or wholesome cooperativeness and security.

The manner of speech—the use of expletives, halting and fumbling, restless movements, blushing, or, on the other hand, a relaxed attitude, mild criticism of one's own performance—provides valuable clues to the testee's personality.

Character disorders may be indicated by impetuous and uncritical responses that are incorrect but are given with assurance and pretentiousness.

The subject's ability to direct his attention toward, to concentrate upon, and to organize a task are often revealed by his mode of approach to a test problem.

The selective character, if any, of a person's vocabulary and information (two subtests widely used) will shed light upon his experiences, interests, cultural background.

A personality trait such as compulsiveness (as opposed to desirable thoroughness and self-criticism) may be revealed by excessively detailed responses and by numerous and unnecessary alternative responses.

Some types of responses indicate pathological or psychotic states: erroneously bizarre responses by an otherwise intelligent person (for example, London is in Africa; the population of the United States is 1,500,000); disjointed and irrelevant responses; and distorted interpretations of the task or problem.

Organic damage may be detected through selected kinds of subtests; for example, disturbance of the visual-motor function as indicated by the diamond copying test (Stanford-Binet) and the object assembly test (Bellevue), among others.

Scatter analysis (discussed in detail in Chapter 14) is essential to the discernment of superior, inferior, and impaired psychological functions.

Sensitized observations on the part of the examiner will enable him, in general, to evaluate *how* the subject proceeded in both success and failure.[12]

The findings on a test—whether it is of general intelligence, specific aptitude, personality, or school learning—indicate the present status of

[12] Illustrations of these qualitative interpretations will be given in Chapter 14, on clinical aspects.

each person examined. They do not, however, tell the psychological examiner by what course the person arrived there; nor do they indicate specifically what factors were operative in his development. The clinical approach, while accepting and utilizing standardized tests and norms, insists upon viewing and evaluating any given individual's performance and status in the light of a variety of other measurements, observations, and activities of that individual, and upon interpreting the objective quantitative data according to the part they have in the total. For instance, children who have suffered from prolonged and serious nutritional disturbances or deficiencies or who are suffering from severe anemia will appear listless, apathetic, and deficient in mental capacity. Other children, of apparently retarded mental development, may be suffering from serious deficiencies of vitamin B complex, while still others may measure at a level of retardation because of emotional pressures and "blocking." [13] Furthermore, the performance of some children on standardized tests is inferior because they developed under conditions of psychological impoverishment, whereas test norms are based on the assumption that all individuals being examined have had approximately equal opportunity, in the grosser aspects of environment, for mental development. Often, of course, that is not the case. These facts, and others of the same kind, indicate that in the case of some individuals, performance and consequent relative status may be impaired by nutritional deficiencies, by emotional handicaps or by other unfavorable environmental conditions.

The fact that psychologists are placing increased emphasis upon individual patterns in test performance (especially in diagnosing cases of behavior and educational maladjustment) and upon the individual as a whole does not mean that statistical and group studies are unnecessary. Such studies are essential in providing norms against which any individual's performance may be projected, in giving more precise meaning and significance to any single score, in demonstrating the great range of human variability in any trait or function, and in providing the means of more precise study of interrelations among psychological traits and functions.

Difference between Norms and Standards

Norms, as already explained, are average scores or values determined by actual measurement of a group of persons who are representative of a specified population; for example, all 12-year-old boys, all fourth-grade children, all native-born male adults. Norms, therefore, are

[13] A condition in which the functioning of mental abilities is impeded because of the individual's emotional state or a mental conflict.

averages *obtained under prevailing conditions*—good, poor, or indifferent. These norms may well ". . . reflect all the sins of omission or commission in their [the people's] nurture and must be critically examined lest we set up as desirable norms for achievement what are but accidental outcomes of our unsystematic and unenlightened nurture of children . . ." (6, p. 9). In other words, a norm of psychological performance or of a physical trait is not necessarily one with which we should be satisfied; for it reflects development under conditions that may be, and often are, much less than optimal. As an example, consider the average vocabulary of eighth-grade pupils. The average, or norm, of this group will depend in part upon these pupils' opportunities for the acquisition and use of language from earliest childhood. Their opportunities might have been extremely poor, moderately satisfactory, very good, or at any other level between these three. Norms of performance in respect to some of the psychological processes measured by means of tests of intelligence and of specific aptitude are likewise dependent upon conditions and opportunities present during the course of development. Norms of height, weight, and other body measurements will also reflect past conditions of nutrition and health.

It is necessary, therefore, to distinguish between norms, on the one hand, and *standards,* on the other; for a standard is the *desired* goal or objective, which may well be above the obtained norm and can be achieved only under improved conditions of development. It is possible that grade norms for reading rate and comprehension are below what they could be under improved educational conditions and teaching methods; that age and grade norms for numerical ability are below what they might be; that universal nursery school and kindergarten experience would promote children's perceptions of form and color and would improve their motor skills, and hence raise the norms; that universal optimal nutrition would raise age norms for height and weight, and so forth.

Psychological tests measure traits and functions as they exist under present conditions. They do not provide psychologist and educator with an index of what *ought* to be, except by implication and to the extent that obtained results might raise certain suspicions, doubts, and queries in the minds of investigators.

Psychological Measurement Contrasted with Physical Measurement

The indexes thus far presented make clear the fact that basically all psychological tests yield results that rank individuals in relation to their fellows. The raw scores obtained on psychological tests are not comparable with or similar to the values obtained in the measurement of physical traits or phenomena, as, for example, length, weight, or light intensity. In the physical realm, the units of measurement are fixed and constant throughout the entire scale. An inch, a pound, a candle power— each has the same value and physical significance at whatever place on the scale it is measured. Psychological measurement, by contrast, is more difficult and is confronted by special problems. In the first place, it is not possible to determine the inherent difficulty of an item in a psychological test in terms of constant units, as it is possible to find the length or weight of any object. Whereas in the measurement of physical phenomena it can be found that a given object is of X length and Y weight, and hence, let us say, twice as long and three times as heavy as another object with which it is being compared, no such *direct* measurement and comparison are possible in psychological testing. In this realm, the measurement value of a test item is dependent basically upon the percentage of persons able to pass the item in the population group for whom the test is intended.

If in the testing of a particular ability, one item is passed by only ten percent of a group, whereas another item is passed by fifty percent, it cannot be said that the first is five times as difficult as the second, because "percent passing" is not a unit in the sense that an inch or a pound is. What can be said is that an individual able to deal successfully with the first item belongs in the highest decile group, while one who cannot pass the first but is able to pass the second falls at the midpoint or average level of the group in respect to that item of the test. This interpretation is significant psychologically and educationally. Or, to use another instance, in the case of the Stanford-Binet scale, the age level at which an item is placed—and hence its value in the scale—is determined by the age group in which average individuals pass that item. Thus, anyone able to solve a reasoning problem placed at the 10-year level, for example, but failing to pass reasoning problems at the 11-year or higher levels, may be said to have typical 10-year-old ability in respect to that mental task.

This leads directly into the problem of the meaning of "mental age" and other "age" units. *Mental age* is an index showing one's level of mental development, corresponding to the level of mental development of average persons of the coinciding *chronological age*. Thus, if a child's mental age is 10, he has reached the level of mental development attained by the average 10-year-old child, regardless of the actual life age of the child being tested.

Now, suppose there are four individuals having mental ages, respectively, of 5, 6, 12, and 13. Is the difference between mental ages 5 and 6 the same as that between mental ages 12 and 13? It is not; for, as measured by mental tests, the rate of mental development at 5 and 6 years of age is more rapid than subsequently; hence, the increment between the earlier years is greater. Figure 6.5 is the curve accepted by most psychologists as representing rate of mental development. The outstanding feature of that curve, for the problem under consideration, is the fact that it rises at a *decreasing rate* with increasing age. The curve is "negatively accelerated." Or, psychologically speaking, with each succeeding year, until maximum development is attained, the amount of increment in mental growth is less than in the preceding year.

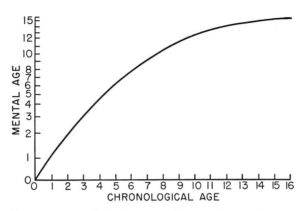

FIG. 6.5. Hypothetical curve of mental growth, illustrating decreasing yearly increments

It is obvious, therefore, that each successive year of mental age added to an individual's level represents something less in measurable growth than the preceding year's increment. In other words, mental age units are not uniform; they rank an individual with respect to the average mental capacity of an age group. The same principle—nonuniformity of age units—applies also to all other types of psychological tests that translate their scores into age equivalents.

Although psychological testing would be easier and more precise if its measuring units were fixed and uniform, available indexes of *relative* rank are, nevertheless, essential in evaluating an individual's mental development, his educational progress, his particular aptitudes, his social maturity, and even certain nonintellective aspects of personality. Experimentally, too, these same indexes have been indispensable in studying a host of practical and theoretical problems, such as sex differences, effects of environmental conditions, inheritance of intellectual capacity and of special aptitudes, occupational differentiation, racial differences, relationships between physical and mental development, and others.

Essential Considerations in Selecting a Test

By way of summary, the following factors are given as those to be considered in selecting a psychological test.

NORMS. The test must provide appropriate and accurate norms, whether they be in the form of age, grade, percentile rank, standard score, or any other type. Norms should be meaningful with regard to the purposes for which the test is intended and to the groups of persons with whom it is to be used.

ADMINISTERING AND SCORING. The procedures of administering the test should be objective and the test items should be amenable to relatively objective and simple scoring, insofar as the nature of the instrument permits. Individually administered tests, like the Stanford-Binet, at times require insightful judgment in scoring responses. Interpretation and evaluation of responses are even more significant in the scoring and analysis of projective techniques for assessing personality.

TIME REQUIREMENTS. The length of the test should not be so great as to produce boredom, satiation, or negativism; for when these set in, the subject does not perform at his best level. Specific time limits cannot be prescribed for all tests or for all types of testees; but in general, shorter time requirements are indicated for younger children and for the mentally retarded. In the case of both of these groups of subjects, the attention span is relatively brief; hence, it may be necessary at times to complete an examination in two sessions.

INTEREST LEVEL. Test items should be of sufficient interest to motivate the individuals for whom they are intended. Particular items and types of problems devised to measure given functions must be suitable to the age levels of examinees. Thus, in constructing an intelligence test for the entire range of adult capacity, from very low to very high, it is necessary that even the items placed at the very low levels be of the sort that will interest an adult rather than a child, even though these low-level adults may be inferior in mental capacity to some children.

THE POPULATION SAMPLE. The manual of a test should state in detail the nature of the population sample on which the instrument was standardized and upon which norms are based. The information given should include the following: total number of cases, age range and number at each age level, number of each sex, geographic distribution, socioeconomic status, and number in each category. For some tests, it will be relevant, indeed necessary, to have information on some of the following: school-grade distribution, number of years of schooling completed, amount and kind of special training (especially for tests of specific aptitudes), special or abnormal adjustment problems and history (especially for tests of personality). In short, the prospective user of a test must be certain that the test has been standardized on an appropriate sample of the population and for the same or similar purposes as those contemplated by the prospective user. This principle seems axiomatic; yet it is not always given due consideration.

THE FUNCTIONS OR TRAITS MEASURED.   The test manual should not only state the purpose of the instrument; it should also provide, so far as possible, an analysis (psychological and statistical) of the functions or traits being measured.

RELIABILITIES.   Coefficients of reliability should be provided not only for total scores but for part scores as well, wherever possible. Also, reliability coefficients are desirable for each of the several age levels and ability levels included within the range of the test. Furthermore, the manual should state which method or methods have been used in calculating the test's reliability. Here, the prospective user of a test must look for information that will help him answer the question: "Reliable for whom and for what purposes?"

VALIDITY.   Data on validity are of several kinds, in addition to coefficients of correlation; for example, expectancy tables, known groups, significance of differences between age levels. The test manual should explain the characteristics of the criterion *groups,* the nature of other criteria used, the validity of the total test, and the validity of the subtests. It is desirable, also, to have data regarding validity at each of the several age and ability levels. Here again, an answer must be sought to the question: "Valid for whom and for what purposes?"

REPORTS OF EXPERIMENTS.   The ideal test manual (subsequent to the first or earliest editions) includes summaries, findings, and interpretations of the most important experimental studies to which the test has been subjected by psychologists. Such information will help users to understand more fully the nature of the test and the factors affecting performance on it, thus making for sounder interpretation of results obtained by those who use it. For example: What is the influence of cultural factors? Of practice? Of time limits? Of psychotherapy or counseling?

Psychological tests are scientifically constructed instruments based upon psychological and statistical principles. Familiarity with these principles should provide students with a sounder comprehension of both the values and the limitations of tests than they would derive from using and interpreting them in a mechanical manner. It is also true that human subjects are being tested; they do not behave like mechanisms under complete control, with all environmental forces likewise under control and measurable. On the contrary, human behavior is often subtle and the psychological forces motivating or influencing persons in a test situation may be elusive and difficult of evaluation. Furthermore, since the quantitative data of psychological testing are not as definite, precise, and uniform as are the data of physical measurements, the interpretation of test findings is more difficult. For these reasons, we have emphasized not only the well-defined scientific principles and procedures of testing, but also the *qualitative* and *clinical* aspects that are essential if test findings are to be of the greatest value to the individuals examined.

References

1. Bennett, G. K., *et al. College Qualification Test: Manual.* New York: The Psychological Corporation, 1957.
2. Brown, A. W., *et al. The Chicago Non-Verbal Examination: Manual of Directions.* New York: The Psychological Corporation, 1936.
3. Chaille, S. E. Infants: their chronological progress. *New Orleans Medical and Surgical Journal,* 1887, *14,* 893–912.
4. Comrey, A. L. Mental testing and the logic of measurement. *Educational and Psychological Measurement,* 1951, *11,* 323–334.
5. Flanagan, J. C. Units, scores, and norms. *Educational Measurement,* E. F. Lindquist (ed.). Washington, D.C.: American Council on Education, 1951, ch. 17.
6. Frank, L. K. Research in child development: history and prospect. In *Child Behavior and Development,* R. G. Barker *et al.* (ed.). New York: McGraw-Hill Book Company, Inc., 1943.
7. Franzen, R. The accomplishment ratio. *Teachers College Record,* 1920, *21,* 432–442.
8. Froehlich, C. P., and J. G. Darley. Statistical methods of summarizing the results of a single test or measuring device. *Studying Students.* Chicago: Science Research Associates, 1952.
9. Guilford, J. P. *Fundamental Statistics in Psychology and Education.* (3rd ed.) New York: McGraw-Hill Book Company, Inc., 1956.
10. Hart, I. Using stanines to obtain scores based on test data and teachers' ranks. *Test Service Bulletin,* New York: Harcourt, Brace & World, Inc., 1957, no. 86.
11. Jacobs, J. N. Aptitude and achievement measures in predicting high school academic success. *Test Service Bulletin,* New York: Harcourt, Brace & World, Inc., 1959, no. 94.
12. Kuhlmann, F. A revision of the Binet-Simon system for measuring the intelligence of children. *Journal of Psycho-Aesthenics,* Monograph Supplement, 1912.

13. McCall, W. A. *How to Measure in Education.* New York: The Macmillan Company, 1922.
14. Otis, A. S. *Self-Administering Test of Mental Ability: Manual.* New York: Harcourt, Brace & World, Inc.
15. Seashore, H. G., *et al. Test Service Bulletin,* New York: The Psychological Corporation, Sept. 1954, no. 47.
16. Stern, W. *The Psychological Methods of Testing Intelligence* (Translated by G. M. Whipple). Educational Psychology Monographs, 1914, no. 13.
17. Stern, W. Der Intelligenz Quotient als mass der Kindlichen Intelligenz. *Zeitschrift für Angewandte Psychologie,* 1916, *11,* 1–18.
18. Walker, H. M., and J. Lev. *Elementary Statistical Methods* (Rev. Ed.). New York: Holt, Rinehart and Winston, Inc., 1958.

7.

DEFINITIONS AND ANALYSES
OF INTELLIGENCE

Psychological testing began, it will be recalled, with efforts to devise scientific instruments for the measurement and study of individual differences in intelligence. Measurement and analysis of this complex mental process has continued to be the most important and widespread type of psychological testing. It is desirable, therefore, to examine the definitions and theories of intelligence, both for their historical value and their current significance in test construction and utilization. Knowledge of these will give the student a fuller understanding of current tests.

Definitions

Three Types. A variety of definitions have been given by psychologists; but as a matter of fact, each can be classified into one of three groups.

One group of definitions places the emphasis upon *adjustment or adaptation of the individual to his total environment,* or to limited aspects of it. According to definitions of this type, intelligence is general mental adaptability to new problems and new situations of life; or, otherwise stated, it is the capacity to reorganize one's behavior patterns so as to act more effectively and more appropriately in novel situations. Thus, the more intelligent person is one who can more easily and more extensively vary his behavior as changing conditions demand; he has numerous possible responses and is capable of greater creative reorganization of behavior, whereas the less intelligent person has fewer responses and is less creative. The more intelligent person, accordingly, can deal with a greater number and a greater variety of situations than the less intelligent; he is able to encompass a wider field and to expand his area of activity beyond that of the less intelligent.

A second type of definition states that intelligence is the *ability to learn*. According to this definition, then, a person's intelligence is a matter of the extent to which he is educable, in the broadest sense. The more intelligent the individual is, the more readily and extensively is he able to learn; hence, also, the greater is his possible range of experience and activity.

Still others have defined intelligence as the *ability to carry on abstract thinking*. This means the effective use of concepts and symbols in dealing with situations, especially those presenting a problem to be solved through the use of verbal and numerical symbols. Binet's conception of intelligence belongs largely in this category, for he maintained that it is the capacity to reason well, to judge well, and to be self-critical.

It should be apparent that the three foregoing categories of definitions are not, and cannot be, mutually exclusive. For the most part, their authors differ in emphasis. Obviously, ability to learn must provide the foundation for adjustment and adaptation to changing or new conditions. And a person may be expected to have learned more or less from situations he had encountered and to which he had previously made adjustments. For if this were not the case, he would have to start anew in every situation which confronted him; there would be no difference between the behavior of an experienced person and that of a novice.

There are, of course, individual differences in respect to learning capacity and in ability to retain, interpret, organize, and apply what has been learned; thus previous experiences will have different significance and different learning value for different persons. And it is learning capacity that constitutes the basis of adjustment and adaptation, although, as will become apparent in later chapters, important nonintellective factors affect adjustment and adaptation.

Yet learning capacity, in the sense only of acquisition of information and knowledge, is not a sufficient criterion for the evaluation of a person's intelligence. Psychologists and laymen alike agree that a person who can reorganize and apply what he has acquired for the purpose of dealing with varied and novel situations is more intelligent than one who is capable of little beyond repeating what he had previously acquired, or than one whose behavior follows stereotyped patterns without insight into the essential elements and relations of each new situation. Thus, a definition of intelligence as the capacity to behave appropriately and effectively in new situations and a definition of intelligence as the ability to learn represent, in fact, two aspects of the same process.

The third type of definition is also inseparable from the other two. A person *learns* abstractions—principally verbal and numerical—through experience, through contact with and perception of the objects, events, qualities, or relationships for which the symbols stand. Thus, the word "dog" has meaning for a child because it has come to represent a class of objects with which he has become familiar. The word "green" represents a quality he has perceived as an aspect of a variety of objects. The word "charity," for the individual who has developed sufficiently to understand the concept, has a certain connotation because he has experienced events that have been labeled as charitable. The number "five" is meaningful to a person when, as a result of experience with concrete objects, he apprehends the term as representing not only ordinal position but summation as well. Furthermore, if it is to be said that an individual has fully learned to deal with the symbols of abstraction, then it must be true that he understands that the *word is not the thing or the quality* for which it stands. He understands that words and numbers are abstractions that represent objects, events, qualities, or relations, but which, in thinking, can be dealt with *as if* they were the things themselves. This aspect of intelligence—the ability to use symbols—is itself the result of an individual's development and learning. And in turn, the mastery and utilization of symbols promotes further learning—for it is hardly necessary to labor the point that without language and number, the range of one's learning would be seriously restricted.

Ability to carry on abstract thinking, it is easy to see, contributes to a person's ability to adjust or adapt to changing or new situations, because through the use of symbols we are enabled to think through a problem without spending time and effort on sheer trial and error in action; we can marshal, evaluate, and deal with past experiences; and we can project our thinking forward. In other words, through the use of symbols and abstract thinking, man is able to enlarge his range of behavior, to extend his horizons, and to transcend the immediate concrete and specific situation.

Two Comprehensive Definitions. Two definitions of intelligence have been presented which, in effect, combine and extend the three views already presented. One writer states: "Intelligence is the aggregate or global capacity of the individual to act purposefully, to think rationally and to deal effectively with his environment" (19, p. 3). The reader can readily compare this definition with those already presented and analyze it with a view to discerning similarities and differences. It will be noted, of course, that this definition encompasses the other three. Although learning ability is not mentioned, it is surely implied. Two new aspects, however, are added. The definition specifically states that an individual's intelligence is revealed by his behavior as a whole ("global"), and that intelligence involves behavior toward a goal, which may be more or less immediate ("purposefully"). A third aspect is presented by the author in his elaboration of the definition; namely that "drive" and "incentive" enter into intelligent behavior. This aspect is probably included and implied in capacity "to act purposefully" and "to deal effectively" with one's environment, as stated in the definition.

The inclusion of "drive," "incentive," and the like as aspects of intelligence is of doubtful validity; their inclusion would confuse the issue, the testing instrument, and the results obtained. It is true, of course, that effective utilization of a person's intelligence depends upon the extent and degree to which he employs it. Nevertheless, a single testing device that attempts to combine the measurement of intellectual with nonintellectual traits without providing for differentiation between the two would not succeed adequately in either respect.[1] This is not to say that in assessing an individual's intelligence and personality as a whole we should ignore "drive," "incentive," "interest"; for the competent psychological examiner does evaluate these and other nonintellectual traits in presenting his test results. Furthermore, as will be seen in later chapters of this book, special psychological instruments are available for the evaluation of nonintellectual traits of personality, which the clinician may use to supplement results of intelligence tests if he believes they are necessary.

Stoddard offers the following definition: "Intelligence is the ability to undertake activities that are characterized by (1) difficulty, (2) complexity, (3) abstractness, (4) economy, (5) adaptiveness to a goal, (6) social value, and (7) the emergence of originals, and to maintain such activities under conditions that demand a concentration of energy and a resistance to emotional forces" (8, p. 4). Here again, the reader will note that this definition does in fact include the first three types presented; but it goes beyond these in several respects. The author specifies the several attributes of intelligence, and in his enumeration are several not included in earlier definitions.

Degree or level of difficulty is implied in all definitions; but Stoddard's contribution here lies in the fact that he rightly insists we must, in testing, distinguish between true differences in degree of difficulty and

---

[1] The Rorschach test attempts to measure both nonintellectual and intellectual traits of personality. This test is discussed in Chapter 25. The point of view stated here does not exclude the possibility of drawing inferences from an individual's performance on a scale such as the Stanford-Binet and the Wechsler regarding some of his nonintellectual characteristics.

differences that only seem to exist, as between two or more test items, whereas, in fact, there are no inherent differences in difficulty. For example, the accumulation of rare information and the ability to define unusual words are not in themselves true measures of difficulty; they may reflect only differences in experience. On the other hand, however, over and above disparity in experiences between various age groups, true differences in difficulty do exist between *problems* that can be solved, let us say, by a group of average 10-year-old children, and those that can be solved by an average group of 8-year-olds or 9-year-olds.

"Complexity" refers to the number of different kinds and varieties of tasks that can be dealt with successfully. According to this attribute of intelligence, the individual who is able to deal successfully with several different kinds of tasks, at a given level of difficulty, is more intelligent than a person who can successfully undertake fewer kinds of tasks at the same level of difficulty. "Complexity," however, means not simply the addition of one type of performance to others; on the contrary, it means the capacity to assimilate new abilities, to integrate them with others, and thus to reorganize one's patterns or forms of intelligent behavior.

"Abstractness"—that is, operating with symbols, especially at levels of analysis and interpretation—has already been discussed. For Stoddard, this attribute "lies at the heart of intelligence as defined."

"Economy" refers to the rate at which mental tasks are performed and problems solved. Assuming that the problems are solved equally well, that the solutions are equally effective, the individual working more rapidly would be regarded as the more able, according to this attribute. Acceptance of "economy" as an attribute of intelligence means that tests would impose time limits that should differentiate among individuals in respect to their rates of performance of tasks and solutions of problems at given levels of difficulty and degrees of complexity.

"Adaptiveness to a goal" implies an approach that is more than aimlessly meeting and solving new situations as they arise. This attribute means that intelligent action is directed toward a goal or a purpose. The more comprehensive the goal and the larger and more complete the purpose, the more is intelligent action required.

The student, after examining representative tests of intelligence, might well question whether they do, or even could, satisfactorily test this last attribute; or whether the problems and tasks included in the tests are rather oversimplified and segmental examples of problems and courses of action that a person has to confront and deal with in actual life situations. If the test items are of the latter kind, then their value and validity as measures of intelligence must be shown by the fact that they do indeed predict to an adequate degree the manner and effectiveness with which the testee will deal with and solve actual life situations of broader scope. In other words, what are the predictive values of the items, tasks, and problems included in a test?

The inclusion of "social value" as an attribute of intelligence is of doubtful validity, and debatable at best; for this criterion is essentially moral or ethical, or a matter of subjective evaluation. The basis of "social value" is group acceptability. If this attribute were applied in evaluating intelligence, we should have to minimize our estimates of the intelligence of individuals whose thinking and solutions of problems are not necessarily consistent with accepted social forms, though they might be "ahead of their time"; and of individuals who are capable of difficult and complex mental operations, but whose mental activities lead to no apparent or demonstrable practical and social values. While we may value more highly the individual whose mental operations culminate in desirable, acceptable, and useful social outcomes, the inclusion of "social value" as an attribute of intelligence would confuse attempts to measure the other, and valid, attributes by injecting largely subjective conceptions of what is socially acceptable, unacceptable, or indifferent. It will be seen later that "social value" is hardly present in current tests of intelligence; although, of course, some psychologists, like Stoddard, take the position that it should be.

"The emergence of originals" as an attribute of intelligence is the ability to create something new and different; it is a characteristic of a high order of thinking and of individuals at the superior end of the distribution of intelligence. Examples of this attribute in operation are the development of a new scientific principle, the discovery of unique relationships in observed data or phenomena, the development of a new machine design, the development of a new technological process, the new organization and new interpretation of historical or social facts, a creatively original painting or musical composition. It is true that current tests of intelligence provide little opportunity for the measurement or emergence of originals. The question, then, so far as these tests are concerned, is whether this attribute, creative originality, is really dependent upon a combination of abilities that are actually measured by available tests and whether the results obtained by means of the tests are indicative of the degree to which a person possesses this attribute. Some psychologists, Stoddard among them, believe that at present the tests of intelligence do not satisfactorily discern and rate an individual's intellectual originality. Others maintain that the hierarchy of abilities established by means of the tests enables us to identify the persons who possess originality in greater or lesser degree.[2]

[2] The observation of psychologists is that persons who show creative originality, almost without exception, score high or very high on intelligence tests; but many persons may

Stoddard's last two conditions of intelligent behavior—"concentration of energy" and "resistance to emotional forces"—are subject to the same criticism as Wechsler's inclusion of "drive" and "incentive." Motivation and ability to exert sustained effort are usually regarded as nonintellectual aspects of activity and are certainly recognized as playing highly important roles in one's general effectiveness. But to introduce them into a test of mental ability would be to confuse and probably to invalidate efforts to arrive at a reasonably valid measure of the level of intelligent activity at which a given person is *able to operate,* whether or not he actually does operate at that level in all situations.

Although tests of intelligence do not directly measure motivation and concentration of energy on the solution of problems, the psychological examiner does in fact try to develop or encourage conditions wherein the persons being examined will operate at their maximum levels of ability. This can be more nearly achieved in individual testing than in group testing. Furthermore, if an individual is not adequately motivated, is not expending a maximum of energy during the test, or is handicapped by emotional factors, these conditions can be discerned much more readily during the examination of one person at a time than during the examination of a group all at once. Indeed, during group testing there may be instances of persons whose test results are vitiated by the effects of these unfavorable conditions, unknown to the examiner. This possibility is a disadvantage of group testing.

No single test or series (battery) of tests can provide an unfailing index or a guarantee of motivation, energy output, or freedom from emotional blocking in all future situations requiring intelligent behavior. For man is not a static being; nor does the environment in which he lives remain static. Long-term motives and immediate incentives will change; values and interests will change. The affective (emotional) quality of a person's experiences will influence his subsequent behavior, including situations requiring the utilization of intelligence. Tests of intelligence now in use are not intended to determine the extent to which an individual will in the future concentrate his energy on problems demanding the use of his intelligence, or to determine whether it is probable that he will be able to remain free from emotional blockings. A variety of personality rating scales and inventories and projective techniques have been devised to evaluate these nonintellectual traits. Although tests of intelligence will be improved so that greater demands will be made upon concentration of attention and sustained effort than is the case with some tests at present, psychologists believe that a qualified examiner will be able to determine

---

score very high on these tests without having exceptional powers of originality. We need tests of originality, but in view of the very nature of the concept and its expressions, such tests cannot very well be standardized.

whether or not a given person's performance on an *individual* test represents his maximum level at that time. They believe, also, that most persons can be motivated to perform at their best levels when taking a *group* test. When groups are tested, this condition must be reasonably well assured as well as being assumed.[3]

Although intelligence tests are not designed to measure a person's emotional status and other nonintellectual aspects of personality, clinically oriented psychologists analyze an individual's test performance for evidence of emotional states, personality "mechanisms" and for "differential diagnosis" (that is, for evidence of neurosis, psychosis, or other atypical states). This aspect of test interpretation, which demands sensitive clinical insights, is discussed in Chapter 14.

Implications for Test Design and Content

Definitions of intelligence are of more than theoretical importance. The conception of intelligence that a psychologist holds will affect, to some extent at least, the content and organization of the test he develops. Yet, at the same time, an examination of a representative group of tests reveals the fact that although some are different from others in certain aspects, they all have much in common, nevertheless. It would be incorrect to say, for instance, that certain tests exemplify exclusively the definition that intelligence is the capacity to learn. Because psychologists emerge with tests having considerable similarity, although they may start with different definitions, it follows that their definitions differ largely in respect to *emphases* and that, as already pointed out, they are interdependent.

Early experimenters in mental testing attempted to measure general intellectual capacity by means of a single type of test that measured only a single capacity, usually a sensory process, or association, or attention. Thus they identified general intellectual capacity with a single function. Their efforts were fruitless. Later, however, experiment showed that a *variety of test materials* yielded more accurate and more useful results when validated against accepted criteria of intelligent activity. Psychologists, in seeking to encompass a greater variety of items in their tests,

---

[3] The "catch" lies in the fact that in any large group of persons being tested it is not unlikely that there will be a few, at least, who are not adequately motivated or who are handicapped by emotional difficulties. Herein is a source of error in group measurement. The discovery of these nonmotivated or blocked individuals will depend upon whether or not each one's rating on the test is scrutinized and evaluated in the light of other, and perhaps conflicting, evidence. Where there is reason to believe that group-test performance is spuriously low in the case of a given individual, it is desirable to re-examine, using an individual rather than a group test.

and thus to produce more useful and successful instruments regardless of the exact definition with which each one started out, found that inevitably their testing instruments were broader than their definitions. Current tests, as a result, have more than a little in common in spite of differences in details of their content. Inspection of their content will show that in varying degrees they are measures of some aspects of learning in what is assumed to be a reasonably uniform environment for all persons,[4] that novel situations and problems are presented, and that ability to carry on abstract thinking is tested through the utilization of symbols and ideas. Inspection will demonstrate also that most of the tests fail to meet the more comprehensive and long-term attributes suggested in Stoddard's definition.

So far as available tests are concerned, it is important to bear in mind that the French psychologist Binet (the "father" of modern mental testing) took the position that it made little difference what specific tasks and items were incorporated into a test, provided that in some degree each part was a measure of the individual's general capacity. Whether or not this condition is met will depend, of course, upon the definition of intelligence regarded as most adequate by the designer of a test and upon the criteria of intelligent activity against which test results are validated. In spite of some differences in definition and in spite of some differences in external appearances, psychologists believe that their tests are reasonably sound because they are related to, and have value in, predicting the likelihood of intelligent activity in life situations.

Three "Kinds" of Intelligence

Some psychologists believe that several kinds of intelligence should be distinguished from one another. Noteworthy among them is E. L. Thorndike, who has divided intelligent activity into three types: (1) social intelligence, or ability to understand and deal with persons; (2) concrete intelligence, or ability to understand and deal with things, as in skilled trades and scientific appliances; (3) abstract intelligence, or ability to understand and deal with verbal and mathematical symbols.

The merit of this classification of types of intelligent activity, for psychological testing and diagnosis, is that it indicates several realms in which persons might be functioning and implies that separate and sufficiently specialized tests might be devised to measure how effectively persons are functioning in each.

Although it is true that any given person's scores on a test using verbal

---

[4] This raises the much-debated problem of heredity and environment as factors in the development of intelligence.

and numerical abstractions might differ appreciably from those attained by him on a test of social relationships and insights, or on one of "concrete" intelligence, it is also true that, when a *representative group* of individuals is tested, the correlations between the types of tests are found to be positive and significant, both statistically and psychologically. For example, correlations between tests of verbal and of concrete abilities vary from about .25 to about .45, the average being about .30–.35. Although this is a somewhat low average correlation, it still indicates that some communality of function is being measured. This index, being so far from unity, also means that there are numerous individuals whose relative scores do not correspond closely or whose two relative scores may be discrepant. This fact points up the important psychological principle that the data and status of any single person may be inconsistent with the *general trend*. Study of the individual, and the ways in which and the reasons why he deviates from or exemplifies general trends, is one concern of the clinical psychologist.

Of the three kinds of abilities enumerated above, abstract intelligence is the one that receives greatest weight and is most pronounced in current tests of intelligence—that is, whenever the test is designed for use with persons who are presumed to have reached a level where they may be expected to have developed facility in dealing with concepts and symbols.

Even tests that present the subject with "things" rather than with ideas and symbols are not devoid of demands upon ability to conceptualize and make abstractions, although testees need not necessarily state these in the form of language and number. For example, when a subject is required to arrange a series of pictures into a sequential and meaningful whole, he must at some stage form a concept of "the whole" if his response is to be correct by some means other than pure chance. He must do this, also, in assembling parts into an integrated unit (called "object assembly"). The same is true of the child who is asked which is the "prettiest" of two pictures ("esthetic comparison"), for he must have a concept of "prettiness," however unarticulated it may be. There are in use many other types of test items that deal with things but still require more or less ability in concept formation. Among these are object classification, tracing the shorter of two routes in a maze, identifying objects by use, and supplying missing parts in the drawing of a human figure. In short, the fact that some types of test items do not employ language or number does not necessarily signify that they make no demands upon ability to reason at a level of concept formation and abstraction.

At the earliest developmental levels there are tasks that depend upon visual-motor skill, such as tying a bow knot, grasping a ring, holding a

pencil and scribbling, and manipulating cubes. These types of tests, however, are restricted principally to the first eighteen months of life. They
are useful as developmental indicators, but they have only slight predictive value for later development of mental abilities, as measured by
tests at more advanced levels.[5]

The role of ability to deal with ideas and symbols (words and numbers) as a measure of concept formation and abstraction is of increasing
importance in tests of general ability (intelligence) as age level increases.
Proportions of verbal and numerical tests, on the one hand, and nonverbal, nonnumerical, on the other, undergo change at different age
levels [6]; some tests include a larger proportion of the latter than do
others, even at the adolescent and adult levels.[7] These differences are not
haphazard, nor are they matters of individual whim; they depend upon
the purposes of the test and the test author's conception of intelligence
and its constituent parts. It will be seen in later chapters that the correlations between various tests of general ability are quite marked—and at
times high or very high—thus indicating that to an appreciable degree in
these tests the verbal and numerical items on the one hand, and the nonverbal, nonnumerical on the other, are measuring the same or closely
related functions.[8] High intercorrelations do not always mean that the
same functions are being measured by the tests concerned; such correlations may reflect other common factors that affect the tests being correlated. This, however, is quite improbable as an explanation of test
intercorrelations.

Analyses of Mental Ability

The definitions of intelligence thus far discussed are functional
in character; that is, they state how intelligence operates: through learning, adaptation, abstract thinking. But, in addition, psychologists have
been concerned to know the "structure" of intelligence. They have made
analyses in an effort to determine its underlying *factors*. Or, otherwise
stated, the purpose of these analyses has been to discover, if possible, the
elements, or components, of intelligence, not only for a better theoretical

[5] See Chapter 13, "Scales for Infants and Preschool Children," in which this problem
is discussed at length.
[6] See the revised Stanford-Binet scale below the age-5 level; also the Merrill-Palmer
scale, the Minnesota Preschool Test, the Detroit Kindergarten Test.
[7] See the Otis tests, the Kuhlmann-Anderson tests, the Wechsler-Bellevue Intelligence
Tests, the Pintner-Paterson scale, and the Lorge-Thorndike tests.
[8] The statements in this paragraph do not mean that the nonverbal materials in the
tests are measures of mechanical ability. Generally, they are believed by the authors
of the tests to measure the same psychological processes as do the verbal materials, but
by means of different content.

understanding of this complex process, but also to learn what might be the implications for the design and construction of mental tests.

It is not to be inferred, however, that the dynamics of intelligent activity can be adequately understood merely by enumerating and characterizing the components, whatever they might be. Whatever the components, they do not operate independently or in isolation. Understanding the dynamic aspects of mental activity requires some means of characterizing the organization of factors, their interrelationships, and their relation to motivational forces.

Essentially, the experimental method followed is this: a rather large number of separate tests, more or less diverse in character, are given to an adequate sampling of the population. The results of each type of test are correlated with those of all the others. The coefficients of correlation are then subjected to various techniques of statistical analysis in an effort to discover the extent of common ground between them (technically known as *communality*) and their degree of independence. These statistical methods are known as *factor analysis*.[9] The particular theory or structure of intelligence educed from the statistical operations will depend upon the expert's interpretation of the analysis; and the experts differ to some extent in their interpretations. These differences, however, need not invalidate the use of well-standardized psychological tests; for, as will be seen, theoretical differences thus far have not had far-reaching consequences as regards the kinds of intelligence tests constructed.

The Multifactor Theory. Thorndike's multifactor theory of intelligence is at one extreme of the interpretations regarding the nature of mental organization. As the name of the theory indicates, intelligence is said to be constituted of a multitude of separate factors, or elements, each one being a minute element of ability. Any mental act, according to this theory, involves a number of these minute elements operating together. Any other mental act also involves a number of the elements in combination. Hence, if performances on these two mental tasks are positively correlated, the degree of correlation is due to the number of *common elements* involved in the two acts. If two types of mental activities, *A* and *B*, are more highly correlated than are *A* and *C*, the reason, according to the multifactor theory, would be that the first pair has more elements in common than does the second pair. According to this theory, then, there is really no such factor as "general intelligence"; there are only many highly specific acts, the number of such depending upon how refined a classification we might wish to make and are capable of making.

Thorndike's is really an "atomistic" theory of mental ability. He adds,

[9] Discussed later in this chapter.

however, that certain mental activities have so many of their elements in common that it is useful to classify these tasks into separate groups to which special names are given; for example, verbal meaning, arithmetical reasoning, comprehension, visual perception of relationships, and others. Consequently, in constructing a mental test, it appeared to Thorndike himself that his "atomistic" theory and the multitude of minute elements of ability are of less practical significance than the conception that many of them operate together in any situation demanding intelligence. This is illustrated by Thorndike's test designed to measure ability to deal with abstractions. His test is composed of four parts: sentence completion (C), arithmetical reasoning (A), vocabulary (V), and following directions (D). This instrument is known as the *CAVD test*. It is not claimed by Thorndike that these four sets of items encompass the entire range of abstract intelligence. They represent and sample only certain parts; but because of the significant correlations between all types of measures within the tested range, it is held, the other aspects of abstract intelligence can be estimated with satisfactory accuracy from those portions that are actually measured by this test.

The Two-Factor Theory. Opposed to Thorndike's theory of the nature of intelligence is Spearman's two-factor theory, which stands at the other extreme of interpretations. According to Spearman, all intellectual activity is dependent primarily upon, and is an expression of, a *general factor* common to all mental activity. This factor, designated by the symbol *g*, is possessed by all individuals, but in varying degrees, of course, since people differ in mental ability; and it (*g*) operates in all mental activity, though in varying amounts, since mental tasks differ in respect to their demands upon general intelligence. Spearman characterized this general factor as mental energy, because in the realm of intelligent activity, he maintained, it has a role similar to that of physical energy in the physical world. Like all other scientific concepts, the general factor can be observed and known only through its specific manifestations —in this instance, through psychological tests. After analyzing tests with varying amounts of the general factor, from high to low, Spearman concluded that the principal distinguishing characteristic of tests highly "loaded" with *g* is that they require insight into relationships—what he called "the eduction of relations and correlates." For example, in solving an arithmetical problem, the subject has to grasp the relationships between the data presented, organize them with reference to the propositions given in the problem, and deduce a correct answer. The *g*-content in this task is high. By contrast, if the subject merely has to repeat a table of multiplications or add a few numbers—both of which can be learned by rote—no insights are necessary and no relationships need be grasped. In this task, the amount of g involved is very small.[10]

Spearman postulated the g factor, in the first place, to explain correlations that he found to exist among diverse sorts of perceiving, knowing, reasoning, and thinking, as illustrated in Table 7.1. That is to say, he

TABLE 7.1

INTERCORRELATIONS OF SUBTESTS

	1	2	3	4	5	6	7
(1) Analogies		.50	.49	.55	.49	.45	.45
(2) Completion	.50		.54	.47	.50	.38	.34
(3) Understanding paragraphs	.49	.54		.49	.39	.44	.35
(4) Opposites	.55	.47	.49		.41	.32	.35
(5) Instructions	.49	.50	.39	.41		.32	.40
(6) Resemblances	.45	.38	.44	.32	.32		.35
(7) Inferences	.45	.34	.35	.35	.40	.35	

SOURCE: C. Spearman (6, p. 149). By permission. Spearman's method of statistical analysis is presented later in this chapter.

concluded that all mental activity is to some extent dependent upon, and an expression of, this general factor; and the magnitude of the correlation coefficient found between any two forms of mental activity reveals the extent to which this g factor is operative in each, and common to both. Thus, the amount of the general factor operating in each activity will determine the size of the correlation between the two mental activities being measured. The types of materials used in current tests of intelligence—word meaning, arithmetical reasoning, sentence completion, reasoning by analogy, paragraph interpretation, perception of relationships in geometric forms, picture completion, and others—all show significant degrees of positive correlation with one another. Spearman and his supporters at first ascribed this fact to the presence of g, in greater or lesser amount, in all of them. Later researches led them to conclude that certain "group factors" are also present in some mental activities. These are the factors that occur in more than one type of test item, but in less than all of any given set of tests. The general factor, however, still remains the primary and pervasive one.

[10] When using an individual test, like the Stanford-Binet or the Bellevue, it has often been observed by examiners that a subject who is unable to solve an arithmetical *problem*—unable even to make a start toward a solution—may still be able to perform the separate arithmetical *processes* involved. In Spearman's terms, such an individual is unable to educe the necessary relations and correlates, for lack of the necessary amount of g.

Since the intercorrelations are by no means perfect, Spearman postulated the existence of specific factors, called *s* factors, each of which is specific to a particular type of activity. Thus, the two-factor theory states that all mental activities have in common some of the general factor; each mental activity might also be a member of a "group"; and each has also its own specific factor. Of the kinds of factors, the general one is regarded as the essential measure of intelligence; accordingly a sound test of intelligence is one that will sample adequately the *g* factor in a variety of activities, and the best test materials are those that call for the largest amount of the general factor. And the largest amounts of the general factor are believed to be demanded by those types of test materials that have the higher intercorrelations with one another.

As a matter of fact, since the beginning of modern mental testing, psychologists have proceeded, at least implicitly, on the assumption that all forms of mental activity have something in common—that they are similar in certain basic respects. Otherwise, psychologists could not have justified their practice of testing together in a single instrument such diverse mental activities as defining words, solving arithmetical problems, finding similarities and differences, repeating digits forward and backward, completing sentences in a meaningful manner, and perceiving geometric forms. All of these, and the others used, must have been regarded as being measures, to a greater or lesser degree, of general intelligence. From the total performance on these tests, it was believed that an individual's level of general intelligence would emerge. Therefore, psychologists believed they were justified in adding up the test items correctly passed in the several types of activity and deriving a single total score to represent an individual's general intelligence level.[11] This is the actual practice in nearly all tests, including individual as well as group scales of mental ability.[12]

The practical implication of the Spearman two-factor theory is clear, so far as test construction is concerned. A test conforming to this theory would be one whose materials and several parts are saturated with the

[11] While this practice is not being discontinued, and should not be, increased emphasis is now being placed on the desirability of representing each individual by means of a test profile, where possible, as well as by a general index. There are some psychologists, however, who would abandon the use of all indexes of general level and would substitute a profile representing the individual's relative rank in each of the specific types of test materials being used, such as numerical ability, word meaning, spatial perception, and the like.

[12] In addition to *g* and *s*, Spearman and others have found by further analysis of experimental results that there are some nonintellectual factors—such as volition, interest, persistence—that influence a person's effectiveness. Spearman and adherents of his theory have also discerned a few *groups* of factors that are intermediate between *g* and the highly specific *s*. They suggest that musical aptitude and mechanical aptitude are of this type.

general factor, so that measurement thereby would cause the testee's level and quality of g to emerge, while the effects of specific factors (s) would be canceled out. Thus, the net result of the test would be a measure of g. To achieve this would require a skillful selection and development of test problems and parts that are significantly intercorrelated, which at the same time satisfy the practical criteria of intelligent activity. Such a test, presumably, would yield an index that reflects the caliber of a particular mentality working as a whole.

The Group-Factor Theory.   Intermediate between the theories of Thorndike and Spearman are the group-factor theories; prominent among them is that of Thurstone. His work has received the most attention and has resulted in the construction of a set of measures called *tests of primary mental abilities.*

According to the group-factor theory, intelligent activity is not an expression of innumerable highly specific factors, as Thorndike claimed. Nor is it the expression primarily of a general factor that pervades all mental activity and is the essence of intelligence, as Spearman held. Instead, the analyses and interpretations of Thurstone and others led them to the conclusion that *certain* mental operations have in common a "primary" factor that gives them psychological and functional unity and that differentiates them from other mental operations. These mental operations, then, constitute a "group." A second group of mental operations has *its* own unifying primary factor; a third group has a third; and so on. In other words, there are a number of groups of mental abilities (the number being as yet undetermined), each of which has its own primary factor, giving the group a functional unity and cohesiveness. Each of these primary factors is said to be relatively independent of the others.

After administering a large variety of test materials to college students and to high school and eighth-grade pupils, and after making correlational and factorial analyses of the results, Thurstone and his collaborators concluded that six primary factors emerged clearly enough for identification and use in test design and construction. They are, briefly, the following (17): [13]

The Number factor (N): "ability to do numerical calculations rapidly and accurately."

The Verbal factor (V): "found in tests involving verbal comprehension."

The Space factor (S): "involved in any tasks in which the subject manipulates an object imaginally in space."

---

[13] Some modifications of factors have been introduced in recent issues of these tests for younger subjects. The six named here are regarded as established. The primary mental abilities do not include the entire range of human abilities. They do not include, for example, mechanical, musical, or artistic aptitudes. The primaries are among those required in abstract intelligence and in academic learning.

The Word Fluency factor (W): "involved whenever the subject is asked to think of isolated words at a rapid rate."

The Reasoning factor (R): "found in tasks that require the subject to discover a rule or principle involved in series or groups of letters." Although it is believed both induction and deduction are involved, it seems that induction is the more significant here.

The Rote Memory factor (M): involving "the ability to memorize quickly."

Although primary mental abilities (or factors) were originally said to be functionally independent of each other, it was actually found that they are positively and significantly intercorrelated, as shown in Table 7.2.

TABLE 7.2

INTERCORRELATIONS OF SUBTESTS

	N	W	V	S	M	R
N						
W	.41					
V	.40	.54				
S	.28	.17	.16			
M	.31	.36	.35	.13		
R	.53	.49	.59	.29	.39	

N, number facility; W, word fluency; V, verbal meaning; S, spatial perception; M, rote memory; R, reasoning.
SOURCE: L. L. and T. G. Thurstone (17). By permission.

This must mean that the primary and presumably independent factors are not the only factors at work in the mental activities required by the tests. There must be some other factor, or factors, to account for the common ground (as shown by the positive correlations) that exists between the various psychological tests intended to measure these primary factors. In other words, it seems that the test authors have not been able to devise test materials that will sample the primary mental abilities in pure form. The Thurstones, therefore, concluded that in addition to the primary abilities, there is a "second-order general factor." They also stated, in their earlier test manual, that "If further studies of the primary mental abilities should reveal this general factor, it may sustain Spearman's intellective factor" (17, p. 7).

Subsequent studies of the primary mental abilities do tend to reveal a general factor. The more recent intercorrelations found among the several tests that make up the PMA [14] batteries are quite marked, especially at the

[14] Primary Mental Abilities.

lower age levels (when abilities are less differentiated through education and interest than they will be in later years).

For the tests at the 5- to 7-year level, the intercorrelations range from .46 to .67 (average equals .55). For tests at the 7- to 11-year level, the range of coefficients is from .41 to .70 (average equals .50); while for ages 11 to 17, the range of coefficients is from .13 to .59 (average equals .30+). It appears, therefore, that the group-factor adherents have found it necessary to posit the operations of a general factor; but at present they regard it as being of a "second order."

In evaluating the group-factor hypothesis we need not question the soundness of the statistical methods used or the comprehensiveness of the experimentation.[15] Several observations are necessary, however, to enable the reader to make a fuller assessment of the hypotheses. In the first place, intelligence is not an entity that operates in a vacuum; it is not something "given," even in the sense that some physical traits are "given," such as the color of eyes and hair, the number of digits. Intelligence is, rather, a name for certain kinds of activity; we can know of it only through its manifestations in behavior. Intelligent behavior develops and is manifested in one kind of environment or another; hence, the particular form of expression that intelligent activity takes will depend upon the sort of functions developed and fostered in a given cultural environment. In our own and similar cultures, verbal and numerical abilities are essential; they are fostered from earliest childhood, and they receive greatest attention and emphasis in our schools. Consequently, there is a relationship between this cultural emphasis and the fact that three of Thurstone's six primary factors are concerned with words and numbers. It is probable also that the "Space" factor emerges from statistical analyses because of our experiences with things in three-dimensional space. The two remaining factors, "Reasoning" and "Rote Memory," are characteristic, in greater or lesser degree, of all persons regardless of the particular culture; we should therefore expect to find them as factors of intelligent activity in any analysis. Furthermore, the "Reasoning" factor is quite similar to Spearman's g, although the latter has been presented as having several aspects.[16] In effect, then, the point is that some of the *particular* factors through which intelligence is expressed are developed by experience and education; and these particular factors—such as the six primaries—may well be conceived of as particular manifestations of a *general* ability rather than as primary abilities.

[15] Some psychologists have criticized adversely Thurstone's methods and his interpretations of his findings.

[16] Apprehension of one's own experience, the eduction of relations, and the eduction of correlates.

The proponents of the group-factor hypothesis do not claim that the exact number of primary mental abilities is known. Hence, we must caution the reader against assuming that there is a finality about the present number. For example, a factor of "Speed" will not appear in a statistical analysis of test results unless speed of performance is, first, a variant in the population being measured and, second, a requirement within the tests themselves. The same can be said of "Persistence" or "Mental Fatigue." Similarly, "Originality" would appear as another factor, *if* it could be measured.

These observations do not invalidate the tests that have been or might be designed on the basis of the group-factor hypothesis. As a matter of fact, the contents of such tests thus far published, though differently organized, are not radically different in their essentials from those designed on the basis of either of the two other theories of the nature of intelligence.

For our present purposes, two consequences of group-factor analyses are indicated. First, the conceptual framework has resulted in more clearly specified and defined test categories and types of test items than was the case previously. Second, several batteries of tests have been constructed on the basis of group-factor theory.

The early versions of the PMA tests did not yield an over-all index of performance, such as mental age, intelligence quotient, or an over-all percentile rank. Instead, they gave, for each subject, separate percentile ranks to represent his performance level in each of the primary factors. These ranks were then used to make a "profile" for each person for educational and vocational guidance. While they granted that the single index (mental age and IQ), based upon a variety of mental activities, is useful for many practical purposes, group-factorists originally maintained that their method of finding separate ratings for each of the primary factors enables the examiner more readily and adequately to recognize a testee's marked mental abilities and disabilities, the degree of uniformity or lack of uniformity.[17]

There is merit in this contention; yet, at the same time, there is no good reason why the group-factor type of test should not also yield an over-all rating (such as MA or IQ) as well as indexes of relative rank for

---

[17] This can be done by a competent examiner when another group test or the Binet or the Bellevue is used. In the case of the last two, the "scatter" of test performance is studied. In the case of group tests, the individual's performance on each of the several parts can be compared with his performances on the other parts. The disadvantage here is that the usual group test does not provide separate scores and norms for each of the parts.

A weakness of the group-factor type of test is that the breakdown into separate factors ignores the fact that intelligence expresses itself in behavior as a combination, a unity of functions, not as a series of independent factors.

each of the specified factors. While mental age and intelligence quotient should never be interpreted and used mechanically and uncritically, or in disregard of the specific performances that have contributed to them, they do nevertheless have considerable significance and valuable connotations for the qualified examiner and interpreter.

The group factorists have apparently recognized this point in their more recent interpretations of test findings. Equally important to them is the fact that their correlations and factorial analyses have persistently yielded results that could not be explained in terms of group factors alone, and that the g factor was indicated. As a result, the most recent editions of the PMA tests provide IQ equivalents for the scores on the scale for ages 11 to 17, but for the younger age levels both MA units and quotients are provided.

As is so often the case in scientific problems—especially in the relatively new ones—divergent theories in time tend to come into closer agreement. The Spearman Two-Factor Theory now recognizes that some group factors should be posited to explain test findings; but emphasis is upon the g factor. Perhaps the Spearman theory may now be renamed "The General Factor–Group Factor Theory," and the other might be renamed "The Group Factor–General Factor Theory." The narrowing of differences between the two theories represents significant scientific progress.

Factor Analysis

The two-factor and the group-factor theories are the two most prominent examples of doctrines emerging from the methods of factor analysis. Although this subject is highly technical, it is desirable to explain it more fully at this stage.

The technique is essentially a search for the psychological functions that are at the basis of and determine test performance. All techniques of factor analysis are statistical and based upon the correlation coefficient. After the statistical calculations have been made, it is necessary for the investigator to bring to bear his psychological insights to interpret and name his statistical findings. Tests contain a variety of items. What psychological functions do the various types of items have in common? Are there functions in common between various tests of verbal performance? Between verbal and numerical? Between spatial perception and numerical ability? Between reasoning with verbal and with nonverbal materials? These are among the questions the factor analyst seeks to answer. After he has found his answer, at least tentatively, he proceeds to construct a scale in which items are included and so grouped as to measure only, or almost solely, the factors he has segregated from his preliminary testing and statistical analysis.

The factor analyst does not begin with a definite set of preconceived mental functions. He tries to discover which psychological functions, or components, are necessary to explain his data. Yet, it should be noted, he must at the outset have some conception of the kinds of test items to include in preliminary experimentation. Thus, what he ultimately distills out as factors are basically dependent upon his original conceptions regarding his preliminary items. The factor analyst, in seeking the components of intelligence, for example, does not start with tests of color perception, tone discrimination, or finger dexterity.

Two-Factor Theory. We have already stated Spearman's *two-factor theory*. It will be helpful now to describe in more detail the reasoning that led to the theory. Spearman, in his early experimentation, was impressed by the fact that all the intercorrelations were positive in a table of coefficients for various types of items. He was also impressed by what appeared to be a hierarchy of coefficients in the rows and columns of the table; not perfect gradations, but strong evidence of proportional gradations. He therefore offered a hypothetically perfect table of correlation coefficients to illustrate his point (Table 7.3). Not only are the coefficients

TABLE 7.3

SPEARMAN'S HYPOTHETICAL TABLE OF CORRELATIONS

	1	2	3	4	5
(1) Opposites		.80	.60	.30	.30
(2) Completion	.80		.48	.24	.24
(3) Memory	.60	.48		.18	.18
(4) Discrimination	.30	.24	.18		.09
(5) Cancellation	.30	.24	.18	.09	

SOURCE: C. Spearman (6, p. 74). By permission.

positive and in a decreasing order along rows and columns, but theoretically any two columns (or rows, since the table is symmetrical about the diagonal which contains the self-correlations) are in direct proportion. The criterion of proportionality requires that the following correlational relationships should hold:

$$\frac{r_{13}}{r_{23}} = \frac{r_{14}}{r_{24}} = \frac{r_{15}}{r_{25}}.$$

Taking only the first two ratios,

$$\frac{r_{13}}{r_{23}} = \frac{r_{14}}{r_{24}},$$

and multiplying by the denominators, we have

$$r_{13} \, r_{24} = r_{23} \, r_{14}.$$

Transposing, the result is

$$r_{13} \, r_{24} - r_{23} \, r_{14} = 0.$$

From this *tetrad equation* (so called because the test correlations are dealt with in sets of four) may be obtained what is known as the *tetrad difference*.

The tetrad equation may be written for the combination of any four tests. By rearranging the four coefficients, three tetrad differences may be obtained for every combination of four tests. Thus, using t as the notation for tetrad difference:

$$t_{1234} = r_{12} \, r_{34} - r_{13} \, r_{24}.$$
$$t_{1243} = r_{12} \, r_{34} - r_{14} \, r_{23}.$$
$$t_{1342} = r_{13} \, r_{24} - r_{14} \, r_{23}.$$

Theoretically, the tetrad-difference criterion is satisfied if t is zero. When it is zero, Spearman and others have offered mathematical evidence to demonstrate that a single common factor can account for the relationships among the four tests, or variables. But in fact, the difference is rarely, if ever, zero. However, if the differences are close to zero, we may also conclude the criterion is satisfied, since correlations between tests will be affected by chance errors of measurement and accidental factors [18] (see discussion of reliability in Chapter 4). Furthermore, the correlation coefficients would also be affected by the operations of the *specific* factor in each test. The specific factor was postulated to explain, in part at least, the tetrad differences that were greater than zero.

If more than four tests are being analyzed to disclose the functions involved, we may substitute tests numbers 5 and 6, for example, in the tetrad equations, in place of numbers 3 and 4. Thus, we would be analyzing tests 1, 2, 5, 6. Then if the tetrad-difference criterion is satisfied, it would be concluded that the functions common to 1 and 2 are identical with those common to 5 and 6. Assuming that the tetrad-difference criterion was satisfied also for tests 1, 2, 3, 4, then the same functions (or factor) are said to be common to the six variables. The same reasoning may be applied to any number of tests.

The principal conclusion drawn by Spearman and some others, after their analyses, was that the degree of correlation between any two tests is

---

[18] Formulas are provided for calculating probable errors of tetrad differences; comparison of a tetrad difference with its probable error (PE) enables one to decide whether it differs significantly from zero.

dependent upon the extent to which *g* is involved in each. Subsequent investigations showed, however, that *some* test intercorrelations may include their own factors, common only to *them,* beyond the single common *g.* It was necessary, therefore, to postulate the operations of *group factors,* each group being effective in two or more tests, but not in all of them. Spearman and others recognized such group factors as numerical, verbal, speed, mechanical, imagination, and attention. In addition, Spearman had postulated three nonintellective factors that influence one's mental effectiveness. These are perseveration (*p*); oscillation (*o*), being one's variability in performance in continuous mental activity; and will (*w*), being one's persistence in effort.

The tetrad-difference criterion does not in itself show the relative weight or importance of the common factor in each kind of test. Following the work of Spearman, therefore, methods have been developed for finding the weights (commonly called "loadings") of each factor—general or group—in each of the intercorrelated tests. These methods are known as "factor pattern analysis" (4, 13, 18).

The two-factor theory can account for the universal positive correlation coefficients among the various kinds of test items included in scales to measure mental ability, since every form of test requires the operation of *g* to some degree. Pooling a variety of kinds of tests in a scale is sound practice, according to this theory, because we thereby approximate a measure of pure *g*. Since the *s* factors are uncorrelated within any individual—that is, they may be possessed in varying and random degrees by him—they will be a negligible factor in the total performance in a pooled test of general ability, because the varied *s* factors will tend to cancel out one another.

Sampling Theory. The two-factor theory has been criticized by some statistical psychologists, notably G. H. Thomson and L. L. Thurstone. Thomson offers a *sampling theory* to explain the same tables of intercorrelations (11). Briefly, his view is that the coefficients of correlation are the results of common samplings and combinations of independent factors. The number of common independent factors utilized by two tests will determine the coefficient of correlation between these two. This theory is, of course, the same as Thorndike's, except that Thomson concedes the practical usefulness of a concept like *g*. Thomson also adds that if several tests call upon many elementary factors in common, they will not only have a very marked or high coefficient of correlation, but they will give the appearance of having *one* common comprehensive factor. Also, Thomson's theory maintains that if several tests draw upon a relatively smaller number of the elementary factors in common, these are group factors—that is, a limited number of factors that enter into performance on types of tests which are distinguished by the fact that they have certain mental processes in common but do not share a very large number of elementary factors or a universal *g*.

Although both theories require that a scale measuring general mental ability should pool a variety of tests that differ in content and mental processes employed, the two-factor theory requires subtests (parts of the scale) that have high intercorrelations. The sampling theory, on the other hand, requires subtests having low intercorrelations among themselves but high correlations with the criteria of validity.

Group-Factor Theory.   As already stated, Thurstone and others believe that a *group-factor theory* fits the facts best and is most useful in testing practice. Their view differs from Thomson's in that they reject the theory of a very large number of independent factors. As previously explained, a group factor is conceived of as an operational concept to account for correlations of performance within only a limited group of tests.[19] Several different groups of factors are necessary to account for all mental activity, plus the more recently added second-order *g* factor, which Thurstone states may be more "central" in character and more "universal" in influence.

Thurstone has contributed significantly to the methodology of group-factor analysis; and from his analyses, as we shall see, has emerged a scale to test mental ability. This volume is not the place to present his techniques; we shall merely state his purposes.[20]

Three objectives, according to Thurstone, are to be achieved by factor analysis: (1) determination of the smallest number of primary mental abilities to be postulated as an explanation of tables of intercorrelations; (2) determination of the amount of each primary ability that is involved in each test; and (3) determination of regression equations whereby the amount of a primary mental ability in an individual can be estimated from tests that draw upon that ability. As an illustration, we may consider several tests in which only two group factors are involved. An individual might make a high score in these tests either by having a moderately high level of ability in each of Factor I and Factor II, or by having very much of one and little of the other. Also, if Factor I carries much heavier weight in the tests than does II, then a high level of ability on I is more important for high performance on these tests than is a high level on II. Thus, the Thurstone method would find the relatively few primary or basic mental abilities, devise a scale to measure all of them, and so

[19] Most recently, some group-factor theorists have characterized primary factors as facilities of the mind and as media of expression.

[20] A number of others have made significant contributions to factor theory, especially K. J. Holzinger, H. Hotelling, R. C. Tryon, H. E. Garrett, C. L. Burt, J. C. Flanagan, J. P. Guilford, and P. Vernon.

TABLE 7.4

TABULAR REPRESENTATION OF THEORIES OF MENTAL ABILITY

THE TWO-FACTOR PATTERN

Test	General factor	Specific factors
1	x	S_1
2	x	S_2
3	x	S_3
4	x	S_4
5	x	S_5
6	x	S_6

THE GROUP-FACTOR PATTERN

Test	A	B	C	D
		Group factors		
1	x		x	x
2	x	x	x	
3		x		x
4	x	x	x	
5	x	x		x
6		x	x	

FACTOR THEORIES COMBINED

Test	General factor	A	B	C	Specific factors
			Group factors		
1	x	x			S_1
2	x	x			S_2
3	x		x		S_3
4	x		x		S_4
5	x			x	S_5
6	x			x	S_6

organize and score the subtests as to reveal each individual's relative strength in each factor.

Summary. Methods of factor analysis differ somewhat in their assumptions, and analysts differ somewhat in their interpretations or results, but the general conclusions derived by the several methods of analysis and interpretation do not differ radically. All factorial theories now postulate the presence of group factors, although the groups are not always identical and differ in relative emphasis placed upon them by different theories. Most theories also find a general factor necessary to explain intercorrelations, although here again emphasis upon the general

factor varies. All agree that an individual's mental activities are attributable to the various ways in which the general and group factors combine
in the performance of varied mental tasks. Although several methods of
factorial analysis are possible, basically the choice between them and interpretations derived through them must rest upon psychological theory
and concepts rather than upon statistical methods. Factors should not be
regarded as fixed, predetermined mental entities. The factors that are
found are influenced by the ages of the persons tested, by interests, by experience and training, and by the test items originally employed in the
preliminary investigations. Factorial analysis is a statistical method that
provides the means of improving test construction and of classifying test
performance.

Illustrations of Factors

The following illustrations will assist the student to grasp more
fully the problem of factors in psychological testing. As already stated,
factor analysis techniques depend basically upon test intercorrelations.
Tables 7.5 and 7.6 show the intercorrelations among two sets of four
subtests of the Wechsler scale for children.

Since all the coefficients in Table 7.5 are positive and quite marked, we
conclude that all four tests have much in common, but that Vocabulary,
Information, and Similarities have somewhat more in common with one
another than they do with Comprehension. But since all the coefficients
are far from perfect (+1.00), we should use all four to sample the testee's
mental abilities, rather than only one or two to the exclusion of the
others. The fact that these four tests are not perfectly correlated—or
nearly so—might be due to one of these possibilities: (1) that each test
samples the g factor in different amounts, plus its own specific factor; (2)

TABLE 7.5

INTERCORRELATIONS OF FOUR SUBTESTS OF THE WECHSLER
INTELLIGENCE SCALE FOR CHILDREN

	Vocab.	Info.	Sims.	Comp.
Vocabulary		.74	.66	.60
Information			.67	.61
Similarities				.61
Comprehension				

SOURCE: Manual, The Psychological Corporation.

that the tests have *g* in common but each test samples also one or more group factors, though not necessarily the same ones; or (3) that each has many highly specific factors in common with every other one, as well as unique factors. A technical factorial analysis would go beyond this inspection analysis in an effort to determine which of these three hypotheses is the most plausible one, and to determine to what extent performance on each of the four tests calls upon whatever factors—*g* or others—might be inferred from the statistical analysis.

Table 7.6, by contrast, shows four subtests that have low intercorrelations. Of the six coefficients, only two (.40 and .46) are large enough to suggest that the subtests involved have much in common in psychological functions. The coefficient of .46 between Comprehension and Arithmetic

TABLE 7.6

INTERCORRELATIONS OF FOUR SUBTESTS OF THE WECHSLER
INTELLIGENCE SCALE FOR CHILDREN (*continued*)

	Obj. Assemb.	Comp.	Arith.	Digit Sp.
Object Assembly		.13	.20	.13
Comprehension			.46	.28
Arithmetic				.40
Digit Span				

SOURCE: *Manual,* The Psychological Corporation.

is attributable to the demands that both of these tests make upon reasoning ability, or, more specifically, ability to analyze a set of given material and then reorganize the elements toward the solution of the specified problem. The coefficient of .40 between Arithmetic and Digit Span is attributable, it appears from the characteristics of the two tests, to facility with numbers and ability in immediate recall (as contrasted with delayed recall). The remaining four coefficients are so low as to suggest that the tests concerned have little dependence upon common functions (whether *g* or other factors), and that each makes demands upon some factor or factors not called upon by the others. Here again, an analysis would attempt to identify more precisely the factors involved; but in so doing, the analyst would have to apply his knowledge of psychological functioning to the items that cluster together, as shown by the analysis.

Figure 7.1 shows in graphic form how two and three tests *might be* interrelated. As the number of types of tests increases, the possible factor interrelationships may become more numerous and complex, though it is extremely improbable that *no* overlapping whatever of factors would be found in measuring human abilities by means of two or more different types of tests. In view of the more recent partial reconciliation of the group-factor and the general-factor theories, the illustrated overlappings are most probably attributable to *g*.

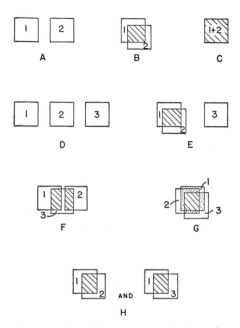

FIG. 7.1. Possible intercorrelations between two and three tests

The possible factor interrelationships of the parts of Figure 7.1 are as follows:

A. Each test is factorially independent of the other. The factor or factors in each are unique to it, either as group factors or as specific factors.

B. The overlapping shaded area indicates a factor or factors common to both tests. This may be *g* or a group factor. The unshaded area indicates factors unique to each, either specific or group, or both. When many diverse tests show some overlapping among all of them, the soundest inference is that a *g* factor accounts for the common ground.

C. In this instance the tests may be measuring only the general factor, or *g* plus the same group factor, or just the same group factor. There are no unique factors. It is extremely improbable, in this situation, that the general factor is not involved. If numerous pairings of different tests showed this relationship, the soundest inference would be that a general factor is being measured.

D. Each of the three tests is factorially independent of the other two. The uniqueness of each may be due to group or specific factors, or to both.

E. The overlapping of 1 and 2 here may be attributable to g or to a group factor. Test 3 is independent of the others. The nonoverlapping segments of 1 and 2 may represent separate group factors or specific factors in each test.

F. In this figure, overlapping between 1 and 2, and between 2 and 3, is attributed to one or more group factors, but different ones in each case, since there is no common ground between all three tests. The unshaded areas would represent special factors or group factors, or both, that are not shared with either of the other two tests.

G. Here there is some common ground in all three tests (shaded area), which is interpreted as showing the presence of the g factor. The dotted areas show group factors shared by only two of the tests. The unshaded areas represent either specific factors or unique group factors, or both.

H. This figure represents three tests that have only the general factor in common. Both tests 2 and 3 have the same amount and the identical area in common with test 1; hence, they have the same amount and identical area in common with each other.

These graphic illustrations of correlations and factor loadings derived from statistical analysis serve three purposes: (1) They demonstrate the complexity of the problem of determining interrelationships of psychological factors. (2) They demonstrate that the same statistical findings are often open to more than one psychological interpretation; and, using the statistical findings as aids, one's interpretation will depend basically upon his psychological analyses of intellectual functioning. (3) The illustrations and their several possible interpretations help to make clear the reasons why the most valid and useful tests within a given category (for example, intelligence) have much in common regarding psychological functioning and the test items themselves.

Finally, Figures 7.2 and 7.3 illustrate elaborate factorial analyses of tests that have been statistically fractionated (2). These indicate the probable quantitative portions of each of the several factors in each of the tests. Such analyses provide insights into the psychological operations that combine in performance on the tests. Test construction is thereby facilitated. It should not be assumed, however, that each of these factors exists or operates independently. We may look at the factors in the Reading Comprehension test as an example. We note that "verbal comprehension" is the largest single factor; then we have, in order, "mechanical experience," "reasoning I," and "reasoning II." It is doubtful that these four factors can, or should be, separated functionally. Mechanical experience

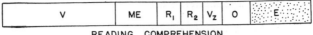

READING COMPREHENSION

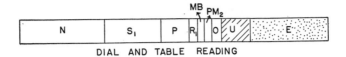

DIAL AND TABLE READING

DISCRIMINATION REACTION TIME

FIG. 7.2. Diagrams of the component variances of three Army Air Force classification tests. From J. P. Guilford (2, p. 86). The letters stand for:

V —verbal-comprehension factor

ME —mechanical-experience factor

R_1—reasoning I (general-reasoning) factor

R_2—reasoning II (common to analogies tests) factor

V_z—visualization factor

O —other common factors, each with variance too small to mention separately

U —unknown common-factor or specific-factor variances

E —error variances

N —numerical factor

S_1—space I (spatial-relations) factor

P —perceptual-speed factor

MB —mathematical-background factor

M_2—memory II (visual-memory) factor

PM_2—psychomotor II (precision) factor

will have been significant in the comprehension of the verbal materials of this test and will have contributed to the verbal competence of the testee in the particular area covered by the test. Reasoning, of whatever kind, is basically a matter of problem-solving ability, whether with the use of concrete objects or with abstractions (words and numbers). In this test of Reading Comprehension, the examinee's ability to reason with the problems presented will depend in part upon his mechanical experience (contributing to his comprehension) and to his knowledge of the terms used in the problems. Conversely, the extent and quality of the vocabulary he

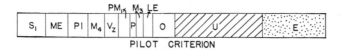

PILOT   CRITERION

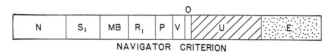

NAVIGATOR   CRITERION

FIG. 7.3. Diagrams of the component variances of pilot and navigator training criteria. From J. P. Guilford (2, p. 86). Letter symbols are as defined with Figure 7.2, except for some additional ones:

PI —pilot-interest factor
M_4—memory IV (content-memory) factor
M_3—memory III (picture-symbol association) factor
PM_1—psychomotor I (coordination) factor
LE —length-estimation factor

acquires and the degree to which he benefits from his mechanical experience will depend in part upon his present and potential reasoning capacity.

Implications

The hypotheses as to the nature of mental abilities have been arrived at by means of several methods of statistical analysis and through partially different interpretations placed upon similar data by different investigators. Regardless of which of the hypotheses an author of a test follows, the instrument he develops will have much in common with those constructed by authors who base their tests on one of the other hypotheses. In many respects, the processes of standardization will be the same; the same basic principles of constructing and testing will have to be observed. A variety of mental activities will have to be sampled; in the case of the multifactor theory, in order to sample an adequate and representative number of the many minute factors; in the case of the group-factor theory, in order to sample the primary abilities and those second-order factors that might be found subsequently; in the case of the two-factor theory, in order to get an adequate sampling of the general factor.

The main practical differences arising from the theoretical differences will be found in the tests based on the group-factor theory, as compared with others. The differences will be as follows:

1. The parts of the test based on group-factor theory must correspond to the factors or primaries and they must try to measure these factors in as pure a form as possible.

2. The subtests in a scale based upon group-factor theory should have low intercorrelations.

3. The test based on group-factor theory will emphasize the separate scores on each of the primaries and will provide a mental profile, even though the group-factor test might also provide an over-all index.

4. The Binet type of test, and other g-factor tests, on the other hand, consists of a variety of test materials that are a composite of abilities, yielding a mental age and an intelligence quotient. Most group tests,[21] while arranging their items according to type (sentence completion, arithmetical reasoning, word meaning, picture completion, form perception), are not organized on the basis of specifically defined factors; and, like the Binet type, they generally yield a single index of relative rank.

Since the several hypotheses regarding the nature of intelligence have thus far produced relatively few differences in practical test construction and application, the reader might well ask: "Why, then, be so concerned with definitions and theories, when the end results are not radically different?" The answer to this question has several aspects. First, the student should be familiar with the thinking of psychologists in this field, as a background for his better understanding of the tests themselves. Second, it is through the interaction of the theoretical and applied that improvements and advances will be made. Third, it is possible that one or more of these theories will have increasing influence, in the future, upon test construction, testing practice, and test interpretation.[22]

Creative Ability

Creativity has long been a subject of interest to psychologists and others. Within about the last fifteen years, psychologists have shown renewed and more vigorous concern with the problem. Answers are being sought to the questions: "What are the intellectual traits required for creative ability?" and "What are the nonintellective personality traits required?"

Numerous introspective reports, written by creative persons in a variety of fields, are available; but they are not particularly helpful in providing clues to the measurement of those human abilities that would enable

---

[21] Excepting the "omnibus" type, in which items of various mental operations are placed in regular or irregular order, instead of being grouped in subtests, each containing items of a single kind.

[22] The student will find additional material on factor analysis in later chapters in connection with specific tests.

psychologists and educators to select the potentially creative artist, scientist, mathematician, musician, or author. In fact, some creative individuals are quite unable to explain their mental processes, even at a descriptive level. One author writes, "I suddenly get an idea for a novel. I start with some characters; others develop spontaneously. In a short time, the central characters have taken hold of me, and I live with them until the book has been finished." [23]

Philosophical and psychoanalytical theories of creativity have been expounded. One principle that seems to be widespread among these writers is that creativity does not occur in a vacuum; it occurs in areas of experience, interest, and work to which the person has been "intensively committed in his conscious living" (1, p. 62). This trait alone is not sufficient, though it is necessary.

Factor analysts, among psychologists, have applied their statistical techniques to test items, with the result that the factors thus far derived appear to be strikingly similar to those found for general ability, productive thinking, and scholastic aptitude. At most, all that can be said of the findings of factor analysis in this elusive and tenuous field of research is that they might identify and name some of the mental tools used by the creative person, but they do not provide insights into how he employs them to produce his results. Furthermore, it is necessary to differentiate among creative abilities in the several fields, each of which has some elements in common with the others; but each also has its own special requirements and elements. Nor have studies of nonintellective personality traits of creative persons succeeded in differentiating them from other groups of superior individuals.

Available psychological tests can only reveal what levels of *general* intellectual ability are demanded and what levels of particularized abilities (verbal, mathematical, spatial, auditory, visual, immediate and remote recall, etc.) are essential in each of the creative fields. In addition, improved personality inventories and projective tests might reveal which traits, if any, are essential to each field and will differentiate individuals in one type of creativity from those in the others. Thus far, these objectives have not been achieved.

Available psychological tests of mental ability have been criticized for not measuring creative ability. The criticism is unwarranted, because these tests are not intended to measure it and because the essential nature of the *standardized* test does not permit individualized or unique responses. Tests of general intelligence, however, have made this contribution: the creative individual is in most cases a person of superior or gifted general mental capacity as measured by sound tests; but not every-

[23] Personal communication.

one who attains the superior or gifted level on tests will prove to be creative. The principal reason for this might be a matter of nonintellectual personality traits. Other than this observation and the reports given by creative persons, educators and psychologists, for the present, will depend largely upon identifying creative children and adolescents by their actual productions.

Probably the most extensive psychological studies of creative persons, in a variety of fields, have been in progress at the Institute of Personality Assessment and Research at the University of California in Berkeley. On the basis of six years of research, D. W. MacKinnon states:

> It is quite apparent that creative persons have an unusual capacity to record and retain and have readily available the experiences of their life history. They are discerning, which is to say that they are observant in a differentiated fashion; they are alert, capable of concentrating attention readily and shifting it appropriately; they are fluent in scanning thoughts and producing those that serve to solve the problems they undertake; and, characteristically, they have a wide range of information at their command. As in the case of any intelligent person, the items of information which creative persons possess may readily enter into combinations, and the number of possible combinations is increased for such persons because of both a greater range of information and a greater fluency of combination. Since true creativity is defined by the adaptiveness of a response as well as its unusualness, it is apparent that intelligence alone will tend to produce creativity. The more combinations that are found, the more likely it is on purely statistical grounds that some of them will be creative.[24]

The intellectual abilities enumerated in this quotation are the same as those specified or implied in the definitions and analyses of general intelligence, as already discussed in this chapter. And as analyses of current tests of intelligence, in later chapters, will demonstrate, these are the mental functions being tested, more or less comprehensively, by the sounder instruments.

References

1. Anderson, H. H. (ed.). *Creativity and Its Cultivation.* New York: Harper & Brothers, 1959.
2. Guilford, J. P. Factorial analysis in a test-development program. *Psychological Review,* 1948, *55,* 79–94.
3. Guilford, J. P. Three faces of intellect. *The American Psychologist,* 1959, *14,* 468–479.

[24] D. W. MacKinnon. "What makes a person creative?" *Saturday Review,* February 10, 1962, p. 16.

4. Kelley, T. L. *Essential Traits of Mental Life*. Cambridge: Harvard University Press, 1935.

5. Loevinger, J. A systematic approach to the construction and evaluation of tests of ability. *Psychological Monographs*, 1947, *61*, no. 4.

6. Spearman, C. *The Abilities of Man*. New York: The Macmillan Company, 1927.

7. Stein, M. I., and S. J. Heinze. *Creativity and the Individual: Summaries of Selected Literature in Psychology and Psychiatry*. New York: The Free Press of Glencoe, Inc., 1960.

8. Stoddard, G. D. *The Meaning of Intelligence*. New York: The Macmillan Company, 1943.

9. Symposium. Intelligence and its measurement. *Journal of Educational Psychology*, 1921, *12*, 123–147, 195–216.

10. Taylor, C. W. (ed.). *The 1955 University of Utah Conference on the Identification of Creative Talent*. Salt Lake City: University of Utah Press, 1956.

11. Thomson, G. H. *The Factorial Analysis of Human Ability*. Boston: Houghton Mifflin Company, 1939.

12. Thorndike, E. L. *The Measurement of Intelligence*. New York: Bureau of Publications, Teachers College, Columbia University, 1927.

13. Thurstone, L. L. *Vectors of the Mind*. Chicago: University of Chicago Press, 1935.

14. Thurstone, L. L. *Primary Mental Abilities*. Psychometric Monograph No. 1., Chicago: University of Chicago Press, 1938.

15. Thurstone, L. L. Psychological Implications of factor analysis. *The American Psychologist*, 1948, *3*, 402–408.

16. Thurstone, L. L., and T. G. *Factorial Studies of Intelligence*. Psychometric Monograph No. 2. Chicago: University of Chicago Press, 1941.

17. Thurstone, L. L., and T. G. *The Chicago Tests of Primary Mental Abilities: Manual*. Chicago: Science Research Associates, 1943.

18. Vernon, P. E. *The Structure of Human Abilities*. New York: John Wiley & Sons, Inc., 1950.

19. Wechsler, D. *The Measurement of Adult Intelligence*. Baltimore: The Williams & Wilkins Company, 1943.

20. Wechsler, D. *The Measurement and Appraisal of Adult Intelligence*. Baltimore: The Williams & Wilkins Company, 1958.

8.

THE BINET SCALES

Binet's Early Work

The historical background of the Binet scales has been presented in Chapter 1. It will be recalled that their development was motivated by the interests of psychologists in measuring individual differences in mental abilities. Galton, whose publications are reported in the first chapter, assumed that simpler measurable sensory capacities would be significantly correlated with intelligence and that if these simple sensory measures were obtained, they would afford a means of judging and predicting an individual's intellectual capacity. Although it has long been demonstrated that measures of sensory capacities have no value for evaluation of the higher, complex processes, Galton's work greatly affected the nature of test experimentation in the United States until about 1900. At that time the influence of Alfred Binet became apparent.

The relatively simple tests of sensory, motor, and memory capacities proved to be of little value as measures to reveal intelligence. In the first place, their *intercorrelations* were very low, ranging generally from zero to only .20. And, in the second place, the results of these tests, when correlated with academic performance, yielded correlation coefficients of much the same magnitude, many of them being less than .10—hence useless for purposes of prediction. As a matter of fact, experimentation in the years that followed the early investigations has consistently confirmed the negligible or very low correlations found to exist between sensory and motor capacities, on the one hand, and the higher more complex functions, on the other.

It is now generally recognized by psychologists that intelligence has little relationship to the elementary sensory and motor processes, and but a very moderate relationship indeed to capacity for rote memory (a correlation of about .30). Many infrahuman animals have keen sensory discrimination. Mentally deficient children in the higher levels of defect and children in the borderline group are not very inferior to normal children in respect to skin sensitivity, visual acuity, auditory acuity, and reaction time. Nor are intellectually gifted children superior to average in these respects. But in the capacities to learn, to organize and direct thinking, to adapt behavior, to comprehend problems and deal with abstractions, in levels of acquired information, in extent of curiosity about one's environment, these groups differ very markedly.

The reader should bear in mind these early kinds of tests, not only for historical purposes, but also in order to compare the early efforts with currently available tests and to be more clearly aware of the direction in which psychological testing has been moving.

The early work of Binet was along the same lines as that of the American and German psychologists mentioned in Chapter 1. He used tests of tactual discrimination, reaction time, visual discrimination, auditory discrimination of time intervals, reproducing letters and numbers from

FIG. 8.1. Alfred Binet (1857–1911)

memory, and so on. But though he experimented with these materials until about 1900, some years earlier he had begun to doubt the value of continuing with them.

Although some of the mental activities that Binet proposed to measure, and with which he was experimenting, were as yet vague, he did nevertheless point out the direction in which mental tests should and in fact did develop.

Binet and his collaborators objected to the kinds of psychological tests that followed Galton's work, on the ground that they were too simple in character and would contribute little to the understanding of differences among persons in respect to the higher mental functions. Binet maintained, furthermore, that intelligence is expressed *not* in the form of simple, segmental responses, but rather as a combined mental operation wherein whatever processes are involved operate as a *unified whole.*

It is in these higher functions that individual differences are most marked; it is these that distinguish individuals most significantly and characteristically in daily activity, whereas it is in the simpler sensory and motor processes that individuals differ least significantly.

The Scales

The 1905 Binet-Simon Scale. The first scale, devised primarily to identify mentally deficient children in the school of Paris, is known by this name.[1] In it we find a fundamental conception underlying all tests by means of which mental abilities of children are measured. *The principle is that we may identify differences in mentality, differences in degrees of brightness or dullness, with differences in levels of development as represented by the average capacities of children of various ages.* Thus, if we know the levels of intellectual performance of typical, or normal, children at each age, we can determine in the case of any individual child the extent to which his mental development is accelerated or retarded, or whether it is just about at the average level for his age at any given time.

In the 1905 scale, this conception was only crudely implemented; but in time it became more precise and has since taken the form of indexes already discussed in Chapter 6: mental age, percentile ranks, decile ranks, standard scores, intelligence quotients, and others.

The thirty items, in order of increasing difficulty, included in the 1905 scale are as follows: [2]

---

[1] Simon was Binet's collaborator. It is called a scale because the items are arranged in order of increasing difficulty.

[2] For a detailed description see References at the end of this chapter (6, p. 475 ff.).

1. Visual coordination—degree of coordination of movement of head and eyes as a lighted match is slowly moved before subject's eyes.

2. Prehension provoked by tactual stimulus—a small cube of wood is placed on back or palm of the subject's hand to see if he grasps it and carries it to his mouth, and coordination of movements is to be noted.

3. Prehension provoked visually—cube of wood is placed within subject's reach by examiner who notes whether subject grasps it.

4. Recognition of food—a small piece of chocolate and a piece of wood of same dimensions are shown successively, and signs of recognition of food and efforts to take it are noted.

5. Seeking food when slight mechanical difficulty is interposed—a small piece of chocolate, wrapped in a piece of paper, is given to the subject, and his manner of separating the food from the paper is noted.

6. Execution of simple directions and imitations of simple gestures.

7. Verbal knowledge of objects—parts of the body (head, ear, nose, etc.) are indicated by the subject, and common objects (key, string, cup) are handed to examiner on request.

8. Verbal knowledge of objects in a picture, as shown by pointing out objects, the names of which are given.

9. Naming of objects designated in a picture.

10. Comparison of the lengths of two straight lines, pointing out the longer.

11. Repeating three digits immediately after hearing the series once.

12. Comparison of weights; identical-appearing blocks of wood weighing 3 and 12 grams, 6 and 15 grams, 3 and 15 grams.

13. Suggestibility—asking the subject for an object that is not present (modification of 7); asking subject to point to a nonexistent object in a picture, designated by a nonsensical word (modification of 8); comparison of lines of equal length (modification of 10).

14. Definitions of familiar objects, such as house, horse, fork.

15. Repetition of sentences having fifteen words each, after hearing each one only once.

16. Giving the differences between two common objects; for example, wood and glass, a fly and a butterfly.

17. Immediate recall of pictures of familiar objects—pictures of thirteen common objects are shown for thirty seconds, after which the subject names as many as he can recall.

18. Drawing from memory two different geometric designs which have been shown simultaneously for ten seconds.

19. Repetition of series of digits, beginning with a series of three and proceeding until the subject's limit is reached.

20. Giving resemblance between common objects; for example, a wild poppy and blood; an ant, a fly, a butterfly, and a flea.

21. Rapid comparison of lengths of lines: a line of 30 cm. is compared with fifteen others varying from 31 to 35 cm.; then a line of 100 cm. is compared with twelve others varying from 101 to 103 cm.

22. Discriminating and arranging in order five weights—3, 6, 9, 12, 15 grams—all being of equal size.

23. Recall of weights—one of the weights in test 22 is removed, the remaining weights are scrambled, and the subject is asked to identify the missing weight or gap in the series.

24. Giving rhymes to selected words.

25. Sentence completion—supplying the correct word to complete a sentence.

26. Devising a sentence to include three given words; for example, Paris, gutter, fortune.

27. Comprehending and giving replies to twenty-five problem questions graded in difficulty—What is the thing to do when you are sleepy? Why is it better to continue with perseverance what one has started than to abandon it and start something else?

28. Reversing the hands of a clock, to be done from memory; for example, giving the time it would be if the large and the small hands were interchanged at four minutes to three. The subjects who succeed are given the more difficult problem of explaining why the precise transposition indicated is impossible.

29. Drawing lines to show the folds and cutout of a piece of paper that has been quarto-folded and from which a triangular piece has been cut.

30. Giving definitions and distinctions between paired abstract terms; for example, sad and bored.

Although this set of tests was not separated into age groups, Binet did indicate several differentiating levels. Question number 6 was the upper limit of idiots (adult); question 9 was the upper limit of ordinary 3-year-old children; number 14 was the limit of ordinary 5-year-old children; number 16, that of imbeciles (adult); test 23, the most probable limit of morons (adult), although test 27 was regarded as having great value in revealing the moron. In addition, the authors reported a number of qualitative and quantitative differences in replies to many of the questions, thus distinguishing between 7- and 9-year levels, on the one hand, and 9- and 11-year levels, on the other.

The order of tests in the 1905 scale was experimentally determined, for it was established after being used with children in the primary schools and in an institution for the mentally deficient (the Salpêtrière). The children in primary school were regarded as normal on the basis of the fact that they were in grades just right for their ages—neither advanced nor retarded. Binet and Simon report that many such children were tested, but norms for the scale were based upon records of only ten cases in each of the following age groups: 3, 5, 7, 9, and 11 years.

While admittedly rather crude and tentative, this first scale enabled Binet and Simon to classify idiots, imbeciles, and morons in a more objective manner than had been possible before.

Furthermore, in the foregoing list of thirty items, the reader will find many types which have since been developed, standardized, and included in a large number of current psychological tests, from those designed for babies to those intended for adult levels.

It is significant to note, also, that while Binet wanted to devise a scale that would yield age ratings, he was equally concerned with the *quality* of judgment and reasoning shown by the subject in the course of the examination. Binet was thus using the test situation as an opportunity for a clinical interview—a practice which is becoming increasingly widespread and of increasing importance in reports of psychological examinations by present-day clinical psychologists.

The 1908 Binet-Simon Scale. Binet and Simon recognized the defects of the first scale. They recognized that an improved scale would have to provide more valid norms, based upon a larger and more representative sampling of children at each age; that tests for each age within the limits of the scale would have to be included to achieve finer units of measurement and greater accuracy. Their own subsequent investigations and those of other psychologists resulted in a new form of the test, known as the 1908 scale, in which the items are grouped at the appropriate age levels, from 3 years to 13 years (2, 3).

Age 3

1. Points to nose, eyes, mouth.
2. Repeats sentences of six syllables.
3. Repeats two digits.
4. Enumerates objects in a picture.
5. Gives family name.

Age 4

1. Knows own sex.
2. Names certain familiar objects that are shown to him (key, knife, penny).
3. Repeats three digits.
4. Perceives which is the longer of two lines 5 and 6 cm. in length.

Age 5

1. Indicates the heavier of two cubes (3 and 12 grams; 6 and 15 grams).
2. Copies a square.
3. Constructs a rectangle from two triangular pieces of cardboard, having a model to look at.
4. Counts four coins.
5. Repeats a sentence of ten syllables.

Age 6

1. Knows right and left; indicated by showing right hand and left ear.
2. Repeats sentence of sixteen syllables.

3. Chooses the prettier in each of three pairs of faces (esthetic comparison).
4. Defines familiar objects in terms of use.
5. Executes three commissions.
6. Knows own age.
7. Knows morning and afternoon.

Age 7

1. Perceives what is missing in unfinished pictures.
2. Knows number of fingers on each hand and on both hands without counting.
3. Copies a written model ("The little Paul").
4. Copies a diamond.
5. Describes presented pictures.
6. Repeats five digits.
7. Counts thirteen coins.
8. Identifies by name four common coins.

Age 8

1. Reads a passage and remembers two items.
2. Adds up the value of five coins.
3. Names four colors: red, yellow, blue, green.
4. Counts backwards from twenty to zero.
5. Writes short sentence from dictation.
6. Gives differences between two objects.

Age 9

1. Knows the date: day of week, day of month, month of year.
2. Recites days of week.
3. Makes change: four cents out of twenty in playstore transaction.
4. Gives definitions that are superior to use; familiar objects are employed.
5. Reads a passage and remembers six items.
6. Arranges five equal-appearing cubes in order of weight.

Age 10

1. Names the months of the year in correct order.
2. Recognizes and names nine coins.
3. Constructs a sentence in which three given words are used (Paris, fortune, gutter).
4. Comprehends and answers easy questions.
5. Comprehends and answers difficult questions.
   (Binet considers item 5 to be a transitional question between ages 10 and 11. Only about one half of the 10-year-olds got the majority of these correct.)

Age 11

1. Points out absurdities in statements.
2. Constructs a sentence, including three given words (same as number 3 in age 10).

3. Gives any sixty words in three minutes.
4. Defines abstract words (charity, justice, kindness).
5. Arranges scrambled words into a meaningful sentence.

Age 12

1. Repeats seven digits.
2. Gives three rhymes to a word (in one minute).
3. Repeats a sentence of twenty-six syllables.
4. Answers problem questions.
5. Interprets pictures (as contrasted with simple description).

Age 13

1. Draws the design made by cutting a triangular piece from the once-folded edge of a quarto-folded piece of paper.
2. Rearranges in imagination the relationship of two reversed triangles and draws results.
3. Gives differences between pair of abstract terms: pride and pretension.

There are several obvious differences between the 1905 scale and that of 1908. In the former, there are thirty test items; in the latter, fifty-nine. The latter does not include the first six items of the 1905 scale, which are at the infant level; some other items of the 1905 scale have been eliminated, and many new ones have been added. As compared with the 1905 scale, the age range extends higher in the 1908 scale. There are specific groups of items for each age (thus permitting a more accurate rating of individuals), and a greater variety of mental processes is tested.

In the 1908 scale, there are also two new and significant contributions to the theory and practice of mental testing and test construction: (1) the tests, after experimentation, were standardized by being grouped into appropriate age levels (Binet's method is explained below); (2) the concept of mental age is employed for the first time.[3]

The principal criterion employed by Binet and Simon in the standardization and age placement of tests was this: in general, a test was placed at the year level where it was passed satisfactorily by two thirds to three fourths of a representative group of children of that age. The *ideal* standard was to place a test at a year level where it was passed by *seventy-five* percent of that age group. Binet's reason for setting this ideal criterion is a sound one and is made clear by reference to a symmetrical bell-shaped curve, which is approximated by most distributions of intelligence-test scores. The middle fifty percent of the group are most nearly alike, most nearly homogeneous in respect to the abilities being measured, as is obvious from the concentration of these fifty percent within a relatively narrow range, or variation, of scores. Otherwise stated, those individuals constituting the middle fifty percent of the distribution

---

[3] Although mental age is employed here for the first time, the concept itself had been proposed by Binet in 1905.

are the *typical* persons of the age group; hence, their test performance should be regarded as typical or normal for their age. If the middle fifty percent of a given age are able to pass a test, then that same test can be passed by the twenty-five percent who are above the middle group in ability, making a total of seventy-five who are able to pass the test.

In actual experience, however, it has been practically impossible to devise tests that will exactly satisfy this criterion of seventy-five percent passing. Fortunately, there are other criteria of validity that are also of primary significance, so that tests are retained if they *approximate* the seventy-five percent criterion, and if they demonstrate their value by also satisfying other demands, such as distinguishing between groups of individuals of known ability (mentally deficient, average, and superior), showing appreciable or significant differences between percentages passing at successive age levels, and correlating fairly well with scholastic achievement. These aspects of validation are more fully discussed in the following chapter, in connection with revisions of the Binet scale.

Binet and Simon standardized their 1908 scale after individual examinations of 203 Paris school children between the ages of 3 and 13 years. Although this number is small and would be regarded as inadequate in present-day test-standardization procedures, the fact is that these French pioneers did set a pattern of standardization that is being followed today, with considerable statistical refinement. For in addition to having suggested the criteria already mentioned, they also, in effect, used the symmetrical bell-shaped curve as a criterion, though without offering precise numerical values. They stated, simply, that the number of children testing above age (superior) should equal the number testing below age (inferior), and the number testing at age, or normal, should be greater than the number who rank as either superior or inferior.

The mental age, with the 1908 scale, was found as follows: first, the subject was credited with the age level at which he passed all tests. To this basic level (now called the "basal year") an additional year's credit was added for every five tests passed at higher levels. The total was the subject's mental age. No credits were given for a fraction of a year; but in the 1911 scale (see below) the calculation of mental age was modified so as to include fractional parts. The reader will note that this method of deriving mental age is essentially the same as that used with the American age-scale revisions.

In spite of its imperfect standardization, in the 1908 Binet-Simon scale and in the publications concerned with it will be found many of the important concepts and practices which have been employed since then in the construction and use of psychological tests.

The 1911 Revision of the Binet Scale. The 1908 scale created considerable interest among psychologists in Belgium, Germany, England, Italy, Switzerland, and the United States. Their interest resulted in a number of valuable applications and evaluations of the Binet scale, accompanied by suggestions for revisions.

For the most part, criticisms and suggestions dealt with the age levels at which various items had been placed. It is not surprising that, in the first age scale devised to measure intelligence, further and extensive applications and analysis of results should have revealed that a number of the items were misplaced. The principal criticism was that the tests at the lower age levels were too easy, whereas those at the higher levels were too difficult, with the result that the former group were rated too high, while the latter were rated too low. In other words, standardization of the test had to be improved. Binet utilized the suggestions and criticisms of other psychologists, as well as the results of his own continued researches on the 1908 scale, the result being the 1911 revision.

Specifically, the major changes incorporated in the 1911 scale were the following: four of the tests at the 11-year level were raised to the 12-year level; all 12-year tests were raised to the 15-year level; the three tests of year 13, plus two new ones, constituted the new adult level. Here and there, also, a few tests were placed in either a higher or a lower age level. No tests were provided for the 11-, 13-, and 14-year levels.[4] In addition to these changes, several tests found in the 1908 scale were omitted from the 1911 scale because they seemed to depend too much on school learning or on incidental information.

At age levels 3, 4, and 5, the tests are the same as in the 1908 version.

Age 6

1. Distinguishes between morning and afternoon.
2. Defines names of familiar objects in terms of use.
3. Copies a diamond.
4. Counts thirteen *sous*.
5. Distinguishes between pictures of ugly and pretty faces.

Age 7

1. Shows right hand and left ear.
2. Gives description of pictures.
3. Executes three commissions given simultaneously.
4. Gives value of three single- and three double-*sous*.
5. Names four colors: red, green, yellow, blue.

[4] Inasmuch as the rate of mental development appears to decrease appreciably after age 10, it becomes difficult to devise tests that will distinguish adequately between yearly levels. This difficulty was encountered also by the authors of the first Stanford revision of the Binet-Simon scale (1916); but in the second Stanford revision (1937), the authors were able to provide tests at yearly levels between ages 10 and 14 (see Chapters 9 and 10).

Age 8

1. Gives differences between two objects (from memory).
2. Counts backward from twenty to zero.
3. States omissions from unfinished pictures.
4. Knows the date.
5. Repeats five digits.

Age 9

1. Makes change from twenty *sous*.
2. Defines names of familiar objects in terms superior to use.
3. Recognizes all nine [French] coins.
4. Gives months of the year in correct order.
5. Comprehends and answers easy problem questions.

Age 10

1. Arranges five blocks in order of weight.
2. Reproduces two geometric designs from memory.
3. Criticizes absurd statements.
4. Comprehends and answers difficult problem questions.
5. Uses three given words in two sentences.

The method of scoring the 1911 scale was modified so that fractions of a year could be used in determining the mental age. Since there were five tests at each age level (except at age 4), each counted as two tenths of a year. Thus, if a child passed all tests at age 6, two at age 7, and one at age 8, his mental age would be 6.6 years.

According to Binet, a child whose mental age is equal to his chronological age is considered "regular" in intelligence; one whose mental age is higher is called "advanced"; and one whose mental age is lower is called "retarded." The degree of advancement or retardation in any instance is dependent upon the extent of the difference. Within about a year, however, William Stern was to suggest the use of the *intelligence quotient,* which has since been widely employed to indicate degree of acceleration or retardation in intelligence.

Binet's scales of 1908 and 1911 provided the stimulation and the basis for several adaptations and revisions in the United States. The authors of American revisions utilized Binet's principles and drew freely on his tests, as well as adding new ones and standardizing their instruments specifically for American children. These revisions are presented in the following chapter.

Summary

At this point we may very briefly summarize Binet's major contributions to the theory and practice of intelligence testing.

1. If a psychologist is to develop a test of intelligence, he should first formulate a working conception and definition of intelligence, and then proceed experimentally. As a result of experimentation, new hypotheses will be developed; these in turn will influence later test construction; thus, both the conception and measurement of intelligence will undergo improvement and refinement. Binet's own conception of intelligence included mainly the following characteristics: ability to reason and judge well, to comprehend well, to take and maintain a definite direction of thought, to adapt thinking to the attainment of a desirable end, and to be autocritical.

2. Intelligence must be measured by testing the higher, complex mental processes rather than the relatively simple sensory and motor activities.

3. Intelligence, being a complex, can be tested only by the use of a diversity of materials devised to evaluate the operations of mental processes as an integrated unit, rather than by measuring the separate elements that might contribute to the complex functioning of intelligence. Though the Binet tests seem to be simple in conception and construction, they actually involve many complex mental activities: memory of several kinds, apperception, free association, orientation in time, language comprehension, ability with numbers, knowledge about common objects, constructive imagination, comparison of concepts, perception of contradictions, understanding of abstract terms, ability to meet novel situations, and combining fragments into a meaningful whole.

4. The tests included must be appropriate to the environment of those for whom they are intended.

5. The tests were arranged in the form of a scale, from easiest to most difficult, and groups of tests were placed at appropriate age levels. The criterion was, ideally, that a test should be placed at a level where it was passed by three fourths of that age group.

6. The concept of mental age was introduced.

7. The tests must be so standardized that the large middle group of average children (in the curve of distribution) will test "at age."

8. Other criteria of validity were introduced, such as known groups, scholastic ratings, and increase in percentage passing a test at successive age levels.

9. The need of establishing the reliability of a test was recognized; Binet, therefore, made a few reliability studies with his 1911 scale.

Not only did Binet make these contributions; he also indicated the extensive uses to which psychological tests could be put in educational, social, vocational, and theoretical problems, for he regarded tests as tools for research and for scientific solution of important practical problems. Indeed, many of the researches and uses to which tests have since been applied are definitely along lines indicated by Binet, including, among others, the testing of prospective soldiers in order to eliminate the mentally unfit.

Binet did not regard his tests as final or as quite satisfactory; he did not claim that they measured all aspects of personality; he emphasized that they must be supplemented by psychological and educational information derived by other means and from other sources. He did claim—and in this he has been supported by extensive subsequent use—that his test, and improved versions that should follow, can provide a very useful and reasonably valid index of an individual's general intelligence, when the tests are administered and interpreted by qualified examiners.[5]

References

1. Binet, A., and V. Henri. La psychologie individuelle. *L'Année Psychologique,* 1896, 2, 411–465. See also vols. 1–17 for most of Binet's contributions.
2. Binet, A., and T. Simon. Le dévelopment de l'intelligence chez les enfants. *L'Année Psychologique,* 1908, *14,* 1–94.
3. Kite, E. S. *The Development of Intelligence in Children.* Baltimore: Warwick and York Incorporated, 1916.
4. Peterson, J. *Early Conceptions and Tests of Intelligence.* New York: Harcourt, Brace & World, Inc., 1925.
5. Varon, E. J. Development of Alfred Binet's psychology. *Psychological Monographs,* 1935, *46,* no. 3.
6. Whipple, G. M. *Manual of Mental and Physical Tests.* Baltimore: Warwick and York Incorporated, 1914, part 1; 1915, part 2.

[5] Alfred Binet died in 1911. His premature death deprived psychology of one of its great pioneers. For a comprehensive study of Binet's psychology, see E. J. Varon (5).

9.

EARLY REVISIONS OF THE BINET-SIMON SCALE

This chapter will be devoted principally to the 1916 version of the Stanford-Binet scale. Although it was the first of three Stanford scales (1916, 1937, and 1960), students, particularly at the graduate level, and those who will use tests or who must be familiar with them in their occupations should be knowledgeable regarding earlier efforts. They will thereby be able to understand more fully the development and progress made over the years. They will have more information regarding the origins of current techniques and procedures; they will be better able to evaluate progress made in current tests.

Four Early Revisions

The two most widely known and used adaptations of the Binet scale in the United States were the Stanford revisions of 1916 and 1937. There were, however, four other revisions that, at one time or another, were of value to psychologists but which today are not employed and are chiefly of historical interest. In 1908, H. H. Goddard published a translation of Binet's 1905 scale; and in 1911 he produced, for use in the United States, a revision of Binet's 1908 version. Yerkes published revisions in 1915 and 1923, in which the several types of items were grouped as subtests in a point scale (for example, memory span for digits, analogies) instead of being placed at age levels. Herring's revision appeared in 1922 and for some years was used as a valuable alternate in place of the 1916

Stanford scale. Kuhlmann's three revisions (1912, 1922, and 1939) were extensive and elaborate in respect to standardization, scoring, and age range covered. Thus, it is clear that a significant amount of psychological work had been done prior to the publication of the 1916 Stanford scale and that several investigators continued their research and improvements on Binet's instrument for some years afterwards.

The Stanford Revision of 1916

The full name of this test, The Stanford Revision of the Binet-Simon Intelligence Scale, is derived from the fact that the revision was made at Stanford University, under the direction of L. M. Terman. The construction of this scale was undertaken for the purpose of providing an instrument that would be adequately standardized and adapted for use in the United States. Its acceptance by psychologists and educators is attested by the fact that it was the most widely used individual scale until the revised Stanford-Binet appeared in 1937.

Although Terman and his collaborators examined approximately 2300 subjects—1700 normal children, 200 defective and superior children, and 400 adults—over a period of several years, the revision of the scale below the 14-year level was actually based upon the results obtained with about 1000 native-born children in California. Each one of these children, representing an unselected group of average social status, was within two months of his birthday.

The 1916 scale includes 90 test items, covering an age range from 3 years to 14 years, with a group of test items added at the "average adult" level and another at the "superior adult" level. Of these 90 test items, 54 were adapted from the 1911 Binet scale, 5 from earlier Binet scales, 4 from other American tests, and 27 were new additions.

VALIDATION. The process of selecting the items involved (1) the comments and notes of the examiners, including the verbatim responses of the subjects to each test item, and (2) the percentage of subjects passing each test at each age level (as an example, see Table 9.1). "The guiding principle was to secure an arrangement of the tests and a standard of scoring which would make the median mental age of the unselected children of each age group coincide with the median chronological age. That is, a correct scale must cause the *average* child of 5 years (CA) to test exactly at 5 (MA), the *average* child at 6 to test exactly at 6, etc." (5, p. 53). Or, in terms of the intelligence quotient employed with this scale, an unselected group of children at each age should yield a median of 100.

Before the desired results were secured and this criterion satisfied, it

TABLE 9.1

PERCENTS PASSING TESTS LOCATED IN YEAR VI:
1916 REVISION

Test	Ages				
	4	5	6	7	8
Right and left	40	50	71	86	95
Mutilated pictures	27	50	65	87	96
Counting 13 pennies	30	46	76	93	86
Comprehension	25	55	70	86	93
Naming 4 coins	25	47	74	91	95
Repeating 16–18 syllables	34	56	69	90	95

SOURCE: L. M. Terman *et al.* (6, pp. 167–168). By permission.

was necessary to prepare three revisions of the scale. This involved the elimination of some test items, the shifting of others up or down in age level, and changes in scoring standards.[1] "As finally revised," Terman states, "the scale gives a median intelligence quotient closely approximating 100 for the unselected children of each age from 4 to 14."

The test items above the age of 14 were based on examinations of 30 businessmen, 150 migrating unemployed men, 150 adolescent delinquents and 50 high school students. These groups are not a representative cross section of persons above 14 years of age in the general population. This fact will help make clear why the 1916 scale was found to be unsatisfactory for use with older adolescents and with adults.[2] The unsatisfactory quality of the scale at the upper ages was due also to inadequate sampling of abilities.

In addition to the criterion of a significant increase in the percent passing a test item at successive ages, the criteria which follow were used in establishing validity of the 1916 scale.

[1] A theoretical or ideal percentage of passes for the placement of a test of a given age level was not used. Terman states, "We had already become convinced . . . that no satisfactory revision of the Binet scale was possible on any theoretical considerations as to the percentage of passes which an individual test ought to show in a given year to be considered standard for that year" (5, p. 54). Accordingly, a "trial-and-success" method was used in order to get the desired median mental age and IQ at each chronological age level. The same practice was followed in standardizing the 1937 revision.

[2] In a personal communication Dr. Terman states that there were three tentative versions of the scale before the final one was published. The businessmen and high school students were used in making the first tentative placement of tests at average and superior adult levels. The other adult groups were then used in subsequent rearrangement of test items.

First, in each age group, all the subjects tested were divided into the following three classes: those testing below 90 IQ, those testing between 90 and 109, and those testing 110 or above. Each test item was then examined to determine whether it was passed by a "decidedly higher" percentage of individuals in the superior IQ group than in the inferior. (The term "decidedly higher" was not defined by Terman.) Only those test items that satisfied this criterion were retained. The data shown in Table 9.2 are illustrative.

TABLE 9.2

PERCENTS PASSING CERTAIN TESTS,
CHRONOLOGICAL AGE CONSTANT

Age	Test	IQs		
		Below 96	96–105	Above 105
6	Counting 13 pennies	40	77	96
7	Describing pictures	48	52	80
8	Giving similarities	44	57	83
9	Making change	39	60	73
10	Comprehension of problem situations	25	64	76

SOURCE: L. M. Terman et al. (6, p. 133). By permission.

Second, after the scale had been developed, the IQs obtained with 504 school children were compared with their scholastic ratings, as graded by their teachers, on a five-point scale; namely, very inferior, inferior, average, superior, very superior. Moderate agreement was found between intelligence quotients and school ratings, the coefficient of correlation being .48—close enough so that Terman and his colleagues concluded there was no justifiable "serious suspicion as to the accuracy of the intelligence scale."

Third, the relation between IQ and grade progress was studied for the children on whom the scale was standardized. A "fairly high" correlation was found, but there were also some "astounding disagreements," inasmuch as a given mental age level was found in a wide range of grades. For example, a mental age of 9 was found in all grades from 1 to 7. Terman states, however, "When the data were examined, it was found that practically every child whose grade failed to correspond fairly closely with his mental age was either exceptionally bright or exceptionally dull. Those who tested between 96 and 105 IQ [the average children] were never seriously misplaced in schools" (5, p. 74).

RELIABILITY.   Following its publication, the Stanford-Binet was subjected to numerous studies in order to determine its reliability by the method of self-correlation. The correlation coefficients, which in such studies will vary with the size and constitution of the experimental group, ranged from about .80 to .95. Such coefficients are regarded as highly satisfactory indexes of reliability.

The Scale.   The reader will have noted that no essentially new concepts or principles have been added in the 1916 Stanford-Binet scale, as compared with Binet's own. Terman and his colleagues did, however, extend, refine, and adapt the Binet scales, so that the 1916 revision was a better standardized, hence more valid and reliable, instrument.

The complete list of tests of the 1916 Stanford-Binet follows.[3] Throughout the scale, those items designated "Al.," instead of being numbered, are alternates, to be used in place of one of the numbered items, where the examiner, for any reason, believes a numbered item to be inappropriate.

Age 3

1. Points to parts of body.
2. Names familiar objects.
3. Enumerates objects in pictures.
4. Gives sex.
5. Gives last name.
6. Repeats six to seven syllables.
Al. Repeats three digits.

Age 4

1. Compares lengths of lines.
2. Discriminates between geometric forms.
3. Counts four pennies.
4. Copies a square.
5. Comprehends and solves problem situations.
6. Repeats four digits.
Al. Repeats twelve to thirteen syllables.

Age 5

1. Compares weights.
2. Names familiar colors.
3. Makes esthetic comparisons of paired drawings of faces.
4. Defines common words: use or better.
5. Puts together a divided triangle.
6. Carries out three commissions.
Al. Gives own age.

[3] Reproduced by permission of Houghton Mifflin Company.

Age 6

1. Knows right from left.
2. Perceives missing parts in pictures.
3. Counts thirteen pennies.
4. Comprehends and solves problem situations.
5. Identifies coins.
6. Repeats sixteen to eighteen syllables.
Al. Knows morning from afternoon.

Age 7

1. Knows number of fingers on each and both hands.
2. Describes pictures.
3. Repeats five digits.
4. Ties a bowknot.
5. Gives differences between paired objects.
6. Copies a diamond.
Al.1. Names days of week in correct order.
Al.2. Repeats three digits backwards.

Age 8

1. Traces path to be followed in a systematic search for a lost object in a field.
2. Counts backward from twenty to one.
3. Comprehends and solves problem situations.
4. Gives similarities between two things.
5. Defines names of objects in terms superior to use.
6. Defines twenty words from a vocabulary list.
Al.1. Identifies six coins.
Al.2. Writes short sentence from dictation.

Age 9

1. Gives date: day of week, month, day of month, year.
2. Discriminates between weights: 3, 6, 9, 12, 15 grams.
3. Makes change in small amounts.
4. Repeats four digits backwards.
5. Makes up a sentence including three given words.
6. Gives rhymes to three words.
Al.1. Names the months of the year.
Al.2. Gives total value of a group of one-cent and two-cent postage stamps.

Age 10

1. Defines thirty words from vocabulary list.
2. Detects absurdities in statements.
3. Reproduces two designs from memory.
4. Reads a short passage and reproduces content.
5. Comprehends and solves problem situations.

6. Names any sixty words by free association.

Al.1. Repeats six digits.

Al.2. Repeats twenty to twenty-two syllables.

Al.3. Fits rectangular blocks into formboard.

Age 12

1. Defines forty words from vocabulary list.
2. Defines abstract words.
3. Traces a path in systematic search (same problem as in year 8, but a superior plan is required here).
4. Rearranges dissected sentences into meaningful sentences.
5. Interprets fables.
6. Repeats five digits backwards.
7. Interprets pictures.
8. Gives similarities between three things.

Age 14

1. Defines fifty words from vocabulary list.
2. Discovers a rule in a paper-folding test (induction test).
3. Gives differences between a president and a king.
4. Integrates given facts and arrives at a conclusion concerning them.
5. Solves arithmetical reasoning problems.
6. Reverses hands of clock, in imagination, and gives the hour.

Al. Repeats seven digits.

Average Adult

1. Defines sixty-five words from vocabulary list.
2. Interprets fables.
3. Gives differences between abstract words.
4. Solves problem of number of enclosed boxes (boxes within boxes) when shown only the large outside box.
5. Repeats six digits backwards.
6. Perceives the pattern of a code and uses it.

Al.1. Repeats twenty-eight syllables.

Al.2. Comprehends problems involving physical relations.

Superior Adult

1. Defines seventy-five words from vocabulary list.
2. Visualizes, imaginally, and draws appearance of a folded and cut piece of paper.
3. Repeats eight digits.
4. Repeats thought of a passage heard.
5. Repeats seven digits backwards.
6. Solves problems involving "ingenuity."

The Scoring Method. Each age level from 3 years through 10, it will be noted, has six test items (plus the alternate which may replace one of the six). Each of these carries credit of two months, so that the tests in each of the age levels provide a year's increment in mental age.

There are no tests at the 11-year level, the reason being that the authors of the scale were, apparently, unable to devise tests that would indicate a one-year difference at this stage of mental development. This gap in the scale, it is believed, is due to the slowing down of mental development, thus decreasing the annual increments and making it more difficult to measure those increments by means of the then-available test items. Since the eight test items at age 12 cover a span of two years, each one carries a credit of three months in order to yield an average mental age of 12, when added to the 10-year level.

The same explanation applies to the six test items at the age 14, each of which gives a credit of four months toward mental age score.[4]

The tests and credits at the average adult level were devised so as to provide a median mental age of 16. Yet each of the six tests at average adult level carries a credit of five months, so that a person who passed all of them would have a mental age of 16.5 years. In his volume describing the standardization of the 1916 revision, in explaining the limit for average adult, Terman states that his data on mental ages of 62 adults, including 30 businessmen and 32 high school pupils, who were over 16 years of age, show ". . . that the middle section of the graph [of the distribution] represents the 'mental ages' falling between 15 and 17. This is the range we have designated as the 'average adult' level" (5, p. 55).

Those persons having mental ages above 17 were designated as "superior adults," the possible maximum mental age on this scale being 19.5. (Six tests, six months' credit each, added to the maximum of 16.5 attainable at the average adult level.)

The method of scoring the 1916 scale is as follows: the examiner goes *down* in the test until the level is reached where the subject passes all items. This is called the "basal year." The examiner then proceeds *upward* in the scale until the level is reached where the subject fails all items. This level is called the "terminal year." As already stated, each test item carries specified credit, in terms of months, contributing to the mental age score. These credits are added to the age value of the basal year; the total is the mental age. For example, assume that in a given instance the basal year is 6; three test items are then passed at the 7-year level, giving additional credit of six months; two are passed at the 8-year level, giving further credit of four months; all are failed at the 9-year level. Thus, this subject's mental age is 6 years, 10 months.

Distribution of IQs. A second rating obtained with the 1916 Stanford-Binet is the intelligence quotient, the calculation and general

[4] The 1937 revision provides a group of tests at age 11 and another at 13.

nature of which have already been explained. Terman not only found the IQ for each individual examined, but he analyzed the distribution of intelligence quotients obtained by the persons on whom the scale was standardized.

Taking those subjects between the ages of 5 and 14 years, the distribution was found to be as shown in Table 9.3. The *SD* of this distribution

TABLE 9.3

DISTRIBUTION OF IQs OF 905 UNSELECTED CHILDREN, AGES 5–14 YEARS

IQ	Percent of total
56– 65	0.33
66– 75	2.3
76– 85	8.6
86– 95	20.1
96–105	33.9
106–115	23.1
116–125	9.0
126–135	2.3
136–145	0.55

SOURCE: L. M. Terman *et al.* (6, p. 133). By permission.

is about 12 points. (Compare this with the *SD* of 16 points of the 1937 revision.)

This distribution, being a fairly symmetrical one, showed that the scale did differentiate among the several levels of mental capacity of the persons examined; at least, so far as concerns the mental processes being tested. It therefore strengthened the belief of Terman and many others that the 1916 Stanford-Binet had considerable validity.

Another method used to represent the frequency with which different degrees of intelligence occur was to indicate the percentage of subjects at and above, or at and below, a given IQ as in Table 9.4. Although the percentages above or below certain IQ levels are not fixed or identical for all tests (for example, the distribution for the 1937 Stanford-Binet is not identical with this one), a table such as this is significant in that it provides one means of determining an individual's relative status in respect to the psychological processes being measured; for, as already explained, the IQ is an index having educational and clinical connotations.

TABLE 9.4

PERCENTAGE DISTRIBUTION OF IQs:
STANFORD-BINET SCALE, 1916

The lowest	1%	go	to	70	or	below
" "	2%	"	"	73	"	"
" "	3%	"	"	76	"	"
" "	5%	"	"	78	"	"
" "	10%	"	"	85	"	"
" "	15%	"	"	88	"	"
" "	20%	"	"	91	"	"
" "	25%	"	"	92	"	"
" "	$33\frac{1}{3}$%	"	"	95	"	"
The highest	1%	reach		130	or	above
" "	2%	"		128	"	"
" "	3%	"		125	"	"
" "	5%	"		122	"	"
" "	10%	"		116	"	"
" "	15%	"		113	"	"
" "	20%	"		110	"	"
" "	25%	"		108	"	"
" "	$33\frac{1}{3}$%	"		106	"	"

SOURCE: L. M. Terman (5, p. 78). By permission.

On the basis of the distribution of intelligence quotients obtained with the 1916 revision, Terman also suggested the classification given in Table 9.5. This classification is reproduced because it has been widely used and because the reader should be familiar with its source. Unfortunately, however, such classifications or labels have frequently been used uncritically, on the erroneous assumption that there was some quality inherent in the classification itself that warranted the designation of "genius," or "superiority," or "dullness," etc. It has already been pointed out, for example, that not all persons of very high IQs have original, creative mentalities; yet these are among the traits of the "genius." The particular IQ intervals and the names attached to them result from the judgment of the specialist making the classification. Some classifiers might choose to place the lower limit of "near genius or genius" at 150 IQ, or the upper limit of "feeblemindedness" at 50 or 60. In short, tables of IQ classifications are essentially statistical tools and conveniences.

Regardless of size of intervals or of their names, a classification is useful chiefly as a convenient device for purposes of research and analysis of data. It should not be used merely to label and pigeonhole an individual who has been examined and for whom an intelligence quotient has been obtained. The trend is away from stating test results in terms of MA and IQ alone; the trend is toward the evaluation of individual performances.

Adult Mental Age and Adult Intelligence Quotient.   Since the 1916 Stanford-Binet includes tests at the levels of average adult and superior adult, it was necessary to make provisions for the calculation of adult mental ages and intelligence quotients. These, however, present special problems.

TABLE 9.5

SUGGESTED CLASSIFICATION OF IQs:
STANFORD-BINET SCALE, 1916

IQ	Classification
Above 140	"Near" genius or genius
120–140	Very superior intelligence
110–119	Superior intelligence
90–109	Normal, or average, intelligence
80–89	Dullness
70–79	Borderline deficiency
Below 70	Definite feeblemindedness

SOURCE: L. M. Terman (5, p. 79). By permission.

We have already quoted Terman's reason for locating average adult performance in the mental age range of 15 to 17, with the assumed midpoint at 16 years. If this is correct, it means that the test performance of the average adult is equal to that of the average 16-year-old individual. Otherwise stated, it means that in the case of an *average* adult, his maximum level of measured intelligence is reached at the age of 16 and that there are no increments thereafter. Terman states that ". . . in so far as it can be measured by tests now available, [intelligence] appears to improve but little after the age of 15 or 16. . . . Although this point [at which intelligence attains its final development] is not exactly known, it will be sufficiently accurate for our purposes to assume its location at 16 years" (5, p. 140). Thus, until the process of decline sets in, *the average adult continues to have a mental age of 16,* according to the 1916 Stanford-Binet.

On the basis of this assumption, then, in the calculation of an IQ for a person who is 16 years of age, or older, the denominator in the formula ($IQ = MA/CA$) is always 16. Otherwise, if his actual CA were used, he would *appear* to be getting less and less intelligent with the succeeding years. For example, an average individual at the age of 16 will have an

IQ of 100 (16/16). At the age of 18, he should still have an IQ of 100 even though, according to the tests being used, there has been no further measurable development of mental capacity; for the formula will still be 16/16. Now if, in the case of this same individual, his actual CA was still used as the denominator, his IQ at age 18 would be shown as about 89 (16/18); at age 20, it would be shown as 80 (16/20), and so on, while as a matter of fact there would ordinarily have been no such decline. Thus, by using the denominator of 16 in the IQ formula for all persons above age 16, if a person of 20 years and one of 60 years have the mental age of 16 years each, then each will be given an IQ of 100.

The reader has also noted that it is possible to attain mental ages above 16 on the 1916 revision, the maximum being 19.5 years at the level of superior adult. If the definition of mental age is borne in mind, it will be apparent at once that a mental-age rating which is higher than that of the *average* adult has been given a new and specialized meaning. It cannot have the same meaning as the term "mental age" does ordinarily. A mental age is defined as the level of mental development of the *average* or *typical group* of persons at that same chronological age. Thus, an MA of 10 represents the test performance and mental level of a group of average children of chronological age 10. Hence, if we assume that *average* or typical adults reach a mental age of 16, then to speak of a "mental age" above 16 is to introduce a new concept; for these latter "mental ages" are not derived from the performance or norms of average or typical persons. They are theoretical and hypothetical indexes devised to enable us to indicate higher than average mental levels and higher than average intelligence quotients.[5] Thus, when a higher-than-average adult "mental age" is used, it is essential that the user be aware of the fact that a new and different concept is being employed.

The fact that the highest possible "mental age" that can be attained on this test is 19.5 years means that the highest IQ an adult can attain is about 122 (19.5/16). This maximum reveals a serious inadequacy of the 1916 revision at the higher levels. What, for example, happens to the IQ of the 10-year-old child who has a mental age of 15, and an IQ of 150 (15/10)? Obviously, to maintain that IQ of 150 at age 16 or older, he must be able to attain a mental age of 24 (24/16); yet the scale permits a maximum MA of only 19.5, with an IQ of 122. The same would be true for this subject after age 16.

Criticisms of the 1916 Stanford-Binet. Experience with the 1916 Stanford-Binet demonstrated that it was inadequate as a measure of

---

[5] In their volume describing the 1916 revision, Terman and his collaborators do not report how they arrived at their mental-age levels above those of average adult. In their 1937 revision this has been done by extrapolation and by providing for a distribution of adult IQs that should correspond to distributions for preadult levels.

adult mental capacity. In fact, experience showed that its usefulness was restricted to ages between 5 and 14 years, the range between 5 and 10 years being the most satisfactory.

This revision was also criticized on several other grounds. First, since the scale was finally standardized on the basis of results obtained with approximately 1000 native-born white children in California, its use with *all* groups of children in *all* parts of the United States seemed to many educators and psychologists to be a practice of doubtful validity; for it was held that the 1000 California subjects were not necessarily representative of the child population of this country. There is merit in the criticism, yet it must be recognized that this scale proved to be very useful in many parts of the United States, when employed and interpreted by examiners who were familiar with its assumptions and construction, and who, at the same time, were familiar with the backgrounds of the subjects they were examining.

Second, the scale was criticized as being much too heavily weighted with verbal and abstract materials, thus penalizing the individual who, for whatever reason, had been handicapped in developing his "verbal intelligence" through the medium of the English language. Terman's reply to this criticism was that intelligence at the verbal and abstract levels is the highest form, the *sine qua non,* of mental ability. Indeed, he defined intelligence as the ability to deal with abstract terms and to do conceptual thinking.

This criticism of the scale was warranted, nevertheless; for children who are handicapped by lack of opportunity to acquire and develop the use of English are at a serious disadvantage and get spuriously low ratings on psychological tests that emphasize verbal intelligence. Such children would include (1) those who have developed in homes where only a foreign language is spoken; (2) those who are handicapped by serious visual or auditory defects; (3) those handicapped by sensory anomalies (reversals, inversions, mirror-writing, poor sound discrimination) that seriously interfere with their learning to read; (4) those who are too young—that is, below age 4 or 5—to be tested adequately by means of verbal materials almost exclusively.

Third, the 1916 scale was found to be defective at some points with respect to procedures in administering and scoring, thus detracting from its objectivity and from the comparability of results obtained by different examiners.

In view of these criticisms, it was to be expected that other scales should be developed, particularly those of the performance and nonverbal types, which would obviate or minimize the second criticism. These are presented and discussed in a later chapter.

It was to be expected, also, that the 1916 Stanford-Binet itself should undergo revision in the light of experience, criticism, and accumulated data. Such a revision, begun about ten years after the original Stanford-Binet appeared, was published in 1937.

References

1. Goddard, H. H. A revision of the Binet scale. Vineland, N.J.: *The Training School Bulletin,* 1911, *8,* 56–62.
2. Herring, J. P. *Herring Revision of the Binet-Simon Tests.* New York: Harcourt, Brace & World, Inc., 1923.
3. Kuhlmann, F. *A Handbook of Mental Tests.* Baltimore: Warwick and York Incorporated, 1922.
4. Kuhlmann, F. *Tests of Mental Development: A Complete Scale for Individual Examination.* Minneapolis: Educational Test Bureau, 1939.
5. Terman, L. M. *The Measurement of Intelligence.* Boston: Houghton Mifflin Company, 1916.
6. Terman, L. M., *et al. The Stanford Revision and Extension of the Binet-Simon Scale for Meauring Intelligence.* Educational Psychology Monographs, 1917, no. 18.
7. Yerkes, R. M., *et al. A Point Scale for Measuring Mental Ability.* Baltimore: Warwick and York Incorporated, 1915 and 1923.

IO.

THE STANFORD-BINET SCALES:
1937 AND 1960 REVISIONS

The 1960 revision of the Stanford-Binet Intelligence Scale is based upon the materials and standardization of the 1937 revision. In the former, the more satisfactory items of Forms L and M of the 1937 version have been retained and combined into a single scale; some individual items have been more satisfactorily located as to age levels; the deviation IQ has been introduced; and several additional improvements have been made. To understand and adequately evaluate the 1960 revision, it is necessary, therefore, to be well-informed on the 1937 scale. Furthermore, since there is a wealth of experimental and empirical information on the 1937 edition which is significant in the interpretation of scores and responses to both revisions, and since many school and clinical psychologists have developed a high degree of sensitivity in its use, it is probable that the 1937 version will continue in use, for a time, in some quarters.

The 1937 Scale

Description. This scale differs from that of 1916 in many details, but it does not differ in its essential and basic conceptions. As the authors themselves state, "The revision utilizes the assumptions, methods, and principles of the age scale as conceived by Binet." They do, however, regard it as a better standardized and more useful scale than its predecessors. The principal differences and modifications follow.

The 1937 scale has two equivalent forms (L and M), each of which contains 129 test items, as compared with the 90 items in the first Stanford-Binet. Items that proved unsatisfactory in the original were eliminated, and new ones were added.

The 1937 scale extends downward to the level of age 2, and upward through three levels of "superior adult" (known as Superior Adult I, II, and III), thus increasing its usefulness.

The levels below age 5 and those above age 14 have been more carefully and validly standardized.

Scoring standards and instructions for administering the tests are improved.

From the age of 2 to age 5, this scale provides groups of test items at half-year intervals. Thus, more accurate and more highly differentiating test results are obtainable. The half-yearly intervals are possible because the rate of mental growth is most rapid in the earlier years and, therefore, the more rapid periodic increments are susceptible to testing.

Groups of tests are provided at ages 11 and 13; there were none at these levels in the 1916 scale for reasons already stated in Chapter 9.

Although the 1937 scale is predominantly verbal in character, it does provide more performance and other nonverbal materials at the earlier age levels, especially through age 4. The performance materials are those with which the subject has to *do* something; for example, build a pattern or make a design with blocks, or fill in a formboard with the variously shaped blocks. Other nonverbal materials include such activities as copying a geometric figure, completing the picture of a man, and discriminating between forms. In all of these, verbal ability is a factor to the extent that verbal directions must be understood. In these tests, verbal ability can also operate if the subject is familiar with the names of the objects or geometric figures and is thus facilitated in his manipulation or classification of them.

The 1937 scale was standardized on a carefully chosen and extensive group of subjects. The base of the standardization population was broadened, and its component members are regarded as more representative of the population.[1] *But only American-born white subjects were used in the standardization of this scale,* the total number being approximately 3000. The subjects were chosen from eleven states in several widely separated areas of the country, and an effort was made to have them from homes which, occupationally and socially, would be representative of the population at large.

Validation.   The test items were chosen on the basis of their validity, ease and objectivity of scoring, economy of time in administer-

---

[1] Up to the age of 5, the number of subjects used was 100 to each half-year level; from 6 to 14 years of age, 200 at each year; from 15 to 18 years, 100 at each year.

ing, interest to the subjects, and need for variation in types of materials.

Of the foregoing, *validity* is of primary significance. In this revision, a criterion of basic importance in judging validity of test items was the increase in percentage of successful performance with increasing age. This criterion was applied in two ways: first, by requiring an appreciable increase in the percent passing a given item in successive ages (as in the 1916 scale); and second, by finding "a weight based on the ratio of the difference to the standard error of the difference between the mean age (or mental age) of subjects passing the test and of subjects failing it" (32, p. 9). Stripped of its statistical terminology, this quotation means that the difference between the average age (chronological or mental) of subjects passing an item, on the one hand, and the average age of subjects failing that item, on the other hand, must be statistically significant. This is essentially an "age criterion." In this connection see Table 10.1.

TABLE 10.1

PERCENT PASSING TEST ITEMS LOCATED IN YEAR VI
(FORM L)

	Ages						
Item	*4*	*1½*	*5*	*5½*	*6*	*7*	*8*
1	3	15	36	50	67	89	97
2	11	29	44	55	70	86	95
3	11	26	46	53	69	86	96
4	3	11	43	48	71	94	96
5	16	29	47	51	73	94	95
6	26	44	52	61	81	91	93

SOURCE: Q. McNemar (23, p. 92). By permission.

A second criterion of major importance in the retention of an item was its correlation with the *total scores* of the individuals of the age level at which the test item is located. Table 10.2 presents the distribution of correlation coefficients (biserial) for both Forms L and M.

The calculated median of the coefficients for Form L is approximately .69; the middle 50 percent of the coefficients fall between approximately .51 and .73. The range for the whole set of coefficients is from .28 (memory for designs, year 11), to .89 (abstract words, year 11; and vocabulary, year 14).

On Form M, the calculated median coefficient is approximately .64; the middle 50 percent of the coefficients fall between approximately .51

TABLE 10.2

DISTRIBUTION OF CORRELATION COEFFICIENTS (BISERIAL)
FOR EACH ITEM WITH TOTAL SCORES

r	Frequency, Form L	Frequency, Form M
.20—	1	2
.30—	5	7
.40—	21	21
.50—	28	23
.60—	32	42
.70—	34	23
.80—	8	9
.90—		2
N	129	129

Based upon data in McNemar (23, Tables 53 and 54.)

and .71. The range for this whole set of coefficients is from .27 (memory for stories, year 13) to .91 (abstract words, year 13).

Of the 258 coefficients, 201, or very nearly 78 percent, are .50 or higher. This fact and the data presented in a later section in this chapter (Analysis of Functions Tested) provide strong evidence that the Stanford-Binet scale measures "general ability" by means of test items that have psychological processes in common to a high degree.

After selection of the tests that were to be used, one other empirical procedure was employed in locating each test item at an appropriate age level. The items were rearranged until it was found that they would yield for each group of subjects a mean mental age that was identical with their mean chronological age, giving a mean IQ as close as possible to 100. Six successive revisions were necessary to achieve this for Form L. Then, ". . . it was possible to achieve at once an equally good result with Form M by arranging its tests so as to match those of Form L at each age level with respect to difficulty, validity, and shape of curves of percents passing by age" (32, p. 23).

Factor analyses of the Stanford-Binet, reported later in this chapter, indicate that this instrument has considerable construct validity, as does the nonstatistical analysis of the mental processes required by the various types of test items, also given later in this chapter.

As was to be expected, the 1937 Stanford-Binet scale has been subjected to numerous studies of its predictive validity for educational purposes, particularly at the elementary and the high school levels, especially within the first several years after it had been made available. For many years, the Stanford-Binet has been regarded as the standard criterion, among psychological tests, for this purpose. (Also since their appearance, the Wechsler scales have been widely used for predicting educability at the elementary and secondary levels.)

In the basic subjects at the elementary school level, correlations of the following magnitudes have been found.

> *Reading:* A majority are .60 or higher.
> The modal interval is .60–.69.
> *Arithmetic:* A majority are .50 or higher.
> The modal interval is .50–.59.
> *Spelling:* A majority are .45 or higher.
> The modal interval is .45–.55.

At the high school level, the Stanford-Binet correlates well with grades in academic subjects, especially with those that are largely verbal. The approximate medians of the correlation coefficients are as follow.

Reading comprehension	.70
Knowledge of literature	.60
English usage	.60
History	.60
Algebra	.60
Biology	.55
Geometry	.50
Spelling	.45
Reading rate	.45

Reliability. Comparing IQs obtained with Forms L and M, Terman and Merrill report reliability coefficients from .90 to .98. The highest coefficients were found for IQs below 70 ($r = .98$), the lowest for IQs above 130 ($r = .90$), and intermediate coefficients for IQs close to 100 ($r = .92$). Age levels above 6 years showed greater reliability ($r = .93$) than those below 6 years ($r = .88$), when coefficients were calculated for separate age groups.

These coefficients are of the same general order as those found by other investigators in subsequent studies. The Stanford-Binet has thus proved to be a highly reliable test, since most of the coefficients reported for different age groups and different IQ levels are very close to .90.

Many test-retest studies of Stanford-Binet reliability, after long intervals, have been made. These researches are generally in agreement that correlation coefficients decrease as the interval between two testings is lengthened. Correlations increase, however, as the children grow older, if the interval between two testings is held constant; for example, one year

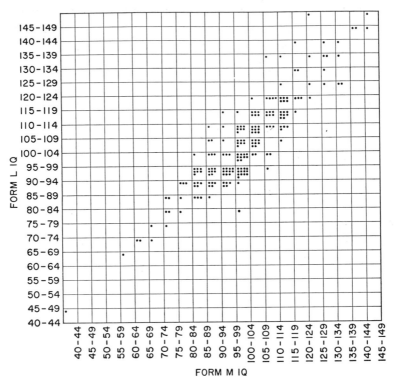

F<small>IG</small>. 10.1. Scatter chart of correlation between Form L and Form M. IQs at chronological age 7. $r = .91$. From L. M. Terman and M. A. Merrill (32, p. 45). By permission.

(6, 30). Test-retest between ages 3 and 4 yielded a coefficient of .83, whereas the coefficients between test results obtained at age 3 and at successive yearly intervals decreased, until between ages 3 and 12, the coefficient was .46. However, between adjacent age levels from 7 to 12, correlations were on the whole much higher. Within these age limits, the coefficients ranged from .73 to .92. Of fifteen coefficients, all but two were above .80. Between adjacent years from 8 to 12, the range was from .81 to .92. The correlations found in this study (30) are in close agreement with those of other investigations cited therein.

Another study reports: "The degree of relationship between the initial composite IQ (Forms L and M) of these subjects when they were in the age range from 2 to 5.5 (mean age 4.0) and Form L IQ when they were in the age range from 26.5 to 32.2 (mean age 29.5) is expressed by a Pearsonian r of .59. This compares favorably with the r of .65 found for the same group in the first follow-up after only ten years. The correlation between the 1941 and the 1956 testings is .85" (6).

Although these findings are cited under the heading of reliability, it is doubtful if test-retest results obtained after such long intervals actually are measures of an instrument's reliability, especially when one set of measures is obtained in early childhood (before age 5). For the findings are the results not only of the test's inherent reliability; they are affected as well by changes in the form, content, and organization of mental activity as age increases during the period of development; by the characteristics of *individual* mental growth curves; by the terminal age of mental development; and by motivation. (See also Chapter 13, Scales for Infants and Preschool Children.) Therefore, when a test's inherent reliability is to be estimated, the testings should take place within a relatively short space of time.

Mental Age and Intelligence Quotient. The scoring method is the same as that used with the 1916 scale for determining mental age and intelligence quotient. There are, however, a few differences in the details.

Whereas the maximum mental age attainable on the 1916 Stanford-Binet was 19 years and 6 months, the maximum on the 1937 revision is 22 years and 10 months. It will be recalled that with the first Stanford-Binet scale, a maximum CA of 16 was used in the denominator to determine the IQ of an individual 16 years of age or older. In the 1937 scale, the maximum CA in the denominator is 15. Thus, the highest possible IQ attainable by a subject who is 15 years of age or older is 152, that is, $(22 - ^{10}/15)$ 100.

In the superior-adult levels, the test items were selected and their credits allotted (in terms of months) in such a manner as to make the IQ distribution of ". . . the older subjects resemble closely those of the younger, as presumably should be the case on an ideal scale" (32, p. 30). In order to achieve this desired goal, it was necessary for the authors to make adjustments in the denominator of the IQ formula, beginning at the age of 13 years and 2 months. The reason given for this adjustment is that it is extremely difficult, perhaps impossible, to escape the effects of selection of subjects at the upper ages in standardizing a scale. The selection generally is such as to include the average range, the higher mental levels, and the moderately retarded, but not the lowest, since less intelligent individuals tend to leave school earlier than others. Hence, *norms* of test performance of the older groups, it is argued, tend to be higher than they should be for an unselected sampling. These higher norms, in turn, tend to reduce the intelligence quotients of subjects in the older groups.

It is this effect that the authors of the scale sought to correct by means of adjusting the denominator.

Although Terman and Merrill believe they minimized the effects of selection, these were not wholly eliminated. Therefore, after a "trial-and-success" process directed toward making IQ distributions of older age groups resemble closely those of younger groups, the procedure adopted was the cumulative dropping of one out of every three additional months of chronological age from age 13 to age 16, and all of it after 16. In substance, this practice is equivalent to saying that average adult mental age, on the 1937 scale, is 15. Table 10.3 gives a few examples.

TABLE 10.3

CORRECTION OF CA DIVISOR: 1937 STANFORD-BINET SCALE

Actual CA	Corrected CA divisor
13–0	13–0
13–3	13–2
14–0	13–8
14–6	14–0
15–0	14–4
15–6	14–8
16–0	15–0

SOURCE: Terman and Merrill (32, p. 31).
By permission.

When, therefore, this scale is used with subjects who are more than 13 years old, it is necessary to refer to the full correction table provided in the manual. Or the examiner may use the tables of IQs provided in the manual, in which the necessary adjustments have already been made.

Distribution of IQs. The mean IQs, for the subjects used in the standardization, are slightly above 100. But this, the authors say, is owing to an "intentional adjustment to allow for the somewhat inadequate sampling of subjects in the lower occupational classes." The adjustment was made by dividing the subjects into seven groups, according to the occupation of the fathers; at each age level the mean IQ was computed separately for each of the seven groups. These means at each age level were given a weight according to the occupational frequencies of each group, as shown by the 1930 census. The weighted means were then combined into a composite mean for each age level from 2 to 18 years, as shown in Table 10.4. The same data are represented graphically in Figure 10.2.

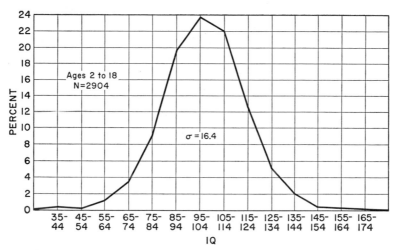

FIG. 10.2. Distribution of composite L-M IQs of standardization group. From Terman and Merrill (32, p. 37). By permission.

In the determination of the equality and comparability of IQs from age to age, not only must the means be very much the same (ideally, identical), but the *variations* should be the same at all age levels. If the differences between the variations of the age groups are large, then the same numerical IQ will have different significance at different chronological ages.

Consider the following hypothetical instance. Suppose a given test of mental ability yields results:

Chronological Age	Mean IQ	Standard Deviation
10	100	14
11	100	20

Accordingly, a 10-year-old child having an IQ of 86 (that is, one standard deviation below the mean) would have a percentile rating of approximately 16—which, it will be recalled, means that this child surpasses about 16 percent of his age group. Now, according to the foregoing data, a child of 11 years whose IQ is 80 (likewise one standard deviation below the mean of *his* group) would also have a percentile rating of about 16, in spite of the fact that his intelligence quotient is six points below that of the 10-year-old in question. While this difference of six points may make little practical difference in the clinical and educational treatment of these children, it is necessary to be familiar with the implications of differences in variations.

Another aspect of the problem is this: taking this hypothetical case of

TABLE 10.4

IQ MEANS ADJUSTED FOR 1930 CENSUS FREQUENCIES
OF OCCUPATIONAL GROUPINGS
COMPOSITE OF FORMS L AND M, STANFORD-BINET

Age	N	Raw	Smoothed
2	76	102.1	
2½	74	104.7	103.3
3	81	103.2	104.1
3½	77	104.3	102.2
4	83	99.2	101.6
4½	79	101.2	100.8
5	90	101.9	100.4
5½	110	98.2	100.0
6	203	100.0	99.8
7	202	101.2	100.8
8	203	101.1	102.0
9	204	103.6	102.7
10	201	103.5	103.0
11	204	101.9	102.2
12	202	101.2	101.6
13	204	101.8	101.0
14	202	100.0	101.3
15	107	102.0	101.3
16	102	101.8	103.3
17	109	103.2	103.8
18	101	106.3	

SOURCE: Terman and Merrill (32, p. 36). By permission.

the 10-year-old boy, if he is to have at age 11 the same *relative rank* he held at age 10, his IQ will have to drop from 86 to 80; and if this happens, the change will give the appearance of lack of IQ constancy; but, if he maintains his 86 IQ at age 11, then his percentile rank will be approximately 24. Here, again, the difference in percentile ranks might have little practical significance; but insight into the effects of differences in group variations will help explain some instances of lack of close agreement in repeated mental measurements. *Furthermore, the professional worker who uses mental tests must know the standard deviations of the instruments employed in order to make as accurate an evaluation of results as possible.*

IQ variability in relation to age, as found in the standardization of the 1937 Stanford-Binet, is shown in Table 10.5. Inspection of this table

TABLE 10.5

IQ Variability in Relation to Age
(Stanford-Binet)

		SD	
CA	N	Form L	Form M
2	102	16.7	15.5
2½	102	20.6	20.7
3	99	19.0	18.7
3½	103	17.3	16.3
4	105	16.9	15.6
4½	101	16.2	15.3
5	109	14.2	14.1
5½	110	14.3	14.0
6	203	12.5	13.2
7	202	16.2	15.6
8	203	15.8	15.5
9	204	16.4	16.7
10	201	16.5	15.9
11	204	18.0	17.3
12	202	20.0	19.5
13	201	17.9	17.8
14	202	16.1	16.7
15	107	19.0	19.3
16	102	16.5	17.4
17	109	14.5	14.3
18	101	17.2	16.6

Source: Terman and Merrill (32, p. 40). By permission.

shows significant fluctuation in standard deviations of the several age groups, especially between the extremes: 12.5 (*SD*) at age 6; 20.6 (*SD*) at age 2½; and 20.0 (*SD*) at age 12. It will be noted, too, that the standard deviations fluctuate around 16 and 17 as a median value. The standard deviation of the composite IQs (Forms L and M) is 16.4 for the entire standardization group of subjects.

In respect to the fluctuations in IQ variability, the authors state: "Notwithstanding our strenuous efforts to correct for . . . errors of sampling, complete success is hardly to be expected, and a considerable degree of irregular fluctuation in the found magnitudes of IQ variability from age to age could reasonably be attributed to these sources of error. . . . Since inspection of the values reveals no marked relationship between IQ variability and CA over the age range as a whole, we may accept 16 points as approximately the representative value of the standard deviation of IQs for an unselected population" (32, pp. 39–40). As evidence to justify this position, the authors of the scale present the graph shown in Figure 10.3. These distribution curves of composite (L and M) intelligence quotients indicate that their variability is approximately the same for the three age-level groupings.[2]

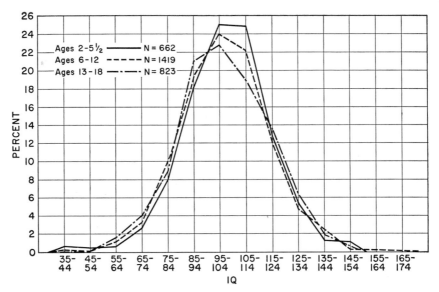

Fig. 10.3. Distribution of composite L-M IQs at three age levels. From Terman and Merrill (32, p. 41). By permission.

Proceeding on the basis of the foregoing reasoning, that the standard deviation of IQs is 16 points and that IQ values are comparable at all age levels, Terman and Merrill provide a table of intelligence-quotient equivalents in terms of standard deviations, using 16 IQ points as equal to one *SD*. Thus, an individual having an IQ of 116 is given a standard score of +1.00; an IQ of 84 is given a standard score of −1.00, etc.[3]

The difficulty presented by unequal sigmas at the different age levels has been overcome in a more satisfactory manner in the 1960 revision by using the deviation intelligence quotient.

Suggested Classification of Revised Stanford-Binet IQs. The classification in Table 10.6 has been provided by one of the authors of

[2] Some critics have not accepted the argument and conclusions of Terman and Merrill. It is our purpose, at this stage, only to present the scale and its rationale.

[3] This practice, apparently viewed with favor, since the table of equivalents was presented, is of questionable validity. It disregards the possibility that individual ranks might be different if standardization of test items were more satisfactory at those age levels where the given *SD*s were appreciably above or below 16.

the 1937 revision (33, p. 18). It will be noted that the nomenclature and
the percents in each of the several categories differ some from those of the
1916 instrument.

Like all such tables, its purpose is primarily descriptive and, also, to
serve as an aid in the ordering and analysis of testing results. The table is
valuable, as well, in showing an approximate distribution of intelligence
quotients throughout most of the range of mental ability.

TABLE 10.6

DISTRIBUTION AND CLASSIFICATION OF COMPOSITE L-M IQS OF THE STANDARDIZATION GROUP

IQ	N	Percent	Classification
160–169	1	0.03	Very superior
150–159	6	0.2	Very superior
140–149	32	1.1	Very superior
130–139	89	3.1	Superior
120–129	239	8.2	Superior
110–119	524	18.1	High average
100–109	685	23.5	Normal or average
90–99	667	23.0	Normal or average
80–89	422	14.5	Low average
70–79	164	5.6	Borderline defective
60–69	57	2.0	Mentally defective
50–59	12	0.4	Mentally defective
40–49	6	0.2	Mentally defective
30–39	1	0.03	Mentally defective

SOURCE: Terman and Merrill (32, p. 42). By permission.

Analysis of Functions Tested.   The items of both Forms L and
M have been analyzed by factorial methods. McNemar, who made the
first and major analysis, concluded that at each of the several age levels the
items test ("are saturated with") a common factor (g), and that this common factor is the same one at all age levels (hence it may be called g).
The *weight* of the common factor differs somewhat among the various age
levels; but the common factor accounts, on the average, for about forty
percent of the differences (variance) in scores—hence for about forty percent of the differences in performance among a group of testees.

The statistical results also suggest the presence of group factors at the
following ages: 2, 2½, 6, 18, and possibly 7 and 11. These are second factors (group factors) that account for from five to eleven percent of the differences; a third factor (another group factor) contributes from four to

seven percent. The group factors do not appear to be identical at all age levels, nor are they at all well defined with regard to the psychological processes involved in them. Tentatively, however, McNemar suggests that several of these group factors, at different levels, might be called "memory for designs," "motor," "verbal." *The most definite and significant conclusion, however, is that one factor, g, is sufficient to account for the intercorrelations of test items, with the few exceptions noted.*[4]

In another factor analysis, the statistics indicated that after the age of 4, the Stanford-Binet scale measures a general factor (16).[5] This same investigator ascribes test performance in the first two years to "sensori-motor alertness." This does not necessarily apply to the Stanford-Binet, the lowest level of which is year 2. Between 2 and 4 years, he finds that a second factor, "persistence," is operative.

On the basis of an inspection of the test items themselves and of psychological analyses of the items, it is hardly possible to accept persistence as the principal factor accounting for test performance between ages 2 and 4; nor sensori-motor alertness as a principal factor, if it persists beyond the age of 2 years.

As a result of McNemar's factor analysis, all items "highly saturated" with the general factor are included in the 1960 revision, although some with lower loadings are also included. Furthermore, biserial correlations of performance on individual test items with total-test score were such as to confirm previous findings that the 1960 scale has high general-factor validity.[6]

When complex and comprehensive ("global") types of test items are used in a scale, as in the Stanford-Binet, it is not surprising that attempts to isolate relatively simple *group factors* through statistical analysis yield results that are indefinite and at best tentative. The reason is that these items, being complex, involve a number of interacting psychological processes, organized in varying degrees. Group and specific factors will be found most clearly when the test items employed are fractionations and small segments of a whole pattern of mental functioning. But such fractionation can destroy "the whole" and can fail to reveal the kinds of mental operations with which the examining psychologist is often most concerned.

The identification of a general factor in a revision of the Binet scale

[4] For an analysis that is not in agreement with McNemar's (23), see L. V. Jones (17).

[5] The author of this study calls the general factor "manipulation of symbols." The meaning of this term is much the same as Terman's concept of ability to carry on thinking with abstract terms; but it is less satisfactory since reasoning and thinking involve more than "manipulation."

[6] "Evidence that this Form [1960] measures the same intellective functions at all parts of the scale is better for the intermediate and upper age levels than for the preschool levels where few changes have been made and our population samples are less good" (33, p. 35).

should not occasion any surprise, for it will be recalled that Binet himself set out to develop an instrument that should test an individual's general intelligence by means of sampling a variety of mental activities that are manifestations of such intelligence. It appears, therefore, that contemporary statistical analyses, applied to the age scale, are confirming Binet's psychological insights.

It was found, also—as Spearman had shown in his earlier analyses—that the various kinds of test items differed in the extent to which they tested (are loaded with) the general factor. The following listing shows which items were found to have high loadings of the general factor, and which had low loadings (23, 33).

AGES 2 TO 4½

High Loadings	Low Loadings
Picture vocabulary	Block building: tower
Identifying objects by name	Block building: bridge
Response to pictures	Three-hole formboard: rotated
Comparison: balls and sticks	Motor coordination
Comprehension	Copying a circle
Opposite analogies	Drawing a cross
Pictorial identification	Three commissions
Naming materials [used in making various objects]	Stringing beads

AGES 5 TO 11

High Loadings	Low Loadings
Pictorial likenesses and differences	Paper folding: triangle
Similarities: two things	Patience: fitting rectangles
Vocabulary	Copying a bead chain
Verbal absurdities	Reproducing a bead chain from memory
Similarities and differences	Picture absurdities
Naming the days of the week	Word naming [free association]
Dissected sentences	Word naming: animals
Abstract words [definitions]	Block counting

AGES 12 TO SUPERIOR ADULT III

High Loadings	Low Loadings
Vocabulary	Problems of fact
Verbal absurdities	Reproducing a bead chain from memory
Abstract words [definitions]	Memory for stories
Differences between abstract words	Enclosed box problem
Arithmetical reasoning	Papercutting [visual imagery]
Proverbs	Plan of search
Essential differences	Repeating digits [forward]
Sentence building	Repeating digits: reversed

Examination of the items that have low loadings reveals that they test only a very limited range of functioning and that, with two exceptions, they involve only the following processes: visualization (space perception and spatial relationships), visual imagery, and rote memory (immediate recall). All of these test items among the low loadings, falling under the foregoing categories, are lacking, relatively, in complexity and would, therefore, not have the differentiating power of the more complex tasks required by the items having high loadings. The exceptions are word naming (random and animals), and problems of fact. The latter is properly considered to be a test of reasoning. Its low loading with g is therefore surprising, but no explanation is apparent or available.[7] Random word naming tests richness of free association; word naming of animals tests controlled association. A possible explanation of their low loadings might be that they are fairly routine tasks that do not require the reasoning (organization, analysis) demanded by the items having high loadings within the same range of ages (5–11).

The foregoing listings are significant for at least two additional and important reasons. First, a knowledge of test items that have high or low loadings of the general factor enables the examining psychologist to make a more thorough analytical and meaningful evaluation of an individual's over-all test performance. The examiner is thus in a better position to evaluate the strength of the general factor in a particular testee. This is particularly valuable if the psychological nature of the general factor has been determined. Second, inspection of the lists of items having high loading strongly indicates that the general, or common, factor is one that involves acquisition of, use of, and reasoning with symbols—namely, language and number—even though the testing of these begins at an elementary level and at times utilizes nonverbal materials in presenting the problem (for example, pictures, sticks). The mental activities required by these test items have very much in common with Spearman's view that intelligence is essentially the ability to educe relations and correlates.

Specifically, the following processes are involved in the test items having high loadings: acquisition and use of vocabulary; verbal analysis of a situation; verbal and numerical concept formation; insights into similarities and differences (also involving concept formation); analysis and synthesis of materials, both nonverbal and verbal; organization and reorganization of materials, both nonverbal and verbal.

The list of items given above (based on statistical calculations) and the indicated psychological functions that are involved provide an illustration of how statistical and psychological analyses work together. They also make it clear that superficial observations of differences between test items

---

[7] It is probable that specific environmental advantages and disadvantages operate here. See test item no. 5, year XI, 1960 revision.

can be misleading as to their essential psychological processes. For example, the test items at early age levels requiring identification of objects by name or use might be regarded simply as tests of information or of specific rote learning, whereas they actually have much in common with items that test "comprehension," and which are more obviously tests of reasoning. Or, at a somewhat later age level, ability to define certain words (vocabulary test) might be regarded simply as the result of specific learning and verbal facility, whereas actually it has much in common with perception of pictorial (as well as verbal) similarities and differences.

It is useful to classify test items as "information," "word knowledge," "perception of forms," "reasoning," etc.; but the point is that such classification does not necessarily signify that each of the subtest classifications measures a distinct group factor or a special factor.[8]

Types of Items. Bearing this important distinction in mind, then, we may indicate the types of items included in the Stanford-Binet scale.[9]

Test Items	Functions Involved
Years 2–5	
Form perception and manipulation (blocks, formboards, stringing wooden beads) / Perception of differences in size and form	Visual perception and analysis
Visual-motor operations	Visual analysis plus motor development
Perception of relationships (in pictures)	Visual perception plus beginnings of concept formation
Rote memory (using digits and sentences)	Immediate recall
Use of words in combination / Identifying objects by name or use / Following directions	Language development and comprehension

[8] McNemar's findings are in close agreement with those of an independent study made in Great Britain. Cyril Burt reports that a common factor accounts for 42 percent of Stanford-Binet test variance, and that two subsidiary factors account, respectively, for 12 percent and 16 percent of test-score differences. The close correspondence obtained in the United States and in England gives additional weight to and confidence in the Stanford-Binet scale as an instrument for measuring intelligence, particularly of children and adolescents. See (10).

[9] Since the Wechsler scale utilizes many of the same types of items as the Stanford-Binet, additional factors affecting test performance on these items will be presented in connection with the Wechsler scale in the next chapter.

Test Items	*Functions Involved*

Years 2–5

Verbal comprehension and word knowledge Understanding of "opposites"	. . . .	Reasoning with abstractions and concept formation

Years 6–12

Form perception	. . . .	Visual analysis
Visual-motor operations	. . . .	Visual analysis plus motor development
Rote memory (using digits and sentences)	. . . .	Immediate recall
Word knowledge (concrete and abstract)	. . . .	Language development and concept formation
Verbal comprehension	. . . .	Reasoning with abstractions and concept formation
Number concepts Arithmetical reasoning	. . . .	Number concept formation and reasoning with abstractions

Year 13—Superior Adult III

Visual analysis and imagery Perception of visual relationships Visual-motor operations	. . . .	Visual perception and analysis plus reasoning with nonverbal materials
Rote memory (using digits, words, and sentences)	. . . .	Immediate recall
Word knowledge	. . . .	Language development and concept formation
Synthesis of verbal materials Problem solving, using verbal materials	. . . .	Reasoning with abstractions
Verbal analysis Arithmetical problems Analysis and comprehension of symbols	. . . .	Concept formation plus reasoning with abstractions

The Short Scale. It is possible to administer an abbreviated form of the scale, the constituent test items having been specified by the authors. A short scale, presumably, is used when the examiner does not need as accurate an index of measurement as it is possible to obtain and when the necessary time is not available for a full-length examination. The use of an abbreviated form, however, should be discouraged, for when it is at all desirable to administer a test of mental ability, it would be unwise not to require the greatest possible accuracy.

The 1960 Revision

Merrill summarizes the changes made and the differences between the 1937 revision and that of 1960 as follows (33, pp. 39–40):

The Stanford Revision in 1960 retains the main characteristics of scales of the Binet type. It is an age scale making use of age standards of performance. It undertakes to measure intelligence regarded as general mental adaptability. The 1960 scale incorporates in a single form, designated as the L-M Form, the best subtests from the 1937 scales. The selection of subtests to be included in the 1960 scale was based on records of tests administered during the five-year period from 1950 to 1954. The main assessment group for evaluating the subtests consisted of 4498 subjects aged 2½ to 18 years. Changes in difficulty of subtests were determined by comparing the percents passing the individual tests in the 1950's with the percents passing in the 1930's constituting the original standardization group. Criteria for selection of test items were: (1) increase in percent passing with age (or mental age); and (2) validity determined by biserial correlation of item with total score. Changes consisted in the elimination or relocation of tests which have been found to have changed significantly in difficulty since the original standardization; the elimination or substitution of tests which are no longer suitable by reason of cultural changes; further clarification of ambiguities of scoring principles and test administration; and the correction of structural inadequacies of the 1937 scale, first by introducing adjustments to make the average mental age that the scale gives more nearly equal to the average chronological age at each age level and second, by providing revised and extended IQ tables that incorporate built-in adjustments for atypical variability of IQs at certain age levels so that the standard score IQs provided are comparable at all age levels.

From the foregoing quotation it is clear that although the 1960 revision is an improved version of the 1937 scales (L and M), one important innovation has been introduced. This is the deviation intelligence quotient, the necessity and meaning of which have already been explained. A second innovation, not mentioned in the quotation, is this: IQ tables have been extended to include chronological ages 17 and 18 because retest find-

TABLE 10.7

THE ASSESSMENT GROUP TABULATED BY AREAS

	Form L item analysis	Form M item analysis	L-M stratified samples	Pretesting modified or substitute items	Total number of subjects
New Jersey	892				892
Minnesota	850	208			1058
Iowa [a]	102				(636)
New York and California				96 + 588	684
Massachusetts	91				91
California	1258	897	200		2355
Totals	3193	1105	200	684	5716
Main sample		4498			

[a] The Iowa total includes 336 cases, tested in 1940–44, for comparison with a similar sample similarly obtained tested ten years later in 1950–54. Both CA and MA breakdowns were made in an attempt to make a study of comparable populations, but the numbers of cases in each CA or MA class were too small to make comparisons meaningful. The number of cases that could actually be used is further reduced by the small numbers at the higher MA categories.

SOURCE: Terman and Merrill (33, p. 21). By permission.

ings indicated that mental development, as measured by the Stanford-Binet, continues at least that long.

Basically, as Terman and Merrill point out, the deviation IQ of the 1960 scale is a standard score derived, theoretically, from a mean of 100 and a standard deviation of 16. As a matter of fact, however, the mean IQs found with the 1937 scale were, with two exceptions, slightly above the ideal of 100 (see Table 10.4). In finding a deviation IQ, therefore, the means (of Forms L and M, averaged and rounded) in Table 10.4 are used. The deviation IQ is calculated by use of the following formula:

$$DIQ = (IQ_x - IQ_m) K + 100$$

where $K = 16/SD$. In this formula, IQ_x is the conventional, or ratio, IQ (MA/CA). IQ_m is the 1937 mean IQ at the age in question, shown in Table 10.4. SD is the smoothed standard deviation of 1937 IQs, derived from Table 10.5.[10] K is the ratio of the accepted standard deviation, 16, to

[10] Details of the smoothing of the conventional IQs are not provided in the Terman-Merrill manual. In a bulletin issued by Houghton Mifflin, S. R. Pinneau states: "The standard deviations were arithmetically smoothed three times and the curve of these

those smoothed for the 1937 scale. It is clear that where, at a given age level, the 1937 *SD* is *greater* than 16, *K* will be less than one, and the variation of IQ_x from IQ_m will be decreased when multiplied by *K*. Conversely, when the 1937 *SD* is *less* than 16, the variation of IQ_x from IQ_m will be increased. Thus, in terms of deviations from their respective means, the DIQs will be comparable at all age levels.

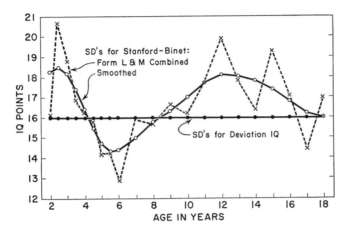

FIG. 10.4. From *Testing Today,* No. 2, Boston, Mass.: Houghton Mifflin Co. By permission.

Consider, for example, the two following instances, using conventional IQs.

CA:	12	CA:	6
MA:	15	MA:	7 years, 6 months
IQ:	125	IQ:	125

The 1937 mean IQ (L and M averaged and rounded) is 102 for age 12 and 100 for age 6. The correction (*K*) for age 12 is .88 (since its smoothed 1937 *SD* is 18.2), while the correction for age 6 is 1.11 (since its smoothed 1937 *SD* is 14.4).[11] When these values are substituted in the formula, we get a DIQ of 120 (rounded) for the 12-year-old and 128 (rounded) for the 6-year-old. In each instance the derived DIQ has the same relation to the *SD* of 16 as its corresponding conventional IQ had to its original *SD* (18.2 or

---

smoothed values was superimposed upon the graph of the raw standard deviations [Forms L and M combined]. . ." (see Fig. 10.4). *Testing Today,* December 1959, no. 2, p. 5. Boston: Houghton Mifflin Co. In a personal communication, Pinneau states: "The standard deviations of Forms L and M for an age level were squared, summed, and divided by two and the square root taken to give the intermediate values which were desired, so they would be equally applicable to Forms L and M."

[11] For the table of the mean conventional IQs and "constants" (*K*), see Terman and Merrill (33, Appendix A).

14.4); but now both deviation IQs are based on a common standard score and may be compared directly. By contrast, although they had the same numerical values, the original and conventional IQ of 125 for the 6-year-old was higher in the distribution of his age group (since the smoothed SD equals 14.4) than was the 125 in the distribution of 12-year-olds (since its smoothed SD equals 18.2).

Essentially, the 1960 scale is the same as that of 1937; but it is an improved version because of relocation of some items, selection of the most discriminative items from Forms L and M, and the substitution of the deviation IQ for the conventional one. It is to be noted, however, that in no case will the former differ so markedly from the latter as to move an individual's revised rating into a significantly different level and category, either upward or downward. The reason for this is that the correction factor (K), for changing conventional IQs into deviation IQs, is no less than .88 and no greater than 1.12 at any age level, while almost exactly fifty percent of the correction factors are between .94 and 1.06.

Evaluations and Criticisms

The Stanford-Binet scales have been subjected to criticism and evaluation on theoretical, experimental, and practical grounds. On the whole, psychologists and educators who have had experience with these instruments are in essential agreement that they have proved to be highly useful in the hands of qualified persons. There are, however, a number of questions to be considered.

Is the age-scale (Binet) type of test preferable to the point-scale type? The standardization of an age scale is much more laborious than that of a point scale. The result is that when experience and experimentation reveal certain defects and inadequacies in an age scale, the difficulties in making the indicated changes are so great as to be a deterrent to early revision. Hence, twenty-one years elapsed between the first and the second versions (1916 to 1937) and twenty-three years between the second and the third (1937–1960), even though some difficulties in interpreting certain responses became apparent after several years, a few items appeared to become obsolete within relatively few years, and the age-level placements of some items were questioned (21). Terman and Merrill report that the 1960 revision is an improvement in these respects. One realizes the difficulties of incorporating suggested improvements and corrections when it is recalled that the authors of the 1937 Stanford-Binet made six revisions of Form L before they were satisfied with the age placement and grouping of test items, so that satisfactory mental ages, intelligence quotients, and IQ distributions could be derived.

In the case of a point scale, on the other hand, it is a much simpler process to revise age norms. All other things being equal, of course, the simpler and easier methods should be employed to achieve a desired goal in psychological testing. But simplicity and ease alone should not be the decisive considerations. The crucial question is whether the age scale or the point scale provides a superior means of obtaining a measure of an individual's mental ability. Thus far, although the views of competent professional persons are not unanimous, it appears that the age scale is preferable for use with children and young adolescents. But when older adolescents and adults are to be examined, it has often been found that point scales (for example, the Wechsler) are preferable (15). Also, the use of point scales having well-defined subtests has been increasing because, in clinical cases, they facilitate "scatter analysis" of scores on the subtests (see Chapter 14).

Does the Stanford-Binet consist of a variety of disconnected tests? This scale has been criticized at times as being only that. This criticism, however, is based upon a failure to take into account the theory of intelligence, the method of measurement, and the basis upon which test items were selected; namely, the sampling of *general ability* by means of a representative variety of types of items, arranged by age level, in order to obtain an adequate estimate of the mental processes involved. The factorial analyses already discussed show that the test items measure primarily a general factor common to all age levels of the scale. Furthermore, the high biserial correlations found between individual items and total scores demonstrate the presence of a common factor. On cursory inspection, the items may *seem* to be unassociated; but psychological and statistical analyses demonstrate that in actuality such is not the case.[12]

Is the composite, or "global," type of scale (such as the Stanford-Binet) preferable to the factorial analyzed type, in which "factors" are separately tested and scored? The final answer to this question will depend upon whether the factorial type of scale proves to be more valid, more accurate, and more useful than the composite type has been in clinical work or in educational and vocational guidance. At present two scales of the global type (Stanford-Binet and Wechsler scales) continue as the most widely used instruments for the measurement of *individual* mental ability (as contrasted with group testing), especially in school and clinical studies of individual "problem cases." At present, also, some "multi-factor" *group* tests are being rather widely employed for purposes of educational and vocational guidance. This type of device is discussed in Chapter 17.

[12] Even those statistical analyses that emphasize *group factors,* rather than a general factor, refute this criticism.

Is the Stanford-Binet scale too heavily weighted with verbal materials?
A criticism heard with some frequency against both the old and the
new revisions is that these scales place a premium upon "verbal intelligence" and that subjects having language handicaps are penalized and
incorrectly rated. In reply to this criticism, Terman and others hold that
the most essential and most significant aspect of higher thought processes
is the ability to do conceptual and abstract thinking; that is, to operate
with language, number, and other symbols. It is maintained, also, that the
vocabulary test, when used with children from homes where English is the
primary language, has higher value than any other part of the scale.

It must be emphasized, however, that this is not so in the case of a child
who, even though he comes from such a home, has reading or language
difficulties due not to lack of capacity but to visual or auditory defects or
anomalies.

In actual clinical practice, the examiner should always supplement
an essentially verbal test of intelligence with one of the nonverbal type
if he has any reason to suspect that the former penalizes the subject.
There will be occasions also when it will be desirable to obtain a rating
for an individual on both types, even where no language handicap is indicated, for the purpose of comparing two or more aspects of a subject's
ability. While the correlation between performance on verbal and on
some nonverbal tests of mental ability is high, coefficients of correlation
reflect *group* trends and relationships; and unless the correlation coefficient is perfect (plus or minus 1.00), there are always individual exceptions from the generalization that can be made on the basis of the
coefficient; hence the need, at times, for the study of the several aspects of
ability in an individual case.

Is the Stanford-Binet scale a test of school learning? As stated in an
earlier chapter, any scale must test mental ability through its manifestations, through activity of some kind. And as Binet originally pointed out,
the tests must be adapted to the environment of the subjects to be rated.
It is reasonable and sound, therefore, that a scale designed to test mental
ability primarily of American children and adolescents should utilize the
effects of common schooling experiences, as well as effects of some other
common experiences. To say that the Stanford-Binet or any other scale is
only a measure of school learning is unwarranted. Differences in quality
and extent of opportunity to learn, in school and out, will have an effect
upon intelligence-test scores; but such differences in opportunity do not
in themselves account for all individual differences in ability that are
found. Good schooling and other good environmental conditions nurture
an individual's mental capacities and provide optimal conditions for his
mental development. Thus, it can be said that the Stanford-Binet and

other scales provide ratings of intelligence, within limits of error, under existing school conditions, general environmental conditions, and clinical conditions. Obviously, therefore, the examiner must know the general developmental background of the individual he is testing, if his interpretation of test results is to be sound.

Several studies of satisfactory and unsatisfactory responses on the Stanford-Binet have found that bright and superior children answer correctly more of the "intellectual" items than do normal or dull children (2, 22). These items include the verbal and numerical, utilizing symbols and abstractions. This finding does not mean that bright and superior children have attained their ratings on mental tests only as a result of schooling. It is to be expected that individuals who are potentially above average in mental ability will be superior in dealing with situations and problems employing language and number; for the greater the capacity of the individual is for mental development, the greater will be his ability to deal with symbols and to handle situations and problems at the level of abstraction. The converse has also long been known; namely, that one of the principal deficiencies of the mentally retarded and mentally defective is their inability to deal with materials and concepts at the levels of abstraction. It will be recalled that one definition states that intelligence is the ability to deal with abstractions. It will be recalled, also, that the educing of relations and correlates extends upward to the use of symbols (language and number).

Are some of the items in the Stanford-Binet scale obsolete?   Since any test utilizes materials from the environment in which it is to be used, and since environments normally undergo change, it is to be expected that some items in any test will in time become culturally obsolete. In the 1937 Stanford-Binet there were a few such items. Some examples follow:

> Identifying a toy steam locomotive by name
> Identifying objects (pictures) by use, such as an old-fashioned kitchen stove
> Response to a picture (Messenger Boy, year 12)

Terman and Merrill state: "In the 1930's . . . 69 percent of the three-year-olds of the standardization group recognized and could name 5 out of 6 items consisting of miniature object reproductions of shoe, watch, telephone, flag, jack-knife, and stove. In the 1950's only 11 percent of children whose mental age on the scale was three years were able to do so" (33, p. 19). This change can be explained by the obsolescence of some of the objects.

There are not many such items in this scale. In the case of some non-obsolete items, however, it becomes necessary, in time, to revise, to some extent, the responses that are acceptable for credit. The following item is an example. "What's the thing for you to do when you are on your way to school and see that you are in danger of being late?" (Year 7).

When scoring an unusual response to an item like this, the qualified examiner is warranted in exercising his judgment as to its correctness; in fact, he has to do that. And his decision will be based upon his familiarity with the psychological processes being tested by the particular item.[13]

Does the Stanford-Binet scale test different abilities at different age levels?   The answer to this question is to be found largely in the preceding discussion of "Analysis of Functions Tested" in this chapter. There it was stated that two major analyses (by McNemar and Burt) found that the scale measures principally a general factor that is common to all age levels, and in addition there appear to be group factors at 2, 2½, 6, 18, and possibly at 7 and 11. It was pointed out that the items having low loadings of the general factor were, with minor exceptions, tests that required the use of visual perception, visual imagery, and rote memory. Emphasis was placed, also, upon the necessity of distinguishing between item-type classifications of tests (vocabulary, arithmetical reasoning, etc.) and basic psychological processes involved in each.

Among the criteria used in the selection and retention of test items for the 1960 revision was the biserial correlation of each item with the total score. Furthermore, inspection of the retained items shows that there are relatively few items with low loadings of the general factor. Thus, the 1960 revision will measure the general factor throughout the scale to a more marked degree than does that of 1937.

Does the scale measure originality and creative abilities?   The answer is that it does not measure these abilities, as such, to an important degree. This aspect of intelligence was discussed in Chapter 7, "Definitions and Analyses of Intelligence." There it was pointed out that the requirement of *objectivity* in standardizing and scoring tests practically excludes tests of creativeness and originality. But, as also stated, while not all individuals who achieve high scores on intelligence tests evidence originality and creative ability, those who are capable of originality and creative mental activity generally do obtain high test scores. It is possible to say, therefore, that persons having creativeness and originality will be found generally in the group who attain superior ratings on the intelligence scales. Furthermore, although originality and creativeness cannot be in-

---

[13] We have had a new and interesting response, resulting from recent scientific developments, to test item 5, year XI, Problem Situation. The problem presented reads: "Donald went walking in the woods. He saw a pretty little animal that he tried to take home for a pet. It got away from him, but when he got home, his family immediately burned all his clothes. Why?" Several boys answered: "Because the animal was radioactive."

cluded in the prescribed objective scoring, a qualified examiner will note responses indicating these traits and will include them in his interpretation and evaluation of the examinee's performance.

Is the Stanford-Binet scale adequate at the adult level? The standardization group of the 1937 scale included individuals of 18 years, but it did not include an adult population. Therefore, the test items at the several adult levels rest upon theoretical considerations already mentioned, rather than upon actual samplings of adult performance. One result, due perhaps to the methods used in standardizing the scale at superior adult levels, has been its frequently observed inadequacy with college students who, as a group, would be ranked above average. The inadequacy of the scale is especially marked when administered to very superior students, for it is not difficult enough at the higher levels of adulthood.

In the 1960 revision, the retained items are an improvement throughout the scale. IQ tables have been adjusted to include ages 17 and 18, because retest findings in more recent years indicate that mental growth continues to age 18. The ratings obtained to age 18, therefore, will be more valid than previously. Consequently, too, the ratings above age 18 should be more valid for the large majority of individuals, with the probable exception of those at the highest levels of mental ability.

Some psychologists have questioned whether certain items and materials included at adult levels are of sufficient interest to persons of their age. The 1960 revision is an improvement in this respect, but it should be clear that it is not possible to provide items which will appeal to the *special* interests of many adults. In fact, it is undesirable to give any group such an advantage. On the other hand, the test items should be at a sufficiently advanced level of maturity, such as will evoke a favorable and cooperative attitude on the part of the examinee.

There is also the question of the soundness of using the mental-age index for individuals who score above the mental level of the average adult. The reason for this question has already been presented. Many psychologists, therefore, prefer to discard the mental age at adult levels in favor of percentile ranks, decile ranks, and standard scores.

Is the Stanford-Binet scale clinically useful? Judging by the extent to which it is employed, the answer must be a strong affirmative. Examiners find the scale useful not only for deriving a mental age and an intelligence quotient, but also as the "framework" within which a psychological interview may be held. If the scale is to serve this purpose, the examiner must have considerable clinical experience and skill to interpret and evaluate a subject's responses and behavior. Nearly all psychologists agree that there is great value to a clinician and to a school psychologist in having available objective and standardized devices which also permit sufficient flexibility to meet the demands of a particular case (34).

As new scales are devised—built, perhaps, upon different conceptions and theories—they will have to be subjected to both experimental investigation and practical use before their value can be compared with that of the Stanford-Binet. A valid judgment cannot be reached on *a priori* grounds. In the meantime, the great value of the Stanford-Binet scale has been demonstrated, and psychologists will continue to use it. They will bring to bear their insights on the interpretation of the *behavior* of the persons being examined and on the interpretation of the *test results* obtained.

References

1. Aborn, M., and G. F. Derner. IQ variability in relation to age on the revised Stanford-Binet. *Journal of Consulting Psychology*, 1951, *15*, 231–235.
2. Baldwin, A. L. The relative difficulty of Stanford-Binet items and their relation to IQ. *Journal of Personality*, 1948, *16*, 417–430.
3. Baldwin, A. L. Variations in Stanford-Binet IQ resulting from an artifact of the test. *Journal of Personality*, 1948, *17*, 186–198.
4. Bayley, N. Consistency and variability in the growth of intelligence from birth to eighteen years. *Journal of Genetic Psychology*, 1949, *75*, 165–196.
5. Bond, E. A. *Tenth Grade Abilities and Achievements.* Teachers College Contributions to Education, 1940, no. 813. New York: Columbia University Press.
6. Bradway, K. P. IQ constancy on the revised Stanford-Binet from the preschool to the junior high school level. *Journal of Genetic Psychology*, 1944, *65*, 197–217.
7. Bradway, K. P. Predictive value of Stanford-Binet preschool items. *Journal of Educational Psychology*, 1945, *36*, 1–16.
8. Bradway, K. P. An experimental study of factors associated with Stanford-Binet IQ changes from preschool to junior high school. *Journal of Genetic Psychology*, 1945, *66*, 107–128.
9. Bradway, K. P., *et al.* Preschool IQs after twenty-five years. *Journal of Educational Psychology*, 1958, *49*, 278–281.
10. Burt, C., and E. John. A factorial analysis of the Terman-Binet tests. *British Journal of Educational Psychology*, 1942, *12;* part I, 117–127; part II, 156–161.
11. Cole, R. An item analysis of the Terman-Merrill revision of the Binet tests. *British Journal of Psychology: Statistical Section 1*, 1948, 137–151.
12. Fisher, G. M., *et al.* Comparability of intelligence quotients of mental defectives on the Wechsler adult intelligence scale and the 1960 revision

of the Stanford-Binet. *Journal of Consulting Psychology*, 1961, *25*, 192–195.

13. Fleming, V. V. A study of the subtests in the revised Stanford-Binet scales, Forms L and M. *Journal of Genetic Psychology*, 1944, *64*, 3–36.

14. Gehman, I., and R. Matyas. Stability of the WISC and Binet tests. *Journal of Consulting Psychology*, 1956, *20*, 150–152.

15. Halpern, F. A comparison of the revised Stanford L and the Bellevue adult intelligence test as clinical instruments. *Psychiatric Quarterly Supplement*, 1942, *16*, 206–211.

16. Hofstaetter, P. R. The changing composition of intelligence: a study of the t-technique. *Journal of Genetic Psychology*, 1954, *85*, 159–164.

17. Jones, L. V. A factor analysis of the Stanford-Binet at four age-levels. *Psychometrika*, 1949, *14*, 299–331.

18. Jones, L. V. Primary abilities in the Stanford-Binet, age 13. *Journal of Genetic Psychology*, 1954, *84*, 125–147.

19. Kagan, J., et al. Personality and IQ change. *Journal of Abnormal and Social Psychology*, 1958, *56*, 261–266.

20. Katz, E. The pointing modification of the revised Stanford-Binet intelligence scales. *American Journal of Mental Deficiency*, 1958, *62*, 698–707.

21. Krugman, M. Some impressions of the revised Stanford-Binet scale. *Journal of Educational Psychology*, 1939, *30*, 594–603.

22. Magaret, A., and C. W. Thompson. Differential test responses of normal, superior, and mentally defective subjects. *Journal of Abnormal and Social Psychology*, 1950, *45*, 163–167.

23. McNemar, Q. *The Revision of the Stanford-Binet Scale*. Boston: Houghton Mifflin Company, 1942.

24. Mitchell, M. B. The revised Stanford-Binet for adults. *Journal of Educational Research*, 1941, *34*, 516–521.

25. Mitchell, M. B. The revised Stanford-Binet for university students. *Journal of Educational Research*, 1943, *36*, 507–511.

26. Mussen, P., et al. Some further evidence on the validity of the WISC. *Journal of Consulting Psychology*, 1952, *16*, 410–411.

27. Parkyn, G. W. The clinical significance of IQs on the revised Stanford-Binet scale. *Journal of Educational Psychology*, 1945, *36*, 114–118.

28. Pintner, R., et al. *Supplementary Guide for the Revised Stanford-Binet Scale (Form L)*. Applied Psychology Monographs, 1944, no. 3.

29. Roberts, J. A. F., and M. A. Mellone. On adjustment of Terman-Merrill IQs to secure comparability at different ages. *British Journal of Psychology: Statistical Section 5*, 1952, 65–79.

30. Sontag, L. W., et al. *Mental Growth and Personality Development: A Longitudinal Study*. Monograph, Society for Research in Child Development, 1958, *23*, no. 2.

31. Stoddard, G. D. *The Meaning of Intelligence*. New York: The Macmillan Company, 1943.

32. Terman, L. M., and M. A. Merrill. *Measuring Intelligence*. Boston: Houghton Mifflin Company, 1937.

33. Terman, L. M., and M. A. Merrill. *Stanford-Binet Intelligence Scale: Manual for the Third Revision: Form L-M.* Boston: Houghton Mifflin Company, 1960.

34. Vernon, P. E. The Stanford-Binet test as a psychometric method. *Character and Personality,* 1937, *6,* 99–113.

35. Wile, I. S. and R. Davis. A study of failures on the Stanford-Binet in relation to behavior and school problems. *Journal of Educational Psychology,* 1941, *32,* 275–284.

II.

THE WECHSLER SCALES

The Binet scale and its several revisions are largely verbal in content, although some nonverbal items are included, especially at the early age levels. There are, however, other scales that are wholly, or in large part, of the performance or nonverbal type. In performance tests, the use of language is eliminated from test content and response, although directions are generally given orally. In a few instances the directions, too, are given without the use of language, by employing pantomime instead.

The test materials of a nonverbal scale consist of concrete objects such as formboards, cubes (to be arranged in specified ways), mazes, geometric figures, pictures (cut up, to be correctly assembled), and others that will be described in later sections. The individual's responses depend upon manipulations, visual perceptions, and interpretations that are implied by what he *does* rather than by anything he says.

Performance tests were first devised as a supplement to or substitute for the Stanford-Binet scale in order to examine deaf, illiterate, or non-English speaking subjects. Since their introduction, the use of nonverbal tests has been extended; for they are now utilized with children who have or are suspected of having reading difficulties, with those who have attended school irregularly and thus might have been handicapped in developing verbal ability, and with persons who might have been handicapped by markedly inferior environmental conditions. Nonverbal tests are used, also, by examiners who, for any other reason, believe that such

a scale will yield a more complete picture of the individual whose capacities are being analyzed and evaluated. The Wechsler scales to be described combine verbal and nonverbal materials within a single instrument to obtain the advantages, comparisons, and contrasts provided by
both types of test items.

Form I (1939)

Range. The first scale, published in 1939, was intended to
test the intelligence of persons from the age of 10 years through 60, although norms were provided beginning at 7.5 years. This, or a similar
beginning level, was necessary if adults and adolescents of inferior mental
levels were to be tested by means of the scale.[1]

Content. The 1939 version (known as the Wechsler-Bellevue
scale), and the 1955 revision (known as the Wechsler Adult Intelligence
Scale), which will be described later in detail, are in part verbal and in
part performance, thus enabling the examiner to obtain three scores and
three intelligence quotients. These are verbal, performance, and full-scale
IQs.

The scales have been constructed in this form on the principle that intelligence involves not only the ability to deal with symbols, abstractions,
and concepts, but also the ability to deal with situations and problems in
which concrete objects, rather than words and numbers, are utilized. The
scales also are put to the pragmatic test of whether a given combination
of items (in this instance verbal and nonverbal) serves the purpose of
individual mental examination and analysis of capacities better than other
combinations.

The types of tests included in this scale are not unique. They were
selected from available sources after a study had been made of a variety of
standardized tests then in use. The objective was the construction of an
effective instrument for adolescents and adults, based upon known and
proved types of psychological materials.

Both Form I and the adult scale of 1955 consist of eleven subtests, six
of them verbal and five nonverbal.[2] The difference between the Stanford-
Binet and the Wechsler scales in regard to arrangement of items is as
follows: in the former, the several types of items are grouped together at
each age level; in the latter, all items of one type are grouped together,
constituting a subtest of the whole. Within each subtest, the intent is to
arrange the items in a sequence of increasing difficulty.[3]

---

[1] A second form was published in 1946.

[2] One of the verbal subtests, "Vocabulary," was originally added as an alternate or
supplement. Now, however, it is used quite regularly.

[3] The eleven subtests will be described later in this chapter.

FIG. 11.1. A 12-year-old girl is shown here taking the block design test of the Bellevue scale. The model of the design to be copied is on the card before her. The examiner is timing her with the stop-watch in his left hand. (Acme Photo.)

Need for an Adult Scale. It will be recalled that Binet's own scales were not suitable for use with adults; nor was the 1916 Stanford-Binet. Although the Stanford-Binet revisions of 1937 and 1960 are better standardized at the upper age levels, they are not intended primarily for adults, whereas the Wechsler scale of 1939 was designed for adolescents and adults, and the 1955 scale is for use with persons above the age of 16 years.

As explained in Chapter 10, it is difficult to use mental ages with above-average adults. The Wechsler scale for adults avoids this difficulty, as will be seen, by not using mental ages at all.

Intelligence testing of adults was begun on a large scale in 1917 with the establishment of a psychological division in the United States Army, in World War I. At that time, the Army Alpha (verbal) and Army Beta (nonverbal) tests were assembled, and with them about 1,750,000 men were tested. This experience in large-scale testing provided the impetus for the development, after the war, of a number of other group tests for adults. But these tests did not prove to be adequate, except for several that were designed for use with selected and limited groups of our population, such as candidates for admission to colleges. (These will be presented in a later chapter.)

The Underlying Theory of Intelligence. The first step was to adopt a theory of the nature of intelligence to serve as a framework within which the test items should fit. The general-factor theory (g) was accepted, requiring that there should be significant intercorrelations among the several subtests of the scale, and that the scale *as a whole* should provide a valid index of an individual's general intelligence.

Having accepted the theory of a general factor, the author of the scale then had to determine which types of test materials should be included in order to measure that factor most effectively. On the basis of past experience, it was decided that both verbal and nonverbal materials, rather than either one alone, provide the most adequate and representative content. Having arrived at this view, the author and his collaborators proceeded to select the particular *types* of subtests that had been used by preceding psychologists, and that experience and experimentation had proved to be valuable. In some instances, specific *items* already in use were included within appropriate subtests; in other instances, it was necessary to create new items for each of the subtests.

Criticisms of Form I. The principal adverse criticism of this scale was directed against the inadequacies and nonrepresentative character of the standardization population. This group consisted of 1081 literate individuals (all white), ranging in age from 17 to 70 years, living in or close to New York City.[4] Since the scale was to provide norms below adult levels, a sampling of school children 16 years of age and younger was also tested. They were selected according to the age–grade distribution of pupils in the New York City schools. The sampling of the school group consisted of 670 white pupils, ranging in age from 7 to 16 years, chosen so as to yield an age–grade distribution that would approximate that of New York City. A small number of institutional mental defectives were also included. This standardization population was considered inadequate both in size and in its geographic narrowness.

When most of the prevailing criteria were used to establish validity (number of years of schooling, teachers' ratings, known groups, range and distribution of IQs, correlation with the Stanford-Binet), the findings, although reasonably satisfactory, were not as numerous and as widespread as they might have been. Nor was the predictive efficiency of the scale demonstrated as convincingly as could be expected, particularly when used with school groups. The probable reason for this is that the scale was developed, to begin with, from psychological work in a hospital clinic. Consequently, its emphasis was on clinical application; research

---

[4] The population sample was an approximation of the occupational distribution of adults, as reported in the United States census of 1930.

publications were heavily weighted on differential diagnosis and other clinical aspects.[5]

Reliability studies were surprisingly meager in number and those that were made were concerned almost exclusively with abnormal groups of subjects. Furthermore, reliability coefficients for each of the subtests were not high enough to warrant making differential diagnoses, which are based upon the patterns ("profiles" or variations) of subtest scores. On the other hand, reliability coefficients for verbal IQs (six subtests), perform-ance IQs (five subtests), and full-scale IQs were quite satisfactory, though not as high as those found with the Stanford-Binet.

The Adult Intelligence Scale (1955)

Although it does not introduce any new principles in content, construction, organization, scoring, or IQ deviation, this edition, known as the Wechsler Adult Intelligence Scale (WAIS), has met some of the adverse criticisms of the 1939 version. The principal changes are in its improved content, extension of the standardization population sample, and improved directions for administering and scoring.[6]

CONTENT.   Range of difficulty has been extended, chiefly downward, in order to assure a score for the lower level of mentally deficient subjects. Upward extension in difficulty has been slight. Progression of difficulty from item to item has been improved. Obsolete items have been re-placed. Items having poor "item validity" and those overlapping others in content have been replaced, as have those that were ambiguous. Illus-trations in the "picture completion" subtest have been more clearly drawn. The "vocabulary" subtest has been revised so as to produce a fairly normal distribution of scores for a representative sample of the population. Maximum scores in verbal and nonverbal subtests and in the full scale are reached by the 25–29 year age group.

POPULATION SAMPLE.   Norms are based upon a sample of 1700 persons, 850 of each sex, from four widely separated geographic areas. The sub-jects ranged in age from 16 to 64 years. The age range was divided into seven age groups, within each of which the numbers were proportioned according to the 1950 United States census with respect to geographic area, race (white and nonwhite), occupation, urban-rural, and years of

---

[5] Differential diagnosis is defined as distinguishing between two or more conditions (classifications, categories) by means of the patterns of symptoms (or indicators) that characterize each condition.

[6] The following discussions of revisions are provided not only to describe the new scale itself, but also to enable the student to understand more clearly the processes of test development and improvement.

formal education. Supplementary data were also obtained for a sample
of older persons ($N = 352$) above 65 years of age.

The Subtests: Verbal. The instrument has six subtests constituting the verbal scale.

1. *Information test.* This test consists of items of information covering
a wide range. (For example, "How many weeks are there in a year?")
The assumptions are that the questions cover a wide enough range of
materials to provide an adequate sampling of information acquired by
a person who has had the usual opportunities of our society; that the
range of an individual's information is an indication of his intellectual
capacity; and that more intelligent persons have broader interests,
more curiosity, and seek more mental stimulation. *This view can be valid,
however, only if the subjects being tested have had the usual opportunities for experience and learning and if the test items are a valid sampling of the opportunities to acquire information.* It is necessary to keep
this caution in mind in evaluating a test of information. Performance on
information tests is susceptible, also, to variations in individual motivation; that is, some bright, self-absorbed persons or those unreceptive to
the offerings of their environment for emotional reasons have unusually
limited funds of information. Others, for motivational reasons quite removed from general intelligence, exhibit an exaggerated and misleading
fund of information. For just these reasons, however, a test of information
is a useful one for clinical purposes, that is, for purposes of diagnosing
personality traits.

2. *General comprehension test.* This part of the scale consists of problem situations in which the subject must comprehend what is involved
in the situations and provide answers to problems presented. (For example, "Why should people pay taxes?") Success on this subtest, it is
held, depends upon possession of practical information, plus ability to
evaluate and utilize past experience. It appears, also, that ability to
verbalize is a factor contributing to success. Tests of general comprehension are now commonly used in intelligence scales; and, it will be
recalled, they were included in the Binet scales. They have been found
valuable clinically in revealing the thought processes, background, feelings, and emotions of the subject.

3. *Arithmetical reasoning.* This part of the Bellevue scale is designed
to test "mental alertness." The problems, the author of the test states,
do not require "knowledge" (presumably arithmetical *skills*) beyond that
of the seventh-grade level. Problems in arithmetical reasoning are widely
used in tests of intelligence, since they are significantly correlated with
total scores of scales and have high predictive value in respect to future
evidence of mental ability.

4. *Similarities test*. This part of the scale consists of twelve sets of paired words; the subject is required to state in what way the words in each pair are similar (for example, orange–banana). The author of the scale regards the similarities test as one of the most satisfactory, for it appears to sample very well the "general factor" (Spearman's g), or what is commonly called *general intelligence*.

5. *Memory span for digits, forward and backward*. The subject is required to repeat series of digits heard once. The series vary in length from three to eight (backward) and nine (forward). This is a test of immediate memory span. Psychological studies—both experimental and clinical—have consistently shown that tests of immediate recall of digits have a low correlation with other, more valid tests of intelligence. Yet, memory span for digits continues to be used because it is helpful in detecting the mentally defective, whose span is often very short (generally less than five digits forward and less than three backwards), and because very poor span is useful in making certain clinical diagnoses of organic defects. Poor memory span for digits, especially backwards, is also found at times in cases of persons who are unable to apply the attention necessary in solving more difficult mental tasks.

6. *Vocabulary test*. This subtest consists of forty words arranged in the order of increasing difficulty. We have already stated that most psychologists concerned with intelligence testing believe that a vocabulary test is one of the most valuable types of material used in deriving an index of a person's general mental ability, if there have been no unusual developmental or environmental handicaps. Thus, although the vocabulary subtest was originally provided for use as an alternate or supplement, experience and statistical study demonstrated its value, so that it is now used as a regular part of the scale. Also, like Binet and many other psychologists, users of Form I and the WAIS have observed that *qualitative* differences in word definitions, as given by various subjects, have clinical value and educational significance in helping to reveal the nature of an individual's thought processes (depth, extent of analysis, nuances of meanings, cultural background, bizarreness of definitions) and, in some instances, feelings, emotions, and values.

7. *Digit-symbol test*. The subject is shown nine divided rectangles; in the upper half of each rectangle is a digit; in the lower half there is a symbol. The key is followed by seventy-five rectangles (of which ten are practice samples) in which only the numerals are given. In each instance, the subject is required to insert the appropriate symbol. This test, also known as a substitution test, requires the association of symbols, and involves speed and accuracy of performance. It also involves visual memory. The purely motor factor, it has been found, is relatively unim-

portant, except in the case of illiterate persons who are not accustomed to using pencil and paper, and, of course, those who have suffered neuromuscular or other anatomical damage. The following is an item from the digit-symbol test.

8. *Picture completion test.* In this part, there are fifteen cards, each of which shows a picture that is incomplete in some detail (for example, a picture of a face with the nose missing). The testee is required to note and name the missing part.[7] In some pictures the task is quite simple for the ordinary person; but in others the deficiencies of the pictures are somewhat more subtle. It has been found that this material is particularly valuable in testing lower level intelligence, as well as having moderate discriminative value at the intermediate levels. At the higher levels, however, this test is inadequate because it is not difficult enough. On the whole, it is said that this part of the scale ". . . measures the individual's basic perceptual and conceptual abilities in so far as these are involved in the visual recognition and identification of familiar objects and forms. . . . In a broad way, the test measures the ability of the individual to differentiate essential from nonessential details" (74, p. 78).

9. *Block design test.* This subtest utilizes nine identical cubes, some or all of which are used to copy ten given designs. Two sides of each cube are red, two are white, and two are half-red and half-white, divided diagonally. The first six designs utilize four blocks; the last four designs are more complex and utilize all nine. Performance on this subtest involves visual analysis and synthesis. Performance, however, is facilitated and improved if the subject is able to *verbalize* his analyses and syntheses.

10. *Picture arrangement test.* In this subtest of the scale, there are eight series of pictures. Each series is presented to the subject in a disarranged order; but when the pictures in each series are placed in the correct sequence, they tell a story. This type of test measures a person's ability to comprehend and evaluate a total situation without the use of language.

11. *Object assembly test.* This subtest of the scale includes four "figure formboards" that represent familiar objects, each cut into several parts which the subject is required to assemble into the whole. The inclusion of this subtest is justified on the basis that it requires perception of parts

---

[7] Generally this type of test is called "mutilated pictures." It was used by Binet in his scales and is now widely used in group tests, as well as in Binet revisions.

and their reconstruction into a meaningful whole. It has, in addition, clinical value of a qualitative kind; for it contributes to the examiner's understanding of the subject's modes of perception, the degree to which he relies upon trial-and-success methods, and the manner in which he responds to his errors.

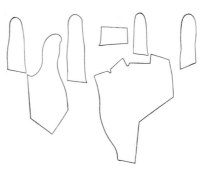

Functions Involved in the Subtests. In each of the eleven subtests, the functions involved may be psychologically analyzed as shown below. These indicate the processes that are operative in the most effec-

Fig. 11.2. The disassembled hand (object assembly test). From the Wechsler-Bellevue Scale. By permission.

tive performance on each of the subtests. This analysis should be distinguished from a factorial analysis. The latter is a statistical technique employed to reduce the number of nonstatistically analyzed functions, on the basis of communality.

Subtest	Functions	Influencing Factors
Information	Long-range retention Association and organization of experience	Cultural environment Interests
Comprehension	Reasoning with abstractions [8] Organization of knowledge	Cultural opportunities Response to reality situations
Arithmetic	Concept formation Retention (of arithmetical processes)	Attention span Opportunity to acquire the fundamental arithmetical processes
Similarities	Analysis of relationships Verbal concept formation	A minimum of cultural opportunities
Vocabulary	Language development Concept formation	Cultural opportunities
Digit Span	Immediate recall Auditory imagery Visual imagery at times	Attention span

[8] "Reasoning with abstractions" generally involves the processes of both analysis and synthesis, with the use of symbols—language and number. The testee must first analyze the relationships existing among the members, or parts, of the whole problem; then he must reorganize and interpret and, at times, create new wholes in order to reach the desired solution.

Subtest	Functions	Influencing Factors
Picture Arrangement	Visual perception of relationships (visual insight) Synthesis of nonverbal material	A minimum of cultural opportunity Visual acuity at times
Picture Completion	Visual perception: analysis Visual imagery	Environmental experience Visual acuity at times
Object Assembly	Visual perception: synthesis Visual-motor integration	Rate of motor activity Precision of motor activity
Block Design	Perception of form Visual perception: analysis Visual-motor integration	Rate of motor activity Minimum of color vision
Digit Symbol	Immediate rote recall Visual-motor integration Visual imagery	Rate of motor activity

While the ability to verbalize and to make abstractions is not necessarily involved in the five nonverbal subtests, nevertheless it has often been observed by examiners that this ability does facilitate and expedite performance. For example, on the Block Design test, it is possible to analyze and formulate the color-and-form realtionships of each design before beginning to reproduce it. In the Picture Arrangement test, some subjects will attempt to discern and state the story told by the group of pictures before placing them in the correct sequence. It is important to recognize this fact in evaluating and analyzing performance on tests that are primarily nonverbal: *even though a test is nonverbal, the ability to verbalize and abstract may be one of the psychological functions involved.*

FACTORIAL COMPOSITION OF THE SCALES. Both scales, 1939 and 1955, have been subjected to a significant number of statistical analyses by the use of the several available techniques. For the most part, they agree in finding the following four factors: a general factor (g), referred to as "eductive" or general reasoning; [9] a verbal factor, or verbal comprehension; a nonverbal organization factor, variously named "nonverbal," "space," or "visual-motor organization"; a general, nonspecialized memory factor. The most significant of these in accounting for variance in test scores is the general factor.[10] Thus, in spite of the differences in types of materials used in each of the subtests, the same or similar mental opera-

[9] This factor appears to be the same as Spearman's eduction of relations and eduction of correlates. See Chapter 7.
[10] See page 161 for a discussion of the meaning of the general factor.

tions are involved to a considerable degree; that is, they show a high degree of "communal variance." Wechsler reports that *g* accounts for about 50 percent of the total contributed by all the tests, and from 66 to 75 percent of the communal variance shared by two or more tests (74, pp. 121–122).

Reliability: SPLIT-HALF. The manual (73) reports split-half reliability coefficients and standard errors of measurement based upon results obtained with three age groups: 18–19 (200 subjects), 25–34 (300 subjects), and 45–54 (300 subjects). There are only slight differences between coefficients found for each group; therefore, only those for one age group are shown in Table 11.1.

TABLE 11.1

RELIABILITY COEFFICIENTS AND STANDARD ERRORS OF MEASUREMENT:
18–19 YEAR AGE GROUP *

Subtest	r	SE_m
Information	.91	0.88
Comprehension	.79	1.36
Arithmetic	.79	1.38
Similarities	.87	1.11
Digit Span	.71	1.63
Vocabulary	.94	0.69
Digit Symbol	.92	0.85
Picture Completion	.82	1.18
Block Design	.86	1.16
Picture Arrangement	.66	1.71
Object Assembly	.65	1.65
Verbal IQ	.96	3.00
Performance IQ	.93	3.97
Full-Scale IQ	.97	2.60

* The standard error of measurement is given in units of the scaled scores. The IQ reliabilities are given, of course, in IQ units. Two of the subtests show more than "slight differences" in coefficients for the three age groups: arithmetic (.79, .81, .86); picture arrangement (.66, .60, .74).
SOURCE: Wechsler (73, p. 103). By permission.

The reliability coefficients for the three types of IQ are highly satisfactory. Their standard errors of measurement, furthermore, indicate high "absolute" reliability; that is, the probabilities are 68 in 100 that an individual's *obtained* IQs on the WAIS are within less than 4 points of his true nonverbal (performance) IQ, within 3.00 of his true verbal IQ, and within 2.6 of his true full-score IQ.

While the subtest reliabilities, on the whole, are not as reliable as the three IQ ratings, they are, however, with three exceptions, high enough to warrant considerable confidence in their results, since eight of the eleven reliabilities are .79 or higher.[11] In making differential diagnoses, based upon patterns of subtest scores, the specific reliability indexes (coefficients and standard errors of measurement) must be taken into account.

TEST-RETEST RELIABILITY. At present, regrettably, no data are available on the test-retest reliability of the WAIS. The data that follow, therefore, are those found with Form I. These are given here on the assumption that the later scale would yield results at least as good, but probably better.

Wechsler's manual reports only meager data on reliability. Fifty-two individuals were retested at intervals of one month to one year, with the results shown in Table 11.2.

TABLE 11.2

RETEST CORRELATIONS FOR FORM I

Ages	N	Rho *	PE
10–13	32	.94	.013
20–34	20	.94	.018

* Rank order correlation coefficient.
SOURCE: Wechsler (73, p. 133).

Since these data were published, the few available reliability studies have dealt almost exclusively with abnormal subjects, principally psychoneurotics and schizophrenics.[12] Table 11.3 shows the range of correlation coefficients found with such groups for each of the subtests and IQ scales.

Examination of Table 11.3 shows (1) that there is considerable variation in reliability among the subtests and that, in general, their reliability is

[11] A coefficient of .79 is not an established cut-off point; but it is practically .80; and .80 is a reasonable reliability coefficient for a subtest. The coefficients in Table 11.1 are superior, with two exceptions, to those obtained for Form I.
[12] Because of the instability of such persons, they are not the most suitable subjects to use for the study of the inherent stability of a measuring instrument.

The ready use of a new and promising clinical instrument is understandable and justifiable, since clinicians, confronted by the immediate, pressing, and persistent problems of living persons, cannot wait until experimental research has subjected the instrument to thoroughgoing tests of reliability and validity.

TABLE 11.3

TEST-RETEST RELIABILITY OF FORM I REPORTED
FOR ABNORMAL GROUPS
(7 STUDIES)

Subtest	Range of coefficients
Information	.56–.99
Comprehension	.12–.78
Digit Span	.59–.77
Arithmetic	.68–.87
Similarities	.38–.93
Vocabulary	.90–.93
Picture Arrangement	.49–.86
Picture Completion	.32–.89
Block Design	.65–.87
Object Assembly	.31–.79
Digit Symbol	.34–.91
Verbal IQ	.76–.91
Nonverbal IQ	.52–.94
Full-Scale IQ	.55–.90

appreciably below that of the scale as a whole; and (2) that in all but one of the reports (in which the subjects were schizophrenics and $r = .55$) full-scale reliability appears to be reasonably satisfactory, considering the instability of the groups used. (Other r values were .87, .84, .84, .87, .89, .90.)

From published reports, it appears, that only one investigation, using a fairly adequate sampling of individuals, has been devoted to reliability of the Bellevue when administered to normal subjects (23). The test-retest method was employed. The age range was 20 to approximately 50 years. One group of sixty subjects was retested after a one-week interval; another group of sixty persons after a four-week interval; a third group of thirty-eight subjects after a six-month period. The major findings were the following:

The mean score for every subtest and for the total scale increased for all three groups.

Increases in scores tend to be somewhat smaller as the retest interval is increased.

The smallest average increase was 0.3 point in weighted score for comprehension retest (after four weeks).

The largest average increase was 2.8 points in weighted score for picture-arrangement retest (after one week).

Largest average increases (2 or more points in weighted score) were found for picture arrangement and object assembly.

Smallest average increases (less than one point in weighted score) were found for information, comprehension, and similarities.

Average changes in IQs were: verbal scale, 4.4 points; nonverbal IQ, 9.1 points; full-scale IQ, 7.6 points.

Retest correlations and standard errors of measurement for all subtests and the three IQs are shown in Table 11.4. It will be noted that for the

TABLE 11.4

Test-Retest Correlations and Standard Errors of
Measurement for Form I
$(N = 158)$

Subtests	Correlations	SE meas.
Information	.86	.68
Comprehension	.74	1.21
Digit Span	.67	1.68
Arithmetic	.62	2.06
Similarities	.71	1.22
Vocabulary	.88	.73
Picture Arrangement	.64	1.82
Picture Completion	.83	.95
Block Design	.84	1.10
Object Assembly	.69	1.31
Digit Symbol	.80	1.06
Verbal IQ	.84	3.96
Nonverbal IQ	.86	4.49
Full-Scale IQ	.90	3.29

Source: G. F. Derner *et al.* (23).

subtests, four of the coefficients are in the .60s (very low reliability); two are in the .70s (low reliability); five are in the .80s (reasonably satisfactory reliability for a subtest).

Comparison of the standard errors of measurement in Table 11.4, for Form I, with those in Table 11.1, for the WAIS, provides an additional basis for estimating the relative reliability of the two versions. In the 1955 edition, standard errors of measurement are slightly smaller in seven subtests, and slightly larger in four. Also, this same index is smaller for the three IQs of the WAIS. There are, furthermore, quite significant differences between the reliability coefficients in arithmetical problems, similarities, digit symbols, and the three IQs. Although, on the whole, the statistics favor the WAIS, one precaution should be noted in comparing and interpreting them. It is that the data for Form I are derived from test-retest scores, and the data for the WAIS are from split-half reliabilities; the latter are expected to be higher and more favorable than the WAIS (see Chapter 4).

Validity: INTERCORRELATIONS OF SUBTESTS. These correlations are always necessary to provide data regarding the presence or absence of a g factor. For this scale, appreciable intercorrelations would be required as one aspect of their validity, that is, *construct* validity.[13] The following coefficients are reported for a group of 300 persons, of ages 25–34 (73, p. 100).

Range is from .30 (Object Assembly with Digit Span) to .81 (Vocabulary with Information).
The range of the highest three fourths of the coefficients is from .46 to .81.
The modal interval is .50–.59.

For a wide range of ages from 18 to 75+ years, classified into seven categories, the median intertest correlations were as follows:

verbal: .59 to .66
performance: .53 to .59
verbal with performance: .41 to .54
all tests: .46 to .57

The preceding correlation coefficients indicate that each of the several subtests has much in common with every other one regarding demands upon the same or similar mental operations, though in varying degrees.

More significant, however, are the coefficients found between scores of each subtest correlated with total scores of all *other* parts of the scale.[14] These coefficients are as follows (74, p. 99):

Range is from .46 (Picture Arrangement) to .84 (Information).
Range of the highest three-fourths is from .65 to .84.
The modal interval is from .70 to .79.

[13] Some writers state this aspect is evidence of the test's *content* validity. A distinction between the two—construct and content—is not always possible. It will be recalled that construct validity has been characterized as "sophisticated content validity."
[14] It is obvious that if scores of a given subtest were correlated with total scores that include those of the subtest in question, the resulting coefficient would be in part a self-correlation, and spuriously high.

These correlations indicate that the WAIS, on the whole, has a reasonably satisfactory degree of construct validity. The findings in regard to the factorial content of the scale, already presented, provide further evidence on its construct validity.

CORRELATION WITH SCHOOLING. Beginning with Binet, the amount of schooling and quality of educational achievement were used as criteria of validity. Hence, the ratings on this scale were correlated with years of schooling for three age groups. These are 18–19 years ($N = 200$); 25–34 ($N = 300$); 45–54 ($N = 300$). The coefficients were, respectively:

> verbal score: .688, .658, .718
> performance score: .597, .570, .614
> total score: .688, .658, .718

These correlations are, on the whole, higher than those found for Form I; and, again, they are reasonably satisfactory for the criterion used.

CHANGES IN SCORES WITH INCREASING AGE. The mean scores of the verbal, performance, and full scales increase moderately and gradually from age 16 to 29 years. Thereafter, they decline moderately and gradually until age 64. These results are consistent with prevailing psychological theory, except that the upper limit, in the 25–29 year age group, is higher than that found with other tests. The standard deviations of the scaled scores, however, are rather close throughout the entire age range, varying from 23.6 (at 16–17 years) to 27.0 (at 45–49 years). With the exception of the two extreme values, all SDs fall between 24 and 26 points (see Fig. 11.3).

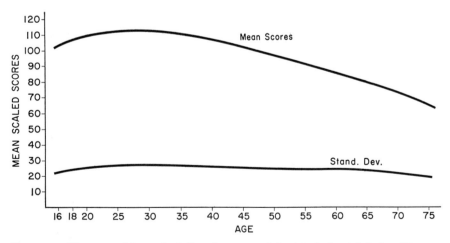

FIG. 11.3. Changes with age in full-scale scores of the Wechsler Adult Intelligence Scale. Ages 16–75 and over.

It is desirable to know the variability of scores not only in terms of standard deviations but also in terms of coefficients of variation, showing the ratio of the *SD* to mean ($SD/M \times$ 100), that is, the *relative* variation of scores at each of the several age levels. These indexes vary from 21.91 at years 25–29, to 28.3 at years 55–59. This index is nearly uniform from age 16 to 44, since it is between 21.91 and 23.57; but after age 44 it ranges from 25.76 to 28.30. The reasons for these differences are not established. They might be defects in the test itself, cumulative effects of specialization of interests in adulthood, or differential effects of advancing age upon mental operations.

RANGE AND DISTRIBUTION OF IQs.   It will be recalled that two of the characteristics of a valid psychological test are that it shall yield a satisfactorily wide range of scores to encompass the large differences in human abilities, and that this distribution shall be a close approximation to the normal (Gaussian) curve. Figure 11.4 represents the WAIS distribu-

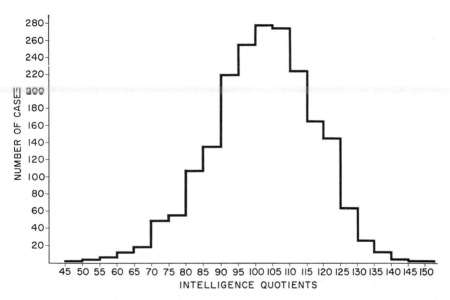

FIG. 11.4. Distribution of Wechsler Adult Intelligence Scale intelligence quotients. Ages 16–75 and over (2052 cases).

tion of IQs for 2052 cases between the ages of 16 and 75 years. The range is from approximately 35 IQ to 155 IQ. This range is wide enough to include almost all cases; but a more comprehensive sampling of the population should yield a very small fraction of one percent of IQs above 155, and a very small fraction of one percent below 35. This distribution, however, does establish that the scale is able to differentiate among most persons, that it measures continuously, and that it does not yield an undue concentration of scores at any of the levels.[15]

CORRELATIONS WITH THE STANFORD-BINET AND OTHER SCALES.   In validating a new scale for testing intelligence, it is common practice to correlate the ratings on the new instrument with those obtained for the same individuals on the Stanford-Binet. This practice is tantamount to accepting the Stanford-Binet as a reasonably valid scale; that is, as one sound criterion of validity against which to evaluate the new scale.

A moderate number of studies have been published—but not as many as might have been expected—on the correlations between Form I (1939) of the Wechsler scale and others. The author of the Bellevue scale reports a coefficient of .82 $(PE = .026)$ between the W-B and the S-B, for seventy-five cases between the ages of 14 and 16 years. Six correlation studies of these two instruments, made by others, yielded coefficients varying from .57 $(PE = .04)$ to .93 $(PE = .01)$. Coefficients of partial correlation, with chronological age held constant, are not given; but it is doubtful if the age range in any of these studies is such as to have raised appreciably the size of the coefficients. In the two instances where the coefficients were below .80, the subjects were college freshmen; hence the relatively lower coefficients (.57 and .62) may be attributable either to the fact that the group is relatively homogeneous, which would result in constriction of range and reduction in correlation, or the fact that the tests are not as reliable at the upper extreme, so that errors of measurement make high correlations unlikely.

For the new edition, the WAIS (1955), only one correlational study with the S-B is reported (74, p. 105). Fifty-two inmates of a reformatory, between the ages of 16 and 26 were tested with both scales, with the following results:

S-B with full-scale IQ = .85
S-B with verbal-scale IQ = .80
S-B with performance-scale IQ = .69

A second correlational study used Raven's Progressive Matrices (a nonverbal test; see Chapter 15) for comparative purposes. The following correlations were found.

----

[15] It is a widely accepted principle among psychologists that the distribution of IQs should approximate the normal (Gaussian) curve. Wechsler states he does not share this view. He apparently interprets the curve in Figure 11.4 as being somewhat skewed at the lower end. This curve is, however, a fairly good approximation to the Gaussian. One reason why it appears slightly skewed is that this sample of 2052 cases does not include IQs above 155; and it also may be that the group above 110 IQ was not an entirely adequate sampling. Tables in the WAIS manual, at some age levels, provide IQ equivalents as high as 179 for maximum-scaled scores.

Matrices with full-scale IQ = .72
Matrices with verbal-scale IQ = .58
Matrices with performance-scale IQ = .70

Table 11.5 summarizes the correlations found between the S-B and the W-B (1939) scales. Although there have been surprisingly few studies comparing the two Wechsler scales and the Stanford-Binet, the available data show that there is substantial correlation between them, especially between full-scale IQs and those of the S-B, and verbal-scale IQs and those of the S-B. On the other hand, as would be expected, correlations between Stanford-Binet intelligence quotients and the performance-scale IQs are only moderate.

It is unfortunate, too, that most of the studies comparing the two instruments have used atypical groups, such as hospital patients, clinic referrals, and prison inmates, to the neglect of individuals who fall within the categories of normal behavior and adjustment.

TABLE 11.5

COEFFICIENTS OF CORRELATION BETWEEN THE STANFORD-BINET
AND FORM I (FREQUENCIES)

r	With full-scale IQ	With verbal IQ	With performance IQ
.90	5	2	
.85	2	2	
.80	1	1	1
.75	2	1	
.70			1
.65			1
.60	1	1	
.55			1
.50			2
.35			1

Since the WAIS is regarded as superior to Form I, it is reasonable to conclude that in comparisons with the S-B, the correlation coefficients found for the latter would be smaller than those found for the former.

Correlation coefficients indicate degree of *relative* agreement of paired scores, but not the *absolute* differences between them. It is necessary, therefore, to know the extent of IQ differences between the correlated values. On the whole, it has been found that the differences are not large, although large discrepancies will occasionally appear at the two extremes of the distribution. In studies of retarded and mentally deficient individuals (say, the lowest decile group), the Wechsler scales yield somewhat higher IQs than the S-B. At the upper level of mental ability, however (say, the highest decile group), the Stanford-Binet yields somewhat higher IQs.

Comparison of IQs is complicated by the fact that age of testees is also a factor. Taking the population samples *as a whole* (rather than only the extreme groups), the following are the general findings. (1) Within the age range of approximately 10 to 19 years, the Stanford-Binet IQs tend to be somewhat higher. (2) From age 19 to about 35, the intelligence quotients tend to be about the same. (3) Above the age of 35, the Bellevue intelligence quotients tend to be somewhat higher.[16]

In the case of any given individual, therefore, comparison of Stanford-Binet and Bellevue IQs must take into account both ability level and chronological age. In a given instance, a person's age and ability level may be such as to increase or decrease the difference between the IQs obtained with the two instruments.[17]

This discussion of the comparison between the S-B and Wechsler scale IQs is based upon results found with Form I of the latter and with the 1937 revision of the former, because no data are available for the most recent versions of either. Because these last versions are improved instruments, and because both now use the deviation intelligence quotient, we should expect closer correspondence between them.

Correlational studies between Form I (or II) and group tests have yielded varying results, depending upon the number and characteristics of the subjects. Coefficients varied from .39 for Thorndike's CAVD Test to .86 for the Army General Classification Test. Most other coefficients were in the .70s.

PROGNOSTIC VALIDITY.   As a test of the validity of Form I, its author applies the pragmatic criterion. He states: "How do we know that our tests are 'good' measures of intelligence? The only honest reply we can make is that our experience has shown them to be so. If this seems to be a tenuous answer we need only remind the reader that it has been practical experience which has given (or denied) final validity to every

---

[16] Number (3) is just what one should expect in view of the method employed in calculating Bellevue IQs. The method is explained later in this chapter.

[17] A definitive answer to the question of the comparability of the IQs of the two scales will have to be based upon an investigation that is representative of the general population, rather than heavily weighted with hospital and clinical subjects, as is now the case. Also, such an investigation must approach the problem in two ways: (1) by analyzing IQs separately for each of the age groups; and (2) by analyzing the IQs separately at each of the ability levels for each of the age groups.

other intelligence test. . . . Empirical judgments, here as elsewhere, play the role of ultimate arbiter. In any case, all evidence for the validity of a test, whether statistical or otherwise, is inevitably of an indirect sort and, in the end, cumulative rather than decisive" (74, p. 127). In other words, it has been found by the author of the scale, and by others, that it works with reasonable satisfaction in clinical practice.

In discussing the validity of the 1955 scale, Wechsler states that it satisfies the following criteria: ratings by selected judges (generally teachers in the case of children); conformity with the normal growth curve of mental ability; and comparisons with over-all socioeconomic achievement (especially in identifying and appraising the mentally deficient). Both versions of the scale, states Wechsler, meet these criteria (74, p. 109).

The foregoing conclusion is based largely upon results found with Form I. For example, teachers' estimates of their pupils' intelligence, rated on a six-point scale, for a group of seventy-four adolescents in a trade school, correlated .52 with IQs derived from Form I. For another group (forty-five in number) in a general high school, the coefficient was .43. These numbers are, unfortunately, not large enough, although they indicate the probable trend.

In one study, two groups were differentiated on the basis of total scores: (1) a borderline group, having IQs between 66 and 79; and (2) a mentally defective group, having IQs between 50 and 65. The problem was to determine whether each of the eleven subtests contributes significantly to the differentiation of the two groups. Since the mean scores on each of the subtests for the two groups did differentiate, and since the differences between the means were in the directions that should be expected, it was concluded that each subtest did contribute to over-all differentiation, although Digit Span and Object Assembly contributed relatively little (69).

A second study used only the verbal subtests with naval recruits as subjects. The problem here was to learn whether these subtests distinguish between (1) the mentally defective and the borderline, or (2) the borderline, the dull normal, and the normal. The findings indicated that each of the verbal subtests contributed to the differentiations between these groups. The Digit Span subtest in this instance, however, proved to be as effective as the others (45).

Extensive research information has not been provided on the predictive validity of the WAIS in educational guidance. It is a reasonable assumption, however, that this more recent instrument, an improvement over the first version, will be at least as effective in these aspects of test validity.

One comprehensive study of 161 college freshmen (55) concludes that the WAIS may be used for educational prediction with more confidence than one of the well-known group tests (The American Council on Education Psychological Examination). In this study the following correlations with grade-point averages were found:

WAIS verbal score	.58
WAIS full score	.53
WAIS performance	.31
A.C.E. linguistic score	.46
A.C.E. quantitative score	.18

In a *clinical situation,* the prognostic value of a psychological test is dependent upon the soundness of the clinical diagnoses with which the test's findings are compared. This fact presents a major problem; for classification into clinical categories is difficult, often unreliable, and subject to the clinician's theoretical orientation. The major exception is the diagnosis of mental deficiency, for the determination of which a sound individual test of general intelligence, when administered and interpreted by a qualified psychologist, is the most valid single instrument. For this purpose, the Stanford-Binet and Wechsler scales have proved to be most valuable. A diagnosis of mental deficiency, of course, is ordinarily not made upon the basis of IQ and MA alone, although in some instances, when the background of an individual is known, the findings with a single test are sufficient because they are clear and unequivocal.

ITEM DIFFICULTY.   The validity of a scaled test depends in part upon the graded difficulty of the items within each subtest. The nine subtests that lend themselves to this type of item analysis (excepting Digit Span, and Digit Symbol) satisfy this requirement in varying degrees; they do not differentiate equally well among the 1700 individuals upon whose performance the data are based. For example, the two easiest items under Information are passed by 100 percent, while the two most difficult are passed by 3 and 1 percent. Between these extremes, the changes in percent passing are gradual and continuous. Much the same is true of the Vocabulary subtest. In the case of the remaining seven subtests, while 100 percent, or nearly that, pass the easiest items, the most difficult are passed by 18 percent (Similarities), 20 percent (Arithmetic), 22 percent (Comprehension and Picture Completion), 24 percent (Block Design), 35 percent (Picture Arrangement), and 67 percent (Object Assembly). With such large portions passing the most difficult test items, if this population sample is typical, these subtests cannot differentiate well among individuals at the lower levels of distribution.

Scoring and IQ Calculation

Scoring. All parts of this scale are scored on a point basis. For some subtests, the earned raw score is simply the number correct, each item being scored either plus or minus (for example, Information). In the subtests of Comprehension or Similarities, the score for each item is 0, 1, or 2, depending upon quality of the response. In other parts, as in Arithmetical Reasoning or Block Design, the earned raw score is based not only upon correct responses, but upon the time taken to solve the problem. Thus, the factor of speed of performance is involved in sections of this scale, especially in nonverbal subtests.

The *raw score* for each subtest is first obtained by addition of the credits on the items in that part. This raw score is converted into a weighted score (a type of standard score), by means of a conversion table. The purpose of this conversion is the customary one of placing all subtest scores on a comparable basis. The weighted scores for all parts of the scale are added to obtain the full score upon which the full-scale IQ is based. Also, the weighted scores of only the six verbal parts are added to get the verbal score, upon which the verbal-scale IQ is based. Similarly, the weighted scores of the five performance tests are added to get the performance score and performance-scale IQ.

The following well-known formula was used for equating each subtest's raw score into *weighted scores.*

$$X_2 = M_2 + \frac{SD_2}{SD_1}(X_1 - M_1),$$

in which

$M_2 =$ an arbitrarily assigned mean of 10
$SD_2 =$ an arbitrarily assigned standard deviation of 3
$X_2 =$ the weighted score to be found
$M_1 =$ the mean of the subtest's raw score
$X_1 =$ the particular raw score to be converted to a weighted score

This formula (1) assigns an arbitrary and *uniform mean score* to all subtests; (2) multiplies each individual score's deviation from its mean by a *constant ratio;* (3) adds the result to, or subtracts it from, the assigned mean.[18] By using this formula, scores are so converted that each individual maintains his relative status on each subtest. And in the case of any

[18] The best way for the student to see how this formula works is to substitute several sets of values in it and to observe the outcome. The logic of the process will then be more readily apparent. For example, if the two following sets of values are substituted in the formula, the process will be clear. Assume the following data for one subtest: mean score $= 12$, $SD = 4$, $X = 15$; while for a second subtest the corresponding values are

given person's subtest scores, differences between scores will be attributable, theoretically, to differences in his performance level rather than
to differences in the weighting of each subtest in the total. It is thus
possible to vary the number of items in each of the several subtests without giving any of them unequal weight in the total score upon which
the IQ is based.

The reason for converting raw scores into weighted scores is that the
possible maximum raw scores vary in the several subtests of the scale.
If, therefore, the raw scores were simply added to obtain an individual's
rating on the scale, each of the parts would carry a different weight in
the total; each part would have the possibility of contributing differently
to the final result—some more heavily than others. The raw-score units
of one part of the scale would not have the same significance as those of
other parts. If this were the case, then implicit in the scoring would be
the assumption that certain of the psychological functions being tested
should be regarded as more important than others in obtaining the total
score and in deriving an index of intelligence. The W-B scale, however,
is scored on the principle that all the functions tested are equally important; hence, the part scores should be equally weighted so that each
may contribute as much to the total as any other.

"The scaled scores for each test are based on a reference group of 500
cases which included the subjects in the standardization sample between
the ages of 20 and 34. The subjects in this age group generally obtained
the highest scores among the various age groups in the sample. . . . For
every subject in the standardization sample, raw scores on the tests were
converted to scaled scores based on the reference group. Consequently,
the scaled scores permit a direct comparison of the test performance of a
subject of any age with the performance of the reference group" (72,
p. 18).

Deriving the IQ. After the scaled scores had been derived,
three separate distributions were made for each of seven age groups (for
the age range 16 to 64 years); one for the full scale, one for the verbal,
and one for the performance. The mean scaled score *for each group* was
assigned an IQ value of 100, and the standard deviation a value of 15 in
each of the three distributions, so that full, verbal, and performance IQs
could be derived. Thus, an individual who obtains the mean score for the
full scale earns an IQ of 100; one whose score is one standard deviation
below the mean earns an IQ of 85; two *SD*s below the mean give an IQ
of 70, and so on, above the mean as well as below. By referring to stand-

24, 8, and 30. The results will show the same weighted score for both subtests (12.25)
because the individual's relative status on each subtest was identical with that on the
other subtest, even though the raw scores differ.

ard percentile distribution tables, it is possible to determine the percentile rank that corresponds to any deviation IQ. Thus, an IQ of 115, being one *SD* above the mean, corresponds to a percentile rank of 84.[19] (See Chapter 6 for a discussion of relative scores.)

In using a deviation IQ, the principle adopted is that an individual's intelligence quotient should indicate the relative extent to which his scaled score deviates from the mean of *his own* age group.

COMMENTS ON THE DEVIATION IQ. The conventional, or ratio, IQ (MA/CA) relates the test score of an adult to the performance level of an average group at a specified maximum age. The 1916 S-B placed this age at 16; the 1937, at 15. The deviation method, at all ages, relates an individual's score to the average (mean) performance of his own age group. This method obviates the necessity of determining the age of "average adult MA"—always a difficult problem and as yet uncertain. (The W-B, Form I, and the WAIS do not use mental age.)

One problem presented by a deviation IQ—and probably a weakness of it—is that the same, or constant, objective performance on the test will give an individual a higher rating with increased age after the maximum level has been reached, since his constant score will be compared with declining age norms.

Norms of the WAIS show a moderate but steady decline after the age interval 25–34. Obviously, after the period of decline sets in (however moderate), as shown by the test scores, an individual's IQ will decline gradually if the ratio IQ is used; whereas, using a deviation IQ, his rating will decline only if his losses are greater than the average losses of his own age group. If his losses are less than the average rate, his deviation IQ will rise.[20]

Deterioration and Scatter

This scale provides a scheme for calculating a "deterioration quotient," based on the premise that certain types of tested mental processes decline more rapidly than do other types; and that the difference between rates of decline, as between these two types, in the case of any

---

[19] Although the standard deviation of the Stanford-Binet is 16, the difference between it and the WAIS *SD* of 15 does not have practical significance.

[20] The reader should note that we have emphasized decline in test score. This does not necessarily mean that on the whole a person becomes progressively less intelligent before the effects of senescence become apparent. While it is true that there is some loss in average test scores after about age twenty-five, it is also true that some mental traits, as yet unmeasured by intelligence tests, increase in effectiveness through an extended period of adulthood and more than compensate for losses in the processes measured by current scales. This view is borne out by the facts regarding ages of maximum achievement of scholars, scientists, writers, and artists.

given person, indicates his relative degree of deterioration. *In other words, there are certain tested functions that hold up with age and others that do not.* This index will be explained in more detail in a later chapter, together with other tests devised to measure deterioration of mental abilities.

A second feature of the scale is its emphasis upon "scatter analysis"; that is, analysis of an individual's performance on the several parts of the scale for the purpose of facilitating clinical analysis of the subject's performance. Such analysis may lead to diagnostic inferences concerning personality characteristics and behavior disorders owing to organic brain disease, psychosis, psychoneurosis, adolescent psychopathy, and mental deficiency. Here again, this application of the scale will be presented in a subsequent chapter on clinical uses and interpretations of tests.

Short Scales. As in the case of the Stanford-Binet, the use of short scales has been suggested by some psychologists. Several have been proposed (12, 24). A short scale is one from which some of the subtests have been omitted in their entirety, and the scores are prorated in order to make them comparable to scores of the full scale for the purpose of obtaining an IQ. The use of a short scale has been proposed as a time-saver.

Although the correlation coefficients found between short and full-scale IQs have been consistently high for the best combinations of sub-tests—usually in the .90s—use of an abbreviated version is not advisable except for rough screening. If decisions are to be made affecting individuals, rough screening is an unwise practice. Furthermore, each subtest constitutes part of a total pattern of performance which is destroyed if parts are removed. Finally, as already pointed out in other connections, an individual test of intelligence provides an opportunity to make valuable qualitative observations of the behavior of the testee, which may differ with different subtests. Thus, reducing the number of subtests reduces opportunities for making significant observations.

Criticism and Evaluation

Was the population sample adequate? Form I was severely criticized because the standardization population was selected from a restricted geographical area. The 1955 version avoided that criticism by being based upon a population from four areas: Northeast, North Central, South, and West. The total number, 1700, was evenly divided between the sexes; and the age groupings are consistent with those used by the Census Bureau. In regard to urban–rural residence, race (white and nonwhite), occupation, and years of schooling completed, the standardization group conforms closely to the percentages reported in the United States census of 1950. In view of data already presented on the several aspects of the scale's internal validity, it appears that this group of 1700 is an adequate one; although the scale's predictive validity has not yet been demonstrated.

Are the subtests a variety of disconnected types?   In view of the findings already presented in this chapter, under the heading of Factorial Composition, the answer to this question must be distinctly in the negative. This answer is supported by the nonstatistical analysis of functions involved in each of the subtests, also discussed in an earlier section of this chapter.

Are the verbal subtests culturally unfair to some persons?   The answer to this question is the same as that given for the Stanford-Binet. In this scale, as in the S-B, the verbal materials under Comprehension, Similarities, and Arithmetic are stated in terms that place little premium upon educational or other cultural advantages. As in all tests of information and vocabulary, success on these parts is dependent, in part, upon opportunity to learn, whether in school, home, or through one's own exploitation of all aspects of the environment.

Are some of the test items obsolete?   Items in all tests must be reviewed periodically for possible obsolescence. In the case of this scale, a number of the items, especially Comprehension, Information, Vocabulary, Picture Arrangement, and Picture Completion, should be re-examined and re-evaluated periodically. Also, the satisfactory, partially satisfactory, and unsatisfactory responses for a number of items should be reviewed and revised in the light of responses that have been obtained since the scale's publication.

Is the factor of speed important?   Unlike the Stanford-Binet, in which very few test items are timed, some WAIS scores are significantly affected by the speed factor. Speed of performance yields additional credits in the subtests that follow: Arithmetic, Picture Arrangement, Object Assembly, Digit Symbol, and Block Design. Thus, in the total score, speed of work is combined with power (or ability level). Although in general, speed and power are highly correlated, it is also a fact that response-time slows down with age. Thus, since this scale is designed for adults, it might measure, to an important degree, decline in speed of response and not necessarily decline in power, particularly in later adult years. This factor must be kept in mind when, in a later chapter, we consider the "decline" of abilities and the suggested use of a "deterioration" index.

Do the nonverbal subtests involve visual acuity?   Although no experimental data are available in answer to this question, several users of the scale have observed that visual acuity might be a factor in some instances. The subtests most likely to make some demands upon visual acuity are Picture Arrangement and Picture Completion. And, of course, color blindness must be considered as a factor in the Block Design subtest.

Are the reliability coefficients satisfactory? Available data indicate that total verbal scores and total performance scores have a satisfactory degree of split-half reliability, as do full-scale scores. While the split-half reliabilities of some of the subtests are high, some are only fair, or low. This fact must be taken into account when response patterns are being used for differential diagnosis or for evaluating deterioration of mental ability. Absence of test-retest reliability data is a significant deficiency.

Should the verbal and the performance scores be combined? The tables of norms show that the maximum verbal norm is reached by the 25–34 year age group, while the maximum performance norm is reached by the 20–24 year group. Some have questioned the practice of combining both scores when the constituents of one do not continue to develop differentially as long as the other. More important, however, is the fact that verbal and performance scores for three age groups (18–19, 25–34, 45–54) correlated .77, .77, and .81, respectively. Some critics have maintained that these coefficients are not high enough to warrant combining the two scores. Whatever the merit of this criticism, the qualified psychological examiner will take note of serious differences between a verbal and a performance IQ in any instance and will try to find the explanation.

Is the scale clinically useful? Judging from its widespread use in clinics and hospitals and from the empirical judgments of many clinicians, it appears that this scale has been of considerable value. Used with scientific judgment and with knowledge of its limitations, the scale is a valuable instrument for estimating intelligence of adolescents and adults.

This scale is a valuable addition to other testing and diagnostic devices, such as the Stanford-Binet, the Arthur Performance Scale, the Babcock test, and others that will be discussed. Between most of these scales there are significant correlations. For the present, and no doubt in the future, psychologists (in schools, clinics, and elsewhere) will use a given scale or a combination of scales as occasion demands and as their clinical insights suggest.

Some psychologists give considerable weight to the fact that the WAIS is so constructed that it is possible to analyze an individual's score in terms of his variations (consistency or inconsistency) on the several parts of the scale, especially since attempts have been made to specify the psychological functions being tested by each of the several parts.

The validity of the Bellevue in identifying personality and behavior disorders has yet to be unequivocally demonstrated. In spite of the fact that this is the area in which most of the evaluative studies of the scale have been made, clinical findings are not definitive.

In attempting to diagnose personality and behavior disorders on the basis of the pattern or profile of scores on the Bellevue or other scales, it must be remembered also that different educational backgrounds and cultural factors, quite unrelated to personality and behavior disorders, could account to some degree for an individual's inconsistency of performance on the several parts of the scale. It has been found, too, that individual variations in interests find expression in different patterns of mental activities and might be reflected in subtest variations. However, the results obtained by means of this scale, plus clinical experience and acumen, provide a valuable combination for study of individual differences and individual mental functioning.

The Intelligence Scale for Children (1949)

Description.   This scale for children from 5 through 15 years of age (WISC) is developed on the same principles and in the same form as the WAIS: verbal subtests, performance subtests, a verbal IQ, a performance IQ, and a full-scale IQ.

The subtest types are identical with those of the older scale, with the exceptions that follow: Digit Span is made optional; an optional maze test has been added; and in place of the Digit symbol test, a coding test has been substituted, in which various lines in varied positions (single, double, circle) are associated with geometric figures (star, circle, triangle, cross, rectangle).

Standardization Population.   The scale was standardized on a sample of one hundred boys and one hundred girls at each of the eleven age levels, each child being tested within one and one-half months of his midyear.

Selection of the 2200 children was based upon (1) rural–urban residence; (2) father's occupation; and (3) geographic area. The proportions in these sampling factors were based upon U.S. census data for 1940, ". . . with some adjustment for the shift of population toward the West." In the final selection of the standardization sample, geographic area percentages are reasonably well satisfied; urban–rural percentages, less well; and father's occupation percentages, moderately.

Reliability.   Split-half coefficients were found for three age groups (7½, 10½, 13½), 200 in each. The findings are summarized in Tables 11.6 and 11.7. It will be noted, from these data, that the subtest reliability coefficients vary markedly, and are, on the whole, only moderate in size. The IQ reliabilities, however, ranging from .86 to .96, fall within the range that is generally acceptable. These data demonstrate again the necessity of distinguishing between reliability of part of a scale and reliability of the whole scale.

TABLE 11.6

RELIABILITY DATA: INTELLIGENCE SCALE FOR CHILDREN

Age group	Range of r's	Subtest		
		Mean	High r	Low r
7½	.59–.84	.67	Block Design	Comprehension and Picture Completion
10½	.59–.91	.76	Vocabulary	Digit Span
13½	.50–.90	.75	Vocabulary	Digit Span
		IQ reliabilities		
	Verbal	Nonverbal		Full
7½	.88	.86		.92
10½	.96	.89		.95
13½	.96	.90		.94
	(Digit Span, Coding, and Mazes are not included.)			

SOURCE: D. Wechsler (71). By permission.

The standard error of measurement indicates the range of scores within which the chances are approximately two to one that a subject's true score will fall in that particular subtest. Thus, the standard error of 1.20 for 7½-year-olds on Picture Arrangement indicates that the probabilities are two to one that an individual's obtained score on this subtest is within 1.20 points of his true weighted score. Likewise, the standard error of 4.25 IQ points (full scale) for 7½-year-olds indicates that the probabilities are about two to one that an individual's obtained IQ on this scale is within 4.25 points of his true IQ.

The split-half reliability coefficients and the standard errors of measurement must be taken into account when scores on the individual subtests are being interpreted or when differences in scores among subtests are being evaluated. The lower the reliability and the larger the standard error, the less is the confidence to be placed in judgments based upon scores of that particular subtest.

Since the reliabilities of the several IQs are at a satisfactory level, on the

basis of the standardization data, it appears that considerably more confidence can be placed in those indexes than in the scores of the individual subtests (with the exception of vocabulary). And because there are
marked differences among reliability coefficients of the subtests for each
of the three age groups, it is highly desirable that separate reliability
studies be made for each of the eleven age groups, especially at the extremes of the age distribution for which the scale is intended.

TABLE 11.7

STANDARD ERRORS OF MEASUREMENT: INTELLIGENCE SCALE
FOR CHILDREN

| Age group | Subtest | | | |
	Range *	Mean	High	Low
7½	1.20–2.45	1.74	Digit Span	Picture Arrange-ment
10½	.90–1.92	1.44	Digit Span	Vocabulary
13½	.95–2.12	1.47	Digit Span	Vocabulary

| | IQ standard errors † | | |
	Verbal	Nonverbal	Full
7½	5.19	5.61	4.25
10½	3.00	4.98	3.36
13½	3.00	4.74	3.68

* Standard errors of measurement of subtests are given in units of the weighted scores.
† Standard errors of intelligence quotients are given, of course, in IQ points.
SOURCE: Wechsler (71, p. 13). By permission.

In a study of the test-retest reliability of this scale, sixty children were
first examined in the fifth grade; after four years they were re-examined
in the ninth (32). The following correlations were obtained: performance-
scale IQ, .74; verbal-scale IQ, .77; full-scale IQ, .77.

Validity. *Subtest Intercorrelations.* In the manual for this
scale, there are no data on the problem of validity as such. There are data
on intercorrelations of the subtests. The assumption is that significant
intercorrelations between subtests would validate the hypothesis that
they and the scale as a whole measure common factors. However, the
intercorrelation coefficients among the individual subtests are, on the
whole, not as high as would be expected. At the 7½-year level, these coefficients are concentrated within the .20s and .30s; at the 10½-year level,
they are concentrated within the .30s and .40s; while at the 13½-year
level, they are distributed within the .20s, .30s, and .40s.

On the other hand *each verbal subtest* correlates quite significantly with *total verbal score,* the range for the three age groups being from .44 to .82, with the coefficients fairly evenly distributed. The *nonverbal subtests* correlate somewhat lower with *total performance scores,* the range being from .32 to .68, with some concentration in the .50s.

The correlation coefficients between *total verbal scores* and *total performance scores* are, respectively, .60, .68, and .56 for these same age groups.

These findings indicate that, on the whole, although each subtest has only a moderate amount of communality with the others taken singly, verbal subtests *combined* have much more communality with each individual verbal subtest.[21] The same is true of *combined* performance and separate performance scores.

Finally, the data indicate that *all the verbal subtests taken as a whole* have considerable communality with *all the performance subtests as a*

TABLE 11.8

CORRELATIONS BETWEEN THE INTELLIGENCE SCALE FOR
CHILDREN AND OTHER SCALES
(5 STUDIES)

Other scale	Subjects	N	r
Arthur point scale	mentally defective	40	.79 (Full scale)
" " "	" "	40	.83 (Nonverbal scale)
" " "	" "	40	.47 (Verbal scale)
Stanford-Binet. L	" "	40	.76 (Full scale)
" "	" "	40	.64 (Nonverbal scale)
" "	" "	40	.75 (Verbal scale)
Stanford-Binet	subnormals	70	.68 (Full scale)
" "	"	70	.69 (Verbal scale)
Stanford-Binet	normals	49–53	.85 (Full scale)
" "	"	49–53	.82 (Verbal scale)
" "	"	49–53	.80 (Nonverbal scale)
Arthur point scale	"	49–53	.80 (Full scale)
" " "	"	49–53	.77 (Verbal scale)
" " "	"	49–53	.81 (Nonverbal scale)
Stanford-Binet, L	"	54	.80 (Full scale)
" "	"	54	.71 (Verbal scale)
" "	"	54	.63 (Nonverbal scale)
" "	"	332	.82 (Full scale)
" "	"	332	.74 (Verbal scale)
" "	"	332	.64 (Nonverbal scale)

[21] Corrections are made to eliminate self-correlation.

whole. Yet, since the aforementioned coefficients of .60, .68, and .56 are fairly distant from unity, the measured abilities in one group (verbal) can be used only for a general approximation of abilities measured by the other group of subtests (nonverbal), and *vice versa.* The reporting, therefore, of verbal, nonverbal, and full-scale IQs with this instrument is essential.

Correlations with Other Scales. Since the appearance of this scale, several reports have been published that deal with the correlations and IQ differences found between it, the S-B, and the Arthur nonverbal tests. The summarized data are given in Tables 11.8 and 11.9.

The data in Tables 11.8 and 11.9 are for the entire group in each instance. At different ages, the correlations between S-B and full-scale IQs vary from .75 to .90; for the verbal scale, between .65 and .90; and for the performance scale, between .50 and .75. The table giving mean intelligence quotients and standard deviations indicates that the Wechsler scale tends to rate subnormal subjects somewhat higher, but not markedly so, than does the Stanford-Binet. At the average level, the reverse is true.

TABLE 11.9

IQs OF INTELLIGENCE SCALE FOR CHILDREN COMPARED WITH TWO OTHER SCALES
MEANS AND STANDARD DEVIATIONS
(5 STUDIES)

WISC	Arthur point scale	S-B	Subjects	N
60(SD6) Full 65(SD13) Verbal 58(SD10) Perform.	65(SD12)	56(SD5)	Deficients	40
66(SD9) Full 67(SD7) Verbal 72(SD11) Perform.		65(SD7)	Subnormal	70
100(SD15) Full 99(SD14) Verbal 101(SD15) Perform.	95(SD16)	105(SD15)	Normal	49–53
102(SD11) Full 101(SD12) Verbal 104(SD11) Perform.		106(SD11)	Normal	54
101(SD13) Full 103(SD14) Verbal 98(SD15) Perform.		108(SD16)	Normal	332

On the basis of the research thus far reported, it is reasonable to conclude that full-scale intelligence quotients and verbal-scale intelligence quotients, on the one hand, and Stanford-Binet IQs, on the other, have considerable communality of psychological functions being measured. The performance-scale intelligence quotients have much less in common with the Stanford-Binet.

A number of other comparative studies have been made, using group tests of both the verbal and nonverbal types. Full-scale IQs of the WISC correlated with these as low as .61 in some instances, and as high as .91 in others (4, 59, 67).

In each study, the coefficient must be viewed in the light of the number of individuals tested, their age range, and their range of ability.

Predictive Efficiency. Validity of a test for school children, especially, should be evaluated in terms of its predictive value in regard to school achievement. Table 11.10 summarizes the results reported in sev-

TABLE 11.10

CORRELATIONS OF WISC SCORES WITH SCHOOL ACHIEVEMENT

Scale	N	Range of r's for separate school subjects	Total achievement test
Full	54	.45–.71	.76
Verbal	54	.48–.60	.62
Nonverbal	54	.41–.64	.65
Full	18–21	.44–.81	—
Verbal	18–21	.47–.74	—
Nonverbal	18–21	.29–.74	—
Full	621	.66–.67	—
Verbal	621	.58–.62	—
Nonverbal	621	.52–.63	—
Full	51	—	.77
Verbal	51	—	.80
Nonverbal	51	—	.54

eral studies in which WISC scores were correlated with objective achievement-test scores.

On the whole, these results compare favorably with the range of correlation coefficients found for other widely used tests of intelligence. Additional systematic validation studies would be valuable at each age and grade level, and for each of the several mental levels (for example, gifted, superior, average, slow, mentally deficient).

Evaluation. This scale is a significant addition to the limited number of instruments available for individual testing. Although one advantage originally claimed for the WISC was that it did not use the mental-age concept, it was subsequently found desirable to supply mental-age equivalents (71); for this concept is a highly useful one when interpreted by a qualified psychologist.

The relatively low reliabilities of some of the subtests indicate that considerable caution must be used in utilizing a test profile for diagnosis or guidance. The full scores and the *total* verbal and total performance scores, however, have yielded reliability coefficients at a satisfactorily high level.

More systematic research is needed on the scale's predictive validity for educational purposes. Available data show that IQ differences between the WISC and the S-B are significant enough in some instances to warrant caution in using the two scales interchangeably in every situation.

The limits of the IQ values given by the WISC full scale are from 46 to 154. This means that the scale is not as accurate when used with individuals who rank above or below these limits, as when used with others. The total number of such individuals is small; but in particular instances this can be a serious limitation.

References

1. Alexander, W. P. Intelligence: concrete and abstract. *British Journal of Psychology,* Monograph Supplement, 1935, no. 19.
2. Alper, A. E., and B. M. Horne. Changes in IQ of a group of institutionalized mental defectives over a period of two decades. *American Journal of Mental Deficiency,* 1959, *64,* 472–475.
3. Altus, G. T. Relationship between verbal and nonverbal parts of the CTMM and the WISC. *Journal of Consulting Psychology,* 1956, *20,* 155–156.
4. Arnold, F., and W. Wagner. A comparison of Wechsler children's scale and Stanford-Binet scores for eight- and nine-year-olds. *Journal of Experimental Education,* 1955, *24,* 91–94.
5. Balinsky, B. An analysis of the mental factors of various age groups from 9 to 60. *Psychological Monographs,* 1941, *23,* 191–234.
6. Balinsky, B., and H. W. Shaw. The contribution of the WAIS to a management appraisal program. *Personnel Psychology,* 1956, *9,* 207–209.
7. Barratt, E. S. The relationship of the progressive matrices (1938) and the Columbia mental maturity scale to the WISC. *Journal of Consulting Psychology,* 1956, *20,* 294–296.
8. Barratt, E. S., and D. L. Baumgarten. The relationship of the WISC and Stanford-Binet to school achievement. *Journal of Consulting Psychology,* 1957, *21,* 144.

9. Birren, J. E. A factor analysis of the Wechsler-Bellevue scale given to an elderly population. *Journal of Consulting Psychology,* 1952, *16,* 399–405.

10. Birren, J. E., *et al.* A factorial analysis of perceptual and mental tests given to healthy elderly men. *The American Psychologist,* 1959, *14,* 350.

11. Carleton, F. O., and C. L. Stacey. An item analysis of the Wechsler Intelligence Scale for Children. *Journal of Clinical Psychology,* 1955, *11,* 149–154.

12. Clayton, H., and D. Payne. Validation of Doppelt's WAIS short form with a clinical population. *Journal of Consulting Psychology,* 1959, *23,* 467.

13. Cohen, J. A factor analytic comparison of intelligence test performance of different neuropsychiatric groups. *The American Psychologist,* 1951, *6,* 334–335.

14. Cohen, J. Factors underlying Wechsler-Bellevue performance of three neuropsychiatric groups. *Journal of Abnormal and Social Psychology,* 1952, *47,* 359–365.

15. Cohen, J. A comparative factor analysis of WAIS performance for four age groups between 18 and 80. *The American Psychologist,* 1956, *11,* 449.

16. Cohen, J. The factorial structure of the WAIS between early adulthood and old age. *Journal of Consulting Psychology,* 1957, *21,* 283–290.

17. Cohen, J. A factor-analytically based rationale for the Wechsler Adult Intelligence Scale. *Journal of Consulting Psychology,* 1957, *21,* 451–457.

18. Cohen, J. The factorial structure of the WISC at ages 7-6, 10-6, and 13-6. *Journal of Consulting Psychology,* 1959, *23,* 285–299.

19. Cooper, J. G. Predicting school achievement for bilingual pupils. *Journal of Educational Psychology,* 1958, *49,* 31–36.

20. Corsini, R. J., and K. K. Fassett. Intelligence and ageing. *Journal of Genetic Psychology,* 1953, *83,* 249–264.

21. Dana, R. H. A comparison of four verbal subtests on the W-B, Form I and the WAIS. *Journal of Clinical Psychology,* 1957, *13,* 70–71.

22. Davis, F. B. A factor analysis of the Wechsler-Bellevue scale. *Educational and Psychological Measurement,* 1956, *16,* 127–146.

23. Derner, G. F., *et al.* Reliability of the Wechsler-Bellevue subtests and scales. *Journal of Consulting Psychology,* 1950, *14,* 172–179.

24. Doppelt, J. E. Estimating the full-scale score on the Wechsler Adult Intelligence Scale from scores on four subtests. *Journal of Consulting Psychology,* 1956, *20,* 63–66.

25. Doppelt, J. E., and W. L. Wallace. Standardization of the Wechsler Adult Intelligence Scale for Older Persons. *Journal of Abnormal and Social Psychology,* 1955, *51,* 312–330.

26. Dunnette, M. D., and W. K. Kirchner. Validation of psychological tests in industry. *Personnel Administration,* 1958, May–June, 20–27.

27. Estes, B. W. Influence of socio-economic status on Wechsler Intelligence Scale for Children. *Journal of Consulting Psychology,* 1955, *19,* 225–226.

28. Fink, G., and F. C. Shantz. Inference on intellectual efficiency from the WAIS vocabulary subtest. *Journal of Clinical Psychology,* 1958, *14,* 409–412.

29. Frandsen, A. N., and J. B. Higginson. The Stanford-Binet and the Wechsler

Intelligence Scale for Children. *Journal of Consulting Psychology*, 1951, *15*, 236–238.

30. Garrett, H. E. A developmental theory of intelligence. *The American Psychologist*, 1946, *1*, 372–378.

31. Gebroth, R. A study of the two forms of the Wechsler-Bellevue Intelligence Scale. *Journal of Consulting Psychology*, 1950, *14*, 365–370.

32. Gehman, I. H., and R. P. Matyas. Stability of the WISC and Binet tests. *Journal of Consulting Psychology*, 1956, *20*, 150–152.

33. Goolishian, H. A., and R. Ramsay. The Wechsler Bellevue, Form I, and the WAIS: a comparison. *Journal of Clinical Psychology*, 1956, *12*, 147–151.

34. Griffith, R. M., and R. S. Yamahiro. Reliability-stability of subject scatter on the Wechsler-Bellevue Intelligence Scales. *Journal of Clinical Psychology*, 1958, *14*, 317–318.

35. Grove, R. Mental age scores for the Wechsler Intelligence Scale for Children. *Journal of Clinical Psychology*, 1950, *6*, 393–397.

36. Hagen, E. P. A factor analysis of the Wechsler Intelligence Scale for Children. *The American Psychologist*, 1951, *6*, 297.

37. Hall, J. Correlation of a modified form of Raven's progressive matrices (1938) with the WAIS. *Journal of Consulting Psychology*, 1957, *21*, 23–26.

38. Hammer, A. G. A factor analysis of Bellevue Tests. *Australian Journal of Psychology*, 1950, *1*, 108–114.

39. Harlow, J. E., Jr., *et al.* Preliminary study of comparison between Wechsler Intelligence Scale for Children and Form L of revised S-B scale at three age levels. *Journal of Clinical Psychology*, 1957, *13*, 72–73.

40. Holland, G. A. A comparison of the WISC and Stanford-Binet IQs of normal children. *Journal of Consulting Psychology*, 1953, *17*, 147–152.

41. Karson, S., *et al.* The effects of scale and practice on WAIS and W-BI test scores. *Journal of Consulting Psychology*, 1957, *21*, 241–245.

42. Klausmeier, H. J., and J. Cheek. Relationships among physical, mental, achievement, and personality measures in children of low, average, and high intelligence at 113 months of age. *American Journal of Mental Deficiency*, 1959, *63*, 1059–1068.

43. Krugman, J. I., *et al.* Pupil functioning on the Stanford-Binet and the Wechsler Intelligence Scale for Children. *Journal of Consulting Psychology*, 1951, *15*, 475–483.

44. Kuenzli, A. E. (ed.). *The Phenomenological Problem*. New York: Harper & Brothers, 1959. (Especially ch. 1, by D. Snygg.)

45. Lewinski, R. J. Discriminative value of the subtests of the Bellevue verbal scale in the examination of naval recruits. *Journal of General Psychology*, 1944, *31*, 95–99.

46. Littell, W. M. The Wechsler Intelligence Scale for Children: review of a decade of research. *Psychological Bulletin*, 1960, *57*, 132–156.

47. Lotsof, E., *et al.* A factor analysis of the WISC and Rorschach. *Journal of Projective Techniques*, 1958, *22*, 297–301.

48. Marks, J. B., and J. E. Klahn. Verbal and perceptual components in WISC performance and their relation to social class. *Journal of Consulting Psychology*, 1961, *25*, 273.

49. McNemar, Q. On WAIS difference scores. *Journal of Consulting Psychology*, 1957, *21*, 239–240.

50. Mundy-Castle, A. C. Electrophysiological correlates of intelligence. *Journal of Personality*, 1958, *26*, 184–199.

51. Mussen, P., et al. Some further evidence of the validity of the WISC. *Journal of Consulting Psychology*, 1952, *16*, 410–411.

52. Nale, S. The children's Wechsler and the Binet on 104 mental defectives at the Polk State School. *American Journal of Mental Deficiency*, 1951, *56*, 419–423.

53. Pastovic, J. J., and G. M. Guthrie. Some evidence on the validity of WISC. *Journal of Consulting Psychology*, 1951, *15*, 385–386.

54. Plant, W. T. Mental ability scores for freshmen in a California state college. *California Journal of Educational Research*, 1958, *9*, 72–73.

55. Plant, W. T., and C. Lynd. A validity study and a college freshman norm group for the WAIS. *Personnel Guidance Journal*, 1959, April, 560–578.

56. Saunders, D. R. On the dimensionality of the WAIS battery for two groups of normal males. *Psychological Reports*, 1959, *5*, 529–541.

57. Saunders, D. R. A factor analysis of the information and arithmetic items of the WAIS. *Psychological Reports*, 1960, *6*, 367–383.

58. Saunders, D. R. A factor analysis of the picture completion items of the WAIS. *Journal of Clinical Psychology*, 1960, *16*, 146–149.

59. Schacter, F. F., and V. Apgar. Comparison of preschool Stanford-Binet and school age WISC IQs. *Journal of Educational Psychology*, 1958, *49*, 320–323.

60. Seashore, H. G. Differences between verbal and performance IQs on the WISC. *Journal of Consulting Psychology*, 1951, *15*, 62–67.

61. Seashore, H. G., et al. The standardization of the Wechsler Intelligence Scale for Children. *Journal of Consulting Psychology*, 1950, *14*, 99–110.

62. Spearman, C., and L. W. Jones. *Human Ability*. New York: The Macmillan Company, 1950.

63. Stacey, C. L., and J. Levin. Correlation analysis of scores of subnormal subjects on the Stanford-Binet and Wechsler Intelligence Scale for Children. *American Journal of Mental Deficiency*, 1951, *55*, 590–597.

64. Stempel, E. F. The WISC and the SRA Primary Mental Abilities Test. *Child Development*, 1953, *24*, 257–261.

65. Stroud, J. B. The intelligence test in school use: some persistent issues. *Journal of Educational Psychology*, 1957, *48*, 77–85.

66. Stroud, J. B., et al. Correlation analysis of WISC and achievement tests. *Journal of Educational Psychology*, 1957, *48*, 18–26.

67. Triggs, F. O., and J. K. Cartee. Preschool pupil performance on the S-B and the WISC. *Journal of Clinical Psychology*, 1953, *9*, 27–29.

68. Viaud, G. *Intelligence: Its Evolution and Forms*. New York: Harper & Brothers, 1960.

69. Wechsler, D., *et al.* A study of the subjects of the Bellevue Intelligence Scale in borderline and mental defective cases. *American Journal of Mental Deficiency,* 1941, *45,* 555–558.
70. Wechsler, D. *The Measurement of Adult Intelligence.* Baltimore: The Williams & Wilkins Company, 1944.
71. Wechsler, D. *Wechsler Intelligence Scale for Children: Manual.* New York: The Psychological Corporation, 1949.
72. Wechsler, D. Equivalent test and mental ages for the WISC. *Journal of Consulting Psychology,* 1951, *15,* 381–384.
73. Wechsler, D. *WAIS Manual.* New York: The Psychological Corporation, 1955.
74. Wechsler, D. *The Measurement and Appraisal of Adult Intelligence* (fourth ed.). Baltimore: The Williams & Wilkins Company, 1958.
75. Weider, A., *et al.* The Wechsler Intelligence Scale for Children and the revised Stanford-Binet. *Journal of Consulting Psychology,* 1951, *15,* 330–333.
76. Wesman, A. G. Standardizing an individual intelligence test on adults: some problems. *Journal of Gerontology,* 1955, *10,* 216–219.
77. Whatley, R. G., and W. T. Plant. The stability of WISC IQs for selected children. *Journal of Psychology,* 1957, *44,* 165–167.
78. Wolfensberger, W. P. Construction of a table of the significance of the difference between verbal and performance IQs on the WAIS and W-B. *Journal of Clinical Psychology,* 1958, *14,* 92.

12.

INDIVIDUAL PERFORMANCE SCALES

Definition and Need

A performance scale is one in which language is used only in the instructions, or not at all when directions are given in pantomime. The task to be performed requires an overt motor response other than verbal. The principal characteristic of the performance test is that a response to, or a solution of, the task does not require the use of language or number. For this reason, the term "performance scale" (or "performance test") is synonymous with "nonverbal test." [1] Although the term "performance" may be applied broadly to anything an individual does overtly, verbal or nonverbal, its use in psychological testing has become specialized and restricted to tests as here defined.[2]

About the time that the final revision of Binet's scale appeared (1911), some psychologists in the United States had assembled a group of performance tests intended to meet practical problems in the study of human abilities and behavior. One of these was the Healy-Fernald group of tests (1911), devised primarily to examine juvenile delinquents. This was an effort to determine their intellectual levels and personality traits

[1] Strictly speaking, then, since the Picture Completion subtest items in the Wechsler scales require a verbal answer, they are not performance tests, although they are included under that heading in the scales.

[2] An individual may verbalize the problem and solution of performance tests and thus facilitate his responses; but the point is that verbalization is not *required* in any language.

as revealed in the course of the examination (18). Unlike tests that were developed subsequently and that are now in use, those of Healy and Fernald were not actually standardized in respect to administration and scoring. This group of tests provided the psychological examiner with situations wherein he could observe, evaluate, and interpret the testee's methods of solving problems and his behavior in test situations. The specific tests were selected on the basis of Healy's and Fernald's judgment and psychological insights as to what constituted intelligent activity; beyond this the value of the results obtained with their tests depended upon the clinical acumen of the examiners, since there were no norms based upon standardization procedures.[3]

Performance tests have proved most valuable when used with persons handicapped by language disabilities, such as the deaf, the foreign-language-speaking groups, the illiterate, and those who have speech or reading disabilities. They are valuable, also, in helping to identify children who are inarticulate or excessively shy because of emotional reasons and who, therefore, might appear at a disadvantage on verbal tests of mental ability.

Used in conjunction with the verbal type, performance tests are helpful in identifying, with increasing certainty, the mentally deficient and the mentally retarded. In cases involving diagnosis of mental deficiency, it is often desirable to supplement the Stanford Binet, the Wechsler, or other verbal scales, with performance tests, in order to determine whether the language factor, cultural handicaps, or poor education, may have adversely affected the testee's score on the types of test materials included in the verbal scales. If a significant difference is found between the two obtained ratings, further study of the individual is indicated.

When performance tests were first used, it seemed as though they would be fairer and more appropriate for testing children and adolescents from culturally underprivileged environments who, therefore, might be handicapped in taking verbal tests.

Originally, then, individual performance scales were devised as *substitutes* for the Stanford-Binet. At present, however, the more general view is that they should be regarded as *supplements* to scales employing largely verbal and numerical materials. The principal reason for this view is that the correlations between performance and verbal scales are only about .50, when chronological age is held constant.

At present, judging from published case reports from schools and clinics, there is little research activity in this aspect of mental testing. We

---

[3] With their performance tests, Healy and Fernald included tests of reading, arithmetic, word opposites, information, and others. All tests referred to are listed in the References at the end of the chapter.

shall, however, present the situation as it is currently, since performance tests are historically significant and are being used, even though they are the subject of research by very few psychologists.

Representative Scales

THE PINTNER-PATERSON SCALE. This group of performance tests, the first to be organized into a scale, is now of interest principally for its historical and background value. Acquaintance with it will also enable the student to see that many of the earliest types of performance tests have survived the years of experimentation and application and have been incorporated into current scales, including the Wechsler.

Pintner and Paterson (1917) standardized some of the Healy-Fernald performance tests as well as several that had been devised by other psychologists and by themselves. The final scale includes fifteen tests that do not require the use of language on the part of either the examiner or the subject. They are intended primarily for use with persons having serious hearing defects and for non-English-speaking individuals. These and similar tests have been found valuable as supplements to verbal scales and with subjects who, although they speak English, have speech defects or reading disabilities.

The subtests in the scale are described below.

1. Mare and Foal Formboard. This, of the picture-puzzle type, is a pictureboard of a mare and foal, in color. Sections of the board are removed to begin with; the subject must replace them correctly. Score is based on time required and number of wrong moves.

2. Seguin Formboard. This is a formboard in which ten common geometric shapes are to be placed. Score is based on the shortest time required in three trials.

3. Five-Figure Board. There are five geometric figures, each of which is divided into two or three parts. The pieces are to be fitted into their appropriate places. Score is based on time required and number of errors made.

4. Two-Figure Board. There are two geometric figures, one cut into four sections and the other into five. These are to be correctly placed in two spaces. Score is based on time required and number of moves.

5. Casuist Board. This formboard—more difficult than the preceding ones—consists of four spaces in which twelve sections have to be fitted. Score is based on time required and number of errors made.

6. Triangle Test. Four triangular pieces are to be fitted into the board. Score is based on time required and number of errors made.

7. Diagonal Test. Five variously shaped sections have to be fitted into a rectangular form. Score is based on time required and number of errors made.

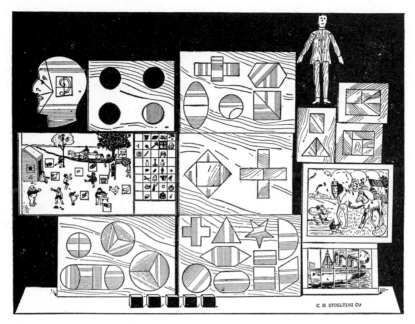

FIG. 12.1. Pintner-Paterson performance tests. C. H. Stoelting Company, by permission.

8. Healy Puzzle A. This consists of five rectangular sections to be fitted into a rectangular frame. Score is based on time required and number of moves made.

9. Manikin Test. Wooden legs, arms, head, and body are to be put together to make the form of a man. Score depends on quality of performance.

10. Feature Profile Test. Wooden sections have to be put together to form the profile of a man's head. Score is based on time required.

11. Ship Test (originated by H. A. Knox). This is a picture of a ship cut into ten sections, all of the same size and shape, to be inserted properly in a rectangular frame. Score depends on quality of performance.

12. Healy Picture-Completion Test I. This is a large picture from which ten small squares have been cut out. The missing parts are to be selected from among forty-eight squares identical in size. Score depends on the quality of completion within a limit of ten minutes.

13. Substitution Test. A page of rows of geometric figures (five different shapes) have to be marked with appropriate digits, to correspond with a key at top of page. Score is a combination of time and errors made.

14. Adaptation Board. This is a formboard having four circular blocks and holes; three are 6.8 cm. in diameter, and the fourth is 7 cm. The subject is shown that one block fits the larger hole. He is then required to keep his attention fixed and to fit this larger block into the correct space when the

board is moved into four different positions. Score is based on the number of correct moves.

15. Cube Test. Four cubes (one inch) are placed before the subject. They are tapped in a specified order by the examiner with a fifth cube. The subject is asked to imitate the order of tapping. The sequence becomes longer and more complex. Score is the number of sequences correctly imitated.

For general testing purposes, the authors of this performance scale recommend the use of a short scale that includes ten of the fifteen parts. These are numbers 1, 2, 3, 4, 5, 9, 10, 11, 12, and 15 of the preceding list.

The age range of the Pintner-Paterson scale is from 4 years to 15. However, this does not mean that every test in the series has discriminative value throughout. For example, the Sequin Formboard is not valuable, ordinarily, beyond age 10, while the Feature Profile Test is generally not useful below age 10.

THE CORNELL-COXE SCALE.   For their scale, these authors selected tests from a variety of sources. This scale includes seven types of test materials, two of which (Manikin and Digit Symbol) are utilized in the Pintner-Paterson and will, therefore, not be repeated here. The remaining five types are the following. (Note that the Cornell-Coxe does not include any formboards.)

1. Block Designs. These are the familiar Kohs colored-block designs, five of which were included. They are scored for accuracy and time required.

2. Picture Arrangement. This includes ten series of pictures which, though different in subject matter, are the same in principle as those in the Wechsler scale. They are scored for accuracy only.

3. Memory for Designs. This test includes five cards, on each of which is a geometric design. The subject is asked to reproduce each design after it has been shown for ten seconds. This type of test is similar to that used by Binet. The score depends upon quality of reproduction.

4. Cube Construction. This test utilizes blocks having some sides painted and others unpainted. The examiner presents models of cube construction and asks the subject to duplicate them. The score depends upon both accuracy and time.

5. Picture Completion. (This is an optional substitute for test 3.) The Healy Picture-Completion Test II was selected. The score depends upon accuracy only. (This test is the same in principle as Picture-Completion I; but its theme is different and it is on a higher level of difficulty.)

THE ARTHUR POINT SCALE.   This scale provides two forms. Form I is a restandardization of eight tests used in the Pintner-Paterson. They are Knox Cube; Seguin, Two-Figure, and Casuist Formboards; Manikin;

Feature Profile; Mare and Foal; Healy Picture Completion I. Two tests, the Porteus Maze and The Kohs Block Design, were added.

The Porteus test consists of a series of mazes of increasing difficulty, each printed on a separate sheet. The subject is required to trace, with pencil, the course from entrance to exit. The Kohs test consists of the same set of blocks used in The Wechsler-Bellevue scale, but the subject reproduces different designs.

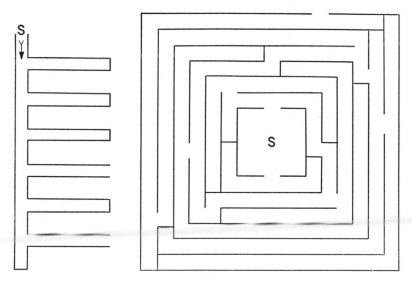

FIG. 12.2. Porteus Maze tests—years 5 and 14. C. H. Stoelting Company, by permission.

Form II serves as an alternate when retesting is necessary. This version utilizes four of the test types already described. These are Knox Cube, Seguin Formboard, Porteus Mazes, and Healy Pictorial Completion II. The only new type of material not thus far described is the Arthur Stencil Design (see Fig. 12.3.) This test employs twenty designs, presented singly, that are increasingly complex and more difficult to reproduce. The testee is given six square, colored cards and twelve colored stencils that are cut within square cards. Each design is to be reproduced by placing the appropriate cards and stencils one upon another, so as to duplicate the original in both form and color. For example, a practice design requires merely that a red octagonal stencil be laid over a white card to get the desired result.

FORMBOARDS. Several performance tests serve a specific and limited purpose by using formboards only. The *Ferguson Formboards* (1920; re-

FIG. 12.3. The Arthur Stencil Design Test. The Psychological Corporation, by
permission.

vised 1939) consist of a series of six, used as a unit and progressing in difficulty (12, 41). These were standardized on subjects ($N = 364$) ranging from
children in grade one to college seniors. These tests were intended for use
with individuals having educational problems; for they were validated
against grade placement ($r = .81$), teachers' estimates of intelligence
($r = .50$), and class standing ($r = .56$); and they were largely utilized, apparently, with individuals who had come to a school guidance clinic for
assistance.

The Kent-Shakow Formboard Series (1952) is probably the most widely
known. Since the original was made available, a modified series appeared,
in 1928, in two forms, one for clinical use and the other for industrial (21,
34). This series of formboards was developed as a clinical instrument. It
was, therefore, standardized on a clinical population. (Revised adult
norms were published in 1939.) No attempt was made to validate this
series against other tests. The intention was, apparently, to provide a
clinical device that would measure manipulative skill and, more important, visual analysis and synthesis of form. At the same time, the test

provides a means of observing the subject's modes of dealing with a problem.[4]

The Carl Hollow-Square Scale, intended for use primarily with adults, is of interest because the problems of analysis and organization it presents are quite complex for this type of test; that is, more than the usual number of variables are involved in each situation. The blocks are of varying sizes and forms, having straight and beveled edges; and they are truncated in several ways. The series of twenty tasks becomes progressively more complex and difficult.

Since the subject must follow different and more complex instructions as he progresses with the tasks in the scale, Carl believes that auditory memory span is involved, as well as the mental operations necessary in other performance tests. He believes that although this formboard test measures mental operations involved in concrete and practical aspects of

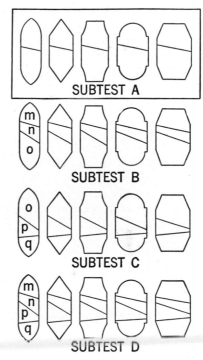

FIG. 12.4. Modified Kent-Shakow Formboard Series. By permission of William R. Grove.

activity, it is also a measure of general rather than special ability, because of its significant correlations with verbal tests ($r = .50$ to $.80$).

Other Types

The Leiter International Performance Scale (1948) differs from others in this category since, for the most part, it does not employ the usual types of test materials. It is intended to be a nonverbal scale to measure general intelligence. As such, it utilizes materials of the kind included in: (1) nonverbal group scales (of the paper-and-pencil type); (2) *forms* of materials included in verbal tests; and (3) a few of the conventional performance tests. In the Leiter scale, however, all tests are presented through a nonverbal medium. Items representing (1) above are, for example, concealed cubes, matching pictures and forms, picture and

[4] In 1939, W. R. Grove made available a modified form of the Kent-Shakow series, Industrial Model. See Figure 12.4.

form completion. Under (2), above, are similarities, number series, and classification of objects. Under (3) are included a number of tests requiring matching of designs and colors, completing block designs, and form completion (see Figs. 12.5 and 12.6).

This series of tests is graded in difficulty, beginning at age 2 and continuing through age 18. It is thus intended, presumably, for use with adults as well as with children.[5]

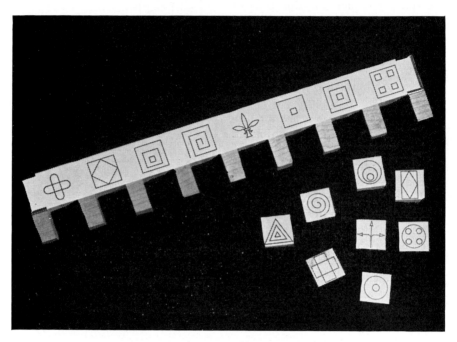

Fig. 12.5. Selection of analogous designs, 9-year level. From The Leiter International Performance Scale. By permission.

Studies of reliability have yielded quite satisfactory results, the coefficients being in the low .90s. Validating correlations with the S-B and the WISC, however, present inconclusive results. When the S-B was used as a criterion, the coefficients varied from about .65 to .80. Since these correlations were derived from the testing of heterogeneous groups, their significance is not clear. The Arthur adaptation, correlated with the WISC, yielded the following coefficients: verbal scale, .40; performance scale, .79; full scale, .77. The coefficient of .40 presents a serious question regarding the similarities or comparability of mental functions required by these two scales.

[5] An adaptation for children has been prepared by Dr. Grace Arthur. It was devised to measure ability of children from 3 to 8 years of age (4, p. 4).

One of the advantages often claimed for performance and other non-verbal tests is that they are "culture free." There are, however, no culture-free tests. Examination of the content of the Leiter and other nonverbal scales shows clearly that the specific materials included are derived from our culture. The aim of these and other tests *intended for the general population* can only be "culture fairness"; that is, to give no segment of the population advantages over others.

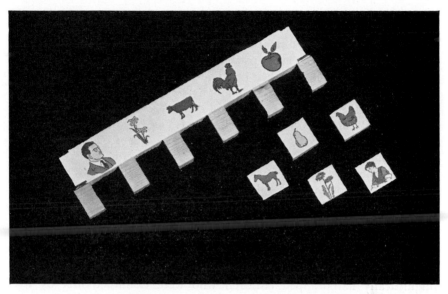

FIG. 12.6. Classification by genus, 5-year level. From The Leiter International Performance Scale. By permission.

The Goodenough Drawing Test (1926) is intended to evaluate a child's intelligence by means of his drawing of a man. It is used with children from the age of 3½ to 13½ years. The child is instructed to make a picture of a man as best he can. He is told to work carefully and to take his time. Scoring is based not upon esthetic quality but, rather, upon the presence of essential details and the correctness of their relationships, which presumably indicate the individual's level of perception and analysis of a familiar object in his environment.

A revision of the Goodenough test is now being prepared for publication (16, 17). This revision is based upon the same principles as the original; but the standardization process was more thorough and, as a result, the norms (for ages 5 to 15) should be more reliable. An innovation is this: the child is asked to draw a picture of a woman and one of himself, in addition to that of a man. Also, consistent with the current trend, point scores on this test are converted to deviation IQs (mean = 100; $SD = 15$).

Reliability coefficients of the Goodenough test vary from about .70 to about .90, depending in part upon the method used. Agreement among different scorers of the same drawings is high, with correlations close to .90.

Validity studies, in terms of correlations with intelligence tests, have yielded varying results. Coefficients—found principally with the Stanford-Binet—are between .40 and .80. Some of these coefficients, of course, are too low to warrant the substitution of the Goodenough for the S-B or any of the other intelligence tests used. But even in the case of the higher coefficients—assuming they are representative—substitution of the Draw-A-Man Test for the S-B, or other intelligence tests in common use, would not be sound, because the Goodenough test does not provide any opportunity for the qualitative analysis of content, or for the observation of an individual's modes of behavior when he is faced with a variety of tasks of increasing difficulty. Nor does it provide the means of testing several forms of mental operations, such as the other tests require. The Draw-A-Man Test, however, is a useful device as an adjunct to verbal tests when mental retardation is suspected.

The Columbia Mental Maturity Scale (1954; revised norms, 1959), designed for the mental age range of 3 to 12 years, is intended primarily, though not solely, to test mental ability of children handicapped by cerebral palsy or other defects of motor or verbal functioning. Also, like other performance tests, this scale may be used in checking on ratings, of linguistically handicapped children who were examined first by tests using verbal materials. The child's response can be restricted merely to pointing, or to pointing plus any verbal additions he wishes and is able to make.

This scale consists of one hundred 6- by 19-inch cards presenting problems graded in difficulty, each with a series of three to five drawings. The child selects from each series the one drawing that is unrelated to the others on that card. That is, he must discern the principle relating the other drawings to one another. These tasks require what Spearman called "the eduction of relations." The student will find that this form of reasoning, from the quite simple to the highly complex problem, is commonly employed, whether the test materials are verbal or nonverbal, in both group and individual tests, including those intended for use with persons whose mental functioning has been impaired by injury or by psychological disorder.

As in the case of nearly all other tests of intelligence, the Columbia scale was validated against the 1937 S-B (Form L) as the criterion. The authors derived separate correlation coefficients for IQs of each yearly group, from age 3 to 12. The coefficients varied from .66 (for age 8) to .88 (for age 11); for the entire group combined, the correlation with S-B intelligence quotients was .78. Reliability coefficients are high for four separate age groups, ranging from .89 (age 4) to .92 (age 10).

FIG. 12.7. Test items from the Columbia Mental Maturity Scale. Reproduced by permission.

This technically well-conceived scale demonstrates that with children it is possible to obtain a reasonably dependable rating, when necessary, through the use of a single type of material of a sound kind. This is not to say, however, that under normal conditions a single-type scale should be used in preference to one, like the S-B or the WISC, that employs several types of test materials.

Functions Tested by Performance Scales

This discussion will supplement the analysis that was presented in connection with the nonverbal parts of the Stanford-Binet and the Wechsler scales. The reader should refer to those for more detail.

Since all performance tests involve visual perception and manipulation of objects, the number of types of items is relatively limited. It is not surprising, therefore, to find that the range of psychological functions is also restricted. This is one reason why the correlations between performance scales and scales of the Stanford-Binet type are not higher than they are, since the latter can sample a much wider range of mental operations.

If the reader will re-examine the descriptions of the fifteen subtests in the Pintner-Paterson scale, and the few other types introduced in later scales, it will be readily apparent that, except for the Goodenough test, they may be classified in one of the following categories:

> geometric formboards, with variations, from the very simple to rather complex.
> picture formboards (also known as picture completion) of various degrees of complexity.
> block designs from simple to the complex.
> recall of geometric designs.
> picture arrangement.
> block building.
> cube sequences (imitating the order of tapping a series of cubes).
> digit symbol.
> mazes from very simple to the complex.
> matching forms.

These tests involve visual perception, plus visual insight requiring analysis and synthesis. Performance on all types is a measure also, in varying degrees, of motor speed. Performance is facilitated by visual imagery, that is, by ability to analyze and synthesize a pattern imaginally before actually going through the movements. In all performance tests, visual-motor integration, affecting the speed and accuracy with which a person responds, is a factor.

Many clinical psychologists believe that performance tests provide an estimate of the subject's attention span, especially in the case of mentally retarded and deficient individuals. Attention span, however, is not a process in the sense that visual analysis, memory span, etc., are. Attention is, rather, an *attribute* of the situation in which an individual is placed. If the person is interested in the task at hand, and if the test is within the range of his comprehension, he will be attentive. If he does not understand the task, and if he is unable to make any progress with it and is confronted by repeated failure, he will probably become inattentive.

It will be noted that these test items, with the exception of the Leiter scale, make few or no demands upon abstraction, concept formation, or the necessity for transcending the immediate concrete situation. For this reason, performance tests are regarded as having limited value as measures of general capacity, particularly for testing individuals who are above average level.

Evaluation of Performance Tests

Validity. Although performance tests were originally devised to serve as substitutes for verbal scales, comparative studies have shown that it is sounder to regard them as supplements. The reason is that when the factor of chronological age is held constant, in almost every instance the coefficients of correlation fall at .50, or lower. Hence, although verbal and performance tests measure some functions in common, or are in other ways interrelated, each type also measures functions different from those of the other.

The Pintner-Paterson scale, for example, yielded coefficients of .43 and .23, respectively, when correlated with the S-B, for a group of dull children and one of superior children (28). The r of .23 indicates that these performance tests are inadequate for differentiating among levels of superior individuals.

A fairly large number of studies have been published reporting higher correlations between performance-test ratings obtained with the Pintner-Paterson and similar tests and those obtained with revisions of the Binet scale. Coefficients in the range of .70 and .80 were not uncommon, whereas others were as low as .50. These coefficients, however, cannot be interpreted as necessarily indicating considerable community of function between these types of tests. It appears that to an appreciable degree the correlation coefficients are the result of the wide age range of the subjects tested, with the result that the coefficients reflect the fact that the psychological functions being tested by both types increase with age. An ordinary group of 10-year-old children will get higher scores on both types of tests than will a similar group of 9-year-olds, who, in turn, will score higher on both than an ordinary group of 8-year-olds; and so on. This is to be expected; for the tests have been so constructed as to yield progressive increases in age norms as chronological age increases.

Another example of the effect of age range on correlations is found in the correlations between intelligence ratings and height, or weight, or dentition. For a wide age range, these are in the neighborhood of .50 and .60, because older children generally are taller, heavier, and have more permanent teeth. But within a single age group the correlation coefficients between these physical traits and intelligence-test ratings drop to negligible levels. Similarly, when age is held constant, or very nearly so, the correlation coefficients between results obtained with the Pintner-Paterson and similar performance tests, on the one hand, and verbal tests, on the other, drop to between .40 and .60.

Cornell and Coxe, who took the position that a performance scale should be supplemental to the verbal type, report a correlation of .79 with the S-B, for a wide age range. Yet when CA was held constant, the partial correlation coefficient dropped to .38. Intercorrelations of the parts of their scale varied from .50 to .75, over a wide age range; but, again, with CA constant, the coefficients dropped to .20–.60.

Since the Arthur scale was devised as a substitute for the Binet revisions, in cases where a verbal scale is inappropriate, it is pertinent to examine the correlations found between the two scales. Table 12.1 shows

TABLE 12.1

CORRELATIONS OF STANFORD-BINET IQs AND ARTHUR IQs

Age	N	r
5	35	.70 ± .06
6	54	.77 ± .04
7	50	.68 ± .05
8	44	.74 ± .05
9	41	.80 ± .04
10	40	.51 ± .08
11	44	.68 ± .05
12	31	.80 ± .04
13	27	.21 ± .12
14	27	.07 ± .13
15	16	−.10 ± .17

Calculated from data in G. Arthur, *A Point Scale of Performance Tests.* New York: The Commonwealth Fund, 1933, 2, 54–61.

the coefficients between S-B (1916) and Arthur intelligence quotients.

Most of the coefficients in Table 12.1 are quite significant between the ages of 5 and 12 years, except at age 10. The coefficients at later ages, however, are so low that they may be regarded as zero, for all practical purposes. If the table of coefficients is representative of the correspondence existing between Stanford-Binet IQs and Arthur performance IQs at ages above 12, then we must conclude that the latter scale is incapable of differentiating among individuals at those age levels.

Although the coefficients for ages 5 to 12 are quite marked, and in several instances high, they are, nevertheless, not close enough to unity (+1.00) to warrant the use of the Stanford-Binet and the Arthur scales interchangeably. For clinical purposes, the Arthur scale is valuable within the age range of 5 to 12 as a supplement to verbal scales of the Stanford-Binet type.

This conclusion is further supported by validating data obtained subsequent to the publication of Arthur's manual. These later studies, using both the 1916 and 1937 revisions of the Stanford-Binet, can be summarized as follows:

Stanford-Binet and Arthur IQs correlate variously, from about .50 to about .80.

In a large majority of cases, the Arthur scale IQs tend to be somewhat higher than the S-B at levels below 90 IQ.[6]

At the levels above 90 IQ, the S-B tends to yield somewhat higher ratings.

The means of the differences between the IQs of the two scales have been found to range from about 5 to 10 points.

Dr. Arthur's position appears to be that the appreciable extent of agreement between S-B ratings and those of her performance scale indicates rather even development and manifestation of psychological functions in general. She believes that if the results of these two scales disagree significantly in the case of a given individual, this is due to unevenness in development and expression of functions, or to some complicating non-intellectual factors.

In the case of any individual, the actual interpretation of performance-test results, taken in conjunction with verbal-test findings, will depend upon all information available with regard to the person concerned and upon the interrelations of all relevant facts and data. If the two scales used give discrepant results, the psychologist's task is to discover the reasons for whatever significant differences are found. His analysis and interpretation of test results are thereby enriched and have greater validity.

The correlation coefficients cited above for the three performance scales are representative of those generally found with this type of testing material. A factorial analysis of results obtained with thirty-four commonly used performance tests suggests one reason for the low or only moderate correlations between these and verbal tests (29). This analysis indicates that the principal factors measured by the performance tests studied may be identified as perceptual speed, spatial, and induction. Perceptual speed is defined as the readiness to discover and identify perceptual detail (mainly visual). The spatial factor is the ability to manipulate objects in space. Induction, of course, means reasoning from the particular to the general. Although the first two of these factors are involved to some ex-

---

[6] Dr. Arthur reported that for 435 clinic cases who had S-B intelligence quotients of less than 95, there was no group trend in the direction of higher ratings on her scale (2, *1*, revised, p. 14; also 3).

tent in many verbal tests of mental ability, they are of relatively minor significance in the determination of an individual's rating on these.

Reliability. So far as reliability is concerned, performance tests stand up reasonably well individually, although, as a group, not as well as the better verbal scales. The Cornell-Coxe scale, for example, reports coefficients for each of the parts varying from .66 to .89, while for the total score the reliability was .929. Forms I and II of the Arthur scales were correlated at each age level from 6 to 16 years. The coefficients, with CA constant, varied from .55 (*PE* ± .06) at age 8, to .70 (*PE* ± .06) at 10 and 15. The median coefficient was .61 (*PE* ± .06). These low coefficients are possibly evidence of the nonequivalence of the two forms rather than of the unreliability of either. In another study, 61 institutionalized mentally deficient boys (mean Stanford-Binet IQ = 67) were tested with the Arthur scale and retested after two years. The reliability coefficient was .85 for total scores, and .69 to .80 for part scores. However, the mean gain on the Arthur scale was ten points in IQ, as contrasted with a mean loss of only one point on the S-B during the same interval (30).

The mean gain of ten points may be attributed to one, or both, of two factors. (1) Scores on the performance type of test are more susceptible to practice (learning) than are those on the verbal type; or (2) residence and training in a soundly conceived and operated institution encourages the development and utilization of the *potentialities* of the mentally deficient beyond levels attained under ordinary circumstances. The latter factor is not synonymous with specific practice and learning effect. It is, rather, a result of general training in more effective behavior.

Advantages and Disadvantages

During the many years the Pintner-Paterson and other performance scales have been used for clinical and experimental purposes, the following evaluations of them have been made. They are more susceptible to practice effects, and chance successes are more frequent than is the case with verbal tests; hence, the reliability coefficients of performance tests are not as high as those of the verbal. The performance scale is most useful with normal young children, and with older children and adults who are mentally retarded. The scale also has clinical significance in the case of an older child when there is marked discrepancy in performance on the several subtests. The several parts of the performance scale examine processes that are more specific than those examined by verbal tests. This is indicated by the scatter of scores on the several parts and by the lower correlation coefficients found when ratings on each of the parts were correlated with ratings for the whole scale.

Performance tests, as already stated, are limited in range of mental functioning tested; because of this, they do not differentiate well among above-average individuals. These performance scales are most useful, on the whole, at the lower age levels and the lower mental levels, as well as for testing persons who have language handicaps.

Geometric formboards, picture-completion boards, object assemblies, etc., are within almost universal experience of American school children; and since these tests make demands upon the mental processes already indicated, they may be regarded, in some degree, as measures of intelligence at these earlier age levels. However, as performance tests go higher in age and difficulty levels, they present specialized problem situations which the subjects have not had comparable backgrounds for handling. This is especially true of the more complex and subtle formboards (for example, the Carl hollow square), performance on which is facilitated by training and experience in tasks requiring spatial perception, as in some types of engineering, cabinetmaking, and the like. Since these conventional performance tests do not require much use of the ability to make abstractions and to deal with concepts, they fail to measure some of the most important aspects of mental activity.

Among the advantages reported for performance tests are these: (1) since the tests do not require the use of language, individuals do not "block" as a result of feelings of inadequacy resulting from lack of formal schooling; (2) since all elements of the problem are visually present, some individuals proceed with greater confidence.

Psychologists are agreed that, where indicated, the use of performance scales can provide more information than only a rating in the form of a numerical index. These tests provide an opportunity to observe qualitative aspects of behavior under standardized conditions in a variety of problem situations. A subject's approach to a problem might reveal, for example, a state of depression or agitation; hesitation or impetuousness; thoughtful deliberateness, bull-headed persistence, or easy discouragement; an insightful approach or one of haphazard trial and error.

The reader will have noted that not all authors of performance tests agree as to what the characteristics of such a scale should be. The Arthur scale was constructed to provide a nonverbal substitute for the Binet revisions. Hence it was expected to have a highly significant correlation with these revisions, and standardization proceeded on that principle. The Cornell-Coxe scale is intended not as a substitute for Binet revisions but as a supplement to them. Thus, this performance scale was constructed on the principle that there should be a relatively low correlation between it and the verbal type of intelligence tests. The Leiter scale, on the other hand, differs from these and other conventional performance tests in that, for the purpose of measuring much the same mental processes as do the verbal tests, it employs a rather distinctive technique with a variety of materials, some of which have been adapted from nonverbal group tests of the paper-and-pencil type, while others have been specially devised.

Experimental evidence indicates that the usual performance scales (for example, Pintner-Paterson) are best used as supplements to verbal scales. The former are instruments with which we may test development of insightful behavior involving visual perception, instead of by the use of symbols (language and number) that are essential for abstractions, concept formation, ideational reasoning, and ability to deal with problems extending beyond one's immediate, concrete environment.

References

1. Ansbacher, H. L. The Goodenough Draw-A-Man Test and primary mental abilities. *Journal of Consulting Psychology,* 1952, *16,* 176–180.
2. Arthur, G. *A Point Scale of Performance Tests.* New York: The Commonwealth Fund, 1930, *1;* 1933, *2;* 1943, *1,* revised.
3. Arthur, G. The relative difficulty of various tests for sixty feeble-minded individuals. *Journal of Clinical Psychology,* 1950, *6,* 276–279.
4. Arthur, G. *The Arthur Adaptation of the Leiter International Performance Scale.* Washington, D.C.: Psychological Service Center Press, 1952.
5. Blank, L., and M. L. Rawn. An experimental method to measure intellectual functioning with verbal and motor factors minimal. *Journal of Psychology,* 1956, *41,* 119–126.
6. Burgemeister, B. B., *et al. Columbia Mental Maturity Scale.* New York: Harcourt, Brace & World, Inc., 1954.
7. Carl, G. P. A new performance test for adults and older children: the Carl hollow square scale. *Journal of Psychology,* 1939, *7,* 179–199.
8. Cooper, J. G. Predicting school achievement for bilingual pupils. *Journal of Educational Psychology,* 1958, *49,* 31–36.
9. Cornell, E. L., and W. W. Coxe. *A Performance Ability Scale.* New York: Harcourt, Brace & World, Inc., 1934.
10. Cruickshank, W. M. (ed.). *Psychology of Exceptional Children and Youth.* Englewood Cliffs, N.J.: Prentice-Hall, Inc., 1955 (especially chs. 3, 4, 6).
11. Doll, E. A. (ed.). *The Oseretsky Tests of Motor Proficiency.* Minneapolis: Educational Testing Bureau, 1946.
12. Ferguson, G. O. A series of formboards. *Journal of Experimental Psychology,* 1920, *2,* 47–58.
13. Goodenough, F. L. *Measurement of Intelligence by Drawings.* New York: Harcourt, Brace & World, Inc., 1926.
14. Goodenough, F. L., and D. B. Harris. Studies in the psychology of children's drawings: II, 1928–1949. *Psychological Bulletin,* 1950, *47,* 369–433.

15. Grove, W. R. Modifications of the Kent-Shakow Formboard Series. *Journal of Psychology*, 1939, *7*, 385–397.

16. Harris, D. B. *Harris-Goodenough Test of Psychological Maturity*. New York: Harcourt, Brace & World, Inc. (in press).*

17. Harris, D. B. *Measuring the Psychological Maturity of Children: A Revision and Extension of the Goodenough Draw-A-Man Test*. New York: Harcourt, Brace & World, Inc. (in press).*

18. Healy, W., and G. M. Fernald. Tests for practical mental classification. *Psychological Monographs*, 1911, *13*.

19. Holden, R. H. Improved methods in testing cerebral palsied children. *American Journal of Mental Deficiency*, 1951, *56*, 349–353.

20. Jones, A. W., and T. A. Rich. The Goodenough Draw-A-Man Test as a measure of intelligence in aged adults. *Journal of Consulting Psychology*, 1957, *21*, 235–238.

21. Kent, G. H., and D. Shakow. Graded series of formboards. *Personnel Journal*, 1928, *7*, 115–120.

22. Kohs, S. C. *Intelligence Measurement*. New York: The Macmillan Company, 1923.

23. Leiter, R. G. *Part II of the Manual for the 1948 Revision of the Leiter International Performance Scale*. Washington, D.C.: Psychological Service Center Press, 1952.

24. Leiter, R. G. Part I of the manual for the 1948 revision of the Leiter International Performance Scale. *Psychological Service Center Journal*, 1959, *11*, 1–72.

25. Lowenfeld, M. *The Lowenfeld Mosaic Test*. London: Newman Neame, 1954.

26. May, W. T., and H. W. Perry. The relationship between the Stanford-Binet (Form L) vocabulary and the Columbia Mental Maturity Scale in a group of mentally retarded children. *American Journal of Mental Deficiency*, 1957, *62*, 330–333.

27. McCarthy, D. A study of the reliability of the Goodenough test of intelligence. *Journal of Psychology*, 1944, *18*, 201–216.

28. MacMurray, D. A. A comparison of gifted children and of dull-normal children measured by the Pintner-Paterson scale against the Stanford-Binet scale. *Journal of Psychology*, 1937, *4*, 273–280.

29. Morris, C. M. A critical analysis of certain performance tests. *Journal of Genetic Psychology*, 1939, *54*, 85–105.

30. Patterson, R. M. The significance of practice effect upon re-administration of the Grace Arthur performance scale to high grade mentally deficient children. *American Journal of Mental Deficiency*, 1946, *50*, 393–401.

31. Pintner, R., and D. Paterson. *A Point Scale of Performance Tests*. New York: Appleton-Century-Crofts, Inc., 1917.

32. Porteus, S. D. *The Maze Test and Clinical Psychology*. Palo Alto, Calif.: Pacific Books, 1959.

33. Scherer, I. W., *et al.* Psychological changes over a three-year period following prefrontal lobotomy. *Journal of Consulting Psychology*, 1955, *19*, 291–298.

* Tentative title.

34. Shakow, D., and B. Pazeian. Adult norms for the K-S clinical formboards. *Journal of Applied Psychology,* 1939, *23,* 495–502.
35. Shontz, F. C. Evaluation of intellectual potential in hemiplegic individuals. *Journal of Clinical Psychology,* 1957, *13,* 267–269.
36. Sievers, D. J., and R. D. Norman. Some suggestive results in psychometric testing of the cerebral palsied with Gesell, Binet, and Wechsler scales. *Journal of Genetic Psychology,* 1953, *82,* 69–90.
37. Sloan, W. The Lincoln-Oseretsky Motor Development Scale. *Genetic Psychology Monographs,* 1955, *51,* no. 2.
38. Strauss, A. A., and L. E. Lehtinen. *Psychopathology and Education of the Brain-Injured Child.* New York: Grune & Stratton, Inc., 1947.
39. Tate, M. E. The influence of cultural factors on the Leiter International Performance Scale. *Journal of Abnormal and Social Psychology,* 1952, *47,* 497–501.
40. Wallin, J. E. W. A comparison of the Stanford 1916 and 1937 (Form L) test results with those from the Arthur performance scale (Form I) based on the same subjects. *Journal of Genetic Psychology,* 1946, *69,* 45–55.
41. Wood, L., and E. Kumin. A new standardization of the Ferguson formboards. *Journal of Genetic Psychology,* 1939, *54,* 265–284.

13.

SCALES FOR INFANTS AND PRESCHOOL CHILDREN

In this chapter we shall present several representative scales devised to evaluate mental development of children ranging in age from one *month* to six *years*. Some of these scales, for the most part, are not tests as that term is commonly understood. They are, rather, norms and inventories of development and behavior, grouped at their respective average age levels, derived from observation of children's behavior and from experimentation in a variety of situations. All are administered individually. The content of these scales is presented in some detail, so that the student may become acquainted with the scales' characteristics in order to make meaningful comparisons with tests used at later ages.

The Gesell Scales

The Gesell scales provide tests at two levels; one is *The Infant Schedule* and the other is *The Preschool Schedule*. They are the products of systematic study of infants and preschool children at the Yale Clinic of Child Development. The first schedule (1925) provided rather crude norms at the following age levels: 4, 6, 9, 12, 18, 24, 36, 48, and 60 months (9).

At each level the inventory was divided into four categories of behavior: (1) *motor,* (2) *adaptive,* (3) *language,* (4) *personal-social.* Although the normative schedules themselves have undergone considerable revision and refinement since their first appearance, these four categories, with some minor variations in terminology and analysis at times, have remained throughout. Motor behavior is said to be of value ". . . because it has so many neurological implications, and because motor capacities of the child constitute the natural starting point for an estimate of his maturity." In adaptive behavior ". . . we reckon with the finer sensori-motor adjustments to objects and situations: the coordination of eyes and hands in reaching and manipulation; . . . the capacity to initiate new adjustments in the presence of simple problem situations which we set before the infant." Language behavior, broadly used, includes ". . . all visible and audible forms of communication, whether by facial expression, gesture, postural movements, vocalizations, words, phrases, or sentences. [It] includes mimicry and comprehension of the communications of others." Personal-social behavior "comprises the child's personal reactions to the social culture in which he lives [bladder and bowel control, feeding abilities, sense of property, self-dependence in play, cooperativeness, responsiveness to training and social conventions]" (11, p. 5).

The Infant Schedule was devised for the examination of children between the ages of 4 and 56 weeks. At the 4-week level, the inventory of behavior includes analysis of head control, arm-hand posture, leg-foot posture, body posture and progression, regard, prehension, language and social behavior. At the 56-week level, the inventory includes body posture and progression, prehension, manipulation and adaptation, language and social behavior. Each of these categories of behavior is evaluated, in the case of a particular infant, by observing him in a number of situations.[1] Each situation is broken down into a number of possible activities that detail the manner in which the infant might respond. Since the enumerated responses follow diverse trends with age, they have been designated as follows: (1) *decreasing trend,* if at ascending ages there is a progressive decrease in percentage of infants showing that behavior; (2) *increasing trend,* if at ascending ages there is a progressive increase in percentage showing that behavior; (3) *focal trend,* if at consecutive ages there is an increase, followed by a decrease in percentage giving that response. The "increasing" and "decreasing" behavior items were allocated to age levels on the basis of fifty percent frequency. The "focal" behavior items were placed at age levels at which they are most frequently observed.[2]

The infant's responses are scored plus or minus, depending upon whether or not he manifests the enumerated behaviors. The score on

[1] For example, activity with a ball, a bell, rattle, cubes, cup, spoon, formboard, mirror, boxes, pellet and bottle, dangling ring, paper and crayon; patterns of body posture; locomotion; spontaneous activities in various daily situations, such as in toilet, bath, and crib; kinds of play; responses to people; kinds of vocalization.

[2] For a detailed account of the scoring method, see Gesell and Thompson (12, pp. 209 ff.).

TABLE 13.1

DANGLING RING BEHAVIOR (4 WEEKS–28 WEEKS)

RD	Behavior items	4	6	8	12	16	20	24	28
1	Regards after delay	77	54	64	65	27	13	14	5
2	Regards immediately	26	46	36	35	68	97	96	95
3	Regards momentarily	53	85	71	38	35	—	—	—
4	Regards prolongedly	47	43	29	62	87	47	38	5
5	Regards consistently	—	—	—	—	17	26	59	90
6	Disregards in midplane	77	39	46	46	14	—	—	—
7	Regards in midplane	29	61	54	54	86	—	—	—
8	Regards in midplane (long head)	22	25	12	50	83	—	—	—
9	Regards in midplane (round head)	32	75	70	56	88	—	—	—
10	Regards ring in hand	—	—	—	—	66	82	100	100
11	Regards string	—	—	—	—	7	13	46	53
12	Shifts regard	94	100	100	96	93	46	38	41
13	Shifts regard to surroundings	75	68	61	35	13	16	14	5
14	Shifts regard to Examiner's hand	28	64	61	77	48	—	—	—
15	Shifts regard to Examiner	41	54	57	65	64	27	24	27
16	Shifts regard to hand	0	4	7	8	19	5	3	—
17	Follows past midplane	44	62	50	58	84	—	—	—
18	Follows past midplane (lg. h.)	20	33	25	37	83	—	—	—
19	Follows past midplane (rd. h.)	55	75	60	67	77	—	—	—
20	Follows approximately 180°	16	43	46	50	68	—	—	—
21	Follows approximately 180° (lg. h.)	0	11	25	25	83	—	—	—
22	Follows approximately 180° (rd. h.)	36	55	55	61	62	—	—	—
23	Approaches	0	0	11	12	62	89	96	100
24	Approaches after delay	—	—	—	—	58	30	19	9
25	Approaches promptly	—	—	—	—	32	66	81	91
26	Arms increase activity	0	4	11	42	64	—	—	—
27	Arms separate	0	0	4	15	17	19	7	—
28	Approaches with one hand	0	0	4	12	20	24	39	55
29	Approaches with both hands	0	0	0	0	50	76	82	77
30	Approaches with arms flexed	0	0	0	12	44	60	54	14
31	Hands come together	0	0	0	8	20	38	11	5
32	Contacts ring	3	4	4	15	43	81	100	100
33	Dislodges ring on contact	3	4	4	8	20	35	28	5
34	Grasps	0	0	0	8	22	73	96	100
35	Grasps after delay if grasps	—	—	—	—	—	75	46	14

TABLE 13.1 (*Continued*)

RD	Behavior items	4	6	8	12	16	20	24	28
36	Grasps interdigitally	—	—	—	—	—	61	45	7
37	Retains entire period	—	—	—	—	20	19	40	65
38	Holds with both hands	—	—	—	—	10	33	56	67
39	Hand opens and closes on ring	—	—	—	—	30	11	10	14
40	Brings ring to mouth	—	—	—	—	38	58	82	74
41	Free hand to midplane	—	—	—	—	25	51	56	84
42	Transfers	—	—	—	—	3	18	41	74
43	Drops	—	—	—	—	78	56	41	32
44	Drops immediately	—	—	—	—	42	32	7	0
45	Regards dropped ring if drops	—	—	—	—	10	37	43	100
46	(If drops) pursues dropped ring	—	—	—	—	7	16	29	100
47	(If drops) resecures dropped ring	—	—	—	—	7	5	29	60
48	Rolls to side	3	4	8	4	35	42	38	18
49	Frets	9	14	4	8	27	23	32	21

SOURCE: Gesell and Thompson (12, p. 127). By permission.

each item of behavior is then noted on a record sheet in accordance with the categories listed above. The infant's "distinctive" (modal) level of behavior is found by observation; from this level, responses showing greater or lesser degrees of maturity are counted; an algebraic sum of the deviating responses is found; this sum is then related to the distinctive level in order to determine whether the trend is in a plus or minus direction. Finally, a rating is assigned the infant in each of the categories, thus providing a profile of development.

Scoring of the items in the several categories as plus or minus demands considerable clinical experience in observing and evaluating infant behavior. Also, once having scored the *items,* an appreciable element of subjectivity enters into the reading and interpretation of the *scoring record sheet.*

The Preschool Schedule extends from the age of 15 months to 6 years (10). Norms are provided at age levels of 15, 18, 21, 24, 30, 36, 42, 48, 54, 60, and 72 months. For illustrative purposes, the schedules at the two extremes are given.

15-Month Level

Motor:

      Walks: few steps, starts and stops
      Walks: falls by collapse
      Walks: has discarded creeping

Stairs: creeps up full flight
Cubes: tower of two
Pellet: placed in bottle
Book: helps turn pages

Adaptive:

Cubes: tower of two
Cup and Cubes: six in and out cup
Drawing: incipient imitation stroke
Formboard: places round block
Formboard: adapts round block promptly

Language:

Vocabulary: four–six words or names
Jargon: uses
Book: pats picture
Picture card: points to dog or own shoe

Personal-Social:

Feeding: has discarded bottle
Feeding: inhibits grasp of dish on tray
Toilet: partial toilet regulation
Toilet: bowel control
Toilet: indicates wet pants
Communication: says "ta-ta" or equivalent
Communication: indicates wants (points or vocalizes)
Play: shows or offers toy to mother or examiner
Play: casts objects playfully or in refusal

72-Month Level

Motor:

Jumps from height of 12″, landing on toes only
Advanced throwing
Stands on each foot alternately, eyes closed
Walks length of 4-cm. board
Copies diamond

Adaptive:

Builds three steps with cubes
Draws man with neck, hands on arms, and clothes
Draws man with two-dimensional legs
Copies diamond
Adds nine parts to incomplete man
Discriminates five weights, no error
Detects missing parts of pictures
Repeats four digits
Gives correct number of fingers on single hand and on both
Adds and subtracts within five

Language:

    Binet items are used here

Personal-Social:

    Ties shoe laces
    Differentiates A.M. and P.M.
    Knows right and left or complete reversal
    Recites numbers up to the thirties

These schedules are not scored quantitatively. They are a clinical guide intended for use in estimating the developmental status of a child in respect to the four designated categories of behavior.

EVALUATION.   These schedules were not subjected to the usual tests of validity; for there were no data on maturity levels to be used as criteria. Gesell and his collaborators do, however, present the following rationale of their Infant Schedule as the basis of validity. "Fundamentally the validity of the schedule here offered depends on the validity of the norms, the legitimacy of the category classifications, the appropriateness of each item for the category to which it is allocated, the soundness of the concept of maturity level, and the justness of using a sample of the child's behavior to indicate that level . . . Our conclusions regarding them [the foregoing issues] go beyond experimental data and are based on years of clinical experience. We are justified in claiming their general soundness and practical applicability until contrary evidence is revealed" (12, p. 218).

The authors of the schedule also maintain that reliability cannot be determined by the usual statistical methods presented in connection with other types of tests. Gesell and Thompson state, "It is the systematic error [of testing] which we have tried to reduce by basing the schedule on a carefully planned and controlled study of infant behavior . . . the accuracy of the schedule resolves in last analysis to the question of the accuracy of each item of the norms" (12, p. 219). And they believe that the percentages at different age levels passing and failing various behavior items, as shown in their normative studies, are reliable to a satisfactory degree.

In discussing the validity of the Preschool Schedule, Gesell and his collaborators do not present statistical evidence beyond percentages passing at the several age levels. They state, however: "Application of the schedules is a simple matter of determining how well a child's behavior fits one age level constellation rather than another, by the method of direct comparison. . . . There is nothing mathematical in this determination, neither is there anything mystical about it. It amounts to matching, which is neither calculation nor intuition; . . ." (10, p. 320). Performance and developmental status are reported separately for each of the four categories of behavior in terms of the four approximate age levels.[3]

Inspection of the Infant and Preschool Schedules shows that each evaluates a combination of some aspects of mental development (as usually understood), of motor development, sensory development and perception, and of personal habits (often called social development).

The schedule for infants (4 weeks to 56 weeks of age) has value for the experienced psychologist, since it provides experimentally derived means for estimating, nonquantitatively, specific aspects of a child's development within the first year of life. But as a group of psychological tests, this schedule does not satisfy the demands of standardization in terms of norms, reliability, and validity. The population sample was small (forty-nine boys and fifty-eight girls) and restricted (from a homogeneous middle-class background). On the positive side, it can be said that superior experimental techniques were used, and careful observation, experience, and behavioral insight went into the derivation of the schedule. For these reasons, it is useful, when applied by skilled observers, in appraising an infant's developmental status as it appears *at the time of the examination*.

For the same reasons stated above, the Preschool Schedule is of questionable value. For this group of children, especially those 2 years of age and older, there are other scales that have been standardized and can be used with more confidence. With some of these, the reader is already familiar (for example, the Stanford-Binet); others will be described in the following pages.

Cattell Developmental and Intelligence Scale

The Cattell scale, of superior merit, covers the range from 2 to 30 months. Its test items are adaptations of many that were developed and included in earlier tests, notably those of Gesell and his associates. Cattell states that the scale ". . . has been so constructed as to constitute an extension downward of Form L of the Stanford-Binet tests. Between the ages of twenty-two and thirty months Stanford-Binet items are intermingled with other items. Thus, using the infant test items for the early months and the Stanford-Binet tests for the older ages with a mixture of the two between, one continuous scale from early infancy to maturity has been attained" (6, p. 24). The test items are grouped at age levels as they are in the Stanford-Binet. Groupings are provided at each month from 2 through 12; at two-month intervals in the second year; and at

---

[3] While there should be (and is) nothing mystical about validity and reliability of psychological tests, subjective comparisons should not be substituted for external criteria, if such are available. Gesell and his collaborators were applying what, at present, would probably be called "construct validity."

27 and 30 months. The following three age levels illustrate the nature of the items and their arrangement.

2 Months

1. Attends voice
2. Inspects environment
3. Follows ring in horizontal motion
4. Follows moving person
5. Babbles
Alt. a. Follows ring in vertical motion
Alt. b. Lifts head in prone position

10 Months

1. Uncovers toy
2. Combines cup and cube
3. Attempts to take third cube
4. Hits cup with spoon
5. Pokes finger in holes of peg board
Alt. Picks up spoon before cup

30 Months

1. Differentiates bridge from tower
2. Imitates drawing lines and circles
3. Stanford-Binet three-hole formboard rotated
4. Folds paper
5. Stanford-Binet identifying objects by use
Alt. a. Identifies picture from name
Alt. b. Concept of one

The scale was standardized by longitudinal testing; 1346 examinations were made on 274 children at the ages of 3, 6, 9, 12, 18, 24, 30, and 36 months.[4]

In the process of standardization, it was Cattell's purpose, among other things, to improve on earlier scales by (1) improving objective procedures for administering and scoring; (2) eliminating items of the personal-social category, which are markedly influenced by home training; (3) eliminating items that are indicators of large motor control; (4) providing more accurate age scaling; (5) providing an adequate age range, so that continuity of development can be studied; (6) providing a more nearly equal distribution of items over the age range covered.

[4] Although the scale was standardized only on these age levels, groups of items are provided at certain age levels between them. The placement of items between the standardization levels was estimated. Dr. Cattell states, however, that the indications are that the scale may be used with only a little less accuracy with children between the standardization ages. At the same time, she urges the exercise of caution in interpreting test results at ages between the standardization levels.

Fig. 13.1. Regards cube. Age 3 months.

Material: A 1-inch cube painted bright red.

Procedure: As the child is sitting in an upright position before the table, the cube is placed on the table within easy view of him. The cube may be tapped on the table or moved about to attract the child's attention.

Scoring: Credit is given if the child observes the cube. His eyes must remain

on or return to the cube after the examiner has removed his hand. In other words, the examiner must make sure that it is the cube and not his hand which is observed.

From P. Cattell, *The Measurement of Intelligence of Infants and Young Children,* Psychological Corporation, by permission.

The method of scoring is the same as that used with the Stanford-Binet. Each item is rated as either plus or minus, no partial credits being given. Since there are five test items at each age level, the credit assigned to each is one fifth of the interval covered by the particular series of tests. Thus, in a series spanning a one-month interval, each item carries a credit of two tenths of a month, when the interval is two months, the credit is four tenths; with a three-month interval, it is six tenths. Like the Stanford-Binet, the Cattell scale uses a basal age, adds the credits at higher levels to obtain a mental age, and from that, a ratio IQ.

VALIDITY AND RELIABILITY. Although the presence of significant increase in percent passing each item at successive ages was used as significant evidence of validity, the principal criterion was the correlation be-

Fig. 13.2. Picks up spoon. Age 5 months.

Material: Teaspoon.

Procedure: The spoon is placed directly in front of the child (sitting position) within easy reach.

Scoring: Credit is given if the child makes a definite effort to reach for and pick up the spoon and succeeds, but if the spoon is picked up by reflex closure of the hand on chance contact, it is not credited. Accurate reaching, however, is

not to be expected at this age.

From P. Cattell, *The Measurement of Intelligence of Infants and Young Children,* Psychological Corporation, by permission.

FIG. 13.3. Places round block in form-board. Age 16 months.

Material: The formboard is similar to Gesell's. It is made of a three-eighths-inch board 36 × 16 cm., stained dark green. Three holes are cut in the board equidistant from each other and from the edges. From left to right the holes are a circle 8.7 cm. in diameter; an equilateral triangle, with sides 9.3 cm., and a square with sides 7.5 cm. The inserts are made of wood 2 cm. thick and painted white. The circle is 8.5 cm. in diameter, the sides of the triangle 9 cm., and those of the square 7.3 cm.

Procedure: The formboard is placed before the child with the circle on his left and the base of the triangle toward him. The circle is placed in its recess and the child is allowed to take it out, then he is asked (with appropriate gestures) to "Now put it back."

Scoring: Credit is given if the child replaces the round block. If it is done with an evidently purposeful act, one trial is enough, but if there is some doubt as to whether or not it was a chance replacement, no credit should be given unless it is placed a second time. (Credit is given for replacing the round block in the reversed board at eighteen months.)

From P. Cattell, *The Measurement of Intelligence of Infants and Young Children,* Psychological Corporation, by permission.

tween Cattell IQs, obtained to the age of 30 months, and Stanford-Binet IQs of the same children at the age of 36 months. These coefficients are shown in Table 13.2.

If we accept the Stanford-Binet as the criterion, it appears that the

TABLE 13.2

VALIDITY COEFFICIENTS: CATTELL AND STANFORD-BINET SCALES

No.	Ages at examination	Coefficients
42	3 mos. and 36 mos.	.10 ± .10
49	6 " " " "	.34 ± .08
44	9 " " " "	.18 ± .10
57	12 " " " "	.56 ± .06
52	18 " " " "	.67 ± .05
52	24 " " " "	.71 ± .05
42	30 " " " "	.83 ± .03

SOURCE: Cattell (6, p. 49). By permission.

predictive coefficients are negligible for tests given during the first 9 months of life. In this respect they are much the same as other current scales. For the later ages, up to 30 months, the coefficients increase appreciably, and are on the whole superior to those found with most other scales designed for these age levels.

In spite of the low predictive value of the coefficients at the earlier ages, Cattell has found, from study of individual cases, that the tests may be of considerable assistance to the clinician in appraising infants who are marked deviants from the norm. This is the case especially with infants who get a high quotient; for, Cattell reports, they have markedly better than average chances of earning a high rating at the age of 2 or 3 years.

Reliability of the scale was calculated by the odd-even method and corrected by the Spearman-Brown formula. Coefficients ranged from a low of .56 ± .05 at the age of 3 months, to a high of .90 ± .01 at 18 months. The median coefficient was .86 ± .02. These coefficients compare favorably with those found for other scales.

Minnesota Preschool Scale

The Minnesota scale, in two forms, is an adaptation and restandarization of test items chosen from the earlier work of a number of psychologists, plus some original additions. It is designed for use with children from 18 months to 6 years.

The scale includes the following twenty-six tests: pointing out parts of the body; pointing out parts in pictures; naming familiar objects; copying a circle, triangle, and diamond; imitative drawing (vertical and horizontal strokes and a vertical cross); block building; response to pictures; Knox cube imitation (tapping a series of cubes in a given order); obeying simple commands; comprehension ("What should you do when you are hungry?"); discrimination of geometric forms; naming objects from memory, recognition of forms, color naming; tracing a form; picture puzzles (object assembly); incomplete pictures; digit span; picture puzzles, diagonal series (more difficult object assembly); paper folding; absurdities (verbal); mutilated pictures; vocabulary; word opposites; imitating position of clock hands; speech (length of sentence spoken by child during examination).

The norms are so arranged that it is possible to obtain three separate scores for children above 30 months of age: a verbal, a nonverbal, and a total score. For a child under 30 months of age, only the total score is used because the authors of the scale were unable to work out a system of differentiated scoring for these earlier levels. A rough analysis is possible, however, to determine whether a pronounced difference between verbal and nonverbal responses exists. If such a difference is found at any age within the range of the scale, then, as the case may be, handicap or acceleration, in respect to language or perceptual-motor ability, may be inferred.

VALIDITY AND RELIABILITY. The manual of the Minnesota scale does not provide data specifically designated as evidence of validity. We may infer, however, that the authors regarded the following facts as their basis of validity (1) the adaptation and use of types of test items considered by many psychologists, over a period of years, to have validity; (2) a standardization group of 900 children, ranging in age from 18 months to 6 years (100 in each of nine half-year age groups), who were balanced equally as to sex and whose fathers were representative of the distribution of occupational levels in the general population.

In a later publication, data relevant to the scale's validity are available (15). Children who had been tested originally with the Minnesota scale at various ages during their preschool years were retested with the 1916 Stanford-Binet in some instances, or with the 1937 revision in others. The intervals between tests and retests varied from a few months to about ten years.

When the 1916 revision was used in retesting and the results were correlated with the total scores of the Minnesota, the range of coefficients for the various groups was from a low of .25 to a high of .75.

When the 1937 Stanford-Binet was used in retesting, the correlations with original Minnesota scale total scores yielded coefficients from .15 to .76.

Table 13.3 shows the median correlations between orginal Minnesota IQ equivalents, found at various ages, and the retest Stanford-Binet IQs at ages ranging from 4½ to 13½ years.

TABLE 13.3

CORRELATIONS BETWEEN MINNESOTA PRESCHOOL AND
STANFORD-BINET IQs

Age in months at taking Minnesota*	Correlations	
	1916 S-B	1937 S-B
Under 36	.45	.21
36–47	.64	.61
48 and over	.65	.68

* The number of cases in each group was large, ranging from 141 to 841.
SOURCE: Goodenough and Maurer (15, Part II).

If the S-B scales are accepted as significant criteria of validity, as they have been by many psychologists, then the conclusion follows that the Minnesota scale has low validity below the age of 36 months, but that it has much higher validity for children above that age.

In this connection, two considerations are relevant. First, it has been found that all scales devised for use with children below the age of 18 months show a low or moderate correlation with retest results in later childhood. The probable reasons for this fact will be presented later. Second, correlation coefficients between results of testing and retesting the same subjects with even the *same* scale tend to decrease somewhat as the time interval between examinations increases.

Reliability data of the Minnesota scale are variable at different age levels. Coefficients between scores on the two forms, with intervals of one to seven days, were .68 to .94 for the verbal tests, .67 to .92 for the non-verbal tests, and .80 to .94 for the total scores. The average reliability coefficients for a single form, within an age range of 6 months, were .86 for the verbal, .82 for the nonverbal, and .89 for the total scores.

The Merrill-Palmer Scale of Mental Tests

Although the norms of this scale are based up on 691 cases rang-ing in age from 18 to 27 months, it is not recommended for use with children below 24 months, or above 63 months of age.

The scale consists of ninety-three items arranged in order of difficulty. There is no attempt to group these according to types of function or behavior involved. The age norm for each item is given, this being the age at which fifty percent of the children were successful. Although there are ninety-three items, only thirty-eight are *different* items. Some (twenty-one) recur several times, at different age levels; at later ages a higher level of performance is required (in terms of quality or quantity of re-sponse, or in rate of activity) if credit is to be earned. Other items (seven-teen) occur only once.

The scale tests some language (for example, "What runs?" "What scratches?" These are known as action-agent tests. There are also simple questions, such as "What does a doggie say?"); manipulation of the body (opposition of thumb and fingers, crossing feet); motor skills and coordination (throwing a ball, buttoning); visual insights (building with blocks, copying a circle and a cross, completing formboards and picture puzzles); and recognizing familiar objects and colors.

Stutsman provides and suggests the use of a "Guide for Personality Observations" in connection with this scale. Although these observations do not affect the scoring, they are, nevertheless, useful to the clinician in interpreting a child's responses during the examination. The following traits are observed and rated during the testing period: self-reliance, self-criticism, irritability toward failure, degree of praise needed for effective work, initiative and independence of action, self-consciousness, spontaneity and repression, imaginative tendencies, reaction type (slow and deliberate, calm and alert, quick and impetuous), speech development, dependence on parent, and others. Value of these observations and ratings, obviously, will depend on the skill and experience of the examiner. These and similar observations, as already pointed out, are desirable, in fact essential, in the complete report on and evaluation of any individual's test performance.

VALIDITY AND RELIABILITY. Criteria of validity were those generally used: (1) known groups, (2) ratings by nursery-school staff, (3) small overlapping of distribution of total scores between age groups, (4) correlation with chronological age ($r = .92 \pm .004$), and (5) correlation with the Stanford-Binet ($r = .79 \pm .019$ for 159 children in the standardization group, between 3 and 6 years of age). The correlation coefficient for the last criterion must be interpreted in the light of the fact that the age range was three years.

In the guide describing the Merrill-Palmer scale and its standardization, no data on its reliability are provided. Subsequent studies, however, furnish information from which we may infer its reliability. When Stutsman retested a group of seventy-seven children (ages 2 to 5 years) after an interval of two months, she found a correlation coefficient of .72 between the two sets of scores. Wellman (29), retesting a group of forty-four children (ages 20–62 months) after an interval of one week, found a coefficient of .92 between the two sets of scores.

Other Scales

Several other scales for infants and preschool children are also available. They need not be described, however, since their content has been derived and adapted from their predecessors. Two of these, both intended for use within the first year of an infant's life, are the California First-Year Mental Scale (2) and the Northwestern Intelligence Tests (13). Kuhlmann's revision of the Binet scale (1922) provided test items from the age of 3 months to 15 years; his 1939 revision began at 4 months (20, 21). One, the Nebraska Test of Learning Aptitude (18) for the ages of 4 to 10 years, was devised primarily for use with deaf children. Two of the scales prepared in England are the Griffith Mental Development Scale for Testing Babies from Birth to Two Years (17) and Valentine's Intelligence Test for Children, for ages from $1\frac{1}{2}$ to 15 years (27).

Although considerable thought and effort have been devoted to the preparation of these scales, they all suffer, more or less, from defects and deficiencies of standardization. They are, for the most part, deficient in regard to validation and evidence of reliability. Population samples are, in some instances, inadequate or nonrepresentative, or both. The order of item difficulty is questionable in some instances. Some of the test items used in earlier scales have been modified, but the reasons are not stated. In this group, the scales that suffer least from these defects and deficiencies are the Kuhlmann and the Griffith.

Critics of these and similar scales appreciate the difficulties inherent in any process of standardizing an individual scale, particularly at these early levels. Yet those who construct such instruments have an obligation not to present them for general use until they are supported by a reasonably sound standardization process and findings.

Evaluation of the Scales

TECHNICAL PROBLEMS. Speeded scales should not be used in tests for the lowest age levels. The measurement of rate of performance is inadvisable and can be misleading, for at least two reasons: (1) speed of performance has not yet become a motivating factor in very young children; (2) the shifting attention of children at these age levels can obscure their true levels of skill and insight.

The grouping of test items according to types of activity, as in the Gesell schedule, has the advantage of readily indicating functions that are retarded, and those that are accelerated, in the child being examined. While this kind of analysis is not so immediately apparent in an age scale, such as Cattell's, it is nevertheless possible.

Since most of the usual validity criteria are not available in standardizing tests for infants and young children, this technical problem can be solved only through longitudinal studies, following the same individuals over a considerable span of years and correlating early test performance with later acceptable criteria of validity. Some efforts have been made in this direction.

Determination of item and subtest reliability, within a scale, presents difficulties too. If the odd-even method is used, the results can be affected by the fluctuating attention of the subject. If the test-retest method is used, the results can be affected by irregularity of growth tempos, when the time interval is significant. Significance of the time interval varies with the age of the subject: the younger the child, the shorter the significant interval. The desirable procedure would be to make retests within a week.

Although most scales for these early age levels extend upward beyond the 2- and 3-year levels, the use of the Stanford-Binet from age 2 is often recommended because of its more adequate standardization. Since the Cattell scale is an extension downward of the Stanford-Binet, and since it overlaps with the latter, it is a desirable alternate for the Stanford-Binet. The Merrill-Palmer has also been found to be quite useful to the age of 3 or 3½ years.

USES. Psychological tests at these early ages are used for two main purposes: (1) to determine a child's developmental status with respect to the behaviors being evaluated at the time of examination; and (2) to predict future developmental and ability level, particularly in the cases of infants who are being considered for adoption. Most psychologists agree that the first purpose is reasonably well satisfied by the sounder of these scales. As for the second purpose, with one possible exception, the scales used with infants below the age of 18 months have proved inadequate; for when ratings obtained within this period were correlated with ratings subsequently obtained with the S-B and other scales, the derived coefficients were so low as to be negligible. A recent, careful study of this question, in which the Yale (Gesell) scales were used, further supports this commonly held view (30). Therefore, when a child is examined within the first 18 months of life, for the purpose of predicting future mental development, little weight can be given to the *numerical* rating, except in the cases of infants who deviate markedly in either direction from the average. The qualified psychologist, in evaluating and reporting test results, will note and interpret the qualitative aspects of the child's performance and general behavior.

Cattell's scale is superior in regard to predictive value. The first three coefficients (.10 to .34) in the table showing validity coefficients of this scale are characteristic of those generally found for the first year of life. But the remaining coefficients of validity are higher than those of other preschool tests. In general, the predictive value of scales for preschool children increases after the age of 18 months or 2 years. While correlational studies published on preschool groups aged 18 months or more show coefficients varying over a considerable range, many of them fall in the .40s, .50s, and .60s, with relatively few higher or lower. In general, the higher the preschool age at the initial test, the higher will be the relationship of initial scores to those on retests.

In spite of their low predictive value for infants, available scales are of assistance to an experienced clinical psychologist in appraising a child's behavioral and mental development when attention is given to analysis of performance on each of the various parts rather than to numerical scores alone and when the analysis is used in conjunction with other clinical data. Developmental and intelligence tests for preschool children must be used with more than ordinary caution, for the value of the findings is exceptionally dependent upon the skill of the examiner in eliciting the child's best efforts and in being able to appraise his behavior during the examination.

There are several reasons why results of tests in infancy and the earlier preschool periods do not have more value in predicting future mental status. Scoring must often be quite subjective, depending upon the examiner's evaluation of behavior. Resistance to examiner, shyness, failure to exercise maximum effort, and other emotional conditions are undoubtedly operative in some instances. A fundamental problem, however, is the fact that there are changes and irregularities in the tempo of development of numerous young children. It has been found that successive examinations of some infants show fluctuations over two or three levels; or they may show a consistent trend downward or upward before leveling off to variations within a relatively narrow range of ratings. These fluctuations and trends in rate of development may be the result of changes in mental organization; that is, of differences in the age of appearance of various functions and differences in their rates of development—appearance of new functions and changes in rates being especially rapid in the first two years of life.

Closely allied to these reasons is the fact that tests included in infant scales are dissimilar to those used at later age levels so that little correlation is to be expected. The reader will have observed that tests used in appraising the development of an infant in the first 18 months of life are, for the most part, of relatively simple motor activities and of sensory perception. These have never been found to correlate significantly with tests used at later age levels, which increasingly involve the higher and more complex mental functions. It may be that psychologists will not be able to devise infancy tests having greater predictive value; for those functions which are subsumed under the term "intelligence" do not reach measurable magnitude until a later age. That is, intelligence, as psychologically understood and defined, does not emerge sufficiently during the earliest phases of development.

When tests are used with children below the age of 18 months, emphasis should be placed upon an analysis of performances and upon evaluation of the child's *present* status. Thereafter, the scales increase in value for the purpose of predicting later mental level. Bayley, after surveying her own and other researches, concluded that tests given between 2 and 4 years of age will predict 8- and 9-year intelligence-test performance with moderate success ($r = .55$), and tests given at 4 years of age will predict 8- and 9-year performance much more satisfactorily ($r = .75$). These conclusions, however, were written before the publication of Cattell's scale with its validity data. It appears, therefore, that, as Cattell has shown, it is possible to devise scales of significantly higher predictive value for use with preschool children who are more than 18 months old.[5]

References

1. Anderson, J. E. The prediction of terminal intelligence from infant and preschool tests. *39th Yearbook, National Society for the Study of Education.* Bloomington, Ill.: Public School Publishing Company, 1940, Ch. 13, part I.

2. Bayley, N. *The California First-Year Mental Scale.* Berkeley: University of California Syllabus Series, 1933, no. 243.

3. Bayley, N. Consistency and variability in the growth of intelligence from birth to eighteen years. *Journal of Genetic Psychology,* 1949, *75,* 165–196.

4. Bayley, N. On the growth of intelligence. *The American Psychologist,* 1955, *10,* 805–818.

5. Catalano, F. L., and D. A. McCarthy. Infant speech as a possible predictor of later intelligence. *Journal of Psychology,* 1954, *38,* 203–209.

6. Cattell, P. *The Measurement of Intelligence of Infants and Young Children.* New York: The Psychological Corporation, 1947.

7. Cavanaugh, M. C., *et al.* Prediction from the Cattell Infant Intelligence Scale. *Journal of Consulting Psychology,* 1957, *21,* 33–38.

8. Doll, E. A. (ed.). *The Oseretsky Tests of Motor Proficiency.* Minneapolis: Educational Test Bureau, 1947.

9. Gesell, A. *The Mental Growth of the Preschool Child.* New York: The Macmillan Company, 1925.

10. Gesell, A., *et al. The First Five Years of Life.* New York: Harper & Brothers, 1940.

11. Gesell, A., and C. S. Amatruda. *Developmental Diagnosis* (revised). New York: Paul B. Hoeber, Inc., 1947.

12. Gesell, A., and H. Thompson. *The Psychology of Early Growth.* New York: The Macmillan Company, 1938.

13. Gilliland, A. R. *The Northwestern Intelligence Tests.* Boston: Houghton Mifflin Company, 1951.

14. Goodenough, F. L., *et al. Minnesota Preschool Scales.* Minneapolis: Educational Test Bureau, 1940.

15. Goodenough, F. L., and K. M. Maurer. *The Mental Growth of Children from Two to Fourteen Years.* Minneapolis: University of Minnesota Press, 1942.

16. Griffiths, R. *The Griffiths Mental Development Scale for Testing Babies from Birth to Two Years.* London: Child Development Research Center (47 Holycroft Avenue), 1955.

---

[5] It is regrettable that psychologists are devoting so little of their research funds, time, and energy to studies of the significant problems associated with testing of infants and preschool children.

17. Griffiths, R. *The Abilities of Babies: A Study in Mental Measurement*. New York: McGraw-Hill Book Company, Inc., 1954.
18. Hiskey, M. S. *Nebraska Test of Learning Aptitude*. Author: 5640 Baldwin, Lincoln, Neb., 1955.
19. Hofstaetter, P. R. The changing composition of intelligence: a study in T technique. *Journal of Genetic Psychology*, 1954, *85*, 159–164.
20. Kuhlmann, F. *A Handbook of Mental Tests*. Baltimore: Warwick and York Incorporated, 1922.
21. Kuhlmann, F. *Tests of Mental Development*. Minneapolis: Educational Test Bureau, 1939.
22. Maurer, K. M. *Intellectual Status at Maturity as a Criterion for Selecting Items in Preschool Tests*. Minneapolis: University of Minnesota Press, 1946.
23. McCarthy, D. A. Measurement of cognitive abilities at the preschool and early childhood level. *Proceedings, 1958 Invitational Conference*. Princeton, N.J.: Educational Testing Service, 1959.
24. Nelson, V. L., and T. W. Richards. Studies in mental development. *Journal of Genetic Psychology*, 1938, *52*, I, 303–325; II, 327–331; 1939, *54*, III, 181–191; 1939, *55*, IV, 299–318.
25. Simon, A. J., and L. G. Bass. Toward validation of infant testing. *American Journal of Orthopsychiatry*, 1956, *26*, 340–350.
26. Stutsman, R. *Mental Measurement of Preschool Children*. New York: Harcourt, Brace & World, Inc., 1931.
27. Valentine, C. W. *Intelligence Tests for Children*. London: Methuen & Co., Ltd., 1958.
28. Wakelam, B. B. The application of a new intelligence test in an infant school and the prediction of backwardness. *British Journal of Educational Psychology*, 1944, *14*, 142–150.
29. Wellman, B. L. *The Intelligence of Preschool Children as Measured by the Merrill-Palmer Scale of Performance Tests*. Iowa City: University of Iowa Studies in Child Welfare, 1938, *15*, no. 3.
30. Wittenborn, J. R. A study of adoptive children. *Psychological Monographs*, 1956, nos. 408, 409, 410.

I4.

INTELLIGENCE TESTS AS CLINICAL INSTRUMENTS

      Clinical psychology involves, among other procedures, the intensive psychological study of individuals and uses testing, interview, observation, and history-taking as tools, in whole or in part. The purpose of such study, in some instances, is to determine the causes of each individual's malfunctioning and to prescribe suitable educational and psychological measures to deal with the problem. These measures may include educational changes and adaptations, manipulation of the person's environment in one or more of several ways, vocational guidance, counseling, or psychotherapy.

      Not all persons coming to a psychological clinic, however, present problems of maladjustment. Some may be individuals seeking objective and psychologically valid information concerning their general and specific abilities, interests, and personality traits.

      All types of tests have become indispensable instruments in the broad practice of clinical psychology. Every test can be clinical in a literal sense, since it helps to analyze an individual's abilities, to obtain a more nearly complete description of his strength and weaknesses. In this chapter we shall deal mainly with only two of the intelligence tests widely used in clinics—the Stanford-Binet and the Wechsler scales—but will consider briefly several other instruments devised particularly for the determination of mental abnormality or deterioration. In a later chapter we shall present some tests of personality and their clinical uses. Although tests of specific aptitudes and educational achievement are often essential in the study of some individuals, they do not present the clinical problems and possibilities found in intelligence and personality tests. The clinical uses of aptitude and achievement tests, especially in cases of educational and vocational counseling, are much more obvious and direct. Nor shall we deal here with tests for infants and preschool children. These are not used in so wide a variety of clinical problems as are the Stanford-Binet and the Wechsler. Their organization, furthermore, is such that they readily lend themselves to analysis of performance in terms of sensory, motor, perceptual, language, and social development.

Factors Affecting Test Performance

Before specific tests are discussed, it is necessary to point out the factors that can affect an individual's performance on any psychological examination. These are of two general kinds: *intrinsic* and *extrinsic*. By the former, we mean factors *within the subject himself;* by the latter, we mean those *outside the subject.* Lack of IQ constancy, in some instances, must be evaluated in the light of the following factors.

INTRINSIC FACTORS. Factors from within the subject that may affect test performance include (1) organic difficulties, such as defective hearing or vision; disability or enervation due to malnutrition or localized or generalized infections; glandular dysfunctions; acute or chronic illnesses that lower an individual's level of performance; brain damage (2) emotional conditions as evidenced by lack of interest, lack of seriousness, deliberate deception, negativism; inhibition due to shyness or lack of confidence; hyperactivity and restlessness; neuroses and the more severe forms of mental disturbances; (3) language handicaps; and (4) speech defects.

The presence or absence of organic difficulties may be inferred from the subject's history or from reports provided by observers, such as teachers; but their existence and degree can be adequately determined only through physical examination. During the process of testing, however, the experienced examiner is often led to suspect, or infer, the presence of organic difficulties. The report of the psychological examination, in such instances, includes a description of the subject's behavior and performance that gave rise to the suspicion or inference.

The psychological examiner must also be able to discern the presence of emotional factors in the subject's behavior or, where the nature of the instrument permits, in his actual performance on various parts of the test itself. This latter aspect will be discussed specifically in connection with the several tests to be presented in this chapter. The discernment of negativism, deception, shyness, lack of interest, and lack of seriousness is a form of subtle clinical insight that can be developed only through

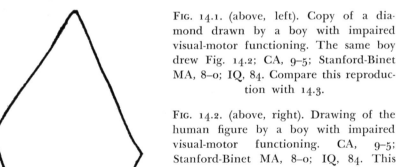

FIG. 14.1. (above, left). Copy of a diamond drawn by a boy with impaired
visual-motor functioning. The same boy
drew Fig. 14.2; CA, 9–5; Stanford-Binet
MA, 8–0; IQ, 84. Compare this reproduction with 14.3.

FIG. 14.2. (above, right). Drawing of the
human figure by a boy with impaired
visual-motor functioning. CA, 9–5;
Stanford-Binet MA, 8–0; IQ, 84. This
drawing, according to the norms of the
Goodenough scale (Measurement of Intelligence by Drawings), gives this boy a
mental-age rating of 6–3, and an IQ of
66. See also Fig. 14.1.

FIG. 14.3. (left). Copy of a diamond by
a mentally deficient boy. CA, 13–2;
Stanford-Binet MA, 8–4; IQ, 63. Compare
with Fig. 14.1.

the experience of testing a variety of individuals who manifest these traits in varying degrees, and of others who do not manifest them at all. Such contrasting individuals provide the necessary basis of comparative evaluations.

EXTRINSIC FACTORS. The extrinsic category includes the following: (1) accidental factors, such as errors in time limits, broken pencils, distracting noises; (2) scale errors inherent in the tests themselves owing to imperfect standardization; (3) scoring errors as a result of the examiner's judgment or the marginal character of the response—that is, a response on the border line between the acceptable and nonacceptable; (4) skill of the examiner, who must not only be thoroughly familiar with the instrument being used, but also must be able to establish the rapport necessary to elicit the subject's best performance. These sources of error imply that the examiner must be highly qualified and must know the standardization and limitations of his instrument.

Administering a psychological test provides a situation in which the subject is psychologically observed as well as being scored in accordance with objective standards. In addition, analysis of an individual's performance on subtests and specific items often yields significant information concerning his mental status and mode of functioning. The following sections will be devoted to this aspect of test interpretation.

The Stanford-Binet Scale

USES. In schools, guidance centers, and clinics, the problems for which intelligence tests are being widely used are as follows:

1. Diagnosis of mental deficiency and mental retardation.
2. Determination of mental levels of delinquents.
3. Diagnosis of intellectual disturbance and deterioration.
4. Differential diagnosis (that is, mental traits and psychological profiles of various clinical groups).
5. Evaluation of the intelligence of maladjusted children.
6. Evaluation of the intelligence of children with special disabilities in learning.
7. Determination of mental superiority.
8. Educational guidance for children and others who are not "problem" cases.
9. Vocational guidance, for which the determination of intelligence level is essential.

Functional Analysis. For these and other clinical problems, it is not sufficient to find only the mental age and the intelligence quotient, since an individual's performances on the several parts of an intelligence test are not entirely uniform. He will be above his general average on some, and below it on others. The MA and IQ are composites, whereas in the analysis of an individual case, we must also determine the components that have yielded these indexes. The reader should recall that tests are standardized on the basis of performances which are characteristic of representative *groups* of persons at particular age levels; but it seldom happens that a given individual conforms to his age group in all respects. Two identical mental ages may differ functionally in terms of their components, as inspection of the results on two Stanford-Binet tests will reveal. For example, two children, each with a mental age of 10, may vary in respect to basal year, extent of scatter (see below), and items passed or failed at each of the several levels.

Functional analysis of Stanford-Binet test results is not readily apparent because the items are grouped according to age levels rather than according to uniform types of subtests, or factors. (Compare the Stanford-Binet, for example, with the Wechsler scales [Chapter 11] and the Chicago Tests of Primary Mental Abilities [Chapter 17].) It is possible, however, to draw inferences about an individual's strengths and weaknesses through analysis of his responses to the various test items. For example, levels may be determined in the following functions: visual perception of form (three-hole formboard, copying a square and a diamond); visual imagery (copying a bead chain from memory, and paper-cutting test); visual memory (reproducing geometric designs); thinking (absurd sentences and arithmetical problems); memory span and attention (recall of digits and of meaningful sentences); ability with abstractions (verbal similarities and differences); reasoning (plan of search, picture absurdities, and picture interpretation); word knowledge (vocabulary); concept formation (definitions of abstract words). Analysis of successes and failures in these or similar terms will assist the examiner in determining the psychological components of average or superior mental-age rating, or the deficiencies responsible for an inferior rating.

Analysis is valuable in detecting the causes of specific learning disabilities, as in reading. For example, the test items may reveal deficient perception and recall of visual patterns, defective visual recognition, poor copying and reproduction of form, and short memory span—all of which are causes of confusion and difficulty in learning to read and in the mastery of other school subjects (see Figs. 14.1, 14.2, and 14.3). When such defects are revealed by the Stanford-Binet scale, further intensive examinations, with special tests of vision and of the functions required in reading, are indicated.

As illustrations of evaluations of Stanford-Binet performance, the following reports are cited.

Range of Allen's performance extends from the 8-year level to his CA level (10 years). His comprehension and reasoning with abstractions are at the level of his chronological age. *Relative to his average level,* Allen is generally superior in dealing with verbal abstractions. Comprehension of problems, analysis of absurdities, and problems of logical fact rank relatively high in his performance. He is weak in dealing with number concepts; cannot make change accurately. Visual perception and visual memory are inferior to chronological age expectancy. Memory for verbal materials is somewhat inferior to CA level. Vocabulary is inferior; he fails to pass at 10-year level; failed rhymes; word association is poor; reads with difficulty. (IQ about 90.)

Lois' test performance was not consistent. She did well on visual items requiring form discrimination and identification, but completely failed esthetic comparison. She was unable to reproduce a square correctly, although hers was a close approximation; and she completely failed to grasp the concept of man-completion. However, she was able to copy folding of paper into a triangle and she did pass maze tracing. She consistently failed on items requiring memory; she could not remember either digit spans or sentences, although her speech difficulty may have been a major influence, especially in the latter. She seemed unable to grasp concepts as a whole; she often misunderstood directions and gave the impression that she occasionally made correct responses accidentally, rather than as a result of understanding. She was self-critical on the drawing items, which she did painstakingly and with self-appraisal and subsequent erasures. She also was critical of her paper triangle and took another piece of paper after saying, "That's wrong," of her first attempt. She did not seem to be aware of her failures in other respects. (IQ about 55.)

Nancy was a very cooperative subject. She was somewhat apprehensive when she came into the testing room, but quickly relaxed and entered actively into the tasks. She had a long attention span and was not distracted by outside stimuli. She thought carefully before answering difficult questions, and was self-critical, for she sometimes thought aloud and corrected herself as she thought. She was rather self-confident and failure on items, some of which she recognized herself, did not seem to bother her. She laughed occasionally, but on the whole was serious most of the time, giving all her attention to the test. (IQ about 125.)

SCATTER ANALYSIS.[1] There are several methods of measuring scatter: (1) the number of age levels, from and including the basal year, up to the highest level where any items are passed; this is known as *range of scatter;* (2) the number of items passed above the individual's mental-age level and number failed below; this is known as *area of scatter;* (3)

[1] Scatter analysis means the distribution of successes and failures over the several levels of difficulty, or the extent to which test items passed or failed by an individual spread over different levels of difficulty.

a combination of range and area, whereby the number of successes and failures at each level is weighted according to the distance of that level from the mental-age level. If only one method is to be used, the first of these is preferable because it covers the entire range of performance and expresses the situation in the most direct and simple manner.

Investigators have reported that psychotic persons show greater scatter than do normal individuals or the nonpsychotic mentally deficient. Many reports state also that excessive scatter is a useful diagnostic sign, particularly in the case of organic psychoses, which apparently yield the greatest degree of scatter.

In addition to general scatter, analyses have been made of "selective scatter"; that is, the effects of specific psychotic conditions upon ability to pass specific kinds of test items. For example, schizophrenics are said to be less proficient than normal persons in detecting absurdities, interpreting fables, solving the "purse and field" test, memory for designs, and passing problem questions. On the other hand, they are said to be relatively proficient in arithmetical reasoning.

These views on both general and selective scatter are tentative. There are several reasons for disagreement among the published findings, one or more of which might operate in any given investigation. These include inadequate control groups, inadequate control of mental age and chronological age of compared groups, divergent techniques of scatter analysis, and errors of psychiatric diagnosis.[2]

In view of inconsistent data, we must conclude that numerical measures of general scatter on the Stanford-Binet scales are, at present, of limited use as clinical aids, so far as most individual cases are concerned. On the other hand, *extreme* degrees of scatter have been found diagnostically valuable often enough so that analysis of scatter on the Stanford-Binet continues as a clinical technique.

Regarding selective scatter, there is a greater degree of agreement; for the published researches deal mainly with schizophrenics, among whom there are a number of different syndromes that affect test performance. Other abnormal groups have also been studied. Although investigators have not been in complete agreement regarding the several abnormal groups, all reports show that schizophrenia involves *selective impairment* of the mental functions tested. It is to be expected that the particular functions impaired, and the degree, will vary with the particular type of schizophrenic disorder; but in this group as a whole, test performance tends to be inferior more often and more markedly in parts requiring practical reasoning and judgment (What is the thing to do when . . . ?), in abstract reasoning (arithmetical problems), and in perceptual organiza-

---

[2] For a comprehensive bibliography on scatter, see D. Rapaport (51, pp. 554 ff.).

tion. Inferior performance is revealed not only in the lower scores, but in the quality (that is, bizarreness, irrelevance) of responses, and inconsistencies (failing easy items and passing more difficult ones).

In the cases of most delinquents and mental defectives—nonpsychotic atypical groups—a quite different pattern of performance was found. Their vocabulary and Stanford-Binet scores were low, while their performance-test ratings were higher. Some individuals in these two groups however, had relatively low performance-test ratings; but they were found to be the least likely to make a satisfactory social adjustment.

It also has been reported that among maladjusted children, most of those with relatively high performance-test ability were individuals referred to clinics as "delinquents"; whereas children with significantly lower performance than verbal ratings were mostly those having personality defects (psychoses, neuroses, emotional instability).

Several important statistical facts should be considered in connection with the interpretation of scatter on the Stanford-Binet scales. The first is that the percentages of the standardization population passing each item at any given age level are not all equal. For example, at age 7 (Form L), the percents passing vary from 51 to 70; at age 8, from 57 to 67; at age 12, only from 61 to 69. These differences signify that the items at a given age level are not all of equal difficulty; hence uniformity of performance is not to be expected. It will be recalled that placement of items was made on the basis of several considerations, only one of which was percent passing.

Other technical factors that might affect scatter are the reliability of each item; low intercorrelations between items, some of which might make demands upon a more or less specialized ability; or items incorrectly placed in the age scale. These technical factors may account for part of the scatter found; however, they cannot account for all of it.

CONTENT ANALYSIS. Psychologists have been increasingly interested in analyzing verbal responses to test items for their possible significance regarding the testee's experiences and personality traits. That is to say, the Stanford-Binet, and other individual scales, have some value as projective tests of personality. (See Chapters 25 and 26.)

The word-naming item (year X, item 5) may reveal current interests, family conditions, school relationships, and so on. One 10-year-old boy (IQ 133) interpolated the following words in his list: *school, ugh, arithmetic, dull, stupid.* In spite of his high mental level, he was having difficulty with his studies (particularly arithmetic) and with his teacher. That the school was a source of anxiety to him was clearly revealed in a sentence-completion test and in the Thematic Apperception Test. Other psychologists report words of violence, ambition, unsatisfied needs, and so forth. Verbal responses may thus reveal more or less deeply rooted emotional conditions.

Word definitions may reveal experiences and centers of interest. For example: when "puddle" is defined as "dirty water that you should not go into"; or "lecture" as "a lot of yak-yak from a grown-up." There are also times when definitions will be concentrated in a special area (for example, sensory), so as to suggest special interests. Some give definitions attended by compulsiveness, uncertainty, or overelaboration.

Values and behavior patterns also are revealed at times. For example, under "Comprehension," one of the questions is this: "What is the thing for you to do if another boy hits you without meaning to do it?" A common, and expected, answer is: "Nothing. He didn't mean it." But at times a boy replies: "Hit him back," or "Go home and tell my mother (or teacher)."

Picture interpretations also may offer an opportunity to gain insight into aspects of behavior and personality. The responses to pictures may be moralistic, or submissive, or hostile, or anxious, etc. Or they may be of the ordinary, expected variety.

Some children who give ready and assured responses to routine materials, such as recall of digits and sentences, may be anxious, hesitant, and tentative when dealing with items that require their own judgment and evaluation, thus suggesting dependence or submissiveness.

"EXTRA-TESTING" PROCEDURES.   While testing, it is possible for experienced examiners to utilize certain practices not prescribed in the manual, nor even contemplated by the test's author. As examples, the three following practices are cited. After the formal testing has been completed, it is sometimes desirable to check on selected item-failures to determine whether failure was because of lack of capacity, verbal handicap, or inability to understand instructions. The probing may be done by giving *actual instruction* on some items, then testing the individual further on the same types of items. The results, of course, do not change the subject's score on the test; but the procedure and its results should be noted in the report. For example, if the child has failed on Similarities and Differences (year VIII, item 4), when testing has been concluded the examiner might return to that item, explain the terms and the nature of the problem, and even give the correct answer to one of the four parts. He then asks the subject to give the answers to the remaining parts to determine if there has been any learning.

A second form of extra-testing procedure is intended to discover *how far* a testee has been able to proceed on an item he has failed, as in arithmetical problems. The examiner returns to the problem; he leads the testee through the solution step by step, at times suggesting the procedure, or even the basic process to be used. Thus, it is often possible to discern the nature and extent of a subject's deficiencies.

If a child has failed to copy the diamond satisfactorily (year VII, item 3), the examiner may want further information on whether the inability might be due to disturbed visual-motor functioning or to defective perceptual analysis. He may, then, make three copies of the diamond, of varying quality, one of which is a duplicate of the testee's own copy. The testee is then asked to select the "best" one. It has been found that the child whose poor copy is consistent with his general mental level will not select the examiner's superior reproduction, or will select at random; but a subject whose general mental level is higher than that suggested by his own copy can make the correct selection, even though he still will not be able to produce a satisfactory copy on subsequent trial.

These are three illustrations of extra-testing procedures that enable the examiner to prepare a richer and more analytical report.

ORDER OF ITEM ADMINISTRATION. The order in which items of the Stanford-Binet should be presented has been under examination and discussion in recent years because clinicians have found that order of presentation in some instances influences performance of maladjusted subjects. Three methods have been used: (1) standard, or consecutive; (2) serial; (3) adaptive. Using the first of these, the examiner presents the items in the order in which they appear in the scale. Using the second, he follows through on *one type* of item, to the more difficult ones, until the subject fails: for example, Memory Span for Digits, Memory for Sentences, Similarities and Differences, Comprehension, and so on. If the third method is used, the examiner starts with easy items and alternates these with difficult ones of the same type. When employing the adaptive method, the examiner begins at a level below the subject's expected mental age (to insure success) and moves up and down in an effort to establish the maximal (or terminal) and the basal levels as early as possible. The principal justification given for the adaptive method is that some individuals are discouraged by a series of consecutive failures when they reach higher and more difficult levels; they might, therefore, fail items that they could otherwise pass. The adaptive method is intended to scatter failures among successes.

The sparse experimental data available support the use of the adaptive procedure. It has been found that there is little difference between results obtained by the standard and the adaptive methods when a *well-adjusted group* is tested. Thus, the norms established by Terman and Merrill through standard testing are applicable when the adaptive method is used. One study reports a correlation of .93 between results obtained when the two methods were compared, using Forms L and M. The test-retest differences between IQs were just about what Terman and Merrill reported in their standardization data: approximately five points.

With the adaptive method, *maladjusted children,* especially the more serious cases, achieved higher IQ ratings than they did by the standard order of testing. One study reports a mean gain of eleven points when the adaptive method was used, as compared with the standard consecutive method (15, 33).

Insofar as an adapted method of procedure contributes to a fuller and more valid understanding of a subject's performance, without violating the basic principles of the scale being used, its use in appropriate cases is warranted.[3]

The Wechsler Scales

Clinical Diagnosis. For the purpose of analysis of functioning and performance, the Wechsler scales have an apparent advantage over the Stanford-Binet, since the items are grouped into subtests, each examining mental operations that might be susceptible to different forms of personality maladjustment. Arrangement into subtests not only facilitates the preparation of analytical profiles for individuals; it also permits the ready analysis of subscore interrelations, which can be studied for any bearing they might have on clinical uses. Many investigations have been published, detailing differences found among normal and abnormal groups of persons. These researches deal with differences in extent of scatter among the several groups and differences among subtest scores within groups, emphasis being placed upon the latter.

The published studies are devoted principally to the determination of group trends and group patterns. Results obtained from study to study are not always in agreement; nor are the results of a particular report always unequivocal. These researches are mentioned here, however, because they indicate efforts being made to determine the analytical and clinical values of the Wechsler scales.

Among these studies are those especially concerned with the extent of

---

[3] Terman and Merrill state: "It probably could be demonstrated that the order of giving the tests could be adapted in various ways to the needs of some particular subject or group of subjects, to secure maximal motivation or to avoid frustration, and obtain higher IQ ratings. The adaptive method . . . seems to us to offer inadequately demonstrated advantages to offset the complications introduced by so many individual variations. The method imposes upon the examiner many additional subjective judgments concerning choices and suitability of test sequences to be used. Its gains were found for a poorly adjusted group, but no advantage was demonstrated for the method when adaptive testing was tried with public school children."

"The accepted practice is to limit changes in test order to *practical* requirements of testing" (*Stanford-Binet Intelligence Scale,* p. 48).

deterioration, or deficit, in intelligence suffered by members of each of several groups: alcoholics, schizophrenics, manic depressives, paranoiacs, psychoneurotics, and others. One method commonly used has been to compare the averages of mental ages and the measures of variation of a sample of abnormal persons with corresponding indexes found for a sample of normal persons. The theory is that inferior status of an abnormal group, as compared with one that is normal, is a result of the mental disorder. On the whole, results indicate that groups suffering from organic psychoses (for example, alcoholism, paresis) show the greatest loss; those suffering from functional psychoses (schizophrenia, paranoia) show less; while those in the psychoneurotic group give no evidence of deficit. The published studies do not agree as to the average amount of deterioration in each group. Furthermore, within each category of mental illness, there are marked individual differences in the degree of deterioration (32, 51).

Because of these variations and the overlapping of group distributions of ratings, the validity and clinical use of *group deficits* have been seriously questioned in making *individual diagnoses*. Investigations of group deficits have been valuable insofar as they have demonstrated that some degree of deterioration of mental functioning accompanies mental disorder. Since clinical practice, however, is concerned with each person as an individual rather than as a member of a specified group, it is necessary to determine individual rather than group characteristics or group losses of mental ability.

On the other hand, for the use of scatter analysis in making diagnoses, it may be stated on the positive side that the test "signs" of a particular syndrome will often correctly identify a small, but nevertheless significant, percentage of cases.[4] Furthermore, the examining psychologist has available information about the individual (the case history) in addition to results from the objective test. The psychologist's diagnosis and decision will be based upon these several sources of information and upon their interrelations.

Scatter Analysis. Brown, Rapaport, *et al.* first suggested an *intraindividual* measure of scatter (51). This consisted of: (1) calculating,

---

[4] "It is almost inevitable that when one looks for unique patterns which are both highly reliable and valid, any selected combination will detect only a small percentage of the individuals tested. This fact has led the writer to turn increasingly, in his attempt at psychological diagnosis, to what may be termed the *method of successive sieves*. The method . . . is based on the hypothesis that one can arrive at diagnostic combinations more easily by dealing successively with selected parts of one's data than by trying to deal with them as a whole. Such approach . . . will reduce the number of individuals . . . detected by any one test pattern. But the possible number that may be eventually detected can be increased considerably by successive applications of second, third and fourth sieves [criteria] to the same population" (64, pp. 167--168).

for each individual, the deviation of *each* subtest score from the *mean of all* his subtest scores; (2) computing the deviation, for each individual, of each verbal-subtest score from his verbal-subtest mean; (3) computing the deviation of each performance-subtest score from the performance-subtest mean.

Scatter of subtest scores was further investigated, resulting in a table of test characteristics, or patterns, of several clinical categories: organic brain disease, schizophrenia, anxiety states, adolescent sociopaths (delinquents), and mental defectives (64, pp. 171–172). For example, the pattern of organic brain disease shows *relatively* high scores on Information, Comprehension, and Vocabulary (very high); but moderately low scores on Arithmetic and Similarities; while the scores on Digit Span, Digit Symbol, Block Design, and Object Assembly may be very low, relatively. The pattern of adolescent delinquents is characterized by relatively high subtest scores in Picture Arrangement and Object Assembly; moderately high scores in Picture Completion, and Block Design; relatively low scores in Information, and moderately low or average scores in the remaining subtests.[5]

The explanation of these and other patterns is, presumably, that mental defect, each major type of personality disorder, and mental illnesses are associated with characteristic deficits or losses of psychological functioning. Mental defectives are individuals whose mental development has been *arrested* at a relatively low level, though not uniformly in respect to all functions. A personality disorder or a mental illness produces impairment in the individual's mental abilities, but the resultant losses are not uniform; apparently some functions are more adversely affected than others. Thus, if a psychological test is able to measure and portray these differential deficits and losses, it can assist significantly in making a clinical diagnosis.

In Rapaport's investigation, discussed at the beginning of this section, essentially two forms of scatter analysis were employed.

1. Vocabulary scatter. This is the difference between a person's score on a particular subtest and his score on the Vocabulary subtest. The reason for using Vocabulary as the base of comparison is that it has rather consistently been found to be the psychological test least vulnerable to impairment by personality disorders or mental disturbance. It is the Vocabulary score, therefore, from which the individual's original, unimpaired intelligence level is inferred. Degree of loss in other functions can thus be estimated from the differences between ratings on each of the subtests and the rating on Vocabulary.

[5] In each instance, each subtest score is high, low, or average with reference to an individual's own average score; not in relation to average performance of a group.

2. *Mean scatter.* This is the difference between the rating on any single subtest and the average of the ratings on all the remaining subtests.[6] The mean scatter, which may be positive or negative for a given subtest, measures the relationship of a single measured function to the average of all other functions measured by the test. It is thereby possible to find out whether an individual's level of achievement and functioning on any of the subtests has deteriorated more or less than on the remaining ones.

Mean scatter can be calculated for the entire test, including both verbal and nonverbal subtests, or it can be found separately for the six verbal and the five nonverbal scores.

A third procedure—one that supplements scatter analyses and is regarded as essential—is the comparison of *pairs* of subtest scores. Any two subtest scores may be compared for the purpose of finding out how the subject's functioning in one compares with his functioning in another. For example, how does his retention of Information (remote learning) compare with his Memory Span for Digits (immediate recall and attention)? How does his Arithmetic score (reasoning and habitual responses) compare with his score on Similarities (concept formation)? Thus, it is possible to obtain, in considerable detail, an analysis of the subject's achievement levels on the several parts of the scale, their interrelationships, and evaluations of general and special mental impairment.

The profile in Figure 14.4 illustrates the method we have been discussing. We quote, also, from the interpretation of this case not only to clarify the profile, but also to emphasize the fact that mechanical scatter analysis is inadequate and to illustrate how the psychological rationale of the scale may be utilized in interpretation.

It is true, unfortunately, that not all clinical cases present clear-cut patterns of test performance upon which a differential diagnosis may be made. In an appreciable number of cases, scatter and subtest analyses have been found definitely diagnostic; in other cases, the analyses, though not conclusive, provide indications of the probable diagnosis; in still others, the scatter profile and analyses are inconclusive. Although test analysis does not provide a definitive diagnosis in all cases, the practice is warranted because it is as efficient as other diagnostic procedures. Such analyses are interpreted in conjunction with results obtained with other psychological tests (for example, projective methods) and other clinical and developmental evidence.

In drawing inferences from a scatter analysis, it is necessary to consider

---

[6] In calculating mean scatter, Rapaport omitted Digit Span and Arithmetic. This omission, he states, ". . . was warranted by the fact that impairments [of these functions] were so general in most of the clinical and control groups, that their inclusion would have vitiated the representativeness of the mean as a central tendency of the scores" (51, p. 53n).

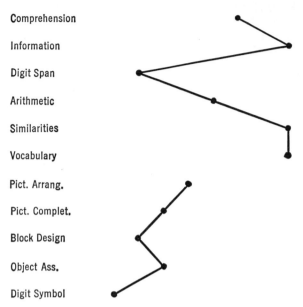

Neurotic Depressive

	6	7	8	9	10	11	12	13	14	15	16	17

Comprehension

Information

Digit Span

Arithmetic

Similarities

Vocabulary

Pict. Arrang.

Pict. Complet.

Block Design

Object Ass.

Digit Symbol

FIG. 14.4. "Outstanding in the scatter is the great discrepancy between the verbal and the performance subtest scores, and this discrepancy we have found to be a statistically significant, and therefore diagnostic, indication of depression. The rationale of this finding is the following: depression becomes manifest in intellectual functioning by a retardation of perceptual and associative processes. The relatively complex visual organization and visual-motor coordination required by the performance subtests put too great demands upon the slow-downed depressive. Furthermore, in contrast to the untimed verbal subtests, the performance subtests have time limits on each item and even give extra credit for speed. Consequently, depressives not only do not obtain extra credit, but exceed the time limit on many items. For this case, item analysis confirms the retardation by showing that, on Picture Completion and Block Design, a number of items were failed only because they exceeded the time limit . . . the impairment of Digit Span or attention is also striking and reflects the presence of intense anxiety accompanying the depression. The mild impairment of Arithmetic is referable to an inability to meet the time limits and gain time bonuses on the items of this subtest. In verbalization, much self-depreciation, as well as indirect criticism of the test and the examiner, are evident." R. Schafer (56). By permission.

the possible influence of environmental predilections or pressures, which may enhance or detract from certain forms of test achievement. In such an event, the diagnostically distinguishing features of intelligence tests will be affected and probably invalidated. Thus, before drawing diagnostic inferences from intelligence-test results, the psychological examiner must know whether, in the case under consideration, there have been educational, cultural, or other environmental factors that might account for any of the ratings and seemingly diagnostic criteria.

Another aspect to consider in evaluating the significance of subtest differences is their reliabilities. It will be recalled that the reliability coefficients of the eleven subtests are not consistently high; thus, only large differences in weighted (scaled) scores may be accepted with confidence.

Qualitative Aspects of Responses. Scatter analysis and subtest comparisons should be accompanied by a qualitative analysis of the subject's verbalizations and general approach to the test problems. Qualitative analysis reveals characteristics of the individual's mentality in operation, such as excessive doubt, indecision, self-criticism, impulsiveness, bizarre notions, obsessions, compulsiveness, and random guessing. Certain qualitative characteristics are frequently associated with clinical groups. Thus, a person's mode of approach to test problems is significant in the interpretation of his behavior and understanding of his personality. Classification and labeling are less significant, in an individual case, than a description and analysis of behavior and functioning, as shown during the test period and as reflected in the test results.

A person's mode of approach will affect his performance differently on each of the various types of subtests, depending on whether the subtest makes demands on habituated responses, for example, or on those requiring flexibility and reorganization. Individuals with brain damage— as a case in point—show rigidity, inability to shift attention, inability to change their mode of responding, inability to ignore superficial or extraneous stimuli, and difficulty in organizing material into a pattern or a meaningful logical sequence. Inspection of the subtests will show that performance on them would be variously affected by behavioral traits such as these.

Failure to respond correctly to a test item is not the only matter of importance. While correct and acceptable responses to test items are fixed by research and by agreement of psychologists regarding the interpretation of findings, incorrect responses are not fixed; nor is the *manner* of responding. To illustrate: current scales have sets of items testing "Comprehension," "Similarities," and "Arithmetical Reasoning." The first are of the "when" or the "why" type; that is, "What is the thing to do when . . . ?" or "Why is it desirable (or necessary) to . . . ?" The second, "Similarities," requires understanding of basic likenesses—for example, "In what way are ——— and ——— alike?" The arithmetical problems range from the simplest to fairly complex. A person's response to any of these may be right or wrong; but his speed and confidence in answering, his anxiety or blandness about incorrect responses often reveal significant personality traits. When, in a test of Information, an otherwise intelligent person blandly replies that Tokyo is in Turkey, or in a test of Similarities, that a dog and a lion are alike because both have digestive organs, and gives other bizarre responses, personality disturbance is indicated.

Personality difficulties of the obsessive kind, for example, must be considered when a subject feels compelled to offer four or five explanations of courses of action in reply to a "Comprehension" item; or when he mentions three, four, or more likenesses on some of the "Similarities" items; or when he gives elaborate and often quibbling definitions of words in the Vocabulary test. Of if the person persists in guessing blindly on test items that are clearly beyond his level of ability, his test behavior may be indicative of an uncritical impulsiveness.

The previous examples illustrate the role of language with respect to certain *types of items*. Some personality patterns or categories may, however, be inferred from the manner in which the person deals with the test in general and as a whole. A few illustrations follow.

In the obsessive-compulsive individual, verbalization of responses is over-detailed and doubt-laden. For example, in response to the question: "What does 'stanza' mean?" the ordinary person who has the information would probably say, "A group of rhymed lines," or something similar. A characteristic obsessive-compulsive response, however, would be comparable to this: "A stanza of rhymed lines forming one of a series of similar divisions in a poem. Two rhymed lines form a couplet. A four-lined stanza is a quatrain, a six-lined one is a sestet," etc. One or a few such replies do not warrant the characterization of the respondent as "obsessive-compulsive"; but when this kind of answer is "idiomatic" of the individual, such characterization is indicated.

Persons in an anxiety state also frequently give responses that are typical of that group. In general, their behavior is characterized by restlessness, apprehensiveness, impaired attention and concentration, and bodily expressions (such as tics, nail-biting, fidgeting, coughing). This psychological state is manifested, in the test situation where language is required, through difficulty with finding words, impulsively blurting out unfinished, unchecked, or inappropriate replies, or fumbling about for adequate formulations. For example, when the question is: "How many weeks are there in a year?" the anxiety-ridden person may reply: "There are 48 weeks in a year; no . . . let's see . . . or is it 50? . . . wait a minute . . . let's see . . . 12 months . . . 4 weeks in a month . . . yes, that's right, 48." Or consider the question: "Why should we keep away from bad company?" The person in an anxiety state may give a reply of the following sort. "If I was in bad company, I'd get away quick. I wouldn't want to be with them in the first place. They . . . er . . . are unlawful . . . and . . . ah . . . get you in trouble. . . . I don't think a person should be in bad company; that is, . . . er, ah . . . if he was brought up right. Anyhow, I'd leave them!"

The test responses of psychotic persons, also, are quite significant for diagnostic purposes; but the subject of psychotic responses is a complex one. One aspect may be indicated here—disorganization of thinking and bizarreness of responses typical of schizophrenics—both, of course, being indicated in the language of their answers. For example, the former teacher of history who cannot correctly give Washington's birthday, or the clergyman who cannot define the word "vesper" are instances that indicate disorganization of memory and loss of previous knowledge. Similarly, in replying to the "bad company" question, when one gives an emotionally intense and moralistic response, and explains, irrelevantly, why people should be "good," such a response suggests serious impairment of judgment. Or, in the Vocabulary test, when a subject gives impulsive replies, such as defining "belfry" as "a kind of bellboy"; or "repose" as "to pose over something." These bizarre answers indicate an impulsive "clang association."

DETERIORATION QUOTIENT. A procedure for estimating the approximate amount of mental loss is provided in the WAIS manual. This index is based upon observations that some of the functions tested decline more rapidly than do others. The difference between the rates of impairment of the two types of functions is regarded as the indicator of an individual's degree of deterioration. The tested functions that decline most markedly with advancing age are placed in the "Don't Hold" category. Those that decline least are in the "Hold" category. The subtests in the latter group are Vocabulary, Information, Object Assembly, and Picture Completion. In the "Don't Hold" category are Digit Span, Similarities, Digit Symbol, and Block Design.

Since some loss of tested abilities is generally expected with advancing age, this factor is taken into account in calculating the deterioration quotient, as shown in the following expression:

$$\text{Deterioration Quotient} = \frac{\text{Hold–Don't Hold}}{\text{Hold}} \times 100$$

For example, assume that a man 35 years of age has the following scores: Hold = 50; Don't Hold = 35. Substituting these values in the formula yields a quotient of 30. The quotient is then compared with the norm for the individual's age group to determine whether his loss is significantly greater or smaller than that expected for his age.

Published researches on this index do not agree on its merit and validity. Some support the technique; others do not; still others are equivocal. The criticism is that the concept of functions which "Hold" or "Don't Hold" might apply to some age groups and clinical categories but not to others, and that with many persons selective rather than over-all loss is the rule.

The soundness of this technique depends, also, upon a high reliability of each subtest and upon the adequacy of standardization at each age level. It is reasonable to conclude that the deterioration index is most significant where the extent of decline is considerable but not apparent. In conception, this index, or a similar one, provides an important technique in estimating changes in mental abilities, since it is seldom possible, when the subject is an older person, to obtain mental-test ratings that were found at his maximum level of development.

A Report Outline

The following is an example of the type of outline used in teaching graduate students to prepare reports of intelligence tests administered by them under supervision. Such outlines help to clarify and emphasize the significance given to qualitative aspects of test performance.

Psychological Examination

Name: (last, first, middle)   Date:
Age: (in years and months)   Date of birth:
Referred by:

I.   Introductory Statement
         a. by whom tested
         b. reason for testing
II.   Name (in full) of the test used
III. State the individual's general attitude and response to the test situation and to the examiner.
IV. Test findings:

Stanford-Binet	WAIS or WISC
a. Mental Age	a. Verbal IQ
b. Intelligence Quotient	b. Performance IQ
c. Basal Year	c. Full-Scale IQ
d. Terminal Year	d. Classification
e. Classification (average, superior, etc.)	

V.   Test evaluation
    a. Analyze the performance on:
        1. verbal materials
        2. nonverbal materials
    b. Compare the MA and IQ with the Vocabulary test score.
    c. Point out the quantitative and qualitative aspects of the results:
        1. strengths
        2. weaknesses
        3. scatter analysis
        4. quality of language (word definitions, use of language, grammar, richness of vocabulary, nuances, etc.)

VI. A summary statement of test performance

VII. Subject's behavior while being tested
    a. Reaction time:
        1. Were responses delayed, blocked, irregular?
        2. Was there any indiction of negativism?
        3. Were responses given quickly or impulsively?
    b. Nature of responses:
        1. Are some nonsensical, immature, childlike?
        2. Are they, on the whole, of good quality; or are they inconsistent?
        3. Is there confabulation?
        4. Does the subject ask for help?
        5. Is the subject critical of his responses?
    c. Depth of responses:
        1. Are they "surface" responses?
        2. Do they show depth of understanding?
        3. Does the subject try to appear penetrating?
        4. Does the subject adopt a "playful" (defensive) attitude?
    d. Self-references:
        1. Is the question or answer referred to the self? (Describe and analyze the references.)
        2. Are the responses in terms of the subject's own or immediate experiences, or in terms of someone else's?
        3. Does the individual give expression to his feelings during the testing (orally or by body movements)?
    e. Evidence of confusion or doubt:
        1. Do test questions have to be repeated?
        2. Does the subject change his answers? (Under what conditions?)
        3. Are questions misunderstood or misinterpreted? If so, explain in what way.
    f. Verbalization:
        1. Is the subject verbose?
        2. Is he spontaneous in responding?
        3. Does he have peculiarities of speech?

g. Organizational methods:
1. Is the individual careful or overmeticulous?
2. Does he plan and work systematically? Or is his a random approach?
3. Does he make many false starts?
4. Does he generalize readily?
5. Is there evidence of perseveration?
h. Adaptability:
1. Does the subject shift readily from one test to the next?
2. Is his interest sustained in all types of test items?
i. Motor coordination:
1. Are the gross and finer movements skillful or awkward?
2. Can he smoothly execute bilateral movements?
j. Effort:
1. Is the subject cooperative?
2. Does he give evidence of trying hard?
3. Does he attend with ease or difficulty?
k. Mood:
1. Was the individual readily upset, irritable, argumentative, stuporous, happy, sad, depressed?
2. Were there any emotional outbursts?
3. Did his mood undergo change during the testing?
4. Was he, on the whole, cheerful?
5. In what mood was the individual when he left the testing room? [7]

Tests of Mental Impairment

In this section, we present brief descriptions and evaluations of several highly specialized testing procedures developed primarily for the clinical study of patients. Where used, they are employed in conjunction with other instruments, particularly the Stanford-Binet, the Wechsler scales, and projective tests.

The Bender Visual-Motor Gestalt Test consists of nine figures characterized chiefly by their patterning (that is, their *Gestalt*). The subject is simply instructed to copy each figure, without time limit. The test, clearly, is not one of visual memory and imagery; it is one of perception and visual-motor functioning.

The figures used were devised by Max Wertheimer—one of the founders of the Gestalt school of psychology—in his experimental work on perception. The underlying principle utilized in the Bender test, as expounded by Wertheimer and others, is that organized wholes (structured

---

[7] I am indebted to my former graduate student and assistant, Dr. Joanna Byers, who collaborated importantly in the development of this form.

units) are the primary forms of perception in man. Loss of integrative perception, therefore, might be a psychopathological manifestation. Perceptual behavior is regarded, in the test, as involving sensory reception of the figures, interpretation at the central levels of the nervous system, and motor performance (drawing). This total process of perception and reproduction can be distorted by neural injury, by emotional maladjustment in the perceiving individual, and by variations in the intellectual level of performance. Hence, the test's possibilities were explored by investigating "gestalt functions" in cases of aphasia, organic brain disease, schizophrenia, manic-depressive psychoses, mental defectives, psychoneurotics, malingerers, and normal children.

Pascal and Suttell (46) provide a standardized and quantitative system of scoring the reproductions of adults. Essentially, the scoring procedure was arrived at in this manner. (1) The reproductions of psychiatric patients were compared to those of normal persons. (2) The drawings of abnormal persons tended to deviate from the originals more than did those of normal subjects. (3) Deviations (differences between originals and reproductions) that discriminated between normal and psychiatric subjects were isolated. (4) A de-

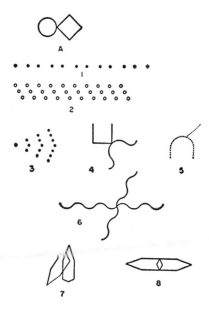

Fig. 14.5. The Bender Visual-Motor Gestalt Test. A visual-motor Gestalt test and its clinical use. *Research Monograph,* American Orthopsychiatric Association, 1938, no. 3.

viation was retained if item analysis showed that it discriminated significantly between the two groups, or if it occurred in the reproductions of abnormals but "practically never" in those of normals. (5) Deviations were weighted according to discriminative value between the two groups. (6) "Score reliability" was determined ($r = .90$; $N = 120$). (7) Norms were found for a nonpatient population of 474 subjects (271 males; 203 females) varying in age from 15 to 50 years, most of whom were attending evening classes at the high school or college level.

After the scoring method had been evolved and the norms determined, validity was studied by (1) "blind" matching of scores with group classification (normal, neurotic, psychotic) and (2) prediction of improvability of patients receiving therapy, who were tested on admission. The test was fairly effective in distinguishing between normals and psychotics, and between normals and neurotics; but it discriminated only slightly between psychotics and neurotics. As between patients who were described, upon discharge, as "improved" or "unimproved," under (2), the mean scores for the two groups showed significant differences. The results under both (1) and (2) were sufficiently discriminating to encourage the use of the Bender-Gestalt as one possible source of significant evidence in the diagnosis of normal and abnormal personalities.

As in all such situations, it must be noted that although the mean scores and standard deviations for the *groups* are significantly different, there is still appreciable *overlapping* of scores of the three groups (normals, neurotics, psychotics). Overlapping of scores within different groups, classified for various purposes, is the usual psychological phenomenon. In dealing with an individual, therefore, in respect to a particular trait or function, it is always necessary to consider the possibility that he might deviate from the central tendency of his group. The scores in Table 14.1 illustrate this point.

TABLE 14.1

BENDER-GESTALT TEST MEANS AND RANGES OF SCORES

	*Mean scores**	*Middle 60%*	*Range*
Normals	50	47–60	32–79
Neurotics	68	53–80	32–139
Psychotics	81	65–100	40–155

* Values are in terms of Z scores; mean equals 50, standard deviation equals 10. The higher scores are the more unfavorable. Based upon data in Pascal and Suttell (46, pp. 30–31).

More recent researches have provided promising evidence showing that this test may be used diagnostically with emotionally disturbed children (11), that it differentiates organics from other categories (61); and that it has been used with some success to differentiate between delinquents and nondelinquents (67). On the other hand, some findings are inconsistent and equivocal in studies on differences between *psychotic* and nonpsychotic groups (60).

The Babcock test is based upon the widely employed principle that intellectual impairment or deterioration of an individual can be estimated by using his vocabulary score to represent his mental capacity as it was prior to the onset of mental disturbance (3, 38). The individual's scores on the several other subtests are compared with the scores made on the same subtests by a normal group of the same "vocabulary age." When this technique is used, the implication is that one's vocabulary withstands best the adverse influences of advanced age and mental illness, and that vocabulary score may, therefore, be regarded as an index of the affected person's previous intellectual level. His performance on other subtests is, therefore, compared with the performance of normal persons of the same vocabulary level, on the principle that in a normal population there is a high correlation between vocabulary scores and those of other mental functions.

The Babcock test provides a measure of mental "efficiency." This index is based upon tests emphasizing information, recall of meaningful materials (nonrote) rote memory (meaningful and meaningless materials), motor speed (rate of writing, tracing, digit symbol substitution), and simple learning (immediate reproduction of paragraph, paired associates, drawing designs from memory). The subtests are arranged into several groups; the score for each group is the average of the subtests that constitute it. The "Efficiency Score" is the total of the *group averages*. The subject's "vocabulary age" is based upon the score he obtains on the vocabulary test of the 1937 Stanford-Binet.

An individual's rating is derived in this way. (1) The vocabulary score is converted into a "vocabulary age." (2) The *expected* average level of performance on the other subtests, *corresponding to this vocabulary age,* is found in the given table of norms; this value is called the *expected average.* (3) The *actual* scores are averaged; this average, called the total efficiency score, is the *obtained* average. (4) The expected average is subtracted from the obtained average, yielding an *efficiency index,* either positive or negative.

The efficiency index has been used as a diagnostic device. For instance, in a group of paretics, an average index of −4.8 was found. The size of the index corresponded in general to the degree of mental deterioration. A group of schizophrenics had a median index of −3.5. Results obtained by other investigators agree, in the general trend, with those reported by Babcock for abnormal groups.

Efficiency indexes, presumably characteristic of the several groups, are *averages.* Inspection of the Babcock and Levy table of norms shows that while the differences between median indexes of the several clinical groups may be reliable, there is still a large amount of overlapping of scores between any two groups. This means, of course, that the efficiency index is not in itself adequate for diagnosis and classification, but must be used as one of several converging lines of evidence.

Some clinical investigators have gone beyond the use of the efficiency index alone. They have sought patterns of impairment and performance, the principle being the same as in the case of the Wechsler scale. Schizophrenics, for example, perform worst on tests of immediate and delayed recall of meaningful materials, their responses being characterized not only by a small number of correct recalls but also by serious distortions and introduction of bizarre material (51, p. 379 ff). However, on rote repetition of digits schizophrenics do relatively well. This difference between the two types of recall is regarded as significant. Since schizophrenics maintain their efficiency on some types of tests, but are markedly inefficient on others, *total* scores will suggest only an intermediate degree of impairment, which is inconclusive and can be misleading. The importance of subtest analysis, both quantitative and qualitative, is thereby illustrated.

This instrument is intended to measure mental functioning regarded as "crucial in the maintenance of stability in our present social environment." Babcock and Levy, therefore, have attempted to isolate aspects of intelligence that remain stable under most mental disorders and that measure level of "abstract ability" (in actuality, vocabulary). Other mental processes, however, are impaired during mental disorders. Therefore the tests are designed to measure impairment of efficiency in the following functions: speed of perception and response in simple well-learned experiences, and in the less familiar and more difficult; rate of learning; psychomotor responses, memory in several stages and aspects; and smoothness in sustained effort.

Not all psychologists agree that these tests measure the functions named. For example, some maintain that the tests measure, among others, attention, concentration, coherence of thought processes, and visual imagery. Nevertheless, regardless of the final determination of the precise functions measured, these tests have demonstrated their usefulness for clinical purposes when the numerical index is supplemented by an analysis of specific impairment and a qualitative statement concerning noteworthy aspects of the subject's performance.

Tests of Concept Formation. These tests are based upon the principle that emotional disturbances and personality disorders interfere with thinking processes, particularly with ability to form abstract concepts. The purposes of these tests are, therefore, to help the psychologist observe the subject's thought processes and to discover the extent to which maladjustment or mental illness has impaired his conscious thinking, as revealed in efforts to solve problems requiring the formation of concepts.

In particular, these tests are intended to evaluate the subject's ability to deal with objects and situations on the abstract or conceptual level, as compared with the concrete. Ability to form concepts implies conscious reasoning at the abstract level; that is, transcending the immediate specific sensory situation, abstracting the common property from particular instances, analyzing and synthesizing, shifting from one aspect to another, keeping in mind several aspects simultaneously, planning ideationally, and self-criticism. An individual's behavior at the concrete level, on the other hand, lacks these characteristics. The individual is then unreflective; he responds to the immediately given object or situation as something unique; he does not perceive an object or situation as one instance of a general class or category.

The Goldstein tests are of several kinds. A Cube Test (devised in collaboration with M. Scheerer) estimates the subject's ability to copy colored designs, using variously colored cubes. The twelve designs are, with one exception, those of the familiar Kohs series. It is maintained that reproduction of designs may be achieved through either a concrete or an abstract approach. In the former, the subject merely perceives the model as a whole and attempts, without analysis or reflection, to copy it. In the latter approach, the subject perceives the design reflectively and attempts to reproduce it while employing deliberate analytical reasoning directed toward a discovery of the relations of the parts of the designs (presumably, the principles underlying its construction). If the subject fails to reproduce the design correctly on the first attempt, the examiner presents the same design in a graded series of modified forms, each of which is less difficult to apprehend than the preceding form. Each step is intended to facilitate the solution through: (1) enlargement of the model to actual block size; (2) emphasis upon delineation of part relations; or (3) use of actual block models.

Abnormal subjects, it was found, did not benefit from the presentation of graded concrete aids, whereas normal subjects did. Those in one group were unable to learn; the other group did learn to solve the problem at the level of abstraction. For the normal group, the aids are said to be a means of learning to succeed at the abstract level on later designs. For abnormal persons, the aids are concrete presentations without possibility of transfer value to subsequent situations. If the subject being tested

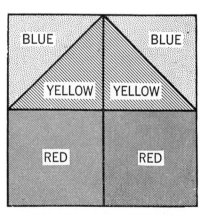

FIG. 14.6. From the Goldstein-Scheerer Cube Test. The subject is required to construct this pattern from a set of blocks, variously colored. The Psychological Corporation, by permission.

cannot benefit from the modified and simplified aids, impairment of abstract behavior is indicated.

A Color-Sorting Test (A. Gelb, collaborator) is also used to estimate levels of abstract and concrete behavior. This requires the use of color *concepts,* if the response is at the level of abstraction. In one test, woolen skeins of different hue and tint are presented at random, and there are twelve different shades of each color hue. The subject selects one and is then asked to pick out all others that go with it. In the second test, three skeins are presented; two are of the same hue but different in brightness and saturation; the third is of a different hue, but the same in brightness as one of the first pair. The subject is expected to make a selection either according to hue or brightness.

Gelb and Goldstein report that abnormal persons with functional behavior disturbances are incapable of using abstraction. In varying degrees, they appear to be unable to shift from concreteness of matching to the abstract thinking required in selecting and classifying.

The third in this group is an Object-Sorting Test (A. Gelb, E. Weigl, M. Scheerer, collaborators). This consists of a group of about thirty objects common to everyday experiences, one group for males and one for females. Its purpose is "to determine whether the subject is able to sort a variety of simultaneously presented objects according to general concepts." Ability so to classify is evidence of the abstract approach; inability is evidence of the concrete approach. Classifications may be made on the basis of use (tools), color, form, materials, situational membership (implements for setting a dinner table), and pairings.

The fourth, a Color-Form Sorting Test (Scheerer and Weigl, collaborators), employs the same principle as that in the others of this group. The subject is required to sort a variety of differently colored geometric figures according to color or form. There are four equilateral triangles, four squares, and four circles. In each of these forms, one is red, one yellow, one green, one blue, while the reverse sides are all white. Conceptual behavior is indicated by the subject's ability to arrange the figures on the basis of color or form and to verbalize his act to confirm its conceptual character. Concrete perception and behavior are generally characterized by typical responses, such as a strong tendency to build patterns following structural lines; an inability to *account* for a grouping or to grasp the *meaning* of sorting; dependence upon sensory aspects and an inability to shift voluntarily from one sensory impression to another; inability to generalize from one performance to another. Inability to approach the test at the abstract level is indicative of disturbance of cortical functioning.

A Stick Test completes the series (in collaboration with Scheerer). This is intended to examine the subject's ability to: (1) *copy* relatively simple geometric figures composed of sticks that are 3.5 and 5.5 inches in length; and (2) *reproduce* these same figures from memory, after exposure of five to thirty seconds. The sequence in which the thirty-four figures are presented represents something of a scale in terms of number of sticks involved and increasing complexity of the model. At the level of abstraction, the subject is expected to survey the pattern and analyze it into its parts and part relationships (spatial and directional). Reference to the stimulus figure as being associated with, or representative of, an *object* in actual experience is regarded as a concrete response. Thus, to reproduce the figure $\wedge$ and call it a "roof" is to perceive at the concrete level. It is reported that this test is particularly suited to cases of marked mental defect or deterioration.

The authors of this series of tests do not present the type of statistical information upon which evaluations are usually based. In fact, there has been no attempt to standardize their tests with respect to the usual criteria of validity and reliability; nor are scoring standards provided. Their emphasis is placed entirely upon qualitative evaluation of the subject's responses as an aid in the diagnosis of mental impairment or of mental arrest. There is no doubt, however, that the clinical value of the tests would be enhanced if quantified or scaled ratings could be had, not necessarily to obtain percentile or standard scores or the like, but to facilitate an over-all estimate of an individual's responses and to increase the objectivity of the tests' interpretation. At the present time, these devices appear to be valuable in the hands of an experienced psychologist for detecting cases of marked intellectual impairment or arrest, by presenting tasks involving abstraction; tasks which are rather simple for persons of average ability who are functioning normally. In fact, the difficulty levels of some parts of this series are such that most 7-, 8-, or 9-year-old children can achieve a solution at the abstract level. Hence, in most instances, the failure of an adult readily to offer a solution at the abstract level may well be regarded as a significant symptom of serious loss of intellectual level and efficiency.

The Hanfmann-Kasanin test [8] consists of twenty-two blocks, each block in one of five colors, six shapes, two heights, and two widths. The problem for the subject is to discern how the blocks may be divided into four categories; tall-wide, flat-wide, tall-narrow, and flat-narrow figures.

The subject is shown the entire set randomly arranged. The examiner selects one as a sample and directs the examinee to pick out all others that are of the same kind. It is obvious that the subject might at first make his selection according to color, shape, or size. Each type of block

[8] This test is a modification of the Vigotsky tests. See E. O. Miller (44).

has a nonsense name on the bottom, concealed from the subject (for example, *bik* for flat-wide). After each grouping, the examiner shows the subject one of the wrongly selected forms by revealing that it carries a different name. The procedure is to continue this kind of aid until the subject discovers the predetermined classification, if it is at all possible for him to do so.

Fig. 14.7. Hanfmann–Kasanin test blocks. C. H. Stoelting Company, by permission.

Performance is analyzed and scored in respect to interpretation of the task, nature of the attempts at solution, and discovery of the correct solution. In each of these, three levels of performance are distinguished—the primitive, the intermediate, and the conceptual—these being scored 1, 2, and 3, respectively. The scoring method is based upon the nature of the subject's approach to the problem, his ability to conceptualize, and his ability to verbalize his performance.

In developing this test, Hanfmann and Kasanin were concerned principally with schizophrenics and their clinical differentiation. Rapaport (51, Chapter 4) found their test clinically useful in obtaining evidence of the subject's modes of thinking and response to difficult and frustrating problem situations, rather than for diagnostic differentiation. For example, different individuals may show the following modes of response in varying combinations and degrees: *fluidity* (lack of direction); *flexibility* (varying the approach, but keeping the end in view); *rigidity* (resistance to modification of behavior); *persistence* (continuity of behavior). These qualitative descriptions, therefore, obtained with the Hanfmann-Kasanin test, are of the kind that are valuable as a supplement to numerical ratings in obtaining a more nearly complete description of a person's mental functioning.

Although the authors themselves used a scoring plan, the weights of the assigned values have not been experimentally determined. They are, rather, arbitrarily assigned scale values; they may, therefore, be more properly designated as numerical indicators. As such, they are useful in obtaining an over-all evaluation of an individual's performance on the test.

The problem situations presented in the test are at a more difficult and higher level of abstraction than those in the Goldstein series. Since these problems make greater demands upon persons of higher mental levels, they may reveal deterioration in conceptual thinking that would still be unapparent in the subject's long-established responses for meeting familiar situations and for dealing with familiar problems. The Hanfmann-Kasanin test provides a means of observing behavior in a controlled situation and of obtaining information of some significance, to be added to other psychological data.

The Hunt-Minnesota Test for Brain Damage was devised as an aid in detecting organic brain damage. It is intended for use with individuals 16 years of age or older. The instrument consists of these three major divisions: the Vocabulary test of the 1937 Stanford-Binet, which has been found relatively *insensitive* to brain damage; six memory and recall tests, considered to be *sensitive* to brain damage; and nine interpolated tests that serve as "validity indicators."

The six deterioration tests involve memorizing and retention of paired designs and of paired words presented orally. Both types are used to test immediate and delayed recall. A series of paired designs is exposed, without interruption, for six seconds each, after which the subject is shown one of each pair, in sequence, and is required to identify the design associated with it (immediate recall). In the word test, a series of ten pairs of words is read; after this, the first word of each pair is given singly, and it is the subject's task to name its paired word (immediate recall). There are three tests of designs and three of words.

The Vocabulary test, as in the case of other clinical instruments, is regarded as a measure of a relatively stable function that holds up against deterioration. The vocabulary score, which is the number of words correctly defined according to the Stanford-Binet standards, is taken as the base for the determination of the deterioration score, from which presence or absence of brain damage is inferred.

The interpolated tests consist of the following: information; naming the months of the year; counting from 1 to 20; counting from 3 to 30 by 3s; tapping on the table every time the number 3 is read in a long series of digits (attention test); counting backwards from 25 to 1; repeating digits backwards; naming the months in reverse order; subtraction of 3s from 79 to 1. These items are included as "validity indicators," since persons unable to perform them are too uncooperative, or too disturbed, or too deteriorated to be tested; hence testing them will not yield valid results. Critical scores are provided for each of the interpolated tests, these having been reached, or exceeded, by 90 percent of the brain-damaged persons used in standardizing the test. The test's author reports that individuals whose scores fall below the critical levels in three or more of the interpolated items cannot be validly tested.

This test was standardized in several state hospitals upon a small number of patients (only thirty-three) who had been diagnosed as suffering from organic cerebral damage, excluding congenital conditions, birth injuries, and childhood brain injury. They ranged in age from 16 to 70 years. The control group consisted of forty-one cases in state institutions, neuropsychiatric wards, or war veterans' hospitals, who were *not* diagnosed as cases of organic brain damage.

When twenty-five cases from each group (brain-damaged and control) were equated on the basis of only their vocabulary scores, striking differences were found on the deterioration tests, and much smaller differences on the interpolated items. The total overlapping of deterioration scores of the two groups was 50 percent, while total overlapping of interpolated scores was 90 percent. These data indicate that the former tests are much more discriminative between the two groups than the latter, and presumably, therefore, much more sensitive to effects of deterioration. The fact, however, that there is a 50 percent total overlap indicates that the test results must be viewed not in isolation, but in conjunction with other evidence in each case.

The correlation between deterioration scores and vocabulary scores was found to be —.51; between age and vocabulary, .07; between age and deterioration score, —.37. Multiple correlation of deterioration score with age and vocabulary was —.65.

This instrument, like all others in this difficult area of psychological testing, needs to be more clearly validated by further application and experimentation. It is well, therefore, to view it at present—as suggested by its author—as additional evidence in reaching a conclusion as to the presence or absence of brain damage. At the same time, the more extreme deterioration scores have greater diagnostic value. Although few relatively recent research studies have been published on this test, available data indicate that it is clinically useful, if its results are carefully analyzed, qualitatively as well as quantitatively (65).

In addition to the instruments briefly described above, other more recent devices have been made available; but these are in rather early experimental stages. One of these is the *Grassi Block Substitution Test,* which requires the subject to construct patterns, the designs of which are presented to him (20). Other experiments have been made with sorting of words, cards (14), and geometric forms (66). These newer experimental efforts, however, utilize essentially the same basic psychological principles as those employed by their predecessors.

Evaluation. Psychological tests in this area are based upon the principle that old, well-established habits and modes of behaving (such as word knowledge) show *relatively* little loss, whereas new learning, newly acquired associations, performing new tasks, and solving new types of problems are impaired in cases of brain damage and other forms of mental disturbance.

As a group, these tests have not been adequately standardized, so far as norms, scoring, and interpretation are concerned. Standardizing tests for extremely deviant and often uncooperative populations is, however, an extraordinarily difficult task. Since these tests are intended primarily for adults, their standardization and interpretation are further complicated by the fact that allowance should be made for normally expected loss at advanced ages; and individual differences in cultural, educational, and occupational backgrounds must be considered in evaluating a subject's performance. Validation is made the more difficult, too, since psychiatric diagnoses and classifications are generally used as one criterion of validity; and these are themselves sufficiently inconsistent and lacking in reliability as to introduce an important source of error in the validation process.

These tests do not, as yet, provide a self-sufficient method of measuring mental deterioration, except in the more marked cases. However, clinicians who have used them are in substantial agreement that they are valuable in providing opportunities for observation of mental operations under controlled conditions in which prescribed materials are used. In such situations, an experienced psychologist is able to make important qualitative observations, in addition to deriving, at times, quantitative values for the subject's performance. The particular qualitative observations that can be made will depend upon the content and technique of the test. Qualitative observations might include descriptions of the subject's thought processes, estimates of levels of abstraction or concreteness, bizarre responses, degree of self-criticism, fluctuations of attention, degrees of rigidity or flexibility of thought processes, level of immediate and delayed recall compared with recall of remotely learned materials, and evaluations of the subject's performance in the light of his former educational and occupational status. To make these observations, of course, requires a background of experience with a sufficiently large and varied number of subjects, including, for comparative purposes, persons within the normal range of behavioral adjustment and performance.[9]

References

1. Abrahamson, H. A., *et al.* Lysergic acid and diethylamine (LSD-25). XIII. Effects on Bender-Gestalt test performance. *Journal of Psychology,* 1955, *40,* 341–349.
2. Anderson, A. L. The effect of laterality localization of brain damage on Wechsler-Bellevue indices of deterioration. *Journal of Clinical Psychology,* 1950, *6,* 191–194.
3. Babcock, H., and L. Levy. *The Revised Examination for the Measurement of Efficiency of Mental Functioning.* Chicago: C. H. Stoelting, 1942.
4. Beck, H. S., and R. L. Lam. Use of the WISC in predicting organicity. *Journal of Clinical Psychology,* 1955, *11,* 154–158.
5. Bender, L. A visual-motor Gestalt test and its clinical use. *Research Monograph,* American Orthopsychiatric Association, 1938, no. 3.
6. Bijou, S. W. The psychometric pattern approach as an aid to clinical analysis —a review. *American Journal of Mental Deficiency,* 1942, *46,* 354–362.
7. Bijou, S. W., and B. R. McCandless. An approach to a more comprehensive analysis of mentally retarded pre-delinquent boys. *Journal of Genetic Psychology,* 1944, *65,* 147–160.
8. Billingslea, F. Y. The Bender-Gesalt: an objective scoring method and validating data. *Clinical Psychology Monographs,* 1948, no. 1.
9. Boyd, F. A provisional quantitative scoring with preliminary norms for the

[9] There is renewed interest in the Porteus Maze Test, since it was found to be of value in the assessment of brain damage resulting from "psychosurgery." Subsequently, research findings indicated its value in assessing mental deficits accompanying continued use of a tranquilizing drug. Porteus reports also that the maze test is useful as an experimental device in studying flexibility and rigidity as aspects of habit formation. See Chapter 12, on performance tests; also S. D. Porteus, *The Maze Test and Clinical Psychology.* Palo Alto, Calif.: Pacific Books, 1959.

Goldstein-Scheerer Cube Test. *Journal of Clinical Psychology*, 1949, *5*, 148–153.

10. Carter, J. W., and J. W. Bowles. A manual of qualitative aspects of psychological examining. *Clinical Psychology Monographs*, 1948, no. 2.

11. Clawson, A. The Bender visual-motor Gestalt test as an index of emotional disturbance in children. *Journal of Projective Techniques*, 1959, *23*, 198–206.

12. Corotto, L. V., and R. H. Curnutt. The effectiveness of the Bender-Gestalt in differentiating a flight group from an aggressive group of adolescents. *Journal of Consulting Psychology*, 1960, *24*, 368–369.

13. Feifel, H. Qualitative differences in the vocabulary responses of normals and abnormals. *Genetic Psychology Monographs*, 1949, *39*.

14. Fey, E. T. The performance of young schizophrenics on the Wisconsin card-sorting test. *Journal of Consulting Psychology*, 1951, *15*, 311–319.

15. Frandsen, A. N., *et al.* Serial versus consecutive order administration of the Stanford-Binet intelligence scales. *Journal of Consulting Psychology*, 1950, *14*, 316–320.

16. Garfield, S. L. A preliminary appraisal of Wechsler-Bellevue patterns in schizophrenia. *Journal of Consulting Psychology*, 1948, *12*, 32–36.

17. Goldman, R., *et al.* Use of the Bellevue-Wechsler scale in clinical psychiatry with particular reference to cases with brain damage. *Journal of Nervous and Mental Diseases*, 1946, *104*, 144–179.

18. Goldstein, K., and M. Scheerer. Abstract and concrete behavior: an experimental study with special tests. *Psychological Monographs*, 1941, no. 239.

19. Grant, D. A. Perceptual versus analytical responses to the number concept of a Weigl-type card sorting test. *Journal of Experimental Psychology*, 1951, *41*, 23–29.

20. Grassi, J. R. *The Grassi Block Substitution Test: For Measuring Organic Brain Pathology*. Springfield, Ill.: Charles C Thomas, Publisher, 1953.

21. Griffith, R. M., and V. H. Taylor. Incidence of Bender-Gestalt figure rotations. *Journal of Consulting Psychology*, 1960, *24*, 189–190.

22. Gutman, B. The application of the Wechsler-Bellevue scale in the diagnosis of organic brain disorders. *Journal of Clinical Psychology*, 1950, *6*, 195–198.

23. Haggard, E. A. *Interclass Correlation and the Analysis of Variance*. New York: Holt, Rinehart and Winston, Inc., 1957.

24. Hanfmann, E., and J. Kasanin. Conceptual thinking in schizophrenia. *Nervous and Mental Disease Monographs*, 1942, no. 67.

25. Hanfmann, E., and J. Kasanin. A method for study of concept formation. *Journal of Psychology*, 1946, *3*, 521–545.

26. Harrower, M. (ed.). *Recent Advances in Diagnostic Psychological Testing*. Springfield, Ill.: Charles C Thomas, Publisher, 1950.

27. Harrower, M. *Personality Change and Development*. New York: Grune & Stratton, Inc., 1958.

28. Heilizer, F. The effects of chlorpromazine upon psychomotor and psychiatric behavior of chronic schizophrenic patients. *Journal of Nervous and Mental Diseases*, 1959, *128*, 358–364.

29. Hoch, P. H., and J. Zubin (eds.). *Relation of Psychological Tests to Psychiatry.* New York: Grune & Stratton, Inc., 1952.

30. Hunt, H. F. *The Hunt-Minnesota Test for Organic Brain Damage.* Minneapolis: University of Minnesota Press, 1943.

31. Hunt, H. F. A note on the clinical use of the Hunt-Minnesota test for organic brain damage. *Journal of Applied Psychology,* 1944, *28,* 175–178.

32. Hunt, J. McV., and C. N. Cofer. Psychological deficit. *Personality and the Behavior Disorders* (J. McV. Hunt, ed.). New York: The Ronald Press Company, 1944, ch. 32.

33. Hutt, M. L. A clinical study of consecutive and adaptive testing with the revised Stanford-Binet. *Journal of Consulting Psychology,* 1947, *11,* 93–103.

34. Jackson, C. V. Estimating impairment on Wechsler-Bellevue subtests. *Journal of Clinical Psychology,* 1955, *11,* 137–143.

35. Juckem, H., and J. A. Wald. A study of the Hunt-Minnesota test for organic brain damage at the upper levels of vocabulary. *Journal of Consulting Psychology,* 1948, *12,* 53–57.

36. Kent, G. H. *Kent Series of Emergency Scales.* New York: The Psychological Corporation, 1946.

37. Kingsley, L. Wechsler-Bellevue patterns of psychopaths. *Journal of Consulting Psychology,* 1960, *24,* 373.

38. Lewinski, R. J. Vocabulary and mental measurements: a quantitative investigation and review of research. *Journal of Genetic Psychology,* 1948, *72,* 247–281.

39. Louttit, C. M., and C. G. Browne. The use of psychometric instruments in psychological clinics. *Journal of Consulting Psychology,* 1947, *11,* 49–54.

40. Magaret, M., and C. W. Thompson. Differential test responses of normal, superior, and mentally defective subjects. *Journal of Abnormal and Social Psychology,* 1950, *45,* 163–167.

41. Malamud, R. F. Validity of the Hunt-Minnesota test for organic brain damage. *Journal of Applied Psychology,* 1946, *30,* 271–275.

42. McNemar, Q. On WAIS difference scores. *Journal of Consulting Psychology,* 1957, *21,* 239–240.

43. Meehl, P. E., and A. Rosen. Antecedent probability and the efficiency of psychometric signs, patterns, or cutting scores. *Psychological Bulletin,* 1955, *52,* 194–216.

44. Miller, E. O. New use for the Vigotsky blocks. *Journal of Clinical Psychology,* 1955, *11,* 87–89.

45. Olin, T. D., and M. Reznikoff. Quantification of the Bender-Gestalt recall: a pilot study. *Journal of Projective Techniques,* 1957, *21,* 265–277.

46. Pascal, G. R., and B. J. Suttell. *The Bender-Gestalt Test.* New York: Grune & Stratton, Inc., 1951.

47. Plumeau, F., *et al.* Wechsler-Bellevue performances of remitted and unremitted alcoholics and their normal controls. *Journal of Consulting Psychology,* 1960, *24,* 240–242.

48. Ptacek, J. E., and F. M. Young. Comparison of the Grassi block substitution

test with the Wechsler-Bellevue in the diagnosis of organic brain damage. *Journal of Clinical Psychology*, 1954, *10*, 375–378.

49. Rabin, A. I. Test-score patterns in schizophrenia and non-psychotic states. *Journal of Psychology*, 1941, *12*, 91–100.

50. Rabin, A. I., and W. H. Guertin. Research with the Wechsler-Bellevue test: 1945–1950. *Psychological Bulletin*, 1951, *48*, 211–248.

51. Rapaport, D. *Diagnostic Psychological Testing*. Chicago: Year Book Publishers, Inc., 1945.

52. Rapaport, D. The status of diagnostic psychological testing. *Journal of Consulting Psychology*, 1948, *12*, 1–3.

53. Riggs, M. M., and K. A. Burchard. Intra-scale scatter for two kinds of mentally defective children. Vineland, N.J.: *The Training School Bulletin*, 1952, *49*, 36–44.

54. Sarason, S. B., and E. K. Sarason. The discriminatory value of a test pattern in the high grade familial defective. *Journal of Clinical Psychology*, 1946, 2, 38–49.

55. Sarason, S. B., and E. K. Sarason. The discriminatory value of a test pattern with cerebral palsied, defective children. *Journal of Clinical Psychology*, 1947, *3*, 141–147.

56. Schafer, R. The expression of personality and maladjustment in intelligence test results. *Annals of the New York Academy of Sciences*, 1946, *46*, 609–623.

57. Schafer, R. On the objective and subjective aspects of diagnostic testing. *Journal of Consulting Psychology*, 1948, *12*, 4–7.

58. Schneider, J. H., and R. E. Kantor. Wechsler's deterioration ratio in psychoneurosis and schizophrenia. *Journal of Consulting Psychology*, 1949, *13*, 108–110.

59. Stewart, H., and S. Cunningham. A note on scoring recalled figures of the Bender-Gestalt test using psychotics, non-psychotics, and controls. *Journal of Clinical Psychology*, 1958, *14*, 207–208.

60. Tamkin, A. S. The effectiveness of the Bender-Gestalt in differential diagnosis. *Journal of Consulting Psychology*, 1957, *21*, 355–357.

61. Tolor, A. Further studies on the Bender-Gestalt test and the digit-span test as measures of recall. *Journal of Clinical Psychology*, 1958, *14*, 14–18.

62. Trehub, A., and I. W. Scherer. Wechsler-Bellevue scatter as an index of schizophrenia. *Journal of Consulting Psychology*, 1958, 22, 147–149.

63. Tucker, J. E., and M. J. Spielberg. Bender-Gestalt test correlates of emotional depression. *Journal of Consulting Psychology*, 1958, 22, 56.

64. Wechsler, D. *The Measurement and Appraisal of Adult Intelligence*. Baltimore: The Williams & Wilkins Company, 1958.

65. Winfield, D. L. Intellectual performance of cryptogenic epileptics, symptomatic epileptics, and post-traumatic encephalopaths. *Journal of Abnormal and Social Psychology*, 1951, *46*, 336–343.

66. Zaslow, R. W. A new approach to the problem of conceptual thinking in schizophrenia. *Journal of Consulting Psychology*, 1950, *14*, 335–339.

67. Zolik, E. S. A comparison of the Bender-Gestalt reproductions of delinquents and non-delinquents. *Journl of Clinical Psychology*, 1958, *14*, 24–26.

15.

NONVERBAL GROUP SCALES OF MENTAL ABILITY

Beginnings

The original Binet scale and its several revisions are administered to one person at a time; hence they are called individual scales. This is true, also, of the performance scales already described. Individual scales, obviously, are time-consuming and require that the examiner be highly skilled in administering them, in interpreting responses, and in evaluating the subject's behavior during the course of the examination. Impelled, perhaps, by the prevailing urge for "efficiency" and mass production, and by a desire to investigate large-scale problems, American psychologists undertook to develop tests that could be administered to a group of persons—large or small—all at one time.

World War I provided the occasion for the organization of the first group test. Prior to 1917, psychologists had been experimenting with test items and organization with a view to group examination. Shortly after the United States entered World War I, a psychological branch was formed in the army, to develop and use group scales for the general classification of soldiers on the basis of mental ability. A few other devices were developed for use in the army—for example, trade tests—but in the army of World War I, psychologists' contributions were made largely in the area of testing general ability.

Although the 1916 Stanford Revision and the Yerkes Point Scale were employed to some extent, as well as an individual performance scale, the main task in the army was one of testing large numbers of men in a short space of time. Consequently, the Army Alpha scale (verbal) and the Army Beta scale (nonverbal), both group scales, were organized. These were actually the product of the contributions of individual psychologists, notably Arthur S. Otis, who pooled their experience, experimental results, and resources.

About 1,750,000 men were tested in the army of World War I. The scales were not highly satisfactory instruments; then, too, the men were often examined under unfavorable conditions. However, the results were of some assistance in the selection of men for advanced or special training, on the one hand, and of men of such inferior ability as to be unsuited for military training, on the other.

The use of psychological testing in World War I had many outgrowths, some of which were unforeseen by the psychologists themselves. The data were reported and analyzed in a huge volume (31). On the basis of these data, many periodical articles and books appeared on such subjects as racial and national differences in intelligence, geographic differences in intelligence within the United States, differences between occupational groups, relationship between educational status and intelligence, and the general intellectual level of the American adult. Not only were many of these data of doubtful validity, but some of the interpretations and publications based upon them gave rise to serious misapprehensions in regard to these problems, which are loaded with social and educational implications. Another result of psychological testing in the army was the impetus it gave to the development of group tests for civilian purposes, notably in educational work at all levels, from kindergarten through university. Also, it set a precedent, for in World War II psychological testing was conducted on a vast scale in all departments of the armed forces.

The types of test materials included in the army group scales and in the numerous group scales subsequently developed were not all innovations. For example, tests of memory, sentence completion, free and controlled word association, arithmetical computation, vocabulary, classification of objects, and following directions had been in process of experimentation in the United States and Europe, during the last quarter of the nineteenth century.

Characteristics of Group Tests of Mental Ability

Most group tests—implicitly or explicitly—are constructed on the principle that intelligence is a general capacity and that it should be measured by sampling a variety of mental activities. Inspection of the scales shows, therefore, that they include, in various combinations, such items as following directions, arithmetical problems, practical judgment (in connection with "common-sense" problems), word meaning, disarranged sentences, completion of number series, completion of sentences, verbal analogies, information, mazes, three-dimensional visualization and counting of cubes, digit-symbol combinations, picture absurdities, picture arrangement, geometrical construction ("paper formboard"), and geometric pattern analogies. Samples of each of these will be presented later when some scales are described.

In most group scales, the items of each type (for example, number series) are placed together in separate subtests or parts, beginning with the easiest and progressing by intervals—as nearly equal as may be achieved—to the most difficult. The principle involved here is as follows. By means of such an arrangement of items, every individual for whom the test is intended should be able to get some items correct and proceed to his level of maximum difficulty in that type of mental activity.

It will be found, however, that items in a scale are arranged, at times, in "spiral omnibus" fashion; that is, items of various types are presented in regular or irregular order, instead of being grouped separately in subtests. Thus, there may be a sequence of this kind: one item each in number completion, arithmetical problem, vocabulary, information, analogies, etc.; then the same kinds of items, increasing in difficulty, repeated in the same or in a different order.

Every group scale is standardized for a specified range of ages or school grades. Thus, the particular types of items used and the levels of difficulty within a scale will depend upon the group for which the scale is intended. For example, a group scale designed for children from kindergarten through the second grade will be almost entirely nonverbal in character, except for directions; one designed for pupils in the intermediate grades will include an increasing portion of abstract and conceptual items (verbal and numerical); and tests of intelligence for high-school pupils and college freshmen are largely, sometimes entirely, of the verbal and numerical kind.

On many group scales, an individual's score is first obtained in terms of the number of points earned; that is, a raw score. From a table of norms, this score is converted into a mental age, from which an intelligence quotient is calculated. The manuals of some group scales also provide tables necessary to find an individual's percentile rank for his age or grade, or both. Other group scales dispense with mental ages and intelligence quotients and give only percentile-rank equivalents for the range of point scores. And, increasingly, authors of group tests are using the deviation IQ.

Group scales are scored more rigidly and more objectively than those individually administered, such as the Stanford-Binet.[1] In the former, the correct response or responses are supplied for each item, so that they can be scored by clerks or machines. In the case of the Stanford-Binet and similar scales, although specimens of satisfactory and unsatisfactory responses are supplied, it is frequently necessary for the examiner himself to evaluate some and decide whether or not credit should be given. This necessary exercise of judgment, however, does not invalidate the scales; correlational studies have shown that there is close agreement between experienced examiners as to the scoring of given responses.

Most group scales impose time limits for each of the several subtests, or parts. Whether this fact makes a scale a test of speed of response, solely or largely, or whether the scale measures "power" (level of difficulty the individual is capable of reaching) is a question to which answers have been provided by experiment. The imposition of time limits does not necessarily make a scale a test of speed of performance; the significance of the speed factor, in affecting the total score of a person, varies with the scale used.

Some group scales are entirely nonverbal in content; others are entirely verbal; still others combine the two types of items. In this chapter we shall describe several representative scales of the nonverbal variety.

Tests for Kindergarten and Primary Levels

Most group scales are devised for use within a limited range of ages or school grades. A few of these instruments are intended for use from the kindergarten level through the second or third grade. It is possible to give a group test at these levels if the number is small enough (a maximum of twenty) to permit close observation by the tester and their teacher, to be assured that the children are paying attention, following instructions, and not having accidents that might affect their scores adversely. Except for instructions, the tests at these age levels are entirely nonverbal in some scales; in others a relatively small amount of verbal and number-test materials is introduced at the third grade level (for example, Kuhlmann-Anderson tests). At the early levels, especially kindergarten and first grade, it is important that the child's responses should not require skill in writing or using a pencil. Responses, therefore, are made by a mark (a circle, straight line, or an X).

---

[1] This does not mean that the group scales are superior instruments. In fact, inflexible scoring is a disadvantage if the examiner's purpose is to study an individual clinically and to analyze test results qualitatively as well as quantitatively.

The Pintner-Cunningham Primary Test (1923–1946) is one of the early and well-known scales in this group.[2] It will be briefly described, since the contents of all tests at this level are similar in form and types of items, although they differ in details. It includes the following seven subtests.

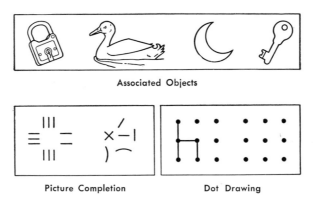

Associated Objects

Picture Completion   Dot Drawing

FIG. 15.1. Items from the Pintner-Cunningham Primary Test. Copyright 1946 by Harcourt, Brace & World, Inc. Reproduced by permission.

Common observation: identifying objects commonly found in the ordinary environment, and belonging in a specified category (for example, selection of feathered animals, objects and animals that fly).

Perception of esthetic differences: the "prettiest" of three drawings of the same object is marked (for example, girl, curved lines).

Identification of associated objects: recognition of objects that belong together (for example, lock and key, star and quarter-moon).

Discrimination of size: matching items of clothing with a pictured girl.

Perception of the parts of a whole: analyzing a series of pictures of increasing complexity. A "stimulus picture" is given; adjacent to it are a number of parts of that picture. The task is to mark those parts that constitute the whole.

Picture completion: noting the missing parts in each of a series of pictures and marking, from several choices, the missing part in each.

Copying designs: using a square of dots to reproduce a given design.

The Chicago Nonverbal Examination (1936–1947) is another early and well-known scale. Although, unlike the Pintner-Cunningham, it was designed for use with individuals from the age of 6 years through adulthood, it has been used principally with young children. The types of items are similar in most respects to those in the other scales; but several

[2] All tests referred to are listed in References at the end of this chapter.

types, though familiar in general psychological testing, are not included in the other scales at the primary level, described in the summary that follows.

Digit-symbol: the familiar test.

Perception of similarities and differences of objects: crossing out the one object that is of a different class from the others in the group.

Three-dimensional visualization: counting the number of blocks in a picture.

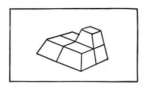

Block Counting

"Paper Form Board"

Matching Figures

Picture Sequence

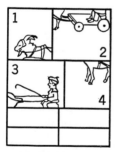

Picture Arrangement

FIG. 15.2. Items from the Chicago Nonverbal Examination. The Psychological Corporation, by permission.

Paper formboard: marking the parts that constitute a whole geometric figure.

Visual perception of detail: matching geometric designs that have more or less internal detail.

Picture arrangement: numbering parts to indicate how they must be placed to form a whole.

Logical sequence: numbering pictures in their correct order to represent a sequence of events.

Picture absurdities: noting missing or superfluous parts.

Picture matching: relating a part to a whole picture.

Digit symbol: a second subtest of this type, but more complex than the first.

Other representative and more recent scales, intended for use with children of kindergarten and primary grade ages, are the lower levels of the California Test of Mental Maturity (latest edition, 1957); the Kuhlmann-Anderson Intelligence Tests (1952 and 1960); the Lorge-Thorndike Intelligence Tests (1957); and the SRA Tests of General Ability (1959). Their subtests are described briefly below to illustrate similarities and differences in content.

California (grades 1, 2, 3):

Memory: immediate and delayed.

Spatial relationships: sensing right and left and manipulation of areas.

Logical reasoning: opposites, similarities, analogies, and inference.

Numerical reasoning: number concepts and number quantity.

Verbal concepts: associating pictures with words.

All of these subtests use drawings, but verbal and/or numerical concepts are more or less involved in each.

Kuhlmann-Anderson, sixth edition (Test C, for grade 3):

Completion: completing rows of symbols in a sequence that has to be perceived.

Classification: selecting the correct item from a series, to match a given category in pictures.

Number concepts: counting dots in squares and writing the number.

Digit-symbols: the familiar task of writing a digit in various simple geometric figures, according to a code.

Following directions: one series of squares and one of circles, of varying sizes, in each of which the pupil is instructed to make a specified mark (for example, a dot, an X) or to make some other mark showing ability to understand and retain directions (for example, to draw a line from the biggest square to the smallest circle).

Spatial perception: selecting two parts of a whole geometric figure which, when put together, will match the given figure.

Scrambled words: writing the correct word after each set of scrambled letters of the word.

Substitution: substituting letters of the alphabet for series of digits, each of which will spell out a word (Fig. 15.3).

1	2	3	4	5	6	7	8	9
A	E	U	B	D	G	C	F	H

Examples:

(A) 1 6 2

(B) 8 1 7 2

(1) 5 3 6

(2) 9 1 5

(6) 9 3 6 2

(7) 4 2 1 5

(11) 4 2 5 1 3 4

(12) 5 2 4 1 3 7 9

FIG. 15.3. From the Kuhlmann-Anderson Intelligence
Tests. By permission.

Perceptual analysis of geometric patterns: completing each partially drawn figure to match the other member of the pair.

Word classification: eliminating the one word that does not belong in a series of five, the other four of which are in a single category (for example, toys, food, plants).

Lorge-Thorndike (grades 2 and 3):

Identification: pictured objects, animals, and humans are identified by name (read out by the tester).

Classification: categories of pictured objects, animals, and humans are to be perceived, the irrelevant one being marked out.

Associated objects: two of five drawings in each row are to be marked, being related according to a common characteristic (for example, musical instruments).

The SRA Tests of General Ability consist of a graded series of scales, each intended for three grade levels from kindergarten through the twelfth. The scale for kindergarten to grade 2, and the one for grades 2 to 4, have two parts, identical in form and type of materials, but differing in content and difficulty. The two subtests are the following:

Identification of familiar objects: placing an X on one of five items, as directed by the examiner (for example, "Find the thing that is used to hit a ball.").

Perception of similarities: identifying one drawing in five that does not "follow the rule" of that particular row.

Evaluation. As in the case of most carefully constructed group scales, those described have quite satisfactory reliability. The Pintner-Cunningham coefficients vary from .83 to .94; for the Chicago Nonverbal, they range between .80 and .90. The California test manual reports reliabilities at .90 or above. The Kuhlmann-Anderson reliability coefficient at the third-grade level is .91; for the Lorge-Thorndike, at grades 3 and 4, the reliabilities are .90 and .86 (retest with alternate forms).[3] The median of the reliabilities of the Tests of General Ability is .87. On the whole, therefore, it may be said that these scales have demonstrated their reliability at an acceptable level. In examining the soundness of a scale, however, one should look, also, for data on standard errors of the scores. The Kuhlmann-Anderson, for example, reports a mean IQ difference of less than 2 points between the first and second testing; but the *SD* of the differences is 9 points. Flanagan reports a standard error of about 7 IQ points "for IQs around 100," for the Tests of General Ability.

In studying their validity, the several authors have used the familiar criteria: correlation with the Stanford-Binet and with measures of school achievement; increase of scores in successive age groups; scores achieved by known groups (especially differentiation of the mentally retarded from the normal group); a symmetrical distribution of scores along the normal curve; intercorrelations among subtest scores and correlations of subtests with total scores. Some of these scales (for example, Kuhlmann-Anderson) have been validated against most of these criteria; others against few. This fact emphasizes the need to know which validity criteria were used with a particular scale and to view the results found with each of the several criteria in relation to each other. The results found with the Chicago Nonverbal Examination provide a case in point. This scale found a mean IQ of 61 (*SD* = 12) for ninety-nine mentally deficient children, as compared with a mean of 62 (*SD* = 6) obtained with the Stanford-Binet. The mean difference between the Stanford-Binet and the Chicago Nonverbal ratings, however, was 9.0 points (disregarding signs; correlation coefficients were not given). Thus, although the two means are practically identical, the standard deviations and the mean of the differences are such as to indicate that in many individual instances there were significant discrepancies between ratings obtained on the two scales. These discrepancies are probably attributable to the differences in content of the scales; and they suggest, further, that the two scales should

---

[3] Odd-even reliability for grades 2 and 3 was only .59. About this, the authors say: "At this level, odd-even reliability is really not meaningful, since there is a systematic alternation between geometric and pictorial items in subtests 2 and 3" (16). This fact illustrates the necessity of using a method suitable to the materials. It seems, however, that an adaptation of the split-half method could have been devised, instead of following the odd-even technique.

be used to supplement each other, rather than as substitutes, when an individual's mental abilities are being analyzed and evaluated.

The SRA Tests of General Ability and the Lorge-Thorndike tests are based in part upon the concept of construct validity (see Chapter 5), although the manuals provide data on some of the other validating criteria as well. The manual of the former states: "The validity of the TOGA series rests primarily on its definition of intelligence as basically involving verbal and reasoning abilities, and its emphasis on test materials that do not require school-learned skills." The items do not require skill in reading, arithmetic, or other specific skills. They do depend, however, upon word knowledge and upon familiarity with objects commonly experienced. The Lorge-Thorndike manual states that the aspects of intelligence to be measured are: ability to deal with abstract and general concepts; interpretation and use of symbols; relationship among concepts and symbols; flexibility in organizing concepts and symbols; using experience in new patterns; power rather than speed (see Chapter 7; "Definitions and Analyses of Intelligence").

All these scales, especially the more recent ones, meet the technical specifications in regard to population sampling, as regards both numbers and representativeness. The one type of adequate evidence lacking is that pertaining to their validity in predicting *future* school performance. However, since they do correlate well with current school performance,[4] we may infer that these scales have reasonably satisfactory predictive value, inasmuch as quality of school achievement in one grade correlates well with quality in later grades. Correlation between Lorge-Thorndike IQs and Stanford Reading Grade Equivalents was .87; with Stanford Arithmetic Grade Equivalents, it was .76. Flanagan reports correlations from .52 to .72, with a median of .60, with the Science Research Associates Achievement Series; and .74 to .81, with a median of .78, with the Iowa Tests of Educational Development.

"Culture-Fair" Tests

The nonverbal tests of intelligence thus far described are intended for use with young children in the United States who have had the advantages, at least, of developing in an ordinary environment. Some psychologists and educators have maintained, however, that any test which depends upon even as little word knowledge as those already described are not "culture-fair" to all children. And some have maintained, also, that tests completely free of demands upon language would be desirable for testing those segments of the adolescent and adult population who

---

[4] The newer term for this form of validity is "concurrent validity."

might be handicapped by even a minimum of verbal test items. The scales described in this section are examples of those regarded as culture-fair by their authors.

The Davis-Eells Test of General Intelligence, characterized as a test of problem-solving ability, was an interesting innovation in the testing of intelligence. It is unusual in respect to its content and rationale, and in respect to its frank rejection of statistical validation with other tests. In place of such validation, the authors substituted intensive interviews with children to disclose the "mental problems of a kind found in most of the basic areas of children's lives: school, home, play, stories, and work. The specific problems resulted from intensive observation and detailed interviewing of children in many areas of activity. . . . The extent to which the items in the test deal with problem situations which seem real to children of the age levels for which the test is planned may best be judged by examining the test with this criterion in mind." The

FIG. 15.4. The task is to select the one statement that best explains the situation shown in the picture.

    1. The boys want to wash the man's window and sidewalk.
    2. The man is making the boys wash his window and sidewalk.
    3. You can't tell from this picture why the boys are washing the window and sidewalk.
From Davis and Eells (8), by permission.

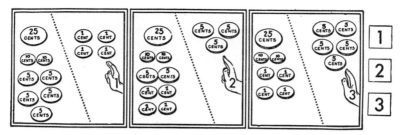

FIG. 15.5. The task is to select the picture in which a given sum of money can be made, beginning with the right-hand side of the dotted line and completing from the left side. In this problem, the sum to be made is forty cents. From Davis and Eells (8), by permission.

FIG. 15.6. The task is to place the bottles in the black box in such a way that the white box may best be placed on the black one. From Davis and Eells (8), by permission.

items selected for initial tryouts and experimentation were based upon the "insights of a number of educators and sociologists familiar with the characteristic modes of living and child upbringing at different socio-economic levels, and in part upon systematic observation of children in free-time activities (on playgrounds, in neighborhood groups, in schools, etc.)"

This instrument was completed after six tryouts with large numbers of children from widely different socioeconomic backgrounds, in several sections of the United States. Forms for two levels are available: Primary, for grades 1 and 2; and Elementary, for grades 3 through 6. They are regarded by Davis and Eells as culturally fair to all socioeconomic groups in *urban* areas.

The scales consist of the following four subtests:

Best way: In each item, three pictures show the beginnings of attempts to perform a given task or solve a given problem. The child indicates the picture he believes will lead to the best solution.

Probabilities: Each picture shows a situation in which certain elements are present. The child has to select, from three statements, the one that presents the most probable explanation of what is happening in the picture.

Picture analogy: This is the familiar type of item in which two related objects are shown. The child is required to select a similar relationship in a given set of pictures.

Money: In each item, two sets of coins are shown in three different combinations, each of which is incomplete. The problem is to discern which of the three combinations will yield a stated sum.

As is the case with many tests, reliability is often more easily established than is validity. Split-half reliability coefficients were from .81 to .84 at all grade levels, except the first, where it was .68. This last is too low for predictive purposes. The remaining indexes are moderately high, but they are not as large as optimally desirable. Test-retest reliabilities, after two weeks, were .72 (grade 2), and .90 (grade 4).

Although Davis and Eells do not attempt to establish validity of their tests upon correlations with earlier and more conventional scales, they present, for informational purposes, some correlations with the Otis Quick-Scoring Tests, obtained in grades 3 through 6. Of the sixteen coefficients, seven are in the .50s; the remainder are rather evenly distributed from .39 (lowest) to .66 (highest). The authors believe these coefficients are what should be expected, since they indicate that the abilities measured by their tests bear a substantial relationship to those measured by the other tests, yet theirs and the others do not measure exactly the same factors.

Correlations with standardized school-achievement tests are also reported. They are: reading, .43; arithmetic, .41; language, .40; spelling, .24. These coefficients are lower than those generally found with the more usual types of individual and group scales, but this is to be expected because of the nature of the Davis-Eells tests. The authors' position is that several significant factors, other than problem-solving ability, contribute to success in school achievement.

Validity studies published subsequent to this test's appearance have shown quite consistently that it does not correlate as well with school achievement nor predict later school achievement as successfully as do the earlier and more usual types of test materials. These investigations include correlations with standardized achievement tests and with teachers' ratings of pupils' abilities. Other data indicate that the Davis-Eells tends to rate children lower, and that it differentiates as much among high and low socioeconomic groups as do the verbal and other nonverbal tests, which were not regarded by Davis and Eells as being culture-fair.

The Davis-Eells test is based upon the concepts of content and construct validity. The authors' objective was to devise an instrument that presents situations and problems in forms that are within the common experience of all children in the groups for whom they were intended.

This meant the elimination of cultural factors—including language (except in the directions, given orally)—that might favor one group and handicap another. Although nonverbal tests are not new, the kinds of situations presented, excepting picture analogies, are novel. Furthermore, the psychological functions to be sampled were determined and specified after interviews and psychological analysis, rather than by statistical methods. The functions specified are association, insight, reasoning, and organizational ability (method of attacking a problem). After the items for these tests were developed, each child in a group was interviewed to determine whether the problems evoked the mental processes that the tests seek to measure. It was found that 92 percent of the children who answered analogy problems correctly also explained the analogy relationship correctly. And nearly all pupils explained the relationships correctly in solving the other types of subtest problems.

Although we may accept the authors' view that this test measures the specified functions, research results have demonstrated the superiority of the long-established types of test items that employ verbal and numerical materials, and pictorial materials requiring concept formation.

The Raven Progressive Matrices Tests (1938–1956), developed in England and widely used in the British armed forces during World War II, are nonverbal scales designed to evaluate the subject's ability to apprehend relationships between geometric figures and designs, and to perceive the structure of the design in order to select the appropriate part (from several) for completion of each pattern or system of relations. The several scales, for use with persons 5 years of age and older, are regarded by the author as being a test of innate eductive ability; that is, a measure of the general factor (g). The tests are intended to evaluate the person's ability to discern and utilize a logical relationship presented by nonverbal materials. The problems require, in varying degrees, analytical and integrating operations of the kind called "insight through visual survey." Verbalization and abstraction of relationships are also possible factors, if the subject is able to analyze and synthesize by these means. Factorial analysis suggests that the matrices tests are measures largely of a "general factor," with a small loading of a spatial-perception factor. Raven interprets the first of these factors as being essentially the same as Spearman's eduction of relations and eduction of correlates.

The PM tests have been subjected to extensive research in several countries and with a wide variety of groups: children, adolescents, and adults, both normal and abnormal. Numerous reliability coefficients reported by Raven vary from the low .80s to the low .90s. Coefficients reported by other investigators, using the split-half method, ranged from .70 to .90. The differences in correlations are attributable to differences in the constitution of the group: age range, mean and range of ability, number in the sample, and socioeconomic and educational levels. These split-half coefficients are, on the whole, creditable under the circumstances. The test-retest reliability coefficients, however, are appreciably lower for scores of the youngest children (below age 7), although with older children and adults the test-retest coefficients vary within approximately the same range as those found by the split-half method.

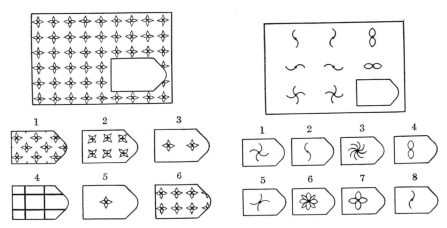

FIG. 15.7. Specimen items from the Raven Progressive Matrices Tests. By permission.

Validity of the Progressive Matrices tests has been studied in a variety of the usual ways. When the Stanford-Binet was used as the criterion, correlations varied from .50 to .86. Correlations with the WISC ranged from the low .50s to .91. Most of the coefficients of correlation with these two widely used criteria were in the .60s and .70s. The tests correlate as well with educational achievement as do many group tests (verbal and nonverbal), but not as high as the Stanford-Binet and the WISC.

The PM tests were correlated against verbal and other nonverbal group scales. Using the former, the resulting coefficients varied rather markedly: from .40 to .67. It is particularly interesting to note that the coefficients found between scores on the PM tests and those on other nonverbal scales (such as Columbia Mental Maturity, Pintner Nonlanguage, Porteus Maze, Chicago Nonverbal) are considerably lower (being in the .30s, .40s, and .50s) than those found when the S-B and the WISC were used as validating criteria. This fact signifies, among other things, that the Progressive Matrices items come closer to measuring the forms of abstract and conceptual intelligence tested by these two individual scales than they do to measuring the functions involved in other nonverbal scales. On the whole, the PM type of tests appears to be among the most promising of the nonverbal group. Since it employs only one type of test material, however, it should not be regarded as a substitute for the Stanford-

Binet and the WISC, both of which provide the testee with greater opportunities for flexibility and versatility of mental activity, and the examiner with more sources of qualitative interpretation of responses and behavior. But the PM tests are of considerable value as a supplement to the S-B and the WISC and as a primary instrument for examining the deaf and others who labor under speech or language handicaps.

The Pattern Perception Test, devised in England under the direction of L. S. Penrose, employs a single type of nonverbal material that be-

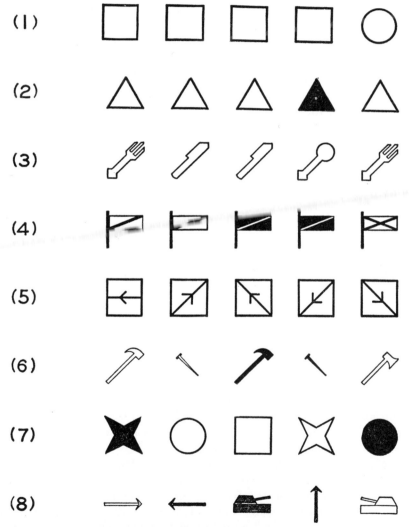

Fig. 15.8. Items from the Penrose Pattern Perception Test. Galton Laboratory, University of London, by permission.

comes quite complex at the higher levels. Intended for use only with adults, its higher level solutions and correct responses require subtle visual insights and reasoning.

The scale includes sixty-four items (or problems), each of which consists of a row of five designs; the task is to discern the four designs that form a pattern and to cross out the inappropriate one. There are eight sets of items, each set arranged in order of increasing difficulty. In each, the problems begin with an elementary presentation of a theme, or pattern, which is developed with increasing complexity in subsequent sets.

Reported test-retest reliabilities vary between approximately .80 and .90. Validity coefficients, using job ratings in the British army and navy as criteria, varied widely, owing to the varying degrees of reliability of ratings and to the effects of selectivity in various jobs. The mean coefficients for each of a number of army and navy branches ranged from .30 to .47. Correlations with other standardized tests ranged from a low of .43 for 67 medical students (a rather homogeneous group) to .73 for a random sample of 597 men in the British army.

Although there are few research reports on this interesting test, it deserves serious attention because it represents a type of nonverbal material that might prove valuable for use with adults of a wide range of ability, with cultural advantages and disadvantages minimized. The test has been found, for example, to be effective in identifying men at the lower and the upper ends of the distribution of mental ability. It may prove, also, to be of value in the diagnostic examining of psychotic persons and those suspected of psychosis, for reports indicate that these groups of individuals perform relatively poorly on items requiring verbal insight and constructive thinking. The Pattern Perception Test might prove significant in identifying individuals capable of a fairly high level of conceptual thinking, but who are handicapped for one reason or another in dealing with verbal or quantitative concepts.

The Pintner Nonlanguage Series (Intermediate Test), for grades 4 through 9 (originally devised for use with deaf children), utilizes no verbal situations and is independent of word knowledge and language facility, except insofar as these are involved in understanding directions. The author also provides directions for administering the scale in pantomime when this is desirable, as in the case of subjects who suffer from language handicaps or from defective hearing.

The tests consist entirely of materials of a diagrammatic nature, intended to provide "relatively independent" measures of the "spatial factor," "perceptual ability" (visual), and "reasoning" (without use of language). This Pintner scale, therefore, is one of those which specifically utilize some of the "factors" enumerated by psychologists who adhere to the group-factor theory of intelligence. Yet, interestingly enough, though tables for separate standard score ratings are provided for each of the subtests, no attempt is made to indicate which of the factors is being measured by means of each of the six subtests. In fact, the author states that, "No claim is made that the subtests tap primary or independent abilities, and little is known as to the significance of the separate subtest

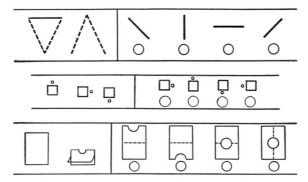

FIG. 15.9. Items from the Pintner Nonlanguage Series (Intermediate Test). Copyright 1945 by Harcourt, Brace & World, Inc. Reproduced by permission. At top are *Reverse* drawings. After looking at the sample pair to the left of the bar, the subject looks at the first drawing to the right of the bar and finds its reverse among the next three drawings. For the middle series, *Movement sequence,* he finds which of the four drawings at the right completes the series started at the left of the bar. For the bottom series, *Paper folding,* he indicates which of the items at the right of the bar shows the way the folded paper at the left of the bar would look if it were opened up.

scores. . . . Only large deviations (from the median) should be given any credence in guidance of individuals." Apparently, then, the inference that this scale measures the spatial factor and perceptual and reasoning abilities rests upon an a priori basis.

The Cattell Culture-Free Test is another attempt to provide a measure of general mental ability free from verbal materials and from "the acquired skills of most performance tests." The subtests are, nevertheless, of much the same kinds as some already described: classification, completion of a series, matrices, and spatial perception, called "pool reflections" (see Fig. 15.10).

These Pintner and Cattell tests employ the usual methods of estimating

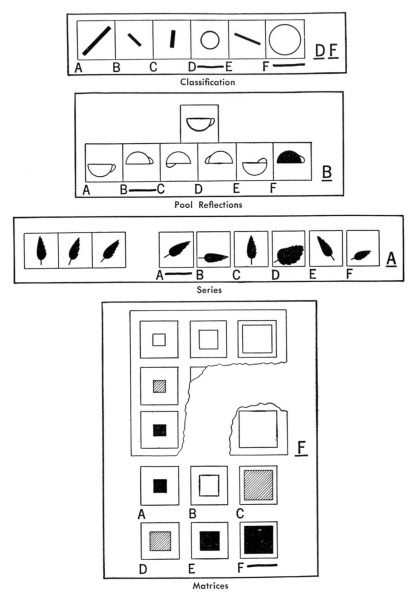

FIG. 15.10. Items from the Cattell Culture-Free Test. The Psychological Corporation, by permission.

reliability and validity. As is generally the case, their reliability coefficients are within the satisfactory range. But evidence of their validity is not so strong. The Pintner test correlates moderately with verbal scales, as does the Cattell; but in neither case are the correlations high enough to warrant using these nonverbal tests interchangeably with the verbal. The coefficients for the Cattell, for example, average in the .50s.

A more recent instrument for culture-free testing is the *IPAT Culture Free Intelligence Test* (1933–1958),[5] available for three levels: Scale 1 for ages 4 to 8 and for mentally deficient adults; Scale 2, for ages 8 to 12 and for unselected adults; Scale 3, for the range from high school pupils through superior adults. Actually only four of the eight subtests in Scale 1 are regarded as culture-free, since the other four involve verbal comprehension and information acquired in our culture. Three of the four nonverbal subtests are of the familiar type: series, classifications, and matrices. The fourth, called "conditions," is said to involve a novel type of "topological reasoning," although the functions it tests are the same as in some other nonverbal tests: visual analysis, reasoning and concept formation. The subtests are the following.

> Series: selecting one of several drawings to complete a series.
> Classification: crossing out the one irrelevant drawing in each row.
> Matrices: marking the one drawing, of several, that correctly fits the incomplete pattern.
> Conditions: inserting a dot in the appropriate one of several designs, the structure of which is consistent with the "conditions" given in the sample design.

Here again, reliability coefficients are, on the whole, reasonably satisfactory when the split-half method was used and when retesting took place within a very short time. These scales in regard to validity, however, present the uncertainties so common to nonverbal tests. Validity data are given principally in terms of factorial analysis, indicating "saturation" with the general factor (g). But the scales' concurrent and predictive validities (see Chapter 5) have not been demonstrated. And since test findings, in and of themselves, are not the primary or major concern of most psychologists who use tests, except in certain theoretical problems, this deficiency is a serious one. On the other hand, studies have shown that these scales are culture-fair, when population samples in the United States, France, Britain, and Australia were tested; for no significant group differences were found among these national groups, all of them essentially of Western culture. In other and dissimilar cultures, the obtained norms were significantly below those found in the process of standardization. If these data are representative, we must conclude that not only is

[5] IPAT are the initials for Institute for Personality and Ability Testing, Champaign, Ill.

it highly improbable that culture-*free* tests can be developed, but that tests should be labeled "culture-*fair*" only when used in countries whose cultures are essentially similar.

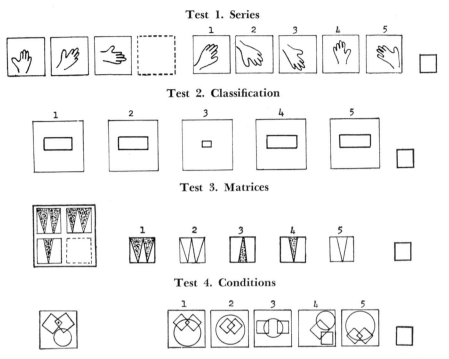

Test 1. Series

Test 2. Classification

Test 3. Matrices

Test 4. Conditions

FIG. 15.11. Practice items from the IPAT Culture Free Intelligence Test. Scale 2, Form B. Copyright, The Institute for Personality and Ability Testing. By Permission.

Evaluation of Nonverbal Group Scales

Uses. A survey of available nonverbal scales shows, for the most part, that they are valuable primarily with children who have had limited educational opportunities or impoverished social backgrounds, with young children who have not yet learned to read, with older pupils who are handicapped by reading or language difficulties, and with illiterate or non-English-speaking adults. Possible exceptions to this statement of limited usefulness are the Pattern Perception and the Progressive Matrices.

Nonverbal tests are valuable, also, for the better diagnosis of persons who, on verbal tests, have intelligence quotients between about 60 and 75, and who, therefore, would be considered as subjects for special educational treatment or possibly institutional care. The examining psychologist might be in doubt with regard to such borderline cases; but if the results of the nonverbal tests confirm those of the verbal, he has reason to allay his doubts. However, if the rating on the nonverbal tests is significantly higher, then the case will require further study to account for the discrepancy.

Nonverbal tests can be clinically useful, also, with individuals whose intelligence quotients are higher than 75; that is, for individuals who, on verbal tests, *appear* to be significantly less capable than there is reason to believe they actually are, on the basis of other information about them. In this connection, they are particularly useful in population centers having large numbers of non-English-speaking people.

In whatever situation nonverbal tests are used, the examiner must realize that defective vision or slow psychomotor responses can be a handicap. The first of these handicaps points up the importance of clear drawings—a condition that is not always satisfied.

Tests of mental ability have had widespread use in schools, where they have been utilized for purposes of educational and vocational guidance, as well as in the diagnosis of learning difficulties. Nonverbal group tests have been found valuable in efforts to determine aptitude and promise in shopwork, mechanical drawing, architectural drafting, and occupations of a mechanical or quasi-mechanical nature—all of which make demands upon psychological operations that involve geometric perception and reasoning with the concrete rather than with the abstract.

Validity.   Studies of the validity of nonverbal scales show that although most of them correlate significantly with scales of the verbal type (individual and group), the coefficients are far enough removed from unity to warrant using the two types as supplements rather than as equivalents. When scores on verbal and on nonverbal scales are correlated, for children in the earlier grades (approximately through grade 6) the coefficients obtained are usually in the .60s and .70s, with relatively few in the .80s. But when the subjects tested are pupils in the later grades, the coefficients usually fall in the .50s and .40s, with a few lower and a few higher. These generally lower coefficients, in the case of pupils in the later grades, result from the inability of most available nonverbal tests to discriminate sufficiently among individuals in the upper levels.

Functions Measured.   The reader will recall that most, though not all, authors of nonverbal tests of mental ability seek to measure the same mental processes as those tested by means of verbal scales. Some of these authors are unequivocal in maintaining that the nonverbal tests require essentially the same type of mental operations as those required by the abstract symbols of language and number. They hold that the problems presented in diagrams, pictures, charts, and geometric forms closely parallel those presented by means of language and number. For example: picture arrangement is regarded as being similar in function to disarranged sentences; picture analogies similar to word analogies; picture completion similar to sentence completion; reasoning with geometric patterns similar to reasoning with numbers and words; perceiving similarities, differences, and part-whole relationships in pictures and patterns similar to such relationships in language form. Many nonverbal tests, however, suffer from their attempt to assess general ability by means of a single type of item or by a limited number of subtests.

The coefficients of correlation found between verbal and nonverbal tests of intelligence demonstrate that there is merit in the view that the two types are, in some degree, measuring the same or associated functions. But this does not mean that verbal and nonverbal tests are equivalent; for one type involves certain functions not involved in the other, or one may demand a higher level of the same functions being tested than does the other.

Language and number are symbolic systems that *represent* something else: for example, objects, qualities, events, actions. Development of abilities in language and number facilitates intelligent behavior, since the use of these symbols expands the individual's range of experience beyond the limits of the immediate situation. Development of language and number makes possible a finer discernment of forms and objects in the world surrounding the individual; for with the use of language and number he is able to analyze, synthesize, classify, and organize his perceptions. Objects and events, at first vague, are more sharply defined; likenesses and differences are accentuated; evaluations are refined. Language and number also enable individuals to organize their thinking into larger and more comprehensive, unified patterns.

Because the use of language and number requires the individual to go beyond the immediate concrete situation, and because he thereby can engage in more complex and subtle mental operations, many psychologists regard the ability to deal with symbols as a higher form of intellectual activity than the ability to deal with concrete objects. They prefer, therefore, to test intelligence, whenever possible and appropriate, by means of verbal and numerical materials. However, they would use nonverbal tests when these are made necessary by developmental immaturity, or language or cultural handicap, to gain the insights that these tests provide if they are adequately scaled in difficulty.

Cultural Influences. Emphasis upon verbal and quantitative aspects of intelligence in many of the individual and group scales has given rise to a misapprehension regarding the nonverbal scales—that these latter are culture-free. Inspection of the items in the several scales reveals that they utilize many objects that children and older persons learn about through experiences in their environments. These experiences are as dependent upon culture as is development of verbal and quantitative abilities. The differences are matters of degree of cultural influence and universality or near-universality of experience. Consequently, it is preferable to speak of "culture-fair" tests when referring to those whose materials do not handicap or favor any segment of the population for whom the device is intended.

The presence of cultural influence in a test that *appears* to be culture-free was demonstrated in a study made with several tribes of North American Indians (13); the Goodenough Draw-A-Man Test was used. In a group of Hopi Indians, the mean IQ for boys was 123, while for girls it was 102. Zias also showed appreciable differences in favor of boys, whereas in a group of Navahos, the means of boys and of girls were very nearly equal (107 and 110). Sex differences within a tribe are attributed to sex differences in training and experience. Boys and girls are trained to observe different aspects and details of their environment and are taught different types of drawing. The two sexes have different functions in their group; these functions are reflected in differentiated training; the differences in training are reflected in differences in performance.

Since every person must develop in an environment of some kind, his skills, information, repertory of responses, modes of thinking, and so on, are to some extent culturally determined. Some psychological tests are more culture-fair than others. At this point we recall again Binet's principle that a test of intelligence should be consonant with the milieu of those who are to be measured by it.

References

1. Altus, G. T. Some correlates of the Davis-Eells tests. *Journal of Consulting Psychology*, 1956, 20, 227–232.
2. Angelino, H., and C. L. Shedd. An initial report of a validation study of the Davis-Eells Tests of General Intelligence or problem-solving ability. *Journal of Psychology*, 1955, 40, 35–38.
3. Brown, A. W. *Chicago Noverbal Examination*. New York: The Psychological Corporation, 1947.
4. Burgemeister, B., *et al. Columbia Mental Maturity Scale* (revised norms). New York: Harcourt, Brace & World, Inc., 1959.
5. Burke, H. R. Raven's Progressive Matrices: a review and critical evaluation. *Journal of Genetic Psychology*, 1958, 93, 199–228.
6. Cattell, R. B. *Culture-Free Test*. New York: The Psychological Corporation, 1944.

7. Cattell, R. B., and A. K. S. Cattell. *IPAT Culture Free Intelligence Test.* Champaign, Ill.: Institute for Personality and Ability Testing, 1949–1960.

8. Davis, A., and K. Eells. *Davis-Eells Test of General Intelligence.* New York: Harcourt, Brace & World, Inc., 1953.

9. Eells, K., *et al. Intelligence and Cultural Differences.* Chicago: University of Chicago Press, 1951.

10. Flanagan, J. C. *Tests of General Ability.* Chicago: Science Research Associates, 1957–1959.

11. Foulds, G. A., and J. C. Raven. An experimental survey with progressive matrices (1947). *British Journal of Educational Psychology,* 1950, *20,* 104–110.

12. Haggard, E. A. Social status and intelligence: an experimental study of certain cultural determinants of measured intelligence. *Genetic Psychology Monographs,* 1954, *49.*

13. Havighurst, R. J., *et al.* Environment and the Draw-A-Man Test: the performance of Indian children. *Journal of Abnormal and Social Psychology,* 1946, *41,* 50–63.

14. Keir, G. The progressive matrices as applied to school children. *British Journal of Psychology,* Statistical Section, 1949, *2,* 140–150.

15. Kuhlmann, F., and R. G. Anderson. *Kuhlmann-Anderson Intelligence Tests.* Princeton, N.J.: Personnel Press, 1952.

16. Lorge, I., and R. L. Thorndike. *The Lorge-Thorndike Intelligence Tests.* Boston: Houghton Mifflin Company, 1957.

17. Love, M. I., and S. Beach. Performance of children on the Davis-Eells Games and other measures of ability. *Journal of Consulting Psychology,* 1957, *21,* 29–32.

18. Ludlow, H. G. Some recent research on the Davis-Eells Games. *School and Society,* 1956, *84,* 146–148.

19. Papania, N., *et al.* Responses of lower social class, high-grade mentally handicapped boys to a 'culture fair' test of intelligence—the Davis-Eells Games. *American Journal of Mental Deficiency,* 1955, *59,* 493–498.

20. Penrose, L. S. An economic method of presenting matrix intelligence tests. *British Journal of Medical Psychology,* 1944, *20,* part 2, 144–146.

21. Penrose, L. S. *Pattern Perception Test.* London: Galton Laboratory, University of London, 1947.

22. Penrose, L. S., and J. C. Raven. A new series of perceptual tests, preliminary communication. *British Journal of Medical Psychology,* 1936, *16,* 97–104.

23. Pintner, R. *Nonlanguage Series: Intermediate Test.* New York: Harcourt, Brace & World, Inc., 1945.

24. Pintner, R., B. V. Cunningham, and W. N. Durost. *Pintner-Cunningham Primary Test.* New York: Harcourt, Brace & World, Inc., 1946.

25. Porteus, S. D. *The Maze Test and Clinical Practice.* Palo Alto, Calif.: Pacific Books, 1959.

26. Raven, J. C. *Progressive Matrices Test*. London: H. K. Lewis & Co., 1938–1958. (Distributed in the U.S. by The Psychological Corporation.)

27. Sperrazzo, G., and W. L. Wilkins. Further normative data on the Progressive Matrices. *Journal of Consulting Psychology*, 1958, *22*, 35–37.

28. Sullivan, E. T., *et al. California Test of Mental Maturity*. Monterey: California Test Bureau, 1957.

29. Tate, M. W., and C. E. Voss. A study of the Davis-Eells test of intelligence. *Harvard Educational Review*, 1956, *26*, 374–387.

30. Vernon, P. E. Research on personnel selection in the Royal Navy and the British Army. *The American Psychologist*, 1947, *2*, 35–51.

31. Yerkes, R. M. *Psychological Examining in the United States Army*. Memoirs of the National Academy of Sciences, 1921, *15*, Washington, D.C.: Government Printing Office.

16.

GROUP SCALES OF INTELLIGENCE: ELEMENTARY, SECONDARY, AND HIGHER LEVELS

Some of the early group tests, designed for use from grade 4 through grade 12—and their corresponding chronological ages—consisted largely of verbal and numerical items; for example, the Henmon-Nelson, National Intelligence Test, Otis scales. Others included, in addition, an appreciable portion of nonverbal materials; for example, the Pintner General Ability Test and the Dearborn Group Tests.

The more recent practice in a number of instances is to give the nonverbal subtests considerable weight, in addition to the verbal and numerical, as in the Lorge-Thorndike, the California Test of Mental Maturity, and the Kuhlmann-Anderson (though to a lesser extent in this last scale). The revised Henmon-Nelson (1957), by contrast, is still predominantly verbal and numerical, whereas the SRA Tests of General Ability (described in Chapter 15) are entirely nonverbal at all levels.

It is our purpose, in this chapter, to describe representative group scales constructed for use at the elementary, secondary, and higher educational and age levels. Since there are a fairly large number of scales that come within these categories, it is neither possible nor necessary to describe and evaluate all of them. A sufficient amount of material will be presented, however, to acquaint the student with their quality, characteristics and content, similarities and differences, and with the psychological processes they test.

Elementary and Secondary School Levels

Several of the scales discussed in the preceding chapter provide tests at levels above the primary grades. Only those parts of their content (subtests) that differ from the materials used at the primary level will be presented here.

THE CALIFORNIA TEST OF MENTAL MATURITY. This instrument provides scales for use throughout the primary, elementary, and secondary educational levels, and for adults. The types of mental operations to be tested are regarded as the same throughout the entire age range. Whereas at the primary level the test items are almost entirely nonverbal, the successive levels employ increasingly difficult verbal and numerical materials, although pictorial items, also of increasing difficulty, are included throughout. The numerical and verbal subtests at levels above the primary, are as follows:

Inferences. Each item contains two premises; the logical conclusion based upon these premises must be selected from among several given choices. For example:

> Joe is shorter than Harold
> Harold is shorter than Sam
> Who is the shortest: Joe, Harold, or Sam?

Number series. (1) Each of one type of item consists of a number series that increases or decreases according to a pattern; the testee is to select in each sequence the one number that does not follow the principle (for example, 1, 3, 5, 8, 7, 9); (2) the second type of number series requires the testee to select from several alternatives the three numbers that have been omitted from each series.

Numerical quantity. (1) The individual indicates from several alternatives, how many coins of each denomination are required to make up a specified sum; (2) part two consists of a series of increasingly difficult arithmetical problems.

Verbal concepts. This is the familiar test of word similarities. The task is to select, from four choices, the one word that is synonymous with the key word, or nearly so.

The subtests of these scales are so arranged that it is possible to obtain separate mental ages and IQs for the verbal, nonverbal, and total scores. It is possible, also, to provide a profile of the twelve subtest scores; but since individual subtest scores are neither as reliable nor as valid as either the full verbal or the full nonverbal scores, or as valid as the total-test scores, the profile has limited value, except in instances of marked discrepancies between subtest scores.

HENMON-NELSON TESTS OF MENTAL ABILITY (1957).[1]   This instrument provides tests at four levels: grades 3–6, 6–9, 9–12, and college.[2] The items are arranged in "spiral omnibus" form; that is, the several different types of items are distributed throughout the scale instead of being grouped by subtest type (for example, number series, word meaning). Successive items of each type are of increasing difficulty. When one uses such a test, it is obvious that only one over-all score can be derived. This is what the authors intend; for their instrument is based essentially on the general-factor theory of mental ability. They state that these scales are intended to measure ". . . those aspects of mental ability which are important for success in academic work and in similar endeavors outside the classroom."

Mark an X in the answer box that you think should be marked :

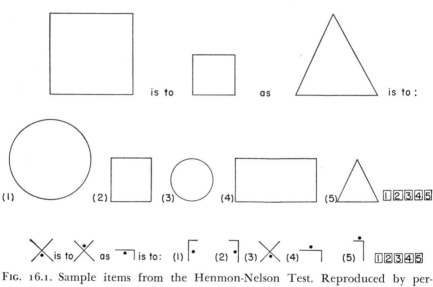

FIG. 16.1. Sample items from the Henmon-Nelson Test. Reproduced by permission.

The test items included are of the familiar types which, over many years, have become established as valuable for the stated purpose, although several of these are not commonly used in other tests at present (for example, scrambled words, scrambled sentences). The types are the following: figure analogies, word analogies, number series, reasoning ("My sister's daughter is my father's _____"), word classification,

[1] Revised by T. A. Lamke and M. J. Nelson. Names of publishers of tests are given in References at the end of the chapter.
[2] The scale for college level was revised in 1961, with P. C. Kelso as coauthor.

scrambled words (hncul: lunch), scrambled sentences, information, vocabulary, proverb interpretation, arithmetical problems.

Although a well-standardized scale of the omnibus type, as the Henmon-Nelson is, can have considerable general value in measuring mental ability and estimating educability, its drawback is the fact that analyses and comparisons of functioning with different types of materials, for diagnostic purposes, are very difficult to make. One might want to make such analyses, although the scale is intended to measure the g factor.

In support of their position, the authors of these scales report research findings which indicate that "factored" (multiscored) tests do not predict success in schoolwork more effectively than a single over-all score. Hence, if a single index and predictor of school success is wanted, a soundly standardized scale of the Henmon-Nelson type will serve very well. On the other hand, if several areas of ability need to be differentiated to reveal strengths and weaknesses, for purposes of diagnosis and remedial instruction, a sound scale arranged in the form of subtests, or a battery of tests, each restricted in scope, would be preferable. ("Factored" and multiscored scales are discussed in the next chapter.)

KUHLMANN-ANDERSON TESTS (1952). This series of scales, of which there are nine, graded according to school level, includes thirty-nine subtests. Each subtest *as a whole* is placed according to its over-all relative difficulty in the age range; and the items *within* each subtest are placed in order of *their* difficulty. Since intelligence levels vary considerably within any single age group, and since there is overlapping among different age groups, there is also duplication of subtests from one scale to the next. Thus, the scales for the adjacent levels include the subtests as indicated below:

kindergarten,	subtests	1–10
grade 1,	subtests	4–13
grade 2,	subtests	8–17
grade 3,	subtests	12–21
grade 4,	subtests	15–24
grade 5,	subtests	19–28
grade 6,	subtests	22–31
grades 7–8,	subtests	25–34
grades 9–12,	subtests	30–39

The subtest types are not unusual, since they utilize the familiar nonverbal and verbal materials, some of which have already been described in the preceding chapter. The verbal and numerical subtests, beginning with grade 4, are as follows: scrambled words, substitution of letters for numerals (word building), word classification, word meanings (and information), word opposites and similarities, word analysis, accuracy of perception (using the alphabet), scrambled sentences, number series, arithmetical problems, perception of details, following increasingly complex verbal instructions, logical analysis of brief statements.[3]

Test Number 12: Completion

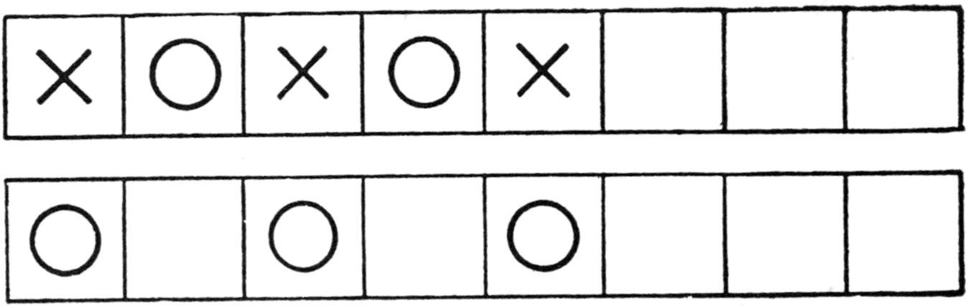

Test Number 14: Counting   Test Number 20: Reproducing Figures

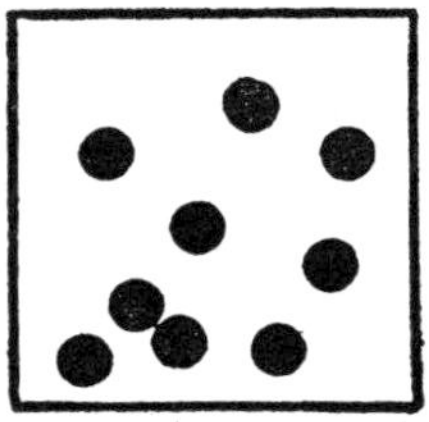

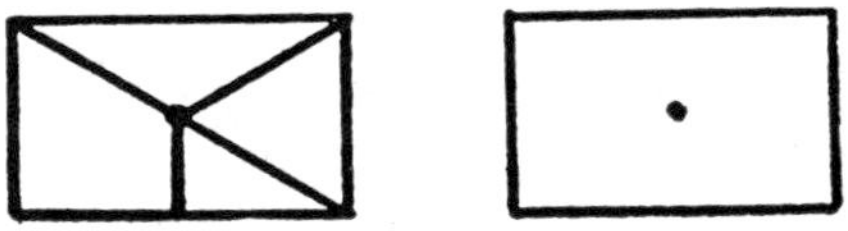

Test Number 27

A B C D E F G H I J K L M N O P Q R S T U V W X Y Z

Examples:

The third letter of the alphabet is .... ————

The second letter before the sixth letter is ————

Test Number 28: Perceiving and Writing the Correct Word

O-C-A-T C

U-E-O-H-S .... H

Test Number 32: Perceiving the Logical Sequence
and Marking the Middle Member

one   multitude   few   none   many

FIG. 16.2. Specimen items from the Kuhlmann-Anderson Tests. Reproduced by permission of The Personnel Press, Inc.

[3] The Kuhlmann-Finch tests (1951–1957) are modeled after the Kuhlmann-Anderson tests. A 7th edition (1960–61) of the Kuhlmann-Anderson, adapted for machine testing, is available. It yields verbal-aptitude, quantitative-aptitude, and total scores. It is not intended to displace the 6th edition.

From the description of the subtests, given in the preceding chapter, and from the foregoing list, it is clear that these, like the Stanford-Binet and the Wechsler scales, combine a variety of materials with increasing emphasis upon the verbal and abstract, as one goes up into successively higher levels. To a considerable extent, there is, from age to age, overlapping of functions measured by these subtests, as there is also in the Stanford-Binet, with which the Kuhlmann-Anderson has a high correlation. This is quite consistent with the purpose of the scales, that is, to measure the levels of general mental development needed to succeed in schoolwork. In this connection, it should be noted also that the authors do not recommend the use of subtest scores as measures of separate psychological functions or for guidance purposes. But they do suggest that *significant* inconsistencies among scores on separate subtests furnish evidence of erratic performance, for which causes and explanations should be sought. Implicit in this position of Kuhlmann and Anderson is the acceptance of the general-factor theory of intelligence. This acceptance is later made explicit by them in their validation.

THE LORGE-THORNDIKE INTELLIGENCE TESTS (1954). The types of subtests utilized in this scale at the level for grades 2 and 3 are presented in the preceding chapter. The whole series includes five levels, extending from kindergarten through grade 12. The first two levels, as already described, use only nonverbal test items, while the higher levels include both verbal and nonverbal subtests, from which two separate ratings can be obtained. The verbal series of subtests include the familiar types; these are word knowledge, sentence completion, verbal classification, verbal analogies, and arithmetical reasoning.

The authors of these scales state that these are tests of abstract intelligence, which they define as the ability to work with ideas and the relationships among ideas. "The tests are based on the premise that most abstract ideas with which the school child or the working adult deals are expressed in verbal symbols, so much so that verbal symbols are the appropriate medium for the testing of abstract intelligence." Thus, these scales, in conception, are consistent with the definitions and analyses of intelligence that have been advanced by Terman and Spearman (see Chapter 7).

Since the very young child, the poor reader, and the poorly educated cannot be expected to deal with verbal materials, a "parallel set of nonverbal tests" has been developed, also as indicators of abstract thinking ability. As is customary, the use of both the verbal and the nonverbal scales is recommended, and for the usual reasons: to reveal discrepancies that might explain reading difficulties or other school deficiencies, and for vocational guidance (at the higher levels) as predictors of aptitudes for certain types of occupations.

TERMAN-McNEMAR TEST OF MENTAL ABILITY (1949). This instrument is intended for use primarily in grades 7 through 12, though norms are provided from the age of 10 years through 19 years, 11 months. Its content is homogeneous in that it is entirely verbal in character; for, consistent with Terman's definition of intelligence, this scale is devised to measure ability to deal with items utilizing symbols and abstractions.[4] The scale consists of seven subtests: information, synonyms, logical selection, classification, analogies, opposites, and best answer.

The authors subscribe to the general-factor (g) theory of intelligence. They hold that the general factor is best tested by means of materials using symbols and abstractions. In order to achieve a high degree of homogeneity in test materials, they omitted from their scale arithmetical and numerical types of subtests, which also are widely regarded as good tests of the general factor. The authors state the reason for their selection of materials as follows: "More homogeneous material has been used in order to have a test more highly saturated with a common factor or ability. Thus, the exclusion of arithmetical and numerical subtests means that the scores of any two individuals are more nearly comparable qualitatively; i.e., they lie along the same continuum. This continuum may be characterized as general verbal intelligence." The usefulness of this scale, therefore, is restricted to subjects who are not laboring under a language handicap and to situations wherein "verbal intelligence" is required as the major ability.

Items from

Terman-McNemar Test of Mental Ability
(Harcourt, Brace & World, Inc. By permission)

Information:

Polo is a kind of
    (1) disease   (2) work   (3) bear   (4) game
    (5) language

Synonyms:

Comic—(1) clumsy   (2) laughable
          (3) universal   (4) tricky
          (5) peculiar

Logical selection:

An orchestra always has
    (1) violinists   (2) piano   (3) musicians
    (4) saxophone   (5) singers

---

[4] This scale is a revision of the Terman Group Test of Mental Ability, published in 1920. This first version included also numerical and arithmetical tests.

Classification:

  (1) Catholic   (2) Methodist   (3) Presbyterian
  (4) Republican   (5) Baptist

Analogies:

  Zoo is to animal as aquarium is to:
    (1) birds   (2) fish   (3) bees   (4) statues
    (5) butterflies

Opposites:

  Exit: (1) emit   (2) transcend
       (3) entrance   (4) origin
       (5) arrival

Best answer:

  The saying, "Idle brains are the devil's workhouse," means
    (1) The devil is lazy.
    (2) People who are idle get into trouble.
    (3) Many hands make light work.
    (4) The devil works with his brains.

Reliability and Validity. The group tests described thus far in this chapter do not present any unfamiliar problems or findings. Their indexes of reliability are high, as shown in Table 16.1. Also, the "errors of measurement" presented in the manuals are all within a satisfactory range of reliability.

TABLE 16.1

RELIABILITY COEFFICIENTS OF FIVE GROUP SCALES

Scale	Range of coefficients	Method
California	.87–.95	split-half
Henmon-Nelson	.90–.95	odd-even
	.91–.93	alternate forms
Kuhlmann-Anderson	.88–.95	odd-even
	.90	test-retest
Lorge-Thorndike	.76–.90	alternate forms
	.88–.94	odd-even *
Terman-McNemar	.96	split-half
	.95	alternate forms

* At level 2, the nonverbal reliability coefficient was .59. Of this, the authors say: "At this level, an odd-even reliability coefficient is really not meaningful, since there is a systematic alternation between geometric and pictorial items in subtests 2 and 3."

As is always the case, validation of a scale is a more complex and difficult task than is establishing its reliability. Each of the group scales described used several of the well-established criteria of validity, as indicated below.

California:

Correlations with the S-B, the Wechsler, and several other group scales: coefficients as usual varied from moderate to high, depending upon the number of individuals and range of ability they represented.

Intercorrelations of subtests: these varied from .25 to .60, of which 70 percent were below .50 and 50 percent below .40.

Correlations with tests of school achievement: these were low at the primary levels; the language subtests at later levels correlated from .42 to .81 with the various school subjects.

IQ distribution: a mean of 100 and a standard deviation of 16 were established.

Henmon-Nelson:

Item analysis: items were analyzed in terms of known groups (inferior, average, superior), as indicated by the composite scores on three "well-known group tests of mental ability."

Correlations with another group test of mental ability (the California): *r*s varied from .74 to .86.

Correlations with educational achievement tests: *r*s varied from .64 to .85, most being in the .70s.

Correlations with composites of school grades: *r*s varied from .68 to .72.

Kuhlmann-Anderson:

Subtest intercorrelations: two thirds of these are in the .40s and .50s.

Subtest intercorrelations with total scores: two thirds are between .50 and .81.

Correlations with school achievement: coefficients range from .60 to .80.

Differentiation among average, retarded, and accelerated pupils.

Relative uniformity of means, standard deviations, and ranges of IQs at the several grade levels.

Lorge-Thorndike:

Construct and content validity: to test abstract ability, defined as ability to work with ideas and relationships among ideas. This ability is divided into six aspects to be tested.

Biserial correlation of each item with scores on the subtest of which it is a part. (See Chapter 5 for discussion of biserial correlation.) The median coefficients ranged from .43 to .70.

Correlations with performance in school subjects: one study yielded a coefficient of .87 with reading, and one with arithmetic yielded .76.

Correlations with four other group tests: forty-six of fifty-two coefficients were .60 or higher.

Correlations with S-B and WISC: these were from .54 to .77.

Intercorrelations of subtests: these ranged from .30 to .70; eight of the coefficients were .50 or higher; five were in the .40s.

Correlation of verbal with nonverbal scores separately for each grade: coefficients varied from .54 to .70, all but two being in the .60s.

Terman-McNemar:

Item analysis: percentage of pupils passing each item in successive grades was the principal criterion.

Item analysis: the correlation was found for each item with total score.[5] No item yielding a coefficient of less than .30 was retained. Ninety percent of the items yielded coefficients of .40 or higher, the mean being .53.

Correlations with school achievement tests: median coefficients were .62 with reading, .66 with language, .54 with mathematics, .66 with social studies, and .64 with science.

Evaluation. The five group-testing instruments described above are representative of the sounder scales of their type. From the lists of their subtests, one can readily perceive which types of materials and test problems have become established, through use and research, as most valuable for educational and psychological purposes. The reliabilities of these and similar scales are high, so that they may be used with a considerable degree of confidence, as far as this aspect of testing is concerned. The numbers of individuals in the standardization groups were large, numbering many thousands; and they were geographically and otherwise satisfactorily stratified. The statistical techniques used in their construction, in determining reliability and validity, give assurance of thorough analysis of data. Technically, they are on a high level of test construction.

From the itemized lists of validating criteria, one can readily see the extent of common practice in validating group scales, which criteria are most frequently used, and which are emphasized by each of the several tests' authors. The data on external criteria of validity (correlations with schoolwork, with grade placement, and with other scales, both individual and group) are not as full or as extensive for some of these scales as for others. Each device, therefore, must be evaluated with respect to the specific use to which it is to be put. On the whole, it is desirable that the reliability and validity of each group scale should be determined for every grade level, or age level, for which it is intended. This ideal, ex-

---

[5] For this purpose the "tetrachoric-correlation" technique was used. See Chapter 5. For a fuller discussion, the student should consult a textbook in statistics.

tremely difficult to satisfy or approximate, is not met by even the soundest of current tests.

Group Scales for College Freshmen and Adults

Some tests of intelligence have been constructed for the specific purpose of appraising abilities with special reference to the intellectual demands of curricula in liberal arts colleges, engineering schools, and teachers' colleges. Several of these will be described briefly, principally to familiarize the student with the types of materials included. These scales do not present any new or unfamiliar principles in respect to construction, organization, or interpretation.

A few group scales are also available for use with the general adult population, while others have been designed for use primarily with graduate students and with adults at the superior levels of intelligence. Several of these will also be described.

Scales for College Students. One of the earliest and most widely used of these was the *American Council on Education Psychological Examination for College Freshmen* (1924–1954). This scale yields two scores: the Q-score (quantitative) and the L-score (linguistic). Each of these subdivisions consists of types of subtests with which the student is, by now, quite familiar: arithmetical reasoning, figure analogies, and number sequences, which give the Q-score; same-opposite, vocabulary completion, and verbal analogies, which give the L-score. Their items differ from those used at lower levels, not in form but in degree of difficulty. This ACE test, as it is known, has been displaced by more recent instruments. It is important historically, however; for probably more research has been published on it than on any other in its category. And although the more recent tests at this level are regarded as improvements, they are not radically different in conception or essentials of content.

Another instrument among those long in use is the *Ohio State Psychological Test* (1919–1958), standardized for grades 9–12 and for college freshmen. This scale, consisting entirely of verbal subtests (same-opposite, word analogy, reading comprehension), is intended to select prospective college students in general, without regard to specialization in particular courses of study. Although the scale is well standardized, having been continually improved over the years, some critics justifiably recommend that it be supplemented with tests of quantitative reasoning, especially for students entering the technical and quantitative sciences.

The Scholastic Aptitude Test of the College Entrance Examination Board, in use since 1926, appears in a somewhat revised form annually for use with high school seniors as one of the college admission criteria. It includes three sections that utilize familiar types of verbal items (completion, opposites, analogies, paragraph meaning) which yield a verbal score; and two sections, including problems in arithmetic, algebra, and geometry, that give a mathematics score. The SAT is a test of "abstract intelligence," devised to estimate the potential for higher education of the upper ability levels among high school seniors. This scale, it appears, does so more effectively for prospective students entering colleges of liberal arts than for those entering technical schools. Authors of a test designed to differentiate among individuals within a selected group at the upper levels are faced with the difficult problem of devising an instrument that is sensitive enough to measure finer differences. For this purpose, the SAT is among the most useful of its category. Its usefulness is enhanced by the fact that separate norms are provided for public and private schools, as well as for all schools combined; for boys and girls; and for students in several types of curricula (for example, liberal arts, engineering).

COLLEGE QUALIFICATION TESTS (1955–1958).   In recent years, a number of new scales to test ability for college work have appeared. Increased concern with this level of ability and of education is due, in part, to the steadily rising numbers of college applicants and the consequent desire to utilize objective criteria of admission. Of these more recent instruments, two will be described

The CQT —as the above-named tests are known—were developed to select college freshmen and to predict degrees of success in college courses. Like almost all other scales at this level, these tests provide a verbal, a numerical, and a total score. Some of the subtests included in these are the familiar types, already enumerated in connection with other college scales. But, in addition, the CQT contain seventy-five items of information, dependent upon learning opportunities. They represent a broad range of school subjects in the physical and biological sciences and in the social studies. From these, separate scores may be found for information in science and in social studies, as well as a total information score.

Since the information subtests are unusual in scales at this level, the authors of the CQT state: "The Information test . . . represents the conviction that a measure of educational background which the student brings to college will be indicative of his future learning. . . . the Information test has therefore been prepared to provide a uniform survey of the students' academic knowledge. . . . General proficiency in the fields of science and social studies can . . . be assessed through the small samplings from component subjects. The parts of the Information test are designed to provide this assessment as well as over-all indication of range of knowledge which the total Information score yields." (Manual, 1957, p. 4.) The authors might have added, also, that scores on a test of information are significantly correlated with other measures of the g factor of intelligence.[6]

COOPERATIVE SCHOOL AND COLLEGE ABILITY TESTS (1955–1957). In keeping with the justifiable current practice of designating long-named tests by their initials, these are known as the SCAT. Although there are five levels, covering the range from the fourth grade through the college sophomore year, and all are identical in conception and mental processes tested, we shall be concerned only with the college level. The subtests are of the familiar type, devised to obtain the now familiar verbal and quantitative, as well as total, scores. The purpose of the SCAT is to measure "school-learned abilities" and thereby to estimate individuals' capacities to undertake additional schooling.

Although these scales contain test items said to be specifically related to areas of study in the high school, and although use of the term "intelligence" is avoided, their content is not markedly different from that of other tests. When we test the intellectual potentialities of a selected population for continued education in liberal arts colleges and in higher technical schools, we are assessing their intelligence at the levels of abstract ability, whether we do so by means of test items that might be directly related to high school studies in some degree, or whether we attempt to measure mental operations through test items that are relatively independent of formal instruction. For differences in what has been learned and retained and can be utilized in organized thinking are indications of differences in intelligence, assuming in this instance that the testees have had reasonably comparable secondary school opportunities. As a matter of fact, close examination of the test items in the SCAT shows that they closely resemble other tests in both form and content. Two representative items from the verbal tests follow.

Sentence Meaning (Select the most appropriate word.)

Since the two questions were completely _____, it was necessary to consider them separately.

        f. irrelevant   *g*. confused   *h*. unrelated
        j. irrational   *k*. theoretical

Word Meaning (Select the word or phrase closest in meaning.)

Recur

        a. hold in bounds   *b*. alternate   *c*. revolve
        d. happen again   *e*. save

---

[6] Predictive validity is discussed in a later section of this chapter.

In addition to the several scales described above, there are others that have been constructed through equally careful planning and adherence to principles of sound test development. Such principles include, among others, extensive research and trial prior to making the tests available for use. Among these scales are the *College Qualifications Test* (1955–1958) and the *Henmon-Nelson* (1961) for college level, both of which are similar in content to the others.

Reliability and Validity. Techniques of construction are now so well developed that it is possible to prepare tests of mental ability having a high degree of reliability. The several scales used for the selection of college freshmen discussed herein—and a number of others, as well—all show high coefficients of reliability. For total scores, these range from the high .80s to the mid .90s; while for separate subtest scores, the coefficients at times drop to the low .70s, although most are appreciably higher, rising to the low .90s.

In the SCAT, an additional and unusual device for indicating reliabilities of scores has been included. This is called the "percentile band," intended to replace the familiar percentile ranks in reporting relative levels of scores. This device is used as a method of showing the probable errors of measurement of obtained scores for each of the separate grade levels. Thus, consider a twelfth-grade boy who has the following scores (see Fig. 16.3): verbal, 297; quantitative, 304; total, 300. On the "band," the first falls between the 75th and the 89th percentiles of his group; the second, between the 65th and 82nd percentiles; the third, between the 79th and 86th percentiles. In each instance, these data are interpreted to mean that the probabilities are approximately 2 to 1 (68 in 100) that this student's true score in each of the three measures falls within the indicated percentile limits. Although the bands overlap somewhat, he appears to be somewhat higher in verbal than in quantitative mental activity. He is, however, well above the average of his group in both; and the band of his total score indicates the probabilities are very high that his combined score ranks him within the highest quarter of his group.[7]

From what has already been said and quoted with regard to each of the foregoing scales, we may infer that the authors, at the outset, were guided by the principles of content and construct validity in developing their tests (see Chapter 5). In addition, however, these scales must have

[7] The soundness of using percentile bands has been questioned by some critics, principally because the bands are based upon standard errors of measurement that may be spuriously small, since these measures were found with reliability coefficients of speeded tests, computed by a Kuder-Richardson formula. This formula is not recommended for speeded tests. See Chapter 4 on methods of estimating reliability of speeded tests.

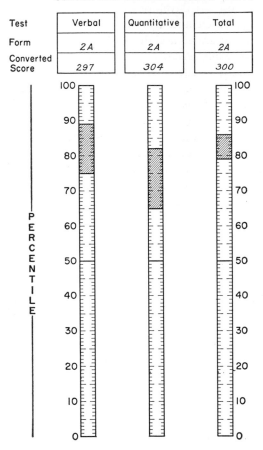

Fig. 16.3. A percentile band. Reproduced by permission.

adequate predictive validity, since their purpose is to identify those students who give promise of ability to learn at levels beyond the secondary school. That is, the test scores must correlate well with grades earned at the college level. Table 16.2 shows these correlations for a group of representative scales.

The wide range of validity correlations for a given scale cannot be fully explained without knowing the variations in scholastic ability represented in each study, the admissions criteria and the scholastic standards of each institution in which the study was made, and the curricula in which the students were enrolled. In view of the differences in correlation coefficients of prediction, it is essential that a scale's predictive validity be separately determined for each of the several types of institutions. Ideally, it would be desirable for each institution to cross-validate a scale for its own purposes. Associated with this is the desirability of providing separate norms for different types of institutions. This has been done in some instances.

TABLE 16.2

PREDICTIVE VALIDITY CORRELATIONS OF SCALES FOR COLLEGE FRESHMEN

Scales	Criteria	Coefficients
American Council (ACE)	.25–.60	Total point average
College Placement Test (CPT)	.57	Freshman grades
College Qualification Test (CQT)	.26–.67	Junior college; first term grades
	.35–.68	Publicly controlled colleges; first semester grades
	.34–.71	Privately controlled colleges; first semester grades
Henmon-Nelson	.54	First semester grades
Ohio State University	.58–.65	Freshman grades
Scholastic Aptitude Tests (SAT)	.45 *	Verbal scores with freshman average
	.58 *	Math. scores with freshman average
SCAT	.43–.68	Freshman grades

* These are average correlation coefficients for a large number of studies.

In Table 16.2 most of the correlation coefficients are based on over-all scholastic averages. The student should be aware of the fact, however, that the coefficients found between the tests and individual subjects of study may, and often do, differ significantly. It is desirable to be familiar with the efficiency of total scores and part scores (for example, verbal and quantitative) in predicting performance in the several areas of study as well as in general. For example, in one investigation, using the SAT, verbal scores correlated with grades in physics from .28 to .36, while the mathematics (quantitative) scores correlated from .48 to .59 with the same grades. Verbal scores and scholastic averages for the freshman year correlated .45, while the scores of the quantitative tests correlated .58. It is to be expected, and it does so happen, that the linguistic tests will usually yield higher coefficients than the quantitative, when correlated with grades in social studies and the humanities, while the reverse will be true when test scores are correlated with grades in mathematics and the physical sciences.

It will have been noted, also, that the correlational studies deal, for the most part, with the college freshman year and only occasionally with the sophomore. In many institutions, the coefficients will be significantly higher for these first two years than for the last two. In one college of liberal arts in a large university, the coefficients dropped gradually from .48 in the first semester of the freshman year to .18 in the second semester of the senior year. The students, as a group, become less heterogeneous in successive years; nonintellectual factors (social, emotional, economic) can become increasingly important; the several areas of study and specialization are not of equal difficulty; grading may be less differentiated at the higher course levels; as students become immersed in a subject of study, smaller differences in ability are not significant, hence do not affect grades.

Coefficients of correlation are significant, of course, in estimating the predictive validity of tests. It appears, however, that too much emphasis has been put upon them, often to the exclusion of another statistical technique that can provide even more significant data; that is, expectancy tables, of which there are several types (see Chapter 5). These two techniques, each used to supplement the other, will provide much more insight into the validity of a test than either used alone. It would be highly desirable to have expectancy tables provided in test manuals.

Evaluation.   As a group, current tests for the selection of college freshmen have met high technical standards in the statistical analyses of their data and in the choice of items. They have utilized types of test items that have best survived years of research and experimentation; so much so, in fact, that there is considerable similarity, from one test to another, in general content and psychological constructs employed.

A major criticism against some available scales is that their norms and studies of predictive validity are based upon results found in too few institutions, not adequately representative of the nation's colleges and technical schools. Therefore, in the study of a particular instrument's possible value for a particular institution, it is essential that the characteristics of the institutions and population upon which the scale was standardized be examined to determine the scale's appropriateness to the situation.

Test scores at the college freshman level do not differentiate well among individuals within the middle range of the distribution (approximately the middle 60 percent) for the purpose of predicting scholastic achievement. There are several reasons for this: the middle group is less heterogeneous than those at other levels of the distribution; the tests are not sufficiently refined to discern the small differences within this group; the numerous nonintellectual and chance factors that affect students' course marks can be more significant in their influence upon correlations between test scores and scholastic achievement than is the case at the upper and lower levels. For example, one study showed that the scale had considerable value in predicting quality of course work and duration of attendance for the highest 20 percent and the lowest 20 percent. Predictions for the middle 60 percent were unreliable. Even this limited usefulness warrants the use of the sounder tests, when the results are interpreted by qualified persons, since in this way the most promising and the least promising prospective students may be recognized. The soundest practice at present, however, is to use the test score as one of two or three primary criteria, the others being the secondary school record and scores on entrance examinations (educational achievement tests). On the whole, college tests of mental ability show up very well when one considers the uncontrollable variables affecting course grades, with which test scores are correlated. Some of these are subjectively determined high school and college grades, fluctuations and variations in motivation, factors of health, economic pressures, personality traits, and emotional problems of late adolescence.

Tests for Graduate Students and Superior Adults. The use of tests of mental ability has been extended, rather widely, to graduate and professional schools. One of these, the Graduate Record Examination (GRE), will be described in a later chapter dealing with educational achievement tests; for it includes sections designed to measure learning and mastery of subject matter in the several areas of undergraduate study as well as subtests which, though on a higher level, are much the same in form and purpose as those used in measures of mental ability for college work. The most widely used measure of general mental ability for prospective graduate students is the Miller Analogies Test. Another instrument, devised specifically for use with superior adults, is Terman's Concept Mastery Test. Both of these will be described to show the direction being taken in testing at the higher levels of mental ability.

MILLER ANALOGIES TEST (1926–1960). Originally devised in 1926, this test has been developed to measure scholastic aptitude at the graduate school level. It consists of a large number of items, with a time limit of fifty minutes; but the speed factor is said to be of negligible importance. The test includes analogies covering a wide variety of fields of learning and specialization. Although quantitative as well as verbal materials are used, the items are predominantly verbal in character. The logical relationships to be discerned within each of the items are not uniform; thus the subject must reorient his analysis with each item. (It is not possible to illustrate or describe the items, since the test is not circulated, and its use is strictly controlled.) The material in the test is often abstruse; and many of the analogies are complex. Consequently, this test has a very high upper level of difficulty, regarded by some as probably the most difficult among tests of abstract ability.

Since the intellectual levels of graduate students are not uniform from university to university, nor among the several departments within a given university, percentile norms are provided for each of the several fields of study, for each of a group of universities, and for a few professional schools. The differences among some of these groups are appreciable; as, for example, when the median (50th percentile) score in one subject-matter group is equal to the 80th or 90th percentile score of another.

So far as reliability is concerned, this is a well-constructed test. Odd-even reliability coefficients are in the low .90s; alternate forms correlate between .85 and .89.

Validity has been estimated largely, but not solely, by the instrument's ability to predict grades in graduate courses and on comprehensive graduate examinations. Findings on predictive validity at the university graduate level are affected by the same determinants as those at the college level, that is, subjectivity of marking standards, differences in intellectual demands made by different courses and areas, differences in standards among institutions, and individual motivation. Correlations at the graduate level are probably depressed, also, by the greater homogeneity of the students in regard to level of ability, as compared with the generality of undergraduates. Correlation coefficients of validity, with course grades and comprehensive examinations, have varied from about .30 to the high .70s, most being in the .40s and .50s. When correlated with the subject-matter sections of the GRE, the coefficients were, for the most part, between .75 and .80; while with the "verbal factor" of the GRE (that is, the verbal part of the test of general mental ability), the coefficients were in the low .80s.

In view of these high coefficients between the Miller test and the GRE, one might ask why both are often required by some university departments or why the latter should be given at all, since it takes several hours while the Miller requires less than an hour. This question has been answered, in some instances, by requiring only the GRE, because it combines educational achievement tests with tests of general mental ability. Those who use both, do so, presumably, because of the subject-matter content of the GRE and the high degree of difficulty at the upper level of the Miller test; and also because one instrument can supplement the other.

Ability to learn verbal and quantitative concepts and course materials is an important factor in successful graduate study. The Miller Analogies Test can make an important contribution to assessment of this ability among individuals in a selected group.[8] More extensive information would be desirable, however, regarding its predictive value in each of the several areas of graduate study: social studies, physical sciences, biological sciences, and the humanities; and perhaps even in each of the departmental divisions within each area. Cross-validation by each university, for its own guidance, is also desirable.

What the analogies tests do not evaluate—nor do they purport to do so—is creative research ability and originality in constructive thinking, both of which should rank high in graduate study.

CONCEPT MASTERY TEST (1956). Developed under the direction of L. M. Terman, this test was devised as a measure of ability to deal with abstract ideas at a high level. Its purpose is to measure intellectual functions similar to the Stanford-Binet; thus, it would be "highly saturated" with the general factor (g). The original form was constructed to measure mental ability of superior and gifted individuals, in early maturity, in the long-term longitudinal studies conducted under Terman's direction. A new instrument was necessary for this group because the Stanford-Binet and other available scales did not advance to a high enough level of difficulty to test and differentiate among them. A later edition (Form T) was developed for use with the gifted group and was released for use with college students at the junior-year level and higher, and for other adults at the upper levels of mental ability.

The content is of two familiar types—identification of synonyms and antonyms, and completion of analogies. The analogies employ both verbal and numerical concepts; and they draw on a wide variety of subject-matter fields.

The CMT, like other carefully constructed tests, has a high degree of reliability. Alternate forms, used with four groups, gave coefficients from .86 to .94. Two of these groups (undergraduates and graduate students at Stanford) were retested at intervals of one day to one week. Two others (gifted subjects and their spouses) were retested after an interval of eleven

[8] A similar test at a high level of difficulty, called the Advanced Personnel Test, has been prepared by Miller. It is a measure of verbal reasoning ability for use by business, industry, and government "for employment and upgrading of management and research personnel." The Doppelt Mathematical Reasoning Test has been prepared "in response to a need expressed by the users of the Miller Analogies Test and the Advanced Personnel Test for a comparable high-level measure of numerical reasoning ability." The Miller and the Doppelt tests, both restricted, are distributed by The Psychological Corporation.

to twelve years. The high reliability coefficients for these two groups (.87 and .92), after such a long period, attest not only to the test's reliability but also to the relative stability of mental functioning by individuals at the highest levels of mental ability.

Validating a test of intelligence for use at the superior adult level presents more than the usual difficulties, because satisfactory external criteria are not readily available, nor are they as reliable as those used in validating tests for children and adolescents. Terman and his colleagues employed a number of criteria that provide favorable evidence. Intercorrelations of parts I and II (synonyms–antonyms with analogies), for two groups, were high: .75 and .76. For a small group ($N = 59$) the CMT and the SAT correlated .70. The mean and the standard deviation of the CMT classified individuals in a manner consistent with Stanford-Binet IQs obtained in childhood. Mean scores of the CMT progressed in conformity with the IQ distribution obtained in childhood. For a group of gifted persons and their spouses, the mean score on the CMT is significantly associated with levels of higher education achieved. The same was true of a group of U.S. Air Force captains. When correlated with grade-point averages of a group of undergraduates ($N = 97$), a coefficient of .49 was found.[9] Again, and as stated in connection with other tests, an instrument such as this, intended for a highly selected segment of the population, should be validated for each institution and situation in which it is to be used, unless reasonable conformity with the standardization group is assured.

Representative Scales for Adults

It is not a common practice to test adults in general, as is the case with children, adolescents, and college students who are tested for purposes of educational selection and vocational guidance. When adults are tested, it is for specific reasons, such as preliminary screening of business and industrial personnel; screening in the armed forces; and upgrading of individuals.[10] When tests of general ability are given for these purposes, they are usually supplements to tests of specific aptitudes (see Chapters 17, 18, and 19). Both kinds are used as predictors of ability to

[9] The grade-point averages were correlated also with CMT scores for a group of 124 undergraduates who were seen at the university's counseling center. The coefficient was only .37. This index, however, should not be regarded as representative of the test's differentiating ability, since students who seek the help of a counseling center are, as a group, having more than the usual personality problems and difficulties of adjustment to college work.

[10] Individual tests of mental ability are used with adults, of course, in hospitals, clinics and in the private practice of psychology.

learn specific types of materials and as predictors of performance in a specified type of occupation.

Two of the scales already described in other connections, the California and the Kuhlmann-Anderson, provide tests at the adult level. It would be possible, also, to use a scale (for example, the Lorge-Thorndike or the Henmon-Nelson) that provides norms through grade 12 or higher; but if that were done, adults would be rated only with reference to grade and age norms within the scope of each scale.

Some instruments, however, have been constructed specifically for adult use. For example, among the older scales are the Pintner Advanced Test, which begins with the ninth grade and continues through adult levels; the Otis Self-Administering Test of Mental Ability: Higher Examination; and the Army General Classification Test (AGCT), based upon the Army Alpha, which was used in World War I. A more recent adaptation is the Modified Alpha Examination, Form 9. This last-named instrument follows the currently common practice of providing a total score and separate scores for the numerical and for the verbal test items. All of these scales include types of items with which the student is already familiar. Perhaps the only type to which attention should be called is block-counting (spatial perception) in the AGCT, now infrequently used in adult tests of general mental ability.

Since the end of World War II, there has been a tendency to develop and use brief or abbreviated scales in adult personnel selection. There are, for example, the Thurstone Test of Mental Alertness (1943–1953) (twenty minutes), the Wesman Personnel Classification Test (1946–1951) (twenty-eight minutes), and the Wonderlic Personnel Test (1939–1945) (twelve minutes). Occasionally, a special brief screening test is devised for a specific business or industry. The form of the content and the mental operations involved are the same as those used in scales intended for use with a more general segment of the population; but the specific items are related to the type of business in which the test is to be used. For example, the American Stores Company uses its own Personnel Selection Test (constructed in collaboration with staff members of The Psychological Corporation). This test, naturally, is heavily loaded with items related to the grocery business.

The adult scales available for general use, by authorized professional persons, are not interchangeable. One (for example, the Wonderlic) may have its highest validity in the selection of personnel for certain types of clerical work; another may be more valid in selecting individuals for higher level rather than lower level employment (for example, the Wesman). It has been found that validity data vary considerably with the levels and types of work, the characteristics of the sample of persons tested, and the criteria used. In these respects, adult tests used for screening and selection are comparable with those used in educational institutions at all levels. The problem of obtaining a representative sample of the general adult population, however, is a more difficult one than getting one of children, adolescents, or college students. It is most essential, therefore, that reliability and validity of tests for adults be determined quite specifically as to population samples and types of occupation.[11]

Evaluation of Group Scales

COMPARISON WITH INDIVIDUAL SCALES. Group scales were developed to permit the testing of large numbers of persons at one time. On the whole, therefore, they are not so useful as are individual scales in studying an individual case. For when a group scale is used, it is not possible to observe a person's approach to the solution of problems, nor his behavior under success and failure. Nor is it possible to evaluate the *qualitative* characteristics of his responses, since group scales are scored quite rigidly. Furthermore, it is difficult—in fact, practically impossible—to know whether an individual is exerting his maximum effort when taking a group examination. It is possible to report the test results only in terms of numerical indexes (plus profiles, at times), whereas during an individual examination the psychologist is able to make behavioral and qualitative observations of considerable value.

Practically all group scales below college level have been validated against individual scales—especially the Stanford-Binet—as one of the principal criteria. This fact in itself is a recognition of the merit of the individual scale, the quality of which the group scale is trying to approach as closely as possible. Other criteria of validity are the familiar ones discussed in this and earlier chapters.

In discussing the definitions and analyses of intelligence, it was stated that one deficiency of all tests is that they do not measure the creative aspects of intelligence; nor do they directly measure the insights that come from experience ("wisdom," "judgment"), or productive thinking, or the intellectual originality of an individual. This deficiency is more marked in group than in individual scales, because of the rigidity of scoring the former.

THEORETICAL AND STATISTICAL BASES. Most of the earlier group scales are based, implicitly at least, upon the general-factor theory of intelligence. A number of the more recent instruments are also based upon

---

[11] In this connection, the student should consult various issues of *Personnel Psychology* for information on validity and normative data as they relate to these tests.

this theory, it appears, even though they yield separate scores of verbal and quantitative aspects of mental ability. Several scales are based upon the group-factor theory. This latter type will be described and discussed more explicitly in the next chapter.

Since many group tests, of varying quality, have been published, it is essential that prospective users examine the manuals closely to determine which of these satisfy the standards that should be demanded of them. The reader is already familiar with the standards and methods of establishing reliability and validity. These should be rigorously applied to group tests. In this connection it is essential that the manual state which method was used in determining reliability, especially if the speed factor seems to be a significant one.

Since group tests for children and adolescents are used primarily to assist in dealing with educational problems, it is essential that the scale's predictive efficiency, with regard to schoolwork and progress, be reported as one criterion of validity. Group tests devised primarily for use with adolescents and adults in occupational selection should also provide specific information regarding their predictive validity.

Scores on a scale as a whole are more reliable and more valid than subtest scores. A distinction should be made, therefore, between subtest reliability and validity, on the one hand, and total-scale reliability and validity, on the other. This distinction is especially pertinent when a scale's subtest scores are to be used for differentiating and diagnostic purposes.

The manual should give not only the size of the standardization population sample, but the characteristics of that sample should be specified, such as geographic and socioeconomic distributions, range of ages, range of ability levels, range of school levels, and sex distribution. Similar pertinent facts should be provided with tests designed for use with adults.

Criteria of Evaluation. In evaluating a group scale with a view to its probable usefulness in a given practical situation or in the study of a theoretical problem, it is customary to use the following criteria.

1. It must be sufficiently *valid* and *reliable*.

2. The range of *norms* must be adequate for the group for which the scale is devised.

3. The *item difficulty* in each subtest must be of sufficient range to differentiate among the various levels of ability. Individuals at the lowest and highest levels should be able to obtain scores that represent their levels.

4. In general, the *range of ability* to be tested (ages, school grades, occupations) should be restricted rather than all-inclusive. If the range is restricted, a given number of items and a given length of time can be used

for a more thorough and accurate examination than if a scale of the same length were employed to cover a wider range. In the latter instance, the test items would have to be spread more thinly.

5. *Length of the scale* must be adequate. In time required, group scales vary from about one-half hour to three hours, depending upon levels for which they are intended. The great majority of scales require one and one-half hours or less. Increase in length, to an optimal point, adds to validity and reliability, since errors of measurement are decreased (better sampling) as length is increased to an optimal point. Judging from current practices, based upon experiment, optimal lengths appear to be about a half hour at the level of kindergarten and primary grades, about forty-five minutes at the level of elementary grades, and up to about an hour, or an hour and a half, at higher levels.

6. *Simplicity of responses* is frequently regarded as an asset in group tests. For some purposes—when group trends are sought, rather than individual performance—this is an asset simply because scoring is facilitated. But, as already pointed out, such simplicity and consequent rigidity may limit the value of tests when evaluation of an individual's responses is desired.

7. *Simplicity of scoring* is also frequently considered to be an asset, since it is actually a result of simplicity of responses. The same comments apply here as above.

8. *Ease of administering* a group scale is desirable. Frequently, group scales have to be given by relatively inexperienced persons; it should, therefore, be possible to train them in a brief time to administer the scale accurately and with precision. Also, simplicity of instructions and procedures in giving an examination to a group reduces the possibility of confusion and misunderstanding on the part of individuals in the group.

9. The *examiner's manual* should be clear and complete in respect to standardization procedures and results, nature of the content, directions for administering and scoring, norms, and interpretation of results.

10. The *content* of the tests should be *interesting* to the groups for whom intended.

11. The *content* of the tests should be *appropriate* to the subjects being examined. That is to say, the psychologist must determine whether or not, in a given instance, it is desirable to use a scale that is entirely verbal, or entirely nonverbal, or verbal and quantitative, or mixed. His choice of scale will depend upon *who* is to be tested and the purpose for which the test is being given.

Uses of Group Scales

Without going into details, the ways in which group scales have been used will be given.

In schools, they have been used for purposes of general survey, ability classification of pupils, and guidance. Under general survey, studies have been made of the range and distribution of mental ability; age and grade overlapping of ability; differences among pupils in various schools within the same community; differences among pupils in different school systems; differences among pupils in the several high school curricula; the effects of different methods of instruction upon pupils at the several levels of ability; relations between intelligence-test ratings and school achievement in general, and in specific school subjects; and comparisons of city, town, and rural children.

In classifying pupils according to ability level for the purpose of differentiated instruction, a test of mental ability is, of course, basic, though it should not be the only criterion.

Since relatively few schools include a qualified psychological examiner on their staffs, and since extensive individual examination is costly and time-consuming, group scales are being used for most guidance purposes. However, in view of the fact that group-test ratings may indicate only the approximate level of an individual's mental ability, they must be used in conjunction with other available evidence obtained from school records, teachers' reports, objective achievement tests, and interviews. But psychological-test ratings, correctly obtained and interpreted, tell us much more about a pupil's mental level and organization of abilities than could be ascertained without their use.

Group tests have been applied extensively to a large number of theoretical and practical problems of psychological, educational, and sociological significance, such as individual differences in relation to sex, racial, and national membership; mental levels and characteristics of special groups, such as the mentally deficient, the gifted, and the delinquent; employee selection for jobs requiring different levels of ability; family similarities and the inheritance of intelligence; effects of changed environment upon mental level; the nature and course of mental development; the nature and organization of intelligence; constancy of the IQ and prediction of later ability; and problems of theory and technique, such as the relationship between "speed" and "power" as aspects of intelligence. Then, of course, there was the vast use of group scales in the armed forces, during World War II, for screening and classification of enlisted and commissioned personnel.

The foregoing enumeration is not complete; but it suffices to show the wide range of application of group tests of mental ability; and it helps to explain why tests should be under continual scrutiny in an effort to increase their validity and reliability.

References

1. Allen, R. M., and H. Bessell. Intercorrelations among group verbal and nonverbal tests of intelligence. *Journal of Educational Research,* 1950, *43,* 394–395.
2. American Council on Education. *Psychological Examination for College Students.* Princeton, N.J.: Educational Testing Service, 1954.
3. Baier, D. E., and R. D. Dugan. Tests and performance in a sales organization. *Personnel Psychology,* 1956, *9,* 17–26.
4. Barthol, R. P., and B. A. Kirk. The selection of graduate students in public health education. *Journal of Applied Psychology,* 1956, *40,* 159–163.
5. Bayley, N., and M. H. Oden. The maintenance of intellectual ability in gifted adults. *Journal of Gerontology,* 1955, *10,* 91–107.
6. Bennett, G. K., *et al. College Qualification Tests.* New York: The Psychological Corporation, 1958.
7. Brandt, H. Development and construction of the Armed Forces Qualification Test: I. rationale, item content, and construction. *The American Psychologist,* 1949, *4,* 239. (Abstract.)
8. Burt, C. The structure of the mind. *British Journal of Educational Psychology,* 1949, *19,* 100–111, 176–199.
9. College Entrance Examination Board. *Scholastic Aptitude Test.* Princeton, N.J.: Educational Testing Service, Annual.
10. Cooperative Test Division. *Cooperative School and College Ability Tests.* Princeton, N.J.: Educational Testing Service, 1958.
11. Doppelt, J. E. *Mathematical Reasoning Test.* New York: The Psychological Corporation, 1958.
12. Englehart, M. D. Obtaining comparable scores on two or more tests. *Educational and Psychological Measurement,* 1959, *19,* 55–65.
13. Finch, F. H., *et al. Kuhlmann-Finch Intelligence Tests.* Philadelphia: Educational Test Bureau, 1953.
14. Harper, B. P., *et al.* Development and construction of an Armed Services Qualification Test: II. item analysis and item selection. *The American Psychologist,* 1949, *4,* 239–240. (Abstract.)
15. Henmon, V. A. C., and M. J. Nelson. *Henmon-Nelson Tests of Mental Ability.* Boston: Houghton Mifflin Company, 1950.
16. Holt, W. G., *et al.* Evidenced relationships between the ACE and the Wesman Personnel Classification Test. *Journal of Educational Research,* 1957, *51,* 71–77.
17. Holzinger, K. J., and F. Swineford. The relation of two bifactors to geometry and other subjects. *Journal of Educational Psychology,* 1946, *37,* 257–265.
18. Juola, A. E. Predictive validity of college-level academic ability tests at one institution. *The Personnel and Guidance Journal,* 1960, *38,* 637–641.
19. Justman, J., and J. W. Wrightstone. Comparison of pupil functioning on the Pintner Intermediate Test and the Henmon-Nelson Test of Mental

Ability. *Educational and Psychological Measurement,* 1953, *13,* 102–109.

20. Klugh, H. E., and R. Bierley. The school and college ability test and high school grades as predictors of college achievement. *Educational and Psychological Measurement,* 1959, *19,* 625–626.

21. Kuhlmann, F., and R. G. Anderson. *Kuhlmann-Anderson Intelligence Tests.* Princeton, N.J.: Personnel Press, 1952.

22. Lamke, T. A. The revision of the Henmon-Nelson tests of mental ability. *Twelfth Yearbook, National Council on Measurements Used in Education,* 1955, 78–80.

23. Lamke, T. A. The standardization of the Henmon-Nelson revision. *Thirteenth Yearbook, National Council on Measurements Used in Education,* 1956, 42–44.

24. Lamke, T. A., and M. J. Nelson. *The Henmon-Nelson Tests of Mental Ability.* Rev. ed. Boston: Houghton Mifflin Company, 1957.

25. Lennon, R. T., and R. E. Schutz. *A Summary of Correlations between Results of Certain Intelligence and Achievement Tests.* Test Service Notebook, No. 18. New York: Harcourt, Brace & World, Inc., 1957.

26. Lorge, I., and R. L. Thorndike. *The Lorge-Thorndike Intelligence Tests.* Boston: Houghton Mifflin Company, 1957.

27. Manuel, H. T. Aptitude tests for college admission. *Fourteenth Yearbook, National Council on Measurements Used in Education,* 1957, 20–27.

28. Miller, W. S. *Advanced Personnel Test.* New York: The Psychological Corporation, 1950.

29. Miller, W. S. *Miller Analogies Test.* New York: The Psychological Corporation, 1960.

30. Otis, A. S. *Otis Self-Administering Tests of Mental Ability.* Harcourt, Brace & World, Inc., 1929.

31. Personnel Research Branch, Department of the Army. The army general classification test. *Psychological Bulletin,* 1945, *42,* 760–768.

32. Personnel Research Section, Classification and Replacement Branch, Adjutant General's Office. *Personnel Classification Tests.* Technical Manual, TM 12-260 rev. Washington, D.C.: Government Printing Office, 1946.

33. Personnel Research Section, Adjutant General's Office. *Army General Classification Test: First Civilian Edition.* Chicago: Science Research Associates, Inc., 1948.

34. Pintner, R., et al. *Pintner General Ability Tests: Verbal Series.* New York: Harcourt, Brace & World, Inc., 1946.

35. Science Research Associates. *College Placement Test.* Chicago: 1957.

36. Sullivan, E. T., et al. *California Tests of Mental Maturity.* Monterey: California Test Bureau, 1957.

37. Taylor, D. W. Variables related to creativity and productivity among men in two research laboratories. In *The Identification of Creative Scientific Talent* (C. W. Taylor, ed.). Salt Lake City: University of Utah Press, 1958.

38. Terman, L. M. *Concept Mastery Test*. New York: The Psychological Corporation, 1956.
39. Terman, L. M., and Q. McNemar. *Terman-McNemar Test of Mental Ability*. New York: Harcourt, Brace & World, Inc., 1949.
40. Thorndike, E. L. *Institute of Educational Research Intelligence Scale, CAVD*. New York: Teachers College, Columbia University, 1925.
41. Thorndike, E. L. *The Thorndike Intelligence Examination for High-School Graduates*. New York: Teachers College, Columbia University, 1936.
42. Thurstone, T. G., and L. L. Thurstone. *Thurstone Test of Mental Alertness*. Chicago: Science Research Associates, 1953.
43. Toops, H. A. *Ohio State Psychological Test*. Columbus: The Ohio State University Press, 1958.
44. Votaw, D. F. Validity estimates of success in graduate school based on Miller analogies test scores. *Fifteenth Yearbook, National Council on Measurements Used in Education,* 1958, 150–156.
45. Weeks, J. S. The predictive validity of ACE and SCAT. *The Personnel and Guidance Journal,* 1959, *38,* 52–54.
46. Wells, F. L. *Modified Alpha Examination, Form 9*. New York: The Psychological Corporation, 1951.
47. Wesman, A. G. *Personnel Classification Test*. New York: The Psychological Corporation, 1951.
48. Williams, N. A study of the validity of the verbal reasoning subtest and the abstract reasoning subtest of the differential aptitude tests. *Educational and Psychological Measurement,* 1952, *12,* 129–131.
49. Wonderlic, E. F. *Personnel Test*. New York: The Psychological Corporation, 1945.

17.

MULTIFACTOR TEST BATTERIES

Characteristics

Multiple-factor batteries are those scales that are intended for the independent measurement of each of several kinds of mental operations and that provide a separate score for each.[1] Ordinarily, a single index (IQ, MA, Z-score, etc.) is not obtained for the entire battery of tests. The kinds of mental abilities tested are described in the following pages.[2]

These instruments stand in contrast to other tests of mental abilities, such as the Stanford-Binet, the Wechsler scales, the Kuhlmann-Anderson, the Henmon-Nelson, and the Lorge-Thorndike, which provide a single index and whose items and subtests are so selected as to yield a unitary and internally consistent measure of intelligence. This is the case, even though separate verbal and numerical scores or verbal and performance scores may be derived from some of these scales, in addition to an over-all rating. In the multifactor batteries, the objective is to obtain a number of separate scores in order to differentiate, if possible, among the several abilities within each individual. In terms of correlations, the authors of over-all tests of general intelligence strive to develop items and subtests that have significant positive intercorrelations, while authors of multi-

[1] These are known, also, as multiple-factor and multiple-aptitude batteries, and as differential-aptitude tests.

[2] Tests constructed to measure specific aptitudes, as in music, graphic arts, mechanical skills, and professions, employ different types of materials in part or entirely. They are discussed in Chapters 18 and 19.

factor batteries aim to devise parts that have as little intercorrelation as they can achieve. Otherwise stated, multifactor tests generally are intended to measure each of several pure factors or each of several combinations of a few closely related factors, with minimal overlapping of abilities measured by each part of the battery. (See Chapter 7, "Definitions and Analyses of Intelligence.") From these efforts have emerged a number of terms to designate psychological functions, such as spatial visualization, perceptual speed, and verbal facility.

There are two principal reasons for the growth of interest in this type of test battery, especially since the termination of World War II in 1945. Some psychologists were impressed by the variations within some individuals (intraindividual variations) in their performance on the several parts (subtests) of measures of intelligence. In other words, they were more impressed, it seems, by the absence of very high correlations among some subtest scores than by the fact that intertest coefficients have always been found to be positive and at a quite significant level, statistically and psychologically. A second reason for interest in multifactor batteries is the desire of the educational and vocational counselor, and of the personnel psychologist, to have tests of this type for use in counseling students and in selecting personnel in business, industry, government, and the military forces.

The rationale of multifactor-test batteries, then, is this: since most of them aim to measure relatively independent factors, each part of the battery (each type of test) can provide its own norms and can be validated for each of a variety of occupations and curricula. Thus, it is maintained, an individual's potentiality in a number of academic and vocational areas can be analyzed and appraised by means of a series of relatively brief tests. The merit of this view rests, of course, upon the ability of each of the several types of test materials in the battery to differentiate significantly among capacities required for successful performance in different occupations or courses of study.

Several of the multifactor batteries will be described and evaluated.

Representative Batteries

TESTS OF PRIMARY MENTAL ABILITIES. The Thurstones have published a series of multifactor tests originally known as The Chicago Tests of Primary Mental Abilities (published by the American Council on Education, 1941–1947). Later editions are named the SRA Primary Mental Abilities.[3] Of the latter, there are three levels: ages 5–7, 7–11, and

---

[3] The initials "SRA" stand for Science Research Associates, Inc., of Chicago, the publishers at present.

11–17. For the most part, but not entirely, we shall deal with the scale for ages 11–17. All scales in this series are based upon the same psychological and statistical principles, that is, the group-factor theory of mental ability, the factors having been inferred through the use of factor analysis. At the 11–17 age level, the following factors are tested:

Space

Look at the row of figures below. The first figure is like the letter F. *All the other figures are like the first but they have been turned in different directions.*

Now look at the next row of figures. The first one looks like the letter F. *But none of the other figures looks like an* F *even if they were turned right side up. They are all made backward.*

Some of the figures in the next row are like the first figure. Some are made backward. The figures like the first figure are marked.

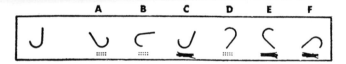

Reasoning

Study the series of letters below. What letter should come next?

a b a b a b a b   a b c d e f

The next letter in this series should be a. *The letter* a *has been marked in the answer row at the right.*

Now study the next series of letters and decide what the next letter should be. Mark the letter in the answer row at the right.

c a d a e a f a   a c d e f g

You should have marked the letter g.

FIG. 17.1. Practice items from the SRA Tests of Primary Mental Abilities. Science Research Associates, by permission.

Verbal meaning. This test is measured by the familiar synonyms type of item; to test "ability to understand ideas expressed in words."

Space (spatial perception). Test items use various simple designs and geometric figures, differently rotated, to test perception of the relations of an arrangement of objects in space; to test "ability to visualize objects in two- or three-dimensional space."

Reasoning. Each item consists of a series of letters arranged according to a pattern, or rule, which has to be recognized; to test "ability to solve logical problems."

Number. This test consists of simple, two-column problems in addition, to which answers have been given; some are right, others are wrong; the answers are to be marked accordingly; to test "ability to work with figures— to handle simple quantitative problems rapidly and accurately."

Word fluency. The test requires the writing of as many words as possible, begininng with a given letter, in a specified time; to measure "the ability to produce words easily."

At the lower levels, three other types of tests are also used. These are *perceptual speed,* ability to recognize likenesses and differences between objects and symbols; *quantitative,* ability to understand the meaning of numbers and to recognize quantitative differences; *motor,* ability to coordinate eye-and-hand movement.

Since this battery is intended to differentiate among the several kinds of mental operations, the first question to ask is this: how low are the intercorrelations among the parts? Table 17.1 provides an answer, as reported in the 1958 Manual.

TABLE 17.1

MEDIAN INTERCORRELATIONS OF PMA SUBTESTS: SIX GROUPS
(EACH SUBTEST WAS CORRELATED WITH THE OTHER FOUR.)

Subtests	*Range of medians*
Verbal meaning	.24–.50
Space	.13–.34
Reasoning	.34–.50
Number	.17–.35
Word fluency	.13–.37

Of the ten intercorrelations, five are in the .30s, two in the .20s, two in the teens, and one in the .50s. The two lowest, .17 and .13, both involve spatial perception, which is not surprising, considering the nature of the test. On the whole, these coefficients are low; thus, they lend reasonable support to the rationale of this battery, although abilities required by the five subtests are not independent of one another, since six of the ten coefficients are above .30 (to take an arbitrary cut-off value). From these data, however, we may conclude that the PMA tests have a reasonable degree of factorial validity. Whether the mental operations involved in these tests are significant aspects of the complex mental processes of intelligence, or whether these tests have significant predictive validity are other questions.

Validity of this battery was studied by the usual methods: correlations with other tests of intelligence, tests of specific aptitudes, educational achievement tests, and school grades, with the over-all results shown in Table 17.2.

TABLE 17.2

PMA VALIDITY CORRELATIONS

Criteria	Correlations
Otis Test	.71 (multiple R with subtests)
Kuhlmann-Anderson	.63 (multiple R with subtests)
GATB *	.16–.77 (range of highest rs with subtests)
ITED †	.13–.73 (with subtests)
Grade averages (9th grade total grade averages)	.27–.55 (with subtests)
Grade averages (total averages in 9th and 10th grades)	.29–.60 (with subtests)
Grades in high school courses	.16–.51 (with subtests)

* General Aptitude Test Battery, U.S. Employment Service. Described later in this chapter.
† Iowa Test of Educational Development.

Since, for educational purposes, these correlations are, on the whole, no higher and often lower than those found with tests of general mental ability, the advantages of using this instrument are not apparent. This reservation is especially relevant because the authors of the PMA battery conclude that the tests of verbal meaning and of reasoning yield the most satisfactory correlation coefficients with criteria of school success. These two subtests are similar to those included in scales designed to measure general mental ability. Furthermore, tests of general ability include items which, in complexity and structure, approximate better than do the PMA the kinds of mental activity actually required in school work.[4]

[4] Reliability data of this and the other multifactor tests are presented in a single table later in this chapter.

THE DIFFERENTIAL APTITUDE TESTS. This battery of tests is a most ambitious instrument. Its statistical data on standardization and on analysis of later studies are exceptionally thorough and comprehensive. Although the tests are intended for use in grades 8 through 12, in educational and vocational guidance, they may also be used with unselected adults. Several guiding principles were followed in developing the several parts.

All eight tests of the battery were standardized on the same population. Thus the norms and percentile values for each test have the same relative significance as those for all the other tests in the battery; for the ranges of age, aptitude, school grade, and nonintellective personality factors were constant in the standardization process. Psychological profiles, therefore, are more meaningful for interpretation of differences *within* an individual. The published norms are based upon a population sample of 47,000 boys and girls in grades 8 through 12, from communities throughout the country. Separate batteries and norms are available for boys and girls.

Each of the abilities represented should be independently tested.

Each test should measure level of ability; that is, power rather than speed of performance, with the exception of the part testing clerical speed and accuracy.

The battery of tests should yield a profile in terms of percentile ranks, all of which will be comparable for a given individual since they have been derived from the same population sample (see Fig. 17.4).

Usefulness in practical counseling is of primary concern. Although theoretical concepts and findings, including factor analysis, were taken into consideration, the parts of the battery are not intended to be "factorially pure."

The battery includes the following eight tests.

EXAMPLE Y

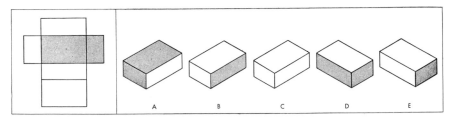

FIG. 17.2. Space relations item from the Differential Aptitude Tests. The examinee selects the three-dimensional figures that can be made by folding the two-dimensional figure at the left. The answer is figures A, C, and E. The Psychological Corporation. Reproduced by permission.

Each row consists of four figures called *Problem Figures and five Answer Figures. The four Problem Figures make a series. You are to find out which one of the Answer Figures would be the next, or the fifth one in the series.*

Abstract reasoning practice item. *Study the position of the black dot. Note that it keeps moving around the square clockwise: upper left corner, upper right corner, lower right corner, lower left corner. In what position will it be seen next? It will come back to the upper left corner. Therefore, B is the answer, and you would mark your Answer Sheet like this:*

A	B	C	D	E
::	▮	::	::	::

TEST ITEMS				
V.	AB	AC	AD	AE	AF
W.	aA	aB	BA	Ba	Bb
X.	A7	7A	B7	7B	AB
Y.	Aa	Ba	bA	BA	bB
Z.	3A	3B	33	B3	BB

SAMPLE OF ANSWER SHEET				
V.	AC	AE	AF	AB	AD
	::::	::::	::::	▬	::::
W.	BA	Ba	Bb	aA	aB
	::::	::::	▬	::::	::::
X.	7B	B7	AB	7A	A7
	▬	::::	::::	::::	::::
Y.	Aa	bA	bB	Ba	BA
	::::	▬	::::	::::	::::
Z.	BB	3B	B3	3A	33
	::::	::::	::::	::::	▬

Fig. 17.3. Clerical speed and accuracy items from the Differential Aptitude Tests. In each row of the Sample Answer Sheet, the examinee marks the combination that matches the underlined combination in the corresponding left-hand row. The Psychological Corporation, by permission.

Verbal reasoning. Verbal analogies of the familiar type are used to measure ability with more or less complex verbal concepts and relationships. (Since this test includes only a limited area of verbal reasoning, a more appropriate designation would be "verbal analogies.") [5]

Numerical ability. Numerical relationships and facility with number concepts are tested. These are essentially computational, rather than problem solving. Some of the items test only proficiency in the four fundamental processes; others require understanding of quantitative concepts and relationships.

Abstract reasoning. Ability to reason with nonverbal materials is tested.

[5] Compare with the Miller Analogies Test and the Terman Concept Mastery Test, in Chapter 16.

The series of designs presented in each item requires understanding of an operating principle in producing changes in members of the series (see Fig. 17.3).

Space relations. Ability in spatial visualization is tested by presenting two-dimensional geometric figures (variously shaded). These are imaginally manipulated, each to form a three-dimensional figure. The purpose is to test ability to visualize constructed figures, variously rotated (see Fig. 17.2).

Mechanical reasoning. Mechanical comprehension is tested by means of a series of pictorially presented situations involving mechanical and scientific principles. Each picture is accompanied by a brief and simply worded question about the principle involved (see Chapter 18, on tests of mechanical aptitude).

Clerical speed and accuracy. Speed and accuracy of responses to letter-and-number combinations are measured. This test requires the matching of various combinations, emphasizing perception of detail and rate of response. The items are intended to "approximate the elements involved in many clerical jobs."

Language usage. Part I is a spelling test. Some words are correctly spelled, while others are misspelled. The testee indicates, for each word, whether it is correctly or incorrectly spelled.

Language usage. Part II consists of sentences in which the examinee is required to distinguish faulty from correct grammar, punctuation, and word usage. Parts I and II are included in the battery as basic skills necessary in many vocations.

Validity of the DAT has been studied in three ways: prediction of course grades, of achievement-test results, and of vocational and educational success. The manual of this battery contains hundreds of correlation coefficients in these three categories.[6] Table 17.3 presents, in summary form, some of the major over-all findings when course averages in grades 8–12 were used as criteria; that is, "concurrent validity."

DAT scores were correlated also with course averages in each of several subjects of study, obtained from six months to three and one-half years after the test scores were obtained. These coefficients of predictive validity are of the same general order as those shown in Table 17.3. When DAT scores were correlated with course averages of college freshmen, however, the results, as reported in the manual, were not promising. It appears, therefore, that the DAT should not displace the scales intended specifically to select college freshmen, discussed in Chapter 16.

When DAT scores were correlated with scores on standardized achievement tests, also as indexes of predictive validity, the results generally are somewhat better than those found with course grades. This is particularly true of Verbal Reasoning and Numerical Ability, and to a lesser degree of Abstract Reasoning and Language II. As a result of their validation studies, the authors of the DAT justifiably conclude that the tests of

[6] Students should consult and analyze these tables.

TABLE 17.3

VALIDITY CORRELATIONS FOUND WITH THE DAT
AND COURSE GRADES: ALL PARTS
(BOYS AND GIRLS)

School subject	Range of median r values for each of the separate parts	Lowest median	Highest median
English	.21–.53	Mechanical reasoning	Language, Part II
Mathematics	.16–.52	Clerical	Number ability
Science	.24–.55	Clerical	Verbal reasoning
Social Studies and History	.21–.52	Clerical and mechanical reasoning	Verbal reasoning

Verbal Reasoning, Numerical Ability, and Abstract Reasoning measure functions associated with general intelligence and, it should be added, are most useful as measures of scholastic ability. For example, the authors of the DAT report that the sums of scores on Verbal Reasoning and Nu-

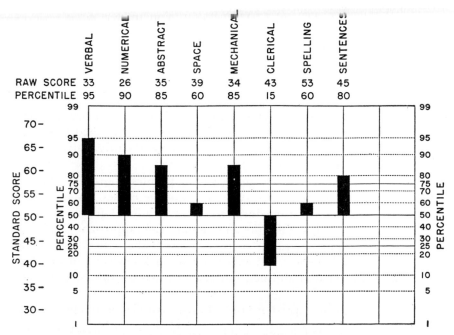

FIG. 17.4. Differential Aptitude Tests. A profile of scores. The Psychological Corporation, by permission.

merical Ability correlate with later schoolwork from .70 to .86. These are
high and speak well for the tests. Thus, although the more recent tests
are technically sounder than some of their predecessors, we find once again
that verbal, numerical, and other types of test items requiring abstract
reasoning, of the kinds long since in use in psychological testing, are prov-
ing to be most valuable in measuring general ability and educational
promise.

The manual of the DAT, unlike that of most other tests, provides data
on a follow-up study of 1700 individuals who were tested as high school
juniors and seniors. Later information obtained from them concerned
their educational and vocational careers since leaving high school, the
purpose being, again, to study the predictive value of the tests in the
battery. On the whole, the battery does not differentiate significantly
among individuals entering different types of higher education or different occupations, *except on the basis of general level of performance.*
Students in premedical, science, and engineering courses have the highest
average scores, with liberal arts students next in order. But there is considerable overlapping of scores among these groups and variation of
scores among the members of each group. Nor is there a clear pattern of
scores to characterize each of these groups. It is significant to note, also,
that the above-mentioned groups, and salesmen, beauty operators, reg-
istered nurses, stenographers, and secretaries, had higher average scores
in Space Relations and Mechanical Reasoning than did mechanics in the
electrical and building trades. This state of affairs is not necessarily attributable to defects in the tests, since many years of research and experience with psychological and educational tests have repeatedly yielded
the same general results, because human abilities are significantly interrelated, even if not uniform. Differences in curricular and occupational
preferences and performance must, in most cases, be attributed to special
sensory traits, motor skills, and nonintellectual personality traits, as well
as to differences in general mental ability.

There are individuals, of course, whose profiles show marked discrepancies. These discrepancies can have various causes. In using the
results of a multifactor test in educational and vocational guidance, therefore, the counselor must take the individual "case approach." This approach depends upon adequate comprehension of the battery's statistical
evidence and psychological rationale, and upon knowledge of development not only of mental abilities, but also of interests, values, and other
personality traits.[7]

FLANAGAN APTITUDE CLASSIFICATION TESTS.   An elaborate approach to

---

[7] The authors of the DAT provide, in this connection, a useful casebook. See reference 1.

multifactor testing is found in this battery (FACT, for short), intended primarily for vocational counseling and employee selection. Norms were established for grades 9 to 12. Flanagan lists twenty-one relatively independent "critical job elements" which, in different combinations, are said to contribute to success in different types of occupations. How are these job elements discerned? Flanagan states: "The first step . . . is to develop a comprehensive list of the critical behaviors involved in the job or jobs being studied. These critical behaviors are obtained by determining systematically which behaviors really make a difference with respect to on-the-job success and failure. The critical behaviors are then classified into job elements in terms of initial hypotheses regarding the precise nature of the aptitudes involved. The next step is to test the hypotheses that specific types of variation in job performance are correlated with variation on the related aptitude" (9, p. 2). "Each job element has been so defined as to be general in the sense that it is included in a number of occupations, but specific or relatively unique in the sense that it measures something different than the other job elements included in the list" (23, p. 67).

Paper-and-pencil tests have been prepared for nineteen of the twenty-one elements; the remaining two, "Carving" and "Tapping," are performance tests. These twenty-one elements and their corresponding tests constitute a rather heterogeneous assortment, involving quite different functions. Sensory, motor, memory, verbal, numerical, general vocabulary, and logical reasoning, and English usage, are among them. The following are several of the elements, with the rationale given by the test's author.

Inspection: measures ability to spot flaws or imperfections quickly and accurately in a series of drawings of objects. (A test of visual perception of detail.)

Assembly: measures ability to visualize how an object would look when a number of given parts are put together. (A test of three-dimensional space relationships.)

Judgment and Comprehension: measures ability to read with understanding and to use good judgment in practical situations. (A test of paragraph meaning.)

Ingenuity: measures creativity or inventiveness in devising ingenious procedures, equipment, or presentations. (A reasoning test, based on a stated problem.)

Alertness: measures ability to size up a situation and notice that a dangerous situation exists, or that some specific action is needed. (A test of perception of details in a picture and their interrelations.)

Other types of FACT tests are briefly as follows:

Coding: speed and accuracy in coding typical office information.

Memory: recall of codes learned in the coding test.

Precision: speed and accuracy in making small finger movements.

Scales: speed and accuracy in reading scales, graphs, and charts.

Coordination: ability to coordinate hand-and-arm movements.

Arithmetic: proficiency in the four fundamental processes.

Patterns: ability to reproduce simple pattern outlines.

Components: ability to identify important component parts in line drawings and blueprint sketches.

Tables: reading two types of tables: one using numbers, the other using words and letters of the alphabet.

Mechanics: ability to understand mechanical principles.

Expression: ability to communicate ideas in writing and talking.

Although each of the twenty-one tests is scored separately, the scores of various tests are combined to predict success in a variety of specific occupations, ranging from the professional to the farmer, policeman, and skilled worker. Since the separate tests represent such a diversity of functions and have been shown to be only weakly interrelated, the practice of combining their scores is seriously questioned.

As for the validity of the tests of this battery, it appears that their author employed construct validity, to begin with, although some psychologists would consider the initial step, in the quotation above, as being similar to face validity. Flanagan regards the job-element approach as a method intermediate between analysis into primary (or pure) factors, on the one hand, and the job-sample method, whereby the essential elements of the real job are simulated in the test, on the other. In addition, however, statistical data are provided on validity.

Since the elements are regarded as relatively independent, their intercorrelations should be low. In a ninth-grade group the range was from −.02 to +.57, with a median of +.20. In a twelfth-grade group the range was from −.03 to +.62, with a median of +.31. This aspect of internal validity, then, is reasonably well satisfied. Table 17.4 presents validity correlations found with schoolwork (concurrent validity). The data in this table are not such as to encourage the use of the individual tests for educational guidance of ninth-grade or twelfth-grade pupils. Although the combined scores of the nineteen parts of the battery yield quite significant multiple-correlation coefficients, the testing time required to obtain these scores is more than seven hours. The same results have been achieved with fewer tests requiring much less time.

After a five-year period, follow-up studies of college performance of students in a variety of fields of study, who were tested in high school (predictive validity), yielded correlations ranging from .04 to .65, with a median of .39. The lowest coefficient was for "clergyman, missionary, social worker," while the highest was for "social scientist" (which includes six vocations; for example, psychologist, lawyer, historian). In addition, a fairly large number of correlations are reported between individual tests and ratings in a number of occupations. Although there are occasional coefficients in the .50s and .60s, most are considerably lower; in some instances they are extremely low, approximating zero. In view of the correlations with achievement in school courses and of those with later educational and occupational ratings, the vocational-guidance counselor will have to exercise considerable caution in the interpretation and application of scores obtained with the tests of this battery.[8]

TABLE 17.4

VALIDITY CORRELATIONS OF THE FACT
(INDIVIDUAL TESTS)

Criteria	Median correlations	Range of correlations
9th grade English	.28	−.05–.48 (R = .63) *
9th grade social studies	.25	−.03–.41 (R = .58)
9th grade science	.27	.01–.42 (R = .60)
9th grade mathematics	.28	−.04–.45 (R = .62)
12th grade English	.34	−.02–.61 (R = .74)
12th grade social studies	.32	.03–.57 (R = .67)
12th grade science	.28	.03–.52 (R = .62)
12th grade mathematics	.31	.02–.52 (R = .61)

* R in each case is the multiple correlation of the entire set of nineteen tests with the criterion.

GENERAL APTITUDE TEST BATTERY. This battery (abbreviated GATB) was first published in 1947 by the U.S. Employment Service, to be used by counselors in the State Employment Services. It is based upon the assumption ". . . that a large variety of tests can be boiled down to several factors and that a large variety of occupations can also be clustered into groups according to similarities in the abilities required. This makes it feasible to test all of a person's vocational abilities in one sitting and to interpret his scores in terms of a wide range of occupations" (5, p. 22). The battery has twelve tests that yield nine "aptitude scores," and requires a little more than two hours to administer. These nine, which follow, were identified by factor analysis.

Intelligence (G): measured by the combined scores on three tests: three-dimensional space, vocabulary, and arithmetical reasoning.

[8] Guidance counselors and other advanced students of tests and testing should make a thorough study of the latest *Technical Report* of FACT.

Verbal Aptitude (*V*): the familiar test of synonyms and antonyms.

Numerical Aptitude (*N*): includes computation and arithmetical reasoning of the usual sort.

Spatial Perception (*S*): tests ability to visualize three-dimensional objects when they are presented in two dimensions.

Form Perception (*P*): tests ability to match drawings of tools in one part, and of geometric forms in another.

Clerical Perception (*Q*): requires the matching of names.

Motor Coordination (*K*): measures coordination by requiring individual to make specified pencil marks in a series of squares.

Finger Dexterity (*F*): tests proficiency in assembling and disassembling rivets and washers.

Manual Dexterity (*M*): measures hand dexterity by using both hands, and then the preferred hand, in placing pegs in a pegboard.

This battery is intended for use in counseling individuals who are looking for occupations or who want assistance in the choice of vocational training. An individual's scores on each of the nine separate parts are matched against the minimum scores (cut-off scores) found to be desirable for each group of occupations. On the basis of standardization statistics, Occupational Ability Patterns (OPA) were established. Each pattern consists of three "key aptitudes" required by a "family of similar occupations." One pattern, for example, consists of Intelligence (G), Numerical Ability (N), and Spatial Aptitude (S). Occupations covered by this pattern are those in "Laboratory Science Work and Engineering and Related Work." Basically, the inclusion of a particular "key aptitude" in any pattern and "family" of occupations depends primarily upon its correlation with performance in those occupations, using as criteria the commonly employed ratings on the job (for example, production records, earnings, work samples, supervisors' ratings).

Regarding validity, the results of a very large number of statistical studies are available (5). The findings are briefly summarized below.

Since the GATB is a set of factored tests, the nine "aptitudes" should show low intercorrelations. They do this fairly well, the coefficients ranging from .03 to .81 for several groups, while the medians were from .29 to .34. It is to be expected, of course, that high correlations were consistently found between G and each of V, N, and S, since the G tests are the same kind as those used in the other three (see above).

Tetrachoric correlations[9] were calculated between aptitude-pattern norms and a large number of job criteria. These coefficients are, on the whole, fairly high; but for many of the jobs listed, the number of cases is small; consequently the standard errors of the coefficients are often too large to permit definite conclusions to be reached.

[9] For this statistic, see Chapter 5. The use of this correlational method has been criticized as being less appropriate than others for the problem at hand.

GATB scores were correlated with grade averages for a fairly large number of college students in a variety of courses of study, using both concurrent and predictive validity. On the whole, these coefficients are poor. The highest obtained were, of course, with G; but even these were inferior to correlations found with other scales, specifically devised for prospective college students. The GATB, therefore, cannot be regarded as a satisfactory substitute for testing such students.

Quite aside from the vast amount of careful statistical analysis of data and its other technical aspects, merit and value of the GATB are found in the fact that they have been, and continue to be, validated against actual occupational criteria in a large number of specific jobs, each of which is placed in a "family" of occupations. Since the tests are intended to select persons for placement in groups of occupations, the parts, or factors, to be included in the battery must be relatively small in number, and each must provide a significant measure for a number of specific occupations. The data on this battery, now available, are sufficient to warrant its use in vocational counseling, provided the testing is followed by thorough interview, since some groupings of jobs include occupations that require abilities different from those tested by the battery, as well as requiring different nonintellectual traits of personality, which can prove to be important determinants of satisfaction or dissatisfaction, success or failure, in a given occupation.

OTHER REPRESENTATIVE BATTERIES. The batteries thus far described present a comprehensive view of the instruments in this category; and they are among those that have received widespread attention. There are also a number of others that, like those described, have been constructed on technically sound bases. However, there is no need to present their content, since the test materials are of the same psychological types, although there are some differences in the specific items and in scoring. Their criteria of validity and methods of estimating reliability are much the same as those used in the other batteries. The major differences seem to be the extent to which emphasis is placed upon "factorial purity" (factorial validity) and the extent to which claims are made for the differential validity of each battery. Some of the claims are moderate and warranted; others are excessive and unwarranted, on the basis of results found.

Among the batteries emphasizing "relatively unique" factors are the *Guilford-Zimmerman Aptitude Survey,* the *Holzinger-Crowder Uni-Factor Tests,* and the *Multiple Aptitude Tests* (by D. Segel and E. Raskin).[10] But the hope of devising tests that would measure distinct abilities, un-

---

[10] Students who are especially interested in multifactor batteries should study the manuals of these three, as well as of those discussed in the preceding pages, for their similarities and differences, and for their statistical details.

related to one another, has not been realized; for examination of intercorrelations of the several types of tests shows the coefficients are appreciable, particularly between the verbal, numerical, and reasoning factors. However, as the author of one of the multifactor batteries recog-

Test 8: Figure Changes

Directions. Study Sample V, the first row of figures on the page. First, look at the figures in columns 1 and 2. The figure in column 1 is a white square, and the figure in column 2 is a black square. Therefore, to change the figure in column 1 into the figure in column 2, you change the color—in this case—from white to black. Now look at the figure in column 3. It is a white circle. If you change its color in the same way, which of the three choices—a, b, or c—will it look like? It will look like "b," the black circle. Therefore, in Sample V, the answer space under "b" has been filled in. Sample V is at the bottom of the second column of your Answer Sheet, under the heading "Figure Changes Samples."

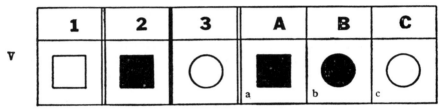

Now study the samples below.

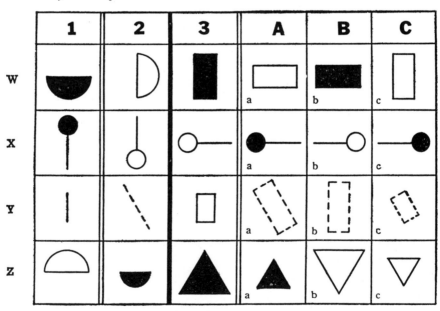

FIG. 17.5. Specimen items from the Holzinger-Crowder Tests. By permission.

nizes, this is to be expected, since individuals tend to be similar in the mental abilities being tested. This, of course, is the reason many other psychologists believe that educational potentiality and the general level of one's vocational expectancy are best measured and estimated by means of a test of general intelligence.

Evaluation

As always, in evaluating tests, we must know their reliabilities. Table 17.5 summarizes the data presented in the manuals. It will be noted

TABLE 17.5

MULTIFACTOR-TEST RELIABILITIES

Battery	Range of coefficients	Method
DAT		
Boys	.85–.93 *	Split-half †
Girls	.71–.92 *	Split-half
Boys: clerical speed and accuracy	.77–.93	Alternate forms
Girls: clerical speed and accuracy	.84–.91	Alternate forms
FACT		
Grade 9	.52–.86	Separately timed halves
Grade 12	.65–.86	Split-half
Grades 9 and 12	.83–.93	Split-half; combined "occupational scores"
GATB	.70–.95	Test-retest after an interval; and equivalent forms close together
Guilford-Zimmerman	.89–.96	Split-half
	.88–.92	Alternate forms
	.74–.94	Kuder-Richardson formula
Holzinger-Crowder	.76–.95	Alternate forms
	.88–.95	Split-half
MAT	.75–.94	Kuder-Richardson formula
PMA	.87–.96	Split-half
	.72–.90	Separately timed halves

* Mean coefficients for grades 8–12, excluding Clerical Speed and Accuracy. Coefficient of .71 is for Mechanical Reasoning. All others are .85 or higher.

† Corrected with Spearman-Brown formula. This is also true of other batteries in the table.

again that there is considerable range of subtest reliabilities within each battery. In some instances, the differences do not raise serious questions about the reliabilities of certain parts; in other instances they do. In all batteries, however, when the scores of two or more subtests are combined for purposes of guidance or selection, the reliability coefficients will rise.

It is clear that these batteries differ in conception from tests of general intelligence. The latter are devised to sample types of complex and varied mental activities essential in situations for which the tests are regarded as suitable. The former, on the other hand, aim to isolate specific and limited psychological operations regarded as or found to be necessary in certain courses of study or in specified types of occupations. Concern with "factorial purity" has led, in some instances, to the inclusion of relatively simple test items having limited value in the measurement of the complex mental operations necessary in learning and in some occupations. Perhaps to overcome this defect, in some of the multifactor batteries, scores are combined in various ways for different purposes. This practice seems to be a recognition of the fact that specific factors or aptitudes function in an organized form of more or less complexity, rather than in isolation.

It appears that, for employee selection in a given organization for specific jobs, specially built tests are superior to those standardized for general use. This is understandable, since these "custom-built" instruments can be made as specific or as general as each occupation may require. For vocational counseling of students and job seekers, however, tests standardized on a varied sample of individuals in relevant occupations and educational institutions are useful. It is for this purpose that some of the multifactor tests have been devised. The DAT, the Holzinger-Crowder, and the PMA, however, were constructed for the purpose of *educational* guidance and selection.

Since multifactor tests are intended to differentiate among individuals with respect to their educational or occupational fitness and promise, counselors should carefully examine the *differential validity* of a battery before using it. They will find that certain subtests are generally valuable predictors for a variety of purposes (for example, verbal ability, numerical reasoning, other forms of abstract reasoning), and others are generally poor predictors (for example, perceptual speed). In this connection, counselors should be aware of the fact that the manuals of some batteries place undue emphasis upon *average* differences of subtest scores among occupational or curricular groups (for example, law, medicine, engineering) while neglecting the considerable overlapping of scores between groups. Students of engineering or medicine, for example, have much in common, and therefore have similar multiple-factor test patterns; but there are also differences in both mental and nonintellectual traits that are not revealed by these data. As another example, consider the test patterns shown by the FACT battery for three professions. These are college teachers of the humanities, physicists, and psychologists, all three of which are said to require the same high level of median-percentile rank for the tests within each pattern. Included in the patterns of all three are only the two following "aptitudes": Judgment-Comprehension and Expression. For only the first of the three professional groups are Vocabulary and Memory included. Psychologists' and physicists' patterns have in common, in addition, Reasoning, Planning, and Ingenuity. Only the physicists' pattern includes Scales. It would seem that Vocabulary, Reasoning, Memory, Planning, perhaps even Ingenuity, would be essential in all scientific and scholarly occupations. The psychological reasons for the differences in patterns are not given; nor are they readily apparent. Furthermore, the marked correspondence between the test patterns of physicists and psychologists clearly indicates that much remains to be done, by way of counseling, after patterns have been determined and groups of occupations identified.

References

1. Bennett, G. K. et al. *Counseling from Profiles: A Casebook for the Differential Aptitude Tests.* New York: The Psychological Corporation, 1951.
2. Bennett, G. K. The DAT—a seven year follow-up. *Test Service Bulletin,* 1955, November, no. 49. New York: The Psychological Corporation.
3. Bennett, G. K., et al. *Differential Aptitude Tests: Manual.* New York: The Psychological Corporation, 1959.
4. Berdie, R. F. The differential aptitude tests as predictors in engineering training. *Journal of Educational Psychology,* 1951, *42,* 114–123.
5. Bureau of Employment Security. *General Aptitude Test Battery:* Section III, *Development: Guide.* Washington, D.C.: U.S. Department of Labor, 1958.
6. Burt, C. The differentiation of intellectual ability. *British Journal of Educational Psychology,* 1954, *24,* 76–90.
7. Dvorak, B. J. Advantages of the multiple cut-off method. *Personnel Psychology,* 1956, *9,* 45–47.
8. Dvorak, B. J. The general aptitude test battery. *The Personnel and Guidance Journal,* 1956, *35,* 145–152.
9. Flanagan, J. C. *Flanagan Aptitude Classification Tests: Technical Report.* Chicago: Science Research Associates, Inc., 1959.
10. Gaier, E. L., and M. C. Lee. Pattern-analysis: the configural approach to predictive measurement. *Psychological Bulletin,* 1953, *50,* 140–148.
11. Ghiselli, E. E. *Measurement of Occupational Aptitude.* Berkeley: University of California Press, 1955.

12. Green, R. F., *et al.* A factor-analytic study of reasoning abilities. *Psycho-metrika,* 1953, *18,* 135–160.
13. Guilford, J. P., and W. S. Zimmerman. *Guilford-Zimmerman Aptitude Survey: Manual.* Beverly Hills, Calif.: Sheridan Supply Co., 1956.
14. Holzinger, K. J., and N. A. Crowder. *Holzinger-Crowder Uni-Factor Tests: Manual.* New York: Harcourt, Brace & World, Inc., 1955.
15. Kettner, N., *et al.* A factor-analytic investigation of the factor called general reasoning. *Educational and Psychological Measurement,* 1956, *16,* 438–453.
16. Mapou, A. Development of general working population norms for the USES general aptitude test battery. *Journal of Applied Psychology,* 1955, *39,* 130–133.
17. Michael, W. B., *et al.* The description of spatial-visualization abilities. *Educational and Psychological Measurement,* 1957, *17,* 185–199.
18. Miles, R. W. Predicting success in industrial arts. *SRA Guidance Newsletter.* Chicago: Science Research Associates, Inc., 1957, October.
19. Rummel, J. F. A simplified method for determining the proportion of differences in excess of chance proportions used in differential prediction. *Educational and Psychological Measurement,* 1953, *13,* 145–149.
20. Samuelson, C. E. The general aptitude test battery in predicting success of vocational school students. *Journal of Educational Research,* 1956, *50,* 175–182.
21. Segel, D., and E. Raskin. *Multiple Aptitude Tests: Technical Report.* Monterey: California Test Bureau, 1959.
22. Super, D. E. The use of multifactor test batteries in guidance. *The Personnel and Guidance Journal,* 1956, *35,* 9–15.
23. Super, D. E. (ed.). *The Use of Multifactor Tests in Guidance.* Washington, D.C.: American Personnel and Guidance Association, 1958. (A Reprint Series from *The Personnel and Guidance Journal,* 1956–1957.)
24. Thurstone, L. L., and T. G. Thurstone. *SRA Primary Mental Abilities: Manual.* Chicago: Science Research Associates, Inc., 1958.
25. Vernon, P. E. *The Structure of Human Abilities.* London: Methuen & Co., Ltd., 1960 (rev. ed.).
26. Wellman, F. E. Differential prediction of high school achievement using single score and multiple factor tests of mental maturity. *The Personnel and Guidance Journal,* 1957, *35,* 512–517.
27. Wolking, W. D. Predicting academic achievement with the differential aptitude and the primary mental abilities tests. *Journal of Applied Psychology,* 1955, *39,* 115–118.

18.

APTITUDE TESTS

Definition

An aptitude is a combination of characteristics indicative of an individual's capacity to acquire (with training) some specific knowledge, skill, or set of organized responses, such as the ability to speak a language, to become a musician, to do mechanical work. An aptitude test, therefore, is one designed to measure a person's *potential ability in an activity of a specialized kind and within a restricted range.*

Aptitude tests are to be distinguished from those of general intelligence and from tests of skill or proficiency acquired *after* training or experience. They should be distinguished, too, from educational achievement tests, which are designed to measure an individual's quantity and quality of learning in a specified subject of study after a period of instruction.

The reader should note that aptitude is differentiated from skill and proficiency. *Skill* means the ability to perform a given act with ease and precision. *Proficiency* has much the same meaning, except that it is more comprehensive; for it includes not only skills in certain types of motor and manual activities, but also in other types of activities as shown by the extent of one's competence in language, bookkeeping, history, economics, mathematics. We may speak of one's degree of proficiency in any type of performance. On the other hand, when we speak of an individual's *aptitude* for a given type of activity, we mean the capacity to *acquire* proficiency under appropriate conditions; that is, his potentialities at present, as revealed by his performance on selected tests that have predictive value.

Furthermore, when we speak of a person's aptitude for a specified activity, we do not make any assumptions regarding the degree to which it depends upon innateness or acquisition. An aptitude test is given to an individual in order to obtain a measure of his promise or essential teachability in a given area. Although they make no assumptions regarding the roles of "nature versus nurture" in this matter, clinicians and guidance counselors cannot ignore a person's past experience in evaluating his performance on aptitude tests. For example, one method of measuring mechanical aptitude is by means of a mechanical assembly test, utilizing various common objects such as a bicycle bell and a door lock. It is inconceivable that a boy who in the past has had opportunity to manipulate such objects will not achieve a higher score than if he had not had such experience. Testing instruments measuring engineering aptitude include, for example, tests of simple mathematical relationships, scientific vocabulary, common scientific principles, and problems of practical mechanical insight. Here again, an individual's performance will be influenced by his previous experience. This aspect of aptitude testing and interpretation will become clearer as the reader becomes acquainted with the nature and content of aptitude tests.

The principles underlying aptitude tests are the same as those employed with tests of intelligence in respect to sampling of performance, population samples, and standardization techniques. Therefore, we shall not present the several aptitude tests in statistical detail. It will be our purpose, rather, to describe the kinds of activities or functions most commonly examined by available tests of this type.

Tests of Vision and Hearing

Quite aside from the obvious desirability of having good vision and hearing, there are numerous occupations and forms of learning for which one or both, at a high level, are essential; thus, they are aspects, or elements, of certain aptitudes. Sensory deficiencies, furthermore, can adversely affect an individual's achievements in schoolwork or in his social and emotional adjustment. In some instances, therefore, these deficiencies might be significant in clinical work and in vocational and educational guidance. The handicaps imposed upon pupils by defective hearing or defective vision are too obvious to be detailed.

As was indicated in Chapter 1, a large part of psychological experimentation in the nineteenth and early twentieth centuries was devoted to research on sensory acuity and discrimination. The purpose of these studies in almost all instances, it will be recalled, was not to reveal the extent and nature of individual differences, but to establish general principles and laws. Although interest in this type of experimentation has continued, there is today much more concern than heretofore with applied experimental research for military and industrial purposes, involving both sensory and motor aptitudes. This type of research is now called "industrial psychology" and "engineering psychology" or, in some instances "human-factor analysis." The purposes of these researches are (1) to learn which sensory and motor resources are necessary, and to what degree, for certain specified types of occupations; and (2) to adapt designs of equipment of all kinds—military, industrial, household—for their most effective and facile use by persons who operate or utilize them. To achieve these ends, knowledge of human sensory and motor abilities and their variations is essential.

At present, psychologists and educators are interested, also, in research in vision and hearing, insofar as these may provide information on the processes involved in learning to read, in working in the graphic arts, and in undertaking certain types of vocational education.

Tests of vision and hearing are used in the selection of industrial and military personnel, in order to select those having the necessary degree of visual or auditory acuity, or of color vision. They are useful, too, in eliminating those below the specified levels, in order to reduce job turnover, accidents, errors, and waste of materials, as well as in improving quality and quantity of production. Also, tests of vision, as well as those of motor skill, now have an important part in studies of automobile accidents and their prevention.

Tests of Visual Acuity. Several opthalmological instruments are available for large-scale testing of the following visual characteristics and for the detection of anomalies in them. These provide measures of near-acuity, far-acuity, depth perception (distance perception), and muscular balance. These instruments are being used by some industries as one job-screening device. They are used in some schools, also, for the detection of anomalies that can interfere with learning. Among the instruments are the Protometer (Freeman Technical Associates), the Ortho-Rater (Bausch and Lomb), the Sight-Screener (American Optical Co.), and the Telebinocular (Keystone View Co.). The Protometer, for example, is designed for rapid and comprehensive testing of vision where numerous individuals are involved. It provides data on monocular acuity, binocular acuity, and muscle balance, for both near- and distance-vision, under conditions of viewing and illumination maintained at a constant level. This instrument, in addition, detects cases of serious impairment of vision where the trouble is not with acuity but with the failure of both eyes to work in coordination. The results of the series of tests indicate either satisfactory vision or deficiencies requiring referral for professional examination.

Most persons have taken tests of visual acuity, the most familiar device being the crude Snellen chart. On this chart are printed rows of letters, varying in size, to be read by the subject. Each row and size has been standardized as recognizable at a specified distance by the "normal eye." Visual acuity is expressed as a fraction. The numerator is the distance the subject stands from the chart (usually twenty feet), and the denominator is the "distance value" of the smallest letter that can be read by the person being tested. Distance value of a given size is the distance at which a letter of that size can be read by the normal eye. Thus, if the smallest letter read by a person standing at a distance of twenty feet is read by the normal eye at forty feet, that person's vision (in that eye) is given as 20/40. The present Snellen chart, though still used, is a very inadequate test; for it will detect myopes (the near-sighted) but not the hyperopes (the "long-sighted" who can see distant objects with less muscle strain than near objects), or presbyopes (those whose eye accommodations are changing with advancing age), or those badly handicapped by muscle imbalance.

No one need labor the point that good vision is highly desirable. Hence, in schools and industry there should be screening by means of a dependable device to find those whose vision needs correction or whose color deficiencies must be given consideration in their education.

It is not unexpected that the data obtained by means of various testing devices have been factor analyzed (44). The factors inferred from the results are given as retinal resolution (ability to distinguish points in the visual field; an attribute of acuity), accommodation, depth perception, lateral and vertical muscle balance, convergence efficiency, brightness discrimination, and form perception. These characteristics of vision will not occasion surprise among persons familiar with physiological optics; for, as a matter of fact, they are the aspects of vision which the various tests and instruments were designed to measure.

Tests of Color Vision. All such tests depend upon the principle that color-deficient persons confuse certain groups of hues, *inter se,* while a person with normal color vision distinguishes among them. Thus, one set of charts is so devised that persons with unimpaired color vision should see certain bars, or arms, radiating from the centers of the circles. In one of the circles, for example, a person having unimpaired color vision will see two radiating arms, one green and one red. A red-blind eye will see only the green, a green-blind eye only the red, and the red-green blind eye will see neither. Another set of charts is so devised that one with normal color vision will see certain numerals, whereas the color-deficient will not. These are called "pseudoisochromatic" charts, or plates. The weakness of these tests lies in their requirement of a standard illuminant for testing—a condition which almost never exists. For example, in the Navy, during World War II, about 50 percent of all color-deficients remained undetected after one to five medical examinations, despite instructions to examiners to exercise great care with illumination.[1]

More recently, however, an illuminant-stable color-vision test has been made available (20), designed to overcome the errors produced by variations in illumination, color fading, and card soiling. This test will yield stable results under varying conditions of illumination. Two other fairly recent tests are designed to differentiate among the colorblind, the moderately color defective ("color-weak"), the normal, and the superior in color discrimination (12, 13). A differentiation finer than a twofold classification is desirable, since color-weak individuals can do satisfactory work when only gross discriminations are needed.[2]

Since examinations of men in the armed services have shown that almost 10 percent of all males are color-deficient in some degree, it is desirable to test all school children very early for this function. Deficients could be diverted, for example, from trying to become artists, geologists, clothes designers, etc. It is wise, also, to use a dependable color vision test in personnel divisions of department stores and of some industries; in the stores, to avoid placing color-deficient sales persons in the wrong departments; in industry, to avoid placing colorblind individuals on, for example, radio or other wiring that requires discrimination of a color code. For a job in which some color deficiency can be tolerated, the demands of the job in regard to color discrimination should be determined, as well as the candidate's degree of deficiency.

Auditory Tests. This function is measured by means of whispered words testing the hearing of consonants and vowels (for example, the Andrews Whispered Speech Test); or, preferably, by means of an audiometer. The first of these consists of numbers that are whispered at a specified distance. An individual's score is the percentage of numbers correctly heard, divided by the normal percentage. It is obvious that this type of test is unreliable because of the uncontrolled variables in the testing situation: for example, quality and intensity of the tester's voice, acoustical properties of the room, external sounds.

Audiometers, of which there are several types, provide much more accurate and reliable measures of acuity, for they are unaffected by any of the disadvantages mentioned above. The subject wears headphones that shut out external sounds, and each ear is tested individually. Some audiometers use pure tones as stimuli; others reproduce recorded num-

---

[1] An early and gross test of color vision was the Holmgren yarns. These require matching small skeins of assorted colors against large sample skeins of green, red, and rose.

[2] There are a number of other tests of visual acuity and of color vision, most of which do not provide adequate standardization and validating data.

bers, words, or sentences. In both types, the sound intensity of the stimulus is gradually decreased at small uniform intervals until the individual's minimum perceptible intensity is reached. The minimum level is
also checked by starting with a sound below the individual's threshold
and increasing it until he is just able to hear it. When pure tones are
the stimuli, different frequencies (number of cycles per second) are used
at each of the various intensity levels in order to test for differential
loss of hearing, if any exists. For example, a person's hearing may be
within the normal range in the lower frequencies but defective in the
higher.

In order to facilitate the testing of large numbers of school children,
group-testing equipment is available, using both speech and pure tones.
Of the two, the latter are superior since they test at different levels of
both frequency and intensity, whereas the former test only for intensity.

It is not necessary to dwell on the importance of hearing in school
learning (especially in reading and language) and in other forms of
activity; yet its significance is sometimes overlooked. It is customary,
therefore, in clinical cases of children and adolescents who present problems in learning, to check on the individual's hearing and vision, as a
matter of routine.

It is obvious that tests of vision and hearing do not measure a person's
aptitude for specific types of learning and activity. For certain kinds of
learning and activity, however, a given degree of visual or auditory
acuity is essential. In that sense, then, these devices may constitute a part
of a battery of tests used to measure a particular aptitude.

Motor and Manual Tests

STRENGH OF GRIP.   One of the oldest instruments for the measurement
of individual differences in the psychological laboratory is the hand
dynamometer for measuring *strength of grip*. The instrument consists
of an inner and an outer handle, a dial, and a pointer. The subject grips
these handles so that the second phalanges of the fingers press against
the inner handle, while the outer handle presses against the heel of the
hand. The subject then squeezes as hard as possible. Strength of grip is
measured in kilograms. After many experiments, it appears that in psychological work this instrument is useful principally as one device for determining degree of handedness and rate of fatigue. Since these two traits
are involved in certain activities and occupations, they are relevant to
some aspects of aptitude testing.

REACTION TIME.   This is the time interval between the onset of a
stimulus and the beginning of the person's overt intentional response.
The particular stimulus and response to it are prearranged in an experimental situation. For example, the subject may be instructed to tap

a telegraph key immediately upon perceiving a red light, the elapsed time between stimulus and response being electrically recorded in thousandths of a second. It is possible to devise a variety of tests, their particular character depending upon which sensory and motor functions are to be measured. This type of test obviously is intended to measure speed of response in situations demanding immediate reaction, as in certain machine operations and in driving an automobile.

MANUAL DEXTERITY. To achieve competence in activities requiring manual dexterity, speed of gross movements of hand and arm, manual rhythm and coordination, and finger control and coordination are necessary in varying degrees. For each of these purposes several tests have been devised, which vary in detail but are fundamentally alike. Gross movements of hand and arm may be measured in terms of the speed with which the subject picks up and places cylindrical blocks in holes in a board. Finger dexterity and coordination, necessary in rapid and accurate manipulation of objects, may be tested by measuring the rate at

FIG. 18.1. The plier dexterity test shown here is useful in evaluating skill in the use of small tools and, in general, in evaluating aptitudes involving finger dexterity. The tray contains metal pegs which must be placed in the small holes in a prescribed order. The score is based upon the time required to complete the task. Sometimes the time required to remove the pegs also is included in the score. (Acme Photo.)

which an individual, with fingers or tweezers, is able to pick up small metal pins or wooden pegs, of different shapes, and place them in the holes of a tray (see Fig. 18.1). Hand precision is measured by the accuracy with which a metal stylus can be placed into holes of small diameter cut in metal and electrically connected. Contacts of the stylus with rims of holes are electrically recorded and constitute the measure of inaccuracy. Occasionally, also, a paper-and-pencil test includes tasks designed to measure hand precision, such as speed and accuracy of tracing a path, speed of tapping, and placing a prescribed number of dots within a small circle (26).

Other tests of manual dexterity follow the same general form, but some are more complex. For example, the *Crawford Small Parts Dexterity Test* consists of a metal plate having two sets of thirty-six holes in each (six rows and six columns). One set of holes is threaded and the other is smooth. The testee uses forceps to place a pin in each smooth hole, then a collar over the pin. In the threaded holes, the testee places a small screw, then tightens it down with a screwdriver (Fig. 18.2). The stated purpose of this test is to measure a combination of perception and dexterity, in terms of rate of performance.

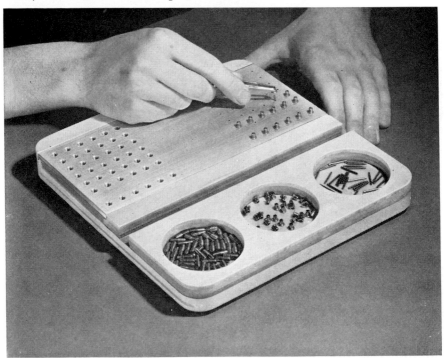

Fig. 18.2. Crawford Small Parts Dexterity Test. The Psychological Corporation, by permission.

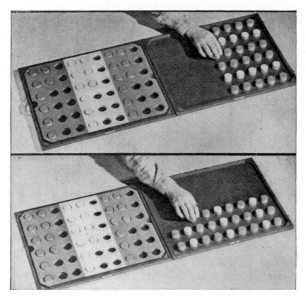

FIG. 18.3. The Stromberg Dexterity Test. The Psychological Corporation, by permission.

The Stromberg Dexterity Test also is a device whose purpose is more complex than the simple measurement of manual dexterity. It consists of a tricolored formboard (six rows and nine columns), into which flat, cylindrical disks, variously colored, are to be placed in a prescribed order (Fig. 18.3). It appears that this test involves not only manual dexterity, but also gross color perception and a rather elementary level of nonverbal classification. *The Minnesota Rate of Manipulation Test* is similar in conception.

Since manual dexterity scores on tests of this type are affected, in varying degrees, by the subject's lateral dominance (the preferred use and superior performance of one side of the body or the other), it is often desirable to use tests of eye-and-hand dominance. This procedure is particularly indicated if we are concerned primarily with analyzing and understanding the person being tested, rather than with making selections among candidates for a particular job (22).

The Purdue Pegboard measures gross movements of hands, fingers, and arms, as well as finger-tip dexterity required in small assembly jobs. It utilizes pins, collars, and washers that are to be assembled, using each hand separately, then both hands in coordination.

Although the stated purpose of the *Bennett Hand-Tool Dexterity Test* is to measure proficiency in the use of wrenches and screwdrivers, it is also a measure of manual and finger dexterity. The task is to take apart twelve fastenings, placed in an upright board, according to a prescribed sequence, and to reassemble the nuts, bolts, and washers, with the use of a screwdriver and several wrenches.

Coordination and rhythm of hand movements have been tested by a card-sorting test in which the subject drops playing cards through slots, using one hand at a time or both hands together. Another device is the two-hand coordination test in which the individual attempts to move both handles of a mechanism simultaneously in such a way as to keep an upper disk over the lower one, which moves in an unpredictable manner. Another two-handle device is employed in testing a subject's ability to follow an irregular path without touching the sides.

During World War II, numerous psychomotor tests were used by army and navy psychologists to assist in the selection of men for specific types of training, especially in the Air Force. These tests involved more difficult operations than those described above, often requiring rapid and complex sensory-motor coordination, such as the following: the use of both hands simultaneously in manipulating two lathe-type handles to follow a target that moves in an irregular path; obtaining patterns of lights by manipulating stick and rudder in a simulated airplane cockpit; reacting to four different relative positions of a red light and a green light by pushing one of four switches arranged in a square pattern before the subject; moving a wheel, resembling an airplane control, in and out of its shaft, in order to hold a horizontal bar in the center of a circular aperture; causing a beam of light to follow a given course when the horizontal movement is controlled by one lever and the vertical by another.

Evaluation.   Tests of sensory capacity and those of motor and manual dexterity have been moderately useful in selecting persons for specific types of training or for particular jobs. The functions and activities measured by these sensory and motor tests are practically unrelated, it appears, to the mental functions measured by tests of general ability; for the many correlational studies made between sensory and motor tests, on the one hand, and tests of intelligence, on the other, have yielded coefficients that are low, some being negligible. It has been concluded, therefore, that these two types of psychological instruments measure functions that are largely independent of one another.

Factor analyses of data obtained with tests of motor activity have produced results that are consistent with what would be expected by one who is familiar with these devices. The more significant factors appear to be the following.

Fine coordination: finely controlled motor adjustments, using large muscles.
Arm-hand steadiness: unspeeded, precise coordinated movements of arm and hand.
Manual dexterity: speeded arm-hand movements with large objects.

FIG. 18.4. The Discrimination Reaction Time Test.

This test was designed to measure how quickly individuals make differential manual responses to visual stimulus patterns differing from one another with respect to the spatial arrangement of their component parts. The test requires that the candidate react by pushing one of four toggle switches in response to the lighting of a red and a green signal lamp. The position of the red lamp with respect to the green determines which of the four switches should be pushed.

A front view of a single test unit, with designations of lights and switches, is shown in the figure. The four stimulus lamps, two red and two green (L1, L2, L3, L4), are arranged in the form of a square on the vertical panel facing the candidate. The stimulus to which the candidate must react by operating one of the four toggle switches is the simultaneous lighting of one of the red lights and one of the green lights. If he operates the correct switch, the white signal lamp (which lights on every trial) is extinguished immediately, signaling the candidate that he has made the correct response. The colored lights do not go out until they have been on for 3 seconds, regardless of how quickly the correct switch has been pushed.

The four spring-return toggle switches (S1, S2, S3, S4) are so set that the candidate must push each one in a different direction. The four directions of movement correspond to the four signal patterns formed by the lighting of the red and green lamps. Thus, if L1 and L4 are lighted, the red is "up" with respect to green, and the upper switch, S1, must be pushed up. If L3 and L4 are lighted, the red is to the right of the green, so the switch on the right, S2, must be pushed to the right. The time taken to operate the correct switch on each of a series of test trials is accumulated on an electric stop-clock and constitutes the candidate's score.

From *Apparatus Tests,* Report No. 4, Army Air Forces Aviation Psychology Program, edited by A. W. Melton. U.S. Government Printing Office, 1947.

FIG. 18.5. The Two-Hand Coordination Test.

The Two-Hand Coordination Test was designed to measure a candidate's ability to coordinate the movement of both hands. He is required to control the movements of a target-follower in response to a visually perceived target moving at varying rates along an irregular pathway.

A single test unit, as seen from the candidate's position, is shown in the figure. Two handles which he manipulates are seen in the foreground and at the left. Rotation of the upper handle causes a contact point, which is mounted on the leaf of a microswitch, to move toward the candidate with counterclockwise rotation and away from the candidate with clockwise rotation. Rotation of the lower handle in a counterclockwise and clockwise direction causes the contact point to move to the left and right, respectively. Rotation of both handles simultaneously causes the contact point to move in any desired direction in the plane of movement of the target. A candidate's task is to manipulate the controls in such a way as to keep the target-follower on top of a round brass button (the target) as it moves along an irregular clockwise path. When the contact point is on the target button, the microswitch is closed and current flows to an electric clock located on a remote control desk. The time which is accumulated on the clock during a series of eight 1-minute trials indicates the efficiency of the candidate's performance.

From *Apparatus Tests*, Report No. 4, Army Air Forces Aviation Psychology Program, edited by A. W. Melton. U.S. Government Printing Office, 1947.

Finger dexterity: digital manipulation of small objects; controlled finger movements.

Wrist-finger speed: measured by the well-known tapping test, using both large and small areas in which dots are placed.

Rate of arm movement: rate of gross arm movements.

Multilimb coordination: coordination of gross movements, using limbs in combination.

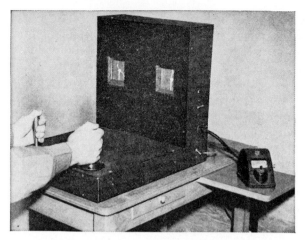

Fig. 18.6. Bi-Manual Planned Pursuit Test.

The Bi-Manual Planned Pursuit Test was designed and developed to measure ability to coordinate the activities of both hands by a systematic shifting of attention. The test consists of an irregular polished brass pathway which moves beneath two pointers. The pointers are separated by a distance of 8 inches. The pointers are adjustable by the candidate by means of two vertical handles, the candidate being required to keep the pointers (one with each hand) in contact with the moving pathway. In view of the fact that a limited amount of the pathway is visible prior to reaching the contact pointers, it was believed that a certain amount of planning could occur and would in part determine the score on the test. The test consists of six 1.5-minute trials. Rest periods of unspecified duration, probably about 30 seconds, occurred between trials. The score is the length of time during which both pointers are on the pathways.

From *Apparatus Tests*, Report No. 4, Army Air Forces Aviation Psychology Program, edited by A. W. Melton. U.S. Government Printing Office, 1947.

> *Rate control:* continuous motor adjustments to changes in speed and direction of a moving target.
> *Reaction time:* the well-known rate of response to a given stimulus.
> *Response orientation:* selection of the correct response under speeded conditions; a complex of sensory-motor behavior.

Although these derived factors do not add new aspects of, or insights into motor activity, they should contribute to the development of specific motor tests that could be applicable to various types of occupations. The predictive validity of new tests based upon this or similar analyses will have to be established.

Thus far, reliability data have not been as high as they should be, the coefficients being, for the most part, in the .70s and .80s. These low indexes result, in part, from practice effects. This fact suggests that the usual correlational methods of estimating reliability are not altogether appropriate with these operations. It would be more useful to evaluate initial scores on motor tests in terms of expectancy tables; that is, to answer these questions: "In certain kinds of individuals, how much improvement may be expected in these functions after specified amounts of training?" and "At what level can cut-off points of initial scores be set, below which an individual is a poor risk for training?" Answers to these questions will have a bearing upon both reliability and validity of the tests. The reason is that validities of motor tests found with criterion tasks have been shown to be most satisfactory in jobs requiring only routine assembly and machine operations; that is, the types of work in which there is little room for improvement with practice. Some of the more complex types of work, which require sensory-motor skills, also require a higher degree of mechanical comprehension and general mental ability; thus, they provide opportunity for improvement with training. For these occupations, sensory-motor tests, in themselves, are inadequate as predictors. Expectancy tables could indicate the minimum initial motor-test scores acceptable for occupations at the several levels in which sensory-motor skills are involved. It is probable, too, that the determination of such cut-off scores could be used in the guidance of high school pupils, as well as in screening applicants for jobs.

Tests of Mechanical Aptitude

The capacity designated by the term "mechanical aptitude" is not a single, unitary function. It is a combination of sensory and motor capacities, such as those already described, plus perception of spatial relations, the capacity to acquire information about mechanical matters, and the capacity to comprehend mechanical relationships. Thus, tests of mechanical aptitude are designed to measure capacity and performance on a higher level of organization than those of sensory-motor capacity and dexterity.

The *Assembly Test of General Mechanical Ability* devised by J. L. Stenquist (1923), the first of its kind and now of little more than historical interest, was intended to measure a person's ability to put together the parts of mechanical devices, among them a bicycle bell, a double-action hinge, a door lock, and a mousetrap. This test, consisting of three series, was constructed for use with individuals covering the age range from children in the lower grades through adulthood.

The Stenquist tests have been revised and extended at the University of Minnesota (1930) and are known as the *Minnesota Mechanical Assembly Test*. In principle, these are essentially the same as Stenquist's tests, some of the same mechanical devices having been retained, with new ones added. Performance on these tests—scored in terms of rate and accuracy of work—has been found useful in predicting success of junior high school boys in shop courses. Also, facility in these assembly tests has been found by some investigators to be one significant indication of a person's aptitude for a number of occupations such as machinist and auto mechanic.

The *Minnesota Spatial Relations Test* (1930) consists of a series of four boards, each of which has 58 cutouts of various shapes, many of them unusual. The subject's task is to replace these in their correct holes in the board. Evidence indicates that persons engaged in mechanical occupations tend, as a group, to earn higher scores than do persons in nonmechanical occupations. This fact, it appears, is a principal justification for use of the test as a measure of mechanical aptitude. Some critics

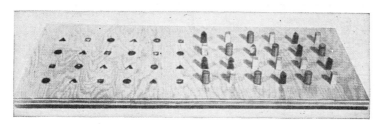

Fig. 18.7. Triform Pegboard Test. Reproduced from (31).

Fig. 18.8. Minnesota Spatial Relations Tests. The upper and lower parts represent the formboards that are filled with the pieces represented in the middle part. Educational Test Bureau, by permission.

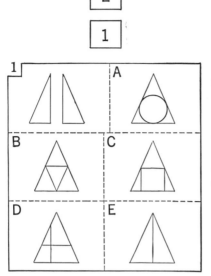

"First look at Problem 1. There are two parts in the upper left-hand corner. Now look at the five figures labelled A, B, C, D, E. You are to decide which figure shows how these parts can fit together. Let us first look at Figure A. You will notice that Figure A does *not* look like the parts in the upper left-hand would look when fitted together. Neither do Figures B, C, or D. Figure E *does* look like the parts in the upper left-hand corner would look when fitted together, so E is PRINTED in the square above ⌐1⌐ at the top of the page."

FIG. 18.9. Specimen item from the Revised Minnesota Paper Formboard Test. The Psychological Corporation, by permission.

of the test have concluded that it is adequate as a measure of speed and accuracy in responding to details of spatial relations and that it yields a measure of an individual's capacity to work with a variety of details in handling objects and concrete materials. On the other hand, it is not adequate for measuring resourcefulnes in solving problems of a mechanical nature, nor for measuring capacity to manipulate small objects with precision.

The *Revised Minnesota Paper Formboard* (1948) is, as its name indicates, a test that reproduces in printed form the same type of problems as those presented by actual formboards. In each problem, the subject is shown two or more parts of a geometric figure; when correctly assembled, the parts will make the complete figure. It is the subject's task to identify the correctly assembled figure from among five choices. This test is designed, it appears, to measure one's capacity to visualize and imaginally manipulate geometric forms. Reported research has shown this paper formboard test to have a moderately good correlation with quality of mechanical performance and a moderate-to-low correlation with success in mechanical drawing and descriptive geometry. Criteria included grades in engineering, technical, shop, and mechanical courses; supervisor's ratings; and production records. As a group, students in engineering and mechanical vocations obtain higher scores than do other groups of students. Available evidence, however, demonstrates that this test does not have high enough predictive value to be used exclusive of other criteria and information.

Several pencil-and-paper tests are intended to evaluate mechanical aptitude by testing for specific mechanical information, specialized vocabulary, and ability to perceive and deal with practical mechanical problems. It will have been noted that the paper formboard type of test and its variants are measures of spatial perception, a psychological function commonly included in multifactor batteries, discussed in Chapter 17.

The *Tests of Mechanical Comprehension* (Bennett *et al.*) present mechanical problems in pictorial form. In each instance, accompanying the picture is a statement of the problem depicted, with two or three answers from which to choose the correct one. These tests, on three levels of difficulty, are designed to measure one's understanding of the operations of physical and mechanical principles in relatively simple situations. One form is designed for use with high school students, engineering school applicants, and, in general, with relatively untrained and inexperienced persons. A second, and somewhat more difficult form, is intended for use with engineering school candidates and applicants for technical courses or employment in technical jobs. The third form was

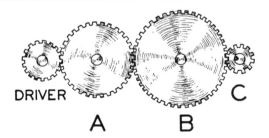

FIG. 18.10. "Which gear will make the most turns in a minute?" From the Bennett Test of Mechanical Comprehension. The Psychological Corporation, by permission.

devised for use with high school girls and women. Since the items should be appropriate to the level and experience of each group of examinees, many of those included in the test for women are related to household activities, involving objects and devices used in a home rather than in a shop.

Unlike some other tests of mechanical comprehension, this one does

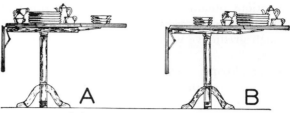

Which table is more likely to break?

Fig. 18.11. Specimen item from the Test of Mechanical
Comprehension by G. K. Bennett and D. F. Fry. The
Psychological Corporation, by permission.

not require specific knowledge, such as matching the parts of a tool;
nor does it require verbal knowledge of tools, processes, or materials. The
items show objects that are almost universal in American life, such as
airplanes, ladders, stairs, wheels, gears, and pulleys. The principle used
is that answers to the problems presented by the test do not depend upon
specific information or training but can be arrived at by analysis of the
materials shown. The extent to which this hypothesis is satisfied varies
among the sixty items. For example, familiarity with principles of physics
or actual experience will be helpful in answering questions involving
pulleys and leverage. Yet, individuals without these advantages, whose
analytical ability is adequate to the task, should be able to answer correctly.

From time to time, new tests have appeared in this area, but they have
not introduced new concepts or new techniques. The *Mellenbruch Mechanical Motivation Test,* for example, is a picture test requiring recognition of and information about certain objects commonly encountered
in our environment (for example, faucet, electric razor, towel rack, pulley
wheel). The task, actually, is to match pairs of objects that belong together. The assumption underlying this test is a very simple one: that
individuals with mechanical interest and capacity, more than others, will
observe the uses, parts, and relationships of these objects. "Mechanical
motivation" is thus inferred.

Another relative newcomer is the *SRA Mechanical Aptitudes Test.* Its
three subtests are devised to measure mechanical information (names
and uses of tools), form perception and spatial visualization (similar to
the Minnesota Paper Formboard), and solution of problems in shop
arithmetic (including use of tables and diagrams). These three subtests
were selected on the basis of face validity; for they are regarded by their
authors as significant in, and hence applicable to, a variety of mechanical
jobs.

The *Employee Aptitude Survey* (Ford *et al.*) utilizes the same types of subtests as the tests already described in this and the preceding chapters. Its tests of visual perception, however, include one of "visual pursuit," which is uncommon (see Fig. 18.12). The authors regard this as a significant measure of perceptual ability for such persons as draftsmen, design engineers, electronics technicians, ". . . and other personnel whose work requires the use of complex schematic diagrams."

Look at the example below. The problem is to follow each line through with your eyes from its number at the right to the box where it comes out on the left. The first three items have been marked to show you how. Line 1 has been drawn extra heavy so that you can trace it more easily. Trace lines 1, 2, and 3 for yourself, to make sure that the correct answers have been marked.

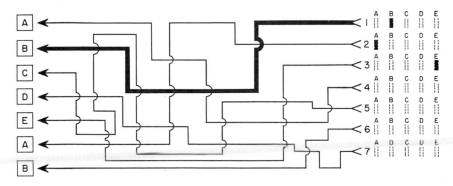

Fig. 18.12. Sample of visual pursuit item from Employee Aptitude Survey. By permission.

Evaluation. It is evident from the previous descriptions that mechanical aptitude should be regarded as a complex of several functions in the measurement of which some tests are limited to only one or two aspects, while others are more comprehensive.

On the whole, the tests of mechanical aptitude are statistically reliable, the correlation coefficients being, for the most part, in the .80s. As usual, of course, the indexes for some subtests are lower than for the tests as a whole. The modal interval of their validity coefficients, when reported, is .40–.50, but evidence of validity, in some instances, is quite inadequate. If we regard marks in high school shop courses, scores of occupational and educational groups (mechanic versus nonmechanic), and low correlations with tests of general intelligence as criteria, then we can say that some of the available tests in this field have a reasonable degree of validity for purposes of educational guidance. On the whole, by comparison with tests of intelligence, those of mechanical aptitude are inferior in respect to technical level of standardization and predictive value in actual performance.

The Wrightstone and O'Toole test may be cited for its relatively favorable statistical evidence. Its reliability is high, about .90. Intercorrelations of subtest scores range from .30 to .70, with a median of .55. Correlations of subtest scores with total scores vary from .52 to .77, with a median of .70. Evidence of validity is offered in two ways: in terms of face validity and of correlations with instructors' ratings in a training course for aviation mechanics. In the first instance, the test's authors state that their device measures the skills prescribed as necessary in eleven mechanical occupations. In the second instance, the coefficients of contingency [3] vary from .60 to .78, with a median of .67. These coefficients are among the highest in this area of investigation, and considerably higher than most others.

Numerous studies have been published in which tests of mechanical aptitude have been intercorrelated. The reported coefficients are almost uniformly low (below .50). A few of the reported coefficients are moderate; that is, somewhat above .50. The reasons for these relatively low coefficients—unlike those found between the sounder tests of intelligence —are to be sought in the following factors. (1) Some of the tests are much more comprehensive in scope than others that are relatively restricted and homogeneous in content; hence, the former measure a greater number of functions, some of which may have little communality with the latter. (2) Not all of these tests are calibrated for the same levels of difficulty; hence they do not have equal differentiating value at a given level. (3) Some of the tests are much more dependent upon experience and specialized information than are others. (4) Performance levels on several tests may reflect different degrees of interest and motivation in special areas.

In connection with (1), above, study of the content of tests of mechanical aptitude shows that they sample, more or less, the following functions: visual-motor integration, spatial visualization, perceptual speed, manual dexterity, and visual insights (analysis). In addition to these, some of the tests measure specialized information, knowledge of techniques, arithmetical problem-solving ability, and technical vocabulary. Some of the functions are measured by means of apparatus tests (Figs. 18.4, 18.5, 18.6), others by means of performance-type materials (formboards, etc.), and still others by means of pencil-and-paper tests. It is not surprising, therefore, that intercorrelations between these tests are low, even though they are placed within the same category.

---

[3] This coefficient is derived from data arranged in several categories rather than in intervals of scores of a variable.

On the whole, tests of mechanical aptitude show moderate correlations with actual job performance. This fact does not necessarily signify that the tests themselves are defective, for many nonmechanical factors affect both the job ratings and the actual performance on the job. These factors include subjective judgments of the raters, as well as the worker's health, motivation, and personality traits that may facilitate or impede performance.

Although the foregoing considerations lower the correlation coefficients, it is highly improbable that they are solely accountable for the findings. It is essential, therefore, that a given test of mechanical aptitude be studied for each type of occupation for which its use is being considered, in order to establish its validity, not only in terms of correlation coefficients but, more significantly, in terms of critical cut-off scores and of expectancy tables for each of several levels of test performance. As in the case of some multifactor batteries, too much emphasis is placed on correlation coefficients, while the overlapping of scores among criterion groups and the probabilities that could be shown in expectancy tables are neglected.

Some of the tests of mechanical aptitude are useful when vocational or educational guidance is the problem at hand, for they are valuable supplements to other kinds of information. For example, the several tests of mechanical comprehension are quite useful for selection in situations where understanding of machines is necessary. And it has been found, in fact, that this type of test material is one of the most satisfactory for selective and predictive purposes in this area.[4] In any case, in guidance work it would be desirable to administer more than one test of mechanical aptitude, since intercorrelations of the several instruments are not high enough to warrant their use interchangeably. The particular combination of tests used in any given situation should depend upon the nature of the problem presented by the individual concerned and upon the kinds of jobs under consideration.

Tests of Clerical Aptitude

Description. Clerical aptitude, like mechanical, is not a unitary function. The tests consist of several kinds of items, some of which correlate quite highly with scores on tests of general intelligence but differ from the latter in that they contain selected materials that are significant in clerical occupations.

---

[4] Since tests of mechanical comprehension involve visual analysis of, and insights into, nonverbal materials—facilitated by verbalization—they appear, also, to be testing general mental ability through the use of mechanical and scientific materials.

It will be recalled that two of the multifactor batteries (the DAT and the GATB, described in Chapter 17) include subtests intended specifically to measure clerical aptitude. In this chapter, several instruments, restricted to this aptitude, will be presented. All the clerical tests have

TABLE 18.1

SUBTESTS IN SIX TESTS OF CLERICAL APTITUDE

Test	Subtests
Detroit	handwriting: rate and quality checking: rate and accuracy simple arithmetic motor speed and accuracy knowledge of simple commercial terms disarranged pictures classification: rate and accuracy alphabetical filing
General Clerical	matching: detecting errors in names and numbers alphabetizing and filing arithmetic: simple calculations arithmetic: locating errors in addition arithmetical problems spelling reading comprehension word meaning language usage: grammar
Minnesota	number comparison name comparison
Purdue	spelling computation checking: speed word meaning copying: accuracy reasoning
Short Employment	numerical operations word meaning classification and filing
Turse	verbal skills number skills written directions checking: speed classification and sorting alphabetizing

much in common, both as to functions being measured and as to actual content. These facts are evident in Table 18.1. The principal differences are the scope and the detailed information provided by each test. The Detroit and the General Clerical are the most comprehensive; the Minnesota is the most restricted.

The more comprehensive instruments attempt to measure a variety of specific operations, whereas the Minnesota attempts to measure only perceptual speed and accuracy, which is only one aspect of clerical work. Restricting a clerical test thus rests upon the finding that these functions are basic to clerical work. But since the designation "clerical work" covers such a diversity of jobs, both in range and level of aptitude, it is desirable to use tests that include measures of other essential mental operations (and manual dexterity, if necessary) as well. Thus, as in the case of

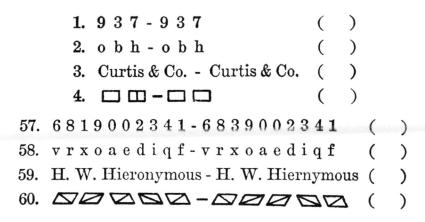

FIG. 18.13. Rate and accuracy in perceiving similarities and differences. From the Detroit Clerical Aptitudes Examination. Public School Publishing Company, by permission.

mechanical-aptitude tests, those of clerical aptitude should be validated against specific types of clerical occupations; and, indeed, it will be desirable, at times, to validate an instrument for use in individual companies.

Analysis of the subtests generally included in these devices yielded the following three factors: comprehension of verbal and numerical relations, perceptual analysis, and rate of making simple visual discriminations. In view of the content of current clerical aptitude tests (Table 18.1), the emergence of these factors should occasion no surprise.

Evaluation. On the whole, results obtained with clerical-aptitude tests, if critically interpreted, will contribute to a better understanding of a pupil's capacities and to his guidance in the selection of a high school course, although the tests correlate only moderately with marks in commercial courses (generally from about .30 to .50). But moderate correlations between test results and school marks are the rule rather than the exception, for the size of the coefficients is affected by several factors external to the tests: pupils' lack of interest or incentive in their courses; interference of nonintellectual factors, such as poor health, economic pressure, emotional forces, and extracurricular activities; and the variability of teachers' marks.

Although their *reliability* coefficients are generally within the satisfactory range, tests of clerical aptitude do not provide unequivocal evidence of their *general* value for the prediction of competence and quality of performance on the job itself. *Validity* correlations generally fall between .20 and .45. However, as so often happens even when validity correlations are low, the tests are useful in identifying those persons at the higher levels and those at the lower. Here again, cut-off scores and expectancy tables can be more revealing than correlation coefficients.

Authors of these tests provide, among other data, norms for a variety of groups—for example, high-school seniors in commercial courses, office workers, nonoffice workers, different classes of clerks, employed and unemployed office workers. Norms for each of these several groups indicate the expected average and range of scores in each instance. The range of scores within each of the groups, however, and the extent of overlapping of scores between any two groups are so considerable, and the validity correlations are low enough, so that in any individual case a detailed analysis of test results must be made, not in isolation but in conjunction with other information concerning the individual under study.

Not all available tests of clerical aptitude are of equal technical merit. The norms of some are inadequate as to numbers in or diversity of the standardization population, or both. Some present quite inadequate validation data. On the whole, tests of clerical aptitude have not reached the technical standards of tests of general intelligence. Prospective users, therefore, should carefully scrutinize the manual of any clerical aptitude test they contemplate using.

In view of the rapidly changing nature of clerical work in large organizations because of the introduction of machine calculators and other forms of automation, it will be necessary to reanalyze many types of clerical jobs and to revise existing tests accordingly, or probably to create new and different ones.[5]

[5] For a comprehensive list of tests of mechanical and clerical aptitudes see O. K. Buros (ed.). *The Fifth Mental Measurements Yearbook.* Highland Park, N.J.: The Gryphon Press, 1959.

References

1. Andrew, D. M., *et al. Minnesota Clerical Test*. New York: The Psychological Corporation, 1933–1959.
2. Bair, J. T. Factor analysis of clerical aptitude tests. *Journal of Applied Psychology*, 1951, *35*, 245–249.
3. Baker, H. J., *et al. Detroit General Aptitudes Examination*. Bloomington, Ill.: Public School Publishing Company, 1938–1954.
4. Barrett, R. S. The process of predicting job performance. *Personnel Psychology*, 1958, *11*, 39–57.
5. Bennett, G. K. *Hand-Tool Dexterity Test*. New York: The Psychological Corporation, 1946.
6. Bennett, G. K., and R. M. Cruikshank. *A Summary of Manual and Mechanical Ability Tests*. New York: The Psychological Corporation, 1942.
7. Bennett, G. K., and R. M. Cruikshank. *A Summary of Clerical Tests*. New York: The Psychological Corporation, 1949.
8. Bennett, G. K., and M. Gelink. *The Short Employment Test*. New York: The Psychological Corporation, 1951–1956.
9. Bennett, G. K., *et al. Test of Mechanical Comprehension*. New York: The Psychological Corporation, 1940–1954.
10. Crawford, J. E., and D. M. Crawford. *Small Parts Dexterity Test*. New York: The Psychological Corporation, 1946–1956.
11. Dorcus, R. M., and M. H. Jones. *Handbook of Employee Selection*. New York: McGraw-Hill Book Company, Inc., 1950.
12. Farnsworth, D. *The Farnsworth-Munsell 100 Hue Test for the Examination of Color Discrimination*. Baltimore: Munsell Color Co., 1942–1957.
13. Farnsworth, D. *The Farnsworth Dichotomous Test for Color Blindness*. New York: The Psychological Corporation, 1947.
14. Fleishman, E. A. Dimensional analysis of psychomotor abilities. *Journal of Experimental Psychology*, 1954, *48*, 437–454.
15. Fleishman, E. A. Psychomotor selection tests: research and application in the U.S. Air Force. *Personnel Psychology*, 1956, *9*, 449–468.
16. Fleishman, E. A. Factor structure in relation to task difficulty. *Educational and Psychological Measurement*, 1957, *17*, 522–532.
17. Fleishman, E. A. Dimensional analysis of movement reactions. *Journal of Experimental Psychology*, 1958, *55*, 438–453.
18. Ford, J. S., *et al. Employee Aptitude Survey*. Los Angeles: Psychological Services, Inc., 1956.
19. Freeman, E. An illuminant-stable color vision test. I. *Journal of the Optical Society of America*, 1948, *38*, 532–538; II. *Ibid.*, 971–976 (with M. A. Zaccaria).
20. Freeman, E. *The Illuminant-Stable Color Vision Test*, 2nd ed. Sarasota, Fla.: Freeman Technical Associates, 1954.

21. Ghiselli, E. E. *Measurement of Occupational Aptitude*. Berkeley: University of California Press, 1955.

22. Harris, A. J. *Tests of Lateral Dominance*. New York: The Psychological Corporation, 1947–1958.

23. Hirsh, I. J. *The Measurement of Hearing*. New York: McGraw-Hill Book Company, Inc., 1952.

24. Lawshe, C. H. *Purdue Clerical Adaptability Test*. West Lafayette, Ind.: Purdue University Bookstore, 1949–1956.

25. Likert, R., and W. H. Quasha. *Revised Minnesota Paper Form Board*. New York: The Psychological Corporation, 1941–1948.

26. MacQuarrie, T. W. *MacQuarrie Tests for Mechanical Ability*. Monterey, Calif.: California Test Bureau, 1925–1943.

27. Mayer, J. J., and M. A. Zaccaria. The evaluation of a color-naming test for color blindness. *Journal of Applied Psychology*, 1955, *39*, 160–163.

28. McCormick, E. J., and R. L. Brown. *Purdue Mechanical Performance Test*. Lafayette, Ind.: Lafayette Instrument Company, 1957.

29. Mellenbruch, P. L. *Mellenbruch Mechanical Motivation Test*. Chicago: Psychometric Affiliates, 1957.

30. Melton, A. W. The selection of pilots by means of psychomotor tests. *Journal of Aviation Psychology*, 1944, *15*, 116–123.

31. Melton, A. W. (ed.). *Apparatus Tests. Army Air Forces,* Aviation Psychology Program, Research Reports, no. 4. Washington, D.C.: Government Printing Office, 1947.

32. Paterson, D. G., *et al. Minnesota Mechanical Ability Tests*. Minneapolis: University of Minnesota Press, 1930.

33. Paterson, D. G., *et al. Minnesota Spatial Relations Test*. Minneapolis: Educational Test Bureau, 1930.

34. Psychological Corporation Staff. *General Clerical Test*. New York: The Psychological Corporation, 1944–1950.

35. Richardson, Bellows, Henry and Company. *SRA Clerical Aptitudes*. Chicago: Science Research Associates, Inc., 1947–1950.

36. Richardson, Bellows, Henry and Company. *SRA Mechanical Aptitudes*. Chicago: Science Research Associates, Inc., 1947–1950.

37. Robinson, H. M. Visual screening tests for schools. *Elementary School Journal*, 1953, *54*, 217–222.

38. Ryan, V. A critical study of visual screening. *American Journal of Optometry*, 1956, *33*, 227–257.

39. Staffs, Psychological Research Unit No. 2, and Department of Psychology, School of Aviation Medicine. Research program on psychomotor tests in the Army Air Forces. *Psychological Bulletin*, 1944, *41*, 307–321.

40. Stenquist, J. L. *The Assembly Test of General Mechanical Ability*. Chicago: C. H. Stoelting Company, 1923.

41. Stenquist, J. L. *Measurement of Mechanical Ability*. Columbia University, Teachers College Contributions to Education, 1923, no. 130.

42. Stromberg, E. L. *Stromberg Dexterity Test*. New York: The Psychological Corporation, 1947–1951.

43. Turse, P. L. *Turse Clerical Aptitudes Test*. New York: Harcourt, Brace & World, Inc., 1955.

44. U.S. Department of the Army. TAGO, Personnel Research Branch. *Studies in Visual Acuity*, P.R.S. Report no. 742, 1948.

45. Watson, L. A., and T. Tolan. *Hearing Tests and Hearing Instruments*. Baltimore: The Williams & Wilkins Company, 1949.

46. Wrightstone, J. W., and C. E. O'Toole. *Prognostic Test of Mechanical Abilities*. Monterey, Calif.: California Test Bureau, 1947.

47. Ziegler, W. A. *Minnesota Rate of Manipulation Test*. Minneapolis: Educational Test Bureau, 1946.

19.

APTITUDE TESTS: FINE ARTS AND PROFESSIONS

Aptitude in Music

Since scores on tests of general ability and grades in the usual school subjects are not well correlated with the specific psychological requirements in music or in the graphic arts, it is necessary to have special measures for them. In view of the current emphasis upon identifying elementary and secondary school pupils of superior intellectual promise for higher education in the sciences, mathematics, technologies and in the humanities, it would be desirable to have instruments to assist in identifying pupils of superior promise in the fine arts. A relatively small number of tests are available for assessing aptitudes in music and the graphic arts, but they are not so well developed as those of general intelligence or of educational achievement. Nor does there seem to be wide interest, among psychologists, in developing them. Perhaps two reasons for this state of affairs are the difficulties inherent in defining these aptitudes, and the highly subjective judgments in evaluating them and their products. The tests that are available, however, have made a contribution and can be of assistance.

The earliest tests in the field of music are the *Seashore Measures of Musical Talent,* intended for use from grade 4 through the college level. The six aspects of hearing, measured by means of phonograph recordings, are as follows:

458

Pitch discrimination: judging which of two tones is higher, graded from readily discernible differences to very fine ones.

Intensity or loudness discrimination: judging loudness of pairs of notes, with gradation differences.

Time discrimination: judging whether the duration of a note is longer or shorter than the duration of the same note sounded a second time.

Discrimination of timbre: judging whether two tones are the same or different in quality.

Judgment of rhythm: paired rhythmic patterns to be discerned as being the same or different.

Tonal memory: paired tonal patterns are played; ability to perceive the difference between the members of each pair is tested.

Total scores for the six parts are not used to represent an individual's rating; instead, a profile representing the scores on each of the six auditory aspects is prepared.

Seashore approached the development of his measures from a point of view different from that of authors of most other types of aptitude tests. Instead of making a "job analysis," in an attempt to discriminate levels of musical aptitude on an empirical basis, he made a theoretical analysis of musical talent into its sensory components. Thus, he employed the principles of content and construct validity. Some of the components, he held, can be measured objectively, whereas others cannot. The six capacities listed are among the measurable ones; but as Seashore indicated, they do not provide measures of all components of musical aptitude. The tests measure auditory aspects regarded by him and others as fundamental to the development of musical proficiency.

For the purpose of validation, results of the Seashore measures have been compared with teachers' ratings of musical ability, with musical achievement, and with quality of work in schools of music. The obtained correlations have indicated that these tests of auditory perception are not sufficiently valid in predicting various levels of musical talent. Seashore himself, however, has objected to attempts at an over-all validation of his measures. He maintains that each of the six tests should be separately validated against different kinds of specialized musical activity. For example, the test of pitch discrimination should be validated especially for players of string instruments.

This much at least may be said: the Seashore tests identify those persons whose auditory capacity is so deficient that they could not successfully engage in the formal study or performance of music.

The *Wing Standardized Tests of Musical Intelligence,* for the ages of 8 years onward, is intended, among other uses, to overcome a frequent objection to the Seashore tests: that the latter are "atomistic" and thus do not represent an actual musical experience. The Wing tests measure seven aspects of musical perceptiveness, yielding a score for each. Test performance is represented, however, by a single total score, since "musical intelligence" is regarded as a unitary, though complex, aptitude.

The seven aspects are chord analysis, pitch change, memory, rhythmic accent, harmony, intensity, phrasing. These are held to be more closely associated with the actual teaching of music than are the Seashore tests, since Wing's are standardized upon individually constructed types of tests employed by teachers and examiners in music. The Wing tests, therefore, are considered by many teachers of music to be more relevant to the selection and training of individuals in that art.

The *Drake Musical Aptitude Tests* measure two aspects: musical memory and rhythm. The first of these tests ability to remember two-bar melodies, and the second to maintain mentally and silently a metronomic beat. These, also, are intended for use with individuals of 8 years and older.

The *Aliferis Music Achievement Test* differs from those already described in that it has been devised for use with entering college-freshmen students of music. The functions tested are not unusual; they are "auditory-visual discrimination of melodic, harmonic, and rhythmic elements and idioms."

Evaluation.   The foregoing tests of aptitude in music are reasonably reliable measures *of the functions they include, when total scores are considered.* The *part-score* reliabilities (split-half) of the Seashore, however, vary from a low coefficient of approximately .60 to a satisfactory high of about .90. These data signify, of course, that the part scores often are not reliable enough to discriminate, except grossly, among the several sensory functions within an individual. The part scores, however, may still be valuable for identifying those having a high level of auditory perception and discrimination and those having a low level.

The Wing and the Aliferis tests, on the other hand, using total scores, report quite satisfactory reliability coefficients. For the first of these, the indexes (split-half and test-retest) vary from .85 to .95; while for the second, the reported coefficient is .88. The reliabilities of the Drake tests, each part taken separately, are in the .80s and .90s.

It is difficult to validate a test of musical aptitude against a criterion of achievement, because grades in music are fragmentary or nonexistent, grading is exceedingly subjective, training opportunities are markedly unequal, and interest and motivation are highly variable from person to person. Thus even after the years the Seashore tests have been in use, many psychologists believe their predictive value has not been sufficiently demonstrated. Available Seashore validity coefficients vary from low to moderate. Seashore himself, however, maintained that content and construct validity are most appropriate and adequate for tests such as his.

The Wing tests present stronger evidence of validity. With the first edition, in a study of above-average, average, and below-average students of musical instruments (ages 14–16; $N = 333$ boys), it was found that 40 percent of the lowest group had discontinued their musical studies, as compared with 27 percent of the average and 2 percent of the highest. A finer classification would have defined the failures more precisely. Teachers' ratings correlated .60 or above with scores on these tests. These validity data are very encouraging in this difficult area of testing.

The Aliferis and the Drake tests also stand up reasonably well in regard to validity; the total scores of the former correlate between .50 and .60 with grades in music courses. The manual of the Drake test reports a median coefficient of .59 when scores were correlated with "talent" as rated for performance and learning music.

On the whole, it appears that the sounder tests of musical aptitude are helpful in identifying individuals with poor prospects and those with high prospects for profiting from instruction in music, so far as these essential psychological functions are involved. In spite of differences in hypotheses and scoring, it appears from factorial analyses that the several testing devices are measuring the same or similar functions to a significant degree. It appears that there is a general factor operating in the several tests, accounting for 30 to 40 percent of the variance in scores. This general factor is identified as perception of a complex of the sensory aspects of musical aptitude. Since this appears to be the case, it would be desirable to measure these aspects by means of tests that demand complex perceptions, rather than by testing separate and isolated auditory perceptions. The former method of testing is indicated, especially because teachers of music and others in that field maintain that the separate sensory functions do not operate in learning and performing as they do in controlled and isolated laboratory situations. The atomistic test, however, can serve a useful purpose in the case of an individual who is found to be deficient in one or more of the complex functions, and whose deficiency is to be analyzed in more detail in order to learn what is lacking.[1]

Aptitude in the Graphic Arts

Testing aptitude in the graphic arts encounters much the same kinds of difficulties as testing in music, in regard to content and validity criteria. Several of the current tests will be described and evaluated for illustrative purposes.

[1] It is unfortunate that among contemporary psychologists, research on psychological problems in music—other problems, as well as those in testing—gets little attention or interest. In fact, the entire field of esthetics is rather neglected by psychologists.

The *Graves Design Judgment Test* is intended to measure the degree to which an individual ". . . perceives and responds to the basic principles of aesthetic order—unity, dominance, variety, balance, continuity, symmetry, proportion, and rhythm" (construct validity). This is done by presenting ninety pairs, or triads, of abstract designs in each of which one is organized in accordance with the eight principles listed above, whereas the other design or designs violate one or more of the principles. An individual's selection of preferred designs ". . . would prove to be a criterion of his esthetic perception and judgment" (Fig. 19.1). Representational art was not included because it is believed judgments of such

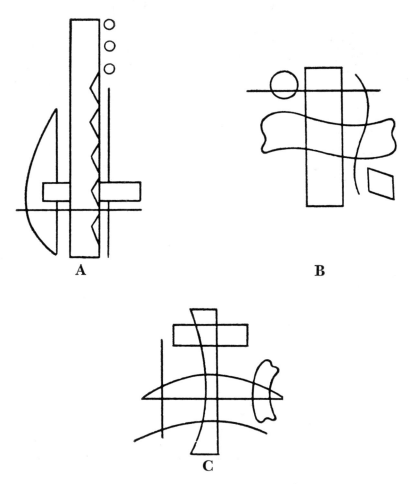

FIG. 19.1. From the Graves Design Judgment Test. The preferred design is to be selected. The Psychological Corporation, by permission.

pictures could be influenced by individual experiences, feelings, prejudices, and conceptions of art. Relatively pure esthetic choice is therefore emphasized.

The Graves test is devised to evaluate a unified, complex perceptual function, rather than to make separate analyses of elements that enter into esthetic judgment. In this respect, it is consistent with the Wing test in music, and with the principle of a general factor in intelligence testing.

The *Meier Art Judgment Test* is another device intended to measure esthetic judgment in a "global" manner. Unlike the Graves, however,

FIG. 19.2. One of these pictures represents an artistic work of established merit. The other is an adaptation of that work, and esthetically inferior. In this pair, the subject is required to select the original and esthetically superior work on the basis of the shapes of the bowls. From the Meier Art Judgment Test. Bureau of Educational Research and Service, State University of Iowa, by permission.

it consists of one hundred pairs of representational pictures in black and white. One member of each pair is a reproduction of a recognized masterpiece, while the second member has been altered from the original in an important aspect so as to make it inferior to the original. Testees are informed regarding which aspect has been altered (for example, shape, angles), but they are not told which is the original. Each individual is required to indicate his preference in each pair (Fig. 19.2). Meier maintains that esthetic judgment is the "key capacity," the most trustworthy and significant index to talent in art and to success in a career in art. The soundness of this view is seriously questioned, although few would deny that esthetic judgment is one of the principal capacities required for a career in art. If it were true that esthetic perception and judgment constitute the "key capacity," rather than the capacities to execute and create, we should then expect art critics and other writers on art to be talented in actual production. Such, of course, is not the case.

Two tests that require and evaluate samples of production in the graphic arts are the *Knauber Art Ability Test* and the *Horn Art Aptitude Inventory.* The first of these, for use in grades 7 to 16, sets the following tasks: drawing a design from memory; drawing, from memory, figures within space limitations; drawing a stereotyped character, such as Santa Claus; arranging a specified composition within a given space; creating and completing designs from supplied elements; spotting errors in drawn compositions, such as incorrect perspective, misplaced details, incorrectly proportioned details, incongruous or inconsistent elements; production of compositions intended to show creative imagination, ingenuity, ability to represent a concept symbolically, or to plan and execute a universal idea.

Measurements of these complex capacities represent a large undertaking for a single test. Performance on some parts, it appears, is dependent upon mastery of stereotypes and traditional problems and upon tasks presented in art instruction. This being the case, the Knauber test would be useful primarily in evaluating school progress in art, quality of observation, and, to some extent, creative imagination. That is, the test would be in large part a measure of learning rather than a measure whose primary usefulness is with individuals who have not had the benefits of some formal instruction.

The Horn inventory was devised for use with applicants for admission to schools of art.[2] It is a test primarily of creativeness, using a quite flexible and simple prescription, or guide, for each drawing. First, however, in Part I of the test, the examinee is required to sketch twenty familiar objects (circle, house, book, fork) within short time limits and on a quite small scale. He is required, also, to create simple abstract designs, starting with a given set of triangles, rectangles, etc. A much higher and more complex level of creativeness is required in Part II, "Imagery." The examinee is given a set of twelve rectangular cards; each one has several lines that must serve as the basis or beginnings of a picture to be drawn (Fig. 19.4). Drawings are judged essentially on the basis of creative imagination and technical quality (for example, order, clarity of thought, shading, quality of line). And in order to minimize

[2] There is no reason, however, why this test and others cannot be used with other individuals whose aptitude is to be assessed.

PROBLEM 3
This is a test of accuracy and observation.

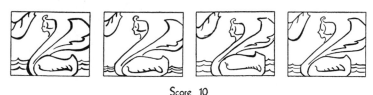

Score 10

These drawings are good in proportion and quality of line. Details are accurately observed.

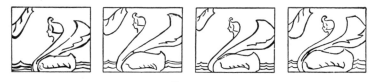

Score 6

The proportions in these drawings are not as good, and the lines are weaker.

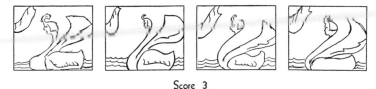

Score 3

These drawings are poor in proportion and in execution. They indicate a lack of careful observation.

FIG. 19.3. From the Knauber Art Ability Test. The subject is shown a design, in the examination booklet, which he is to copy. This item is a test of accuracy and quality of reproduction. By permission.

subjectivity of judgment in scoring, examples are provided of drawings rated as excellent, average, or poor.[3]

Evaluation. Once again, even in this highly subjective area of psychological testing, we find reliability coefficients varying from somewhat low to satisfactory and high, as shown in Table 19.1. In most of these reliability studies, the groups were relatively homogeneous. For example, in the Graves studies, for third-year students of "illustration" the coefficient was .81; for first-year engineering students it was .93.

[3] Other tests are listed in the references at the end of this chapter.

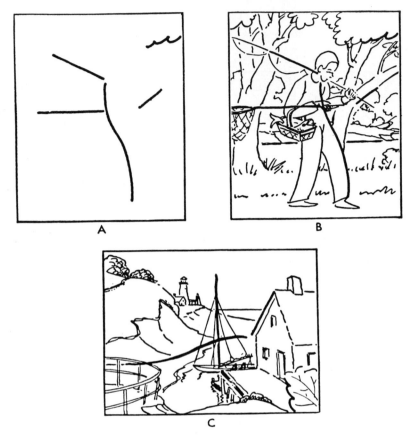

FIG. 19.4. From the Horn Art Aptitude Inventory. The person being tested is given card *A*. With the given lines as a beginning, he must make a completed drawing. *B* and *C* are completed samples. By permission.

TABLE 19.1

RELIABILITIES OF FOUR ART APTITUDE TESTS

Test	Correlations	Method
Graves	.81–.93	Split-half
Horn	.83–.86	Ratings of the same papers by two teachers of art
	.76	Alternate forms rated by two teachers of art
Knauber	.95	Split-half
Meier	.70–.84	Split-half

To evaluate validity, the authors of these devices followed familiar practices. Scores were expected to differentiate significantly among the several age and grade groups; art students and those who had had art education were expected to get significantly higher scores than others (for example, art faculty members *vs* nonart faculty; art students *vs* nonart students). The usual correlational validity studies were made, using small groups, and the results in Table 19.2 are representative.

TABLE 19.2

VALIDITY COEFFICIENTS OF TWO ART APTITUDE TESTS

Test	Coefficient	Criterion
Horn	.53	Mean rating in a 3-year art course
	.66	Grades in a high school senior art course
Meier	.40–.69	Grades in art courses and ratings on creativeness

Authors of tests in this area (for example, Graves and Knauber) used the principle of content validity in developing their instruments. Graves, for example, cites these three criteria in deciding whether or not to retain an item: (1) agreement among teachers of art as to the preferred design in a pair or triad; (2) greater preference of a design by art students than by nonart students; (3) greater preference for a design by high scorers on the whole test than by low scorers. (Percentage of agreement among teachers and degrees of differences in the latter two criteria are not stated in the manual.)

It is evident that the authors of tests of aptitudes in the graphic arts are not in complete agreement regarding the capacities to be measured, although there is some common ground. N. C. Meier, after years of study and experiment, identified six interrelated traits that characterize those having aptitude in the graphic arts, though not all are found in everyone with such aptitude. Meier's conclusions are based upon studies of high school and college students (39).

1. Manual skill.

2. Energy and perseveration. (This trait is much the same as the one that Francis Galton called "zeal," in characterizing the work of gifted men and women.)

3. Esthetic intelligence. This refers to the application of one's general intelligence to the field of art.

4. Perceptual facility. "The relative ease and effectiveness with which the

individual responds to and assimilates experience which has potential significance for present and future development in a work of art."

5. Creative imagination. "The ability to visualize vivid sense impressions effectively in the creation (organization) of a work havng some degree of aesthetic character."

6. Esthetic judgment. "Ability to recognize aesthetic quality in any relationship of elements within an organization."

The tests are of two general types: those that evaluate esthetic judgment and those that require the production of drawings. Since aptitude in esthetic judgment is not equivalent to aptitude in the production of art, a combination of both types should have greater predictive and selective value than either one alone for the purposes of education and guidance.

It is not surprising that tests in this category differ in content, for experts in the highly subjective field of art often disagree regarding the basic criteria or principles to be employed in the selection of superior designs or pictures; that is, they disagree on esthetic judgment. It is more than ordinarily difficult, therefore, to establish universal criteria for the selection and scoring of test items and for the validation of test scores, once the items have been selected.

Closely related to this problem is the inevitable result that different teachers and critics of art, employing varying criteria in their evaluations, will rate art productions differently. Consequently, there are relatively few data on the predictive efficiency (validity) of tests in the fine arts with regard to level and quality of performance in educational and vocational activities. Available tests are useful, however, when the criteria are specified, in identifying individuals of unusual capacity and in evaluating esthetic judgments in general.

As already stated, these tests distinguish quite consistently between art students and nonart students, as groups; the differences between their mean scores are significant, and the respective standard deviations of their scores indicate a significant difference in the location on the scale, or the limits, of their score distributions. For nonart students, the tests can be useful in evaluating capacities that are essential in esthetic appreciation, as a basis for nonvocational education in the fine arts.

Finally, the available tests of esthetic judgment assume, apparently, that this capacity is generalized and transferable from the evaluations of pictures and of relatively pure designs, to architecture, furniture, clothing, sculpture, and industrial products. This assumption may be warranted and actual demonstration of its validity would be of significance in school and college courses that offer instruction designed to cultivate esthetic judgment. Definitive research has yet to be done on this psychological and educational problem.[4]

[4] The graphic arts, like music, have been neglected by contemporary psychologists.

Aptitude in Medicine

Background. The first of the aptitude tests for medicine appeared in numerous revised editions over a period of about twenty years, under the direction of F. A. Moss, sponsored by the Committee on Aptitude Tests for Medical Students, Association of American Medical Colleges. It is interesting to note the functions tested by these, and later to compare them with the content of the instrument now current.

The earlier devices included the following subtests: visual memory, memory for subject-matter content, scientific vocabulary, understanding of printed material, scientific definitions, and logical reasoning. These subtests were based upon an analysis of aptitudes believed, by experts, to be necessary for the study of medicine; namely, content validity. The subtests were justified on the following basis. First, it is essential to have sufficient mental alertness to learn quickly and to organize the material learned, so that it can be retained and utilized in later work. A sampling of medical materials was used in the test to examine this capacity. Second, past scholastic performance may be expected to indicate future learning. Inasmuch as all premedical students have had elementary courses in chemistry, physics, biology, and English, sections of the test are devoted to questions in these subjects to determine the extent of the candidates' learning in them. Third, the capacity to make correct interpretations and deductions from given data was considered essential. Hence, the test included a passage of difficult reading, using medical subject matter. The testee is required to make certain interpretations and deductions based upon the passage, to which he may refer at any time. Fourth, since medical students and practicing physicians are expected to draw conclusions and make diagnoses from given facts, a subtest was devised to evaluate "logical reasoning." This consists of a set of premises and conclusions drawn from them, the student's task being to determine whether or not the conclusions are warranted.

In 1946, the committee, which Moss directed, was discharged; subsequently and for a number of years, the development of tests of medical aptitude was taken over by the Educational Testing Service. Currently, these tests are being administered and studied by staff members of The Psychological Corporation. Although in the more recent devices some of the materials differ in specific content from the committee's instruments, inspection of the items that follow will show that the psychological and educational premises are the same.

The reader has surely observed that the mental capacities measured by means of the foregoing types of test materials are not peculiar to the study of medicine. They are, indeed, capacities required in all fields of higher education and in all professions. These devices, therefore, though called aptitude tests, are actually tests of general mental capacity, *utilizing, in part, selected materials included in or closely associated with the materials studied in medical schools.* In other words, the *forms* of mental activity being tested are the same as in any other professional field, but the *content* is in part specialized. It is in this sense that these are "aptitude tests," as the term has been defined.

Medical College Admission Test. The purpose of this aptitude test was stated to be the provision of highly dependable measures of the advanced student's *general ability* and of his *achievement in a special field of study.* The tests are predicated upon the principle that a significant aspect of potentiality for a specialized field of study at the graduate and preprofessional level may be measured by testing the candidate's general scholastic ability and his achievement in a special field that is prerequisite to advanced study in the same or a closely related field.

In the addition, a test of "understanding modern society" (now called "general information") has been included in the battery. This part includes current history, economics, political science, and sociology, the purpose being to evaluate alertness to and interest in social issues, rather than materials retained from college courses in these fields of study.

The total test consists of four parts, described in the following terms:

Verbal ability: a test of vocabulary strength and ability to perceive verbal relationships; it is indicative of ability to handle postgraduate study.

Quantitative ability: a measure of ability to reason through and understand quantitative concepts and relationships; with verbal ability, it is indicative of general academic aptitude.

Understanding modern society (general information): a test broadly covering the subjects of history, economics, government, and sociology as they pertain to the contemporary scene; it measures social awareness; it does not presuppose specific college courses in these subjects.

Science: a test covering a wide sampling of concepts and problems taken from college courses in biology, chemistry, and physics.

The following are sample items.[5]

Verbal ability
Choose the word which is most nearly opposite in meaning to the word in capital letters:

SPORADIC: (*A*) immediate   (*B*) regular   (*C*) affiliated
(*D*) conflict   (*E*) replete

Each sentence below has one or more blank spaces indicating a word has been omitted. Choose the one word or set of words which, when inserted in the sentence, best fits with the meaning of the sentence as a whole.

[5] From the 1961 announcement of the test, issued by The Psychological Corporation.

The manufacturing of small machinery is profitable for the nation lacking mineral resources, inasmuch as _____ can be exploited in place of _____
(A) quantity . . . quality (B) power . . . efficiency (C) skills . . . quality (D) alloys . . . ores (E) skills . . . materials

Each question below consists of two words which have a certain relationship to each other followed by five lettered pairs of related words. Select the pair of words which are related to each other in the *same* way as the pair of words in capital letters.

ASHES : FIRE :: (A) extinction : life   (B) repentance : sin
(C) disaster : jealousy   (D) depression : prosperity
(E) relics : civilization

Quantitative ability
Solve each problem and then indicate the one correct answer.
If a motor launch goes 3r miles on 2t gallons of fuel, how many miles will it go on 6 rt gallons?

In questions 14 and 15 it is not necessary to solve the problems, but simply to show what information is needed to solve each of them. Read carefully each question and the two facts which follow it, then choose

   A if fact (1) alone is sufficient but fact (2) alone is not sufficient to answer the question,
   B if fact (2) alone is sufficient but fact (1) alone is not sufficient to answer the question,
   C if facts (1) and (2) together are sufficient to answer the question but neither fact alone is sufficient,
   D if either fact (1) alone or fact (2) alone is sufficient to answer the question.
   E if more information is needed to answer the question.
Be sure to decide on the *minimum* facts which are necessary to answer each question.

   14. Can line segments XZ, XY, and YZ form the sides of a triangle XYZ?
     (1) $XZ = YZ$
     (2) $XZ = \frac{3}{4} XY$
   15. Is X greater than Y?
     (1) $3X = 2k$, $4Y = 3k$, k is positive
     (2) $X + Y = 5$

Understanding modern society
Each of the following questions or incomplete statements is followed by five choices. Select the choice that best answers the question or completes the statement.

   16. Of the following, which is the best measure of public interest in a particular election?
     (A) The number of offices to be filled

(B) The size of the popular vote
(C) The amount of campaigning preceding the election
(D) The importance of the issues at stake
(E) The amount of money spent by the opposing parties for campaign purposes

17. In the majority of cases, the residential distribution of families in a city is governed chiefly by the
(A) length of residence in the city
(B) ability to pay for housing and transportation
(C) scale of values concerning the most desirable quarter of the city
(D) topographic features of the city
(E) location of hospitals and schools

Science

Each of the following incomplete statements is followed by five suggested completions. Select the one completion which is best in each case.

The nucleus of an atom consists of
(A) electrons and protons
(B) protons and neutrons
(C) electrons, protons, and neutrons
(D) electrons and neutrons
(E) protons only

Each of the following questions consists of an incomplete analogy with five suggested completions. Select the one word or phrase which best completes the analogy and indicate your selection in the appropriate space on the answer sheet.

26. ohm : resistance : : watt : _____
(A) electricity (B) work (C) power (D) current
(E) potential

27. atom : molecule : : element : _____
(A) electron (B) mixture (C) isomer (D) isotope
(E) compound

28. yolk : egg : : _____ : bean seed
(A) hypocotyl (B) epicotyl (C) cotyledon (D) testa
(E) endosperm

The following paired statements describe two entities which are to be compared in a quantitative sense. Choose
A if (A) is greater than (B)
B if (B) is greater than (A)
C if the two are equal or very nearly equal

29. (A) The total resistance of two given resistances in series
(B) The total resistance of the same two resistances in parallel

30. (A) The volume occupied by one gram-molecular weight of helium at standard conditions

(B) The volume occupied by one gram-molecular weight of oxygen at standard conditions

The passage below is followed by a series of statements. Read the passage and then classify each of the statements under one of the following categories:

(A) The statement is warranted by information given in the passage
(B) The statement is true but not warranted by the passage
(C) The statement is contradicted by the passage
(D) The statement is contradicted by established evidence but not by the passage.

From a nutritional standpoint, proteins are classified as complete and incomplete. A complete protein is one which contains all the eight amino acids essential for growth and maintenance; an incomplete protein is deficient in one or more of the essential amino acids. A person on a diet consisting mainly of incomplete proteins soon develops a negative nitrogen balance, loses weight, and experiences a lowered resistance, with impaired physiological processes. A vegetarian diet must be supplemented with milk, dairy products, or eggs to maintain a positive nitrogen balance in the human body. Most animal proteins, except gelatin, contain all the essential amino acids for normal growth and maintenance, but certain plant proteins are deficient in one or more of the essential amino acids.

32. A gram of protein when oxidized in the body tissues yields about 4 calories of heat energy.

33. Gelatin is deficient in one or more of the essential amino acids.

34. Incomplete amino acids contain no nitrogen.

35. A diet made up entirely of fruits and vegetables will supply all the amino acids necessary for growth.

Evaluation. The purpose of these tests is to provide an improved basis for predicting quality of performance in medical studies, not in medical practice. In some instances, the test scores have been better predictors than have premedical course grades; in other instances the reverse has been true. But in all cases, the best criterion is a combination of the two. For example, in one validating study, the following coefficients were found for a group of students who were not selected on the basis of test results as one criterion: premedical course grades with medical school averages, .67; test scores with medical school averages, .64; medical school averages with test scores and premedical grades combined (multiple correlation), .81. These are very satisfactory results. Other correlational studies yielded higher simple coefficients in some instances, but lower in others.

When medical students are selected on the basis of test scores as one criterion, however, it is to be expected that for them the correlations with grades (predictive validity) will be lower than those reported above, since the ranges of test scores and course grades have been narrowed. (See discussions of correlation in Chapters 2 and 5.) In such studies, the correlations have been .40 and below (6, 22). The low coefficients found for restricted groups do not necessarily invalidate the tests.

Variations in correlation coefficients between test scores and medical school grades, found in different studies, are not attributable solely to inadequacies of the medical aptitude tests. Differences among coefficients also reflect differences in medical school grading standards, inequalities of undergraduate preparation (which to some extent can be compensated for in medical school courses), and personality traits, which tend to produce inconsistencies between promise and performance. It would be highly desirable, also, to study the validity of these aptitude tests when the scores on General Information are omitted and those of the other three sections are combined. The reason is this: it appears that medical students and practicing physicians have little interest in general problems of human and social welfare, strange as that may seem (22).

Expectancy statistics have also provided useful findings regarding test scores. For example, one study reports that only 1 percent of the students in the highest decile group failed in medical school, whereas 18 percent of those in the lowest decile group failed. These findings provide an argument for admitting all top-decile students, but *not* for refusing admission to those in the lowest. Another study reported that the lowest decile group contributed 25 percent of the failures—that is, two and one half times its quota, in proportion to the total group of students.

Reliabilities of the verbal and science sections of the tests are approximately .90; for the quantitative section the reported coefficient is .82, and for that on modern society it is .84.

Although these aptitude tests are not intended to predict effectiveness in medical practice, which, like other professions, is dependent upon a complex of factors, the tests appear also to have some value in forecasting medical students' levels of success in internships. When a group of interns were rated on a five-point scale by their hospital staffs, the results showed that the tests have some selective value in identifying students who prove to be the most satisfactory interns.

With study in professional schools, including medicine, now within the prospects of large numbers of students, continued research leading to the development of increasingly effective testing instruments is essential. It would be desirable to have thorough studies made of such factors as effects of coaching and cramming upon the medical-aptitude test scores; relationships between test scores and ratings on interest inventories; relationship of test scores to drop-outs, in the form of expectancy tables (that is, value of the tests in predicting survival in the professional school; not in predicting grades alone); correlations between test scores and interview ratings; role of personality traits in medical school performance and survival (that is, degree of emotional stability, degree and type of motivation, introversion–extroversion, dominance–submission, kinds of strengths of values, and so on). Research on these and other personality traits would be difficult and time-consuming, but they could prove significant.

Aptitude in Law

Tests in this field are aptitude tests in the same sense as are those in the field of medicine. Psychologists and others concerned with the problem of testing aptitude for the study of law agree that the following abilities are most important: reading rapidly and comprehending relatively difficult material, memorizing and accurate recall, reasoning by analogy, discriminating between the relevant and the irrelevant in a mass of facts, reasoning inductively and deductively, and facility in acquiring and using a vocabulary. Legal aptitude tests thus far constructed attempt to measure most or all of these abilities in some degree. The device described in the following pages is the one currently required of all applicants by a large number of law schools in the United States.

Law School Admission Test. This instrument was introduced in 1948. The authors state the tests are designed to measure capacity to read, to understand, and to reason logically with a variety of verbal, quantitative, and symbolic materials; to measure knowledge of the mechanics of writing, ability to organize a piece of prose, ability to improve a badly written passage, and knowledge of basic information in the fields of humanities, sciences, and social studies. To measure these abilities, the following subtests are included.

Principles and cases: the examinee judges the relevance of stated principles to given cases.

Data interpretation: a measure of quantitative reasoning, including the use of tables, charts, and graphs.

Reading comprehension: passages with general content, followed by questions based on the content (stated or implied).

Reading comprehension and recall: this differs from the preceding subtest in that the questions are to be answered from recall of the content of the passage.

Writing ability: ability to recognize errors in written English, as in diction, verbosity, grammar; and ability to correct a poorly written brief passage ("interlinear exercise").

Organization of ideas: sets of statements, each of which is to be classified as a central, main supporting, or irrelevant idea, or as an illustrative fact.

Figure classification: a nonverbal perception and reasoning test, similar in principle to those used in nonverbal group tests of intelligence (see Chapter 15 and Fig. 19.5).

Directions. Each of these problems consists of two groups of figures, labeled 1 and 2. These are followed by five lettered answer figures. For each problem you are to decide what characteristic each *of the figures in group 1 has that* none *of the figures in group 2 has. Then select the lettered answer figure that has this characteristic.*

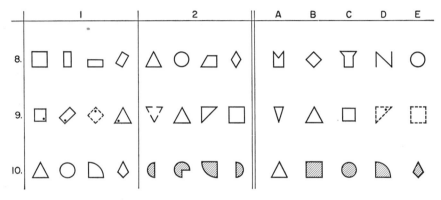

(In sample problem 8 you will note that all the figures in group 1 are rectangles but none of the figures in group 2 is a rectangle. In sample problem 9, all the figures in group 1 include a dot but none of the figures in group 2 includes a dot. The figures in group 1 sample problem 10 are all white figures, but none of the group 2 figures is white.)

FIG. 19.5. Sample of Figure Classification, from the Law School Admission Test. Educational Testing Service, by permission.

General background: multiple-choice questions in the fields of the humanities, physical and biological sciences, and social studies.

Evaluation. It is essential to note, first, that these tests are intended to predict quality of scholastic achievement in law schools; they do not claim to be useful in predicting performance or degree of success in the professional practice of law.

Reliability coefficients of the LSAT were high when the Kuder-Richardson formula was used; they were in the low .90s. The tests have been rather widely studied in regard to prediction of scholastic achievement. The two most valuable criteria for prediction are grades in pre-law courses and test scores. Some investigators have found the former yield higher correlations, and a few report that the latter do so. For either of these two criteria, in studies of earlier versions of the Law School Admission Test, the correlation coefficients with first-year marks in law schools were mainly between .40 and .60. However, when prelaw college grades and law-aptitude test scores were combined, coefficients of multiple correlation with law school grades were raised to the high .60s, and in some instances well into the .70s.

Subsequent studies, with later versions, have yielded much the same results (29, 33, 45, 59). The correlations obtained with first-year grades, over a period of ten years, were as follows:

Prelaw record: median coefficients for each of the four years ranged from the middle .30s to low .40s.

Test scores: median coefficients ranged from the high .30s to high .50s.

Median multiple correlation coefficients for the two criteria ranged from the high .40s to middle .60s.

Modal interval for prelaw record is the .30s.

Modal interval for test scores is the .40s.

Modal multiple-correlation interval is the .50s.

The use of expectancy tables provides additional evidence of the value of the LSAT. When the data for four law schools were combined, they showed that:

of those in *highest* 4 percent on test scores, 96 in 100 earned average or better than average first-year grades;

of those in the next 12 percent, 86 in 100 earned average or better than average grades;

of those in the *lowest* 4 percent on test scores, only 4 in 100 earned average or better than average first-year grades;

of those in the next 12 percent, only 14 in 100 achieved average or better than average grades.[6]

In spite of the fact that third-year students in law schools are a somewhat more selected group than first-year students, the test scores correlate just about as well with averages for the three years as they do with only first-year averages.

There are several reasons why the coefficients of predictive validity are not higher than those reported above. First, students admitted to most law schools are a group selected on the basis of prelaw college grades and admission-test scores. The result is restriction in range of scores on the

[6] Obviously, these data represent performance of the students ranking approximately one *SD* or more above the mean test score and those approximately one *SD* or more below the mean.

aptitude tests and of grades in law school courses. This situation, as explained in Chapters 4 and 5, lowers the coefficient.

A second factor is the disparity among academic and grading standards that prevails among colleges that provide prelaw education. Consequently, college grades do not offer a consistent basis for correlation with law school grades. A third factor contributing to lowered coefficients is variation in standards and in grading among the law schools themselves. These three considerations are adequate reasons for establishing *specific* rather than *general* validity. That is, validity should be determined for each law school individually with regard to prelaw grades and test scores.

Tests for the selection of students of law are sufficiently developed to warrant their use in conjunction with prelaw course grades. This conclusion is indicated by the validity coefficients found in some universities, by the quite significant multiple correlations with prelaw grades and test scores combined, and by the ability of the tests to identify a large percentage of candidates who have high promise and of those whose promise is low.[7]

Aptitude for Teaching

It is extremely difficult to devise tests for the selection of teachers because their preparation is not so clearly defined as in the case of law and medicine, since the contents of professional courses of the same name will differ considerably, and since teaching encompasses such a wide range of subject matter and educational levels. Of equal importance with general mental ability and competence in subject matter to be taught are the personality traits essential in successful teaching. As yet, no definitive psychological studies of those traits are available. From the descriptions that follow, it will appear that tests of aptitude for teaching should, strictly, be included in the chapter on tests of educational achievement and of proficiency. They are included here, however, because they deal with the selection of personnel for one of the professions.

The *National Teachers Examinations* are essentially subject-matter tests (including problems and applications) to evaluate the adequacy of preparation of candidates for teaching positions in elementary and secondary schools. The two major divisions are (1) common examinations and (2) optional examinations. The first includes sections on professional information, general information (social studies, literature, fine arts, science and mathematics), English expression, and nonverbal reasoning (similar

---

[7] The LSAT was preceded by several other law aptitude tests, for example, the Ferson-Stoddard Law Aptitude Examination (1927), the Iowa Legal Aptitude Test, by M. Adams *et al.* (1943–1948). See References at the end of this chapter.

to the nonverbal subtests in measures of general intelligence). The optional examinations include eleven tests in specialized fields of teaching, from among which the candidate elects one or more. These eleven fields include subject-matter specialties (for example, biology, music, English, mathematics) and general educational levels (for example, elementary school, early childhood education).[8]

Another set of tests, *Teacher Education Examination Program*, is much the same as the examinations in the NTE. Another device, the *Graduate Record Examinations Advanced Tests: Education*, however, serves a different purpose. It is intended to evaluate college graduates' qualifications for graduate work in education. For this purpose, the examination consists of 200 items that sample the several fields of professional study in the preparation of undergraduates for teaching (for example, educational philosophy and psychology, curriculum and methods).

Efforts are being made to devise tests that will provide information regarding the candidate's knowledge of and insights into nonintellectual aspects of the behavior of children and adolescents, the belief being that such knowledge and insights increase the probabilities of one's success in teaching. Noteworthy here is *The Case of Mickey Murphy: A Case Study Instrument in Evaluation* by W. R. Baller (5). This is an actual case record, in great detail, of a 14-year-old boy. Interspersed are 150 questions on interpretation of data, conclusions to be drawn, and formulation of plans.

Evaluation. In one very important respect, these tests differ from those in law and medicine. Whereas the last two are administered *before* professional education is begun, teaching aptitude tests are administered *during* or *after* professional education, to evaluate the professional knowledge and understanding the candidate has already acquired. Although the general and professional information and judgments being evaluated are essential to teaching success, authors of these tests recognize that knowledge of subject matter to be taught, understanding of teaching methods, a sound educational philosophy, and psychological information about human behavior do not necessarily indicate one's ability to apply these in actual teaching. Other aspects of the candidate's personality need evaluating if future classroom effectiveness is to be estimated. These include motives for teaching, emotional stability, social values, ability to communicate, ability to establish rapport, attitude toward and concept of one's self. These traits, admittedly, are difficult to assess and would require, at best, a procedure tantamount to clinical assessment or, at least, the use of a series of self-rating personality inventories. Probably the most feasible procedure is to use the tests described above to supple-

[8] An earlier device was the Coxe-Orleans *Prognosis Test of Teaching Ability* (10).

ment the "work sample" method; that is, practice teaching by the candidate, rated by an experienced critic on a soundly devised rating scale (see Chapter 21).

From the technical point of view of test construction, these examinations stand up well in regard to reliability (where reported), the correlations being .85 and higher. In the absence of predictive validity (performance in actual teaching), the criterion has been content validity; for the tests are based upon the judgments of professionally qualified individuals.

Although these examinations are not employed in a large percentage of American school systems in selecting teachers, their use is steadily increasing as the nature of their contribution, and of their limitations, is recognized.

Aptitudes in Science and Engineering

Aptitude in science is not a special talent in the same sense that musical aptitude, for example, is said to be. Scientific aptitude is the application of general intellectual capacity to scientific materials and problems. A test of scientific aptitude, therefore, should be regarded as a device intended to estimate probability of success in scientific and engineering occupations, without implying that it measures psychological functions that are essentially different in form from those required in other types of mental activity.

An early illustration of this type is the *Stanford Scientific Aptitude Test* (1930) which was intended for high school seniors and college students. Its author stated that the subtests evaluate experimental bent; clarity of definition; suspended *versus* snap judgment; reasoning; inconsistencies; fallacies; induction, deduction, and generalization; caution and thoroughness; discrimination of values in selecting and arranging experimental data; accuracy of interpretation; and accuracy of observation. At present, this test is only of historical interest, having been displaced by the Scholastic Aptitude Test and others of the same type (see Chapter 16).

The *Engineering and Physical Science Aptitude Test* (B. V. Moore *et al.*) consists of a group of previously developed and standardized tests. The six subtests are: mathematics (algebra), formulation of scientific relationships in algebraic terms, physical science information, arithmetical reasoning, scientific vocabulary, and comprehension of mechanical relationships and problems (presented in pictorial form). The authors present statistical details which show that their test has a reasonably high degree of validity when college grades in introductory engineering subjects are taken as criteria. The highest validity coefficients were found with grades in physics and chemistry, whereas the lowest were found with those in "manufacturing processes" and drafting. This fact suggests that the instrument tests aptitude in the scientific subjects more than in the applied engineering subjects of study.

Correlations with grade averages for each of the eight semesters ranged from .58 (first semester) to .26 (eighth semester), the decline in coefficients being steady from semester to semester, with one minor exception. To account for the decline from a coefficient of moderate magnitude to one that is very low, the usual influencing factors may be operative. These are increasingly homogeneous groups of students, reduction of individual differences resulting from earlier handicaps or advantages, increasing professional interest and motivation in students, unreliability of grading, etc. But here again is an instance in which expectancy tables would provide more information than correlation coefficients and probably would indicate that this aptitude test has greater predictive value than the correlations suggest (see Fig. 19.6).

The *Pre-Engineering Ability Test* (Educational Testing Service) has only two parts: comprehension of scientific materials and general mathematical ability. The first part requires reading and answering questions on scientific selections, tables, and graphs. The items in mathematics include arithmetic, algebra, and geometry (including analytic geometry). Although it is maintained by the authors of this test that specific factual knowledge is not needed for the comprehension items, there is no doubt that familiarity with some of the materials, vocabulary, problems, and concepts in the physical sciences is an advantage.

The *Minnesota Engineering Analogies Test* was constructed for use with candidates for jobs and for admission to graduate schools. As its name indicates, in form it is like the Miller Analogies Test. Emphasis, of course, is upon mathematical and scientific materials, the content having been selected largely from courses taken by all engineering students in their first two years of undergraduate study. Correlations with grades and faculty ratings in undergraduate and graduate courses varied from .40 to .60, while correlations with salaries and ratings on the job were in the neighborhood of .30. The latter coefficient is probably to be explained by the fact that this analogies test purports to measure only a limited though important aspect of the traits required in the successful practice of engineering, that is, logical reasoning with scientific and mathematical materials.

Another example of the measures in this field is the *Advanced Test in Engineering,* a Graduate Record Examination. This, also, is for use with candidates for admission to graduate study. Each GRE in a special field, such as engineering, is intended to measure what the candidate has

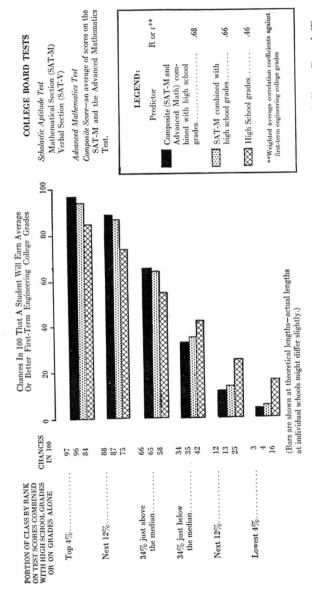

COLLEGE BOARD TESTS

Scholastic Aptitude Test
Mathematical Section (SAT-M)
Verbal Section (SAT-V)

Advanced Mathematics Test
Composite Score—an average of scores on the SAT-M and the Advanced Mathematics Test.

LEGEND:

Predictor	R or r**
■ Composite (SAT-M and Advanced Math) combined with high school grades.................	.68
▦ SAT-M combined with high school grades........	.66
▨ High School grades........	.46

**Weighted average correlation coefficients against first-term engineering college grades

Chances In 100 That A Student Will Earn Average Or Better First-Term Engineering College Grades

PORTION OF CLASS BY RANK ON TEST SCORES COMBINED WITH HIGH SCHOOL GRADES OR ON GRADES ALONE	CHANCES IN 100
Top 4%...............	97 / 96 / 84
Next 12%...............	88 / 87 / 75
34% just above the median...............	66 / 65 / 58
34% just below the median............	34 / 35 / 42
Next 12%...............	12 / 13 / 25
Lowest 4%.............	3 / 4 / 16

(Bars are shown at theoretical lengths—actual lengths at individual schools might differ slightly.)

Fig. 19.6. Prediction of scholastic success in a group of five engineering colleges by College Board Test scores combined with high school grades. Educational Testing Service, by permission. Data, courtesy of Dr. W. B. Schrader, for 721 enrolled engineering freshmen during their first week in the fall of 1948 at Carnegie Institute of Technology, Cornell University, Lehigh University, Rutgers University, and the University of Pennsylvania.

learned in his field (information, principles, problem solving). It is, thus, an educational-achievement test that is regarded as having value in estimating aptitude for graduate study.

Evaluation. The purposes of instruments in this field of testing are to measure the most important elements of aptitude significant in the guidance and selection of pre-engineering students and graduate students. Some of the current tests measure a fairly large variety of elements believed to be associated with success in the study of science and engineering. Others measure only a few. The tendency now is to reduce the number of subtests and to improve these, so that the smaller number have as much predictive value as the larger.

These aptitude tests correlate less well with term grades in engineering schools (usually .55 or lower) than they do with tests of general ability (.70 or higher). And the latter themselves have as high a predictive value in engineering as the former. The two types thus have much in common. Yet they are not perfectly correlated; nor will each type necessarily be as effective as the other in the case of any specific student. Better results, therefore, will be obtained if both types are administered, one to supplement the other, and if, in addition, the reasons are sought for significant discrepancies that might be found between the two scores of any candidate.[9]

The desirability of investigating *specific* institutional validity is indicated for these tests, just as in the case of law and medical school tests; for the complex problems of intellective and nonintellective behavior are encountered in all areas when psychologists deal with learning, schooling, motivation, standards, and so forth.

Results obtained with current tests of engineering and scientific aptitude can be most helpful when analyzed and interpreted by a qualified professional counselor or psychologist. It is not always the total score alone that is useful. A profile representing scores on subtests can be even more valuable; but it is necessary to go still further in the analysis of an individual's performance. That is, a detailed analysis of performance on each type of subtest and item may reveal an individual's strengths and weaknesses that can then be evaluated in an interview with the subject, in the light of other available educational and psychological information regarding him. Although numerical ratings obtained on some engineering and scientific aptitude tests will be of significance, greater value will be derived from them in counseling by a qualified person who interprets the

[9] Students should consult the discussions of multifactor scales (Chapter 17), especially with reference to their tests of space relations, mechanical reasoning, and quantitative reasoning ability. Also, consult Chapter 16 with reference to tests of general ability for high school seniors.

results in the light of his educational, psychological, and occupational insights. This is a subjective approach in part; but sole dependence should not be placed upon aptitude-test scores. Furthermore, every type of counseling and guidance involves a subjective element, insofar as the counselor interprets, collates, and draws conclusions—as he must.

Evaluation of Aptitude Tests

Differences among Tests. Various testing devices have been described, beginning with those that measure limited sensory perception and motor response, continuing to those that measure more complex and more varied functions as in mechanical and clerical performance, and culminating with those involving even more complex processes intended to predict capacity for learning the types of materials taught in the arts and in professional schools of medicine, law, engineering, and education.

It should be clear from the descriptions that the several types of instruments designated as "aptitude tests" satisfy the definition of the term in varying degrees. On the whole, those measuring the more limited and precise kinds of performance—sensory and motor—come closer to satisfying the definition than do those designed to measure the complex mental operations involved in learning the content of professional courses of study. These latter devices are aptitude tests largely in the sense that they employ a selected and specialized content, performance on which is intended to forecast scholastic achievement within a limited and specialized range of studies.

Reliability and Validity. Most current tests of aptitude have shown satisfactory reliability. Their validity, so far as performance on the job is concerned, has not always been adequately demonstrated, though there is appreciable variation among tests. Nevertheless, in each field discussed, validity of the sounder tests is high enough in predicting aptitude *to learn* to warrant their use in conjunction with other criteria. Some of the reasons for the difficulties in establishing higher validity coefficients have already been indicated in the course of the discussions.

The value attached to aptitude tests will depend upon the purpose for which they are being used. If they are to be used for the guidance of an *individual,* who is the primary concern of the counselor, then their degree of validity is a matter of primary importance; and it is essential that their results be supplemented with school records, intelligence-test performance, evidence of interests, and interviews.

If, on the other hand, an aptitude test is being used by a personnel manager whose primary concern is the filling of *a job*—and who is only incidentally concerned with individuals as such—though he will be interested in validity, he will evaluate a test in terms of the extent to which it enables him to select employees who have the best chances of succeeding on the job. That is to say, the personnel manager may want to identify, in a large group of persons, a smaller group who, *on the average,* will excel the larger group in the trait being tested. This procedure means that among those persons selected for employment some will fail, while among those rejected some would have succeeded. The purpose of such a procedure is to raise the percentage of successful selections. Admissions officers of colleges and professional schools can also employ the same principle if they are satisfied with a mechanical and impersonal procedure. For this purpose, tests of even relatively low validity (coefficients of .30 or .40) have some value when supplemented by expectancy tables.

In this connection, the "selection ratio" (SR) is often used (53). The term is defined as the ratio of the number of persons selected to the number tested. Thus, if 200 individuals were examined for a specified type of employment or for admission to a professional school, for example, and if only the highest 100 were to be selected, the ratio would be .50. Whenever there is a reliably established positive correlation between the test scores and the criterion of performance, any degree of selectivity will to some extent yield a group of persons whose promise is greater than that of the whole group, the degree of superiority depending upon the size of the test's validity coefficient. For example, assume we have an aptitude test that correlates .50 with the criterion (for example, level of performance in a professional school). Assume also that of the candidates for selection, only one half will be chosen. The SR, therefore, is .50. We might ask ourselves the following questions, among others. What are the probabilities that the scholastic performance of those in the selected group will place them in the upper half of the levels of performance of an unselected group? In the present instance the chances are 67 in 100.

Any validity coefficient of a test and any selection ratio may be used in combination to predict the probable *average* performance of a selected group at any level of success. Assume that only the upper 50 percent of an unselected group are to be chosen. What percent of those retained are likely to prove satisfactory if the validity coefficient is of a certain size? For example, if the coefficient is .20, the percent satisfactory will probably be 56; if the coefficient is .30, the percent is 60; if the coefficient is .40, the percent is 63; if the coefficient is .70, the percent is 75. Tables of relationships have been calculated for combinations of selection ratios ranging from .05 to .95 and coefficients of validity from .00 to 1.00. These tables provide a useful general index for estimating the probable value of a test of given validity in a given situation.

It is desirable to re-emphasize that this technique yields indexes applicable to groups, but it does not show what will necessarily happen in the case of a particular individual within that group. The utilization of the selection ratio does, however, add to the utility of aptitude tests when group trends and a minimum of elimination from a job or course of study are the first concerns. When the individual himself is the first concern—as he is to clinician and counselor—aptitude-test results should be used only as one source of information in a total picture.[10]

References

1. Adams, W. M., *et al. Iowa Legal Aptitude Test.* Iowa City: Bureau of Educational Research and Service, University of Iowa, 1948.
2. Adams, W. M. Prediction of scholastic success in colleges of law. *Educational and Psychological Measurement,* 1943, *3,* 291–305 and 1944, *4,* 13–19.
3. Adams, W. M., and D. B. Stuit. The predictive efficiency of the 1946 revision of the Iowa Legal Aptitude Test. *Educational and Psychological Measurement,* 1949, *9,* 23–29.
4. Aliferis, J. *Aliferis Music Achievement Test: College Entrance Level.* Minneapolis: University of Minnesota Press, 1954.
5. Baller, W. R. *The Case of Mickey Murphy: A Case Study Instrument in Evaluation* (3rd ed.). Lincoln: University of Nebraska Press, 1955.
6. Buckton, L., and J. E. Doppelt. Freshman tests as predictors of scores on graduate and professional school examinations. *Journal of Counseling Psychology,* 1955, *2,* 146–149.
7. Burnham, P. S., and A. B. Crawford. Law school prediction at mid-century. *Journal of Legal Education,* 1957, *10,* 201–207.
8. Buros, O. K. *The Fifth Mental Measurement Yearbook.* Highland Park, N.J.: The Gryphon Press, 1959.
9. Cook, W. W., *et al. Minnesota Teacher Attitude Inventory.* New York: The Psychological Corporation, 1951.
10. *Coxe-Orleans Prognosis Test of Teaching Ability.* New York: Harcourt, Brace & World, Inc., 1930.
11. Crawford, A. B., and T. J. Gorham. The Yale Legal Aptitude Test. *Yale Law Journal,* 1940, *49,* 1237–1249.
12. Douglass, H. R. *University of Minnesota Studies in Predicting Scholastic Achievement, Part II.* Minneapolis: University of Minnesota Press, 1942.
13. Drake, R. M. Four new tests of musical talent. *Journal of Applied Psychology,* 1933, *17,* 136–147.

[10] In this and the preceding chapter, aptitude tests of only a few occupations, including professions, have been described and evaluated. There are available, of course, tests for numerous other occupations in business, industry, and the professions; as for example, typewriting, selling, nursing, dentistry, pharmacy, veterinary medicine. Since the problems and technical procedures in devising aptitude tests are basically the same in all vocations, it is unnecessary to deal with all of them specifically. For a comprehensive listing of aptitude tests, see O. K. Buros (8).

14. Drake, R. M. The validity and reliability of tests of musical talent. *Journal of Applied Psychology*, 1933, *17*, 447–458.
15. Drake, R. M. *Drake Musical Aptitude Tests*. Chicago: Science Research Associates, Inc., 1957.
16. Dunnette, M. D. *Minnesota Engineering Analogies Test*. New York: The Psychological Corporation, 1955.
17. Farnsworth, P. R. An historical, critical and experimental study of the Seashore-Kwalwasser test battery. *Genetic Psychology Monographs*, 1931, *9*, no. 5.
18. Farnsworth, P. R. Rating scales for musical interests. *Journal of Psychology*, 1949, *28*, 245–253.
19. Farnsworth, P. R. *Musical Taste: Its Measurement and Cultural Nature*. Stanford, Calif.: Stanford University Press, 1950.
20. Farnsworth, P. R. *The Social Psychology of Music*. New York: The Dryden Press, Inc., 1958.
21. *Ferson and Stoddard Law Aptitude Examination*. St. Paul, Minn.: West Publishing Company, 1927.
22. Gee, H. H., and J. T. Cowles (eds.). *The Appraisal of Applicants for Medical Schools*. Evanston, Ill.: Association of American Medical Colleges, 1957.
23. *Graduate Record Examinations Scores for Basic Reference Groups*. Princeton, N.J.: Educational Testing Service, 1960.
24. Graves, M. *Graves Design Judgment Test*. New York: The Psychological Corporation, 1948.
25. Graves, M. *The Art of Color and Design* (2nd ed.). New York: McGraw-Hill Book Company, Inc., 1951.
26. Guilford, J. P. Creative ability in the arts. *Psychological Review*, 1957, *64*, 110–118.
27. Holmes, J. A. Increased reliabilities, new keys and norms for a modified Kwalwasser-Dykema Test of Musical Aptitude. *Journal of Genetic Psychology*, 1954, *85*, 65–73.
28. Horn, C. C. *Horn Art Aptitude Inventory*. Chicago: C. H. Stoelting Company, 1953.
29. Johnson, A. P., et al. *The Law School Admission Test*. Princeton, N.J.: Educational Testing Service, 1959.
30. Kandel, I. L. *Professional Aptitude Tests in Medicine, Law, and Engineering*. New York: Teachers College, Columbia University, 1940.
31. Knauber, A. J. *Knauber Art Ability Test*. Chicago: C. H. Stoelting Company, 1932–1935.
32. Kwalwasser, J., and P. W. Dykema. *Kwalwasser-Dykema Music Tests*. New York: Carl Fischer, Inc., 1930.
33. *Law School Admission Test: Summary of Validity Studies*. Princeton, N.J.: Educational Testing Service, June 1961.
34. Lundin, R. W. *An Objective Psychology of Music*. New York: The Ronald Press Company, 1953.
35. Madison, T. Interval discrimination as a measure of musical talent. *Archives of Psychology*, 1942, no. 268.

36. McAdory, M. *The McAdory Art Test.* New York: Teachers College, Columbia University, Bureau of Publications, 1929–1933.

37. McLeish, J. The validation of Seashore's Measures of Musical Talent by factorial methods. *British Journal of Psychology, Statistical Section,* 1950, *3,* 129–140.

38. *Medical College Admissions Test.* New York: The Psychological Corporation, 1946–1961.

39. Meier, N. C. Studies in the psychology of art. *Psychological Monographs,* 1939, *51,* no. 231.

40. Meier, N. C. *The Meier Art Tests. 1. Art Judgment.* Iowa City: Bureau of Educational Research and Service, University of Iowa, 1940–1942.

41. Meier, N. C., and C. E. Seashore. *The Meier-Seashore Art Judgment Test.* Iowa City: Bureau of Educational Research and Service, University of Iowa, 1929.

42. Moore, B. V., *et al. Engineering and Physical Science Aptitude Test.* New York: The Psychological Corporation, 1943–1951.

43. Moss, F. A. Report of the Committee on Aptitude Tests for Medical Schools. *Journal of the Association of American Medical Colleges,* 1942, *17,* 312–315.

44. Mursell, J. L. *The Psychology of Music.* New York: W. W. Norton & Company, Inc., 1937.

45. Pitcher, B., and M. Olsen. *The Law School Admission Test as a Predictor of First-Year Law School Grades.* Princeton, N.J.: Educational Testing Service, 1959.

46. Saetveit, J. C., *et al. Revision of the Seashore Measure of Musical Talent.* Iowa City: Bureau of Educational Research and Service, University of Iowa, 1940.

47. Seashore, C. E. *Psychology of Music.* New York: McGraw-Hill Book Company, Inc., 1938.

48. Seashore, C. E., *et al. Seashore Measures of Musical Talents.* New York: The Psychological Corporation, 1939–1956.

49. Siceloff, M. M., *et al. Validation and Standardization of the McAdory Art Tests.* New York: Teachers College, Columbia University, Bureau of Publications, 1933.

50. Smith, M. Cautions concerning the use of the Taylor-Russell tables in employee selection. *Journal of Applied Psychology,* 1948, *32,* 595–600.

51. Stanton, H. M. *Measurement of Musical Talent.* Iowa City: Bureau of Educational Research and Service, University of Iowa, 1935.

52. Stuit, D. B., *et al. Predicting Success in Professional Schools.* Washington: American Council on Education, 1949.

53. Taylor, H. C., and J. T. Russell. The relationship of validity coefficients to the practical effectiveness of tests in selection: discussions and tables. *Journal of Applied Psychology,* 1939, *23,* 565–578.

54. Tiebout, C., and N. C. Meier. Studies in the psychology of art: artistic ability and general intelligence. *Psychological Monographs,* 1936, *48,* no. 213.

55. Webb, S. C. The prediction of achievement for first-year dental students. *Educational and Psychological Measurement,* 1956, *16,* 543–548.
56. Whittington, R. W. T. The assessment of potential musical ability in secondary school children. *Journal of Educational Psychology,* 1957, *48,* 1–10.
57. Wing, H. D. A factorial study of musical tests. *British Journal of Psychology,* 1941, *31,* 341–355.
58. Wing, H. D. *Wing Standardized Tests of Musical Intelligence* (rev. ed.). London: National Foundation for Educational Research, 1958.
59. Winterbottom, J. A., and A. P. Johnson. *The Law School Admission Test: 1948–1958.* Princeton, N.J.: Educational Testing Service, 1958.
60. Zyve, D. L. *Stanford Scientific Aptitude Test.* Stanford, Calif.: Stanford University Press, 1930.

20.

TESTS OF EDUCATIONAL ACHIEVEMENT

Nature and Scope

A test of educational achievement is one designed to measure knowledge, understanding, or skills in a specified subject or group of subjects. The test might be restricted to a single subject, such as arithmetic matter, yielding a separate score for each subject and a total score for the several subjects combined.

Tests of educational achievement differ from those of intelligence in that (1) the former are concerned with the quantity and quality of learning attained in a subject of study, or group of subjects, after a period of instruction and (2) the latter are general in scope and are intended for the measurement and analysis of psychological *processes,* although they must of necessity employ some acquired content that resembles the content found in achievement tests.

Most educational achievement tests are devoted largely to the measurement of the amount of information acquired or the skills and techniques developed. In recent years, however, an increasing number have been devised to measure such educational results as attitudes and appreciations, ability to solve problems, to draw inferences from subject matter, to apply generalizations to specific situations and problems.

Emphasis upon these more recent types of test materials is clearly illustrated in a publication in which educational objectives are analyzed in detail (3). The authors offer six major classes of objectives. These are knowledge, comprehension, application, analysis, synthesis, and evaluation. Each of these is analyzed into several aspects. For example, knowledge is divided into knowledge of specifics, ways and means of dealing with specifics, universals and abstractions in a field. These, in turn, are broken down further into knowledge of:

      specific information
      terminology
      ways and means of presenting ideas and phenomena
      trends and sequences
      classification and categories
      criteria
      methodology
      major ideas
      principles and generalizations
      theories and structures

Comprehension is divided into three aspects: translation (ability to paraphrase), interpretation, and extrapolation. Analysis is regarded as being of three types: analysis of elements, relationships, and organizational principles. Comparable aspects are given for the other major objectives.[1]

It is apparent that several of these objectives and their divisions engage the higher, more complex mental processes, going beyond only the acquisition and retention of information; although it is also clear that specifics are essential.

Currently, also, emphasis is being placed upon tests that measure educational achievement in broad areas, such as the social studies, natural sciences, and humanities, rather than in the specific and restricted divisions of each of these. The trend is particularly marked in the senior year in high school and at the college level. The newer types of tests are outgrowths of changes in conceptions of curriculum organization, educational objectives, and teaching methods: namely, that courses and units, where possible, should be "interdisciplinary"; they should include the several relevant areas of study rather than being segmental; and they should contribute to the development of complex mental functioning.

Although educational achievement tests, especially those of the newer types, involve some of the psychological processes measured with tests of intelligence, they differ from the latter in that they utilize specific materials from an area of subject matter in which instruction has been provided. Their purpose is to measure how much has been learned in the subject and what specific abilities or skills have been developed. The test of intelligence, on the other hand, is intended to provide indexes

[1] Sample test items are given in a later section of this chapter.

representing an individual's level of general mental development and quality. The line of demarcation between the two is not always sharp; and the correlation between them is quite significant. But there are clear distinctions in regard to details of content, emphasis, and purpose.

The number of tests of educational achievement is very large. They cover almost every subject taught in elementary and secondary schools and colleges; and they vary considerably in merit. Some are broad in range of school grades and extent of subject matter, while others are relatively restricted. Still others are devised not only to measure the amount learned but, also, to diagnose difficulties. For example, some tests in arithmetic are intended to reveal pupils' weaknesses in each of the four fundamental processes or in the several types of skills (for example, fractions, decimals). Some tests in reading, likewise, are used to disclose reading deficiencies as in rate, vocabulary, and comprehension.

The principles upon which tests of educational achievement are standardized are the same as those of the other types already presented; the same principles of definition of aim, sampling, validity, and reliability apply here as elsewhere. A standardized test of educational achievement should be based upon a careful analysis of materials taught in a given field; the test items should be carefully phrased and analyzed for their discriminative value; uniform scoring directions should be provided to eliminate personal judgment. Age norms, grade norms, or both, should be provided, thus making it possible to evaluate on an objective basis any individual's performance in relation to others of his group.

Uses

Tests of educational achievement have been put to a number of uses in educational institutions at all levels, in psychological clinics, in business, industry, and government. In elementary and secondary schools, in particular, they are used to evaluate teachers' effectiveness, when employed in conjunction with tests of intelligence. They have often been used, also, to appraise experimentally the effectiveness of different teaching methods. School administrators and supervisors have found these tests helpful in maintaining standards and in making surveys of pupils' performance and progress for a general evaluation of all or part of a school system. Obviously, for any of these purposes it is necessary to use uniform and objective measuring devices; that is, tests that have been adequately standardized.

Standardized achievement tests provide information for the classification and placement of individuals in relatively homogeneous groups (often referred to as "ability grouping") for purposes of differentiated instruction. The results of the tests may also be used to provide a basis or criterion of motivation for an individual, since he can more readily measure his progress on a standardized scale than by other available means. Thus the progress of pupils can be evaluated over a period of time, by the pupils themselves and by their teachers.

Reliable and valid achievement tests, whether constructed by specialists for widespread use or by a group of teachers for use only in their own school, are indispensable in the guidance of individual pupils; for they enable teachers and counselors to diagnose each pupil's strengths and weaknesses. Such diagnosis is necessary to plan remedial instruction and to assist in the selection of a future course of education to be followed by a given individual.

Selection of pupils and students by institutions for particular types of education is the converse of guidance of the individual himself. Accordingly, many secondary schools, colleges, and universities administer objective achievement tests as one criterion to be considered in their process of selecting and eliminating applicants for admission to various types of education. Many colleges, for example, require that their applicants take the objective tests of the College Entrance Examination Board. Some university graduate schools require applicants to take the Graduate Record Examinations.

The clinical psychologist often uses the results of educational achievement tests when dealing with individuals at the elementary, secondary, or college level. They are individuals whose adjustment problems are associated with deficiencies or inabilities within certain subjects of study. Paradoxically, the problems of some pupils are attributable to superior aptitude or achievement in certain school subjects which, however, are unrecognized and unutilized by their teachers. Results of standardized tests often disclose such a condition. The clinical psychologist might, also, utilize achievement-test results as part of a total case history.

Achievement tests are now widely used outside of educational institutions. State and Federal civil services include objective tests among their requirements for appointment, as do some businesses and industries for certain of their positions. One of the requirements for obtaining a license or a certificate to practice a profession (for example, law, dentistry, nursing, psychology, medicine) is the passing of a state examination (or national, in some professions), at least part of which is of the objective type. Since examination by means of objective tests is widespread and since decisions depend in part upon test scores, it is imperative that these devices be constructed jointly by professional persons of two kinds: (1)

those who are expert in the techniques of test construction, and (2) those who are specialists in the subject-matter area for which the examination is to be prepared.

Derived Indexes

Educational Age and Achievement Age. Scoring of educational tests does not involve unique problems or principles. Their raw scores may be converted into the familiar percentile ranks and standard scores; or into "educational age" or "achievement age," by means of a table of age norms. Raw scores may be converted, also, into grade equivalents, using a table of grade norms.

The reader is already familiar with the concept of the norm and with the method whereby it is derived. Thus, if a pupil's raw score on a standardized test of the four fundamental arithmetical processes gives him a grade equivalent of 4.5, it means that his achievement on this test is equal to that of the average of pupils who have completed half of the fourth grade. By means of this index, obtained for each of the several subjects of instruction, it is possible to get a profile for each pupil and thereby to evaluate his general level of achievement, the evenness or unevenness of his performance, his weakness and strength in the type of learning measured.

The educational age (EA) designates a pupil's average standing in the several subjects in which he has been tested. For example, assume that a pupil has been given a test battery on which his scores were as follow: reading rate and comprehension, 9-year level; arithmetic fundamentals, 10-year level; spelling, 9-year level; language usage, 10-year level. His EA would be the average of these, or 9.5. Each of the separate ages represents the measured average level of educational achievement of the pupils of that age. The EA is a composite, representing a pupil's average achievement. Although the EA is useful in a general way and for group studies, if it is considered alone and without reference to levels of performance on the several subjects of study from which it is derived for a given individual, it may conceal significant inconsistencies, both weaknesses and strengths.

Achievement age (AA) designates a pupil's level of performance in a single school subject. The "subject age" is sometimes used synonymously with AA. Thus, if a pupil gets a rating of achievement age 10 on an arithmetic test, his level is equal to the norm of 10-year-old pupils, as measured by the given test. If "subject age" is used, it would be said that this pupil's "arithmetic age" is 10. At present, it is a matter of personal choice whether to designate a pupil's performance on an arithmetic test as "achievement age (arithmetic)" or "arithmetic age." [2]

Norms.   Grade norms, educational ages, and achievement ages derived for different tests are not always comparable, nor are they always applicable in a given school or community, since the standardization populations of these tests vary in respect to adequacy and representativeness. This is an important problem in achievement testing, since quality of education is far from uniform among various parts of this country. Rather than deriving only national norms, it is much more meaningful to present, in addition, separate norms for different sections of the country, and even for different types of communities (according to population). In connection with norms, it is necessary to recall the earlier distinction made between norms and standards (Chapter 6). Norms, in this instance, will represent the levels of manifested achievement in the subject matter being tested. They do not necessarily represent the level of learning that might be desirable or optimal—that is, a standard of performance.

Educational Quotient and Achievement Quotient.   It is necessary to have a quotient to accompany an educational or an achievement age. Hence, there are two types of quotients used with tests of educational achievement when EA or AA is found; these are the educational quotient (EQ) and the achievement quotient (AQ). The latter is sometimes called the accomplishment quotient.

The educational quotient is the ratio of educational age to chronological age (EA/CA) multiplied by 100 to remove the decimal; that is, the individual's average level of measured learning in relation to what is expected on the basis of his life age. Theoretically, the "normal" EQ is 100; deviations above or below represent, respectively, superior or inferior school learning, as compared with the individual's age group.

The achievement quotient is the ratio of educational age to mental age (EA/MA), multiplied by 100; that is, the individual's average level of measured learning in relation to what is expected on the basis of his mental level. Due to marked individual differences in mental ability in any group of persons of the same life age, the mental age is regarded as a more reliable index of a person's learning capacity than is chronological age; therefore, the AQ is a more valuable index than the EQ in judging whether or not a pupil's school achievement is commensurate with the quantity and quality of learning that might reasonably be expected of him.

[2] At present the term "achievement age" is in disfavor, as is the term "achievement quotient," defined later in this section.

The educational quotient and the achievement quotient have been used not only when the composite EA is derived and taken as the numerator of the ratio, but also when only the age level for a single subject (subject age or achievement age) is used as the numerator. When this is the case, then the quotients should be read as "educational quotient in . . ." (naming the school subject tested; for example, arithmetic); "achievement quotient in . . ."

The wisdom of using the AQ has been seriously questioned, for the following reasons. (1) Since this index is derived from two separate tests, each of which has a certain degree of error or unreliability, it has a lower reliability than an index based upon either test alone. (2) Since the norms of the two tests, one of educational achievement and the other of general mental ability, have in all probability been derived from different standardization groups, they will not be strictly comparable, nor will their measures of dispersion. For example, unless the distributions of scores of the two standardization groups are approximately equal, a given EA (10) and EQ (110) will not be comparable with an MA of 10 and an IQ of 110. Unless the distributions are equivalent, or nearly so, the two sets of apparently identical indexes will have different values, more or less. Hence, an index derived from them will not have the same meaning as either one. (3) Since courses of study in most schools are geared to pupils of average ability, bright pupils will not have an opportunity to learn up to a level consistent with their capacities; hence, they will be penalized and will get AQs of less than 100. Slow pupils, on the other hand, will be working "over their heads," and will more often get AQs above 100.[3] In spite of these criticisms, however, and assuming that one is aware of its limitations, there are occasions when the AQ serves a useful purpose, especially in studying the educational problems of superior children.

Types of Items

Test items may be classified into one or another of the following major types: (1) simple recall; (2) two alternatives, such as true-false, right-wrong, yes-no; (3) multiple-choice; (4) completion; (5) matching; (6) analogies; and (7) check lists. The following examples illustrate these types.

(1) *Simple recall:*

What are the dates of World War I? ....
What are the two main gases found in water? ....

---

[3] This criticism does not seem to have much merit; for what it says, in effect, is that the AQ helps to reveal an undesirable educational situation, so far as superior pupils are concerned.

(2) *Two alternatives:*
NaCl is the chemical symbol for common salt.   T   F
Abraham Lincoln served two complete terms as president of the
United States.   T   F

(3) *Multiple-choice:*
Scrooge is a character in
    1. *Oliver Twist*
    2. *David Copperfield*
    3. *A Christmas Carol.*
An example of an appointed official is a
    1. congressman
    2. senator
    3. federal judge.

(4) *Completion:*
The executive head of the United States government is the _____,
while the federal legislative bodies are the _____ and the_____.

(5) *Matching:*
Directions: After each name write the number of the topic which is
intimately associated with that person.
    1. conditioned reflex   Titchener ....
    2. age scale for testing intelligence   Hall ....
    3. reaction-time experiments   Pavlov ....
    4. psychoanalysis   Cattell, J. M. ....
    5. psychology of adolescence   Freud ....
    6. existential psychology   Binet ....
    7. factorial analysis

(6) *Analogies:*
Executive functions : President : : legislative functions : _____
Hydrogen : H : : sodium : _____

(7) *Check lists:*
Directions: Place a check mark in front of each of the following items
which is part of an automobile:
        throttle   generator
        rudder   distributor
        gear shift   aileron
        periscope   stabilizer

Although these are the principal types of items used in tests of educational achievement, they are not found with equal frequency; true-false,
multiple-choice, and completion are the most common. There are also
variations on some types. For example, tests of paragraph meaning (in
literature, social sciences, physical sciences, and others) are quite common.
The testee reads a paragraph and is then required to answer questions
intended to show the extent to which he has comprehended it. The ques-

tions usually are in the form of true-false, multiple-choice, or completion. In arithmetic and other aspects of mathematics, the items in a standardized test usually are in the same form as those devised by the individual teacher, that is, the student simply provides the correct answer. In tests of some aspects of English, special types of items have been developed, as, for example, in tests of punctuation and capitalization. In the following illustration, the necessary capitals and marks of punctuation are to be supplied.

why did you come home so early mary asked

For purpose of comparison, the following items are presented to illustrate the content of the newer types of test items, although their form is the same as that of other multiple-choice items.[4]

To test knowledge of "conventions":
For computation purposes, forces are frequently represented by
  1. straight lines
  2. circles
  3. areas of a circle
  4. angles
  5. objects of three dimensions

To test knowledge of methodology:
  When a scientist is confronted with a problem, his first step toward solving it should usually be to
  1. construct and purchase equipment
  2. perform an experiment
  3. draw conclusions
  4. use other scientists to cooperate with him in working it out
  5. gather all available information on the subject

To test analysis of elements:
  1. Galileo investigated the problem of the acceleration of falling bodies by rolling balls down a very smooth plane inclined at increasing angles, since he had no means of determining very short intervals of time. From the data obtained, he extrapolated for the case of free fall. Which of the following is an assumption implicit in the extrapolation?
  1. That air resistance is negligible in free fall
  2. That objects fall with constant acceleration
  3. That acceleration observed with the inclined plane is the same as that involved in free fall
  4. That planes are frictionless
  5. That a vertical plane and one which is nearly so have nearly the same effect on the ball

[4] From Bloom (3). By permission. Students are advised to consult this volume to examine in detail the wide range of item types.

To test analysis:

Items 28 and 29 are based on a composition which is played during the test. Number 28 calls for analysis of the systematic arrangement or structure which makes the composition a unit. Number 29 tests such an objective as ability to analyze, in a particular work of art, the relations of materials and means of production to the elements and to the organization.

    28. The general structure of the composition is

        1. Theme and variations

        2. Theme, development, restatement

        3. Theme 1, development; theme 2, development

        4. Introduction, theme, development

    29. The theme is carried by

        1. the strings

        2. the woodwinds

        3. the horns

        4. all in turn

Representative Batteries

Educational achievement tests are extensive in range and number and they vary in merit. Whenever a psychologist or educator has to evaluate the educational achievement of a group or of an individual, the selection of tests must be based upon their appropriateness to the problem at hand and upon the adequacy of their standardization: that is, range of grades covered, aspects and comprehensiveness of subject matter covered, reliability, validity, and population sample from which norms were derived. In this section, we shall list only several of the sounder batteries as representative of the group. When these are compared, it is apparent that they have much in common, both as to areas covered and content, although each has some individuality.

California Achievement Tests (1957): Forms for grades 1–2, 3–4, 4–6, 7–9, 9–14. Tests in reading vocabulary, reading comprehension, arithmetical fundamentals, arithmetical reasoning, mechanics of English, spelling.

Iowa Tests of Basic Skills (1956): Grades 3–9. Tests in vocabulary, reading comprehension, language, arithmetical skills, work-study skills.

Metropolitan Achievement Tests (1959): Forms for grades 1, 2, 3–4, 5–6, 7–9. Tests in vocabulary, reading, arithmetic, science, social studies, study skills.

SRA Achievement Series (1957): Forms for grades 2–4, 4–6, 6–9. Tests in reading, language perception, language arts, arithmetic, work-study skills.

Sequential Tests of Educational Progress (1958): Referred to as STEP. Forms for grades 4–6, 7–9, 10–12, college. Tests in reading, writing, mathematics, science, social studies, listening comprehension, essay writing.

Standard Achievement Test (1953): Forms for grades 1–3, 3–4, 5–6, 7–9. Tests in arithmetic, reading, science, study skills, social studies.

Some batteries are constructed for use only at the high school level: for example, Essential High School Content Battery (1951), Evaluation and Adjustment Series (1950), Iowa Test of Educational Development (1952). These, naturally, place more emphasis upon specific sciences, social studies, and upon general educational development in thinking with and using materials learned.

Evaluation. These and other equally sound batteries of tests have much in common regarding objectives, standardization population, reliability, and conceptions of validation. On the whole, they are technically well constructed. They have been current long enough, having gone through revisions, so that their normative data are based upon the scores of many thousands of individuals. Their reliabilities are high, mostly in the high .80s and low .90s. Validity of achievement tests is given primarily in terms of content and constructs. These criteria of selecting test materials are justifiable. The value of an achievement battery will depend upon (1) the thoroughness with which the test materials were selected; (2) adequacy of item analysis to determine the discriminating power and difficulty level of each (see "Item Analysis," Chapter 5); and (3) adequacy and differentiating value of norms, as between chronological age groups and grade levels.

If an achievement test is valid, it measures what is actually being taught in the schools for which it is intended. The procedure followed in constructing the sounder achievement tests, therefore, is essentially as follows. The widely used textbooks in the subject are thoroughly analyzed; a variety of course syllabi are analyzed; educational objectives of the courses of instruction are defined; information (content validity), skills and intellectual processes (construct validity) to be tested are defined; an analysis is made of research findings relating to pupils' experiences, forms and levels of concepts, and vocabularies at successive ages and school grades. On the basis of these analyses, outlines of test content are prepared, in which proportions are allotted to all the skills, types of information, and understandings that are to be examined. The outlines of content and proportions are then evaluated by subject-matter specialists. After this has been done, the first version of the test is ready for a series of tryouts, involving the usual standardization techniques, during which items are revised, added, and eliminated, until satisfactory reliability and validity are achieved.

These batteries are intended to be analytical to pupil achievement in these ways: (1) they measure continuity of educational growth over several school grades; (2) they reveal group or classroom differences in subject matter, skills, or insights being tested; (3) they reveal differences in competence within a single individual; (4) they identify those pupils who are so markedly deficient in any area as to require more intensive testing, observation by their teachers, and diagnosis of the elements of deficiency, with a view to remedial instruction. The comprehensive survey batteries are not designed primarily for this kind of diagnosis, though they contribute to this end in a limited degree. For example, if a pupil earns a low score on the arithmetic test in the battery (for reasons other than poor general intelligence), a diagnostic test in arithmetic (either standardized or especially devised) should reveal in which of the four fundamental processes, and at which levels, he is deficient; or in which number combinations, or specific skills and understandings, he is weak.

There are several important and complicating considerations that must be taken into account when an educational achievement test is being constructed and when it is being evaluated for use in a particular school. As already stated, the tests are based upon analyses of textbooks, course syllabi, and judgments of experts. For each school or school system however, the appropriateness of the test's content must be judged. The question is: Are the school's courses of study, syllabi, and objectives comparable? If they are not, the pupils' scores will not be valid indexes of what has been taught and learned, except for the purpose of comparison with the schools and the rationale used in the standardization process.[5]

Most sound achievement batteries provide grade norms and percentile norms within each grade. It is highly desirable, also, to provide grade norms for the beginning, middle, and end of the school year; for, obviously, there should be measurable development during the year. Currently, however, the use and interpretation of norms present difficulties. There always have been, and there still are, sectional differences in the quality of schooling provided in the several geographic areas of the country. "National norms," therefore, especially when they stand alone, are of doubtful value; for they might not be representative of any schools or groups of schools in particular. It is desirable, for this reason, to calculate separate norms for geographic areas, or even for individual states, where the population sample has been representative. The meaning of grade norms is further vitiated by the different policies followed in promoting pupils into successive grades. Many schools do not use a standard of achievement ("passing"); pupils are moved along after two years in a grade, regardless of competence. (In this connection, see Chapter 6 on the difference between norms and standards.) Other schools follow different practices. Grade norms, therefore, have a different significance from place to place. Some test authors meet this problem by providing

[5] A well-conceived and soundly constructed test can stimulate improvements in the courses of some schools for whose pupils the content is too difficult or inappropriate in view of what they have been taught.

modal age-grade norms (Stanford Achievement Tests, for example); that is, the norms are based upon the scores of the most common age group in each grade rather than upon the scores of all pupils in the grade.[6] The modal-age group consists of those pupils who are typical of the grade with respect to age; they have been in each grade one year and entered school at about the same age. Furthermore, the age requirement for entering school is approximately the same throughout the United States.

On the whole, soundly conceived and constructed achievement test batteries can contribute much to the study and solution of the educational and psychological problems indicated under the section on "Uses" in this chapter.

Reading Tests [7]

Reading, of all school subjects, is the one to which most research has been devoted and for which the largest number of tests have been devised. This is quite understandable, since ability to read is the foundation of the usual curricula through high school, and also of most courses of study at higher levels. The numerous tests, some more comprehensive than others, have much in common; but they are not of equal quality. Reading tests, for the purpose of classification, may be divided into three groups, although these are not mutually exclusive: achievement, readiness, diagnostic.

Achievement.   The principal objective of these tests is to measure reading rate and level of comprehension. For these purposes, they test sentence comprehension, paragraph comprehension, understanding directions (this, of course, is also a matter of comprehension), word meaning (vocabulary), and recall of details. Less often, the tests include sections on the selection of key words and use of an index or a dictionary. Although time limits are imposed, some are more speeded than others. While tests in this category are intended to measure ability in each of the several aspects of reading, they are intended, also, to provide information regarding sources of pupils' reading difficulties, especially when a higher level of reading competency might be expected of them. All of the educational achievement batteries, already described, include more or less material to test reading achievement. For our present purposes, it will be most useful to describe several tests in each of the two remaining categories: readiness and diagnostic.

---

[6] The authors of the Stanford tests report that approximately 65 percent of the pupils in any grade are in the modal-age group.

[7] In connection with reading aptitude, the student should refer to the discussion of tests of vision in Chapter 18.

Readiness. Children are ordinarily admitted to the first grade on the basis of age, the assumption being that when a child reaches a specified age (usually 6 years), he is ready to begin the study of prescribed first-grade subjects. Extensive research on individual differences has revealed, however, that an appreciable percentage of children is not ready for formal instruction in reading at the prescribed time owing to immaturity of some types of perception, although these children are not necessarily retarded in general mental development. Tests of reading readiness, therefore, are devised to identify children who are not mature enough to benefit from instruction. The tests, the elements of which are listed below, are representative of those found valuable in evaluating a child's status.

American School Reading Readiness Test (1955). Grade 1.
  1. Vocabulary
  2. Discrimination of letter forms
  3. Discrimination of letter combinations
  4. Word selection
  5. Word matching
  6. Discrimination of geometric forms
  7. Following directions
  8. Memory of geometric forms

Gates Reading Readiness Test (1939). Grade 1.
  1. Following directions in marking pictures (ability to listen, understand directions, and remember)
  2. Word matching (identification of visual word patterns)
  3. Word perception (selecting one word from among four)
  4. Rhyming (auditory perception)
  5. Naming letters and numbers

Harrison-Stroud Reading Readiness Tests (1956). Kindergarten and Grade 1.
  1. Making visual discriminations
  2. Using context
  3. Making auditory discriminations
  4. Using auditory clues in identifying items
  5. Using symbols
  6. Giving names of letters

Metropolitan Readiness Tests (1950). Kindergarten and Grade 1.
  1. Word knowledge (selecting pictures that correspond to words)
  2. Understanding of and response to oral directions (selecting pictures in response to sentence-long directions, involving sustained attention)
  3. Information (same as 2, but more elaborate, involving more vocabulary and names of common objects)
  4. Matching (visual perception, involving selection of pairs of identical pictures of common objects)
  5. Knowledge of numbers

> 6. Copying (simple geometric forms and less complex numerals and capital letters)

Tests of reading readiness are based upon empirical observation and analysis of aptitudes involved in children's learning to read, and upon psychological analysis of the functions involved. Inspection of each of the parts of the foregoing tests shows extensive agreement, in spite of different names and emphases. On the whole, reading readiness is assessed in terms of sensory development and acuity, language development and interest, curiosity about the environment (information, vocabulary), and, to a lesser extent, motor control and rate (since learning to write is collateral with learning to read).

These and comparable tests have demonstrated their value. Obtained ratings will indicate whether a child may be expected to experience much, moderate, or little difficulty in learning to read. The scores of the sounder tests are significantly correlated (in the .70s) with later achievement in reading in the lower grades. Analysis of a child's performance on each of the parts can reveal areas of deficiency and possible sources of future difficulty. Conversely, the tests provide information that will enable teachers to identify pupils who are equipped to learn without difficulty.

Diagnostic. These tests are intended to isolate in detail the elements responsible for a pupil's disabilities in reading. The following instruments, and the lists of their parts, are representative.

Diagnostic Reading Tests (1952). Grades 7–13.
  1. Vocabulary: in the fields of English, mathematics, science and social studies
  2. Comprehension: silent and auditory
  3. Rate of reading: general, social studies, science
  4. Word attack: oral and silent—identification of sounds, syllabication

Durrell Analysis of Reading Difficulty (1955). Grades 1–6.
  1. Oral reading comprehension
  2. Oral reading recall
  3. Silent reading
  4. Word and letter recognition
  5. Word pronunciation
  6. Spelling
  7. Handwriting

Gates Reading Diagnostic Tests (1953). Grades 1–8.
  1. Oral reading errors (omissions, reversals, mispronunciations, etc.)
  2. Vocabulary
  3. Phrase perception
  4. Visual perception (syllabication, blending, letter sounds, etc.)
  5. Auditory perception
  6. Spelling

Gilmore Oral Reading Test (1952). Grades 1–8.
1. Substitutions
2. Mispronunciations
3. Assistance in pronunciation
4. Disregard of punctuation
5. Insertions
6. Hesitations
7. Repetitions
8. Omissions

Group Diagnostic Aptitude and Achievement Test (1939). Intermediate Form, Grades 3–9.
1. Paragraph meaning
2. Speed of reading
3. Word discrimination: vowels, consonants, reversals, additions, omissions
4. Letter and form memory (visual)
5. Auditory discrimination
6. Copying text and crossing out letters
7. Vocabulary

Rosswell-Chall Diagnostic Reading Test (1956). Grades 2–6.
1. Word recognition and word analysis
   a. single consonants and combinations
   b. short vowel sounds
   c. rule of silent *e*
   d. vowel combinations
   e. syllabication

Inspection of the preceding lists shows that the several tests have much in common. It will be noted that these and other current diagnostic tests in reading are concerned very little, if at all, with detecting visual anomalies, or with auditory and visual deficiencies that interfere with learning and with progress in reading. Early tests in this field placed more emphasis upon these elements; and, it seems, wisely so.

Evaluation. Of the many tests of reading, too large a percentage are inadequately standardized; they do not provide the essential data on reliability and validity. These deficiencies are especially serious in the case of tests of reading achievement. Although it can be done, it is much more difficult to determine validity of readiness and diagnostic tests, because their effectiveness as predictors has to be estimated in terms of either progress at the earliest stages (readiness) or elimination of deficiencies and handicaps. The degree to which these objectives are achieved will depend upon a number of elusive determinants, such as the child's motivation and general intelligence, the quality of teaching in the regular classroom, the technical skill of the remedial teacher, and the improvability of a particular defect.

The sounder tests are reasonably reliable, and their validity is based upon content or construct validity, or both. When they are based upon thorough analysis of reading materials at each of the several grades, followed by analysis into the psychological processes involved in reading at each of the levels, the tests can have considerable merit. The more analytical and more thorough tests not only require more time to administer, but they demand greater skill and insights in scoring and interpreting. It is possible, however, to get useful clues from a brief and less complex device (for example, the Roswell-Chall), to be followed, if necessary, by a more extensive and analytical examination.

Arithmetic Tests

Characteristics. Since it is a basic and universal area of instruction, the subject of arithmetic has also been widely studied, and a large number of tests have been prepared. Too many of the devices in this field, however, fail to satisfy the criteria of sound test construction. The most satisfactory available objective tests of arithmetical ability are parts of the sounder comprehensive batteries, such as those already described.

A valid test in arithmetic is designed to measure the specified objectives of the teaching of that subject at each of the grade levels. These objectives can be determined only by means of a thorough study of textbooks, syllabi, and research publications. This means, of course, that tests designed for one educational level, or a few successive levels, will differ in content and emphasis from those devised for higher or lower levels. We find, therefore, that in the aggregate, practically all aspects of arithmetical instruction are included in available tests. The following are the understandings and operations most frequently included, both in specialized tests and in comprehensive batteries.

1. The four basic processess in a great variety of combinations
2. Manipulation of whole numbers
3. Manipulation of fractions
4. Manipulation of decimals
5. Manipulation of mixed numbers
6. Arithmetical terms and concepts (for example, average)
7. Percentage and interest
8. Measurement
9. Number meaning
10. Arithmetical reasoning (problem solving)

Types. Objective tests in arithmetic are of two major types, achievement and diagnostic, although, as in reading, they cannot be mutually exclusive. The achievement type, obviously, is intended to measure the amount and level of each testee's learning. To accomplish this end in all respects is extremely difficult; for among the objectives in modern teaching of the subject are understanding of arithmetical principles and generalizations, and insights into arithmetic as a system—an organized and orderly method—of thinking. It is not surprising that most of the available devices are concerned almost exclusively with manipulations of one kind or another and with the solving of the usual types of problems, since it is quite difficult to devise test items that will evaluate the extent to which the more complex aims have been achieved. Thus, in spite of the emphasis, in the last decade and before, upon developing meanings, understandings, and insights in teaching arithmetic, few tests provide adequately for these functions. Some progress, however, has been made. The following are illustrative of items used to test the ability to evaluate the nature and sufficiency of data (41).

Level 4 (Grades 4–6)

Situation: In Tom's school, some children ride bicycles, some walk to school, and some ride the school bus. The pupils on the safety patrol have to come early.

11. Two children from each class in the school were members of the safety patrol. To find how many patrol members there are altogether, what other fact would you need to know?

    A The number of children in the school

    B The number of classes in the school

    C The number of children in each class

    D The number of street crossings

Level 3 (Grades 7–9)

Situation: Mr. Jones has a dairy farm.

8. Three fourths of Mr. Jones' cows are Jerseys. Two thirds of Mr. Brown's cows are Jerseys. Mr. Jones has fewer cows in his herd than Mr. Brown. Which of the following statements about the number of Jerseys they own is true?

    E They have the same number.

    F Jones has more than Brown.

    G Brown has more than Jones.

    H More information is needed to find out who has more.

9. Mr. Jones has two fields of equal size. If he grows corn on $\frac{7}{8}$ of field *R* and $\frac{8}{9}$ of field *S*, which of the following statements is true?

    A Field *R* has more space in corn than field *S*.

    B Field *S* has more space in corn than field *R*.

    C Equal space is in corn on both fields.

    D The spaces in corn cannot be compared.

The following is a type of item devised to test ability to understand the meanings of processes.

Which of these examples will have the same answer as the example in the box? (30, p. 147) (Grades 4–5)

$$\boxed{\tfrac{1}{3} \text{ of } 27}$$

(a) 27   (b) 27   (c) 3/$\overline{27}$ (d) 27
    −3   +3   ×3

Attention to the more complex and generalized outcomes of instruction in arithmetic should not obscure the fact that mastery of the fundamental arithmetical processes and of techniques of calculation are basic and should also be measured both in achievement and diagnostic tests.

Diagnostic tests in arithmetic must be based upon the same principle as those in reading. Each must be specialized and detailed in order to reveal not only areas of weakness and deficiency but also the specific difficulties within each area. Thus, for example, it is not enough to find that a pupil is weak in subtraction; it is necessary to know which specific steps and number combinations are the cause of the difficulty. In working with decimals, the meaning and placement of the point might be the source of trouble; or particular number combinations in multiplication might be troublesome.

When a diagnostic test is given individually, it is desirable for the testee to work his problems and make his operations orally as well as in written form, while the examiner records the pupil's responses step by step. This examination should be followed by an interview. Thus the errors, faulty methods, and incorrect reasoning may be detected and remedial instruction specifically directed.

Ability in arithmetic is a function of general intelligence. In trying to find the cause (or causes) of disabilities in this subject, a test of general mental ability, preferably an individual test, should be administered to determine whether the disability is attributable to an inadequate general mental level or to a specific deficiency that should be readily remediable.

Tests at High School and College Levels

Scope. At the secondary school level, tests are available in nearly all subjects of study. They vary considerably in quality with regard to adequacy of content and technical standardization. As in the case of the tests at the elementary school levels, these largely measure information and skills; but currently understandings, meanings, and insights are receiving greater emphasis.

In the secondary schools themselves, the tests are used to measure progress and development in subject matter. Among these are the *Cooperative Achievement Tests* (Educational Testing Service), the *Evaluation and Adjustment Series* (Harcourt, Brace & World, Inc.) and the *Iowa Tests of Educational Development* (Science Research Associates, Inc.).[8]

The College Entrance Examination Board, as many students already know from first-hand experience, has constructed many editions of achievement tests, in a variety of secondary school subjects, to be used as one criterion of college admission. Some of these measure not only mastery of subject matter, but place emphasis upon ability to apply principles in new situations within the subject-matter area. Thus, they are intended to serve as measures of what has been learned and as predictors of future performance with similar materials in college courses. In addition, the College Board has introduced, within relatively recent years, *Advanced Placement Examinations* for high school seniors. These, in each subject, are based upon content equivalent to a first course at the college level. They thus encourage superior high school students to take advanced work and offer these students an opportunity to enter sooner into more advanced studies, commensurate with their abilities, at the college level.

Since 1937, objective tests of educational achievement for college graduates have been developed. They are the *Graduate Record Examinations* (Educational Testing Service). An increasing number of universities are using these as one of the criteria for admission to their graduate schools. The Examinations consist of three parts: an Aptitude Test, Area Tests, and Advanced Tests. The first of these is a test of general mental ability, yielding separate scores in verbal and quantitative subtests and intended to serve as one predictor of ability to do graduate work. The Area Tests (for the college sophomore year and higher) provide examinations in social science, humanities, and natural science. They constitute a general-achievement battery designed to estimate the level and extent of a student's knowledge and understandings in the major areas of college studies (liberal arts and sciences). The items include some that evaluate the student's ability to solve problems in general fields of study and to exercise judgment based upon familiarity with academic subject matter. The Advanced Tests are specialized examinations to test students in their subjects of major study and intended graduate specialization. Data on the predictive validities of the GRE have shown, as in other comparable situations (for example, law and medicine), that a combination of their scores with undergraduate grades provides a better predictive criterion than either one taken alone (20, 21).

[8] Students should consult Buros (6) for descriptions and evaluations of these series and of numerous others.

Tests of Complex Educational Objectives

Although, as already explained, some tests of educational achievement have been including items that go beyond the measurement of information and rather routine skills, a few have been devised specifically to estimate the more complex and enduring educational objectives. One of the earliest of these is the *Wrightstone Test of Critical Thinking in the Social Studies* (1939). It included items requiring the following three types of operations: (1) obtaining facts, (2) drawing conclusions, (3) applying general facts. The first part requires the student to select certain items from a group of facts in accordance with specific directions. The correct answer is given to each question, the task of the pupil being to match answers and given facts. In this part of the test, the pupil is required to obtain facts from graphs, tables, maps, indexes of a textbook type, and to locate information in books, magazines, and newspapers in the ways required in a library. This is, in short, a test of ability to utilize a variety of kinds of materials in order to acquire information. Part two, called "Drawing Conclusions from Facts," is a reading test that requires the pupil to evaluate a number of conclusions drawn from given data. All necessary information is provided, so that recall is not involved. The procedure consists of reading a paragraph, then matching several given statements with it to determine which of them is appropriately drawn from the paragraph. Part three, "Applying General Facts," is much the same as part two, for the pupil is required to generalize and apply facts presented in a paragraph to be read.

Although this Wrightstone test is rarely encountered now, it was an important contribution to educational testing; for its underlying rationale, different from that of the great majority of tests at the time, has since been incorporated in some of the more recent achievement batteries and is receiving increasing attention.

The Watson-Glaser Critical Thinking Appraisal (1942–1956), for grades 9 through college, is another test of the same general type.[9] It consists of five subtests: (1) drawing inferences, (2) recognition of assumptions, (3) making deductions, (4) making interpretations, (5) evaluating arguments. Although the content of this test does not call specifically upon knowledge acquired in courses, it is intended to evaluate important educational objectives: namely, aspects of critical thinking. Insofar as it is used to evaluate the effectiveness of programs of instruction, which is its stated purpose, it is a test of educational achievement.

A similar type of test was developed by the Committee on Appraisal

[9] Originally called the Watson-Glaser Test of Critical Thinking.

of the Progressive Education Association, in an eight-year study of learning at the high school and college levels. One test, on "interpretations of data," includes a series of exercises that require the student to formulate reasonable generalizations from data drawn largely from the physical and the social sciences. "Application of principles of general sciences," another test, includes a series of exercises requiring the student to explain scientific phenomena in terms of relevant facts and principles. There are also tests dealing with the application of social science generalizations to social problems; others require the drawing of logical conclusions from given premises; still others, in the nature of proof, require the student to identify basic definitions and assumptions and to judge their plausibility. The publications of this committee provided impetus to the newer directions taken in testing educational achievement.

It seems appropriate to include tests of study habits, skills, and attitudes under the title of this section. There are many of these. They assess such matters as motivation for study, attitudes toward academic work, skill in using a dictionary and library index, finding sources of information, interpreting graphs and tables of data, and organizing a set of lecture notes. Since effective levels in all of these aspects are desirable educational objectives, it was to be expected that tests for these skills would be devised.

Prognosis Tests in Specific Academic Subjects

In the fields of mathematics and foreign languages, at the high school level, several tests, intended to predict achievement in these subjects, have been constructed. They are aptitude tests in the sense that they use restricted and specialized types of materials in an effort to predict learning in a limited area.[10] These tests are based upon the well-recognized principle that a sample of learning in a given subject, obtained under standardized conditions, provides significant evidence of future prospects in that subject. Prognosis tests are not to be confused with achievement tests. The former are intended for pupils who have not yet studied the subject; the latter are measures of learning after a period of instruction.

In algebra, for example, two of the well-known instruments are the *Iowa Algebra Aptitude Test* and the *Orleans Algebra Prognosis Test*. The first of these consists of four parts: (1) arithmetical problems involving only numerical manipulations, (2) verbal problems using arithmetic and

---

[10] These are discussed here rather than in Chapter 18 or 19 because they are concerned with learning a particular form of subject matter, whereas the chapters on aptitude tests deal primarily with their usefulness in vocational guidance.

simple algebraic procedures, (3) number-series exercises requiring the examinee to discern the principle used in each series, and (4) exercises requiring understanding of the effect of one value in an equation produced by the variation of another value. Prediction by means of this test, thus, is based almost entirely upon skills and understandings previously learned.

The Orleans test is different in conception, in that algebraic operations have been analyzed and defined (construct validity). It consists of a number of "lessons" in algebra, each followed by a test. The lessons deal with basic elements involved in the study of elementary algebra: (1) use of symbols to represent numbers, (2) substitution of values for symbols, (3) representation of quantities by symbols and use of these, (4) expression of relationships by means of symbols, and (5) combinations of the preceding four in the solution of problems. Prediction by means of this test is based upon the acquisition of *new* understandings and upon "work samples." The *Orleans Geometry Prognosis Test* is constructed upon the same principles as the algebra test.

Similarly conceived prognosis tests have been prepared for foreign-language study. Symonds' *Foreign Language Prognosis Test,* a very early device, attempts to measure this aptitude in "pure" form by presenting exercises in Esperanto that are mainly applications of principles to word and sentence translation and to the formation of parts of speech. The *Modern Language Aptitude Test* (Carroll and Sapon) is much more comprehensive. Like the Symonds tests, it consists of practice exercises in learning several aspects of language, for which it utilizes tape-recorded and paper-pencil materials. The functions tested are the following, as described by the test's authors. (1) Number learning: learning numbers in a foreign language; a test of memory and "auditory alertness." (2) Phonetic script: ability to learn the correspondence between speech sounds and symbols; "sound-symbol association ability." (3) Spelling clues: also "sound-symbol ability"; the scores depend to some extent upon the examinee's knowledge of English, since he is required to associate certain sounds with words. (4) Words in sentences: "sensitivity to grammatical structure." (5) Paired associates: rote memory exercise in learning vocabulary of a foreign language (Kurdish) and the English equivalents.

Since scores on sound tests of general intelligence correlate significantly with high-school grades, the question naturally arises why special prognosis tests have been prepared for elementary mathematics and foreign languages. There are several reasons. The prognosis tests correlate somewhat higher than do intelligence tests with grades in the particular subject for which each is intended, the coefficients being, generally, close to .60. Learning a foreign language involves, among other functions, a complex of the auditory and visual senses that are not significantly correlated with general intelligence. The learning of high school mathematics can be impeded, in spite of adequate mental ability, by poor preparation in arithmetical understandings and by a negative affective attitude. Where feasible, it would be good practice to give prognosis tests in conjunction with tests of general intelligence, not only to determine the multiple correlation (the two tests combined, correlated with grades), cut-off scores and expectancy tables, but—and equally important, if not more so—to find the exceptions among the pupils; that is, those with sufficiently high intelligence-test ranks but with poor ratings on the prognosis tests. Such pupils would be studied individually to determine the causes of the discrepancies and to provide remedies. Where this practice is not feasible, the ratings on tests of general intelligence may be used as measures of expectancy in learning. Pupils whose scholastic learning and achievement are appreciably inconsistent with these measures can then be given special tests, followed by interview, to determine the source of difficulty.[11]

Evaluation of Achievement Tests

The sounder standardized achievement tests, at all levels, are satisfactory so far as reliability is concerned. Their validity may be estimated in one or more of three ways: (1) predictive, (2) content, (3) known groups. In the first instance, test scores are correlated with marks given by teachers, or with teachers' ratings of their pupils on a scale. These correlations are of moderate size, because marks and ratings are subjective. Teachers' marks and ratings are justifiable criteria, however, since competence and success in learning are ordinarily judged by these. Validity may also be estimated by the use of groups of known abilities, the expectancy being that there will be significant differences between them in test scores. Increases in percent passing each item in successive school grades and increases in average total score from grade to grade are also used as validity criteria.

Content validity is a matter of expert judgment. In this instance, the question to be answered is: Does the test, in the judgment of specialists, measure the stated educational objectives of instruction in a given field of study? If it is the stated aim of a course, at any level, to provide individuals only with information, or verbal skills, or numerical skills, then a test designed to measure these educational results will be judged accordingly. On the other hand, if the purpose of instruction in a given subject is to develop ability to evaluate materials, make generalizations, reason deductively, etc., then a standardized educational test will have to be evaluated in these terms. Content validation means, in effect, that

---

[11] We assume that the tests of intelligence have been properly administered, scored, and interpreted. This must be true, also, of the tests used for prognosis or diagnosis.

evaluation of the merit of a test rests ultimately upon the judgment of teachers who are specialists in the subject and also upon the judgment of specialists in test construction.

In contemporary education in the United States, educational objectives emphasize development of concepts and attitudes, critical thinking, analysis and synthesis of subject matter, creativity, and problem solving, as well as the acquisition of essential information and skills. As already pointed out, many tests of educational achievement do not attempt to measure these abilities; and those that do are by their nature limited in the extent to which they are able to measure the attainment of these more complex educational objectives. The more complex tests present a number of problem situations, for each of which the facts are given, as are the possible solutions, inferences, logical explanations, evaluations, or interpretations. It is the examinee's task only to *select* certain of these as being correct, sounder, or more relevant than others. There is very little, if anything, that is creative, original, or spontaneous in such a task; the critical thinking required of the examinee is considerably reduced. These devices test ability, for the most part, to discriminate among arguments, to recognize warranted and unwarranted assumptions, to distinguish between the relevant and the irrelevant, etc. If well conceived and executed, such tests are valuable and are superior to the measurement of information only; but their limitations must be recognized.[12]

Tests of Proficiency

Tests in this category deal principally with achievement in occupational areas rather than in subjects studied in school. They are specialized achievement tests. For this reason they are designated differently and are separately classified.

The first task in devising a test of proficiency is to make a job analysis in order to discern the psychological functions and traits involved. These may be sensory, motor, intellectual, or nonintellectual traits of personality, or any combination of these. The job analysis requires psychological insights into the processes involved, through observations of persons on the job; but the psychologist will also consult with expert workmen (including foremen and supervisors) to learn from them what traits and skills they believe are essential or desirable. After the job analysis, the procedures and technical principles involved in devising a test are the same as in the other areas already discussed.

Specific proficiency tests are available in bookkeeping, shorthand, type-

---

[12] The persons of whom considerable creativity, originality, and ingenuity are demanded are those who select and prepare the test's items.

writing, and for some industrial and mechanical occupations. A battery of proficiency tests may, however, be built from existing instruments that were originally devised for another purpose. For example, analysis of a particular type of office job may show that proficiency in four areas is necessary: arithmetical computation, spelling, perceptual speed, and memory span (immediate recall). As a first step, it might be possible, in this instance, to utilize, in combination, four existing tests already standardized. But specific validation studies for this particular situation would be necessary. On the other hand, the nature of the job might be such as to require the development of new tests adapted to this specific situation.

Another type is the *work sample,* which may be in miniature or a simulation of the actual task; or it may be a full-scale realistic performance. This type requires the candidate to produce a piece of work or perform a task as actually required by the job to be filled. Examples are performance on a replica of a telephone switchboard, operation of an airplane pilot trainer (on the ground), machine operation, typewriting, taking and transcribing shorthand. In work-sample testing, considerable interest has been shown in business education and business itself because, among other reasons, there are aspects of proficiency common to all types of jobs in typewriting, stenography, bookkeeping, and, more recently, business-machine operating.

The *Seashore-Bennett Stenographic Proficiency Test,* used for selecting, training, and upgrading employees, is a *work-sample* test, consisting of five letters dictated at three different rates. The testee then transcribes the letters in a form that might be mailed out. The final product is scored for (1) neatness and cleanness of typing; (2) arrangement of the letter; (3) quality of stroke; (4) typing errors and erasures; (5) errors in English; (6) changes from the original in wording and meaning. The letters to be dictated and transcribed are on records, thus keeping the quality and rate of dictation constant for all testees. Samples of superior and poor transcriptions are provided as guides for scoring.

To have any merit beyond that of a randomly selected task chosen by each employer individually, work samples must be carefully selected to be representative of the job, and scoring must be placed on a clearly defined basis, with subjectivity minimized. To have a fair approximation to uniformity of rating procedure, appropriate check lists and rating scales are used (see Chapter 21).

A third type is the test of *analagous functions.* Instead of producing a sample or working in a situation that is a replica of the job, the candidate is tested in functions analogous to those necessary in the job itself. For example, if manual speed and precision are required, rate of tapping, filling pegboards, and tracing with a stylus might be used as tests. In another situation, two-hand coordination, reaction time, and color discrimination might be measured.

On the whole, the merit of proficiency tests is that, in spite of lack of normative data and adequate validation for widespread use—which is true of many—they have been more carefully and analytically prepared than the usual tests devised by individual teachers, employment personnel, and employers. As in other types of testing, determination of *specific* (rather than general) validity of proficiency tests is necessary.

References

1. Aiken, W. M. *The Story of the Eight-Year Study.* New York: Harper & Brothers, 1942.
2. Blair, G. M. *Diagnostic and Remedial Teaching.* New York: The Macmillan Company, 1956.
3. Bloom, B. S. (ed.). *Taxonomy of Educational Objectives: Handbook I: Cognitive Domain.* New York: David McKay Company, Inc., 1956.
4. Bond, G. L., and M. A. Tinker. *The Prevention and Correction of Reading Difficulties.* New York: Appleton-Century-Crofts, Inc., 1957.
5. Brueckner, L. J., and F. E. Grossnickle. *How to Make Arithmetic Meaningful.* New York: Holt, Rinehart and Winston, Inc., 1947.
6. Buros, O. K. *The Fifth Mental Measurement Yearbook.* Highland Park, N.J.: Gryphon Press, 1959.
7. Carroll, J. B., and S. M. Sapon. *Modern Language Aptitude Test.* New York: The Psychological Corporation, 1959.
8. *Cooperative General Achievement Tests.* Princeton, N.J.: Educational Testing Service, 1951–1956.
9. Davis, F. B. Item analysis in relation to educational and psychological testing. *Psychological Bulletin,* 1952, *49,* 97–121.
10. Dressel, P. L., and L. B. Mayhew. *General Education: Explorations in Evaluation.* Washington: American Council on Education, 1954.
11. Durost, W. N. (ed.). *Evaluation and Adjustment Series.* New York: Harcourt, Brace & World, Inc., 1951–1958.
12. Durost, W. N. (ed.). *Metropolitan Achievement Tests.* New York: Harcourt, Brace & World, Inc., 1961.
13. *Durrell Analysis of Reading Difficulty.* New York: Harcourt, Brace & World, Inc., 1955.
14. French, J. W. *Comparative Prediction of Success and Satisfaction in College Major Fields: Part II.* Princeton, N.J.: Educational Testing Service, 1961.
15. Furst, E. J. *Constructing Evaluation Instruments.* New York: David McKay Company, Inc., 1958.

16. Garrett, H. E. *Testing for Teachers*. New York: American Book Company, 1959.

17. *Gates Reading Diagnostic Tests*. New York: Teachers College, Columbia University, 1953.

18. Gerberich, J. R. *Specimen Objective Test Items: a Guide to Achievement Test Construction*. David McKay Company, Inc., 1956.

19. *Gilmore Oral Reading Test*. New York: Harcourt, Brace & World, Inc., 1952.

20. *Graduate Record Examination: Institutional Testing Program for Colleges and Universities: Handbook for Deans and Examiners*. Princeton, N.J.: Educational Testing Service, 1960.

21. *Graduate Record Examinations Scores for Basic Reference Groups*. Princeton, N.J.: Educational Testing Service, 1960.

22. Green, H. A., and A. H. Piper. *Iowa Algebra Aptitude Test* (rev. ed.). Iowa City: Bureau of Educational Research and Service, State University of Iowa, 1942.

23. Harris, A. J. *How to Increase Reading Ability* (4th ed.). New York: David McKay Company, Inc., 1961.

24. *Harrison-Stroud Reading Readiness Tests*. Boston: Houghton Mifflin Company, 1956.

25. Hildreth, G. H., and N. L. Griffiths. *Metropolitan Readiness Tests*. New York: Harcourt, Brace & World, Inc., 1950.

26. Kelley, T. L., *et al. The Stanford Achievement Tests*. New York: Harcourt, Brace & World, Inc., 1956.

27. Lindquist, E. F. (ed.). *Educational Measurement*, Washington: American Council on Education, 1951.

28. *Monroe Diagnostic Reading Examination*. Chicago: C. H. Stoelting Company, 1930.

29. Monroe, M., and E. E. Sherman. *Group Diagnostic Reading Aptitude and Achievement Tests*. Boston: Houghton Mifflin Company, 1939.

30. National Society for the Study of Education. *The Measurement of Understanding*. 44th Yearbook, Part I. Chicago: University of Chicago Press, 1946.

31. National Society for the Study of Education. *Reading in the High School and College*. 47th Yearbook, Part II. Chicago: University of Chicago Press, 1948.

32. National Society for the Study of Education. *Reading in the Elementary School*. 48th Yearbook, Part II. Chicago: University of Chicago Press, 1949.

33. National Society for the Study of Education. *The Teaching of Arithmetic*. 50th Yearbook, Part II. Chicago: University of Chicago Press, 1951.

34. Nelson, M. J., *et al. The Nelson-Denney Reading Test* (rev. ed.). Boston: Houghton Mifflin Company, 1960.

35. Olsen, M. Summary of main findings on the validity of the CEEB Tests of Developed Abilities as predictors of college grades. *Educational Testing Service, Statistical Report*, 1957.

36. *Orleans Algebra Prognosis Test.* New York: Harcourt, Brace & World, Inc., 1951.
37. *Orleans Geometry Prognosis Test.* New York: Harcourt, Brace & World, Inc., 1951.
38. Pratt, W. E. *American School Reading Readiness Test.* Bloomington, Ill.: Public School Publishing Company, 1941–1955.
39. *Roswell-Chall Diagnostic Reading Test.* New York: Essay Press, 1956.
40. *Seashore-Bennett Stenographic Proficiency Test.* New York: The Psychological Corporation, 1956.
41. *Sequential Tests of Educational Progress: A Brief.* Princeton, N.J.: Educational Testing Service, 1958.
42. Spencer, P. L., and M. Brydegaard. *Building Mathematical Concepts in the Elementary School.* New York: Holt, Rinehart and Winston, Inc., 1952.
43. Strang, R., et al. *Problems in the Improvement of Reading* (2nd ed.). New York: McGraw-Hill Book Company, Inc., 1955.
44. Symonds, P. M. *Foreign Language Prognosis Test.* New York: Teachers College, Columbia University, 1930.
45. Thorpe, L. P., et al. *SRA Achievement Series.* Chicago: Science Research Associates, Inc., 1959.
46. Tiegs, E. W., and W. W. Clark. *California Achievement Tests.* Monterey: California Test Bureau, 1957.
47. Triggs, F. O., et al. *Diagnostic Reading Tests: Their Interpretation and Use in the Teaching of Reading.* New York: Committee on Diagnostic Reading Tests, Inc., 1950.
48. Triggs, F. O., et al. *Diagnostic Reading Tests: A History of Their Construction and Validation.* New York: Committee on Diagnostic Reading Tests, Inc., 1952.
49. Tydlaska, M., and C. White. *SRA Typing Adaptability Test.* Chicago: Science Research Associates, Inc., 1956.
50. Tyler, R. W., and E. R. Smith. *Appraising and Recording Student Progress.* New York: Harper & Brothers, 1942.
51. *Watson-Glaser Critical Thinking Appraisal.* New York: Harcourt, Brace & World, Inc., 1956.
52. Willis, E. P., et al. *American School Reading Readiness Test.* Bloomington, Ill.: Public School Publishing Company, 1955.
53. Wood, D. A. *Test Construction.* Columbus, Ohio: Charles E. Merrill Books, Inc., 1960.
54. Woolf, M. D., and J. A. Woolf. *Remedial Reading: Teaching and Treatment.* New York: McGraw-Hill Book Company, Inc., 1957.
55. Wrightstone, J. W. *Test of Critical Thinking in the Social Studies.* New York: Teachers College, Columbia University, 1939.
56. Wrightstone, J. W., et al. *New York Tests of Arithmetical Meanings.* New York: Harcourt, Brace & World, Inc., 1956.

21.

PERSONALITY RATING METHODS

Definition of Personality

     This term has been variously defined because personalities are complex and inclusive of all traits; hence, there is much room for differences in comprehensiveness of the definition. Those definitions, however, that include only the individual's *social* value to other members of his group (that is, more or less superficial attractiveness or reputation) are inadequate because they are concerned only with overt behavior, while they ignore the *inner* aspects of the personality—the motivation, perceptions, feelings, reactions, attitudes, values, prejudices that are the *basis* of one's behavior. These social-value definitions are concerned only with what a person does and the impression made by him upon others in his social groups. Such impressions and evaluations are, of course, important in an individual's life. They are evaluated by means of *rating scales*, which will be discussed in this chapter. These definitions, however, do not take into account the basic traits of a person, aside from what he *actually does*. His overt behavior may or may not reveal the covert aspects of his personality. Some parts of the *personality inventories*, as distinguished from rating scales, are intended to identify these covert traits in order to provide the psychologist with a basis for a fuller understanding of an individual's behavior. Whether they succeed in doing so is a question to be discussed. Also, *projective tests*, more than any other type of instrument, are intended to reveal the covert, subtler aspects of personality and behavior. These methods will be dealt with in later chapters.

A definition that commends itself is as follows: A personality is the product of the dynamic and characteristic organization within the individual of psychobiological structures, or systems, and their interaction with the environment. It is these two aspects—individuality of the structured organism and the nature of his environment—that determine the individual's particular adjustments to his surroundings.[1] A personality is the individuality that emerges from interaction between a psychobiological organism and the world in which he has developed and lives.

Personality is *described* in terms of an individual's behavior—his actions, postures, words, and attitudes and opinions regarding his external world. But personality may be more basically described in terms of the individual's covert *feelings* about his external world; feelings that may not be apparent or discernible in his overt behavior. It is described also in terms of one's feelings about *oneself*.

One's actual feelings about his external world and oneself may be at the conscious, preconscious, or unconscious level. The same is true regarding the consciousness levels of the *reasons for* these same feelings. In other words, a person may know why he feels as he does (conscious); or the reasons for his feelings may be somewhat below (figuratively) the level of awareness, but they can come into awareness with relatively little effort under appropriate stimulation (preconscious). Or the reasons may be so deeply submerged or blurred that they can be brought to the level of awareness only with difficulty, if at all (unconscious). This being the case then, it is desirable to have tests of personality that can probe the various aspects of personality and the levels of awareness as well.

Several aspects of the foregoing definition need more explanation before the instruments themselves are presented.

By *dynamic organization,* psychologists mean that personality traits do not exist independently or act in isolation. They are interrelated, interacting in an organized and coherent manner. They may, like any other organized system, be in process of change and evolution. *Disorganization* of traits and behavior results in "abnormality." It is in respect to the dynamic organization of traits that one of the greatest difficulties of personality testing is encountered; for it is much simpler to construct an inventory that will give an indication of an individual's tendencies to introversion, or sociability, or self-confidence, or ascendency, etc., than it is to construct one that will evaluate the person as a whole. The reader will note, later, that the available inventories and rating scales actually

---

[1] For excellent discussions of these aspects of personality, see G. W. Allport (2, Chaps. 2 and 3); and G. Murphy (11, Chap. 1).

deal with only smaller or larger segments of the personality, a number of which may be portrayed on a psychological profile; but to be most meaningful, these segments must somehow be organized into a whole by the psychologist who studies the individual case.

The term *psychobiological structures* connotes motives, habits, traits, attitudes, feelings, values, ways of thinking and acting. The word "psychobiological" is used to indicate that personality and its component integrals are neither exclusively mental nor exclusively biological. Rather, they involve psychological processes and functioning, together with their biological correlates.

Interaction with the environment is made explicit in order to emphasize that an individual's personality does not merely grow from within. It is the product of the interaction between himself as a developing organism having certain psychological and biological needs, on the one hand, and, on the other, his environment that has nurtured, influenced, directed, satisfied, or in varying degrees failed to satisfy those needs.

Rating Scales

Purposes. This type of scale is useful chiefly for learning what impression an individual has made on persons with whom he has come in contact, in respect to some specified traits or attitudes. It is a device that rates social value, occupational efficiency, group status, and the like, in certain specified areas; it reflects the impression the subject has made upon the persons who do the rating. The rating of one person by others is among the oldest of practices, the present psychological tools being refinements of the common practice of providing letters and oral recommendations.

For the evaluation of an individual, rating scales are submitted to teachers, counselors, employers, colleagues, parents, and others who have had sufficient contact with the person in question to have formed an opinion based upon evidence derived from observation. Usually, of course, ratings of a particular person are obtained from more than one judge; for validity of ratings is thereby increased, inasmuch as subjectivity of judgment is decreased through the balancing of errors and bias.

Rating scales may be devised for a variety of traits, such as tact, generosity, leadership, cooperativeness, resourcefulness, punctuality, industriousness, honesty, emotional control, study habits, personal attractiveness, and many others, the number of possibilities being virtually unlimited. Each scale usually includes traits to be rated individually, the specific ones depending upon the purposes for which the scale is intended. The terms used to designate each of the several traits being rated are often vague and may have different meanings for different judges. In order to minimize this problem of semantics and to make the rating scales more useful than they would otherwise be, it is necessary to observe certain established principles. The following are the major aspects to be considered in their construction and use.

Characteristics. *Each trait should be clearly defined.* This requirement is essential so that traits may be clearly and uniformly understood by all judges. This end may be achieved by giving explanations, synonyms, or specific instances as behavioral illustrations.

The degree of the trait should be defined. Each trait is rated on a scale, most frequently of five or seven intervals. A larger number of intervals would require refinements of distinctions which are not often possible. Each step on the scale must be clarified in much the same way as the trait definitions themselves. Examples are given in a later section, under "Types."

Reliability depends upon extent of variation of judges' ratings. Judges rating an individual on a specified trait will not always agree as to his score or rank. It is customary, therefore, to take the median or the mean of all the judgments as representing the nearest approximation to the true rating. If this method of averaging is to be meaningful, however, it is essential that the variation of the judges' ratings shall be small, thus indicating reasonably close agreement. A large variation, on the other hand, would indicate unreliability owing to lack of clarity regarding the trait being evaluated, contradictory or unstable behavior of the subject, or undependability of some judges. An average of the judges' ratings without regard to their variation might be misleading or even absurd. For example, if, on a seven-point scale, two judges rated an individual at -3, two at $+3$, and two at zero, the mean rating would be zero (or average level), whereas the probability is that he is not average at all, in view of the wide disparity of judgments. Reliability of ratings is usually dependent upon having a sufficient number of qualified judges, five to seven being the number frequently recommended, but infrequently obtained. The degree of agreement required before a set of judgments may be regarded as sufficiently reliable is, to some extent, arbitrarily determined; but to be statistically reliable, agreement among judges should be three or four times as great, at least, as that obtained by chance. (See Chapter 2, on errors of measurement and of the correlation coefficient.)

At times it is possible to discern, by inspection of the ratings of all judges, which *individual* judges seem to be most dependable. This is done by noting the extent to which each trait rating, of each judge, approximates the average of all ratings on that trait. Similarly, it is possible to identify the subjects who have been most reliably rated, in terms of extent of agreement among the judges. Thus, a rating scale can be useful in some individual cases, whereas the evidence for a group as a whole might be less than satisfactory.

Methods of studying reliability of rating scales most commonly include the following: repeating judgments after a time interval; correlation between ratings of two or more judges; and relationship between judges' ratings and self-ratings. The correlation coefficients thus found are near .50 and .60—much lower than would be acceptable in the case of tests of general intelligence, specific aptitudes, or educational achievement. Occasionally, however, much higher reliability coefficients have been obtained, some being approximately .85.

The relatively low reliabilities are not necessarily attributable to defects in the conception of a scale or in the phrasing of the characteristics to be rated. The coefficients reflect, to a considerable extent, the differences among the judges and their unreliability.

It has already been stated that the traits to be rated and the intervals on the scale should be clearly defined. In addition, it is necessary to instruct respondents with regard to other aspects affecting the reliability of their judgments; that is, the rating of each trait should be made independently of other ratings of the same person (avoidance of the "halo" effect); ratings should be based upon adequate acquaintance with the subject; experience and acquaintance with a broad enough variety of persons to provide bases of judgment are desirable; sincere motivation to provide the most reliable ratings possible is necessary. Of these, the "halo" effect has been shown to be among the most serious causes of unreliability. One tends to overrate a person in all respects if he likes him, or if he is a close acquaintance.

Determination of validity is difficult. There are few, if any, useful criteria of validity, in the usual sense, that can be employed in evaluating a rating scale, because there are only a few measured or measurable behaviors available with which these scales can be compared. The validity of a rating scale is assumed, in actual practice, to rest upon the judges' understanding of the meanings of the traits being evaluated and upon their accuracy in rating them. The principal indication of validity of some rating scales is the fact that persons using them—guidance counselors, personnel officers, employers—find them helpful if the judges are carefully selected and if the ratings are conscientiously made. This last condition cannot always be taken for granted. A rater might be unwilling to devote the time and care necessary for a careful appraisal. It happens, not infrequently, that raters find the task an onerous one and, consequently, respond with superficial evaluations. The respondent might—

consciously or not—identify with the person being rated. Or the judge might want to help this person; or, at least, not injure him. Furthermore, ratings may be in part determined by idiosyncracies, prejudices, and folklore. We still hear and read about the "strong jaw," the "honest face," the "penetrating eye," and the "intelligent brow."

Overt traits are more reliably rated than covert traits. Traits that can be evaluated upon the basis of objective activities, upon actual past or present behaviors known to the judges, are more reliably rated than covert traits. For example, emotional expression, social acceptability, manifest fear and anxiety, aggressive or impulsive acts are rated with greater reliability than those dealing with a person's inner life and feelings about one's self. Although these ratings can be of significance in learning about the subject's status, they are not to be taken at face value so far as basic personality structure and dynamics are concerned. Overt behavior can be misleading. Aggression can be an expression of feelings of insecurity; excessive display may be evidence of strong feelings of inferiority; a high degree of conformity and agreeableness is, in some instances, symptomatic of deep-seated anxiety.

Degree of certainty of ratings should be stated. With each rating, it is desirable to have the respondent state his degree of certainty (that is, very strong, strong, moderate).[2] It has been demonstrated that judges are most confident and in closer agreement on ratings at the extremes. This is understandable because extreme deviants are most clearly distinguishable from others and are most readily characterized by the trait names. Thus, such terms as "cooperative–uncooperative" and "introverted–extroverted" apply most forcibly and clearly to individuals who are manifestly at one pole or the other.

Some persons are more accurately rated than others. On the whole, extroverted individuals are more reliably judged than introverted. The ratings of persons whose traits are characterized by overt behavior, rather than by covertness and inner qualities, will be based upon fuller, more representative, and more clearly perceived behavior samples. Also, it has been found that judges rate more reliably those persons who most resemble themselves, because, it is believed, one can best empathize with persons whose behavior resembles his own.

Reliability of trait estimates is affected by desirability or undesirability of the trait. In self-ratings there is a tendency for individuals to overrate themselves in respect to traits regarded as socially desirable. In rating other persons, especially friends, some judges may be similarly influenced, even while trying to be conscientious. In fact, there is a general tendency toward generosity in ratings, rather than the reverse.

[2] A similar practice is now often used in polling public opinion.

Types of Rating Scales. The two most common forms are the *scoring* and the *ranking* types. When the first of these is used, the subject is rated at a point, or level, on the scale, without direct reference to or comparison with other persons in his group (for example, classroom, fellow workers). Each point or level on the scale carries a specified score. On a scale of five, for example, the "average" person is scored 0; the deviants are scored +2, +1, −1, or −2. Or the scores, to eliminate signs, can all be positive, 1 being the lowest, 3 the average, 5 the highest.

A common variant of the scoring method is the *graphic rating* scale. The several levels, or degrees, of the trait are defined and placed at points along a horizontal line. The judge places a mark anywhere he chooses on this line, between the two extremes. Although a graphic scale theoretically permits scoring at a large number of points, such refinement and spurious accuracy are not warranted. The investigator or compiler of information will, therefore, convert each rating within a given range according to a predetermined numerical scheme.

The following are examples of the numerical rating scale.

How emotional is the parent's behavior where the child is concerned?

_____Constantly gives vent to unbridled emotion in response to child's behavior.

_____Controlled largely by emotion rather than by reason in dealing with child.

_____Emotion freely expressed, but actual practice is seldom disorganized.

_____Usually maintains calm, objective behavior toward child, even in face of trying situations.

_____Never shows any sign of disorganization toward child.

Does he get others to do what he wants done?

_____Displays marked ability to lead his fellows.

_____Sometimes leads in important affairs.

_____Sometimes leads in minor affairs.

_____Lets others take the lead.

_____Probably unable to lead his fellows.

_____No opportunity to observe.

Each rater checks what he believes to be the correct description. The investigator then will convert the check marks into scores. In the first instance, the third item would be the average and would be scored zero; the first and second would be −2 and −1, respectively; the fourth and fifth, +1 and +2, respectively.

The graphic type of item may be illustrated by the following, remembering the necessity of definition of the trait and clarification of levels.

Quality of work

Of doubtful satisfaction.	Not quite up to standard.	Satisfactory.	Superior to general run.	Exception- ally high.

Attitude toward others

Quarrelsome, uncooperative, upsets morale.	At times difficult to work with.	Ordinarily tactful, co- operative, and self- controlled.	Always con- genial and cooperative.	Unusually strong fac- tor in co- operation and group morale.

The *ranking* scale is used with persons who are associated within a single group and who are to be rated relative to one another. The judge arranges the names in serial order with regard to each one's status in a specified trait. Usually, the judge is instructed first to select the individuals to be ranked highest, lowest, and average, and then to place the others in relation to these three. Since intervals between successive individuals are not equal, and since it is impossible by this method to determine the sizes of the intervals, arithmetical and statistical computations are not warranted and should not be attempted. The ranking scale simply provides a method for use with a single group of subjects when, for any valid reason, intragroup comparisons are desired.

Another method, frequently used in rating high school and college students, is to place each individual according to his *percentile or decile* (sometimes quartile or quintile) *position* in his group.[3] Thus, a high school senior applying for college admission, or a college senior applying for admission to a graduate school, might be rated according to the following scheme.

Ranks in the highest 5 per cent of his group.
        in the second highest 5 percent of his group.
        in the highest 25 percent, but not in the top 10 percent.
        in the third quartile group.
        in the second quartile group.
        in the first (lowest) quartile group.

When it is desirable to learn whether certain specified traits or behaviors are present or absent, a *check list* is used. This consists simply of a number of statements; each one that applies to the person being rated is checked. At times, such a list may be scored +1 for a favorable

[3] See Chapters 2 and 6 for explanations of these indexes.

item, −1 for an unfavorable item, and 0 for a neutral one. Scores of check lists, however, have little meaning, except as a gross indication of a trend. Anyone using these devices will find more information and value in analyzing and interrelating the items that have been checked (as present) and those left unchecked (as absent). The Vineland Social Maturity Scale (see below) is a carefully constructed and unusual example of a check list in that it is a standardized scale. The usual list takes the following form.

> Handles others well; gets cooperation.
> Gives evidence of sound decisions.
> Usually well-balanced emotionally.
> Cooperates willingly when others direct.
> Satisfactory standards can be relied on.

A more discriminating type of check list uses statements, such as those above, but provides the respondent with an opportunity to indicate the degree to which he believes each behavior is manifested by the subject. This is done simply by adding to each item a series of qualifying terms, such as: always, usually, occasionally, rarely, never.

FORCED-CHOICE ITEMS. Each item of this type consists of two or more statements or attributes (there may be two, three, or four). The respondent is asked to indicate which one or two of the attributes, in each set, is most descriptive of or appropriate to the person being rated. In each set, of one form, all attributes may be either desirable or undesirable in the situation or occupation for which the subject is being evaluated. Although all statements in each set are descriptive of desirable or undesirable characteristics, they do not have equal discriminative value; that is, they are not equally valid in helping to identify desirable or undesirable personalities for the particular job or educational program under consideration, though they might appear so to the rater. This fact is one of the advantages of the forced-choice method; for it reduces the possible effects of a favorable bias. The following four statements might constitute one item from which the judge is to select two as being most appropriate to the individual being evaluated.[4]

Is well informed in his science
Can apply scientific fact and theory to practical situations
Creates confidence in those with whom he deals
Explains the reasons for his recommendations

In another form of the forced-choice item, within each set of four statements two are favorable and two are unfavorable. Of the two favor-

[4] The forced-choice method is also used in some self-rating scales, such as the Kuder Preference Record and the Edwards Personal Preference Scale. These are discussed in Chapter 23.

able statements, one has greater validity than the other; and the same is true, in a negative sense, of the unfavorable statements. The rater is required to select the one attribute that is most applicable and the one that is least applicable to the subject.

Forced-choice rating scales yield, in general, more valid results than do graphic scales; but of the two forms of forced choice, better results are obtained with items that present four favorable attributes, two being relevant to the criterion, while the other two are significantly less relevant. This is attributable, at least in part, to the fact that respondents prefer the all-favorable type of item, hence cooperate better, and to the fact that faking and distorting are easier on the two-favorable and two-unfavorable type.

The advantages claimed for the forced-choice form are these: Descriptions of behavior and assignment of attributes are kept within a narrower range of standards; generosity in ratings and the "halo" effect do not operate as strongly as with other methods; and rater bias, in either direction, is reduced, since it is difficult for respondents in general to know which of the attributes are the more favorable or the more unfavorable.

This method, however, has its disadvantages. Respondents are often resistant or antagonistic to forced-choice items because of the restrictions imposed upon them and because they believe none of the statements within some sets are really appropriate to the person being rated. Conscientious raters generally prefer the independence and the opportunity to exercise judgment, as provided by graphic scales, numerical scales, and percentage ratings (percentile, decile, etc.).

THE Q-SORT TECHNIQUE. This method may be used for a variety of purposes when a fairly wide range of relative rankings is wanted. The rater might be given, for example one hundred pictures of works of art to be sorted into a specified number of groups (frequently nine or eleven), from most preferred to least preferred. Or he might be given a large number of human traits to sort out according to the degree to which he regards each as desirable or undesirable in persons with whom he must associate. Similarly, when this technique is used to rate a particular individual, the respondent is given a list of behaviors or attributes, each on a separate card, which are to be sorted into a specified number of groups, ranging from those least descriptive of the subject to those most descriptive. The rater is instructed not only to sort these into the specified number of groups, but he is required to place a specified number of items in each group, so that the final result is a symmetrical, normal frequency distribution. Each statement, thereby, is given a score indicating the relative strength, within the subject, of the quality it represents. Obviously, this forced distribution is a variant on the forced-choice procedure. It can have little value, even with only seven groupings, unless the number of items or statements to be sorted is rather large, in order to give the distribution significance.

There are no fixed or standardized lists of behaviors and attributes; individual and particularized lists may be devised for each of many different purposes or situations. Since, in this chapter, the discussion is concerned with ratings of individuals by others, the following statements are given as illustrations of items that might be used in making a Q-Sort (4).[5]

Has a wide range of interests
Behaves in an assertive fashion
Is introspective and concerned with self as an object; frequently self-aware
Has insight into his own motives and behavior.

These statements are not different from those included in check lists or other forms of rating. They are different only in the manner in which they are treated.

The *justifications* offered for the forced distribution are these:

1. It eliminates individual differences in the patterns of response among raters; it is a means of making ratings more nearly objective and comparable by prescribing a pattern.

2. It facilitates the computation of a median or mean score (position) on a set of attributes considered desirable or undesirable in a specified situation.

3. It provides a convenient method for calculating reliabilities of ratings and validities of the items.

4. The method can yield a broad description of an individual if the statements are carefully chosen and are parts of a meaningful whole.

Adverse criticisms are these:

1. Users of the technique assume without proof that a normal distribution best fits the ratings of each person, whereas while statements may have relative applicability and significance for a person, it does not necessarily follow that an arbitrary distribution is the correct or the best fit.

2. The Q-Sort technique provides an estimate of the relative rating for each attribute; it does not give any information about the strength of each attribute within an individual, since each person's own typical behavior is used as the standard of comparison in each instance.

3. The method requires considerable conscientious effort on the part of the rater and is, therefore, not feasible in most practical situations.

4. That the Q-Sort technique yields results superior to those obtained by other rating methods has not been established. It does appear, however, that it is a useful tool in research on groups.

CRITICAL INCIDENT TECHNIQUE. This is a technique that uses detailed descriptions of an individual's behavior, regarded as favorable (effective) or unfavorable (ineffective) in a given situation. The purpose of the

---

[5] This method also may be used to obtain self-ratings. See (13).

method is to find the traits and behaviors that contribute significantly to successful or unsuccessful performance in a certain type of job or undertaking, and upon the basis of the findings, to prepare a list of favorable and unfavorable attributes to be used in subsequent ratings. Flanagan states: "By an incident is meant any observable human activity which is sufficiently complete in itself to permit inferences and predictions to be made about the person performing the act. To be critical, an incident must occur in a situation where the purpose or intent of the act seems fairly clear to the observer, and its consequences are sufficiently definite so that there is little doubt concerning its effects" (8, p. 2). "Essentially, the procedure was to obtain first-hand reports, or reports from objective records, of satisfactory and unsatisfactory execution of the task assigned. The cooperating individual described a situation in which success or failure was determined by specific reported causes" (8, p. 4).

Since this technique originated in the armed forces of the United States, the following example is cited (8, p. 8) .

> This officer (a Capt.) was in charge of a Base Service Section and had one of the hardest jobs on the base. One of the many activities under his section was the Officer's Club—always a headache, and especially when the club officer was no good. This particular club was losing money, service was terrible and the place continually looked dirty and unkempt. In addition the chef and the civilian manager (a woman) feuded from dawn to dusk and the club officer was afraid of the club manager. The Base Service Officer realized that he must take action immediately so he went over to the club and called each of the key people in separately and explained in detail what their duties were and what he expected them to do and how. Then he called them all together and gave them a lecture on tact, cooperation and service. This took care of the personnel angle, so he spent the next three weeks (after his normal duty hours) reorganizing the club's stock control system, purchasing system and many other small club activities. At the end of that three-week period, the club had improved so greatly that the amount of business had nearly doubled.

Following an exploratory study of the use of this technique for application to medical education, a rather lengthy tentative list of attributes (a "first approximation") was suggested. One section of this list follows (5).

E. Communication with patients
1. Taking time to talk over a problem until full understanding is reached
2. Informing patient of operative findings
3. Informing patient that he has cancer
4. Honesty in telling patient what to expect
5. Failure to give clear directions
6. Clear understanding of financial obligations before a procedure is initiated

The value of the critical incidents depends upon the competence and insights of observers who report them and upon obtaining a series of reports that will permit the isolation of a comprehensive list of valid attributes.

Representative Rating Scales. Several scales, representative of the more satisfactory ones and serving different purposes, will be described.

Haggerty-Olson-Wickman Rating Schedules. These are designed for the detection and study of behavior problems and problem tendencies in individuals from nursery school through high school. Schedule A is a behavior-problem record, enumerating fifteen types or sources of problems, such as speech difficulties and defiance of discipline. Each of the fifteen is rated from 1 to 4, depending upon frequency of occurrence. Schedule B is a graphic scale, consisting of thirty-five traits classified into four groups: intellectual, physical, emotional, and social. These traits are scored on a five-point scale. The authors provide better than usual evidence of validity. They report a correlation of .76 with frequency of referral for reasons of discipline or other action by school principals, which may be symptomatic of a variety of adjustment difficulties. They report, also, that only 10 percent of "normal" children reach or exceed the median score of those referred to the psychological clinic.

The Vineland Social Maturity Scale. This scale is unique in having been constructed and standardized on the model of the Stanford-Binet scale. It is designed for use with individuals from infancy to the age of 30 years.

Unlike many other scales, this one is based upon a well-defined rationale and has been systematically constructed. Behavior items are grouped at age levels, as in the Stanford-Binet. The items represent progressive maturation and adjustment to the environment in the following categories: self-help, self-direction, locomotion, occupation, communication, and socialization. The following examples illustrate the several categories.

Self-help: Reaches for nearby objects (age 0–1)
Self-direction: Buys own clothing (age 15–18)
Locomotion: Walks about room unattended (age 1–2)
Occupation: Helps at little household tasks (age 3–4)
         Systematizes own work (age 25+)
Communication: Makes telephone calls (age 10–11)
Socialization: Demands personal attention (age 0–1)
         Advances general welfare (age 25+)

Items are scored after interviewing someone well acquainted with the subject, or the subject himself. A social age is then obtained; this is divided by chronological age, yielding a social quotient (SQ).

Although this social maturity scale shows a high correlation with intelligence-test results (about .80), Doll maintains that it is distinct enough in content and in the behaviors rated to warrant its use in the study of an individual's general development, since social age provides a basis upon which to proceed in his care and training.

Although the scale is intended for use with a normal population as well as with the mentally deficient, it was first conceived as an aid in the diagnosis of feeblemindedness. In the first instance, it was and still is intended to differentiate between mentally deficient individuals who are also socially inadequate, on the one hand, and, on the other hand, the mentally retarded who are competent to conduct their personal and social lives.

The Vineland scale has had wide use in clinics for children and adolescents because, in addition to the uses already indicated, it is a valuable device for interviewing and counseling both parents and children.

The Fels Parent Behavior Scales. This device provides thirty rating scales, in as many aspects, for assessing parental behavior toward their children. Ratings are made by a qualified observer in respect to those aspects of the home environment that the rater has been able to observe and review in a systematic manner, by means of home visits and interviews with parents. Among the rated thirty aspects of child-parent relationships are the following: discord in home, sociability of family, child-centeredness of family, restrictiveness of regulations, readiness of criticism, rapport with child.

In clinical and research work, these scales have been found useful in providing a systematized approach to the detailed analysis of psychological environments in which children are developing. The scales provide a standardized method for describing and estimating the nature of the effect of a child's home upon his behavioral development.

Rating Scale for Pupil Adjustment. Eleven areas of personality, to be rated by teachers, are included in this scale, which was originally intended for use in conjunction with the *Michigan Picture Test* (see Chapter 25). The areas dealt with are: over-all emotional adjustment, social maturity, tendency toward depression, tendency toward aggressive behavior, extroversion–introversion, emotional security, motor control, impulsiveness, emotional irritability, school achievement, and school conduct. From this list of characteristics, it is apparent that the scale is clinically oriented; its use is recommended by schools that provide diagnostic and treatment services; and it is intended to improve the selection of referrals to clinics.

The nature of the traits to be rated on this scale requires more professional information and psychological insights than might reasonably be expected of most teachers, since the ratings often will depend upon the *interpretations* of overt behavior, rather than upon only the *descrip-*

tive characterizations of behavior. To be of most use to a counselor or a clinician, each trait rating should be accompanied by a recorded description of the pupil's behavior in that category.

Wittenborn Psychiatric Rating Scales. This is a highly specialized device, being ". . . a procedure for recording the observed behavior of mental patients and for describing them according to their current symp-

WITTENBORN PSYCHIATRIC RATING SCALES
J. Richard Wittenborn

Copyright, ©, 1955. The Psychological Corporation, 522 Fifth Ave., New York 36, N.Y. Copyright in Canada.

Patient's Name_____ Age _____ Sex _____

Date Observations Began_____ Date of Rating_____

Institution_____ Ward_____ Ratings Made by_____

Instructions to Rater:

    1. Print the requested information in the spaces above.

    2. Each scale consists of three or four descriptive statements. For each scale, select the one statement which best describes the patient's behavior and draw a circle around the number found at the right of that statement.

Scale		I	II	III	IV	V	VI	VII	VIII	IX
1. Gives no evidence of difficulty in sleeping.	0									
Without sedation may have difficulty in falling asleep, or sleep is readily or spontaneously interrupted.	①	/				/				
Without sedation long periods of wakefulness at night.	2									
Acute insomnia; without sedatives gets less than 4 hours sleep in 24.	3									
2. Rate of change of ideas (e.g., topics of conversation) does not appear to be accelerated, nor are changes conspicuously abrupt.	0								2	
Ideas may change *abruptly*.	1									
Ideas are in the process of *rapid* and *constant* change.	②				2					
Ideas change with spontaneous and unpredictable rapidity as to make sustained conversation *impossible*.	3								2	
3. No evidence that he imagines people (who probably are wholly indifferent to him) have an amorous interest in him.	⓪									
Believes (without justification) that certain persons have an amorous interest in him.	1									
Believes (without justification) that a sexual union has occurred or has been formally arranged for him.	2									
4. No evidence for obsessional (repetitive, stereotyped) thinking.	⓪									
Obsessive thoughts recur but can be banished without difficulty.	1									
Patient is able to banish obsessive thoughts but only with difficulty.	2									
Cannot banish or control obsessive thoughts.	3									
5. No evidence that patient considers himself to be particularly unworthy or blameworthy.	0		3							
Patient tends to blame himself or refer to his unworthiness.	1									
Patient blames and criticizes self to an unrealistic and inappropriate degree.	2									
Patient appears to have a *delusional* belief that he is an extraordinarily evil, unworthy or guilty person.	③		3							
Subtotals (p. 1)		7	2		5					

Fig. 21.1. Items from the Wittenborn Psychiatric Rating Scales. The white spaces indicate to which of the nine psychiatric categories the item is relevant and for which it is scored. By permission.

toms. The Scales provide for the assignment of numerical values to indicate the presence and degree of pathological symptoms in a patient"
(16, Manual). Fifty-two symptoms (pathological manifestations) are rated;
each, with a few exceptions, is given a weighted score from 0 to 3; the
scores are then totaled for each of nine psychiatric categories (see Fig.
21.1, in which five of the fifty-two symptoms are rated). Since the symptoms sample behavior "ordinarily considered important by psychiatrists,"
this instrument is based, primarily, upon content validity.

The nine categories are: acute anxiety, conversion hysteria, manic
state, depressed state, schizophrenic excitement, paranoid condition,
paranoid schizophrenic, hebephrenic schizophrenic, and phobic compulsive. The scores for these categories may be viewed as a profile, for the
purpose of making a clinical diagnosis. Significant clues are provided by
high scores; [6] in general, the fifty-two items assist in and focalize objective
descriptions of patients' observable behavior. From the categories listed,
it is quite evident that this scale should be used and interpreted only by
professionally qualified persons.

Other Scales. The reader will have observed that the scales described
above are intended for school and clinical use. The reason for this selection is that the better devices of this type are to be found in schools
and clinics. Numerous rating scales are being used also in personnel
departments of the government, and in business, industry, social agencies,
and counseling centers. In conception, they are similar to those presented;
but relatively few have been subjected to as thorough scrutiny as they
should be.

The following items, used in industry, are presented for illustrative
purposes. They are typical of those that are widely used.

Relations with other supervisors:
    a. Often not satisfactory
    b. Sometimes not satisfactory
    c. Usually gets along well
    d. More satisfactory than average
    e. Exceptionally satisfactory
Knowledge of the characteristics and abilities of subordinates:
    a. Knowledge markedly limited
    b. Knowledge somewhat limited
    c. Knows employees fairly well
    d. Knowledge better than average
    e. Knowledge exceptional
Willingness to make difficult decisions:
    a. Often "passes the buck"
    b. Inclined to "pass the buck"

[6] This fact, the student will recognize, applies to various types of psychological testing.

    c. Usually properly willing
    d. More willing than average
    e. Exceptionally willing
Resourcefulness in meeting difficulties:
    a. Often goes to pieces
    b. Easily discouraged by obstacles
    c. Usually meets the situation
    d. More resourceful than average
    e. Nearly always finds good way out
Ability to learn new work:
    a. Learns with difficulty
    b. Learns somewhat slowly
    c. Learns fairly easily
    d. Better than average
    e. Learns with exceptional ease and speed

In the armed forces during World War II, rating scales were devised to assist in personnel evaluation in a variety of situations. These followed the usual principles and practices already explained.[7]

    Evaluation of Rating Scales. Rating scales are not tests; nor are they precise or objective measures; hence, their reliability cannot be so high as that found for other types of psychological instruments. Rating scales do provide a means of obtaining organized descriptions of behavioral traits from judges who have had ample opportunity to make the necessary observations. If the scale meets the specifications discussed in this chapter, ratings will be based upon greater uniformity of trait-definition and trait-connotation than will purely individual ratings of traits defined by each judge independently.

By means of an organized scale it is possible to obtain ratings on specified traits that are considered essential or significant in the particular setting where the scale is being used. Completely independent, or "unstructured" ratings, by contrast, may fail to provide desired information.

While high reliability of ratings among judges of the same persons would simplify interpretations of results, moderate or even low reliability coefficients do not discredit a soundly conceived scale. The reason for relatively low reliability coefficients may be one or a combination of the following two factors. (1) In spite of carefully defined traits and degrees thereof, ratings are always subject to the judges' biases, values, and standards of performance and behavior. Some degree of influence of these aspects of the judges' own personalities is inevitable. (2) Behavior of the person being rated may be and at times is variable in different types of situations. This is the case even though there is some degree of

[7] See Stuit (14).

trait-consistency within a person. For example, an individual who is "self-confident" in one situation is prone to be "self-confident" in another, whereas a person who is "withdrawn" is prone to behave that way in many settings. Yet that same individual is not equally self-confident or equally withdrawn on all occasions; and, in fact, there may be situations in which his characteristic mode of behavior is not readily apparent. Variability of behavior is especially true of children and adolescents whose personality traits are still in process of formation. In interpreting ratings, it is necessary, therefore, to know the types of situations in which each judge made his observations.

The usual criteria and standards of validity are not applicable to rating scales. Theirs is a matter of construct, or content, validity. The questions to be asked regarding the validity of a rating scale are these: Does it meet the specifications of a sound scale? Are the traits being rated by the scale significant in the setting or occupation for which the individual is being considered? If these two questions are answered satisfactorily, then the ultimate usefulness (that is, predictive validity) of the scale will depend upon the soundness (reliability) of the judges' ratings.

References

1. Allen, R. M. *Personality Assessment Procedures.* New York: Harper & Brothers, 1958.
2. Allport, G. W. *Pattern and Growth in Personality.* New York: Holt, Rinehart and Winston, Inc., 1961.
3. Andrews, G., *et al. Rating Scale for Pupil Adjustment.* Chicago: Science Research Associates, Inc., 1950–1953.
4. Block, J. A comparison between ipsative and normative ratings of personality. *Journal of Abnormal and Social Psychology,* 1957, *54,* 50–54.
5. Diederich, P. B. *The Critical Incidents Technique Applied to Medical Education,* RM-54-9. Princeton, N.J.: Educational Testing Service, 1954.
6. Doll, E. A. *The Vineland Social Maturity Scale.* Vineland, N.J.: The Training School, 1935–1953.
7. *Fels Parent Behavior Scales.* Yellow Springs, Ohio: Fels Institute, 1937–1949.
8. Flanagan, J. C. *The Critical Incident Technique.* Pittsburgh: American Institute for Research, 1953.
9. *Haggerty-Olson-Wickman Rating Schedules.* New York: Harcourt, Brace & World, Inc., 1930.
10. Kelly, G. A. Theory and technique of assessment. *Annual Review of Psychology,* 1958, *9.* Palo Alto, Calif.: Annual Reviews, Inc.
11. Murphy, G. *Personality: A Biosocial Approach to Origins and Structure.* New York: Harper & Brothers, 1947.

12. Richardson, M. W. Forced-choice performance reports: a modern merit-rating method. *Personnel,* 1949, *26,* 205–212.
13. Stephenson, W. *The Study of Behavior: Q-Technique and Its Methodology.* Chicago: University of Chicago Press, 1953.
14. Stuit, D. B. (ed.). *Personnel Research and Test Development in the Bureau of Naval Personnel.* Princeton, N.J.: Princeton University Press, 1947.
15. Super, D. E. Theories and assumptions underlying approaches to personality assessment. In B. M. Bass and I. A. Berg (eds.), *Objective Approaches to Personality Assessment.* Princeton, N.J.: D. Van Nostrand Company, Inc., 1959.
16. *Wittenborn Psychiatric Rating Scales.* New York: The Psychological Corporation, 1955.
17. Wolf, R., and H. A. Murray. An experiment in judging personalities. *Journal of Psychology,* 1937, *3,* 345–365.

22.

SITUATIONAL TESTS

Among the more recent developments in psychological testing are situational tests that either test the individual in action or confront him with situations related to his own life, in response to which he gives expression to his feelings for other persons. The individual's behavior is rated or evaluated by his peers or by judges.

Although situational tests are not as unstructured as the Rorschach and the Thematic Apperception Test, they are in a degree projective methods;[1] for the subject, by means of them, reveals some of his personality traits through his preference for or against certain contacts with others (as in sociometric tests), and through his spontaneous methods of dealing with life situations (preconceived by the examiner) that confront him (as in the psychodrama and in Office of Strategic Services tests).

Sociometric Methods

Description. This method, credited to J. L. Moreno as the innovator (15), may be defined as a technique for revealing and evaluating the social structure of a group through the measurement of the frequency of acceptance or nonacceptance among the individuals who constitute the group. It is an approach to the problem of studying interpersonal relationships. This technique permits the analysis of each person's position and status within the group, with respect to a particular criterion.

[1] For projective tests, see Chapters 25 and 26.

(For example: Name the pupil in your class with whom you would most like to sit at lunch; name your second choice. Name the two persons in your class, in order of preference, whom you would choose as leader on a trip.) The method also reveals the organization of the group, as well as identifying dominant individuals, cliques, cleavages (sex, racial, economic, etc.), and patterns of social attraction and rejection. The reasons for the existing patterns of attraction and avoidance can then be determined if the personality traits of each individual are known and the values of the group as a whole, established.

The method is a very simple one. The sociometric test requires that each individual in a given group choose one or more other persons in that group for a specified purpose. In a schoolroom, the pupils may be asked to name their first and second preferences next to whom they wish to sit, or with whom they wish to attend the movies, or with whom they would like to work on a project. Or they may be asked to name one or more individuals in the group who possess certain specified traits, such as the opposites "talkative–silent," "neat–unkempt," etc. Sociometric tests were used in a state training school for girls to determine with whom each individual would prefer to live or work, and with whom each would not want to live or work (9). The method was adopted for use in the armed forces in an effort to identify individuals for specific assignments requiring, for example, leadership and dependability. Thus, each individual is viewed in his social relationship to the whole group.

It is apparent that a sociometric test may be devised for innumerable groups and situations. The guiding principles are that each one must be relevant to a life situation of the group, and the items or questions must be such as to require each person in the group to make one or more definite selections revealing certain personal preferences, rejections, or values.

As an illustration, we take a class of seventeen pupils—seven girls and ten boys—in a school grade. They are asked to name the two pupils with whom they would prefer to sit at lunch. After the information is obtained, a sociogram is constructed. Of the several kinds of sociograms that have been suggested, the one shown in Figure 22.1 commends itself because it is simply made and easy to interpret. It is known as the "target technique," having been described by Northway (20). There are four concentric circles; acceptability scores, based on total number of choices received by each person, are divided into four groups; the lowest quarter is on the outside of the target and the highest are in the center. Each individual is represented on the target according to his acceptability score. The arrows show which individuals have been selected by whom. Solid and broken lines indicate first and second choices, respectively. It is possible, also, to divide the target in various ways in order to show cleavages. In this figure, the vertical line readily shows the intersex choices.

Usually, an individual's sociometric score is simply the number of mentions he receives, or the percentage of mentions he receives from others in the group.

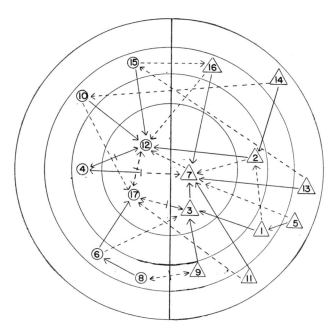

FIG. 22.1. Sociogram of an elementary school class

Another form of sociometry, which has been called an opinion test, is used to obtain individuals' opinions of one another with regard to a number of traits. The test consists of a series of brief "word pictures," each one followed by a blank space in which the child is to write the names of others in the group (for example, classmates), who may be like the "word picture." One may include his own name if he believes the description suits him. Two items are used to describe the extremes of each trait. For example: "Here is someone who finds it hard to sit still in class; he (or she) moves around in his (or her) seat or gets up and walks around." "Here is someone who can work quietly without moving around in his (or her) seat."

In the research reported by Tryon (23), twenty pairs of items were used, describing the extremes of twenty traits, as follows:

restless—quiet
talkative—silent
attention-getting—non-attention-getting
bossy—submissive
unkempt—tidy
fights—avoids fights
daring—afraid
leader—follower
active in games—sedentary
humor (regarding self)—humorless (regarding self)
friendly—unfriendly
popular—unpopular
good-looking—not good-looking
enthusiastic—listless
happy—unhappy
humor (jokes)—humorless (jokes)
assured (with adults)—shy (with adults)
assured (in class)—embarrassed (in class)
grown-up—childish
older friends (preference for)—younger friends (preference for)

An individual's score on a given trait is determined by the number of times he is mentioned by his classmates on the pair of opposed items. The item in each pair designating activity or a favorable trait is given a positive score, whereas the opposed item is given a negative value. An individual's score on each trait is the algebraic sum of positive and negative mentions received. In order to equate for the size of each group, the algebraic sum of mentions received by each child on each trait is converted into a proportion of the class voting for him. (Self-mentions are not included.)

A recent sociometric instrument is the *Syracuse Scales of Social Relations* (6), separate forms of which are available for elementary (grades 5 and 6), junior high school (grades 7–9) and senior high school (grades 10–12) pupils. The scales are based upon, and rate, two important and specific psychological needs at each of the three levels.[2] These are:

elementary:	succorance
	achievement–recognition
junior high school:	succorance
senior high school:	deference
	succorance
	playmirth

[2] These needs, the authors of the scales indicate, were based upon the research of H. A. Murray and his colleagues (18).

These particular needs were selected ". . . because they provide the most vital kind of information . . ."

The procedure is the same at all three levels. Each individual ". . . is asked to rate his classmates as possible sources of aid when he is troubled by some personal problem" (succorance). Under "need-achievement," each pupil ". . . rates each of his classmates as a possible source of support in his effort to attain personal goals whose attainment will bring social approval and commendation." Under "deference," fellow pupils are rated as ideals to look up to; while under "playmirth," they are rated according to the extent to which their company would be enjoyed at a party or other forms of recreation. The evaluations by each pupil are made ". . . with reference to a scale of 'all persons he has ever known' which permits inter-individual and inter-group comparisons of need-satisfaction expectations" (see Fig. 22.2).

The results obtained with these scales are expected to indicate the extent to which each individual feels favorable toward his classmates. The scores are intended to provide answers—at least tentative ones—to such questions as these: Does a particular pupil feel comfortable with his classmates? Does he feel he is part of the group and accepted by them? Are his feelings toward his classmates consistent with theirs toward him? What, in general, are the social relations within the class? Answers to these questions, it is held, should provide a basis upon which to proceed with any remedial measures that might be necessary, to be taken by the parent, teacher, guidance counselor, or psychologist.

Validity and Reliability. The ordinary questions have arisen in regard to reliability and validity of these sociometric devices. Correlational data indicate that mutual ratings and reratings over short intervals of several weeks, are highly reliable, yielding coefficients of about .90. Tryon obtained on each trait, for each subject, two sets of scores by taking the score for one half of the judges (selected at random) and correlating these with the scores of the other half. This split-half method, for the twenty traits, yielded an average reliability coefficient of about .75. The test-retest method (ten-day interval), gave an average correlation between the two sets of scores of about .80. Tryon also reports that only about ten percent of the children and adolescents in her group received disagreeing votes on any pair of items; and most of these individuals were close to the average category in the number of votes received. However, there was rarely any disagreement regarding individuals who clearly deviated from the average category. The foregoing evidence indicates that, among the subjects tested, there is concurrence of opinion regarding one another. Test-retest reliability coefficients obtained with the Syracuse scales varied from .61 to .85, thirteen of the sixteen coefficients being above .70.

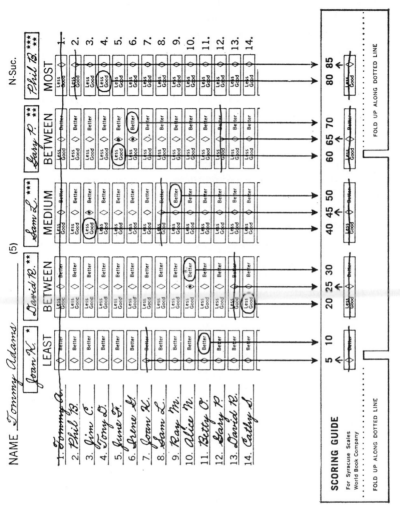

Fig. 22.2. An example of ratings on the Syracuse Scales of Social Relations. By permission.

The usual criteria and standards of validity do not apply to sociometric tests; for they do not set out to determine what are some of the actual personality and behavior traits of the individuals being rated. They are, rather, measures of the *environment of opinion* in which each individual is functioning. When children and adolescents express preferences for, or rejection of classmates, or when they mention classmates in connection with specific traits, they are not necessarily giving their own independent judgments. As a member of the group, each individual acquires, in some degree, the prevailing group attitudes toward his fellows. And as the object of these attitudes, each individual interacts in some manner with these opinions and with the persons holding them. Since the chief purpose of the sociometric technique is not to measure the personality of each individual, but to measure the environment of opinion in which he lives, evidence of validity in the usual psychometric terms is not expected. The discovery of the environment of opinion is none the less important, for such information helps explain his behavior as well as the organization of the group. Generally the sociometric instruments may be regarded as having content validity and, in some instances, construct validity. The Syracuse scales provide some data, also, of concurrent validity; that is, correlations between findings with the scales and ratings of *esprit de corps* and of "group effectiveness" of social fraternities in a university (5, 6). For the first of these, the mean coefficient is .74; for the second it is .32.

Uses. In analyzing a group structure by sociometric means, Moreno and others have used the number of "isolates," "mutuals," "unreciprocated choices," and "stars" as indexes of group coherence. Frequencies of intersex, interrace, internation, interoccupational-level choices may be used as evidence of cleavages.

Sociometric technique has been applied to the study of a variety of social situations in classrooms, factories, camps, fraternities, and residential communities. These investigations have revealed the structures of social groups and have provided the bases upon which remedial procedures were developed or reconstruction undertaken.

Psychodrama

Aside from a degree of mysticism and extravagant claims made for it, the psychodrama is a useful method in the study of personality and in psychotherapy. The technique requires an individual to play *spontaneously* an assigned role in a specified situation. The "drama" involves two or more persons; it deals with a situation significant in the lives of the participants. Each individual may play a role representing either himself or another person with whom he is involved.

The central principle of the psychodrama is *spontaneity,* which has been defined by Moreno as the ability of the subject to meet each new situation with adequacy, as "the most important vitalizer of living structure." In contrast to the act of spontaneity stands the "cultural conserve," which is the creative idea that has become preserved and static, and hence repeated and stereotyped. What the psychodrama aims at, therefore, is to develop in the subject the capacity to play his life roles in a spontaneous and always creative manner that will enable him to meet adequately the demands of new and evolving situations, rather than by employing stereotyped patterns of response.

The psychodrama involves a *director,* who is the therapist or the one studying the personalities in the situation. On the basis of knowledge of his subjects and their problems, he creates the situation, selects the actors, assigns roles, observes and interprets the action, and acts as the link between actors and audience. Emphatic and active participation by the audience is an essential of this technique; for its members are individuals who are, or will be, in situations similar to those being portrayed in the act. The individual who is the subject in the drama (or the patient, in therapy) is called the *primary ego.* He is the one being assisted in the solution of a problem of adjustment, or in learning to live a certain role in life. The *auxiliary ego* is another actor in the drama; he is the agent who provides the assistance needed by the primary ego. The auxiliary ego does so either by (1) acting as the primary ego, identifying with him and representing him toward others or (2) by acting in the role of, and representing another person with whom the primary ego is involved.

The foregoing are the basic procedures. A number of modifications and variations of the technique have been evolved. Where the two persons involved in a conflict (for example, parent and child, husband and wife, employer and employee) are placed in a psychodramatic situation, each may be instructed to act out his own role, or each may be required to act the role of the *other* person, as he perceives that other one in the specified situation.

Briefly stated, the psychological rationale of the psychodrama is the following. In therapy, the subject, by acting, by participating in the reproduction of a life situation significant to him, experiences an emotional catharsis.[3] In the process, while he gains insight into his own behavior, he should learn how to meet a situation adequately (spontaneously and creatively) through observations of himself and through

---

[3] Adherents of the psychodramatic technique maintain that the catharsis derived from it is much more genuine than catharsis derived from the method of psychoanalysis in which the subject verbalizes in a remote situation (the therapist's office), dissociated from other persons involved in the conflict.

interpretations and evaluations given by the therapist (or director) and members of the audience. The psychodrama, thus, is intended to be a *learning procedure* that will teach the subject how to meet each life situation adequately.

In personality evaluation by means of psychodrama, the director and others observe and analyze each subject's characteristic ways of dealing with a situation commonly encountered. A wide range of themes may be used for testing behavior, depending upon the nature of the persons involved: economic problems, family relationships, social status, school status, play activities, levels of aspiration and self-realization, etc. The number and kinds of themes are as varied as life itself.

A variant of the psychodrama is called the *sociodrama*. The latter differs from the former in respect to purpose and emphasis. Whereas the psychodrama deals with interpersonal relations and adjustment problems within the individual, the sociodrama is concerned with group values and group structure and thinking. The sociodrama portrays *social* phenomena and conflicts with which the audience is concerned and to which a solution is being sought.

Although Moreno's book on psychodrama was published in 1946, there is as yet little sound empirical evidence to establish its value as a method of diagnosis and treatment suitable for wide use. The method has yet to achieve a satisfactory level of objectivity and systematic organization in respect to techniques of observation, rating of behavior, and interpretation of responses. Furthermore, the validity of the hypotheses regarding the value of the psychodrama as a technique to develop spontaneous, adequate, and adjusted personalities has not been demonstrated. A serious obstacle to the experimental development and use of the psychodramatic group technique is its heavy requirement of time, personnel, and equipment. Perhaps this accounts for the paucity of research data.

Office of Strategic Services: Assessment Tests

Description and Procedure. During World War II, a group of psychologists and psychiatrists were given the assignment of assessing the traits of men and women recruited for the OSS, as it has come to be known (21). The task was to devise test procedures that would reveal the recruits' personalities and give reliable predictions of their future usefulness in this branch of military service. At the main station, the testing period lasted three days; at another station it lasted one day.

The number and types of jobs in this organization were large and varied. They included script writer, base-station operator, demolitions instructor, field representative, section leader, resistance-group leader, saboteur, undercover agent, liaison pilot, pigeoneer, and others. Very little indeed was known regarding the qualifications essential for successful performance in these jobs. Nor was there time and opportunity to make job analyses, as would be done in the case of an ordinary civilian situation when aptitude and personality tests for a specific occupation are to be devised. The assessment staff decided, therefore, to use the "wholistic" approach: that is, to evaluate each personality as a whole. This meant that some members of the staff would provide an over-all evaluation and description of each individual, based upon interview; each candidate would be tested, observed, and evaluated in respect to specific traits of personality, intellect, and physique. Finally, all information for each individual would be assembled, organized, and interrelated to provide a complete description and evaluation of each candidate. On the basis of their unified conception of each individual's personality traits, the staff estimated the probable level of future performance. For each recruit, then, an assignment was determined upon, using as criteria the statements of the qualifications required for each job as formulated by each branch of the OSS.

Among the variety of devices used in the assessment of the candidates were situational tests, similar in conception to those used in the sociodrama. A few are listed below:

> Upon arriving at the testing station, each candidate was judged according to the ease with which he used the fictious name under which he went (candidates did not know each other's real names, ranks, or civilian status); physical agility in getting off the truck.
>
> The first day, during the welcoming talk, each candidate's attitudes, postures, questions, and comments were noted.
>
> During the first meal, each recruit's conversation was noted (topics revealing identity were prohibited), as was ease of establishing contact with others.
>
> Various other observations were made during the first evening, in the free periods, when the situations were relatively unstructured.
>
> Terrain test: Candidates were told that at noon of the following day they would be tested for ability to observe the terrain of the station and its buildings, and from their observations, to infer the history of the farm.
>
> Crossing a brook: The task was for a group to carry a delicate instrument over a "raging torrent" with "sheer banks" and to return with some material from the other side. Available were a few boards, a log, a heavy rock, lengths of rope, a pulley, and a barrel with both ends knocked out. All members of the group were on an equal footing, no one having been designated as leader. The actual setting was a shallow, quiet stream, about eight feet wide.
>
> Construction: Ostensibly a test of the candidate's ability to direct two

helpers in building with him a frame structure out of simple wooden materials. Actually it was a test of leadership, emotional stability, and frustration tolerance, for the two helpers were junior staff members. The job of one was to act passive, sluggish, and even as an obstacle. The job of the other was to be aggressive, offer poor suggestions, express dissatisfaction and criticism.

Stress interviews: This situation was devised to test the candidate's capacity to tolerate severe emotional and intellectual strain. Strain was created by rapid, confusing cross-questioning under disagreeable conditions with the aim of detecting flaws in a covering-up story which the candidate has been given twelve minutes to invent.

Post-stress interview: Following the stress interview, each candidate, individually, was placed in a relaxed atmosphere, in the presence of a staff member. Casual conversation was started by the latter in an effort to get the candidate to "let down his guard" and thus reveal information about himself and his experiences at the station that should have been kept to himself.

Improvisations: For each candidate appropriate dramatic situations were invented, to which he had to respond realistically in a psychodrama. These improvisations were used to test out and clarify "critical hunches" regarding certain personality traits of each candidate. Leadership quality, moods, attitudes, and modes of conducting interpersonal relationships were evaluated by this method.

After interviewing branch chiefs to obtain their views regarding the necessary traits for successful performance, and after organizing and combining the listed traits, seven major variables emerged; and to evaluate these in each candidate, the several kinds of tests were devised, of which those described above are samples.

The seven general variables considered to be basic to the needs of the OSS were:

1. motivation for assignment: war morale, interest in proposed job
2. energy and initiative: activity level, zest, effort, initiative
3. effective intelligence: practical and efficient utilization of intelligence in dealing with things, people, and ideas
4. emotional stability: steadiness, endurance, control over disturbing emotions, freedom from neurotic tendencies
5. social relations: good will, teamwork, freedom from disturbing prejudices and annoying traits
6. leadership: initiative; ability to evoke cooperation, to organize, administer, and accept responsibility
7. security: ability to keep secrets; caution; discretion; ability to bluff and mislead

To these seven traits, three others were subsequently added for use in selected jobs.

8. physical ability: agility, daring, ruggedness, stamina
9. observing and reporting: observation and accurate recall of significant facts and their relations, evaluation and succinct reporting of information
10. propaganda skills: ability to perceive the psychological vulnerability of the enemy, to devise subversive techniques, and to speak, write, or draw persuasively

Candidates were rated independently, by staff members, on a sixteen-point scale. Staff meetings were held to arrive at an "optimal characterization and evaluation" of each candidate. The entire procedure was a combination of situational and other test techniques, rating scales, and case conferences.

Evaluation of the OSS Tests. Since the task of the staff was to devise tests that would reveal personality traits for the purpose of predicting success in future assignments, it was necessary to appraise the forecasting value of the procedures being used. Even in ordinary civilian situations, where subjects are under frequent or constant observation and where their effectiveness in performance can be judged in terms of relatively concrete outcomes, assigning ratings presents serious difficulties. It was to be expected, therefore, that evaluations of the performance of persons accepted after OSS assessment would be even more difficult and less reliable; for these men and women were not always under close observation in the field; it was not always possible to rate their work, because often the results were intangible and deferred; and, for the most part, the primary judges on the job were inexperienced in making psychological evaluations. The following results should be viewed with these considerations in mind.

Four techniques of appraisal were used: (1) overseas-staff appraisal (2) theater-command appraisal, (3) reassignment-area appraisal, and (4) returnee appraisal.[4] In all instances, by whatever method obtained, appraisal information, rated on a numerical scale, was correlated with over-all *assessment* ratings and with specific trait ratings that had been assigned after the initial testing period at the center. The validity coefficients depend, among other things, upon the reliability of the ratings. In the case of "returnee appraisal," the mean correlation between ratings was approximately .35. As a measure of reliability, this coefficient is poor and indicates there were serious differences among judgments of informants regarding the same individuals being evaluated. When appraisal

[4] The only one of the four types of appraisal needing clarification is the fourth. When OSS men returned from field service they were asked to rate other OSS personnel known to them in their areas of operation. Members of the assessment staff, under type (3), rated field personnel on anxiety, dejection, homesickness, irritability, quarrels, alcoholism, psychosomatic symptoms, and strength of complaints.

ratings obtained by each of the four methods were intercorrelated, the coefficients varied from .46 to .59, and the mean was approximately .52. Members of the assessment staff, however, agreed much more closely when they themselves rated the field performance of individuals on the basis of information they had obtained from several sources about each person. In this instance, the mean reliability coefficient was approximately .80.

Validity of the original *assessment* ratings was estimated by correlating them with the several appraisals. The obtained coefficients were low, ranging from .08 to less than .40, with one exception (.53). The most satisfactory correlations were found between *staff* assessment ratings and overseas *staff* appraisals. This fact is attributable, first, to the staff's professional experience and greater competence in evaluating behavior; and, second, to the fact that as members of the staff they were applying the same criteria in the rating of field behavior as they and their colleagues had applied in their original assessment ratings.

More significant data on the effectiveness of the assessment procedures are the percentages of unsatisfactory cases in the field, found among the men and women who had been passed as satisfactory (high or medium) by the assessment staff. In reports from two centers, the percentages of unsatisfactory individuals from the groups rated high or medium (combined), as found by each of the four types of appraisal were: 14.8 and 6.0 (overseas-staff appraisal); 13.4 and 15.2 (theater commander's comments); 11.3 and 4.5 (reassignment-area appraisal); 16.1 and 3.5 (returnee appraisal).

The authors of the assessment study suggest that data on the predictive value of the assessment procedures employed were not more impressive because of some or all of the following reasons: (1) defects of the appraisal methods; (2) defects of the assessment methods; (3) assessment staff's lack of familiarity with jobs to be filled and conditions under which personnel would work; (4) the shifting and unpredictable conditions under which overseas personnel worked. No doubt, each of these was in an undetermined degree responsible for the unimpressive validity coefficients.

Since the termination of the war, little has been done along the lines of the OSS situational tests, probably because of the difficulties and complexities inherent in the method. One similar project in Michigan was concerned with the selection of graduate students in clinical psychology (11, 12). The subjects studied were 137 men who had already been accepted in a number of universities for preparation in clinical psychology. Although this project followed the principles of the OSS program, adapted to civilian situations, additional forms of psychological evaluation were used, such as projective tests, personality inventories, achievement and aptitude tests, and interest questionnaires. Also, the period of observation was longer than that of the OSS—nine days as compared with three (or at times only one).

The purpose of the Michigan project was to discover, if possible, the traits that contribute to or detract from competence and success in the practice of clinical psychology. Since there were few adequate criteria beyond academic ratings in graduate studies, the findings were inconclusive. This is not surprising, inasmuch as the observed behaviors and the personality traits rated in the situational tests (for example, co-operation, group participation, expressive movements, and ability to empathize) are not necessarily associated with academic and intellectual aspects of professional preparation.

Evaluation of Situational Tests

The several psychological techniques presented in this chapter are not of equal value, nor at comparable levels of development, nor applicable with equal facility. Sociometric methods are furthest along in development, can most readily be applied, and yield results most easily interpreted. They are valuable, in the hands of professional psychologists and other professional groups, for furnishing descriptions of group structures and of individual status within the group. They do not provide information regarding the causes of the structure or status. These can be determined only through close study of the individuals and the community involved.

The psychodrama and the sociodrama are based upon the long-recognized value of psychological catharsis, but catharsis through activity rather than verbalization. The proponents of this technique also claim that it develops spontaneity of behavior, which promotes wholesome development and adjustment. This remains to be demonstrated. The psychodrama, in addition, is so devised as to provide the subjects with opportunities to gain insight into their conflicts and into the attitudes of other persons involved with them in the conflict. In this respect, the psychological rationale appears to be sound. The final test of the validity of any technique of personality diagnosis or therapy is a pragmatic one. And here, although a number of case studies have been reported, final evaluation must be deferred until adequate data are available regarding efficacy of the technique.

The situational tests used in the OSS and elsewhere are basically sound, from the psychological viewpoint, in that they demand activity of the subject in a situation that simulates the actual setting or task to be performed. The tests were devised to yield evaluations of specified personality traits. The creation of situational tests to bring out particular traits, their numerical rating on a scale, and the statistical study of their interrelations demonstrate that situational tests and psychodrama, as testing techniques, need not be entirely a matter of subjective judgment.

It is apparent, of course, that the use of the situational-test technique is, at best, difficult. Often elaborate facilities are required, and a staff of experienced psychologists able to diagnose and interpret behavior is essential. The complexity and difficulty of situational testing is evident from the following necessary characteristics of a system of personality assessment, as advocated by the authors of the OSS report (21, p. 464):

1. Social setting: the whole program to be conducted within a social matrix of staff and candidates, permitting frequent informal contacts and opportunities to observe typical modes of response to other persons.

2. Multiform procedures: many different techniques to be employed; standardized tests, uncontrolled situations, performance tests, projective methods, and interview.

3. Lifelike tasks: in a lifelike environment; complicated tasks requiring organization of thought at a high integrative level, and some of them to be performed under stress and in collaboration with others.

4. Formulations of personality: collection of sufficient data to permit conceptualization of the form of some of the chief components of the personality of each individual; the formulation to be used as the basis in making recommendations and predictions.

5. Staff conference: interpretations of the behavior of each individual at a final meeting of staff members; ratings and recommendations to be reached by consensus.

6. Tabulations of assessments: formulations of personality, ratings of traits, and predictions of effectiveness to be recorded for the purpose of statistical treatment and precise comparisons with later appraisals.

7. Valid appraisal procedures: special attention to be devoted to the perfection of appraisal techniques, to determine the validity of each test in the assessment program and of ratings of each variable.

It is not probable that this ideal program will be achieved even after a long time, or in even a few centers of personality study. In the meantime, approximations have been achieved in some psychological clinics, where all the tests can be administered and conditions met excepting the situational tests themselves. As a substitute for these, psychologists and other qualified persons have made detailed observations and rated behavior of subjects, not in "lifelike" situations but in *actual* life situations: for example, children in the classroom or on the playground, teachers in the classroom, adolescents in clubs and in games, employees at work, a man and wife during a discussion. Obviously, there will always be some personality diagnoses and predictions that will have to depend upon situational tests (simulated, or lifelike) simply because it is impossible to place and observe the individual in the actual situation. For this purpose and for personality study of individuals under controlled conditions, the situational-test technique holds promise.[5]

References

1. Byrd, E. A study of validity and constancy of choice in a sociometric test. *Sociometry*, 1951, *14*, 175–181.

2. Del Toro, J., and P. Corneytz. Psychodrama as expressive and projective technique. *Sociometry*, 1944, *8*, 356–375.

3. Flanagan, J. C. Some considerations in the development of situational tests. *Personnel Psychology*, 1954, 7, 461–464.

4. Flanagan, J. C. *Performance Record for the Personal and Social Development Program*. Chicago: Science Research Associates, Inc., 1956.

5. Gardner, E. F., and G. G. Thompson. *Social Relations and Morale in Small Groups*. New York: Appleton-Century-Crofts, Inc., 1956.

6. Gardner, E. F., and G. G. Thompson. *Syracuse Scales of Social Relations*. New York: Harcourt, Brace & World, Inc., 1959.

7. Gronlund, N. E. *Sociometry in the Classroom*. New York: Harper & Brothers, 1959.

8. Haas, R. B., and J. L. Moreno. Psychodrama as a projective technique. In H. H. and G. L. Anderson, *An Introduction to Projective Techniques*, Englewood Cliffs, N.J.: Prentice-Hall, Inc., 1951.

9. Jennings, H. H. A sociometric study of emotional and social expansiveness. In R. G. Barker *et al.*, *Child Behavior and Development*, New York: McGraw-Hill Book Company, Inc., 1943.

10. Jennings, H. H. *Sociometry in Group Relations: A Work Guide for Teachers*. Washington, D.C.: American Council on Education, 1948.

11. Kelly, E. L. The place of situation tests in evaluating clinical psychologists. *Personnel Psychology*, 1954, 7, 484–492.

12. Kelly, E. L., and D. W. Fiske. *The Prediction of Performance in Clinical Psychology*. Ann Arbor: University of Michigan Press, 1951.

13. Lindzey, G., and E. F. Borgatta. Sociometric measurement. In G. Lindzey (ed.), *Handbook of Social Psychology*, *1*, Reading, Mass.: Addison-Wesley Publishing Company, 1954.

14. Mathews, J. *Research on the Development of Valid Situational Tests of*

[5] For example, a subject has unresolved needs for aggression that cause him to respond to situations on the basis of personalities involved rather than in terms of the issue at hand. This hypothesis might be specifically examined in a specially devised situational test of the discussion type. Or personality organization might be probed by placing subjects in unconventional situations of varying degrees of stress, relatively devoid of cultural cues and barriers, so that culturally controlled and stereotyped behavior are much less likely to be manifested.

    Leadership: 1. Survey of the Literature. Pittsburgh: American Institute for Research, 1951.
15. Moreno, J. L. *Who Shall Survive?* New York: Beacon House, Inc., 1934.
16. Moreno, J. L. *Who Shall Survive? Foundations of Sociometry, Group Psychotherapy, and Sociodrama* (rev. ed.). New York: Beacon House, Inc., 1953.
17. Moreno, J. L. (ed.). *Sociometry and the Science of Man.* New York: Beacon House, Inc., 1956.
18. Murray, H. A., *et al. Explorations in Personality.* New York: Oxford University Press, 1938.
19. Newstetter, W. I., *et al. Group Adjustment: A Study in Experimental Sociology.* Cleveland: School of Applied Social Sciences, Western Reserve University, 1938.
20. Northway, M. L. A method of depicting social relationships by sociometric testing. *Sociometry,* 1940, *3,* 144–150.
21. OSS Staff. *Assessment of Men.* New York: Holt, Rinehart & Winston, Inc., 1948.
22. Selltiz, C., *et al. Research Methods in Social Relations* (rev. ed.). New York: Holt, Rinehart & Winston, Inc., 1959.
23. Tryon, C. M. *Evaluation of Adolescent Personality by Adolescents.* Monograph no. 41, Society for Research in Child Development, 1939.

23.

PERSONALITY INVENTORIES

Purposes and Types

It has been estimated that there are approximately five hundred personality tests and inventories. Obviously, there would be no point in attempting to describe all of them, or even a large number; for they all have much in common; and many of them, inferior in conception and validation, merit no attention. The inventories that are briefly presented in the following pages are among those that have been most widely used and are representative of the group as a whole. The satisfaction of these criteria, however, by no means implies that they are wholly satisfactory instruments. They are useful within limits and in the hands of qualified psychologists.

Rating scales, for the most part, are intended to reveal how other persons (the judges) respond to or have been impressed by the subject; these scales provide evidence of the value placed upon an individual in certain group situations. Personality inventories, on the other hand, are self-rating questionnaires that deal not only with overt behavior (for example, insisting on having one's own way, emotional expression, sympathetic acts), but also with the person's own feelings about himself, other persons, and his environment, resulting from introspection (liking to be alone and living introvertly, need for praise, repression of desires, caution and worry). Insofar as inventories actually evaluate aspects of personality that are beyond impressions made upon observers, and resulting reputation, they are the more valuable instruments.

Personality inventories may be classified into five types: those that (1) assess specified traits (for example, ascendance, conservatism, self-confidence); (2) evaluate adjustment to several aspects of the environment (home, school, community); (3) classify into clinical groups (paranoiac, psychopathic personality); (4) screen persons into two or three groups (psychosomatic disorders *versus* normal); (5) evaluate interests, values, and attitudes (vocational interests, scientific and economic values, attitude toward religion).

An example of the first group is the Bernreuter; of the second, the California; of the third, the Minnesota Multiphasic; of the fourth, the Cornell Index; of the fifth, the Kuder or the Allport-Vernon-Lindzey Study of Values.

Classification into five groups does not signify that the inventories in each have nothing in common with the others. The differences between them are dependent upon purposes, organization, nature of total content, and scoring categories. Fundamentally, nearly all personality inventories are based upon the principle that behavior and personality are, in part, manifestations of certain *traits,* and that the strength of traits can be evaluated by them.

A *trait* may be defined as a generalized mode of behavior or a form of readiness to respond with a marked degree of consistency to a set of situations that are functionally equivalent for the respondent. It is a form of adaptive or expressive behavior employed by the individual in situations that he perceives as having some equivalence. Thus, if a child readily volunteers information and opinions in classrooms but is reticent in all other situations, his school behavior would be regarded as a "habit" rather than as a "trait." However, if this child's classroom self-confidence extends into a variety of situations—that is, if it is generalized—his self-confidence would be designated as a "trait." Also, if a person always votes for candidates of the most conservative party, this might be only a habit; but if conservatism is his characteristic mode of responding to a variety of situations (along a scale of conservatism–radicalism), then conservatism is one of his traits.

Thus, in personality inventories an effort is made to estimate the presence and strength of each specified trait through a number of items representing a variety of situations in which the individual's generalized mode of responding may be sampled. The traits selected for measurement in a particular inventory are those present in varying degrees that can be compared among the members of the population for whom the inventory is intended.

Selection of Content.   Four methods have been used in selecting and developing the content (items) of personality inventories. These methods are not mutually exclusive. They are: (1) content validation; (2) known, or criterion, groups; (3) concept, or construct, validation; (4) factor-analysis techniques.

Content validation was the first procedure used. The Woodworth Personal Data Sheet, the first of the personality inventories, was developed by this method during World War I for use in the armed forces.[1] Its items were based upon (1) behavioral problems and symptoms reported for psychoneurotic cases of various degrees of severity and (2) discussions with psychiatrists regarding behavior and experiences of persons in this group. The purpose of this inventory, used in lieu of time-consuming interviews, was to identify men who would be poor risks in training or combat. Several of the items follow. They are answered either *yes* or *no*.[2]

Do you usually feel well and strong?
Do you usually sleep well?
Are you bothered much by blushing?
Did other children let you play with them?
Do people find fault with you more than you deserve?
Do you think you have too much trouble in making up your mind?

The items in the inventory are concerned with the whole range of symptoms of psychoneuroses: psychosomatic symptoms, excessive fears, sleep disturbances, obsessions, compulsions, motor disturbances, paranoid feelings, sex interests, feelings of unreality, emotional history of family, and other areas in which excessively deviant behavior, experience, and feelings are significant.

The Mooney Problem Check List (1950) is a relatively recent example of content validation. Its items, covering a wide range of interests, activities, and concerns, were derived from case records, counseling interviews, and written reports of their own problems submitted by several thousand high school students. The principal purpose of this check list is to serve as a guide to organized introspection by the respondent and subsequent interview by a counselor.

The use of *known, or criterion, groups* is a familiar method, long used in constructing all types of psychological tests, as the reader already knows. In developing a personality inventory, two or more known groups are selected (for example, delinquents and nondelinquents, hypochondriacs and nonhypochondriacs, schizophrenics and nonschizophrenics). The groups are given sets of questions (items) to answer; group differences in the answers to each question are analyzed in order to find those items that are significantly different statistically for each group.

[1] This inventory was published in 1919, by C. H. Stoelting Co., Chicago.
[2] These items and most of the others in the Woodworth PDS have been used in many of the later inventories.

Examples of inventories that employed this procedure are the Minnesota Multiphasic Personality Inventory and the Cornell Index. The validity of an instrument so devised will depend upon the adequacy of the criterion groups (numbers and representativeness) and upon the soundness of diagnoses or classifications made by psychologists or psychiatrists.

Concept, or construct, validation was explained in Chapter 5. When using this procedure, the psychologist begins with one or more personality traits he has analyzed and defined and which he wants to evaluate. One of the best examples of this procedure is Maslow's Security–Insecurity Inventory. Among other traits similarly evaluated by means of inventories are introversion–extroversion, dominance–submission, confidence, sociability, and neurotic tendencies. When the author of an inventory starts with a conception of a trait, he devises or selects items that he believes fall within his definition and analysis of the trait.

When construct validation is used, responses to the items of each scale (or trait variable) are analyzed in one or both of two ways. The scores may be intercorrelated and factor analyzed in order to identify and select relatively homogeneous items as content of the scale. Or total scores on all the items may be found for all individuals; then the obtained responses to each item are analyzed in relationship to the total scores to find the extent of agreement or disagreement of each item with the over-all trend indicated by the total scores (see Chapter 5 on factor analysis and item analysis).

If *factor analysis* is the method used, to begin with, the psychologist starts with a large pool of items. Although he does not devise and select items at random, he does not proceed within the restrictions set by one who uses construct validation; his items are relatively heterogeneous rather than homogeneous. Examples of inventories based upon this procedure are the Guilford-Zimmerman Temperament Survey and the IPAT High School Personality Questionnaire.

The obtained responses to *each* item are correlated separately with the responses made to each of the other items; that is, all possible *pairs* of items are correlated. The resulting correlation coefficients are then factor analyzed to determine which items cluster together closely enough (have "high loadings") to constitute a "factor." This is followed by examining the content and the apparent characteristics involved in the items within each cluster, in order to determine what aspects of personality they have in common. These items are then given an appropriate name and will constitute a scale for the evaluation of the personality trait identified through the factor analysis.

The factor analyst, in devising personality scales as described above, does not begin with preconceptions of particular traits he wants to measure; nor does he necessarily know beforehand what they may turn out to be, or for which groups or types of persons each trait might be significant. As in other approaches, the factor analyst draws on items devised by his predecessors and creates some of his own. Thus, the factors that emerge for him are bound to have something in common with inventories constructed by other procedures. It is obvious that the number of factors obtained will depend upon one's resourcefulness in the number and variety of items used (and upon the availability of mechanical computers). It also appears that to begin the development of a personality inventory by this procedure is to work without a directing or clear objective. Any scales thus derived must subsequently be widely applied to learn whether they have significance or relevance to this, that, or the other group. From the viewpoints of both personality theory and effective use of personality inventories, factor analysis should *follow* and be an aid to the use of constructs and criterion groups.

Regardless of the procedure employed initially, any scale, to be of significance, must ultimately demonstrate its usefulness and value with certain specified groups of individuals (criterion groups; external validity); and it must be based upon, or develop, psychological concepts (constructs) that will contribute to analyses and descriptions of personalities.

Representative Inventories [3]

The *Bell Adjustment Inventory* consists of questions intended to evaluate the subject's status in respect to home (satisfaction or dissatisfaction with home life); health (extent of illness); social adjustment (extent of shyness, submissiveness, introversion); emotional adjustment (extent of depression, nervousness, ease of disturbance); and (adults') occupational adjustment (satisfaction with work, associates, and conditions). There are two forms: one for students (grade 9 through college) and one for adults. The items are of the usual kind, to be answered as *yes, no,* or *?*. For example: "Are you troubled with shyness?" "Are you often sorry for the things you do?" "Do you daydream frequently?"

The Bell inventory, based on content validity, raises a problem common to all devices of this kind: Do the questions and the scores for each category actually represent separate and distinct aspects of behavior and adjustment? Are these aspects mutually exclusive? Some critics maintain they are not. They hold, on the contrary, that the same personality variables influence adjustment in all situations and, therefore, that the more useful and significant inventories are those that probe the various psychological mechanisms such as hysteria, defense (for example, rationalization

[3] Data on validity and reliability of these inventories are given in Tables 23.1 and 23.2.

and projection) and escape techniques (for example, negativism, suppression), and psychosomatic manifestations. Other psychologists, while recognizing the instrument's inability to reveal the dynamics of behavior, nevertheless believe it is useful in placing the individual relative to a group in respect to the specified areas of behavior, and as a basis for further psychological interviewing. While the first criticism is warranted, the Bell inventory has found wide and justified use for the latter purpose.

The *Bernreuter Personality Inventory* is a questionnaire for use in grades 9 to 16, and with adults. Although the items are not arranged into categories, they are scored for six traits: neurotic tendency, self-sufficiency, introversion–extroversion, dominance–submission, confidence, and sociability. The last two of these were added by J. C. Flanagan after factor analysis. The items themselves and the manner of answering (*yes, no, ?*) are not new. The method of scoring was, however, not typical; each of the responses to each item is regarded as characteristic of several traits, the scores for each item being weighted on the basis of empirically or statistically determined differentiating power. There are thus six scoring scales, one for each of the specified traits.

This inventory, starting with trait concepts, has been criticized for establishing arbitrary categories and for being inadequate for individual diagnosis. The first of these criticisms is not warranted, since the categories are widely recognized and accepted personality traits. Its principal value is as an aid in identifying persons at the extremes of the scale, as an early step in their psychological study. Several sample items follow: "Have you ever crossed the street to avoid meeting a person?" "Are you inclined to study the motives of people carefully?" "Do people ever come to you for advice?"

The California Test of Personality, based on content validity to begin with, is ". . . organized around the concept of life adjustment as a balance between personal and social adjustment." It has five scales: primary, elementary, intermediate, secondary, and adult. The questions, answered either *yes* or *no,* are grouped under the following categories.

> Personal adjustment: self-reliance, sense of personal worth, sense of personal freedom, feeling of belonging, withdrawing tendencies, nervous symptoms.
> Social adjustment: social standards, social skills, antisocial tendencies, family relations, school relations, occupation relations (adult level only), community relations.

This broad twofold division is consistent with a frequent practice of classifying adjustment difficulties into "personality" problems (personal adjustment) and "conduct" problems (social adjustment). But it should not be assumed that any particular focal maladjustment is restricted to only one or the other of these categories; for, in fact, the whole person and his environment are involved in behavioral difficulties or disorders. What these two major categories and their subdivisions do is assist in identifying some of the principal sources of an individual's problems. This inventory, like the Bell, provides an opportunity for responses that may be symptomatic of maladjustment and that can be valuable in subsequent psychological interview and treatment.

Several items from the intermediate inventory follow.

> Do you keep on working even if the job is hard? (self-reliance)
> Do you find that a good many people are mean? (sense of personal worth)
> Is it hard for you to say nice things to people when they have done well? (social skills)
> Do you often visit at the homes of your boy and girl friends in your neighborhood? (community relations)

The *Minnesota Personality Scale,* which has separate forms for men and for women, is intended to rate the following aspects of personality: morale (belief in society's institutions and future possibilities); social adjustment (gregariousness and social maturity); family relations (parent-child relations); emotionality (degree of stability); economic conservatism (degree on a scale from conservatism to radicalism). The inventory is devised for use in the last two years of high school, with college students, and "in some adult cases." An aspect of this instrument infrequently found is the gradation of answers whereby the subject indicates the strength of his responses. Instead of the commonly used *yes, no,* or *?,* the subject in this instance has five choices, such as *strongly agree, agree, undecided, disagree, strongly disagree;* or *almost always, frequently, occasionally, rarely, almost never.* The score of each item is weighted from one to five, corresponding to the degree of intensity represented by the choice of answer.

Perhaps the only parts of this inventory needing special mention are the first and fifth: morale and economic conservatism. Both traits are unusual in personality questionnaires. In the first, whereas high scores are regarded as indicative of belief in society's institutions and future possibilities, low scores "usually indicate cynicism or lack of hope in the future." Sample items on morale are: "No one cares much what happens to you." "Court decisions are almost always just." Two items on the scale of economic conservatism–radicalism are: "On the whole our economic system is just and wise." "Poverty is chiefly the result of injustice in the distribution of wealth."

The particular selection of the five personality aspects tested by the

Minnesota inventory may appear to be a rather strange one. The authors explain their selection as being ". . . the result of . . . work on problems of personality measurement in a clinical personnel program" in the University of Minnesota. The personality aspects sampled with this instrument have been found valuable in identifying ". . . a substantial proportion of adjustment problems in a large scale student personnel program" after a number of traits and attitudes had been experimentally investigated.

The *Minnesota Multiphasic Personality Inventory* is the most elaborate and ambitious instrument in this field. It is not surprising, therefore, that it has been subjected to more research than any other one. The authors state in their manual that the inventory is ". . . designed ultimately to provide, in a single test, scores on all the more important phases of personality. The point of view determining the importance of a trait in this case is that of the clinical or personnel worker who wishes to assay those traits that are commonly characteristic of disabling psychological abnormality." It is intended for persons sixteen years of age or older who are able to read.

The inventory consists of 550 statements, each of which is printed on a separate card. The cards are sorted by the subject into three groups—*True, False,* or *Cannot Say*—depending upon whether he regards the statement as true of himself or not. The statements cover a wide range, including physical condition, morale, and social attitudes. The items have been classified under twenty-six headings—for example, general health, gastrointestinal system, family and marital, religious attitudes, affect (depressive and manic), delusions, phobias, masculinity–femininity interests. Originally, various items were selected and grouped to form separate scales for scoring in nine categories. With one exception (masculinity–femininity), these are clinical classifications; but this exception might also have clinical significance. The nine are: hypochondriasis, depression, hysteria, psychopathic deviate, masculinity–femininity interest, paranoia, psychasthenia, schizophrenia, and hypomania. Since its original publication, scoring has been developed for a new scale from the same 550 items. This is called the Social Introversion (Si) scale, to measure the tendency to withdraw from social contacts with others.

Other psychologists have derived additional scales from the MMPI items; among these are several for evaluating traits of persons within the normal range of behavior. Some of the newer scales might have general applicability whereas others are to be used only with special groups (49). Among these derived scales are:

General maladjustment (Gm)
Social status (St)

Prejudice (Pr)
Dominance (Do)
Ego strength (Es)
Control in psychological adjustment (Cn)
Caudality: that is, clinical discrimination between brain lesions in frontal and parietal regions (Ca)

It is apparent from this list of scales that the Multiphasic inventory was originally concerned exclusively with the clinical problem of differential diagnosis. This is further indicated by the fact that the scales were developed by contrasting normal groups with clinical psychiatric cases. The chief criterion of validity was the prediction of clinical cases against the diagnoses of a hospital staff.

The items that constitute the inventory are not unusual. Its distinguishing characteristics are its comprehensiveness; its large number of scales to diagnose clinical types; the large number of research publications; and four unusual scores, obtained in addition to the diagnostic classifications. These four are a "validity score" (F), a "lie score" (L), a "question score," and a "K-score." [4]

The first of these, the "validity score," is based upon a group of items that serve ". . . as a check on the validity of the whole record. . . . If the [validity] score is high, the other scores are likely to be invalid either because the subject was careless or unable to comprehend the items, or because someone made extensive errors in entering the items on the record sheet. A low [validity] score is a reliable indication that the subject's responses were rational and pertinent." This score is obtained from sixty-four items that have been answered uniformly by about 90 percent of normal persons and by nearly as many miscellaneous abnormal subjects. It has been concluded, therefore, that a marked deviation from these uniform responses is an indication of invalidity of other responses, for reasons given above.

The "lie score" consists of fifteen items on which a high score strongly suggests that the subject has answered them falsely in order to create a favorable impression and thereby place himself in a socially acceptable light. In general, these are statements about one's behavior which, if they apply to the subject (and they do apply to practically everyone), indicate that he is something less than perfect. Though a high lie score does not *necessarily* invalidate the other scores, it may indicate that responses to items in general have been influenced by a tendency to lie, or misrepresent. Thus, the total findings would be open to question. There are,

[4] Although F-scores of a group affect statistical studies of validity and one's estimate of the value and credence to be given to a particular individual's scores and responses to the inventory, the term "validity" is not used in its usual technical sense.

however, instances of individuals whose "lie scores" are not indicative of conscious falsifying, but are symptomatic of personality traits that should be probed; for the individual himself might be unaware of the motivation responsible for his false answers.

The "question score" is the total number of statements placed in the *Cannot Say* category. The authors of this inventory state that a high "question score" invalidates the others; for it is held that such high scores tend to move *high deviate* scores toward the mean. In other words, it appears that persons who tend to deviate from the mean (the normal range) more often classify statements as doubtful, whereas a correct classification would produce an even greater deviant score and rating. Here again, the subject who has a high "question score" is not necessarily aware of the factors responsible for it.

The K-score is a "correction factor" used to obtain increased validity of the scales. Application and interpretation of the inventory revealed that some normal persons got highly unfavorable scores in certain areas; scores that indicate abnormality. An analysis was made of the items that were marked unfavorably by these normal persons (called "false positives"); these items constitute the K correction score. A low K-score is said to indicate that the person was excessively severe in evaluating himself: overcandid, very self-critical, or exaggerated minimal symptoms. A high K-score, by contrast, represents a desire to make a more nearly normal (or favorable) impression: unconscious or preconscious defensiveness against psychological weakness, or deliberate distortion. The authors of this inventory regard the K-score as a subtle measure of test-taking attitude; hence, it is a score that gives further evidence of the over-all validity of the scores on each of the several scales.

The MMPI is one of the several most widely used inventories, both clinically and experimentally. As is to be expected when dealing with the subtle and often elusive problems of personality traits, clinical and experimental findings have not been in complete agreement; and some have been negative.

The authors report in their manual that a high score on a scale correctly predicted the final clinical diagnosis in more than 60 percent of new psychiatric admissions. This is an encouraging finding, in view of the lack of a high degree of agreement (low reliability) among psychiatrists who make the clinical diagnoses and classifications. An instrument's external validity, as already emphasized (Chapter 5), depends in part upon the criterion's reliability. It may therefore be said, at least, that the MMPI is valuable in facilitating diagnosis and in describing and predicting behavior.

Other published studies report significant agreement between scale scores and hypochondriasis, paranoia, schizophrenia, and, in particular, depressions. Also, numerous investigations have reported that scale scores readily distinguish between pathological groups (undifferentiated), on the one hand, and normal persons, on the other. In other words, the Multiphasic inventory is more effective when its validity findings are not affected by the uncertainties and unreliabilities of psychiatric classifications.[5]

Since the MMPI was originally devised as a clinical instrument, it should be used and interpreted with great caution because of the clinical labels attached to its scoring categories. The authors of the inventory have been criticized for using this traditional psychiatric classification which has been found clinically unsatisfactory and has long been questioned—and, in fact, rejected—by specialists in the psychology of abnormal behavior. In partial response to this criticism, code numbers (from 0 to 9) are now used to represent an individual's profile of scores in each of the categories. Although this device does not get away completely from psychiatric labels, it has tended to place emphasis upon profiles, or patterns, of responses and descriptions of behavior rather than upon the name of a category. Thus, "male juvenile delinquents," as a group, get statistically reliable higher scores than nondelinquents on scales 4, 7, and 9 (respectively, psychopathic deviate, psychasthenia, hypomania). The "neurotic triad" consists of scores reliably higher than normal on scales 1, 2, and 3 (hypochondriasis, depression, and hysteria). A clinical case diagnosed as suffering from "anxiety state" scores quite high on scale 1 (hypochondriasis), and above normal, but not so high on scales 3 (hysteria), 7 (psychasthenia), and 8 (schizophrenia). This patient's scores on the inventory are represented in code form thus: 1'378—.

The following two instruments are based in part upon the MMPI. *The California Psychological Inventory,* for ages 13 and older, has 480 true-false items (12 being duplicates), of which somewhat fewer than half are included in the MMPI. Unlike the latter, however, the CPI is devised for use with the "normal," nonclinical population. It provides eighteen scores to represent such aspects as dominance, socialization, tolerance, achievement via conformance, achievement via independence, intellectual efficiency. Its items were selected upon the basis of the familiar external criteria, such as social-class membership, course grades, and leadership, and upon extreme groups with regard to each trait.

The Minnesota Counseling Inventory, for use at the high school level,

---

[5] Psychologists who have reviewed and evaluated published studies on the MMPI do not agree on its merits; some accentuate the positive side, others the negative. One favorable review reports that 71 of 80 studies made significant group discriminations (9). An adversely critical review reports that in 160 studies, significant discriminations were made in 102, or 64 percent (8, p. 166).

has 355 true-false items, many of which are similar to those in the MMPI. It yields scores in seven categories that are similar to the Bell Adjustment Inventory and the California Test of Personality: family relationships, social relationships, emotional stability, conformity, adjustment to reality, mood, and leadership. This device, like many others, was validated against known groups (extreme cases), who were compared with random samples of pupils.[6]

Two inventories based upon factor analysis are *The Guilford-Zimmerman Temperament Survey* and *The IPAT High School Personality Questionnaire* (by R. B. Cattell *et al.*). The first of these provides scores for each of the following traits: general activity, restraint, ascendance, sociability, emotional stability, objectivity, friendliness, thoughtfulness, personal relations, and masculinity. The inventory is intended for use with individuals in grades 9 through 16, and with adults. The particular traits included are the products of factorial analyses made over a period of years by Guilford and his associates.

The statements of these authors regarding the values and characteristics of their inventory are much more restrained and psychologically cautious than those of some other authors of inventories.

The authors of the IPAT Questionnaire state that it ". . . covers *all* major dimensions in any comprehensive view and description of individual differences in personality" (*Handbook,* page 1).[7] Fourteen "dimensions" of personality are measured, some of which are designated by terms already familiar in personality testing while others have been given rather novel names. They are: schizothymia versus cyclothymia (aloof *vs.* sociable),[8] mental defect versus general intelligence,[9] general neuroticism versus ego strength (emotional immaturity *vs.* maturity), phlegmatic versus excitable temperament, submissiveness versus dominance, desurgency versus surgency (sober *vs.* enthusiastic), lack of rigid internal standards versus superego strength, threctia versus parmia (shy and sensitive *vs.* adventurous and insensitive), harria versus premsia (tough and realistic *vs.* esthetically sensitive), dynamic simplicity versus neurasthenic self-critical tendency (liking group action *vs.* fastidiously individualistic),

[6] A questionnaire derived from the MMPI, known as the Taylor Manifest Anxiety Scale, originated in laboratory studies of learning (44). The purpose of the experiment was to test the hypothesis that strength of symptoms of anxiety is associated with strength of drives. A group of five psychologists were asked to select the MMPI items that were overt admissions of feelings of anxiety. Fifty items were so identified. These constitute the anxiety scale. It has not been standardized or published and made available in the usual form, although it has been used in research and in clinics.

[7] Such complete power is claimed for no other inventory.

[8] The terms in parentheses are those given by the authors of this inventory as popular synonyms of the technical terms.

[9] A rather unusual trait to be included in a personality inventory.

confident adequacy versus guilt proneness, group dependency versus self-sufficiency, poor self-sentiment formation *vs.* high strength of self-sentiment (uncontrolled and lax *vs.* controlled and strong will power), low ergic tension versus high ergic tension (relaxed composure *vs.* tense and excitable).

The authors of this ambitious inventory, in summarizing its merits, state that one of its "utilities" is: ". . . omission of no research-demonstrated dimension of personality of importance in clinical, educational, or counseling practice" (*Handbook,* page 4). The statistical and other evidence on this inventory, however, do not justify the assertions in the two preceding quotations. Evidence of convincing functional, external (practical) validity is lacking. Validation data are largely in terms of factorial intercorrelations, which might or might not be significant in counseling or in clinical problems. Additional validating information is provided by "criterion profiles" of different groups. These profiles do not provide sufficient differentiation upon which clinical diagnoses could be made or counseling conducted, especially in view of the low reliabilities of the scales. (See Table 23.2.)

The *Cornell Index* was devised ". . . for the rapid psychiatric and psychosomatic evaluation of large numbers of persons in a variety of situations." The index ". . . was assembled as a series of questions referring to neuropsychiatric and psychosomatic symptoms, which would serve as a standardized psychiatric history and a guide to the interview, and which, in addition, would statistically differentiate persons with serious personal and psychosomatic disturbances from the rest of the population. It was devised as an adjunct to the interview, not as a substitute unless an interview is impractical." This questionnaire, standardized for males only, consists of 101 items. The questions fall into two groups: those differentiating sharply between persons with serious personality disturbances (for example, "Does worrying continually get you down?") and those concerned with significant bodily symptoms (for example, "Do you usually have trouble in digesting food?"). The questions are undisguised and often extreme ("Are you keyed up and jittery every moment?" "Are you a sleepwalker?"). They must be answered either *yes* or *no.*

The authors of the Index report that it has been effective in showing the presence of anxiety states, hypochondriasis, asocial trends, convulsive disorders, migraine, asthma, peptic ulcers, and borderline clinical syndromes. It is to be noted that this inventory, unlike the Bernreuter, the Minnesota, and others, does not provide separate scoring scales and norms for specific personality traits or disorders. Its scores for the entire inventory are intended only to assist in distinguishing between those having serious personality or psychosomatic difficulties and those not having them. The scoring of the inventory is to be followed by an interview, or interviews, after which the diagnosis may be made.

The 101 questions themselves have been classified under the following ten categories, the number of items varying from one to another: defects in adjustment expressed as feelings of fear and inadequacy; pathological mood reactions, especially depression; nervousness and anxiety; neuro-circulatory psychosomatic symptoms; pathological startle reactions; other psychosomatic symptoms; hypochondriasis and asthenia; gastrointestinal psychosomatic symptoms; excessive sensitivity and suspiciousness; trouble-some psychopathy. This is distinctly an instrument for clinical use, chiefly for screening purposes and expediting diagnosis.

Two unusual features characterize the scoring of this inventory: cut-off scores and "stop" scores, both based upon a total of 1000 cases at military installations. Of these, 400 were men who had been rejected for neuro-psychiatric reasons, and 600 were accepted after psychiatric interview. A table of cut-off scores shows (1) the percentage of rejectees, at each score level, who would have been identified by the Index, and (2) the per-centage of those accepted after psychiatric interview, but who would have been rejected by the Index (Table 23.1). Thus, a cut-off score of 13 would have identified 74 percent of those rejected after psychiatric interview, and would have rejected 13 percent of the men passed after interview, as well.

The "stop" questions ("Were you ever a patient in a mental hospital?") are such as would indicate extreme maladjustment or pathology. The "stop" items are to be used for ready identification of men who, pre-sumably, are to be considered immediately for rejection.

The efficiency of this Index in identifying poor personality risks, as shown in Table 23.1, is great enough to warrant its use for the purposes stated by its authors, especially in situations where large numbers of persons must be rapidly screened. In situations where such pressure does not exist, the Index is still useful as a basis for and a guide to subsequent interview and to psychotherapy. The fact that the Index does not identify larger percentages of probable poor risks at some levels, while, at the same time, it rejects a number of "psychiatric accepts," may be attribu-table to some inadequacy of the inventory or errors in psychiatric judg-ments leading to acceptance or rejection after psychiatric interview. It is widely recognized that the brief psychiatric screening interviews during World War II were not optimally conducted; and the psychiatric inter-viewers, in many instances, were inadequately prepared for their tasks.

The *Security–Insecurity Inventory* is an instrument that differs from most others in that it is devised to assess degrees of only one pair of op-

TABLE 23.1

PERCENT OF PSYCHIATRIC ACCEPTS AND PSYCHIATRIC REJECTS*
IDENTIFIED AS REJECTS AT VARIOUS CUT-OFF LEVELS
OF THE CORNELL INDEX

Cut-off level	400 psychiatric rejects	600 psychiatric accepts
0	100%	100%
1	99	82
2	97	67
3	94	54
4	93	46
5	92	39
6	90	32
7	86	28
8	85	24
9	83	20
10	81	18
11	78	16
12	76	15
13	74	13
14	72	12
15	68	10
16	66	9
17	62	8
18	61	7
19	60	7
20	57	6
21	55	5
22	53	4
23	50	4
24	48	4
25	45	3
26	42	3
27	41	3
28	40	2
29	39	1
30	35	1
31	34	1
32	32	1

* In terms of opinion at psychiatric interview at five induction stations.
The table reads: If cut-off score of 7 on Index were used, 86% of those rejected at interview would have been rejected by Index; 28% of those accepted at interview would also have been rejected by Index.
SOURCE: *Manual* of Cornell Index. The Psychological Corporation. By permission.

posed personality traits. The authors of this inventory have selected these particular traits because they believe that security "is almost synonymous with mental health." Security is defined, essentially, as feelings of being liked, loved, and accepted; of belonging and having a place in the group; of safety and of being unanxious.

The S-I Inventory is intended for use with groups for research and survey purposes, and for screening college students who might need psychological therapy or counseling. This is a very good illustration of an inventory designed to evaluate a personality trait that has been defined explicitly and in detail (construct validity).

Evaluation of Personality Inventories

Reliability and Validity. The reliabilities of these inventories, as reported in their manuals, vary considerably from low, unsatisfactory coefficients to some (in the .80s) that are reasonably satisfactory, considering the traits being measured. The methods used are the usual ones with which the student is familiar from discussions of other types of tests, and which were explained in Chapter 4. It is especially important to consider reliability coefficients when one judges the value and soundness of profiles or patterns of scores obtained on an inventory.

It is in respect to validity, however, that personality inventories as a

TABLE 23.2

Reliability Data of Certain Inventories

Inventory	Reliability	Method
Bell Adjustment Inventory	.75–.97	retest
	.80–.89	odd-even
Bernreuter Personality Inventory	.78–.92	split-half
California Psychological Inventory	.70s	Kuder-Richardson formula
	.38–.87	test-retest; separate scales
California Test of Personality	.51–.97	for part scores
	.80–.96	for total scores
Cornell Index	.95	Kuder-Richardson formula
Guilford-Zimmerman Temperament Survey	.75–.85	split-half

Inventory	Reliability	Method
IPAT Personality Question-	.68–.80	test-retest
naire	.36–.60	split-half
	.40–.69	equivalent forms
Minnesota Counseling Inven-	.70–.80	split-half
tory		
Minnesota Personality Scale	.90	odd-even
MMPI	.56–.90	retest; normal subjects
	.52–.89	retest; psychiatric patients
Security–Insecurity Inventory	.84	retest
	.86	odd-even

class present the greatest difficulties and are most vulnerable to criticism. Determination of validity is certainly difficult; yet that must be the most essential requisite of a useful instrument.

In devising their personality measures, the earlier authors began with questions or statements, gathered from a variety of publications and

TABLE 23.3

Validity Criteria of Certain Inventories

Inventory	Validity criteria
Bell Adjustment Inventory	Other inventories; ratings of judges; item analysis; differentiation of extreme groups
Bernreuter Personality Inventory	Other inventories; differentiation of extreme groups; low intercorrelations of part-scores
California Psychological Inventory	Extreme groups; cross validation; other inventories
California Test of Personality	Later clinical findings; experts' judgments of item appropriateness; item analysis
Cornell Index	Neuropsychiatric cases: after interview; normal persons, accepted after interview; civilian groups; other inventories; distribution of scores in a college population
Guilford-Zimmerman Temperament Survey	Low correlations between traits; factor analysis

TABLE 23.3 continued

VALIDITY CRITERIA OF CERTAIN INVENTORIES

Inventory	Validity criteria
IPAT Personality Questionnaire	Factor analysis; criterion profiles
Minnesota Counseling Inventory	Normal group sample; known extreme groups
Minnesota Personality Scale	Item analysis; extreme groups; known groups of adjusted and maladjusted students
MMPI	Diagnosed psychiatric groups; normal subjects; amount of score overlap between nosological groups; differentiation between unselected patients and normal persons
Security–Insecurity Inventory	Other inventories; self-estimate of subjects; known groups; systematic analysis of syndromes, security and insecurity

sources (clinics, schools, colleges, industry and business, home, community), that are symptomatic of neurotic disorders, behavior difficulties, or of normal behavior manifestations. The nature and scope of the items depend, of course, upon the age levels and purposes for which a particular inventory is intended. Authors of later instruments followed the same practice, often utilizing items from several earlier devices, recombining them, and adding some new ones.

METHODS. The following methods and criteria have commonly been used in studying validity: (1) statistically significant differences between average scores of clinically well-defined groups; (2) significant average-score differences between clinical groups and a normal population; (3) ability of each item to differentiate between the two extreme groups in the standardization population; (4) internal consistency of items or parts; (5) comparisons of inventory scores with judgments of counselors and school officials; (6) selection of items from other published tests and correlations with these instruments; (7) factorial analysis; (8) the author's own judgment regarding manifestations which constitute evidence of a specified trait.

1. The first criterion should be employed only when an inventory is designed primarily for clinical use in the diagnosis of personality disorders;

as, for example, in the case of the Minnesota Multiphasic Personality Inventory (depression, hysteria, paranoia, etc.). Measures standardized on this criterion cannot and should not be used for the study of a normal population, except for the purpose of screening out, for further clinical study, individuals at the extremes of maladjustment.

2. The second criterion is likewise used with measures that are intended chiefly for clinical purposes, but in this instance the emphasis is upon segregation of the normal from the abnormal, rather than differentiation among the abnormal themselves.

3. The third criterion evaluates each item in regard to its effectiveness in distinguishing between the extreme groups of a distribution of scores for a single trait (for example, radical–reactionary or ascendance–submission), as shown by the percentage at each extreme answering the item in a specified manner. A test so validated should not be used for a general, representative population because it is not necessarily adequate to differentiate among the great percentage of persons who are located between the extremes.

4. The fourth, internal consistency, differs from the preceding criterion in that each item is correlated against part scores for all subjects, the purpose being to learn whether answers to the individual items are, on the whole, reasonably consistent with the behavior or personality trends suggested by the scores. This is a form of content validity; for basic to it is the assumption that the total or part score actually does measure what it purports to, and that it is the author's task to eliminate those particular items that do not conform to his selected traits and to the test items as a whole. With few exceptions, it is doubtful that internal consistency may be regarded as a measure of validity unless external criteria are used in addition. If this is done, then internal consistency will be sought in an effort to obtain total scores that yield the highest validity coefficients against external criteria.

5. The fifth criterion, employed in constructing inventories to be used principally in schools, assumes that the obtained judgments have adequate validity and that the judges are competent to assess personality traits as well as desirable and undesirable forms of adjustment. In some instances the assumption is warranted; in many it is not.

6. The sixth criterion assumes that items and tests already in use are themselves valid. This practice is frequently not justified and tends to perpetuate inadequacies, errors, and misconceptions inherent in the older inventories.

7. Factor analysis, the seventh criterion, in the work of some investigators, has taken the place of validation against behavioral and psychological analysis. As already explained, these investigators assemble a number of items, administer the inventory to a standardization population, statistically analyze the scores, group the items into a number of categories, and give the categories names of traits that appear to be measured by means of the items they decided should go into the inventory in the first place. This is a form of circular reasoning. Actual behaviors of defined groups of persons must be the ultimate criteria of validity of practically all personality inven-

tories. For personality traits derive their ultimate significance from the role they play in advancing or retarding personal and social adjustment.[10]

8. In using the eighth criterion, an author selects or devises items to suit his own definition of a trait or a theory of personality, without concern thereafter over their behavioral or statistical validity. Starting with theories and definitions is, of course, desirable; but the validation process must go beyond that stage.

RESEARCH FINDINGS.   Only few personality tests have been validated according to all, or even several, of these criteria. Most have been subjected to validation by the method of internal consistency, or correlation with earlier tests, plus, in some instances, the use of known groups, in one form or another. Validation data obtained by correlations of internal consistency have yielded the most impressive results. But this is readily understandable, because items can be retained, modified, or eliminated so as to create the desired internal relationship without, however, giving any assurance that the specified traits are actually being measured. Results obtained by intercorrelations of inventories among themselves, though high or moderate in some instances, have not, on the whole, been satisfactory. Poorest results have been found in studies of validation against competently determined group classifications (known groups). Yet it is this method that is the most significant and crucial one. Using this criterion, experimental studies have yielded contradictory results (15, 16, 17). For example, of nine investigations to validate personality questionnaires with groups of behavior-problem children, the number of correlation coefficients of various sizes were as follows:

> two above .70
> one between .40 and .70
> six below .40

In 75 validating studies, correlating scores of normals and abnormals (diagnosed neurotics and psychotics) with selected criteria, the following coefficients were obtained:

> thirty-six above .70
> nine between .40 and .70
> thirty below .40

---

[10] Cattell (10) states that 18 factors have been found from the use of ratings and 62 from the use of questionnaires (inventories). French (18) brings together comparable factorial analyses and emerges with 49 personality traits. Cattell adds that perhaps twice as many factors could be found by searching further. Since one of the principal justifications and purposes of factor analysis is the reduction of the number of concepts in order to organize and simplify measurement, it does not seem probable that the multiplication of entities will facilitate personality testing.

When inventory scores were validated against ratings by teachers, friends, or associates, the findings were:

> twelve above .70
> ten between .40 and .70
> twenty-two below .40

Validation studies of four group inventories (Bell, Bernreuter, Thurstone Personality Schedule, Woodworth Personal Data Sheet) yielded the following results:

> twenty-five above .70
> eleven between .40 and .70
> forty-four below .40

More consistent and convincing results were obtained when personality tests—principally the Minnesota Multiphasic—were administered individually rather than to groups. The validity coefficients were:

> ten above .70
> three between .40 and .70
> two below .40

These last data suggest that individual testing of personality is superior because subjects may be more highly motivated, owing to clinical rapport; the inventories are more carefully developed; their uses are more limited and more clearly defined.

Somewhat more than half of the coefficients reported above (.40 and higher) are either quite high or moderate as validating data. And somewhat fewer than half are quite low (below .40). Although coefficients below .40 or .50 do not have high predictive value for all individuals within the group, they may, nevertheless, indicate that the inventory has value in identifying individuals who constitute the more deviant groups.

The differences found among the large number of studies summarized cannot be attributed to the inventories alone. Other factors to be considered are the number of subjects, their homogeneity, and their classification; the soundness of the ratings or of the clinical diagnoses that are used as validity criteria; and the purposes for which, and the conditions under which, the inventories were administered.

These findings indicate that inventories for the assessment of personality traits should not be used indiscriminately or uncritically; nor should the sounder among them be rejected uncritically. Personality inventories are more valuable for certain defined populations than for others; they are more valuable in some kinds of situations than in others. One comprehensive survey of published studies between 1946 and 1951 reports ". . . that in most cases inventory scores discriminate significantly when used with psychoneurotic, psychosomatic, alcoholic, age, sex, ethnic, and college groups. . . . and they usually do not give significant group discriminations when used with vocational, academic, socioeconomic, and disabled and ill groups" (16).

ADVERSE INFLUENCES UPON VALIDITY FINDINGS. A number of reasons have been offered in explanation of the equivocal and less satisfactory validity data reported in the many studies published on the subject. The principal reasons are briefly noted here.

The questionnaires sample segments of the person; they do not bring out the whole patterned, or organismic, representation of behavior. Personality cannot be described in terms of separate traits or a mere summation of traits. None of the available questionnaires, rating scales, and personal-history records are able to portray the personality as a complete, dynamic, organized whole. They measure—not very precisely—certain aspects of behavior. They do not actually measure or assess the unit (the organism) that does the behaving.

Many studies of validity have been devoted to correlations with differential diagnoses as criteria; but the psychiatric descriptions and classifications are not always clearly defined or sufficiently distinct; psychiatric diagnoses are often not sufficiently reliable; and many clinical subjects are too unstable or unresponsive in the test situation.

In testing for traits common to a population, attention may be diverted from the individual as a unit to the assignment of a mere rank or index to a segment.

Some inventories purporting to measure two or more separate traits are measuring largely the same trait under more than one name.

Differences in cultural factors will cause subjects to respond differently to the same question.

A given question or statement does not have the same meaning for all subjects, even when clearly stated. It is a fallacy to assume that all persons have similar reasons for giving similar responses to an item.

Misunderstandings of questions are due to vocabulary limitations of some respondents.

Many questions cannot be answered in the *yes, no, ?* form.

There is a general tendency for some subjects to overrate themselves ("self-halo").

Almost anyone can falsify his replies to a questionnaire; and an indeterminate number do so.

Some subjects lack insight into their traits; others fundamentally and unconsciously may be different personalities from their own conscious self-appraisals.

The scoring of answers to items is often based upon the test author's own judgments and set of values.

On some questionnaires, either very low or very high scores, or both, may be significant; but the wide middle range of scores may not be meaningful for differentiation and description.

Statistical assumptions and procedures often take the place of behavior analysis and psychological insights.

POSITIVE CONTRIBUTIONS. On the positive side, interest and research in the development of personality inventories have made the following contributions.

Personality testing is still in process of development.

Efforts to develop measures of personality traits encourage greater uniformity in, and precision of, trait definition and description.

When there is essential agreement in regard to definition of traits and terms, and in regard to behavior and symptoms, the use of standardized inventories increases the objectivity of personality ratings and descriptions.

The use of personality measures encourages analysis of traits into their constituent elements, thus providing a better understanding of each trait. (The elements themselves, taken separately and in isolation, are not, however, the trait.)

In some cases when, consciously or unconsciously, persons misrepresent themselves by their answers on an inventory, the instrument may still be clinically valuable, because the fact that they have misrepresented is significant in understanding their personalities, by means of subsequent interviews.

Psychometric analysis is useful as one of several clinical procedures, when its results are considered in conjunction with other evidence (for example, the individual's history and psychological interview).

Answers to items of a questionnaire may be employed as the starting points of subsequent psychological interviews, since answers to various questions and responses to various statements may be significant in themselves, or they may reveal significant patterns of behavior, attitudes, and feelings. In such instances, the numerical scores and percentile ranks can be disregarded. Pragmatically, at the present time, a useful test of personality is one whose score or responses to individual items assist in identifying areas of actual or potential maladjustment for purposes of further, more intensive study and subsequent treatment. Conversely, they can help in the identification of areas of wholesome adjustment. At their present stage of development, this is one of the most useful ways in which results of personality inventories can be employed.

Personality inventories are useful in the study of *group* trends; that is, in differentiating among groups of adjusted and maladjusted, rather than among individuals.

Concluding Statement. Since personality traits and attitudes may undergo change, it is to be expected that inventories will be less reliable in terms of test-retest scores than, for example, scales measuring intelligence. Yet, the use of inventories as a means of evaluating and studying personality is justifiable, but only by professional persons who know the principles of their construction and their limitations, and who are capable of making insightful analyses of behavior. The instruments are not suitable for widespread or uncritical use with large groups.

More basic research is needed. In addition to showing improved reliability and validity, the traits being evaluated should be more clearly defined, and the relevance of each item in a scale should be established. The meanings of items should be as nearly uniform as possible for all persons; thus, words such as "usually," "rarely," and "generally" should be made explicit. Even words like "headaches," "leadership," "square deal" do not have the same connotations for everyone. Improved, more finely graded means of answering would be desirable, in place of *yes, no, ?*.

The criteria against which personality tests are to be validated should also be made more reliable than they are at present. If, for example, clinical diagnoses are used as a criterion, they should be valid. Too often this is not the case. In some instances "tentative diagnoses" instead of final ones have been employed, or, as frequently happens, diagnosticians do not agree among themselves (3). Again, as another illustration, it is unsound to use a blanket classification such as "delinquency" or "problem behavior" as a criterion, because there are various kinds of delinquents and problem behaviors, differently motivated and occurring under varying conditions.

In this chapter, the student has become acquainted with the range of traits being tested, the general purposes of personality inventories, their similarities and differences, and the types of items being used. But in view of inadequacies of available questionnaires, psychologists have been giving increasing attention to the study of personality by means of projective methods. These are presented in Chapters 25 and 26.

References

1. *Allport A-S Reaction Study*. Boston: Houghton Mifflin Company, 1928–1939.
2. Allport, G. W., and H. S. Odbert. Trait-names: a psycholexical study. *Psychological Monographs*, 1936, *47*, no. 211.
3. Ash, P. The reliability of psychiatric diagnoses. *Journal of Abnormal and Social Psychology*, 1949, *44*, 272–276.
4. Bass, B. M., and I. A. Berg (eds.). *Objective Approaches to Personality Assessment*. Princeton, N.J.: D. Van Nostrand Company, Inc., 1959.
5. Bell, H. M. *The Adjustment Inventory*. Palo Alto, Calif.: Consulting Psychologists Press, 1934–1939.
6. Berdie, R. F., and W. L. Layton. *Minnesota Counseling Inventory*. New York: The Psychological Corporation, 1957.

7. Bernreuter, R. G. *The Personality Inventory*. Palo Alto, Calif.: Consulting Psychologists Press, 1935–1938.

8. Buros, O. K. *The Fifth Mental Measurements Yearbook*. Highland Park, N.J.: Gryphon Press, 1959.

9. Calvin, A., and J. McConnell. Ellis on personality inventories. *Journal of Consulting Psychology*, 1953, *17*, 462–464.

10. Cattell, R. B. *Personality and Motivation Structure and Measurement*. New York: Harcourt, Brace & World, Inc., 1957.

11. Cattell, R. B., *et al. The IPAT High School Personality Questionnaire*. Champaign, Ill.: Institute for Personality and Ability Testing, 1958.

12. Dahlstrom, W. G., and G. S. Welsh. *An MMPI Handbook: A Guide to Use in Clinical Practice and Research*. Minneapolis: University of Minnesota Press, 1960.

13. Darley, J. G., and W. J. McNamara. *Minnesota Personality Scale*. New York: The Psychological Corporation, 1941.

14. Drake, L. E., and E. R. Oetting. *An MMPI Codebook for Counselors*. Minneapolis: University of Minnesota Press, 1959.

15. Ellis, A. The validity of personality questionnaires. *Psychological Bulletin*, 1946, *43*, 385–440.

16. Ellis, A. Recent research with personality inventories. *Journal of Consulting Psychology*, 1953, *17*, 45–49.

17. Ellis, A., and H. S. Conrad. The validity of personality inventories in military practice. *Psychological Bulletin*, 1948, *45*, 385–426.

18. French, J. W. *The Description of Personality in Terms of Rotated Factors*. Princeton, N.J.: Educational Testing Service, 1953.

19. Gilliland, A. R., and R. Colgin. Norms, reliability, and forms of the MMPI. *Journal of Consulting Psychology*, 1951, *15*, 435–438.

20. *Gordon Personal Inventory*. New York: Harcourt, Brace & World, Inc., 1956.

21. Gough, H. G. Diagnostic patterns on the MMPI. *Journal of Clinical Psychology*, 1946, *2*, 23–37.

22. Gough, H. G. *California Psychological Inventory*. Palo Alto, Calif.: Consulting Psychologists Press, 1956–1957.

23. *Guilford-Zimmerman Temperament Survey*. Beverly Hills, Calif.: Sheridan Supply Company, 1949–1955.

24. Hanley, C. Responses to wording of personality test items. *Journal of Consulting Psychology*, 1959, *23*, 261–265.

25. Hathaway, S. R., and P. F. Briggs. Some normative data on new MMPI scales. *Journal of Clinical Psychology*, 1957, *13*, 364–368.

26. Hathaway, S. R., and J. C. McKinley. *Minnesota Multiphasic Personality Inventory*. New York: The Psychological Corporation, 1943–1951.

27. Hathaway, S. R., and P. E. Meehl. *An Atlas for the Clinical Use of the MMPI*. Minneapolis: University of Minnesota Press, 1951.

28. Hathaway, S. R., and E. D. Monachesi. *Analyzing and Predicting Juvenile Delinquency with the MMPI*. Minneapolis: University of Minnesota Press, 1953.

29. Kassebaum, G. G., *et al.* The factorial dimensions of the MMPI. *Journal of Consulting Psychology*, 1959, *23*, 226–236.

30. L'Abate, L. Personality correlates of manifest anxiety in children. *Journal of Consulting Psychology*, 1960, *24*, 342–348.

31. Maslow, A. H., *et al. Security–Insecurity Inventory.* Palo Alto, Calif.: Consulting Psychologists Press, 1945–1952.

32. McKinley, J. C., and S. R. Hathaway. The identification and measurement of the psychoneuroses in medical practice: the MMPI. *Journal of the American Medical Association*, 1943, *122*, 161–167.

33. Meehl, P. E. Profile analysis of the MMPI in differential diagnosis. *Journal of Applied Psychology*, 1946, *30*, 517–524.

34. Meehl, P. E., and W. G. Dahlstrom. Objective configural rules for discriminating psychotic from neurotic MMPI profiles. *Journal of Consulting Psychology*, 1960, *25*, 375–387.

35. Meehl, P. E., and S. R. Hathaway. The K factor as a suppressor variable in the MMPI. *Journal of Applied Psychology*, 1946, *30*, 525–561.

36. Miner, R. W. (ed.). *Non-Projective Personality Tests.* New York: Academy of Sciences, 1946, *46*.

37. Mitchell, J. V., and J. Pierce-Jones. A factor analysis of Gough's California psychological inventory. *Journal of Consulting Psychology*, 1960, *25*, 453–456.

38. Noll, V. H. Simulation by college students of a prescribed pattern on a personality scale. *Educational and Psychological Measurement*, 1951, *11*, 478–488.

39. Osgood, C. E., and G. J. Suci. A measure of relation determined by both mean difference and profile information. *Psychological Bulletin*, 1952, *49*, 251–262.

40. Panton, J. H. MMPI profile configurations among crime classification groups. *Journal of Clinical Psychology*, 1958, *14*, 305–308.

41. Porter, R. B., and R. B. Cattell. *IPAT Children's Personality Questionnaire.* Champaign, Ill.: Institute for Personality and Ability Testing, 1960.

42. Sullivan, P. L., and G. S. Welsh. A technique for objective configural analysis of MMPI profiles. *Journal of Consulting Psychology*, 1952, *16*, 383–388.

43. Taft, R. A. A cross-cultural comparison of the MMPI. *Journal of Consulting Psychology*, 1957, *21*, 161–164.

44. Taylor, J. A. A personality scale of manifest anxiety. *Journal of Abnormal and Social Psychology*, 1953, *48*, 285–290.

45. Thorpe, L. P., *et al. California Test of Personality.* Monterey, Calif.: California Test Bureau, 1939–1953.

46. Thurstone, L. L. The dimensions of temperament. *Psychometrika*, 1951, *16*, 11–20.

47. *Thurstone Temperament Schedule.* Chicago: Science Research Associates, Inc., 1949–1953.

48. Weider, H. A., *et al. Cornell Index.* New York: The Psychological Corporation, 1944–1949.

49. Welsh, G. S., and W. G. Dahlstrom. *Basic Readings on the MMPI in Psychology and Medicine.* Minneapolis: University of Minnesota Press, 1956.

TABLE 24.3

SCORES OBTAINED BY AN ENGINEER FOR ENGINEERING INTEREST;
ALSO SCORES FOR INTEREST IN FIVE OTHER OCCUPATIONS, ILLUSTRATING
THE METHOD OF SCORING THE STRONG INTEREST BLANK

First ten items on the vocational interest blank	Scoring weights for engineering interest			Responses of an engineer to the ten items			Scores for engineering interest obtained by this engineer	Scores obtained by this engineer on interest scales for				
								Lawyer	Life insurance salesman	Minister	secretary YMCA	Accountant
	L	I	D	L	I	D						
Actor (not movie)	−1	0	1	—	—	x	1	−1	−1	−2	−1	−1
Advertiser	−2	0	2	—	—	x	2	1	−1	0	−2	−1
Architect	2	−1	−1	—	—	x	−1	1	1	0	0	0
Army officer	1	0	−1	—	x	—	0	0	0	−1	0	0
Artist	0	0	0	—	x	—	0	0	1	1	1	0
Astronomer	1	0	−1	x	—	—	1	0	0	2	0	0
Athletic director	−1	1	0	—	x	—	1	0	0	1	0	0
Auctioneer	−1	−1	2	—	x	—	−1	−1	0	0	0	0
Author of novel	−1	1	0	—	x	—	1	0	0	0	0	0
Author of technical book	3	−1	−2	x	—	—	3	0	−1	−1	−1	1
Total 10 items							+7	0	−3	0	−3	−1
Total 400 items							+182	+23	−115	−91	−134	−33
Standard score							67	36	10	11	3	16
Rating							A	B	C	C	C	C

SOURCE: E. K. Strong (54, p. 75). By permission.

given group or occupation has a greater chance of finding that type of activity congenial and, hence, of succeeding in it; provided, of course, that he also has the degree of aptitude required. The differentiating value of the Strong inventory is illustrated in Figure 24.3, which contrasts rather markedly divergent occupational groups in respect to interests.

Although the Kuder and the Strong inventories differ in their original and primary conceptions, they have, in their later additions, provided some similarities. The Kuder Preference Record–Vocational is intended

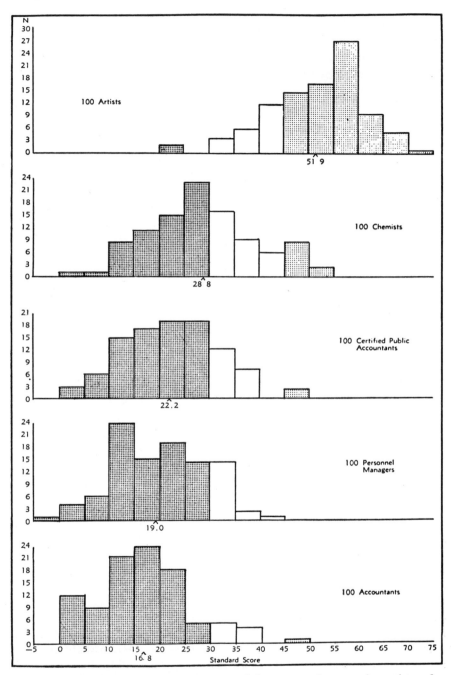

FIG. 24.3. Distribution of standard scores of five occupations on the artist scale. From E. K. Strong (54), by permission.

to identify significant evidences of interests in broad vocational areas. An occupation or a limited list of occupations is suggested by high scores in a given area. Or still another restricted list may be suggested by a combination of the scores in two or more areas. The Strong, on the other hand, aims primarily to provide patterns of preferences that distinguish one specific occupation from others. The Kuder Preference Record–Occupational approximates the Strong in providing scores for each of a large number of occupations; and the Strong somewhat approximates the Kuder in forming clusters of occupations into separate groupings. Each of these instruments, however, continues to be used primarily for its original purpose.

RELIABILITY AND VALIDITY. Reliability coefficients of the ten scores found with the Kuder vocational inventory, in terms of internal consistency, are quite satisfactory, varying from .80 to .95, with an average of about .90. Retest-reliability coefficients, however, after intervals of one to four years, range from about .50 to .80 for men (the average being about .65) and from about .60 to .80 for women (the average being about .68). These retest coefficients indicate that, in some instances, significant changes have occurred over a period of several years. It appears, therefore, that retesting is desirable, from time to time, for counselling purposes. Long-range decisions, based upon scores obtained in grade 9 or 10, will be of questionable validity in more than a few instances. This finding is not necessarily attributable to defects of the instrument; for interests and values undergo change and may strengthen during adolescence, as more information and varied experiences are acquired. In the case of the Kuder Preference Record–Occupational, the internal-consistency coefficients vary from .42 to .82 (with a median of .62), while the retest reliabilities, for unspecified intervals, reported for a high school and a college group, range from .61 to .85 and .77 to .91, respectively.

Reliability coefficients of the Strong inventory for men, using odd and even scores, range from .76 to .94, with a median of .88. Retest scores, after an interval of only one week, yielded an average coefficient of about .85. Persistence of interests was estimated by retesting after varying intervals, with the following correlational results (all males):

first tested as eleventh-grade boys; retested after 2 years .81
"   "   " college freshmen;   "   "   1 year .88
"   "   "   "   "   "   "   19 years .72
"   "   "   " seniors;   "   "   5 years .84
"   "   "   "   "   "   "   22 years .75

These findings indicate remarkably consistent interest trends over long periods.[3] It is not to be assumed, however, that all of the occupa-

[3] No comparable data are provided for women.

tional scales yield equally consistent results (56). For example, the 1959 Manual reports retest results for 663 men, after an interval of 18 years. The coefficients ranged from .48 (public administrator) [4] to .79 (engineer and chemist). Here again, changes in scores are not necessarily attributable to the inventory; they may be the result of changes within the persons answering the questions. This is suggested by the fact that highest retest coefficients were found for men in professions whose interests remain relatively consistent: engineers, lawyers, psychologists. It is not surprising that in more than a few instances changes in relative scores, over a period of years, are found. Many considerations and determinants other than ability and original preferences influence occupational choices which, in turn, have their influence upon subsequent interests and preferences. These determinants are often subtle, unpredictable, and may be unknown to the persons concerned. Under these circumstances, the information provided by these and equivalent inventories is highly creditable.

For the Strong inventory, a number of different criteria of validity were used: mean scores and standard deviations of criterion (specific occupational) groups compared with a general sample; correlations with grades in schools and colleges; completion of occupational training; ratings of success in work; earnings (in sales work); persistence in occupations; job satisfaction; differences between occupational groups; and correlations with other types of psychological tests. Excepting the correlations found with tests of intelligence, educational achievement, personality traits, and with school and college grades, these criteria, all already familiar to the student, have been found to be related significantly to the scores on the Strong inventories.

Three important types of data will indicate the general nature of the findings. When mean scores of each occupational group (male) were compared with mean scores of "men-in-general," the range of percentages of overlapping of scores was from 53 to 15, with an average of 31.5. For women the range was from 43 to 17, with an average of 35.[5]

Of 137 college students who became physicians, 64 percent, as undergraduates, had ratings of A on the physician scale; 13 percent rated $B+$, 10 percent B, 8 percent $B-$, and 5 percent C. The probabilities of subsequently entering the occupation, indicated by inventory ratings obtained for 663 college students as shown by their occupations 18 years after testing, were found to be as follows. For students who scored $A+$,

---

[4] The number of cases scored for this occupation was 248.

[5] The percent overlapping indicates the percentage of one group who reach or exceed the mean of the other. Thus, 15-percent overlap means that only 15 percent of "men-in-general" reached or exceeded the mean score of the particular occupational group being used in this comparison.

the probabilities were 88 in 100; for those scoring $A-$, 74; $B+$, 62; B, 49; $B-$, 36; C, 17.

The foregoing validity data indicate that the Strong inventory has considerable value in vocational guidance with college students. It is not to be assumed, however, that this instrument is equally efficient, as a predictor, at earlier ages. As Strong states in the Manual, the Vocational Interest Blank is "distinctly" applicable to ages 25–55, since occupational interests, it is maintained, change very little during that period. He also states that changes are "relatively slight" between ages 20 and 25. But, he adds, the VIB should be used ". . . below 17 years of age only with relatively mature boys and girls of 15 and 16 years" (54). Regardless, however, of the age of the person being advised, the results of the Strong inventory should be interpreted and utilized only by counselors who are familiar with its rationale and with the techniques used in its construction.

Validity of the Kuder Preference Record–Vocational was estimated in several ways. Profiles of a large number of specific occupations were derived in terms of percentile ranks in the ten areas. Each profile should show significant peaks for those interests regarded as essential and as having differentiating value for each occupation. Kuder found that "mean profiles" for occupational groups ". . . indicate in general that the names assigned to the various scales are appropriate in terms of the type of occupation entered as well as in terms of the activities for which the scale is scored. Chemists are found to be high on the scientific scale, writers on the literary scale . . ." etc.

Scores in each of the ten areas were analyzed in relation to choice of curricula and of occupations; and scores were related to degree of job satisfaction. These criteria yielded reasonably satisfactory results. Scores for the areas were correlated with educational achievement; but the coefficients were, for the most part, in the .20s and .30s, though higher in a few instances. Most significant findings were those showing the relative independence of the ten areas of preferences; that is, their intercorrelations. Of forty-five coefficients, thirty are negative, ranging from $-.52$ (outdoor correlated with persuasive) to $-.03$ (musical correlated with clerical). Of the fifteen positive correlations, the range was from .54 (commercial correlated with clerical) to .03 (artistic correlated with literary) (25).

In validating the occupational inventory, a "differentiation ratio" was used. First the range of scores was divided, arbitrarily, into five parts. The ratio of the two proportions (for the norm group and for the occupational group) falling within an indicated score range, is the differential ratio. This index is used to answer this question: Are the scores of the occupational group significantly higher than those of the norm group? That is, does the inventory differentiate between them? Table 24.4 illustrates the procedure in a case where the scores of clinical psychologists were compared with those of the norm group. It appears that the inventory differentiates well for that profession (26).

TABLE 24.4

DIFFERENTIATION RATIO: KUDER PREFERENCE RECORD–OCCUPATIONAL
SCORED FOR CLINICAL PSYCHOLOGIST

Range of scores	Number in sample of 200 psychologists	Number in sample of 200 from norm group	Differentiation ratio*
56 or higher	153	4	++(10+) †
51–55	23	8	+3
46–50	11	15	=(no difference)
41–45	11	27	−2
40 or less	2	146	— †

* In each instance, the larger number is the numerator. If the number in the occupational group is larger, the sign is plus.
† The ratio is more than 10 on the positive or negative side.
SOURCE: Science Research Associates. Reproduced by permission.

Both inventories were also validated by means of item analysis. Essentially, the problem would be to examine an adequate number of responses to each item by known groups, to determine which of them are selected and rejected most often by persons strongly interested or successful in a given area or occupation. For example: Do high scorers in the "Scientific" area select an item more often than the low scorers in the same area? Do high scorers in a given area tend to choose the same items? How frequently do successful engineers select a particular item?

Scores obtained on the Kuder Preference Record–Vocational and on the Strong have, in general, a low correlation with ranks on tests of general intelligence. These coefficients indicate that there is, at best, but a weak relationship between general mental ability and vocational interests. When, therefore, these or similar devices are used in guidance, they must be supplemented by measures of general ability, among others, especially in attempting to estimate occupational *level;* for example, as between clerk and accountant, machinist and mechanical engineer, technician and scientist.

APPLICABILITY TO DIFFERENT AGE GROUPS. With whom should such occupational and interest inventories be used? Obviously, they can be valid only for persons whose lives have been long enough and varied enough to have included experiences providing a basis for a choice between the alternatives presented by each item in the inventories. The Kuder Preference Record, concerned with broad areas of interest, is standardized for high-school students (beginning with grade 9), college students, and adults at large. The Strong Vocational Interest Blank, concerned primarily with specific occupations, is intended for ages 17 and over. Since the Strong inventory is based upon responses of adult men and women, more valid and useful results will be obtained with adults than with persons in their teens. Since the Kuder record has been standardized with high-school and college students, as well as with adults, it may be used appropriately with adolescents. But even so, the interests, values, and attitudes of adolescents are still in a state of flux and are as yet not fully developed; hence, the results of the preference record, when used for guidance purposes, must be interpreted with this fact in mind.

With either a high-school or a college student, the scores and the profile obtained with the sounder inventories in this category are useful as an introduction to the study of occupations that involve activities of the sort for which he has indicated a preference, and during interview and counseling to check the individual's choice of an occupation against his expressed interests and preferences. For purposes of guidance at the secondary-school and college levels, it appears that the Kuder has the greater value because it is less specific.

Both instruments are intended to provide measures of motivation in various fields of study and work. Their application and usefulness are based upon the premise that release and effective utilization of an individual's general ability and specific aptitudes are strongly affected by motivation and interests, that a person will work best at what he enjoys most. This is a psychologically valid position. However, it is doubtful that adolescents' interests and preferences are actually classifiable into the highly specific occupations. It appears, rather, that they fall into broad categories, each including a group of educational and vocational interests. The method used in the Kuder record, therefore, directed toward identification of general patterns (or profiles) of preferences and interests, seems the more appropriate in the guidance of individuals who have not yet reached adulthood. In any event, anyone who uses these and similar instruments must realize that the profiles do not present simple patterns of strong likes and dislikes. They provide a valuable additional source of information that can be added to results obtained by means of other psychological instruments, educational records, and psychological interviews.

Some critics of preference inventories, and some persons who fill them out, have said that these devices reveal what the subjects already knew about themselves. Although this is true in some instances, the inventories are still useful, for they provide the means of an organized and standardized process of stock-taking and comparison of an individual's scores with norms and percentile scores of known groups.

Attitudes and Values [6]

DEFINITION OF ATTITUDE. An attitude is a dispositional readiness to respond to certain situations, persons, or objects in a consistent manner which has been learned and has become one's typical mode of response. *An attitude has a well-defined object of reference.* For example, one's views regarding a class of food or drink (such as fish and liquors), sports, mathematics, or Democrats, are attitudes. If, however, a person's characteristic behavior is described as self-sacrificing, intellectual, liberal—or the opposite of these—some of his *traits* are being indicated, since these terms represent his *generalized* ways of behaving and viewing situations. The degree or strength of a person's attitude may vary from extremely positive through a gradation to extremely negative. Obviously, it is possible to construct tests of innumerable attitudes.

Methods of Scaling. Tests of attitudes are based upon several assumptions: (1) the scale should deal with a controversial question; (2) an individual's feelings and insights in regard to the question will determine his responses to the various statements that are made pro and con; and (3) the statements can be scaled regarding the degree to which they favor, or are opposed to, the question under consideration.

Thurstone's technique of scaling attitude tests is known as the method of *equal-appearing intervals.* The method is essentially this: statements, both favorable and unfavorable, bearing on a particular problem, question, or institution are obtained from a group of selected writers, other experts, and laymen. These statements are edited. Then they are classified by a large number of judges on an eleven-point scale. This is done by placing each statement in one of eleven piles, presumably forming a continuum, according to degree of favorableness or unfavorableness of each item with respect to the question at hand. The median of the judged locations for a statement (item) is its scale value. Statements that are judged to be ambiguous or irrelevant to the continuum are eliminated.

Before inclusion in the final scale, each question is analyzed for consistency with the general attitudes found by the total scale. For example, on a scale to determine attitudes toward churches, if it is found that many persons having an unfavorable attitude check a statement that is

---

[6] Since attitudes and values are not separable in actual life situations, they are dealt with under a single heading.

apparently favorable, then that item is considered irrelevant and is discarded. Statements having approximately the same values in the scale should show high consistency in degree of endorsement by each subject. This is essentially a simple method of item analysis. Ambiguity of an item is determined by the spread or range of judges' ratings in the original eleven-fold scale, given in terms of Q (quartile deviation). If an item's Q is "high," it is eliminated.

In taking an attitude test scaled in this manner, the respondent checks those statements with which he agrees, his score being the median of the scale values of the items he has marked. Thurstone held that scales constructed for different attitudes by this method permit direct comparison of the scores of any attitudes so measured. The validity of such comparison, however, has been questioned because the defined "neutral points" of different attitudes are not necessarily the same. Nor are the intervals demonstrably equal; they are only equal *appearing*. The Thurstone method is useful if strict comparability of scores is not assumed.

Thurstone and his students developed a series of scales, each consisting of statements from extremely favorable to extremely unfavorable. The topics included in these scales dealt with attitudes—among others—toward Negroes, Chinese, war, censorship, the Bible, patriotism, and freedom of speech. The following statements are from the scale of attitudes toward the church. The scale value of each is given in parentheses, low values being favorable and high values unfavorable, with a possible range from 0 to 11.

> I find the services of the church both restful and inspiring. (2.3)
> I think the church is a parasite on society. (11)
> I believe what the church teaches but with mental reservations. (4.5)
> I think the teaching of the church is altogether too superficial to have much social significance. (8.3)
> I believe in religion but I seldom go to church. (5.4)
> I believe the church is the greatest institution in America today. (1.7)

Likert suggested the use of an attitude-scoring technique that is simpler than the Thurstone method and is regarded by many as at least as reliable. Each item, or statement, in the attitude scale is followed by five responses, one of which is checked by the subject. The responses, indicating degree of strength of attitude, are: *strongly agree* (SA), *agree* (A), *undecided* (U), *disagree* (D), or *strongly disagree* (SD). (Approve-disapprove may be used in place of agree-disagree). Arbitrary scoring weights of 1, 2, 3, 4, 5 were assigned for the respective responses. An individual's score on a particular attitude scale is the sum of his ratings on all items. The principal advantage of Likert's method, obviously, is that it makes unnecessary the use of a group of judges to arrange statements into categories representing degrees of favorableness or unfavorableness. However, since the items are selected on an a priori basis, and since the scoring weights are arbitrarily assigned, the use of the Likert method, like the Thurstone, measures attitudes only in the sense that individuals are given a rank order according to attitude intensity.

The following items from the Minnesota Personality Scale (for men) are examples of the technique suggested by Likert.

SA, A, U, D, SD On the whole lawyers are honest.
"   The future looks very black.
"   Education only makes a person discontented.

Remmers and his collaborators have prepared a series of attitude scales that differ in construction from Thurstone's in that each scale is intended to measure an attitude toward a larger group of objects, persons, or institutions. The scales deal, among others, with national and racial groups, vocations, teachers, social action, and school subjects.

THE SEMANTIC DIFFERENTIAL.[7] This is a technique used to measure the connotations of words representing persons, concepts, organizations, institutions, events, and objects; in fact, anything the experimenter or clinician might regard as relevant. Each word is rated on a seven-point polar scale, and a given word may appear on more than one scale in order to elicit several attitudes (38). For example:

Father

happy   ____ : ____ : ____ : ____ : ____ : ____ : ____ : sad
hard   ____ : ____ : ____ : ____ : ____ : ____ : ____ : soft
intelligent ____ : ____ : ____ : ____ : ____ : ____ : ____ : dull

Woman

fair   ____ : ____ : ____ : ____ : ____ : ____ : ____ : unfair
active   ____ : ____ : ____ : ____ : ____ : ____ : ____ : passive
superior   ____ : ____ : ____ : ____ : ____ : ____ : ____ : inferior

Or

Father: happy   ____ : ____ : ____ : ____ : ____ : ____ : ____ : sad
Woman: fair   ____ : ____ : ____ : ____ : ____ : ____ : ____ : unfair
Success: merit   ____ : ____ : ____ : ____ : ____ : ____ : ____ : chance
FDR: wise   ____ : ____ : ____ : ____ : ____ : ____ : ____ : foolish
Labor Unions: ____ : ____ : ____ : ____ : ____ : ____ : ____ : selfish
  idealistic

---

[7] This technique provides, in some degree, a measure of an individual's projection of his personality. As a matter of fact, all personality tests do that to some extent. The Semantic Differential technique is included here because it most closely resembles scales of attitudes and values.

This method has possibilities of providing information on an individual's traits; and it may add information regarding specific sources of personality difficulties or behavioral conflict. This is so if the stimulus words and the word opposites are skillfully chosen so as to elicit significant responses in important areas. The stimulus words used and the polar words selected for each pair will depend upon their intended purpose (see, for example, 38, p. 43).

Osgood and his colleagues have found, through factor analysis, that the numerous word-opposites they used in their experiments might be classified into three variables (factors).

> Evaluative: good–bad, beautiful–ugly, clean–dirty, fair–unfair, fragrant–foul.
> Potency: large–small, strong–weak, thick–thin, loud–soft, deep–shallow.
> Activity: fast–slow, active–passive, sharp–dull, angular–rounded.

In the case of any individual's responses, of course, these three variables can occur in different combinations and at different degrees of strength.

This technique was developed originally for experimental purposes, not for clinical use; but it has been found to have possibilities also in the latter field. While the three factors named above can be useful in describing and understanding some clinical cases, they are not exhaustive. It is highly probable that clinical use of and experiment with this technique will provide other variables; and the likelihood is that these will be similar to or identical with those found by other methods.[8]

SOCIAL DESIRABILITY. In connection with rating scales (Chapter 21), the forced-choice type of item was explained. It was pointed out that respondents often select descriptive statements because they are socially desirable. It has been demonstrated that when the usual type of item (a single statement) is used, there is a strong tendency to describe oneself in socially desirable terms. Edwards (12) reports correlations in the .80s between the frequency with which descriptive items are selected and their estimated social desirability. This result has been called the "façade effect," since it is attributed to the desire—not necessarily conscious—of most persons to make a favorable social impression. The façade effect, however, is only a partial explanation that does not apply to all persons. Another explanation is the fact that the behavior of most individuals in a given society actually conforms, in greater or lesser degree, to the cultural stereotypes. Their behavior is, thus, not a façade.

Edwards developed a scale to evaluate the effects of the social-desirability factor upon respondents' attitudes toward traits and behaviors listed in personality inventories. He submitted 150 items from the MMPI to

[8] As an illustration of possible clinical use, see (38, pp. 258 ff.) and (39).

ten judges, who were asked to give the socially desirable responses to each. From the viewpoint of a favorable social attitude toward a respondent, how should each item be answered? The judges agreed perfectly on 79 of the 150. On the basis of later statistical analysis, 39 items were selected. These, after experimental tryout, showed the greatest differentiation betwen a high-scoring and a low-scoring group on the 79-item scale.[9] The score an individual earns on this scale is regarded as a measure of his tendency to give socially desirable responses in self-description. The criticism of the concept of façade effect, in the preceding paragraph, should be borne in mind.

Edwards combined the forced-choice type of item with the social-desirability concept to devise the Personal Preference Scale, in which the statements are scaled for degree of social desirability by the method of successive intervals. "This scaling method resulted in a psychological continuum of social desirability on which the statements could be located"[10] (8). The Edwards scale is designed to minimize the influence of social attitudes and values in responses to the statements therein. Two statements representing different personality traits constitute an item. The two statements in each item are equal (or nearly so) in regard to their social values, although they may describe apparently unrelated forms of behavior. "If one is now asked to choose that statement in the pair that is more characteristic of himself, it may be argued that the factor of social desirability will be of much less importance in determining the response than in the case of a *Yes-No* type of inventory" (11).

The author's statistical analysis of this inventory, consisting of 225 paired statements, indicates that it satisfies his assumptions. Subsequent research, however, showed that the very pairing of statements in an item can modify the social desirability score of each in the pair, because of their juxtaposition (6). Other published reports also indicate that individuals can to some extent misrepresent their social values and attitudes by deliberately marking the statements for that purpose (2, 9). To succeed in this, however, requires a degree of social sophistication that is not widespread in the general population.

The Edwards scale is of additional interest since it is intended to measure fifteen "normal personality variables," which are among the

---

[9] In scaling the items for favorableness or the opposite, Edwards used Thurstone's method of equal-appearing intervals and that of successive intervals. In the latter, equality of widths of successive intervals is not assumed, whereas it is in the former.

[10] In the process of developing the scale, these two statements were included: "I like to be loyal to my friends." "I like to avoid responsibilities and obligations." The first was endorsed by 98 percent of a student group and has a scale value of 4.4 (highly desirable); the second was endorsed by 6 percent, with a scale value of .68 (highly undesirable).

needs listed by H. A. Murray *et al.* (34) and which are tested by means of the Murray Thematic Apperception Test (see Chapter 25). The selection of these needs as the basis of the scale gives assurance that it is devised to evaluate aspects of personality which have been derived from extensive research.

TESTS OF VALUES. A test of values, in contrast to one of attitudes, purports to measure *generalized and dominant* interests. The *Study of Values* (Allport *et al.*), for example, is based upon six categories of values, as classified by Spranger (52). The items are intended to measure the relative prominence of the subject's interests, for the purpose of classifying his values. The six categories are: *theoretical, economic, esthetic, social, political,* and *religious.* According to this classification, the dominant interest of the theoretical man is discovery of truth; the economic man is interested in what is useful; the esthetic man values form and harmony most; the highest value of the social type is love of people; the political man is interested primarily in power; and the religious man places the highest value on unity, in an effort to comprehend the cosmos as a whole. This test of values presents forty-five problem situations, under each of which the subject is required to select—from paired alternatives or from multiple choices—responses which are indicative of degrees of the six types of values. For example:

The main object of scientific research should be the discovery of truth rather than its practical applications. (*a*) Yes; (*b*) No.

Do you think that a good government should aim chiefly at—(The following statements are to be ranked in order of preference.)
(*a*) more aid for the poor, sick, and old
(*b*) the development of manufacturing and trade
(*c*) introducing highest ethical principles into its policies and diplomacy
(*d*) establishing a position of prestige and respect among nations

It is not to be assumed that these six are "natural" types, or that they include all possible value groups, or that individuals can be classified entirely under one or another. As a matter of fact, most persons are a mixture of two or more of these value groups, some values being stronger and more dominant than others in each person. The six classifications were employed as starting points for the investigation of complex views of life which, among others, serve to give unity and purposefulness to the mature person.

A different approach to the study of values of high-school and college students and adults is found in the *Sims SCI Occupational Rating Scale.* This scale is devised "to reveal the level in our social structure—i.e., the social class—with which a person unconsciously identifies himself." The scale lists forty-two occupations, representing all levels of socioeconomic status. The subject indicates whether persons following each of the occupations generally belong to the same, or to a higher, or to a lower social class than he does himself. Sims states that ". . . by examining the occupations which the subject indicates are those whose followers belong to his own social class, we are able to determine the position which he assigns himself in our society." This inventory may be regarded as one that estimates one set of social values; for affiliation with a socioeconomic group usually signifies acceptance of the major values of that group.

CHECKLISTS.   In Chapter 21, the use of checklists for rating persons other than one's self was explained. Also available are several check lists for self-rating. Although these are intended to assist the individual himself and his counselor in more readily identifying sources of behavioral and adjustment difficulties, they also serve to indicate the subject's values and his attitudes toward persons, institutions, and other aspects of his environment. The *Mooney Problem Check List* is representative of this type of instrument. Forms are available for junior high school through college, and for adults. Among the areas sampled are the following: [11] health, school, home and family, boy-girl relations, self-centered concerns, morals and religion, finances, economic security, and courtship. The checked items are not scored, but they serve as a basis for counseling or, in some areas, for class discussion.

The areas included in the checklist were selected through an analysis of written statements of problems obtained from several thousand high school students, as well as from counseling and clinical sources. The Mooney list is thus an example of content validity.[12]

BIOGRAPHICAL DATA QUESTIONNAIRES.   With this type of device, the purpose is to sample several areas of a person's experiences that appear to be associated, directly or indirectly, with behavior and success in a particular occupation or situation. These aspects may include the intellectual as well as the nonintellectual; for example, education, religious activities, occupations, interest in athletics, marital record, financial status and interests, specific skills, group affiliations, family relationships, etc. The development of a biographical questionnaire involves a job analysis and experimental determination of biographical areas that are most significant.

Items of a questionnaire are intended to reveal the subject's attitudes and adjustments in terms of significant situations in which he has participated. This approach is not an attempt to measure personality traits. Its major premise is that past behavior, interest, activities, habits, skills,

[11] The areas sampled vary in the several levels: junior high school, seven; senior high school, eleven; college, eleven; adults, nine.
[12] See also the SRA Junior Inventory (46) and the SRA Youth Inventory (47).

attitudes, etc., are indicators of what may be expected in the future. Actually, biographical data questionnaires are variations on the familiar application blank, including a wide range of information, with answers to be given in multiple-choice form.

During World War II, this technique was employed in the armed forces in an effort to improve the selection of personnel for various training assignments. The results were not highly successful; the correlation between questionnaire rating and degree of success as a pilot was .30. These results, however, were regarded as encouraging enough to warrant continued research with biographical questionnaires (20, 57) in civilian situations.

The following is an item from the questionnaire used in the U.S. Air Force during World War II (19, p. 772).

> Mark any of the following types of work which you have done at any time and for which you have received remuneration. (More than one may be marked.)
> *A*. Manufacturing industries (machine operator, factory hand, textile worker, etc.)
> *B*. Technical trades (baker, electrician, radio repairman, etc.)
> *C*. Transportation and communication (truck driver, linesman, deckhand, etc.)
> *D*. Business trades (store clerk, salesman, agent, window dresser, etc.)
> *E*. Public service (fireman, policeman, forest ranger, soldier, etc.)

A recent attempt to devise a biographical questionnaire for selection of educational administrators sampled information in the following areas: childhood and early background; professional preparation; health; interests; early signs of leadership; heterogeneous items (20). Two sample items follow.

> During most of the time before you were 16 you lived:
> *A*. with both parents
> *B*. with one parent
> *C*. with a relative
> *D*. with foster parents or nonrelatives
> *E*. in a home or institution

> How often were you a leader of your childhood "gang" activities up to the age of 12 years?
> *A*. always
> *B*. frequently
> *C*. occasionally
> *D*. seldom or never
> *E*. never a member of a gang; or can't remember

Although this investigation proved of little value for the selection of school administrators, it is reported here as representative of the approach to the problem and of the early stages of a technique that may prove fruitful for purely practical purposes.

Since the introduction of the biographical questionnaire in personality study, efforts have been made to organize the data into patterns and clusters, and to assign trait names. Multiple-choice items are written to sample biographical experiences that will represent these patterns and clusters, from which predictions of subsequent performance might be made. Data obtained with these items are then validated against external criteria to estimate the predictive value of the questionnaire.

The biographical-data method has within it a potentially serious defect. It is a purely empirical procedure, in which an attempt is made to find the predictive value of each biographical datum with respect to "success" in a specific position or in a type of occupation. Since this type of questionnaire does not deal with abilities, skills, and basic personality traits, and since it is validated against job-performance ratings and against "progress" of individuals in an organization, the predictive significance of biographical data is largely a matter of the standards, values, and preferences of raters or of the particular organization. For example, it may be found that being "rural-born" (rather than "city-born") has a fairly heavy positive weight in predicting progress to a school superintendency, or to an executive post in industry. This asset would indicate nothing about the person's abilities for the position, about his personality traits, or about the actual demands made by the position itself. Such a finding would, however, assist in an analysis of the attitudes and values of prospective employers. This criticism will not apply, of course, to all biographical information obtained through the questionnaire.

Evaluation of Tests of Attitudes and Values.   There is little to choose between the methods of attitude testing, so far as reliability is concerned. On the various scales devised, the median reliability coefficient has been about .70; with some below .60, and even below .50, while others were above .80. In a few instances, the coefficients were so low as to be negligible. The two methods of scoring (Thurstone's and Likert's) are themselves very highly correlated (about .90), as shown when the same sets of statements and responses were scored both ways (14).

Validities of tests of attitudes and values are extremely difficult to determine by statistical methods, since the only observable criterion is overt behavior. Obviously, it is practically impossible to obtain objective *behavioral* data on a population sampling with regard to attitudes toward church, the foreign-born, specific minority groups, and the like. Furthermore, overt behavior need not always be correlated with attitude scores.

For example, consider two persons, one of whom is extremely hostile to churches while the other is indifferent to them. Their scores on the scale will differ significantly; but the indifferent person might attend and support a church as little as the hostile one. On the other hand, another indifferent person might attend regularly for social or economic reasons. Similarity of manifest behavior may be demonstrated, also, by one who is hostile to the foreign-born and by one who merely avoids them. The fact that attitudes and overt behavior need not correspond makes validation, in the usual terms, a near impossibility. It is reasonable to conclude, however, that if individuals make a genuine effort to respond according to their own attitudes, these scales are useful in evaluating the beliefs of the respondents, as of the time the responses are given.

As in all other forms of psychological testing, we are interested in knowing whether attitudes and values change over a period of years. Kelly (23) had 300 engaged couples fill out questionnaires during the years 1935–1938 and retested a very large percentage of them in 1954. Scores on the two sets of tests were correlated, with the following results.

Allport-Vernon: religious, .60; theoretical, economic, and esthetic, in the .50s; political, in the high .40s; social, in the low .30s.

Remmers Generalized Attitude Scale: gardening, housekeeping, entertaining, church, in the .30s; rearing children, about .15; marriage, about .07.

When one takes into account the fact that the Allport-Vernon retest correlations after one year (reliability) were .75 or lower, the coefficients obtained after 20 years indicate an impressive degree of stability. The Remmers retest correlations, for Forms A and B, were between .70 and .80. The much higher long-term stability shown by the Allport-Vernon indicates that it is sampling more fundamental aspects of personality than is the Remmers. Furthermore, with the exception of attitude toward "church"—which is not necessarily the same as a "religious" attitude—the Remmers scales measure attitudes that are based upon limited experience, or none at all, or are susceptible to chance experiences of a fortunate or an unfortunate kind. In general, whether retest scores will or will not change significantly after a long interval will depend upon each respondent's experiences, including education, in the interim.

Opinion Polling

Opinion polling is essentially a method of finding out the attitudes and values of a specified population. It has become a specialized field of study and practice. Opinion polling has been concerned also with a great variety of subjects dealing with social, economic, international, military, and other questions, and also with questions of consumer preferences, usually called "market research" and now called, by some, "motivational research."

Although some opinion studies use several questions in surveying an issue, many employ only a single question. The question may be given in one of several forms: some require merely a *yes* or *no* answer; some require a rating of intensity or degree, such as *strongly approve, approve,* etc., or *very much, much,* etc.; at times the respondent is asked to check or rank items in a given list; sometimes the respondent selects one of two alternatives; occasionally the question is of the "open-end" type, in which the respondent completes a statement or sentence to suit himself.

The mailed questionnaire, which had been in use long before opinion polling became popular, is another form of opinion gauging. This form of questioning, however, presents several serious disadvantages, so that it is not as widely used as formerly. Representative mailing lists are difficult to obtain or develop; the percentage answering the questionnaires is often small and atypical of the total group; the questions may not be understood or correctly interpreted by persons at the lower end of the intelligence scale; and the semantic problem is always present.

Opinions are obtained from a sampling of persons regarded as representative of a defined population. This population may be any group that is to be studied; for example, college students, or farmers, or trade-union members, or housewives, or all the voters of the United States. Once the population to be polled has been defined, it may be sampled by one of three most common methods: (1) random sampling; (2) stratified sampling; (3) area sampling.

The first two of these methods were explained in Chapter 2. When *area* sampling is used, the geographic area to be polled is divided into a number of subdivisions of approximately equal population. The characteristics of the population in the various areas are known, so that in the final selection, individuals of the desired characteristics will be included in correct proportions. The particular divisions to be studied are chosen to yield as large and diversified a sampling as may be necessary for the investigation. Each division is further subdivided into much smaller units, each including persons who have the desired characteristics of those to be polled by interview. Then, from among these small subdivisions, a random sampling is made for actual study. Within each of these final units, *every* person is interviewed, even if repeated visits to the homes are necessary.

The area-sampling method is infrequently used because it is so expensive; it requires that relevant information be obtained regarding every family within specified areas and that extremely elaborate files be kept. It is doubtful whether the advantages of the area-sampling method warrant the cost and the attempts to obtain information of kinds that many people will, with justification, regard as an invasion of their privacy.

The major problems and difficulties in opinion polling will be indicated without elaboration.

With any method of sampling, it is extremely difficult to get a completely unbiased sampling because of unknown chance errors, unknown selective factors, and errors of judgment in evaluating traits and responses of some persons.

It is doubtful that opinions can be correctly gauged by a single question, except in special instances such as elections, when the respondent makes a choice between candidates.

Answers to questions may be deliberately falsified or there may be lack of frankness which results in a large number of "undecided" or neutral answers.

All respondents do not necessarily interpret a question or statement in the same way; the same question or statement has varying connotations for different persons.

Some respondents do not understand the *language* or phrasing of the question or statement.

Some respondents do not know or understand the *issue* being dealt with.

Individuals who do not actually have an opinion feel at times constrained to express one anyhow.

Over-all percentages of responses vary with different ways of stating a question.

When the open-end question is used, it is difficult to classify the responses.

Responses are influenced by the training, influence, and possible bias of the interviewer.

Significant differences in status between interviewer and respondents may influence answers: for example, responses of Negroes to Negro may differ from those of Negroes to white.

Verbal expression of an opinion does not necessarily indicate the respondent's actions.

Different persons have different reasons for giving the same responses; and persons giving different responses may do so for a common reason. Psychologically, it is necessary to determine, through skillful interview, the reasons for a response.

Some of these difficulties and problems can be met in part if the questions are stated unambiguously and simply and are easily understood by persons for whom intended; if the respondents are familiar with the issue; if the respondents could reply by "secret ballot" or could be sure of remaining anonymous; if more than one question is used for a given issue.

As psychologists, however, we are primarily concerned with knowing *why* individuals hold certain opinions about the issues that are polled, rather than with learning only that certain percentages of the sampling think thus or so. Why do certain persons choose to vote as they do? Why do a large majority of a certain category of housewives prefer pastel-colored refrigerators to white? Why are some individuals hostile to persons of Oriental origin? Determination of reasons for these and even more subtle behaviors, attitudes, and values requires interviewing by qualified psychologists or other qualified professional persons. So long as opinion polling continues to be a matter of classification of responses and determination of percentages, it remains, aside from technical considerations, a statistical problem of significance principally to political scientists, sociologists, and consumer-research specialists.

References

1. Allport, G. W., *et al. Study of Values.* Boston: Houghton Mifflin Company, 1931–1960.
2. Borislow, B. The Edwards Personal Preference Schedule and fakability. *Journal of Applied Psychology,* 1958, *42,* 22–27.
3. Brayfield, A. H., and W. H. Crockett. Employee attitudes and employee performance. *Psychological Bulletin,* 1955, *52,* 396–424.
4. Comrey, A. L., and W. S. High. Validity of some ability and interest scores. *Journal of Applied Psychology,* 1955, *39,* 247–248.
5. Cook, W. W., *et al. The Minnesota Teacher Attitude Inventory.* New York: The Psychological Corporation, 1951.
6. Corah, M. L., *et al.* Social desirability as a variable in the Edwards Personal Preference Scale. *Journal of Consulting Psychology,* 1958, *22,* 70–72.
7. Corey, S. M. Professed attitudes and actual behavior. *Journal of Educational Psychology,* 1937, *28,* 271–280.
8. Darley, J. G., and T. Hagenah. *Vocational Interest Measurement: Theory and Practice.* Minneapolis: University of Minnesota Press, 1955.
9. Dicken, C. F. Simulated patterns on the Edwards Personal Preference Schedule. *Journal of Applied Psychology,* 1959, *43,* 372–378.
10. Dunkleberger, C. J., and L. E. Tyler. Interest stability and personality traits. *Journal of Counseling Psychology,* 1961, *8,* 70–74.
11. Edwards, A. L. *Personal Preference Schedule: Manual.* New York: The Psychological Corporation, 1954.
12. Edwards, A. L. *The Social Desirability Variable in Personality Assessment and Research.* New York: Holt, Rinehart and Winston, Inc., 1957.
13. Edwards, A. L. *Techniques of Attitude Scale Construction.* New York: Appleton-Century-Crofts, Inc., 1957.
14. Edwards, A. L., and K. C. Kenney. A comparison of the Thurstone and

Likert techniques of attitude scale construction. *Journal of Applied Psychology*, 1946, *30*, 72–83.

15. Fishman, J. A., and I. Lorge. The influence of judges' characteristics on item judgments and on Thurstone scaling via the method of ranks. *Journal of Social Psychology*, 1959, *49*, 187–205.

16. Fordyce, W. E. Social desirability in the MMPI. *Journal of Consulting Psychology*, 1956, *20*, 171–175.

17. Frandsen, A. N., and A. D. Sessions. Interests and school achievement. *Educational and Psychological Measurement*, 1953, *13*, 94–101.

18. Fryer, D. *Measurement of Interests*. New York: Holt, Rinehart and Winston, Inc., 1931.

19. Guilford, J. P. (ed.). *Printed Classification Tests*. Washington, D.C.: Government Printing Office, 1947, Report no. 5.

20. Guilford, J. P., and A. L. Comrey. Prediction of proficiency of administration personnel from personal-history data. *Educational and Psychological Measurement*, 1948, *8*, 281–296.

21. *Guilford-Shneidman-Zimmerman Interest Survey*. Beverly Hills, Calif.: Sheridan Supply Company, 1948.

22. Herzberg, F., and A. Bouton. A further study of the stability of the Kuder Preference Record. *Educational and Psychological Measurement*, 1954, *14*, 326–331.

23. Kelly, E. L. Consistency of adult personality. *The American Psychologist*, 1955, *10*, 659–681.

24. *Kuder Preference Record–Personal*. Chicago: Science Research Associates, Inc., 1948–1954.

25. *Kuder Preference Record–Vocational: Examiner Manual*. Chicago: Science Research Associates, Inc., 1956.

26. *Kuder Preference Record–Occupational: Handbook*. Chicago: Science Research Associates, Inc., 1957.

27. La Piere, R. T. Attitudes vs. actions. *Social Forces*, 1934, *13*, 230–237.

28. Layton, W. L. Theory and research on the Strong Vocational Interest Blank: a conference report. *Journal of Counseling Psychology*, 1955, *2*, 10–12.

29. Lee, E. A., and L. P. Thorpe. *Occupational Interest Inventory*. Monterey, Calif.: California Test Bureau, 1956.

30. Likert, R. A technique for the measurement of attitudes. *Archives of Psychology*, 1932, *22*, no. 140.

31. Mallinson, G. G., and W. M. Crumrine. An investigation of the stability of interests of high school students. *Journal of Educational Research*, 1952, *45*, 369–383.

32. McNemar, Q. Opinion-attitude methodology. *Psychological Bulletin*, 1946, *43*, 289–374.

33. *Mooney Problem Check List*. New York: The Psychological Corporation, 1941–1950.

34. Murray, H. A., et al. *Explorations in Personality*. New York: Oxford University Press, 1938.

35. Nelson, L. W. *Survey of Attitudes and Beliefs.* Chicago: Science Research Associates, Inc., 1954–1955.

36. Nickels, J. B., and G. A. Renzaglia. Some additional data on the relationship between expressed and measured values. *Journal of Applied Psychology,* 1958, *42,* 99–104.

37. Northway, M. L., and L. Weld. *Sociometric Testing: A Guide for Teachers.* Toronto: University of Toronto Press, 1957.

38. Osgood, C. E., *et al. The Measurement of Meaning.* Urbana: University of Illinois Press, 1957.

39. Osgood, C. E., and Z. Luria. A blind analysis of a case of multiple personality using the semantic differential. *Journal of Abnormal and Social Psychology,* 1954, *49,* 579–591.

40. Palubinskas, A. L., and L. D. Eyde. SVIB patterns of medical school applicants. *Journal of Counseling Psychology,* 1961, *8,* 159–163.

41. Parten, M. B. *Surveys, Polls and Samples.* New York: Harper & Brothers, 1950.

42. Powers, M. K. Permanence of measured vocational interests of adult males. *Journal of Applied Psychology,* 1956, *40,* 69–72.

43. Reid, J. W. Stability of measured Kuder interests in young adults. *Journal of Educational Research,* 1951, *45,* 307–312.

44. Remmers, H. H. *Attitude Scales.* Lafayette, Ind.: Division of Educational Reference, Purdue University, 1943–1946.

45. Remmers, H. H. *Introduction to Opinion and Attitude Measurement.* New York: Harper & Brothers, 1955.

46. Remmers, H. H., *et al. SRA Youth Inventory.* Chicago: Science Research Associates, Inc., 1949–1956.

47. Remmers, H. H., and R. H. Bauernfeind. *SRA Junior Inventory.* Chicago: Science Research Associates, Inc., 1951–1957.

48. Remmers, H. H., and E. B. Silance. Generalized attitude scales. *Journal of Social Psychology,* 1934, *5,* 298–312.

49. Schaefer, E. G., and R. Q. Bell. Development of a parental attitude research instrument. *Child Development,* 1958, *29,* 339–361.

50. Siegel, L. A. A biographical inventory for students. *Journal of Applied Psychology,* 1956, *40,* 5–10, 122–126.

51. Sims, V. M. *SCI Occupational Rating Scale.* New York: Harcourt, Brace & World, Inc., 1952.

52. Spranger, E. *Types of Men.* (Translated by P. J. W. Pigors.) New York: Hafner Publishing Company, 1928.

53. Stewart, L. H. Modes of response on the Strong blank and selected personality variables. *Journal of Counseling Psychology,* 1960, 7, 127–131.

54. Strong, E. K. *Vocational Interests of Men and Women.* Stanford, Calif.: Stanford University Press, 1943.

55. Strong, E. K. *Vocational Interests 18 Years After College.* Minneapolis: University of Minnesota Press, 1955.

56. *Strong Vocational Interest Blanks: Manual.* Palo Alto, Calif.: Consulting Psychologists Press, 1959.

57. Stuit, D. B. (ed.). *Personnel Research and Test Development in the Bureau of Naval Personnel*. Princeton, N.J.: Princeton University Press, 1947.
58. Super, D. E. The measurement of interests. *Journal of Counseling Psychology*, 1954, *1*, 168–172.
59. Super, D. E., *et al. Vocational Development: A Framework for Research*. New York: Teachers College, Columbia University, 1957.
60. Terman, L. M., and C. C. Miles. *Sex and Personality: Studies of Masculinity and Femininity*. New York: McGraw-Hill Book Company, Inc., 1936.
61. Terman, L. M., and C. C. Miles. *Manual of Information and Directions for Use of Attitude-Interest Analysis Test (M-F Test)*. New York: McGraw-Hill Book Company, Inc., 1938.
62. Thurstone, L. L. *Scales for the Measurement of Social Attitude*. Chicago: University of Chicago Press, 1930.
63. Thurstone, L. L. The measurement of social attitudes. *Journal of Abnormal and Social Psychology*, 1931, *26*, 249–269.
64. Thurstone, L. L. A multiple factor study of vocational interests. *Personnel Journal*, 1931, *10*, 298–305.
65. Thurstone, L. L. The measurement of values. *Psychological Review*, 1954, *61*, 47–58.
66. Thurstone, L. L., and E. J. Chave. *The Measurement of Attitude*. Chicago: University of Chicago Press, 1929.
67. Tyler, L. E. Distinctive patterns of likes and dislikes over a twenty-two year period. *Journal of Counseling Psychology*, 1959, *6*, 234–237.
68. Webb, S. C. Scaling of attitudes by the method of equal-appearing intervals: a review. *Journal of Social Psychology*, 1955, *42*, 215–239.
69. Weschler, I. R. An investigation of attitudes toward labor and management by means of the error-choice method. *Journal of Social Psychology*, 1950, *32*, 51–62.

25.

PROJECTIVE METHODS:
THE RORSCHACH AND THE
THEMATIC APPERCEPTION TESTS

Definition and Explanation

Psychologically, *projection* is an unconscious process whereby an individual (1) attributes certain thoughts, attitudes, emotions, or characteristics to other persons, or certain characteristics to objects in his environment; (2) attributes his own needs to others in his environment; or (3) draws incorrect inferences from an experience. Projection is not recognized as being of personal origin, with the result that the content of the process is experienced as an outer perception and of external origin.

A projective test, then, is one that provides the subject with a stimulus situation, giving him an opportunity to impose upon it his own private needs and his particular perceptions and interpretations. The several forms of the projective method (pictures, inkblots, incomplete sentences, word associations, one's own writings and drawings, and others) are intended to elicit responses that will reveal the individual's "personality structure," feelings, values, motives, characteristic modes of adjustment, or "complexes." He is said to project the inner aspects of his personality through his interpretations and creations, thereby involuntarily revealing traits that are below the surface and incapable of exposure by means of the questionnaire type of personality test.

Personality inventories are standardized questionnaires that ask how the respondent feels or acts in a variety of representative situations. Projective tests, by contrast, are more or less unstructured; [1] instructions are general and are kept at a minimum to permit variety and flexibility of responses; the responses, which are neither right nor wrong, are the subject's own spontaneous interpretations or creations. Projective tests are expected to elicit responses involving not only cognitive factors (that is, those that relate to what is present to the senses and to which meaning is given), but also affective factors (that is, feelings about what is there).

The most widely used projective techniques (for example, the Rorschach inkblots, the Murray pictures) are, among other things, tests of perception and meaning, both of which are dependent upon individual mental processes.[2] The less clear-cut the situation, the greater will be individual differences in perceiving it. These tests, therefore, provide relatively unrestricted opportunity for the exercise and expression of individual differences in perception; for each subject sees what he himself is disposed to see and does what he is personally disposed to do. In so doing, and through the manner of confronting and responding to the stimulus situation, the individual revels some aspects of his personality.[3]

By contrast with inventories that attempt to evaluate personality traits individually, the results of a projective test are used to interpret and understand a personality as a whole. Although specific meanings may be given to certain partial scores, as Rorschach himself did, the components of the whole test must also be interpreted in their interrelationships. This viewpoint is generally known as the *holistic* or *organismic* theory, according to which the whole and its parts are mutually interrelated, the whole being as essential to an understanding of the parts as the parts are to an understanding of the whole. According to the holistic principle, the measurement and evaluation of components alone does violence to the organized structure of the whole.

The holistic conception of personality has emerged from clinical studies of numerous individuals whose behavior could be understood only in terms of the interrelationships and interdependence of traits, and from

[1] The term "unstructured," as used in projective testing, means that the elements or attributes of the situation do not form a uniform and clearly defined pattern for all who encounter it. The term is synonymous with "ambiguous" in that the stimulus situation can elicit a variety of responses among persons tested, as well as a number of different responses from an individual. Projective tests, it will be seen, differ in the degree to which they are unstructured.

[2] Normal perception is defined as awareness of objects, conditions, and relationships as unified, articulated mental structures. Perception is also defined as a mental complex or integration that has sensory experiences as its core. Disturbances of perception will be shown by lack of integration, distortion, and bizarreness.

[3] This is not to say that each person's perceptions and responses are completely idiosyncratic. To each stimulus situation there are certain responses that are quite frequently obtained from certain groups. But there are also numerous individual variations and combinations which give each person's total response pattern its individuality.

the many experimental investigations of perception and behavior. Projective methods, therefore, are regarded by many psychologists as the most valuable type of personality test because they are concerned with a complex of psychological aspects of the individual.

The Rorschach Test [4]

Description and Procedure. This is the well-known and widely used inkblot test, named after Hermann Rorschach, a Swiss, who began his experimentation with inkblots as a means of stimulating and testing imagination. He was not the first investigator to perceive the possibilities of inkblots in experimental psychology, although his work was the most extensive of any, having continued from 1911 to 1921. He is credited with being the first to develop a technique for their use in personality diagnosis.[5] He also changed the emphasis from content analysis to determinant analysis, which is explained in the following pages. Rorschach developed his test and methods as a practical tool to be applied to clinical cases in the study of unconscious factors in perception and meaning, and to reveal dynamic factors of behavior and personality. He proceeded on the principle that every performance of a person is an expression of his total personality, the more so if the performance is concerned with non-conventional stimulus situations in response to which one cannot wilfully conceal his individuality. In responding to inkblots, the subject is generally unaware of what he reveals by the reports of what he sees. Yet in telling what he perceives, he provides insights into his personality.

The Rorschach Test—used from the nursery-school level through adulthood—consists of ten cards, on each of which is one bisymmetrical inkblot. Five are in black and white with differently shaded areas. Two contain black, white, and color in varying amounts; three are in various colors ("chromatics").

The cards are presented to the subject one at a time and in prescribed sequence. The instructions are very simple; the subject is asked, accord-

---

[4] The purpose of this and the following chapter is to familiarize students with the essential characteristics of the instruments, their psychological rationale, their uses, and the major problems they present. Since the Rorschach and the TAT are prominent not only in psychology but also in anthropology, sociology, education and psychiatry, the student of the general field of tests and testing must have more than a cursory and fleeting glance at these instruments. The materials that follow are minimal for a reasonably adequate understanding of the characteristics and purposes of projective tests.

[5] For a bibliography of early investigations, see J. E. Bell (12, pp. 75–76). See also Buros' several yearbooks on mental measurements, especially the fourth and fifth. The great bulk of research on the Rorschach has been published since 1935. For Rorschach's own thinking see (122). Rorschach's most literal interpreters are Oberholzer (123) and Beck (11).

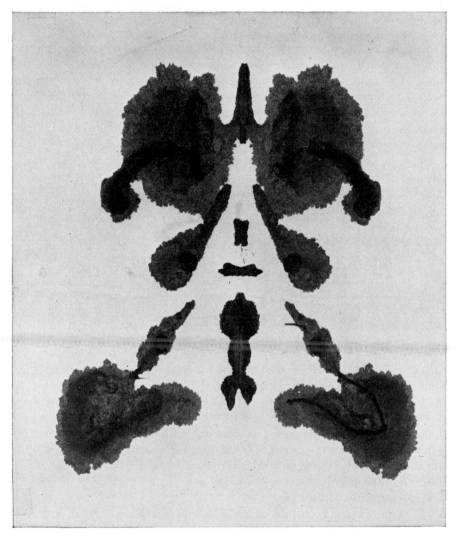

FIG. 25.1. An inkblot similar to the Rorschach blots.

ing to Rorschach's own formula: "What does it look like? What could this be?" Several clinicians and investigators, who have used the test extensively, have somewhat modified the original instructions, though not in their essentials. Klopfer and Kelley, for example, use this formula: "People see all sorts of things in these inkblots; now tell me what you see, what it might be for you, what it makes you think of" (79). The principal differences in the directions of the several specialists who have evolved their own formulas is in the amount of encouragement and urging used to elicit from the subject the fullest possible response to each card.

Rorschach did not impose time limits; nor do present users. Nor is there any fixed number of responses for each card. The examiner makes note of various aspects of the subject's behavior: namely, a verbatim record (so far as possible) of the responses; time elapsed between presentation of each card and the first response to it (reaction time); length of time in long pauses between responses; total time required for each card (response time); position in which card is held for each response (indicating extent of the subject's exploration of the stimulus situation); the subject's extraneous movements and other behavior of significance. The three recordings of time are useful in determining emotional blocking or resistance to what the individual might be perceiving in a particular inkblot.

Directly after all ten cards have been presented for responses, a second phase, the *inquiry,* follows.[6] There are two main purposes of the inquiry. The first is to learn which aspects of the blot initiated and sustained the association process: response to wholes, parts, small details, location, color, shading, apparent movement—all of which are essential items of information for scoring purposes. Second, the inquiry gives the subject an opportunity to add to, or clarify his original responses; but if this is done, it must be completely spontaneous on the part of the subject and without any suggestion from the examiner. The only questions that should be asked are those needed to clarify the scoring, so that the score will include all the significant aspects of the responses. Too many or leading questions by the examiner may elicit answers which do not represent his own perceptions but spring, rather, from suggestions implicit in the questions asked. The only specific questions asked are to determine the exact area or location to which particular responses refer, since this information is necessary for scoring and analysis under the several categories of the test.

Scoring. Following Rorschach's method for the most part, the scoring is based upon four major categories.

LOCATION. The first is the *location,* or the area, which has been perceived as the basis of each response. This may be the entire inkblot, a large portion, a small portion, a minute detail, or part of the white background. The area may be well defined, or merely vague and blurred. Location of responses is the basis of obtaining scores for wholes (called W), large usual details (D), and small usual details (d), unusual detail (Dd),

---

[6] Some examiners prefer to conduct the inquiry immediately after the presentation of each card. Some users of the Rorschach have introduced occasional innovations of their own in administering and scoring, but these will not be described.

and the white spaces (S), which are parts of each person's pattern of response to the entire test. Additional symbols are used to designate other aspects of location; but these five are the major categories.

The locations of responses and the subject's ability to delineate them are regarded as indicative of his perceptual organizing processes, of his ability to analyze and articulate the parts, and of his associations as his perceptions shift within each blot. Analysis of responses in respect to location is said to reveal extent of the subject's perceptual organization or disorganization, measured in terms of agreement with norms of perception, and ability to analyze the whole and synthesize the parts.

DETERMINANTS. The second category includes the *determinants,* or characteristics, of the inkblot as perceived by the subject. The determinants are those aspects or qualities of the blot that have produced the responses to it. These may be *form, shading, color, perspective,* or *motion* —or combinations of them. Forms may be perceived with ordinary accuracy (F); or they may be unusual and clear percepts (F+); or poor percepts (F−). Generally, evaluation of form is a matter of the examiner's judgment, although some investigators have provided normative descriptions and numerical scores (78, 80, 116).

The frequency, intensity, and interpretation of shading noted by the subject are recorded. The manner in which the subject responds to the shading (K) of the blots is said to be relevant to the manner in which he meets and satisfies his own affectional needs; whether by conscious denial of affectional need, or by a repressive mechanism, or by insensitivity and undeveloped affectional relationships with other persons.

With regard to color (C), the examiner records the particular colors reported and the manner in which the subject combines color with form, there being three categories: responses to pure color without form being involved (recorded as C); responses to a combination of form and color, in which form is dominant (FC); and responses to a combination of color and form in which color is dominant (CF).

A score for movement is given by most examiners when the subject perceives something going on in the blot, whereas Rorschach himself restricted the movement score (M) to responses that indicated empathy; that is, a true experiencing of, or identification with, the movement reported (obviously an extremely difficult phenomenon for the examiner to discern). At present a common practice is to reserve the symbol M for human movement, to designate animal movement as FM, and inanimate movement as *m.*

The subject's mention of perspective or depth (FK) is also noted and scored. Parts of the inkblots are perceived as having perspective and being three-dimensional. FK, "in reasonable numbers," is said to be related to good adjustment, through attempts to handle affectional anxieties by introspective efforts.

The foregoing are the principal determinants as developed by Rorschach, and as further developed and modified by Klopfer and his collaborators. Somewhat different sets of determinants have been developed from Rorschach's original ones by several other psychologists, notably S. J. Beck (11). Although there are some differences in symbols used and in details of response classification, the conceptual similarities are much greater than the dissimilarities. One of Beck's categories, in particular, should be mentioned, that is, what he calls *organization* (designated by Z). This determinant, an extension of the concept of the whole (W), indicates ability to perceive (or create) "new and meaningful relations between portions of the figure not usually so organized." Organization is said to be related to level of intelligence. A relatively low Z rating, it has been observed, may be useful in detecting depression, anxiety, or unresponsiveness in persons known to be of superior intelligence.

CONTENT. The third scoring category is *content*. Here the subject's responses are classified into the several more common groups, such as plants, animals, humans, landscapes, man-made objects, anatomy, sex, and others. Content items are not merely classified into groups; they are used by the examiner as a source of ascertaining the subject's personal meanings, attitudes, interests, and even "complexes." Some examiners have interpreted content items, also, as having psychiatric or psychoanalytic meanings. For example, *in some contexts* the response "eyes looking at me"—in some of the cards—is given the obvious interpretation of "paranoid reaction." "Puppets" or "marionettes" perceived in a card are interpreted at times to suggest schizoid tendency, as a feeling of being influenced and directed by hostile persons.

ORIGINALS AND POPULARS. The fourth scoring category is *originality* —also known as "popularity–originality." This has to do with the rating of a response as one that is commonly given (popular), or as one that is uncommon (original). Investigators and interpreters of Rorschach test responses are not entirely agreed as to which responses shall be scored popular and which original, although there are, of course, many about which there is no doubt. However, if users of the Rorschach test are to achieve satisfactory agreement in regard to the significance of their results, this problem of popularity–originality will have to be resolved statistically, in a manner similar to that used in other types of tests. Some normative studies have been made in this area.[7]

Scoring of the responses according to the foregoing categories, or according to any one of the modifications and elaborations thereof, is not

[7] For example, Hertz (58), Thetford (146), Ames (4, 5, 6).

an end in itself. The major purpose of the test is to assess the subject's general adjustment, and to learn whether he is experiencing psychological difficulties—in short, to get insights into his personality, such as could not be obtained ordinarily by direct questioning.

Although considerable experience under supervision is necessary to learn the techniques of administering and scoring the Rorschach, much more experience and expertness are required for the interpretation of scores. With the Rorschach, the two aspects—expertness in a scoring system and skill in psychological interpretation—are essential.

Interpretation. Having scored each response and tabulated the results, the next and significant step is to analyze the *relationships* existing between the frequencies in several categories. For example, the following are among the relationships investigated: the proportion of responses in each of the scoring categories; the ratio of wholes to larger details and to minute details; extent to which form is used with other determinants, such as color and shading—form being dominant; extent to which color is used with other determinants—color being dominant; relationship between color and movement responses; frequency with which color is named apart from other determinants; the ratio of human-movement responses to animal-movement responses; ratio of pure movement responses apart from other determinants to movement plus other elements, especially form; percent of original responses. These and other comparisons and interrelationships indicate the organization and patterned characteristics of the individual's personality, as measured by the Rorschach test. For instance, responses indicative of strong emotion, and thus a sign of *possible* danger, in one record may be regarded as relatively serious; in another record, if there are balancing factors, they may be indicative of satisfactory adjustment.

The frequencies of responses in each of the categories and the various ratios and interrelationships are the bases upon which the subject's personality is delineated.

LOCATION. The locations of responses are used mainly in evaluating intellectual aspects of personality: the manner of approach to a perceptual problem; the preferred mode of apperception. A predominance or large percentage of whole responses (W)—that is, emphasis upon the whole rather than the particular—is regarded as being characteristic of persons of higher levels of capacity for intellectual organization and abstraction. Not only the number of wholes is important here; the originality and appropriateness of the responses must be considered; for simple, popular wholes indicate superficiality and commonplace thinking.

Predominance of common responses of detail (D) is regarded as evidence of concrete, unoriginal, practical mental processes. Responses of unusual detail (Dd) indicate perception of the unusual, associated at times with precise and critical mentalities. But carried to an extreme, rare detail responses may indicate an obsessive preoccupation with the trivial, often accompanying states of anxiety.

Rigidity of approach to problems is said to be indicated by a subject who uses the same procedures with all cards in making his reports, beginning with wholes, then proceeding to larger details, minute details, and white spaces. The reverse of this order is found less frequently. Rigidity is distinguished from *orderliness* of approach, the latter being indicated when a uniform procedure is followed in most location responses, but when, also, variations are used on occasion. Psychotic and some emotionally unstable persons are confused and chaotic in their approach, no order or plan being observable.

FORM. If a person's *form perception* is clear and accurate (F+ or F), he is said to have firm control over his intellectual processes and behavior. By contrast, the schizophrenic, whose behavior is disorganized and whose perceptions are distorted, often reports inappropriate and bizarre forms (F−). A high percentage of form scores independent of other determinants is regarded as evidence of restricted emotional and social adjustment (repression or suppression). Form scores combined with other determinants indicate the degree of intellectual activity.

COLOR. Responses to color in the blots is said to provide the most direct evidence of the subject's impulsive life and emotional relationships to his environment, the combination of color and form, and extreme accent on color alone, being regarded as the most significant signs. Color usually arouses some degree of feeling or emotion in the respondent. The subject may entirely suppress his response; he may spontaneously respond solely to the color without associating it with a form or object; he may combine color and form, one or the other being dominant. The degree to which color is the sole or principal determinant in a subject's responses is viewed as indicative of his emotional intensity. The extent and manner in which he combines color with form is viewed as evidence of the degree of control over emotional impulse. Predominance of form–color responses (FC), perceived as meaningful wholes, implies optimal emotional control, accompanied by a capacity for social adaptability. Color–form responses (CF), in which form is secondary, when dominant suggest a somewhat impulsive, egocentric personality. A large proportion of pure color responses (C) is indicative of emotional impulsiveness.

An additional kind of color response, "color shock," has been observed. This occurs when the respondent is thrown off balance by the presentation of a colored card, especially when it follows a black-and-white blot. Shock is shown by a delay in reaction time, by exclamations, by peculiar responses; or by inability to respond to color. Color shock is believed to imply anxiety neurosis; the person's ability to respond is seriously impaired by loss of emotional equilibrium because of affect produced by color.

The concept of color shock and the actual appearance of the phenomenon, however, have been questioned and subjected to experimental study. Most of the experimental data do not support the original concept. But critics of these statistical studies maintain that this concept and the interpretation of color responses have been dealt with in a mechanical manner, without due regard to the individualized way in which color is handled in the record. They hold that *how* the subject responds to color, if at all, is more significant than statistical counts, in judging the impact of color stimuli upon emotional responsiveness. These critics of the usual statistical analyses point out that the following aspects of response must be evaluated in clinical interpretations of color responses: color selection, color shyness, color denial, color avoidance, and disregard of color accompanied by overt disturbance.

The disagreement noted regarding this area of Rorschach interpretation is an example, in general, of a principal basis of difficulty encountered in efforts to objectify interpretations of responses and to validate the instrument as a whole; that is, the conflict between those who would break down the responses into elements for purposes of statistical analysis and those who maintain that by so doing the significance of each element is destroyed, since each must be viewed in its relationships to the whole. Those in the latter group maintain, also, that available statistical methods are inadequate for handling this problem.

SHADING.   Responses that use shading are said to be related to the manner in which the subject meets his affectional needs. These responses are interpreted as being related to anxiety, depressed attitudes, and feelings of inadequacy.

MOVEMENT.   The movement score (especially human movement), according to Rorschach, is evidence of the richness of one's associative life; the higher the score, the richer the associations and the richer the imaginative life. A large number of reports of human movement, combined with responses to color but not outweighed by them, indicate superior creativeness and giftedness. A high frequency of human movement with little or no color response is said to be characteristic of persons having a rich inner life but little affective response to the outside world. Such persons were named *introversive* by Rorschach. On the other hand, many color responses, accompanied by few reports of human movement, indicate the *extroversive* personality.

Beck, one of the most productive students of the Rorschach, reports that the significance of movement responses differ with various personality organizations. In emotionally stable adults and in some neurotics, it is as stated above. In cases of schizophrenia, movement response is indicative of a highly subjective and personal experience. In adults having adjustment problems but without psychosis, it represents fantasy living; in the manic, it indicates egocentric wish fulfillment.

Klopfer, who has published extensively on the Rorschach, makes a distinction between reports of human movement and those of animal movement (79). In respect to the former, he agrees essentially with Rorschach's interpretation. But a large proportion of animal movement, according to Klopfer, indicates that the person is functioning on a "level of instinctive prompting" rather than at the level of creative activity.

Other clinicians have added still another interpretation to movement responses. They report that a high movement score, combined with satisfactory form, originality, detail, and organization, indicates superior intellectual ability.

CONTENT. The number, proportions, and kinds of things represented in the responses have been variously interpreted as having psychoanalytic significance (fantasy life, symbolic meaning); as showing the amount of stereotyped thinking in the subject; as a sign of maturity or immaturity; as revealing feelings of inferiority; as reflecting the subject's interests, obsessions, and compulsions. Much of this content interpretation is tentative and needs experimental confirmation.

ORIGINALS AND POPULARS. The percentages and number of *original and popular* responses, as might be expected, are taken as evidence of the subject's level of intelligence, though the quality of the originals must be evaluated; for these might be no more than bizarre items or distortions of perception.

INTERRELATIONSHIPS. The relations *within* each of the scoring categories and *among* the several categories provide the materials from which an individual's personality structure and organization are inferred. Various clinicians and investigators have arrived at norms and response proportions, for which they have offered formulas to be used in determining the characteristics of an individual's personality, such as intellectual aspects, emotional control, insecurity and anxiety, introversive, extroversive, or ambiequal "types," and others.

From the foregoing sketch of the possible meanings of various scores it is clear that no single indicator is relied upon exclusively in the determination of the traits of a given personality, and that the major task of the clinician is to interrelate the indicators in such a way as to yield a meaningful whole. It is obvious, also, that scoring techniques among the experts are not uniform, since they are in a state of development. It

should be apparent, too, that there is an appreciable degree of subjectivity in both the scoring and interpretation of responses—and necessarily so, in dealing with an unstructured test. This means, of course,
that skill in the use of such instruments and the attainment of maximum
validity can be achieved only after carefully supervised practice and
experience.

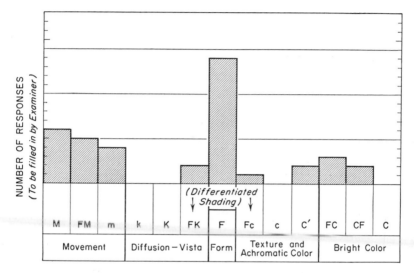

Fig. 25.2. Rorschach response profile. From B. Klopfer and H. H. Davidson, *Individual Record Blank,* New York: Harcourt, Brace & World,
Inc., by permission.

Figure 25.2 is a profile form devised by Bruno Klopfer and Helen H.
Davidson. As reproduced here, it shows the number of responses of an
actual case in each category, to illustrate the manner in which results are
portrayed. Table 25.1, also by Klopfer and Davidson, is shown so that
the student may see more clearly the extent to which the various scores
are interrelated and comprehend more clearly what is meant by interpretation of Rorschach responses as a whole. The information in this
figure and the table provide the starting materials for interpretation.

PERSONALITY STRUCTURE. The Rorschach test is a "multidimensional
instrument" that is intended to yield information on the structure of the
examinee's personality. Three major dimensions are evaluated: conscious
intellectual activity, externalized emotions, and internalized emotions.
Each of these is measured in terms of the several categories already explained. The term "structure" designates the manner in which the various personality traits or aspects are interrelated so as to produce each of

TABLE 25.1: OUTLINE FOR ANALYZING RORSCHACH RESPONSES

RELATIONSHIPS AMONG FACTORS

Total Responses (R) =

Total Time (T) =

Average time per response $\left(\dfrac{T}{R}\right)$ =

Average reaction time for Cards I, IV, V, VI, VII =

Average reaction time for Cards II, III, VIII, IX, X =

$\dfrac{\text{Total } F}{R} =$ F%

$\dfrac{FK + F + Fc}{R} =$ %

$\dfrac{A + Ad}{R} =$ A%

Number of P =

Number of O =

(H + A) : (Hd + Ad) =

sum C = $\dfrac{FC + 2CF + 3C}{2}$ =

M : sum C = :

(FM + m) : (Fc + c + C') = :

$\dfrac{\text{No. of responses to Cards VIII, IX, X}}{R}$ = %

W : M =

Succession:

Rigid   Orderly   Loose   Confused

(Place a check mark at the appropriate point on the scale above)

Estimate of Intellectual Level

Intellectual Capacity	Intellectual Efficiency
....Very Superior	....Very Superior
....Superior	....Superior
....High Average	....High Average
....Low Average	....Low Average
....Dull Normal	....Dull Normal
....Feebleminded	....Feebleminded

Note that this estimate is based mainly on the following:
number and quality of W
number and quality of M
level of form accuracy
number and quality of O
variety of content
succession

Manner of Approach

W(____%) D(____%) d(____%) Dd and S(____%)
or

Enter the location percentages in the spaces above. Compare these percentages with the norms shown in the box below, by placing a check mark opposite the appropriate range of percentages.

W	D	d	Dd and S or
<10% ((W))	<30% ((D))	<5% (d)	<10% Dd S
10–20 (W)	30–45 (D)	5–15 d	10–15 Dd S
20–30 W	45–55 D	15–25 d	15–20 Dd S
30–45 W	55–65 D	25–35 d	20–25 Dd S
45–60 W	65–80 D	35–45 d	>25 Dd S
>60 W	>80 D	>45 d	

SOURCE: B. Klopfer and H. H. Davidson, *Individual Record Blank*. New York: Harcourt, Brace & World, Inc. By permission.

the three major "dimensions," which, themselves, are interrelated in producing the individual's whole personality. The organization, or "structure," of a person's traits is said to indicate how he experiences life around him and how he utilizes some of his experiences. What are his characteristic perceptions, attitudes, and behaviors that result from the organization of his traits? For example, in regard to structure, some of the questions that the Rorschach pattern of responses is intended to answer are: Is the subject's mentality original or stereotyped? Are his abilities creative or reproductive? Is he less adaptable or more adaptable to reality? Is the "inner" or the "outward" life stronger? Or, more specifically, how and to what degree does the individual control his emotions and feelings? Is he prone to anxiety?

Taking one of the three major dimensions—intellectual activity—as an example, it would be appraised by the scores on the following aspects of the responses. Each aspect is accompanied by the factors regarded as significant elements in interpretation of mental level.

Perception of form: quality and percentage of total responses; clearness vs. vagueness; accuracy vs. inaccuracy (F, F+, or F−).

Perception of wholes: number and percentage of total responses: ability to integrate; ability in abstract and theoretical activity.

Perception of major and minor details: number and percentage of total responses; concrete or practical intelligence.

Organization: ability to perceive and create new wholes; creative ability.

Original and popular responses: qualitative richness of response vs. commonplace, stereotyped thinking.

Animal content: "sterility" or immaturity of thought processes (an excess of animal responses) vs. rich and insightful thought processes (perception of forms of a variety of categories).

Productivity: total number of responses; intellectual energy.

Sequence: rigid, or orderly and flexible, or loose, or confused approach to a problem, indicating level of intellectual control.

Movement (mainly human movement): inventive and creative abilities vs. stereotyped thinking.

Reliability. It is undoubtedly true that experienced, skilled clinicians are able to draw remarkably acute and sound inferences from Rorschach protocols; but this is a subjective matter. Ideally, it would be desirable to demonstrate objectively the inkblot test's reliability and validity. Considerable research has been devoted to that end.

There are several problems and principles that should be kept in mind in evaluating studies on the reliability and validity of the Rorschach test. First, while certain part-scores are significant, interpretation is essentially global in character; but as yet there are no satisfactory statistical methods to deal with global patterns of responses. Second, rating or scoring of responses introduces a greater subjective element (than in the case of intelligence tests) because there are no right or wrong answers, the variety of responses is considerable, and normative data are insufficient. As criteria of validity, differential clinical diagnoses are not reliable enough; descriptions of behavior are nonquantitative and subjective to an appreciable degree.

Studies on Rorschach reliability may be classified into the following six types. Each will be briefly explained and evaluated.

1. Parallel series of cards
2. Split-half correlations
3. Test-retest correlations
4. Matching interpretations of Rorschach responses
5. Perceptual and conceptual consistency
6. Attempts to falsify responses and to misrepresent oneself

PARALLEL SETS.   Two parallel sets of cards are used on the assumption that they are analogous to two equivalent forms of the same test. An alternate series of inkblots, devised by Harrower and Steiner, elicit much the same types of responses as do the Rorschach cards, and in similar proportions (49). Detailed analyses of scores are lacking; and results of a sufficient number of comparative studies are not available, so that only general conclusions may be drawn regarding the degree of equivalence of the two sets. It appears, however, that the Rorschach and the Harrower-Steiner sets have yielded sufficiently similar results, for the same subjects, to warrant the use of the latter as a supplementary instrument.

The Behn-Rorschach (30, 161), a parallel series, was used for retesting two groups after a period of 20–21 days. The average correlations of the scoring categories were .56 and .65. With another group of 100 normal subjects and one of 96 abnormal persons, the average coefficients for the scores of the two sets were, respectively, .41 and .52; but the range of coefficients for the separate scoring categories was very wide: from about zero to .86. These results are typical of other studies as well.

Devising two equivalent or closely comparable sets of inkblots is much more difficult than constructing two sets of equivalent test questions or problems; for unless the inkblots are very nearly identical, their stimulus values will differ in some degree. The closer the two sets come to being identical, the more significant might be sheer recall of the responses given to the original inkblots. The difficult problem, then, is to devise a parallel set that will not resemble the original too closely, but will elicit consistent perceptual and conceptual responses.

SPLIT-HALF.   When this method is used to estimate reliability, scores of responses to odd-numbered cards in each of the categories are correlated with those given to even-numbered cards; for example, scores for the number of wholes, good forms, large details, small details, and color. This method has yielded coefficients ranging from approximately .60 to .95 (26, 59).

For several reasons, the use of the split-half method has been seriously questioned; and some clinical psychologists would abandon it. First, the method is inconsistent with the widely held principle that the significance of a Rorschach protocol is to be derived from the whole integrated set of responses; therefore, correlating isolated variables is invalid. This argument is of questionable merit, since isolation of a variable for statistical analysis is one matter, while isolation for interpretation is quite another. The second point is that there are differences in the stimulus value of each of the ten cards; hence, since they are not similar in characteristics or behaviors to be elicited, the odd-even method should not be employed. A third point—one that applies to all quantitative analyses of the Rorschach—is that scoring of responses is too subjective, owing to lack of normative criteria and to the large variety of responses possible. A fourth objection is that the number of responses, in individual protocols and in each category, is often too small to be statistically significant.

TEST-RETEST. This method, using the same cards on two occasions, has also yielded coefficients varying from low to high. One study with young children reports reliabilities of determinants from .30 to .86, after a one-month retesting interval (33). In another study after a twenty-one-day interval, the average coefficient for the several scoring categories was .68 for a group of adults (30). The size of the coefficient varies roughly with the length of the test-retest interval. Swift, for example, retested school children at several intervals with the following results.

> After fourteen days, coefficients varied from .59 to .83 for the several scoring categories.
>
> After a ten-month interval, coefficients varied from .18 to .53 for the several scoring categories.

The findings for the fourteen-day interval are more significant as evidence of reliability (internal consistency) of a projective test, especially with young children who are developing rapidly and in whose lives ten months are a relatively long and significant period.

Another reliability study, using twenty chronic schizophrenics, yielded these reliability coefficients (67).

Location categories:	.50 to .95
Determinants:	.16 to .96
Content:	.36 to .94
Relative scores:	− .17 to .84

On the whole, with a few exceptions, the coefficients ranged from moderate to quite high. Low correlation coefficients, the authors state were due to small numbers of responses and narrow range of the number within each category. An additional reliability test was applied: test and retest tabulation sheets were matched by two experienced Rorschach examiners. They were correct in 85 percent of the selections, this being significant at the 1 percent level. In a study using one hundred college students, fourteen different Rorschach indexes of intelligence, obtained by testing and retesting, were correlated (3). The range of coefficients was from .13 to .93, with a mean of .63.

A different approach, which may have promise, is the use of a scale to rate responses (9). A group of students rated previously obtained responses on a five-point scale according to how well each response corresponded with what he himself was able to see in the blot. The investigators' hypothesis was that there will be a reliable positive relationship between obtained responses and ratings. Split-half reliabilities of the ratings ranged from .74 to .97, with a median of .86. Retest reliabilities, after a two-week interval, of the percentage of responses in each of the categories, were from .51 to .90, the median being .78. While this study is not conclusive, it suggests that higher reliabilities, in general, would be found if more objective scoring methods were used than is usually the case.

The test-retest method should be used with caution. There may be carry-over resulting from recall of previous responses (84). Since the scoring of determinants is dependent in part upon each subject's introspection during the inquiry, this is another possibility of inconsistency in retesting. The subject is not always able to state exactly which determinants were primary or were involved in his perceptions. If the interval between examinations is a significant one, changes in behavior may have taken place as the result of maturation, therapy, or environmental factors. The time interval may be particularly significant in the case of children whose rate of development is rapid. In children, also, attention span and interest are variable from one occasion to another. When parallel forms are used for retesting, reliability correlations are affected by the small number of responses, by possible changes in the examinee's "set" toward the whole situation, and by the possibility that different effects are produced by different examiners (18, 93).

It appears that Rorschach results are more stable for some classes of persons than for others. The question to be asked, therefore, is one of *specific* reliabilities: Reliable for whom and under what conditions? Partial answers have been given to this question; but more definitive research remains to be done.

MATCHING.   As a method of estimating Rorschach reliability, matching is regarded by many experts as most satisfactory, since the whole Rorschach report is kept intact. This is a reliability technique in the sense that it attempts to answer the question: "Do the responses have the same meanings for different experts?" Internal consistency of responses, then, is estimated in terms of consistency of meaning conveyed by the responses; that is, reliability of scoring and of interpretations. Krugman reports, for example, that three judges agreed perfectly in matching twenty Rorschach records with interpretations that had been made by others (81). Also, in this same study it was found that when two independent interpretations of the twenty response records were made, the two agreed essentially in respect to the significance of about 90 percent of the response data, and showed partial agreement on 10 percent. In another instance, when twenty-five records were matched with interpretations, using six judges, the average coefficient of contingency was .87.[8]

Other reports of matching are also favorable, but the number of matched protocols is small. When one evaluates findings in studies of matching, it is necessary to take into account the fact that there may be only partial agreement among the judges, yet other aspects of their individual interpretations, which do not coincide with one another, may be valid too, because each, to some extent, has emphasized different aspects of the responses (76). When general evaluations of degree of adjustment were made on a point scale, based upon the Rorschach records, the results were fairly good (36). Three qualified psychologists rated 146 boys and girls on a four-point scale. The average correlation for their ratings was .67.

Although matching is well regarded as a method, it has been infrequently used, probably because it is most difficult to carry out with large enough numbers of cases rated and interpreted by a large enough number of specialists.

PERCEPTUAL AND CONCEPTUAL CONSISTENCY.   A relatively recent and promising approach to the study of reliability is one whereby responses to the Rorschach blots are compared with responses to altered blots (28, 96) and with responses to other types of tasks which, like the Rorschach, involve perceptual and conceptual tasks (9, 66). The findings thus far indicate that an individual's responses to the several types of stimulus materials are rather consistent in regard to number of responses, variety of interpretations, and use of color. More research of this kind is neces-

[8] The coefficient of contingency is an index of correlation that is used when both variables are classified in two or several categories, rather than distributed quantitatively in the form of continuous or discrete variables. See also Lisansky (91) and Palmer (108).

sary; but the findings reported provide evidence of reliability of the perceptual and conceptual responses evoked by Rorschach inkblots.

ATTEMPTS TO MISLEAD.   Attempts to falsify responses do not appear to be an appropriate method of estimating Rorschach reliability. Some psychologists have called this method "testing the limits of reliability." The results on almost any type of testing device can be distorted by examinees, depending upon their intelligence and degree of psychological sophistication. When this method is used, the experimenter is not actually trying to answer the question of reliability. He is seeking an answer to the question, "Is the Rorschach test resistant to a person's attempts to falsify responses in certain specified ways and to misrepresent his personality?" The answer is that *some* changes in the patterns of response can be effected by deliberate effort; but the amounts and directions of change depend upon several factors, such as relative personality maturity, normality or maladjustment, intellectual level, and amount of knowledge about and definiteness of "set" toward the test (39, 72).

At the same time, other reports indicate that experimental subjects who are simply instructed to try to make a generally good or poor impression do not succeed, in a large percentage of cases, in altering their response patterns. In one study of twenty persons, using the several scoring categories, only three subjects succeeded to an appreciable extent (5-percent level of significance) and only two other subjects to a moderate degree (10-percent level) (19).

SUMMARY.   It appears, on the whole, that the characteristics tested by the Rorschach method have a moderate degree of reliability in terms of internal consistency and retest after a relatively brief interval. When categories are isloated, some scores are found to be more stable than others. The instrument's reliability appears to be greater when the global or patterned character of response records are studied than when scoring categories are isolated. In evaluating the findings of reliability studies on the Rorschach, it is necessary to take into account the complexity of the instrument, the subtleties of interpretation, and the influence of factors extrinsic to the test (for example, "set," motivation, verbal handicaps, previous experience, attitude toward examiner) upon perception. An individual's responses in a test situation are not the product of only his "constant" personality traits reacting to constant test materials.

Available data do not unequivocally demonstrate reliability of the Rorschach test *when the usual methods and standards are used*. It may be that the usual conceptions and criteria of reliability (such as applied to tests of intelligence and specific aptitudes) are not applicable to an instrument like the Rorschach, which is unstructured and thus permits variations in responses not readily quantified, and which has been employed largely to test and describe personalities that are maladjusted or are in a fluid state. Probably the more significant result is the percentage of agreement of judges in the interpretation of responses. In regard to the Rorschach at present, it may be concluded that some researches indicate satisfactory reliability, as usually defined, while others do not; but there is a much higher and a reasonable degree of consistency among experienced Rorschach examiners regarding interpretation of response data.

Validity. Since Rorschach's original work, several validating methods have been used in addition to his own. These may be classified as follows:

1. Known groups
2. Rorschach diagnoses compared with diagnoses by psychotherapists and clinical interviewers
3. Rorschach findings compared with consistent observation of behavior over an adequate period of time
4. Matching Rorschach interpretations with clinical case reports
5. Comparing Rorschach protocols obtained before and after therapy, based upon changes in behavior
6. Single Rorschach variables, or a combination of a few, related to observed aspects of behavior
7. Experimental validation. (a) influencing the subjects; (b) varying the stimulus; (c) relation of Rorschach responses to physiological reactions

Each method will be briefly described and general results briefly noted.

KNOWN GROUPS. Rorschach himself used 288 mental patients who presented clearly discernible extremes of certain traits. In addition, he tested more than one hundred artists, scholars, and persons of average abilities, and also some mental deficients. Among these groups, Rorschach found what he regarded as significant differences in characteristic response patterns. For example, in the neurosis pattern, the following distinguishing signs, among others, are some of the most important reported: very few movement responses, color shock, shading shock, few or no form–color responses, noncombined form responses constituting 50 percent or more of the total number of responses, refusals to one or more cards, small total number of responses. This pattern was interpreted as signifying lack of social adaptability, excessively rigid control, suppression of spontaneity and originality, and anxiety. Since this original work, many similar studies have been published. The results of some of them are reasonably satisfactory and in essential agreement with Rorschach; but many agree only in part.

COMPARISONS WITH CLINICAL DIAGNOSES. Individuals are examined and diagnosed with the Rorschach. Also, another staff member makes a psychiatric diagnosis after interview. Findings are then compared. In one study of 26 children referred to a clinic, the two sets of diagnoses were in essential agreement in 62 percent of the cases before psychotherapy. One year later, the diagnoses agreed in 89 percent of the cases (135). This is one of the more favorable reports. In another study, among the unfavorable reports, only four of thirty-four Rorschach scores differentiated significantly among the several groups of diagnosed patients (129). Among the large number of published studies, a wide range of findings is reported: favorable, indifferent, and unfavorable.

COMPARISONS WITH OBSERVATIONS OF BEHAVIOR.   Behavioral observations of selected individuals are made continuously over a period of time by qualified persons. The subjects observed are usually maladjusted children, adults diagnosed as pathological, or nonclinical school children. These observations are compared with Rorschach findings in respect to certain aspects of personality, such as intellectual functioning, anxiety, emotional expression, etc. The observations may be made in a camp for children, a community or recreation center, in a school, or the like. The results of these studies are not consistent or unequivocal (138). In one of the more favorable reports, teachers' descriptions and ratings of personalities of thirty children (nonclinical cases) were matched with their Rorschach responses. The correspondence found was at the 1-percent level of significance. But here again, other reports of similar studies have not been nearly so favorable.

MATCHING.   A frequently used method of studying validity involves comparisons of Rorschach reports with clinical or other case reports. Some of the studies have used deviant personalities; others have used clinical groups; still others have equated two groups, except for one important factor, the significance of which was to be tested (for example, adolescents in foster homes compared with those in institutions); some have used normal groups.

A study in this area, frequently cited, is Krugman's (81). Rorschach interpretations of twenty-five problem children were matched by five judges with *clinical case reports*. For these 125 pairings, a contingency coefficient of .85 was found. For the five judges, the average of correct matchings was 84 percent. The next step was to compare Rorschach interpretations with case records in regard to each of the following: (1) intellectual aspects; (2) emotional aspects; (3) diagnosis; (4) total personality. Essential agreement was found in 73 percent of the comparisons, fair agreement in 21 percent, and slight agreement in the remainder. These are favorable findings. The results of some other investigations, however, are not so favorable. One (69) reports that only five of fifty

Rorschach reports were correctly matched with descriptions of pupils in private schools, written by their teachers. The marked difference between the findings of these two studies can be accounted for, in considerable part, by the fact that Krugman's cases were a heterogeneous group whose case reports were prepared by clinicial personnel, whereas the private school children were a relatively homogeneous selected group whose personality descriptions were probably on a behavioral level. In still another study, each therapist had to select the Rorschach report of each of his patients from among five others, so chosen as to be varied, but neither very similar nor very dissimilar. Correct selections were made in eleven of the twenty-eight cases.

CHANGES AFTER TREATMENT. When Rorschach reports obtained before and after treatment are compared, the hypothesis is that the test record should reflect personality changes that have taken place in the interim. Two studies—one involving psychoanalysis and the other involving insulin treatment—will be mentioned. In the first, there were thirty-six persons, for all of whom significant changes between the "before" and the "after" Rorschach records were found; and these changes were related to the trends reported by the therapist: for example, improved emotional control, improved intellectual functioning (120, 154). On fourteen outpatient subjects, the Rorschach examiner and the therapist were in essential agreement regarding improvement. In the case of twenty-two hospitalized patients, the two clinicians agreed on ten in regard to direction and degree of improvement; for the remaining twelve, the therapist reported "social recovery" (a nebulous matter), whereas their Rorschach responses showed no improvement.

When insulin treatment was used on schizophrenics, those who showed behavioral improvement also showed improved performance on the Rorschach: increase in speed of reaction and of response, improved verbal form and logical content, clearer perceptions and more relevant responses, and improved emotional control. Changes such as these are not precise and quantitative; but they may still be of clinical and behavioral significance.

SEPARATE VARIABLES RELATED TO BEHAVIOR. Without discussion of the details and tentative findings in this area of validation, the kinds of studies undertaken and the general conclusions will be indicated. This is called the "molecular" approach because, instead of making a global interpretation, only one or a few Rorschach variables are studied in relation to selected aspects of behavior. The Rorschach variables most frequently investigated have been color, movement, and form responses as they are related to certain aspects of behavior, such as introversion–extroversion (as measured by a personality inventory), intellectual capacity (as measured by a test of intelligence). On the whole, the results have been inconclusive; statistically, they have not confirmed some of Rorschach's hypotheses regarding the differentiating significance of some determinants.

EXPERIMENTAL VALIDATION. This method takes several forms. The subjects used may be influenced through experimentally induced tensions, hypnosis or drugs, brain surgery, or electric-shock treatment. When the Rorschach test is administered "before" and "after," it is possible to estimate the effects of the changed conditions. There are two principal obstacles to the employment of this method: first, the number of subjects is necessarily small in each study, because of the great amount of time required by each and the difficulty in obtaining subjects; and, second, the paucity of scientific information as to organic changes in subjects treated by means of surgery, drugs, or electric shock.

Experiments in which the stimulus is varied have been concerned more with color and movement than with other variables. The purpose of the color experiments was to test the stimulus value of color in the cards and the hypothesis of "color shock." Although the results have not been entirely consistent, most researches have raised serious doubts concerning the earlier conceptions of the role of color. In response to the negative results, some clinicians point out that although the reported data are statistically relevant to the isolated stimulus of color, they are not necessarily relevant to the interpretation of color responses in the context of the whole. They emphasize, also, that the statistical findings refer to group trends but do not negate the fact that in some individual cases color has a disruptive influence.

The third experimental approach is to study the relationships between Rorschach responses and changes in physiological activity. For example: What is the relationship between "color shock" responses and galvanometric response? What are the effects of experimentally induced stress on Rorschach responses? Thus far, experimental reports have demonstrated that there is a degree of association between autonomic responsiveness and Rorschach responses. In general, the experimental results indicate the sensitivity of inkblot responses to an examinee's "set" and to temporary emotional states.

SUMMARY. Although approaches to validation have differed in detail, they are essentially of two broad types, experimental and matching—the latter having been the more widely used and the more significant. The matching methods are based upon the principle that descriptions and diagnoses derived from the Rorschach should correspond closely with those obtained by other clinical means—usually those derived from case histories and the long and slow process of clinical study. Such approaches are of three kinds, each differing only slightly from the other two: (1) intercomparisons of Rorschach responses of known *groups;* (2) "blind" diagnoses of *individual* cases, followed by comparisons with diagnoses otherwise determined; and (3) direct comparison, or matching, of an *individual's* Rorschach record with extensive clinical study and diagnosis, to determine areas of agreement and disagreement. If valid, the inkblot test can be used to facilitate a diagnosis in much less time, or to supplement or confirm a diagnosis arrived at by other means. Rorschach specialists maintain that many investigations support the clinical value of their instrument. They have found that results obtained by the several methods indicate the Rorschach test to be useful in revealing threatening or unwholesome trends in personality development before serious difficulties actually appear. If this predictive power of the instrument can be definitely established, the Rorschach will become especially valuable in mental hygiene and preventive psychological treatment. For definite determination of its forecasting quality, an adequate number of longitudinal studies over an appreciable period of the subjects' lives will be necessary. Few of these are as yet available, since their achievement is beset by many difficulties (47, 48).

Other Inkblot Tests. Several group techniques have been devised and are being applied for practical purposes while, at the same time, they are being subjected to experimentation and evaluation.

In one instance, the Rorschach blots—on slides—are projected on a screen, each for a specified time, the subjects being required to write out their responses. They are later asked to mark the blot reproductions on their blanks and to answer a series of questions so that their responses may be scored according to the standard categories.

A second method differs from the preceding in that the subjects are provided with a list of responses for each blot from which to choose (multiple choice). A suggested modification of the multiple-choice item proposes that the several responses (some "normal" and some "neurotic") be rated by the subjects themselves in their order of appropriateness or likeness to the particular blot to which they are attached. The sum of the values assigned to the "neurotic" responses constitutes the score for each blot. Another group procedure being explored is to have the subjects self-administer the test, following prepared instructions.

Group methods have been used with varied degrees of success and inconsistent results. On the whole, they appear to be less successful than the individual method, which permits free, unlimited response and during which the examiner is able to make observations of the subject's behavior and attitudes. While group tests can be used appropriately and successfully in studies of *group* trends and *group characteristics,* the individual may be lost sight of in group findings; a particular individual need not necessarily conform to the trend; and there is overlapping of scores and characteristics among groups.

As is so often the case with projective tests, published research data on group Rorschach tests are not consistently favorable or unfavorable. The reasons for the differences are not always evident, although poor research design and faulty statistical analyses are often said to be the principal ones. Further research is necessary. Such research may reveal not only defects in the group Rorschach but may show, for example, that successful persons in some occupations represent a wide variety of personality patterns, or that reliabilities of the criteria (for example, foreman's ratings, ratings by deans of students) are too low. In the meantime, it can be said that group Rorschach methods have been used effectively by many specialists.

The Holtzman Inkblot Technique is an interesting and possibly promising variation on the original Rorschach method. This technique consists of two alternate forms, each of which has forty-five cards. The noteworthy innovation is that the subject is instructed to give only one response to each card. The principal advantages are said to be (1) the total number of responses is controlled and relatively constant from person to person, yet the number is large enough to be significant; (2) intercomparisons of individuals are more meaningful because the number of responses is relatively constant and large; and (3) alternate forms permit sounder estimates of reliability for each variable.

Many of the reliability coefficients, for the separate variables, are high; others are moderate or low, as shown by the following data.

Intrascorer reliability (72 university students)	.89–.97
Interscorer reliability (72 university students)	.73–.89
Interscorer reliability (40 schizophrenic patients)	.89–.99
Internal consistency (odd-even cards)	.00–.97

Odd-even reliabilities were calculated for ten normal groups of subjects differing in age and occupational status ($N = 60–197$), and for five abnormal groups (mental-hospital patients and mentally retarded; $N = 41–99$). The coefficients vary markedly among these groups and among the variables for which the test is scored. An evaluation of this inkblot test, therefore, must be made for separate groups and for individual variables.

Regarding validity, Holtzman *et al.* state that their correlational data ". . . indicate quite conclusively that the Rorschach and the Holtzman systems have a great deal in common so far as the underlying meaning of their respective variables is concerned" (64, p. 175). As for external criteria of validity, they say: "Although the internal characteristics [factors] of the Holtzman system have been amply documented, the external correlates are still relatively unknown" (p. 253). They add, however, that their data demonstrate highly significant group differences which are "generally consistent with earlier findings using the Rorschach" [9] (p. 253).

Evaluation of the Rorschach Test. The Rorschach inkblot method has been shown to have its greatest usefulness in revealing markedly deviant personalities. Its value in differentiating among individuals within the large groups in the middle ground between extremes is limited, partially for two reasons: (1) differences among individuals within the middle groups are not pronounced, hence they are more difficult to measure or assess; and (2) the instrument is not sufficiently refined to detect finer differences. Other probable reasons are the lack of uniformity in scoring, in determining interrelationships of scores of the several scoring categories, and in the psychological concepts on which various interpretations are based. It is pertinent to add, however, that often the Rorschach test and its specialists are asked by critics to reach higher levels of achievement in application and prediction than are imposed upon other types of psychological tests.

Rorschach exponents recognize that the test needs further clinical and experimental research, especially normative studies for age levels, sex membership, cultural and economic status. More longitudinal studies are also needed. To some extent, progress has been made in these areas (4, 5, 6, 17).

Adverse criticism of the Rorschach has been severe and, at times, hostile. Critics have dwelt on its inadequate objectivity, reliance on personal norms, limited validity, restriction to clinical use, and even "cultism." Although these criticisms are warranted to some degree, Rorschach exponents themselves have not been unaware of the problems and the unanswered questions; for the literature contains many of their own critical publications on the test's reliability, validity, clinical usefulness, guidance value, case studies, and predictive value.[10]

M. L. Hutt has stated the problem reasonably: "Clinical practice is, at present, an art. Art, I believe, will always remain an integral part of clinical practice. However, the scientific aspects of clinical work will, in

---

[9] The *Howard Inkblot Test*, consisting of twelve cards, is available. A considerable amount of careful work has been done in arriving at the final selection of cards and in analyzing the responses of the more than 500 persons, presented in the manual. This test is not intended for use as an alternate to or parallel with the Rorschach. The manual does not provide data on reliability or validity (internal or external), so that this test's practical value cannot be evaluated.

[10] See also Buros, *Fifth Mental Measurement Yearbook*, for four critical reviews of the Rorschach, varying in attitude and substance.

time, become a major portion of this practice as theory, technique and criteria reach a more mature state of psychological development. Meanwhile, I frankly admit the importance of subjective norms, clinical judgment, and subtle influences of intuition. These . . . must be given full play in clinical work in reaching working hypotheses about the [person]. At the same time I rely as much as I can upon all the scientific clues we already have—norms, reliability and validity data, crucial empirical studies, and the like—and utilize these in refining my hunches and delimiting them. Finally, I test these clinical hunches against biographical data, clinical behavior, and all other evidence accumulated about the [person]. In short, I recognize that as a clinician I have two roles to play: the artist and the scientist. I use the former in getting to know the [person] and use the latter to correct my impressions as well as I can. . . . Each role has its place and . . . we must be careful not to confuse the two" (71; see also 43).

Thematic Apperception Test

Description and Procedure.   Commonly referred to as the TAT, this projective method consists of thirty pictures plus one blank card. The cards are used in various combinations, depending upon sex and age. Some are used with all subjects, while others are used with only one sex group or age group. The maximum number of pictures used with any subject is twenty, usually administered in two sessions, ten each time. In actual clinical practice, however, examiners frequently use only ten cards, selected for the particular case.

The person being examined is told that this is a test of imagination, that he is to make up stories to suit himself, and that there is no right or wrong response. The pictures are shown one at a time. The subject is informed that each card shows a scene. He is asked (1) to tell what he thinks led up to the scene; how it came about; (2) to give an account of what is happening and the feelings of the characters in the picture; and (3) to tell what the outcome will be. There are no time limits; in fact, the subject is encouraged to continue for as long as five minutes on a picture. The account should be recorded verbatim if possible.[11] It is recommended that testing be followed by an interview to learn the origins of the stories, seeking associations to places, names of persons, dates, specific and unusual information. This is an important aspect of the process because it enables the examiner to clarify meanings of stories and to evaluate their significance more reliably. The subject's accounts not

[11] As in the case of the Rorschach, some specialists in the use of the TAT have introduced their own variations in giving instructions.

only are a product of his inner personality traits but may be a superficial reflection of cultural forces (radio, television, movies, comics, current events, reading materials, etc.). For instance, a 10-year-old girl made up an unexpectedly large number of stories dealing with crime and mystery. She had been listening regularly to a radio mystery serial. The frequent or compulsive utilization of recent environmental experiences, however, is considered significant in interpreting a subject's reports, because the person *has* utilized them as representing a conflict on the preconscious level, or as a symbol on the unconscious level. Although the TAT pictures are not unstructured to the same degree as inkblots, they are sufficiently ambiguous to permit a wide latitude for individual differences in responses.

There is a basic difference between the TAT and the Rorschach. The latter is intended to reveal the structure and *organization* of an individual's personality, the former is devised to bring out primarily the *content*

FIG. 25.3. A picture from the Thematic Apperception Test. Harvard University Press, by permission.

of one's personality: the drives, needs, sentiments, conflicts, complexes, and fantasies. The test is based upon the principle that when a person interprets an ambiguous situation, he is apt to reveal aspects of his own personality which he otherwise will not admit, or of which he is not aware. The individual, being absorbed in the picture and attempting to construct an appropriate story, becomes much less aware or quite un-aware of himself in the situation. In creating stories based upon ambigu-ous pictures, the individual organizes content of his own personal ex-periences. Everything he says is regarded as having meaning.

Analysis of Stories. Interpretation of TAT stories may be made in one of several ways, depending upon the viewpoint of the ex-aminer and the purpose of the testing. But in all instances, the details of stories must be viewed against facts known about the personality being studied. The stories should not be interpreted *in vacuo.*

In some cases, rereading the stories several times will reveal the sub-ject's basic problems, for repetitive patterns may be found throughout; or it may be found that facts and aspects of different stories constitute a meaningful whole. Or one may make an analysis in accordance with the scheme provided by Murray, or in accordance with modifications sug-gested by others. Two schemes of analysis will be briefly outlined so that students may see more clearly the purpose of the TAT. All schemes, however, have this in common: they are intended to disclose personality content primarily and organization secondarily.

Murray recommends that the content of stories be analyzed into (1) the forces emanating from the "hero" and (2) the forces emanating from the environment. These two divisions are analyzed under the following six categories.

1. *The hero:* the character in each picture with whom the subject identi-fies; in whom the subject is most interested; whose point of view, feelings, and motives have been most intimately portrayed. The heroes are to be characterized by the interpreter according to their principal traits (for ex-ample, solitariness, leadership, superiority, and criminality).

2. *Motives, trends, and feelings of the heroes:* analysis of everything each of the heroes feels, thinks, and does; noting especially the unusual, the high frequencies, the high and low intensities. Under this category, Murray lists traits which are scored on a scale from one to five, on the basis of their strength as expressed through intensity, duration, frequency, and importance in the plot (for example, abasement, achievement, dominance, conflict, dejection).

3. *Forces in the hero's environment:* the nature and details of the situa-tions, especially human, noting uniqueness, intensity, and frequency, as well as objects and persons not in the picture but invented by the subject. The environmental forces are classified according to the effect—realized or

promised—upon the hero. More than thirty such forces have been listed (for example, rejection, physical injury, dominance, lack, loss). The strengths of these are rated on a scale of one to five.

4. *Outcomes:* the comparative strengths of the forces emanating from the hero and the strengths of those from the environment; the amount of hardship and frustration experienced; relative degrees of success and failure; happy and unhappy endings.

5. *Themas:* interaction of a hero's needs with environmental forces, together with the successful or unsuccessful outcome for the hero, constitute a simple thema. Combinations or sequences of these are called complex themas. The thema, simple or complex, is a synthesis of the elements analyzed under the first four categories, the purpose being to view the several forces in their interrelationships and to determine the subject's most prevalent problems arising from internal needs and external forces.

6. *Interests and sentiments:* choice of topics and manner of dealing with them, displayed by the positive and negative appeal of various elements in the pictures (for example, older women who may be mother figures, older men as father figures, same or opposite sex).

S. S. Tomkins has devised another scheme of analysis (149). He differentiates it from Murray's in this way: "Its rationale consists in tapping *varying levels of abstraction* in the hope that significant aspects of diverse types of protocols will be detected by the use of concepts which range from a level of broad generality to a high degree of differentiation." Each story is scored under four main categories: vectors, levels, conditions, qualifiers.

1. *Vectors:* the psychological direction of behavior, drives, and feelings. The ten vectors may have as their objects any thing, person, or idea of interest. Vector means a field of force, or magnitude and direction of force (for example, the vector "against," to attack objects; the vector "toward," to approach or enjoy objects).

2. *Levels:* the "plane" of psychological function involved in the story, seventeen being listed (for example, object description, intention, wish, night dreams).

3. *Conditions:* any psychological, social, or physical state that is not in itself behavior, striving, or wish; that is, conditional qualities of behavior. Two major divisions have been made: (a) states with negative factors or forces—called valences: lacks, loss, danger, inner conditions (depression, anxiety); (b) states with positive or neutral factors: abundance, security, moderation, inner conditions (optimism, certainty).

4. *Qualifiers:* specific aspects of the first three categories: temporal characteristics (past, present, future, duration of an episode); contingency (degree of certainty); intensity (strength of items in story); negation (any type of denial); subsidiation (any means-end relationship); causality (any causal relationship).

Any word or statement in the subject's stories may be classified under one or more of the major categories and their subdivisions. This method of analysis is exceedingly detailed and laborious; but its author states that it often yields insights not otherwise obtainable.

Comparison of these two outlines and comparison of these with other schemes make it obvious that the TAT is not an objective test in the sense that tests of intelligence and specific aptitudes are; first, because the details of the stories are primarily evaluated and classified rather than scored; and second, because there are no uniform standards or criteria which can be objectively applied. We are not maintaining that an instrument like the TAT should or can conform to the standards and criteria of objectivity used in scoring and reporting other types of tests. But the fact that the TAT does not so conform explains why its interpreters report their results in different terms and why its use requires psychological insights on the part of interpreters, particularly into the psychology of needs and motivation.

Regardless of the particular scheme used in making an analysis, the results are interpreted as representing, literally or symbolically, tendencies and traits of the subject's personality, belonging to his past or present, or projected into the future. The results are interpreted, also, as representing, literally on symbolically, effective forces in the subject's environment, his views of the world, his past experiences, his anticipations of the future. The conclusions reached through analysis of the stories should be used as an hypothesis to be checked against other sources of information and as starting points for further psychological interview, counseling, or treatment.

Reliability.   TAT reliability has been studied in three ways:

1. Extent of agreement among interpreters of the same stories in regard to traits of the persons examined

2. Similarities between stories on repeated examinations of the same persons

3. Split-half method, correlating frequency and intensity of needs expressed in the stories.

AGREEMENT AMONG INTERPRETERS.   The first of these methods is dependent, in part, upon the reliability of the interpreters. Published reports indicate that agreement is greater if they have had *similar training and if they use similar systems of analysis and scoring*. This is as it should be, since the interpreters approximate uniformity in their criteria of analysis and ratings. This is an approximation to the prescribed and uniform scoring standards and criteria provided for tests of intelligence and of specific aptitudes.

Studies of agreement among interpreters, using for the most part rank-order correlation and the coefficient of contingency, have reported coefficients ranging from approximately +.30 to +.90.

When the method used was percentages of agreement among interpreters, clinicians have agreed on interpretations of from 50 to about 75 percent of the stories. In addition, there was essential, though not detailed, agreement in from 10 to 25 percent. On the remaining stories there was only partial agreement (44, 46, 94).

In a variation of this method (21), the same judges scored and, after a period of six months, rescored the stories of a large group of college students on ten TAT variables: for example, achievement, aggression, autonomy. The average correlation between the two sets of scores was .89.

Interjudge reliability (contingency coefficients) reported by Henry and Farley varied from .38 to .46; yet, in a pilot study, the coefficients were from .87 to .94. These appreciable differences might be explained by differences between the sets of judges, differences between the groups of subjects, and variable conditions under which the test was given. The authors conclude, on the basis of their detailed analyses, that they ". . . are only justified in declaring . . . that the personality revealed by the TAT expresses the constant needs, dispositions, and attitudes of the subject. About the consistency of test findings from administration to administration . . . and about the consistency of interpretation . . . we can make no unequivocal statement" (56, p. 21). The Q-sort technique was used, in another study (30), to determine the correlations between ratings given by different interpreters to characterizations of the "hero" in TAT stories. The correlations varied from .37 to .88 for various protocols, with an average of .74.[12] A. R. Jensen reports that in fifteen statistically sound studies of interscorer reliability, the coefficients range from .54 to .91, with an average of .71 (16, p. 164).

These data reflect, in part, differences in systems of analysis and differences in ability and experience of interpreters. The results of researches are influenced also by the complexity and often intangibility of elements in the stories. Considering the nature of the problem, the reliability coefficients obtained by this method are encouraging.

TEST-RETEST. Reliability data obtained by the test-retest method are affected by the stability of the personalities being examined and by personality changes as a function of time. The greater the time interval, the lower reliability we may expect, because there will be more opportunity for the influence of intervening forces. Since it is expected that some personalities often will change with time, as developmental conditions change, especially in the case of children, adolescents, and clinical subjects, the more significant reliability data are those based upon extent

[12] See also Little and Shneidman (92).

of agreement of judges and those of test-retest after a brief interval. Tomkins reports a reliability coefficient of +.80 after an interval of two months, for fifteen young women; +.60 after an interval of six months, using a different group of fifteen comparable subjects; and +.50 after ten months for a third group (149). While these last two coefficients indicate significant changes in ratings of some subjects, the indexes represent *group* trends; they do not signify that all subjects showed important changes. It was found that the time intervals between tests had little or no effect upon the ratings of stable personalities.

In another study (90), in which only four cards were used, the subjects were retested after two months. The range of reliability coefficients for fifteen variables was .54 to .91, while the average was .77.

SPLIT-HALF METHOD.   Using the split-half method, Sanford reported reliability coefficients of .48 and .46. The responses were quantified by analyzing the stories for frequencies and rating intensities of "needs" and "press" elicited by the pictures (126). As reliability coefficients, these are ordinarily too low to be significant. Child *et al.* (21) report internal-consistency reliabilities ranging from −.07 to +.34, with a mean of .13 for ten of the variables. McClelland (95), on the other hand, reports a reliability correlation of .70 for the "achievement" need, derived from *selected* pictures. This correlation suggests that reliability is higher when pictures are selected to elicit a single major variable and stories are scored for that purpose. By contrast, the low over-all correlations obtained in some researches are said to be attributable to the inappropriateness of the method, since not all TAT pictures are expected to elicit the same needs and press; each is intended to have its own major stimulus values, and the variables in the theme of one picture are not necessarily additive to those of the others.

Tomkins reported results obtained with *one person* studied intensively for ten months, from whom about four hundred stories were obtained with TAT and other pictures. One interpreter rated the traits revealed in half the stories, while another rated the other half. The obtained correlation coefficient was +.91.

Of the several methods used in studying reliability, interpreter agreement is the most significant; for in employing a projective test, what we want to learn primarily is the content and organization of a personality *at the time of examination*. Whether that personality will remain unchanged and whether we can predict what the personality will be in time will depend upon his degree of stability and upon the determinants in his environment.

Validity.   Essentially, several methods of studying TAT validity have been employed:

1. Comparison with past histories and/or with results obtained through an intensive case study employing a variety of techniques

2. Comparison of characteristics of known individuals or groups with their TAT records

3. Comparison of TAT findings with other clinical materials: the subject's Rorschach record, dreams, or psychoanalytic interpretations

4. Experimentally produced changes

Since most of the studies do not fall exclusively in one category or another, they are not being presented according to this classification.

MATCHING. Of these, the first method has been explored more than the others. Harrison's studies are regarded as among the most significant (44). Forty patients at a mental hospital were given the TAT, without prior knowledge, on the part of the examiner, of their histories. On the basis of their stories and behavior during the testing, Harrison drew his inferences concerning the personality development, traits, attitudes, level of intelligence, personal problems, and conflicts of each subject. These inferences were checked by another person against the hospital records. A correlation of +.78 was obtained between estimated and obtained IQs; 82 percent of the inferences were correct; in somewhat over 75 percent of the cases, diagnostic classification was correct, using the *major* categories; when eighteen cases were classified into clinical *subgroups,* the percentage of agreement with clinical classification was 67. In order to eliminate inferences drawn from observation of the subject's behavior during the testing session, Harrison had another examiner give the TAT to fifteen patients; then he made a blind analysis himself. In this instance, his inferences were 74 percent correct, when compared with already known biographical and personality data. This drop in correspondence (from 82 to 74 percent) indicates the value of using behavioral observations in conjunction with projective-test results.

In another matching experiment, an adaptation of the TAT was administered to groups of Navaho and Hopi Indians. On the basis of their stories, blind interpretations were made of the personality traits of the people of these two cultures. Anthropologists familiar with the two Indian societies found the personality analyses based upon TAT results to be in essential agreement with their facts concerning these Indian cultures.

An investigation in India, using a modified and adapted form of the TAT, yielded promising results regarding the test's applicability to the study of social problems in that culture. The findings make a positive contribution to the question of validity; for a high percentage of the stories dealt with the basic problems of survival (Murray's "succorance"), intrafamily relationships (between the wife and the family of the husband in particular; Murray's "submission"), and the need for education and skills to improve one's lot (Murray's "achievement" and "acquisition").[13]

KNOWN GROUPS.   Satisfactory results were obtained when the stories of diagnosed groups, of known characteristics, were analyzed in detail to determine if significant differences existed among them. The results showed that such differences exist among the following classifications, consisting of individuals who were relatively clear cases in each instance: conversion hysteria, anxiety hysteria, obsessive–compulsive neurosis, brain disease, and head-injury cases (27, 118, 131).

Rapaport, Gill, and Schafer made a qualitative analysis of TAT responses of clinically diagnosed individuals. They found trends in responses that are significant for diagnostic purposes with groups such as the depressive, the paranoid, the schizophrenic (116).

TAT responses were found to have considerable validity in the personality studies of adolescent delinquents in a juvenile court (51). The TAT has been used, also, and with moderately favorable results, for the study of known nonclinical groups. Among these are the selection of potential leaders from among officer candidates in the armed forces (104) and the differentiating TAT responses of prejudiced and nonprejudiced persons (35).

COMPARISONS WITH AUTOBIOGRAPHIES.   Data obtained from autobiographies have been compared with TAT interpretations. Findings demonstrate that some of the pictures (about 30 percent) elicited stories that reflected past history better than did others and that, in this respect, the most useful pictures are those that contain characters with whom the subject is able to identify (23). Critics of this method believe that information obtained from biographies will influence interpretations of stories, even though the interpreter is not aware of the influence.

COMPARISONS WITH DREAMS.   Since psychoanalytic theory holds that dreams are a medium for expressing fears, wishes, etc., that are repressed and inhibited, and since the TAT provides an opportunity for expressing and elaborating these, degree of correspondence between dream content and TAT stories have been investigated. Though not all the themes of the TAT responses appeared in dreams of the subjects thus studied, the few reports available state that the extent of similarity was great enough to give added evidence of TAT validity (127). In this connection, the subjective character of dream interpretation and symbolism must be kept in mind.

AGREEMENT WITH RORSCHACH FINDINGS.   Some investigators have reported sufficiently close agreement between the Rorschach and the TAT

[13] These unpublished studies were made by one of the author's former graduate students, a native and life-long resident of India.

as additional evidence of the validity of the latter (45, 56). This method must be evaluated in the light of the discussion of Rorschach reliability and validity.

INTENSIVE STUDY OF INDIVIDUAL CASES. Morgan and Murray report that the TAT stories of one patient indicated all the major characteristics revealed by five months of psychoanalysis (98). This sucessful outcome is attributable in part to the fact that the psychologists making both the TAT and the therapeutic studies were psychoanalytically oriented. This fact does not necessarily minimize the findings; it emphasizes the possibilities of the TAT when uniform analytical concepts are used with the test and with other forms of behavior.

Tomkins made an intensive study of one person, consisting of seventy-five hours of psychological interview and testing. He concludes that the results of the intensive study disclosed no material inconsistent with his TAT stories and analysis (148). On the whole, it was found that the TAT and other methods supplement one another, that each contributes something to an understanding of the personality not revealed by the others. The usual criticism of studies such as this is that the clinician's interpretations of the stories are "contaminated" by his knowledge about the individual obtained through interviews.

EXPERIMENTAL CHANGES. The use of experimentally produced changes as a technique is based upon the view that validity is shown to the degree that induced changes correspond to changes in TAT responses. In one experiment the need of "achievement" was selected for study with college students. Four pictures were used, administered under experimentally controlled conditions (95). Different subjects performed under conditions called "relaxed," "neutral," "failure," and "success–failure." The "relaxed" state was created by telling the subjects that the test is merely experimental; the "neutral," by urging them to do their best, though the test is experimental; the "failure," by creating a sense of failure on previous paper-and-pencil tests; the "success-failure," by creating a sense of success and of failure on previous pencil-and-paper tests.

The relaxed state was interpreted as being least motivating and the failure state most motivating, in regard to the need for achievement. When this hypothesis was tested relevant to achievement, significant differences under the four experimental conditions were found (at the 5-percent level or better) for many of the categories: for example, increase in achievement reports, deprivation related to achievement, acting to achieve a goal, projecting a goal.

It appears that temporarily induced ego-involving tasks can influence TAT records. There is a basic distinction, however, between experimentally produced, transitory conditions and their effects upon responses, on the one hand, and actual, more or less durable personality traits and content, on the other. The TAT is intended to assess the latter primarily. These experiments, therefore, have limited significance as a method of estimating this instrument's validity. But they can indicate the test's degree of sensitivity to temporary and artificial conditions under which a person performs.[14]

Evaluation of the TAT.   From the viewpoint of psychological theory, the TAT has met with considerable favor among clinicians and students of personality theory. It has also gained widespread use among clinical psychologists because they have found it can make useful contributions to the understanding of individual cases. They continue in this practice even though researches on the instrument's reliability and validity have not produced results that satisfy certain psychometric standards.

While it is used principally in studies and diagnoses of maladjusted and abnormal persons, the TAT is also used with others: for example, selected normal groups, such as college students; groups having particular attitudes, such as racial, economic, or religious prejudices; cultures other than our own. In these areas, the TAT has contributed to a fuller understanding of personality differences. The principal value has been to provide useful material to supplement other sources of information.

In responding to the Thematic Apperception Test situation, the subject is free from social tensions that often accompany early psychological interviews. Consequently, TAT responses provide effective starting places for interview and treatment; thus they can be timesavers and facilitators in the process of diagnosis and therapy.

The range of material in the test—permitting wide quantitative and qualitative individual differences in expressions of wishes, fantasies, frustrations, modes of adjustment—is one of its assets as a projective method. At the same time, this wide range has proved to be a weakness, since procedures in administering, scoring, and interpreting vary, depending upon the conceptual system of the user and the purpose for which he is employing the test. Further use and analysis should determine the most desirable standard procedure and the most valid organization and interpretation of responses. Improvements in analyzing and interpreting responses should contribute to greater validity.

Validity can be improved, also, by more detailed analyses of relations among elements of stories and known behaviors and traits of the subjects; that is, a close study of the *elements* within the stories that contribute to validity and of those that do not. Concurrently, it will be necessary to analyze and describe the kinds of *situations* (the organized "psychological

---

[14] For a useful summary see G. Lindzey (87).

fields") in which the TAT is more or less effective. If such research proves fruitful, we should then be able to indicate validity not only in general but in particular, with respect to certain kinds of situations.

It will be necessary, furthermore, to analyze TAT reports—in fact, all projective test responses—in the light of significant determinants of behavior and personality development of the subjects. Such determinants are age, sex, special occupational training; and social, economic, and cultural status and values (broadly, one's caste and class status). Such analyses might reveal that scoring and interpretations should be modified on the basis of these determinants. It appears, for instance, that separate thematic apperception tests are desirable for children and adolescents. These are described in the next chapter.[15]

References

1. Affleck, D. C., and S. A. Mednick. The use of the Rorschach test in the prediction of the abrupt terminator in individual psychotherapy. *Journal of Consulting Psychology,* 1959, *23,* 125–128.
2. Allen, R. M. *Elements of Rorschach Interpretation.* New York: International Universities Press, Inc., 1954.
3. Altus, W. D., and G. M. Thompson. The Rorschach as a measure of intelligence. *Journal of Consulting Psychology,* 1949, *13,* 341–347.
4. Ames, L. B., *et al. Child Rorschach Responses.* New York: Paul B. Hoeber, Inc., 1952.
5. Ames, L. B., *et al. Rorschach Responses in Old Age.* New York: Paul B. Hoeber, Inc., 1954.
6. Ames, L. B., *et al. Adolescent Rorschach Responses.* New York: Paul B. Hoeber, Inc., 1959.
7. Arnheim, R. Perceptual and aesthetic aspects of the movement response. *Journal of Personality,* 1951, *19,* 265–281.
8. Atkinson, J. W. (ed.). *Motives in Fantasy, Action and Society.* Princeton, N.J.: D. Van Nostrand Company, Inc., 1958.
9. Baker, L. M., and J. A. Creager. Rating scale technique applied to Rorschach responses. *Journal of Clinical Psychology,* 1954, *10,* 373–375.
10. Baughman, E. E. The role of the stimulus in Rorschach responses. *Psychological Bulletin,* 1958, *55,* 121–147.
11. Beck, S. J. *Rorschach's Test: I. Basic Processses.* New York: Grune & Stratton, Inc., 1950.
12. Bell, J. E. *Projective Techniques.* New York: David McKay Company, Inc., 1948.
13. Brody, G. G. A study of the effects of color on Rorschach responses. *Genetic Psychology Monographs,* 1953, *48,* 261–311.

[15] The list of references that follows contains only a small portion of the publications on the Rorschach and the TAT. More inclusive lists are in 2, 12, 16, and 80, among others.

14. Brosin, H. W., and E. Fromm. Some principles of gestalt psychology in the Rorschach experiment. *Rorschach Research Exchange,* 1942, *6,* 1–15.
15. Buckle, D., and N. Holt. Comparison of Rorschach and Behn inkblots. *Journal of Projective Techniques,* 1951, *15,* 486–493.
16. Buros, O. K. *Fifth Mental Measurement Yearbook.* Highland Park, N.J.: Gryphon Press, 1959.
17. Byers, J. *The Relationships between Sub-Cultural Group Membership and Projective Test Responses.* Unpublished Ph.D. Thesis. Cornell University, 1954.
18. Campbell, F. A., and P. B. Fiddleman. The effect of examiner status upon Rorschach performance. *Journal of Projective Techniques,* 1959, *23,* 303–306.
19. Carp, A. L., and A. R. Shavzin. The susceptibility to falsification of the Rorschach Psychodiagnostic Technique. *Journal of Consulting Psychology,* 1950, *14,* 230–233.
20. Carr, A. C., *et al. The Prediction of Overt Behavior Through the Use of Projective Techniques.* Springfield, Ill.: Charles C Thomas, Publisher, 1960.
21. Child, J. L., *et al.* Self-ratings and TAT: their relations to each other and to early childhood background. *Journal of Personality,* 1956, *25,* 96–114.
22. Clark, R. A method of administering and evaluating the Thematic Apperception Test in group situations. *Genetic Psychology Monograph,* 1944, *30,* no. 1.
23. Combs, A. W. The validity and reliability of interpretation from autobiography and Thematic Apperception Test. *Journal of Clinical Psychology,* 1946, *2,* 240–247.
24. Cronbach, L. J. Statistical methods applied to Rorschach scores: a review. *Psychological Bulletin,* 1949, *46,* 393–429.
25. Dana, R. H. Clinical diagnosis and objective TAT scoring. *Journal of Abnormal Psychology,* 1955, *50,* 19–25.
26. Datel, W. E., and J. A. Gengerelli. Reliability of Rorschach interpretations. *Journal of Projective Techniques,* 1955, *19,* 372–381.
27. Davison, A. H. A comparison of the fantasy productions on the TAT of sixty hospitalized psychoneurotic and psychotic patients. *Journal of Projective Techniques,* 1953, *17,* 20–33.
28. Dorken, H. Psychological structure as the governing principle of projective technique. *Canadian Journal of Psychology,* 1956, *10,* 101–106.
29. Dreschsler, R. Affect-stimulating effects of color. *Journal of Abnormal and Social Psychology,* 1960, *61,* 323–328.
30. Eichler, R. M. A comparison of the Rorschach and Behn-Rorschach inkblot tests. *Journal of Consulting Psychology,* 1951, *15,* 185–189.
31. Epstein, S., *et al.* Responses to inkblots as measures of individual differences. *Journal of Consulting Psychology,* 1957, *21,* 211–215.
32. Exner, J. E. The influence of chromatic and achromatic color in the Rorschach. *Journal of Projective Techniques,* 1959, *23,* 418–425.

33. Ford, M. *The Application of the Rorschach Test to Young Children.* Minneapolis: University of Minnesota Press, 1946.

34. Fosberg, I. A. An experimental study of the reliability of the Rorschach psychodiagnostic technique. *Rorschach Research Exchange,* 1941, *5,* 72–84.

35. Frenkel-Brunswick, E. Dynamic and cognitive categorization of qualitative material: I. General problems of the TAT. *Journal of Psychology,* 1948, *25,* 253–260.

36. Friedman, I. Objectifying the subjective: a methodological approach to the TAT. *Journal of Projective Techniques,* 1957, *21,* 243–247.

37. Gardner, R. W. Impulsivity as indicated by Rorschach test factors. *Journal of Consulting Psychology,* 1951, *15,* 464–468.

38. Garfield, S. L., and L. D. Eron. Interpreting mood and activity in TAT stories. *Journal of Abnormal and Social Psychology,* 1948, *43,* 338–345.

39. Gibby, R. G. Stability of certain Rorschach variables under conditions of experimentally induced sets: the intellectual variables. *Journal of Projective Techniques,* 1951, *15,* 3–26.

40. Goldfarb, W. Rorschach test differences between family-reared, institution-reared, and schizophrenic children. *American Journal of Orthopsychiatry,* 1949, *19,* 624–633.

41. Grant, Q., *et al.* Reliability and validity of judges' ratings of adjustment on the Rorschach. *Psychological Monographs,* 1952, *66,* no. 334.

42. Gross, L. Effects of verbal and nonverbal reinforcement in the Rorschach. *Journal of Consulting Psychology,* 1959, *23,* 66–68.

43. Halpern, F. A. *A Clinical Approach to Children's Rorschachs,* New York: Grune & Stratton, Inc., 1953.

44. Harrison, R. Studies in the use and validity of the Thematic Apperception Test with mentally disordered patients. II. A quantitative validity study. III. Validation by blind analysis. *Character and Personality,* 1940, *9,* 122–133, 134–138.

45. Harrison, R. The Thematic Apperception and Rorschach methods of personality investigation in clinical practice. *Journal of Psychology,* 1943, *15,* 49–74.

46. Harrison, R., and J. B. Rotter. A note on the reliability of the Thematic Apperception Test. *Journal of Abnormal and Social Psychology,* 1945, *40,* 97–99.

47. Harrower, M. *Personality Change and Development.* New York: Grune & Stratton, Inc., 1958.

48. Harrower, M. *The Practice of Clinical Psychology.* Springfield, Ill.: Charles C Thomas, Publisher, 1961.

49. Harrower, M. R., and M. E. Steiner. *Psychodiagnostic Inkblots.* New York: Grune & Stratton, Inc., 1945.

50. Harrower-Erickson, M. R. *Large Scale Rorschach Techniques: A Manual for the Group Rorschach and Multiple Choice Test.* Springfield, Ill.: Charles C Thomas, Publisher, 1945.

51. Hartman, A. A. An experimental examination of the Thematic Appercep-
    tion technique in clinical diagnosis. *Psychological Monographs,* 1949,
    63, no. 303.
52. Heimann, R., and J. Rothney. Development and applications of projective
    techniques. *Review of Educational Research,* 1959, *29,* 73–83.
53. Henry, E., and J. B. Rotter. Situational influence on Rorschach response.
    Journal of Consulting Psychology, 1956, *6,* 457–462.
54. Henry, W. E. The Thematic Apperception technique in the study of
    culture-personality relations. *Genetic Psychology Monographs,* 1947,
    35, pp. 3–135.
55. Henry, W. E. *The Analysis of Fantasy: The Thematic Apperception Tech-
    nique in the Study of Personality.* New York: John Wiley & Sons, Inc.,
    1956.
56. Henry, W. E., and J. Farley. The validity of the Thematic Apperception
    Test in the study of adolescent personality. *Psychological Monographs,*
    1959, *73,* no. 487.
57. Hertz, M. R. Rorschach: twenty years after. *Psychological Bulletin,* 1942,
    39, 529–572.
58. Hertz, M. R. *Frequency Tables To Be Used in Scoring Responses to the
    Rorschach Ink-Blot Test.* Cleveland: Department of Psychology, West-
    ern Reserve University, 1946.
59. Hertz, M. R. Current problems in Rorschach theory and technique. *Jour-
    nal of Projective Techniques,* 1951, *15,* 307–338.
60. Hertz, M. R. The Rorschach thirty years after. In D. Brewer and L. Abt,
    Progress in Clinical Psychology. New York: Grune & Stratton, Inc., 1952.
61. Hertz, M. R. The use and misuse of the Rorschach method. *Journal of
    Projective Techniques,* 1959, *23,* 33–48.
62. Holt, R. R. Clinical and statistical prediction: a reformulation and some
    new data. *Journal of Abnormal and Social Psychology,* 1958, *56,* 1–12.
63. Holtzman, W. H. Validation studies of the Rorschach test: shyness and
    gregariousness in the normal superior adult. *Journal of Clinical Psy-
    chology,* 1950, *6,* 343–347.
64. Holtzman, W. H., *et al. Inkblot Perception and Personality.* Austin: Uni-
    versity of Texas Press, 1961.
65. Holzberg, J. D. The clinical and scientific methods: synthesis or antithesis?
    Journal of Projective Techniques, 1957, *21,* 227–242.
66. Holzberg, J. D., and M. J. Schleifer. An experimental test of the Rorschach
    assumption of the impact of color on perceptual and associative
    processes. *Journal of Projective Techniques,* 1955, *19,* 130–137.
67. Holzberg, J. D., and M. Wexler. Predictability of schizophrenic perform-
    ance on the Rorschach test. *Journal of Consulting Psychology,* 1950,
    14, 395–399.
68. Howard, J. W. The Howard Inkblot Test. *Journal of Clinical Psychology,*
    1960.
69. Hunter, M. E. The practical value of the Rorschach test in a psychological
    clinic. *American Journal of Orthopsychiatry,* 1939, *9,* 278–294.

70. Hutt, M. L. The use of projective methods of personality measurement in Army medical installations. *Journal of Clinical Psychology*, 1945, *1*, 134–140.

71. Hutt, M. L. The assessment of individual personality by projective tests: current problems. *Journal of Projective Techniques*, 1951, *15*, 389–390.

72. Hutt, M. L., *et al.* The effect of varied experimental sets on Rorschach test performance. *Journal of Projective Techniques*, 1950, *14*, 181–186.

73. Jensen, A. R. The reliability of projective techniques: review of the literature. *Acta Psychologica*, 1959, *16*, 108–136.

74. Kagan, J. The long-term stability of selected Rorschach responses. *Journal of Consulting Psychology*, 1960, *24*, 67–73.

75. Kaplan, B., and S. Berger. Increments and consistency of performance in four repeated Rorschach administrations. *Journal of Projective Techniques*, 1956, *20*, 304–309.

76. Kelly, E. L., and D. W. Fiske. *The Prediction of Performance in Clinical Psychology*. Ann Arbor: University of Michigan Press, 1951.

77. King, G. F. A theoretical and experimental consideration of the Rorschach human movement response. *Psychological Monographs*, 1958, *72*, no. 458.

78. Klopfer, B., and H. H. Davidson. Form level rating: a preliminary proposal for appraising mode and level of thinking as expressed in Rorschach records. *Rorschach Research Exchange* 1944, *8*, 164–177.

79. Klopfer, B., and D. M. Kelley. *The Rorschach Technique*. New York: Harcourt, Brace & World, Inc., 1942.

80. Klopfer, B., *et al. Developments in the Rorschach Technique*. New York: Harcourt, Brace & World, Inc., 1954, *1*; 1956, 2.

81. Krugman, J. I. A clinical validation of the Rorschach with problem children. *Rorschach Research Exchange*, 1942, *6*, 61–70.

82. Kurtz, A. K. A research test of the Rorschach test. *Personnel Psychology*, 1948, *1*, 41–51.

83. Ledwith, N. H. *Rorschach Responses of Elementary School Children: A Normative Study*. Pittsburgh: University of Pittsburgh Press, 1960.

84. Leventhal, H. The influence of previous perceptual experience on the variance of the Rorschach W & Z scores. *Journal of Consulting Psychology*, 1956, *20*, 93–98.

85. Levitt, E. E., and J. Grosz. A comparison of quantifiable Rorschach anxiety indicators in hypnotically induced anxiety and normal states. *Journal of Consulting Psychology*, 1960, *24*, 31–34.

86. Levy, E. Stimulus values of Rorschach cards for children. *Journal of Projective Techniques*, 1958, *22*, 293–296.

87. Lindzey, G. TAT: interpretive assumptions and related empirical evidence. *Psychological Bulletin*, 1952, *49*, 1–25.

88. Lindzey, G. On the classification of projective techniques. *Psychological Bulletin*, 1959, *56*, 158–168.

89. Lindzey, G. *Projective Techniques and Cross-Cultural Research*. New York: Appleton-Century-Crofts, Inc., 1961.

90. Lindzey, G., and P. S. Herman. Thematic Apperception Test: a note on reliability and situational validity. *Journal of Projective Techniques,* 1955, *19,* 36–42.

91. Lisansky, E. S. The interexaminer reliability of the Rorschach test. *Journal of Projective Techniques,* 1956, *20,* 310–317.

92. Little, K. B., and E. S. Shneidman. Congruencies among interpretations of psychological test and anamnesic data. *Psychological Monographs,* 1959, *73,* no. 476.

93. Masling, J. The influence of situational and interpersonal variables in projective testing. *Psychological Bulletin,* 1960, *57,* 65–85.

94. Mayman, M., and B. Kutner. Reliability in analyzing TAT stories. *Journal of Abnormal and Social Psychology,* 1947, *42,* 365–368.

95. McClelland, D. C., *et al.* The projective expression of needs: IV. The effect of the need for achievement on Thematic Apperception. *Journal of Experimental Psychology,* 1949, *39,* 242–255.

96. McFarland, R. Perceptual consistency in Rorschach-like projective tests. *Journal of Projective Techniques,* 1954, *18,* 368–378.

97. McReynolds, P. Perception of Rorschach concepts as related to personality deviations. *Journal of Abnormal and Social Psychology,* 1951, *46,* 131–141.

98. Morgan, C. D., and H. A. Murray. A method for investigating fantasies: the Thematic Apperception Test. *Archives of Neurology and Psychiatry,* 1935, *34,* 289–306.

99. Munroe, R. L. The inspection technique: a method for rapid evaluation of the Rorschach protocol. *Rorschach Research Exchange,* 1945, *9,* 46–70.

100. Munroe, R. L. Prediction of the adjustment and academic performance of college students by a modification of the Rorschach method. *Applied Psychology Monographs,* 1945, no. 7.

101. Munroe, R. L. An experiment with a self-administering form of the Rorschach and group administration by examiners without training. *Rorschach Research Exchange,* 1946, *10,* 49–59.

102. Murray, H. A. *Explorations in Personality.* New York: Oxford University Press, 1938.

103. Murray, H. A. *Thematic Apperception Test Manual.* Cambridge, Mass.: Harvard University Press, 1943.

104. Murray, H. A., and M. I. Stein. Note on the selection of combat officers. *Psychosomatic Medicine,* 1943, *5,* 386–391.

105. Murstein, B. I. The concept of projection: a review. *Psychological Bulletin,* 1959, *56,* 353–374.

106. Murstein, B. I. Factor analyses of the Rorschach. *Journal of Consulting Psychology,* 1960, *24,* 262–275.

107. Mussen, P. H., and H. K. Naylor. The relationship between overt and fantasy aggression. *Journal of Abnormal and Social Psychology,* 1954, *49,* 235–240.

108. Palmer, J. O. A dual approach to Rorschach validation: A methodological study. *Psychological Monographs,* 1951, *65,* no. 325.

109. Perlman, J. A. Color and the validity of the Rorschach 8–9–10 percent. *Journal of Consulting Psychology*, 1951, *15*, 122–126.

110. Phares, E., *et al.* Instruction variation and Rorschach performance. *Journal of Projective Techniques*, 1960, *24*, 29–31.

111. Phillips, L., *et al.* Rorschach indices of developmental level. *Journal of Genetic Psychology*, 1959, *94*, 267–285.

112. Piotrowski, Z. A. *Perceptanalysis*. New York: The Macmillan Company, 1957.

113. Piotrowski, Z. A., and B. Bricklin. A second validation of a long-term Rorschach prognostic index for schizophrenic patients. *Journal of Consulting Psychology*, 1961, *25*, 123–128.

114. Pope, B., and A. R. Jensen. The Rorschach as an index of pathological thinking. *Journal of Projective Techniques*, 1957, *21*, 439–455.

115. Rae, R. A normative study of Rorschach responses of eight-year-old children. *Journal of Projective Techniques*, 1952, *16*, 56–65.

116. Rapaport, D., *et al. Diagnostic Psychological Testing, Vols. 1 and 2.* Chicago: Year Book Publishers, Inc., 1946.

117. Reisman, J. M. Types of movement in children's Rorschachs. *Journal of Projective Techniques*, 1960, *24*, 46–51.

118. Renaud, H. Group differences in fantasies: head injuries, psychoneurotics, and brain diseases. *Journal of Psychology*, 1946, *21*, 327–346.

119. Rickers-Ovsiankana, M. A. (ed.). *Rorschach Psychology*. New York: John Wiley & Sons, Inc., 1960.

120. Rioch, M. J. The use of the Rorschach test in the assessment of change in patients under psychotherapy. *Psychiatry*, 1949, *12*, 427–434.

121. Roe, A. *The Psychology of Occupations*. New York: John Wiley & Sons, Inc., 1956.

122. Rorschach, H. *Psychodiagnostics*. (Translated by P. Lemkau and B. Kronenberg.) Fourth Edition. Bern: Hans Huber, 1949.

123. Rorschach, H., and E. Oberholzer. The application of the interpretation of form to psychoanalysis. *Journal of Nervous and Mental Diseases*, 1924, *60*, 225–248, 359–379.

124. Rothney, J. W. M., and R. A. Heimann. Development and applications of projective tests of personality. Ch. 5 in "Educational and Psychological Testing." *Review of Educational Research*, 1953, *23*, no. 1.

125. Sandler, J., and B. Ackner. Rorschach content analysis: an experimental investigation. *British Journal of Medical Psychology*, 1951, *24*, 180–201.

126. Sanford, R. N., *et al. Physique, Personality, and Scholarship.* Monograph of the Society for Research in Child Development, 1943, *8*, no. 8.

127. Sarason, S. B. Dreams and Thematic Apperception Test stories. *Journal of Abnormal and Social Psychology*, 1944, *39*, 486–492.

128. Sarason, S. B. *The Clinical Interaction*. New York: Harper & Brothers, 1954.

129. Sarason, S. B., *et al.* Rorschach behavior and performance of high and low anxious children. *Child Development*, 1958, *29*, 277–286.

130. Sargent, H. Projective methods: their origins, theory, and application and personality research. *Psychological Bulletin*, 1945, *42*, 257–293.

131. Saxe, C. H. A quantitative comparison of psychodiagnostic formulations from the TAT and therapeutic contacts. *Journal of Consulting Psychology*, 1950, *14*, 116–127.

132. Schwartz, F., and S. L. Kates. Behn-Rorschach and Rorschach under standard and stress conditions. *Journal of Consulting Psychology*, 1957, *21*, 335–338.

133. Sen, A. A statistical study of the Rorschach test. *British Journal of Psychology*, 1950, *3*, 21–39.

134. Shneidman, E. S., *et al. Thematic Test Analysis*. New York: Grune & Stratton, Inc., 1951.

135. Siegel, M. G. The diagnostic and prognostic validity of the Rorschach test in a child guidance clinic. *American Journal of Orthopsychiatry*, 1948, *18*, 119–133.

136. Siipola, E. M. The influence of color on reactions to ink blots. *Journal of Personality*, 1950, *18*, 358–382.

137. Silverman, L. H. A Q-sort study of the validity of evaluations made from projective techniques. *Psychological Monographs*, 1959, *73*, no. 477.

138. Singer, J. L., and H. E. Spohn. Some behavioral correlates of Rorschach's experience-type. *Journal of Consulting Psychology*, 1954, *18*, 1–9.

139. Stainbrook, E. The Rorschach description of immediate post-convulsive mental function. *Character and Personality*, 1944, *12*, 302–322.

140. Stein, M. I. *The Thematic Apperception Test*. Reading, Mass.: Addison-Wesley Publishing Company, 1955.

141. Steiner, M. E. *The Psychologist in Industry*. Springfield, Ill.: Charles C Thomas, Publisher, 1949.

142. Swift, J. W. Reliability of Rorschach scoring categories with preschool children. *Child Development*, 1944, *15*, 207–216.

143. Swift, J. W. Matchings of teachers' descriptions and Rorschach analyses of preschool children. *Child Development*, 1944, *15*, 217–224.

144. Taft, R. Multiple methods of personality assessment. *Psychological Bulletin*, 1959, *56*, 333–352.

145. TAT issue: a birthday tribute to Henry A. Murray. *Journal of Projective Techniques*, 1958, *22*, no. 2.

146. Thetford, W. N., *et al.* Development aspects of personality structure in normal children. *Journal of Projective Techniques*, 1951, *15*, 58–78.

147. Tolor, A., *et al.* Rorschach card rejection as a correlate of intelligence in children. *Journal of Projective Techniques*, 1960, *24*, 71–74.

148. Tomkins, S. S. Limits of material obtainable in the single case study by daily administration of the Thematic Apperception Test. *Psychological Bulletin*, 1942, *39*, 490.

149. Tomkins, S. S. *The Thematic Apperception Test*. New York: Grune & Stratton, Inc., 1947.

150. Veroff, J., *et al.* The use of the Thematic Apperception Test to assess

motivation in a nationwide interview study. *Psychological Monographs,* 1960, *74,* no. 499.

151. Waller, P. The relationship between the Rorschach shading response and other indices of anxiety. *Journal of Projective Techniques,* 1960, *24,* 211.

152. Watkins, J., and J. Stauffacher. An index of pathological thinking. *Journal of Projective Techniques,* 1952, *16,* 276–286.

153. Williams, M. An experimental study of intellectual control under stress and associated Rorschach factors. *Journal of Consulting Psychology,* 1947, *11,* 21–29.

154. Windle, C. Psychological tests in psychopathological prognosis. *Psychological Bulletin,* 1952, *49,* 451–482.

155. Wishner, J. Rorschach intellectual indicators in neurotics. *American Journal of Orthopsychiatry,* 1948, *18,* 265–279.

156. Witkin, H. A., *et al. Personality Through Perception.* New York: Harper & Brothers, 1954.

157. Wittenborn, J. R. Some comments on confounded correlations among Rorschach scores. *Journal of Consulting Psychology,* 1959, *23,* 75–77.

158. Wright, B. A. Experimentally created conflict expressed by means of a projective technique. *Journal of Social Psychology,* 1945, *21,* 229–245.

159. Young, R. A., and S. A. Higginbotham. Behavior checks on the Rorschach method. *American Journal of Orthopsychiatry,* 1942, *12,* 87–94.

160. Zax, M., *et al.* Some effects of non-personality factors on Rorschach performance. *Journal of Projective Techniques,* 1960, *24,* 81–92.

161. Zulliger, H. *The Behn-Rorschach Test.* Bern: Hans Huber, 1956.

26.

PROJECTIVE METHODS: VARIOUS

It was inevitable that a variety of projective devices should appear after the Rorschach and the TAT had found wide favor and use among psychologists. In this chapter, some of these will be described and evaluated in order to provide a comprehensive view and appreciation of projective testing. Of these, all but one (word association) appeared subsequent to the Rorschach and the TAT. In addition, several other projective methods will be described, although they are not tests in the usual sense. However, they have been employed for many years (play, storytelling, and finger painting, for example) and have proved to be clinically useful.

Word-Association Tests [1]

This method has a long history in psychological experimentation, dating from the work of Francis Galton published in 1879 (36). For many years thereafter, word association was experimentally studied in psychological laboratories. With the growing interest in psychoanalysis after 1900, the word-association method received increased attention as a clinical technique. Jung and other clinicians, beginning about 1906, made extensive use of the technique as a quick means of detecting "complexes" (46).

Jung's list of one hundred words was selected to represent common emotional "complexes." The subject is told that the examiner will speak

---

[1] A general evaluation of the tests discussed is at the end of the chapter.

a series of words, one at a time; after each word, the subject is to reply as quickly as possible with the first word that comes to mind; there is no right or wrong response. The examiner records the reply to each stimulus word, the reaction time, and any unusual speech or behavior manifestations accompanying a given response. Replies to stimulus words that are emotionally toned for the subject generally have a longer reaction time and may evoke physiological changes (in respiration, pulse, flushing, blood pressure), restless movements, coughing, laughing, and mild speech impediments. Jung believed that when a stimulus word was relevant to an emotional disturbance of the subject, an unusual response would be given. Content of the responses, reaction times, and attendant conditions were analyzed for the discovery of emotional tensions, inferred from the classes of words to which noteworthy responses were given. The inferences then are used to initiate further psychological exploration by interview.

The best known of the word-association tests is the one devised by Kent and Rosanoff to differentiate between the mentally ill and the normal (51). Unlike Jung, they used words which were not intended to indicate personal emotional problems but were neutral in character and were to provide diagnostic evidence on the basis of the proportion of common (normal) responses to the uncommon (abnormal). Determination of normal and abnormal replies was based upon the frequencies of word associations of 1000 normal and about 750 psychotic subjects. The table of response frequencies provided the percentages of most common, less common, and uncommon replies. The percentage in each category, it was expected, might differentiate the normal from the abnormal. It was found, however, that word associations did not distinguish clearly enough between the two groups, although the results were at times useful as additional evidence in the study of a particular person. Part of the Kent-Rosanoff word list follows:

table	black	sweet	soldier	justice
dark	mutton	whistle	cabbage	boy
music	comfort	woman	hard	light
sickness	hand	cold	eagle	health
man	short	slow	stomach	Bible
deep	fruit	high	stem	memory
soft	butterfly	working	lamp	sheep
eating	smooth	sour	dream	bath
mountain	command	earth	yellow	cottage
house	chair	trouble	bread	swift

Several other word lists are available. A recent one, which indicates a revival of clinical interest in word association, was constructed by Rapaport, Gill, and Schafer (73). It is intended for use as an aid in diagnosis and in estimating degree of maladjustment and impairment of thought organization. This list is heavily loaded with stimulus words of psychoanalytic significance, especially in regard to psychosexual matters. The words and interpretations of responses are based upon an analysis of what its authors believe to be the psychological processes involved in word association (construct validity). Their rationale includes three aspects of associative responses: (1) memory, as influenced by emotional determinants that affect the process of associative recall; (2) concept formation relevant to the stimulus word; (3) anticipation, in terms of the popular character of the conceptual responses, based upon the subject's ability to adopt a "set" from the examiner's instructions and from the character of the stimulus words themselves, and upon his ability to produce an appropriate response.

A modification of the word association technique is the *homographic* free association test. A homograph is a word spelled exactly like another, but with a different meaning and a different derivation. An example is the word "base," which means "foundation" and, also, "wicked." Thurstone's homographic test, for instance, uses a list of words, each of which has two frequent associations: a social, interpersonal one and a literal, physical one (103). The word "revolution" is an example. The subject is asked to respond to each word with a synonym or a short phrase. A person's associative response to "revolution" can have social or physical relevance: namely, "a political upheaval" or "the turn of a wheel." The purpose of such a restricted list of words would be to identify individuals who are the more strongly oriented toward their social environment. This is shown by the number of responses that are essentially social in nature rather than physical or literal. Similar lists of homographs can be devised for other purposes as well.

The many determinants that influence word associations must be taken into account in utilizing tables of response frequencies and in the interpretation of responses (72, 101). These influences include not only "complexes" and thought impairment, but variations in word usage due to regional, cultural, and socioeconomic differences, and to levels of general intelligence and age. The significance of word associations must be sought in the characteristics and experiences of each individual.

Picture Tests

THEMATIC APPERCEPTION TEST: THOMPSON MODIFICATION. Clinical experience with the Murray TAT convinced some psychologists that Negroes often are unable to identify with the stimulus figures of white persons. These Negroes responded with stories that were chiefly simple, matter-of-fact descriptions of the persons and objects in the pictures. They did not manifest empathy based on the interpersonal relations being portrayed. The value of the TAT depends upon the principle that extent and strength of identification derive from the number and kinds of symbolic elements in the picture, relevant or common to the person being examined. Hence, if a picture does not satisfy this principle, there will be little or no identification and the test will not yield the desired projective information.

Most published research reports on this modification have not confirmed Thompson's position that it has greater clinical value than the original TAT (22, 55, 77). As yet, however, there is too little research from which to conclude whether or not Thompson's modification is superior to the original for use with Negroes. It does appear that the Thompson version is useful in studying racial attitudes and notions of stereotypes in both white and Negro subjects.

CHILDREN'S APPERCEPTION TEST. This test, for children of 3 to 10 years, consists of ten pictures in which all characters are animals. These animals are shown in commonplace *human* situations: eating, sleeping, shopping, being punished, and so on. The assumption underlying the use of animal pictures is that children will more readily identify with them than with humans. In support of this, the authors cite Freud's widely known report on "The Phobia of a Five Year Old."

The authors state in their manual: "The pictures were designed to elicit responses to feeding problems specifically, and oral problems generally; to investigate problems of sibling rivalry; to illuminate the attitude toward parental figures and the way in which these figures are apperceived; to learn about the child's relationship to the parents as a couple . . ." (8). The pictures are intended to elicit, also, the child's fantasies regarding aggression and the adult world, and his methods of responding to and dealing with his problems of growth.

The themes of the pictures are derived primarily from problems and relations suggested by psychoanalytic theory of development and behavior. Interpretations of the stories rest upon the symbolic significance attributed to the content. Although psychoanalytic theory guided the authors of this test in its construction, it is possible to use other principles in the interpretation of responses.

Ten supplementary pictures also have been published (7). These, the authors state, are designed to elicit themes ". . . not necessarily pertaining to universal problems, but which occur often enough . . . in a good many children." These pictures are intended to reveal the following, among others: fear of physical activity or of physical harm, interpersonal problems in school, wishful fantasies about adulthood, regressive tendencies, competitiveness, ideas of body image, fantasies or fears related to the mother's pregnancy.

Although much research remains to be done on reliability and validity, clinicians report that the CAT is a helpful tool in revealing some of the basic traits of a child, while the supplement can indicate transitory characteristics. These, then, can be further investigated by other procedures.

Here, again, we have a useful instrument in the hands of skillful psychologists, but in regard to which several fundamental questions remain to be answered in addition to those of reliability and validity. What will adequate normative data show regarding types and frequencies of stories in relation to age, sex, and socioeconomic status (18)? Do children, in general, actually identify more readily with animals (10)? How are responses influenced by intelligence level (47)? [2]

SYMONDS PICTURE-STUDY TEST. This set of 20 pictures is designed for use with adolescent boys and girls. The cards depict situations and interpersonal relations in which individuals at this stage of development commonly find themselves. The stories told in response to the pictures are analyzed for the psychological forces indicated by them. The forces are among those commonly described in dynamic psychology:

hostility and aggression	ambition and striving for success
love and erotism	conflicts
ambivalence	guilt
punishment	guilt reduction
anxiety	depression, discouragement, despair
defenses against anxiety	happiness
moral standards and conflicts	sublimation

The author's norms indicate that the five themes most frequently obtained are concerned with family relations, aggression, economic problems, punishment, and separation. Informal reports, made shortly after the test became available, suggested that it had possibilities of considerable usefulness; and a follow-up study gives support to this view (97). After an interval of thirteen years (1940–1953), twenty-eight of the original group of forty boys and girls (ranging in age from 25 to 31) were retested. Matchings and qualitative analyses of the two sets of stories ". . . demonstrated the remarkable persistence of personality over a thirteen-year interval and, in particular, the fact that it is possible to

[2] Responding to pictures is a test item long used in the Binet scales and its revisions. At the age of 3 years and 6 months, only "enumeration" is normally expected. The successive higher levels of response are "description" and "interpretation." Since this is the course of development, "identification" may not be expected ordinarily at the first two levels. This view was supported by the findings of Kaake (47).

estimate personality adjustment in later years from facts gathered about a person when he is adolescent" (97, viii). As statistical evidence, Symonds and Jensen report a correlation of .54 between estimates of adjustment made when the subjects were adolescents and those made thirteen years later. They recognize, however, that some of their findings should be regarded as tentative or "fruitful hypotheses." Still, the evaluations of personalities based upon test-retest results indicate that this set of pictures is able to provide significant information (97).

THE BLACKY PICTURES (12). This set of twelve pictures, intended for ages 5 and over, is offered as a "measure of psychosexual development." They are used to learn the degree to which the subject has developed the various psychoanalytic "dimensions" of psychosexual traits. The pictures portray a young dog, Blacky, in situations intended to represent relevant experiences with three other dogs: his father, mother, and sibling. As in the case of the Children's Apperception Test, the Blacky pictures anthropomorphize by presenting the animals in obviously characteristic human situations. The same questions that were raised regarding the CAT may be asked of the latter. The usual methods of estimating reliability of projective tests were employed: matching, interrater agreement, and correlating rating and rerating of the "dimensions" of stories. On the whole, the results showed that the test yields results which are stable to a "modest degree" (38).

Validation studies thus far published suggest "that there is something there . . . but do not necessarily indicate what it is or where it is." Validity is reported in several ways (70):

> Relationships within the theory itself; that is, construct validity: Statistically significant correlations were found among "dimensions"; hence, it was concluded, they are related in some systematic manner.
>
> Responses analyzed for sex differences: Results were in the direction that would be predicted by psychoanalytic theory.
>
> Understanding clinical syndromes: Results were interpreted as a "valid indicator" of psychosexual deviation in a small, selected (clinical) population.
>
> The factor analytic approach: Male subjects produced results consistent with psychoanalytic theory, but the responses of females presented contradictions that could not be explained.[3]

The most prevalent current view is that the Blacky pictures are useful in studies of psychoanalytical theory; their use in clinics and in theoretical analyses of personality traits requires sound preparation in psychoanalytic theory; in individual cases, where relevant, they are useful to indicate aspects of psychosexual development to be investigated.

[3] Also see symposium on validity (98).

MAKE-A-PICTURE STORY (88).   This device, for use with adolescents and adults, combines one feature of the TAT (telling stories) with an innovation: giving the subject an opportunity to construct his own pictured situation with the materials provided by the test. These materials consist of twenty-two "background pictures" (achromatic, on cardboard); some ambiguous, others semistructured, still others definitely structured. Among the backgrounds are, for example:

living room	street	forest
bedroom	camp	cave
bathroom	landscape	schoolroom

There are also sixty-seven cutout figures (sixty-five human and two animal) representing:

male adult	indeterminate as to sex	children
female adult	legendary and fictitious	a dog
minority groups	silhouette and blank faces	a snake

These figures are portrayed in a variety of postures and states.

The examiner selects one background picture at a time, asks the subject to place one or more figures of his own choosing against the background, as they might appear in real life, and then to tell a story about the scene he has created. Any of the figures may be placed against any background. The principle here is that the individual may project whatever actions and relations he wishes upon whatever persons he chooses.

After each story, the examiner conducts an inquiry, as in the case of the TAT. Complete responses are recorded and analyzed according to a rather detailed and elaborate scheme. Essentially, the stories are analyzed primarily for form and secondarily for content. The second of these—content—may be of almost unlimited variety, intended to elicit through these "fantasy productions" the subject's social adjustments and relations. By analysis of form, the test's author means ". . . which figures are chosen, how many are chosen, where they are placed on the background, how they are handled by the subject, and what relationships they bear to each other." Form is analyzed and characterized in terms of forces operating on the subject (goals, drives, conflicts, values, ego ideals) and of modes of behavior (hostility, sexuality, aspiration, autonomy).

Some psychologists think that the stories evoked by this test may be more spontaneous and richer in fantasy than the TAT because the pictured situation has been created by the subject himself (27). On the other hand, it is possible that the subject will evade certain types of situations and problems, significant in his case, with which he would have to deal in one way or another in the TAT type of test.

THE MICHIGAN PICTURE TEST (2). This instrument is the most systematically and solidly constructed thematic apperception test that has
appeared since Murray's TAT. It is intended for use with children from
8 to 14 years of age. The test consists of sixteen pictures, twelve of which
are used with each child. The selection depends upon the subject's sex.
The basic principle is the same as that of the original TAT: revealing
needs through responses to pictures. Construction of the Michigan test
was motivated by reports from child guidance clinics that the TAT was
not entirely suitable for children under 14 and that a special test was
necessary.

The authors state in their manual that the over-all purpose of their
project was to ". . . investigate and measure the emotional reactions of
children in the preadolescent and adolescent stages of development. . . .
It was believed the test should be nontraumatic and yet tap the common
conflict situations for this age group." To do this, they followed the
methods of population sampling, behavior sampling, and response analysis prescribed for and frequently found in the construction of tests of intelligence and specific aptitudes.

Results of the construction process indicated that certain test variables
effectively discriminated between groups of well-adjusted and groups of
poorly adjusted children. These variables constitute: (1) the "tension index," (2) "verb tense," (3) "direction of forces." The tension index is based
upon the following four types of needs (2, p. 66):

> love: verbal expression, positive or negative, indicating affection, affilia-
> tion, attachment, friendship, or admiration
> extrapunitiveness: verbal expression of aggression toward an external
> object
> submission: verbal expression of defeat, resignation, passivity, compliance,
> obedience, acceptance of suffering without opposition
> personal adequacy: verbal reference, positive or negative, of happiness,
> strength, competence, or any reference to the temperament or physical char-
> acteristics of the human or animal figures in the story

"Verbal tense" of responses is scored for frequencies of past, present,
and future tenses. The hypothesis, empirical in origin, is that disproportionate emphasis upon each of the several tenses may indicate behavior as follows:

> past tense: avoidance of conflict
>   a regressive trend
>   schizoid character structure
>   submissiveness or isolation
> present tense: compulsivity or pedantry
>   personality disturbance

effective intellectual functioning

future tense: anxiety

disturbed but relatively mature personality

inefficient intellectual functioning

"Direction of forces" refers to the action expressed in the story:

centrifugal direction (outward action)

centripetal action (inward action)

neutral (no direction indicated)

Well-adjusted children, it was found, express both centrifugal and centripetal directions much more frequently than the poorly adjusted.

A second group of variables, for which the stories are also scored, consists of those ". . . for which trends were indicated, but in which differences were not statistically significant." This group of variables includes the following:

psychosexual level: a measure of psychosexual maturity in orthodox Freudian terms

interpersonal relationships: range and frequency of expressed interpersonal relationships

personal pronouns: frequencies of the three personal pronouns as a measure of self-reference

popular objects: most commonly referred to objects and persons

level of interpretation: degrees of interpretation, from "no response," through enumeration and description to complex interpretation and inference

The results obtained for these four variables were inconclusive as between well-adjusted and poorly adjusted groups; yet they were suggestive enough to warrant further investigation as possible differentiating criteria.

Technical superiority of this Michigan test is owing to the fact that the pictures were designed in accordance with well-defined concepts of psychological development and of significant environmental situations affecting development. As already stated, careful sampling procedures were used. Also, the Michigan test presents extensive data on group differences, norms for each of the scoring variables, and reliabilities.[4] Of the picture tests published since the original TAT, this one appears to be most soundly constructed and promising for the study and assessment of children's personalities within the specified age groups.

ROSENZWEIG PICTURE-FRUSTRATION STUDY. The full name of this test

---

[4] Reliability correlations of the four variables constituting the "tension index" scores obtained by two judges, grade 3: .67, .93, .93, 1.00; grade 5: .91, .97, .97, .98; grades 7 and 9: .70, .81, .98, .98. Fifteen cases in each group. Reliability correlations for "direction of forces" as scored by two judges, grade 3: .95; grade 5: .87; grades 7 and 9: .91. Ten cases in each group.

is "Picture-Association Study for Assessing Reactions to Frustration." Consisting of twenty-four cartoon-like pictures, the test is intended to serve as a projective method for revealing the subject's characteristic patterns of response to common stress-producing situations regarded as important in normal and abnormal adjustment. Two forms are available, one for children of ages from 4 to 14 years, and one for persons older than 14.

Each picture shows two persons involved in a frustrating situation of common occurrence. One person in each picture is represented as making a statement which either helps describe the frustration of the second individual or is itself actually frustrating to the latter. The caption box above the second person is blank. The features and expressions in all pictures are omitted.

The task of the subject is to examine each picture and to write in the blank box the first appropriate response that occurs to him. (Young children give oral responses to be written by the examiner.) The assumption is that the subject identifies himself, consciously or unconsciously, with the frustrated individual in each situation and that his replies are projections of his own ways of acting. Obviously, this picture test differs from others in being relatively structured and in serving a limited purpose.

The situations presented are of two kinds: ego-blocking and superego-blocking. The first are those "in which some obstacle, personal or impersonal, interrupts, disappoints, deprives, or otherwise directly frustrates the subject." The second type of blocking "represents some accusation, charge, or incrimination of the subject by someone else." An inquiry follows the recording of responses, for clarification and elaboration.

Scoring of responses is based upon (1) direction of aggression and (2) reaction type. Under the first of these, three forms of expression are distinguished: (a) extrapunitiveness, in which aggression is turned onto the environment; (b) intropunitiveness, whereby the subject turns the aggression upon himself; and (c) impunitiveness, in which aggression is evaded in an effort to gloss over the frustration. Each type of reaction also has three classes: (a) obstacle dominance, in which the barrier occasioning the frustration stands out in the response; (b) ego defense, in which the ego of the respondent predominates; and (c) need persistence, in which the subject emphasizes the solution of the frustrating problem. In addition to this analysis, the manual gives a sufficient number and variety of responses and examples of scoring to provide this projective test with a relatively objective scoring system.

The responses to the frustration pictures are intended to show the individual's frustration tolerance, which signifies the relative absence of ob-

noyances, likes and dislikes, fears and attractions. Another may be designed to reveal motives, needs, and environmental forces. Still another may be concerned primarily or solely with feelings about one's home, community, friends, occupation, school. Others may be intended to discover psychological mechanisms, such as feelings of rejection, evidence of rationalization, methods of evasion. In other words, each sentence-completion test should be adapted to the particular situation in which it is to be applied.

Several sample items are the following:

> I worry over . . .
> I feel proud when . . .
> Other people usually . . .
> I prefer to . . .
> My father used to . . .
> My hope is . . .
> When I was a child . . .

Two fully described and frequently used instruments are Rhode's *Sentence Completion Test* and *The Rotter Incomplete Sentence Blank*. Each is designed to estimate the subject's degree and areas of maladjustment, if any exist. Although both provide schemes for scoring responses, it appears that this type of test is most useful for identifying areas of behavioral problems and for providing diagnostic clues. For example, the responses of a 10-year-old boy to one set of completion sentences were all neutral and indicative of satisfactory adjustment except those related to his school experiences.

On the whole, it appears that sentence-completion tests evoke personality materials that are closer to the level of awareness than those evoked by the Rorschach and the thematic apperception type (17, 40). Nevertheless, the sentence completions provide a basis for subsequent interviews and counseling.

PROJECTIVE QUESTIONNAIRE. By means of this technique, the subject is given a series of questions to answer in his own way. Unless he is aware of the psychological significance of the questionnaire, he does not grasp the implications of the questions or of his answers. It is thus possible to obtain information regarding the subject's emotional life, his values, his attitudes, and sentiments. Each question is intended to show which dynamisms might be operating in an individual's behavior; for example, suppression, projection, identification. The specific questions to be included will depend upon their purpose and upon the persons for whom they are intended. In any event, the value of this type of test, at present, does not lie in a numerical score; indeed, rating schemes have not yet been devised, since this technique is quite recent and has not been used extensively. The value of the projective questionnaire lies, rather, in the fact that the answers are interpreted as revealing certain traits and serve as a basis for psychological interview.

The following are items included in the questionnaire devised by the psychological staff of the Office of Strategic Services during World War II, to be used, among other tests, in the screening and job assignment of personnel (see Chapter 22).

It seems that no matter how careful we are, we all sometimes have embarrassing moments. What experiences make you feel like sinking through the floor?

What kinds of things do you most dislike to see people do?

What things or situations are you most afraid of?

If you were (are) a parent, what things would you try to guard your children against most carefully?

STORYTELLING AND STORY COMPLETION (11, 86). Although this method has been used informally for some years, the published work on it is meager. Several approaches have been employed, the most common with children being the following:

Retelling of children's popular stories, such as "The Three Bears."

Retelling the story the child likes best of all those ever heard or read.

Stories made up on specified themes, such as on a boy or girl, a father, a mother.

A story especially constructed for the purpose at hand, told to the children by a teacher; reproduced in writing for the teacher, later retold to the therapist, this being the "emotional version." In evaluating such retold stories, the therapist must take into account the common phenomena of memory distortions (6).

Users of these methods report that they are helpful in revealing a child's conflicts, aggressions, anxieties, wish fulfillment, affectivity, and so forth.

Among other methods that have been tried are these:

A situation is set up creating a moral conflict, the effects of which on the child are evaluated through the story he makes up about it and his methods of dealing with the conflict.

The child is asked to invent stories about favorite comic-strip characters; and these stories are regarded as indications of his "retreat into fantasy," on the one hand, or his realistic attitude toward his environment and interpersonal relations, on the other. The child is also asked to invent stories about disliked comic-strip characters as a means of discerning his personality tensions and for subsequent use in therapy, since these stories give evidence of emotional transference and are a means of communicating affectivity.

Storytelling as a projective method has been tried also with adults.

Ordinarily the subject is asked to develop a story on a theme dealing with some aspect, or aspects, of his environment in order to bring out some of his strivings and modes of adjustment.

A little work has been done on combining music and storytelling. Recordings of selected musical classics are played; the subject is told to report the images and themes he associates with these. The expectation is that the respondent's reports will indicate certain psychological states, such as fear, struggle, romance, animation, reverence, and others.

Story-completion techniques are of several kinds.

Dramatic situations are presented briefly and concisely; the subject is required to develop each into a skeleton of a short story.

The outline of a story is provided; it is the subject's task to write a narrative based upon it.

A brief incomplete story is presented, which the subject is to complete.

The individual is given a group of brief statements each of which presents a situation of emotional conflict, followed by two questions on how the central figure in the situation responded to it: "How did he feel?" "What did he do and why?"

An elaboration and systematic development of story completion has been offered by H. D. Sargent, called *The Insight Test,* for men and women (86).

[It] . . . is composed of a series of items . . . in which the bare outlines of a problem situation are stated and to which the subject is asked to respond by telling what the leading character did, and why, and how he felt about it. The nature of the material and the task itself, which is presented as a test of insight or ability to "see into" the motives, actions, and feelings of others is designed to conform to two basic principles of a projective test: ambiguity of stimulus to which the subject must respond in his own personal terms, and direction of attention away from concern with self toward the task of reacting to something external.

This story completion test has the merit of providing a system of analysis and scoring that yields interpretations based upon a set of common principles.

[The scoring system] . . . involves primarily a differentiation between expressions of feeling in response to the [items], and other types of expression which are regarded as serving the purpose of control, defense, and delay of unmodulated emotion. Phrases . . . are categorized both with reference to the fate of the aroused affect and to the mood or content expressed. Several indications of disturbance in thought or feeling are also recorded. Finally, certain relations between expressions supposed to represent affect and defense, and within the quantities of different kinds of expression standing for different sorts of discharge and control, are computed.

As a testing technique, storytelling and story completion present difficulties in evaluation and interpretation; for, with the exception of Sargent's test, the situations are almost completely unstructured and fluid, and the possibilities of categorical analysis are almost unlimited. At present these techniques must be regarded as useful principally for exploratory purposes when viewed against a background of other information on the individual's experiences, traits, and behavior. Some clinicians who have used the Insight Test believe it has possibilities not yet demonstrated by research and practical applications.

Drawing and Painting

If volume of publication is a criterion, then it may be said that drawing and painting (including finger painting) are of increasing interest and significance as projective methods. Psychological studies have dealt with the relations of art to chronological age, general intelligence,

FIG. 26.1. Finger painting. "Sometimes it bleeds! Look!" (Indicates paper painted red.) "Look! Bloody! Like my throat!"

"He smears his hands and arms through the finger paint. And as he pins his thoughts and feelings down on paper he feels, perhaps, more secure. After he has captured them on paper he can handle them a little better." From V. M. Axline, *Play Therapy*, Boston: Houghton Mifflin Company, by permission.

specific aptitudes, and cultural influences. In these studies, the art productions of normal and abnormal groups have been analyzed to discover if there are characteristics that differentiate among normal persons and various atypical groups. In other words, do the productions have diagnostic value? It was thought, also, that drawings and paintings might contribute information to descriptions of normal personalities. In studies of psychotic groups, for example, it is reported that, among other things, their productions are markedly similar to the drawings of children and of some primitives; pronounced stereotypes and mannerisms are typical; representation is extremely nonrealistic; and their meanings may be discovered in a manner similar to analysis of dream content. It is reported, also, that color and movement have diagnostic significance, as do size, line, form, and the symbols used.

Finger painting has much in common with drawing and other forms of painting in personality study; but, in addition, its exponents emphasize the considerable diagnostic value of observing and analyzing the subject's approach to the situation and his behavior throughout.

Methods of obtaining productions vary, as do evaluations and interpretations. In some, considerable free play is given by the interpreter to his particular theoretical concepts. The great needs, before painting and drawing can occupy a reliable position in the area of projective methods, are that their psychological rationale be determined, their underlying psychological processes analyzed, and their validity established.

A quite different projective technique utilizing drawings is the *Draw-a-Person Test* (60). Used with individuals 2 years of age and older, it requires the subject to "draw a person." When the first drawing has been completed, he is instructed to draw a person of the opposite sex. Completion of the drawings is followed by an inquiry, in which the subject is asked to tell a story about each "person" he has drawn, as though that "person" were a character in a play or a novel. The examiner may also ask a series of prescribed questions about the "characters" in order to get added information about environmental factors and personal relations.

Each drawing is analyzed for specified characteristics; intercomparisons of the two drawings are made to discern the subject's attitudes toward himself and toward his own as well as the opposite sex. Analyses and interpretations of drawings are based upon the hypothesis that they represent one's conception of his body in the environment. The drawing of the figure representing one's own sex is regarded as a "body image"— a symbol of the concept of the self, a reflection of self-regard. In drawing the human figure of either sex, it is held, the subject becomes ego-involved; conflicting needs and tensions are expressed through details and organization of the drawn figures.

The nature of the analysis can be better appreciated by noting the structural features that are taken into account: size, background, exactness, degree of completion, detailing, symmetry, mid-line emphasis, perspective, reinforcements, proportions, placement on the page, theme, shading, erasures. Content of the drawing is also analyzed: individual body parts, clothing, accessories, facial expression, posture. Esthetic qualities are not considered.

Several body parts are listed below to illustrate interpretive significance attached to them:

head: intellectual aspirations, rational control, fantasy elaboration of the personality
eyes: uncertainty, paranoid wariness, sexual appeal
nose: masculinity and assertiveness
arms and hands: the primary extensive organs; indicators of degree of power, degree of reaching out, extent of environmental manipulation
bilateral symmetry: degree of obsessiveness–compulsiveness
body points: exaggerated somatic preoccupation

For a number of years, Karen Machover has used and experimented with this device. She has made acute and insightful personality interpretations with it. Other clinical psychologists, also, report that they have made effective use of the technique. The validation of this projective method, however, awaits more extensive study.

Other Noteworthy Projective Tests

In a textbook, it is impossible to describe and discuss every available test, since the number is so large, and many of them have not progressed much beyond their initial stages.[5] There are a few, however, that are regarded by critics as having promise because they are psychologically well conceived, they have proved useful in practical situations, and results of research warrant further experimental and applied study. Among them are the following.

Four-Picture Test (van Lennep) consists of four vaguely drawn colored pictures. The subject is required either to write or to tell one integrated story, using all four pictures. The pictures represent scenes of social groups and of individuals in isolation. This test has undergone a long period of development; careful analyses have been made of the probable psychological significance of responses.

The *Lowenfeld Mosaic Test* uses 456 small wooden (or plastic) squares, diamonds, and triangles of varied colors and sizes. The subject is in-

---

[5] Buros' *Fifth Mental Measurements Yearbook* includes 51 projective tests that are available in English-speaking countries.

structed to make anything he likes with the pieces. Patterns are classified as representational, conceptual, or abstract in design. They are then analyzed as multiform, composite, diffuse, and collective. Further complex analyses are made regarding many details and approaches to the problem for the purpose of differentiating among several age groups and personality categories. This test's complex and laborious method of analysis is a drawback to its wider use.

Raven's *Controlled Projection for Children,* of ages 6 to 12, combines drawing and storytelling. "The method consists of asking the child to draw [anything he wants to] and while he is drawing, to imagine and describe a series of events [in answer to a prescribed set of questions]. The verbal record shows the content of the child's thought and the organization of his ideas at the time of the test, while the drawing shows the way in which he controls and organizes his actions" (74, p. 25). This technique is used to elicit each child's social attitudes, habits, and personal relations in order to evaluate the extent of his social conformity. The method has been widely used in Great Britain for clinical purposes as well as in research. Although Raven's book does not contain the usual statistics of test standardization, it does present complete records of responses of 150 children and detailed analyses of responses given by several types of children. This test is not intended to provide a comprehensive description or measurement of personality. Raven's purpose is ". . . to provide a theory, terminology, and method of comparative study, to describe a technique of collecting information . . ." As such, he believes it can be useful in studies in genetic, social, and clinical psychology.

The *Tomkins-Horn Picture Arrangement Test* consists of 25 plates, each of which has three drawings. The subject is asked to indicate the sequence in which each set of drawings should be arranged to make "the best sense." He is instructed, also, to write one sentence telling the story of each drawing. The test is intended to sample three aspects of personality and behavior: social orientation, optimism–pessimism, and level of functioning. Although it was originally designed for use with industrial personnel, the authors believe this test has general applicability. Large groups of normal and abnormal subjects were examined to obtain normative and unusual, or deviant, responses. In the analysis, by a complex scoring method, emphasis is placed on the deviant responses in making personality evaluations. One of the most interesting aspects of this instrument is the authors' pattern, or global, scoring method. The common view among critics is that this device has much to commend it, but it should be used extensively in research before it becomes an established clinical test.

The *House-Tree-Person Projective Technique* (14), for ages 5 and older, requires the subject to draw a house, a tree, and a person, in that order. While the drawings are being made, the examiner takes notes on sequence of detail, tempo, spontaneous comments, and general behavior. In a second session, an extension initiated by J. T. Payne, the subject is asked to use colored crayons in making drawings of a house, tree, and person. A planned interview, including a set of standardized questions, follows the completion of the drawings. The purpose of the interview is to provide insights into various aspects of the drawings by having the subject describe, clarify, and interpret the objects. At the same time, the interview provides an opportunity for the examinee to free-associate. The methods of scoring and making qualitative interpretations of the drawings and responses are complex; but the objectives and personality traits being evaluated are similar to those of other projective tests: discernment of affective tone, quality of verbalizations, drive, psychosexual level, reactions to one's environment, interpersonal relations, intrapersonal balance, major needs, and major assets. The qualitative analysis is not based upon a single, theoretical system; it utilizes Freudian, neo-Freudian, and other concepts. Since the author of this instrument believes that each drawing arouses both conscious and unconscious associations, each of the objects presumably has symbolic and literal significance. The house relates to the subject's home and those living with him; the tree—highly symbolic—concerns his "life role" and his ability to "derive satisfaction" from his environment; the person represents his general and specific interpersonal relations.

It is obvious that a large part of the information on these aspects of personality would be derived from interpretations of answers to the standard questions in the interrogation. Clinicians who have had considerable experience with the H-T-P technique have found it useful especially with children; but its usefulness is largely a matter of individual and intuitive insights gained from varied experience with it. Other clinicians believe the technique is too time-consuming to administer and analyze and that equally or more valuable results may be obtained with other less complex instruments.

Play

Since play is free of the constraints of ordinary adult activity and free of those imposed by adults upon children, it is useful as a projective technique in the study of less apparent aspects of personality. For it is unstructured, provides opportunity for fantasy and imaginativeness to operate, and gives scope to individuality of expression.

As a method of personality diagnosis and therapy, play is used almost solely with children. It was first tried as a substitute for the free-association technique of psychoanalysis. From that practice, investigators developed the theory that play activity is determined by a complex of factors; it provides an outlet for the release of emotional tensions and for overt or symbolic behavior expressing needs, wishes, desire for experience, and attitudes, without fear of censure or punishment.

FIG. 26.2. Doll play. She began to play with the family of dolls. "This is Tom," she said to the therapist. "Tom is a funny boy. Want to know what happens to Tom?" From V. M. Axline, *Play Therapy,* Boston: Houghton Mifflin Company, by permission.

The play technique commonly used in personality study and therapy consists of this: the child is introduced to a collection of toys which he is permitted to use freely, while the observer notes his activities with respect to the particular items employed, the use made of them, the organization or patterning of toys, attitudes toward each toy, vocalizations, and general behavior in the play situation. The toys themselves must be able to provide insights into a child's personality and needs. The items include dolls representing members of the family, furniture (especially kitchen and bathroom appliances), water, sand, vehicles, animals, building blocks, balloons, sticks, or any other objects that might be relevant in a particular instance.

With play, as with drawing and painting, methods of analysis and interpretation of behavior differ according to the theoretical position and assumptions of the investigator or therapist. However, while the play technique of personality study is a subjective method, numerous case reports attest to its value as a diagnostic and therapeutic procedure.

An effort has been made to standardize and objectify the evaluation of children's play in the therapeutic situation (16). This device, called the World-test, utilizes numerous miniature pieces that represent a large variety of objects and persons in children's environments. The child is instructed to create any setting or situation he chooses. His performance and emotional condition are interpreted in terms of the number and variety of pieces used, the structure of the situation (rigid, flexible organization, chaotic), aggressiveness, etc. (depending upon which pieces are used and how they are used). Although this technique is more formalized and has some objective aspects, the basic value of the method depends upon the interpretation of the child's performance and upon demonstrable relationships between this play activity and children's problems of adjustment.

Evaluation of Projective Tests

Since the Rorschach and the Murray TAT are the two most widely used projective tests and have been subjected to the most thorough research, they were described and explained in some detail. The other projective tests were presented to acquaint the student more fully with psychological thinking in this area, to show how this thinking is being implemented, and to indicate the variety of instruments.

The following paragraphs summarize the present status and the major problems of current projective tests.

The Rorschach and the TAT have proved to be of considerable value, even though much research remains to be done to fulfill all requirements of a soundly standardized test. It should be recalled, however, that many specialists maintain that the usual specifications of standardization cannot and should not be applied to projective tests.

Although progress is being made, *adequate* normative data are lacking for projective tests, even for the Rorschach and the TAT. In some instances, however, no normative data are available. Response norms, both quantitative and qualitative, should be obtained for various groups, according to age, socioeconomic status, sex, educational levels, and clinical classification. More emphasis upon normal populations is needed to provide the proper perspective within which to view performances of clinical groups. The views and interpretations of clinicians have been too strongly affected by their contacts with atypical personalities.

Reliability studies in terms of agreement among several scorers are most significant for these instruments and on the whole have yielded encouraging results. Test-retest reliabilities are of limited value and present special difficulties, as already pointed out. The method of split-half reliability is generally inappropriate for the reasons indicated.

Validity studies of the matching type have proved to be the most satisfactory kind. The use of known groups has been only moderately satisfactory because the criteria are qualitatively and, to some degree, differently defined. Furthermore, the use of these definitions in actual classification is a subjective matter. The relative unreliability of psychiatric classifications has already been noted. Validity studies are often complicated by the fact that interpretation of test data is "global" rather than in terms of limited and measurable elements. Laboratory studies of experimentally induced states or "sets" may be seriously questioned as a validating method; for they do not deal with basic and established personality traits. A possible exception is the use of hypnosis and similar means.

Although instructions and procedures in administering a test do not vary radically among specialists, uniformity is highly desirable.

An examiner's attitude (for example, reassuring or neutral) and his relations, in general, with the subject can influence the individual's responses. If rapport is established with the examiner, the subject is encouraged to verbalize and understand his behavior, attitudes, values, and the environmental forces.

More nearly uniform and objective scoring systems should be developed. Since interpretation must be based upon a theory and an understanding of the dynamics of human behavior, different theories lead to varied interpretations.

More experimental research remains to be done on the nature of the psychological processes involved in some of the projective tests.

Appropriately graded projective techniques are of more interest to subjects than are personality inventories.

Malingering and falsification are more difficult than on personality inventories, though not impossible.

Projective methods—particularly the Rorschach and the TAT—are frequently used by psychologists to supplement information derived from other tests (such as intelligence) in order to understand better the complex of factors operative in behavior at a given time.

Projective methods alone are not the answer to all questions regarding human personality and adjustment—a claim made for them by some enthusiasts. But in the hands of a qualified examiner these instruments assist in obtaining information not otherwise available, except possibly through extended psychological interview and observation.

Interest in projective methods is widespread among psychologists, from the viewpoints of experimentalists, personality theorists, and clinicians dealing with individuals who present every gradation and variety of problem (not necessarily maladjustment) from childhood through adulthood. It is to be expected, therefore, that solutions of the problem of projective methods will, with time, be more nearly achieved and the inadequacies of the instruments reduced.[6]

If the present trend continues, we may expect to have a number of separate projective tests—especially of the thematic picture type—designed for limited age levels, providing relationships and situations significant for that group. The large crop of new devices, among them being some that are promising and insightful, will be "shaken down"; and the "chaff" will be separated from the "wheat."[7]

References

1. Anderson, J. W. Controlled projection responses of delinquent boys. *Journal of Mental Science*, 1954, *100*, 643–656.
2. Andrew, G., *et al. The Michigan Picture Test*. Chicago: Science Research Associates, Inc., 1953.
3. Aronson, M. L. A study of the Freudian theory of paranoia by means of

[6] More research is necessary on the basic problems. A disproportionate number of research publications deal with segmental, unrelated, and limited questions; and they are, therefore, of limited significance. Research on basic problems needs an organized cooperative undertaking costly in time and funds.

[7] Some psychologists are extremely severe in their criticisms of projective tests. One of their most common criticisms is that interpretations of projective findings are not objective, but depend upon the psychologists' intuitions. Since this criticism is based largely upon data that are regarded as inadequate statistical evidence to support the claims made for projective tests, it is pertinent to quote what a mathematician says on intuition. The following quotations are from J. B. Rosser, *Logic for Mathematicians* (New York: McGraw-Hill Book Company, Inc., 1953, pp. 8–11).

". . . much of our discussion in the earlier chapters will be quite intuitive in character and not particularly precise. Gradually, as our symbolic logic crystallizes out of the intuitive background, we shall become more precise, though we shall never lose sight of our intuitive background completely, even after we have finally completely defined our symbolic logic and are proceeding quite mechanically.

"Intuition arises from experience, and so may be expected to have some foundation in fact. However a formal system is merely a model devised by human minds to represent some facts perceived intuitively. As such, it is bound to be artificial.

"We summarize the above points. Although we think that the average mathematician will find that a study of symbolic logic is very helpful in carrying out mathematical reasoning, we do not recommend that he should completely abandon his intuitive methods of reasoning for exclusively formal methods. Rather, he should consider the formal methods as a supplement to his intuitive methods to provide mechanical checks of critical points, and to provide the assistance of symbolic operations in complex situations, and to increase his precision and generality. He should not forget that his intuition is the final authority, so that, in case of an irreconcilable conflict between his intuition and some system of symbolic logic, he should abandon the symbolic logic. He can try other systems of symbolic logic, and perhaps find one more to his liking, but it would be difficult to change his intuition."

the Blacky pictures. *Journal of Projective Techniques*, 1953, *17*, 3–19.
4. Axline, V. M. *Play Therapy*. Boston: Houghton Mifflin Company, 1947.
5. Bach, G. R. Young children's play fantasies. *Psychological Monographs*, 1945, *59*, no. 2.
6. Bartlett, F. C. *Remembering*. New York: Cambridge University Press, 1932.
7. Bellak, L. *The Thematic Apperception Test and the Children's Apperception Test in Clinical Use*. New York: Grune & Stratton, Inc., 1954.
8. Bellak, L., and S. S. Bellak. *Children's Apperception Test*. New York: C.P.S. Co. (Box 42, Gracie Station), 1949–1955.
9. Bernard, J. The Rosenzweig P-F Study: norms, reliability, and statistical evaluation. *Journal of Psychology*, 1949, *28*, 325–343.
10. Biersdorf, K. R., and F. L. Marcuse. Responses of children to human and to animal pictures. *Journal of Projective Techniques*, 1953, *17*, 455–459.
11. Blos, P. *The Adolescent Personality*. New York: Appleton-Century-Crofts, Inc., 1941.
12. Blum, G. S. *The Blacky Pictures*. New York: The Psychological Corporation, 1950.
13. Borstelmann, L. J., and W. G. Klopfer. The Szondi test: a review and a critical evaluation. *Psychological Bulletin*, 1953, *50*, 112–132.
14. Buck, J. N., and I. Jolles. *H-T-P: House-Tree-Person Projective Technique*. Los Angeles: Western Psychological Services, 1946–1956.
15. Budoff, M. The relative utility of animal and human figures in a picture-story test for young children. *Journal of Projective Techniques*, 1960, *24*, 347–352.
16. Buhler, C. *The Toy World Test*. Los Angeles: J. B. Baisden, 4570 Mt. Eagle Place, 1941–1955.
17. Byers, J. *The Relationships between Sub-cultural Group Membership and Projective Test Responses*. Unpublished Ph.D. thesis. Cornell University, 1954.
18. Byrd, E., and R. L. Witherspoon. Responses of preschool children to the Children's Apperception Test. *Child Development*, 1954, *25*, 35–44.
19. Churchill, R., and V. J. Crandall. The reliability of the Rotter Incomplete Sentence Test. *Journal of Consulting Psychology*, 1955, *19*, 345–350.
20. Clarke, H. J., *et al.* The reliability of the scoring of the Rosenzweig Picture-Frustration Study. *Journal of Clinical Psychology*, 1947, *3*, 364–370.
21. Cole, D. The reliability of a single Szondi profile. *Journal of Clinical Psychology*, 1951, *7*, 383–384.
22. Cook, R. A. Identification and ego defensiveness in thematic apperception. *Journal of Projective Techniques*, 1953, *17*, 312–319.
23. Coulter, W. M. The Szondi Test and the prediction of antisocial behavior. *Journal of Projective Techniques*, 1959, *23*, 24–29.
24. David, H. P., *et al.* Qualitative and quantitative Szondi diagnosis. *Journal of Projective Techniques*, 1953, *17*, 75–78.
25. Davids, A., and G. R. Oliver. Fantasy aggression and learning in emotionally disturbed and normal children. *Journal of Projective Techniques*, 1960, *24*, 124–128.

26. Deri, S. K. *Introduction to the Szondi Test*. New York: Grune & Stratton, Inc., 1949.
27. Edgar, C. L., and E. S. Shneidman. Some relationships among thematic projective tests of various degrees of structuredness and behavior in a group situation. *Journal of Projective Techniques*, 1958, *22*, 3–12.
28. Elkisch, P. Children's drawings in a projective technique. *Psychological Monographs*, 1945, *58*, no. 1.
29. Ellis, A. The Blacky Test used with a psychoanalytic patient. *Journal of Clinical Psychology*, 1953, *9*, 167–172.
30. Engel, M. The development and applications of the Children's Insight Test. *Journal of Projective Techniques*, 1958, *22*, 13–25.
31. Engel, M., and W. Rechenberg. Studies in the reliability of the Children's Insight Test. *Journal of Projective Techniques*, 1961, *25*, 158–163.
32. Erikson, E. H. Studies in the interpretation of play: clinical observations of play disruption in young children. *Genetic Psychology Monographs*, 1940, *22*, no. 4.
33. Fleischmann, M. The discriminative power of the Szondi syndromes. *Journal of Consulting Psychology*, 1954, *18*, 89–95.
34. Frank, L. K., *et al.* Personality development in adolescent girls. *Society for Research in Child Development*, 1951, *16*, no. 53.
35. Furuya, K. Responses of school children to human and animal pictures. *Journal of Projective Techniques*, 1957, *21*, 248–252.
36. Galton, F. Psychometric experiments. *Brain*, 1879, *2*, 149–162.
37. Gordon, L. V. A factor analysis of the Szondi pictures. *Journal of Psychology*, 1953, *36*, 387–392.
38. Granick, S., and N. A. Scheflen. Approaches to reliability of projective tests with special reference to the Blacky Pictures Test. *Journal of Consulting Psychology*, 1958, *22*, 137–141.
39. Guertin, W. H. A factor analysis of some Szondi pictures. *Journal of Clinical Psychology*, 1951, *7*, 232–235.
40. Hanfmann, E. Studies of the Sentence Completion Test. *Journal of Projective Techniques*, 1953, *17*, 280–294.
41. Hartwell, S. W., *et al.* The Michigan Picture Test: diagnostic and therapeutic possibilities of a new projective test in child guidance. *American Journal of Orthopsychiatry*, 1951, *21*, 124–137.
42. Holden, R. H. The Children's Apperception Test with cerebral palsied and normal children. *Child Development*, 1956, *27*, 3–8.
43. Holzberg, J. D., and R. Posner. The relationship of extrapunitiveness on the Rosenzweig P-F-S to aggression in overt behavior and fantasy. *American Journal of Orthopsychiatry*, 1951, *21*, 767–779.
44. Hutt, M. L. The use of projective methods of personality measurement in Army medical installations. *Journal of Clinical Psychology*, 1945, *1*, 134–140.
45. Jung, C. G. The association method. *American Journal of Psychology*, 1910, *21*, 219–269.

46. Jung, C. G. *Studies in Word-Association*. (Translated by M. D. Eder.) London: William Heinemann, Ltd., 1918.
47. Kaake, N. A. *The Relationship between Intelligence Level and Responses to the Children's Apperception Test*. Unpublished M.A. thesis. Cornell University, 1951.
48. Kagan, J. The measurement of overt aggression from fantasy. *Journal of Abnormal and Social Psychology*, 1956, *52*, 390–393.
49. Kagan, J., and G. S. Lesser. (eds.). *Contemporary Issues in Thematic Apperception Methods*. Springfield, Ill.: Charles C Thomas, Publisher, 1961.
50. Kamenetzky, J., *et al*. The relative effectiveness of four attitude assessment techniques in predicting a criterion. *Educational and Psychological Measurement*, 1956, *16*, 187–194.
51. Kent, G. H., and A. J. Rosanoff. A study of association in insanity. *American Journal of Insanity*, 1910, *67*, 37–96, 317–390.
52. Korchin, S. J., *et al*. A critical evaluation of the Thompson Thematic Apperception Test. *Journal of Projective Techniques*, 1950, *14*, 445–452.
53. Lasky, J. J., and L. Berger. Blacky test scores before and after genito-urinary surgery. *Journal of Projective Techniques*, 1960, *24*, 57–58.
54. Levin, M. L. Validation of the Lowenfeld Mosaic Test. *Journal of Consulting Psychology*, 1956, *20*, 239–248.
55. Light, B. H. A further test of the Thompson TAT rationale. *Journal of Abnormal and Social Psychology*, 1955, *51*, 148–150.
56. Lindzey, G., and D. Kalmins. Thematic Apperception Test: some evidence bearing on the "hero assumption." *Journal of Abnormal and Social Psychology*, 1958, *57*, 76–83.
57. Lowenfeld, M. The world pictures of children. *British Journal of Medical Psychology*, 1939, *18*, 65–101.
58. *Lowenfeld Mosaic Test*. London: Newman Neame, 1954.
59. Lubin, B. Judgments of adjustment from TAT stories as a function of experimentally altered sets. *Journal of Consulting Psychology*, 1961, *25*, 249–252.
60. Machover, K. *Personality Projection in the Drawing of the Human Figure: A Method of Personality Investigation*. Springfield, Ill.: Charles C Thomas, Publisher, 1949.
61. Machover, K. Human figure drawings of children. *Journal of Projective Techniques*, 1953, *17*, 85–91.
62. Machover, K., and M. Zadek. Human figure drawings of hospitalized in-volutionals. *Psychiatric Quarterly Supplement*, 1956, *30*, part 2, 222–240.
63. McCary, J. L. Reactions to frustration by some cultural and racial groups. *Personality*, 1951, *1*, 84–102.
64. Mira y Lopez, E. *Myokinetic Psychodiagnosis*. (Translated by Mrs. Jacques Dubois.) New York: Logos Press, 1958.
65. Murphy, L. B. Art technique in studying child personality. *Rorschach Research Exchange and Journal of Projective Techniques*, 1949, *13*, 320–324.

66. Murray, H. A., and C. D. Morgan. A clinical study of sentiments. *Genetic Psychology Monographs,* 1945, *32,* 3–311.
67. Murstein, B. I. Nonprojective determinants of perception on the TAT. *Journal of Consulting Psychology,* 1958, *22,* 195–198.
68. Mussen, P. H. Differences between TAT responses of Negro and white boys. *Journal of Consulting Psychology,* 1953, *17,* 373–376.
69. Napoli, P. J. Interpretive aspects of finger painting. *Journal of Psychology,* 1947, *23,* 93–132.
70. Neuman, G. G., and J. C. Salvatore. The Blacky Test and psychoanalytic theory: a factor analytic approach to validity. *Journal of Projective Techniques,* 1958, *22,* 427–431.
71. Norman, R. D., and G. J. Kleinfeld. Rosenzweig Picture-Frustration Study results with minority group juvenile delinquents. *Journal of Genetic Psychology,* 1958, *92,* 61–67.
72. Rapaport, D. *Emotions and Memory.* Baltimore: The Williams & Wilkins Company, 1942.
73. Rapaport, D., *et al. Diagnostic Psychological Testing.* Vol. 2. Chicago: Year Book Publishers, 1946.
74. Raven, J. C. *Controlled Projection for Children.* London: H. K. Lewis & Co., 1951.
75. Rhode, A. R. *Sentence Completion Tests.* Los Angeles: Western Psychological Services, 1957.
76. Rhode, A. R. *The Sentence Completion Method: Its Diagnostic and Clinical Application to Mental Disorders.* New York: The Ronald Press Company, 1957.
77. Riess, B. F., *et al.* Further critical evaluation of the Negro version of the TAT. *Journal of Projective Techniques,* 1951, *15,* 394–400.
78. *Rosenzweig Picture-Frustration Study.* The Author, 8029 Washington St., St. Louis, 1944–1949.
79. Rosenzweig, S. The picture-association method and its application in a study of reactions to frustration. *Journal of Personality,* 1945, *14,* 3–23.
80. Rosenzweig, S., *et al.* Revised scoring manual for the Rosenzweig Picture-Frustration Study. *Journal of Psychology,* 1947, *24,* 165–208.
81. Rosenzweig, S. Revised norms for the adult form of the Rosenzweig P-F-S. *Journal of Personality,* 1950, *18,* 344–346.
82. *Rotter Incomplete Sentences Blank.* New York: The Psychological Corporation, 1950.
83. Rotter, J. B., and B. Willerman. The Incomplete Sentences Test. *Journal of Consulting Psychology,* 1947, *11,* 43–48.
84. Rotter, J. B., *et al.* The validity of the Rotter Incomplete Sentences Blank. *Journal of Consulting Psychology,* 1954, *18,* 105–111.
85. Santorum, A. A cross-validation of the House-Tree-Person drawing indices predicting hospital discharge of tuberculosis patients. *Journal of Consulting Psychology,* 1960, *24,* 400–402.
86. Sargent, H. D. *The Insight Test: A Verbal Projective Test for Personality Study.* New York: Grune & Stratton, Inc., 1953.
87. Schwartz, M. M., and L. Karlin. A new technique for studying the meaning

of performance on the Rosenzweig P-F-S. *Journal of Consulting Psychology,* 1954, *18,* 131–134.

88. Shneidman, E. S. *Make a Picture Story.* New York: The Psychological Corporation, 1947–1952.

89. Shneidman, E. S. Some comparisons among the Four Picture Test, TAT, and Make-a-Picture Story Test. *Rorschach Research Exchange and Journal of Projective Techniques,* 1949, *13,* 150–154.

90. Smith, L. M. The concurrent validity of six personality and adjustment tests for children. *Psychological Monographs,* 1958, *72,* no. 457.

91. Sohler, D. T., *et al.* The prediction of family interaction from a battery of projective techniques. *Journal of Projective Techniques,* 1957, *21,* 199–208.

92. Starr, S., and F. L. Marcuse. Reliability in the Draw-a-Person Test. *Journal of Projective Techniques,* 1959, *23,* 83–86.

93. Stoltz, R. E., and F. C. Coltharp. Clinical judgments and the Draw-a-Person Test. *Journal of Consulting Psychology,* 1961, *25,* 43–45.

94. Sumerwell, H. C., *et al.* The effect of differential motivating instructions on the emotional tone and outcome of TAT stories. *Journal of Consulting Psychology,* 1958, *22,* 385–388.

95. *Symonds Picture Study Test.* New York: Bureau of Publications, Teachers College, Columbia University, 1948.

96. Symonds, P. M. *Adolescent Fantasy.* New York: Columbia University Press, 1949.

97. Symonds, P. M. (with A. R. Jensen). *From Adolescent to Adult.* New York: Columbia University Press, 1961.

98. Symposium. Current aspects of the problem of validity. *Journal of Projective Techniques,* 1959, *23,* 259–289.

99. *Szondi Test.* Bern: Hans Huber, 1947–1952. (U.S. distributor: Grune & Stratton, Inc., New York.)

100. Szondi, L. *Experimental Diagnostics of Drives.* New York: Grune & Stratton, Inc., 1952.

101. Tendler, A. D. Significant features of disturbance in free association. *Journal of Psychology,* 1945, *20,* 65–89.

102. Thompson, C. E. The Thompson modification of the Thematic Apperception Test. *Rorschach Research Exchange and Journal of Projective Techniques,* 1949, *13,* 469–478.

103. Thurstone, L. L. *Word Associations with Homonyms.* Chicago: University of Chicago Psychometric Laboratory, 1952, no. 79.

104. Tomkins, S. S., and J. B. Miner. *The Tomkins-Horn Picture Arrangement Test.* New York: Springer Publishing Company, Inc., 1957.

105. van Lennep, D. J. *The Four-Picture Test.* The Hague: Martinus Nijhoff, 1948.

106. van Lennep, D. J. The Four Picture Test. Ch. 6 in H. H. and G. L. Anderson (eds.), *Introduction to Projective Techniques.* Englewood Cliffs, N.J.: Prentice-Hall, Inc., 1951.

107. Wolff, W. *The Expression of Personality: Experimental Depth Psychology.* New York: Harper & Brothers, 1943.

INDEX OF NAMES

INDEX OF SUBJECTS

Date Loaned
